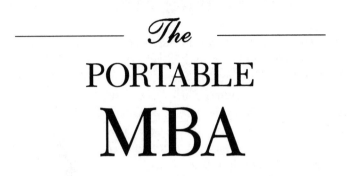

The
PORTABLE
MBA
in
FINANCE AND
ACCOUNTING

The Portable MBA Series

The

PORTABLE
MBA

in

FINANCE AND
ACCOUNTING

THIRD EDITION

Edited by
John Leslie Livingstone
and
Theodore Grossman

John Wiley & Sons, Inc.

Preface

Do you know how to accomplish these important business tasks?

- Understand financial statements.
- Measure liquidity of a business.
- Analyze business profitability.
- Differentiate between regular income and extraordinary items.
- Predict future bankruptcy for an enterprise.
- Prepare a budget.
- Do a break-even analysis.
- Measure productivity.
- Figure out return on investment.
- Compute the cost of capital.
- Put together a business plan.
- Legitimately minimize income taxes payable by you or your business.
- Decide whether your business should be a limited partnership, a C or S corporation, or some other type of entity.
- Take your company public.
- Manage foreign currency exposure.
- Evaluate a merger or acquisition target.
- Serve as a director of a corporation.
- Build a successful e-business.
- Understand and use financial derivatives.
- Use information technology for competitive advantage.
- Value a business.

These are some of the key topics explained in this book. It is a book designed to help you learn the basics in finance and accounting, without incurring the considerable time and expense of a formal MBA program.

The first edition of this book was published in 1992, and the second edition in 1997. Both editions, hardback and paperback, have been highly successful and have sold many, many copies. In addition, the book has been translated into Chinese (Cantonese and Mandarin), French, Indonesian, Portuguese, and Spanish. We are delighted that so many readers in various countries have found this book useful. Now, the entire book has been updated for the third edition. The following new chapters have been added:

- Chapter 1: Using Financial Statements
- Chapter 3: Cost-Volume-Profit Analysis
- Chapter 5: Information Technology and You
- Chapter 6: Forecasts and Budgets
- Chapter 9: The Business Plan
- Chapter 10: Planning Capital Expenditure
- Chapter 17: Profitable Growth by Acquisition
- Chapter 18: Business Valuation

Also, there are eight new authors, substantial revisions of four chapters and complete updates of all remaining chapters. The book consists of valuable, practical how-to-do-it information, applicable to an entire range of businesses, from the smallest startup to the largest corporations in the world. Each chapter of the book has been written by an outstanding expert in the subject matter of that particular chapter. Some of these experts are full-time practitioners in the real world, and others are part-time consultants who also serve as business school professors. Most of these professors are on the faculty of Babson College, which is famous for its major contributions to the field of entrepreneurship and which, year after year, is at the top of the annual list of leading independent business schools compiled by *U.S. News and World Report*.

This book can be read, and reread, with a great deal of profit. Also, it can be kept handy on a nearby shelf in order to pull it down and look up answers to questions as they occur. Further, this book will help you to work with finance and accounting professionals on their own turf and in their own jargon. You will know what questions to ask, and you will better understand the answers you receive without being confused or intimidated.

Who can benefit from this book? Many different people, such as:

- Managers wishing to improve their business skills.
- Engineers, chemists, scientists and other technical specialists preparing to take on increased management responsibilities.
- People already operating their own businesses, or thinking of doing so.
- Business people in nonfinancial positions who want to be better versed in financial matters.
- BBA or MBA alumni who want a refresher in finance and accounting.

- People in many walks of life who need to understand more about financial matters.

Whether you are in one, some, or even none of the above categories, you will find much of value to you in this book, and the book is reader friendly. Frankly, most finance and accounting books are technically complex, boringly detailed, or just plain dull. This book emphasizes clarity to nonfinancial readers, using many helpful examples and a bright, interesting style of writing. Learn, and enjoy!

JOHN LESLIE LIVINGSTONE
THEODORE GROSSMAN

Acknowledgments

A book like this results only from the contributions of many talented people. We would like to thank the chapter authors that make up this book for their clear and informative explanations of the powerful concepts and tools of finance and accounting. In this world of technology and the Internet, while most of the underlying concepts remain fixed, the applications are ever changing, requiring the authors to constantly rededicate themselves to their professions. Our deepest appreciation goes to our wives, Trudy Livingstone and Ruth Grossman, and to our children Robert Livingstone, Aaron and Melissa Grossman, and Michael Grossman. They provide the daily inspiration to perform our work and to have undertaken this project.

J. L. L.
T. G.

Contents

PART ONE

UNDERSTANDING THE NUMBERS

1 USING FINANCIAL STATEMENTS

John Leslie Livingstone

WHAT ARE FINANCIAL STATEMENTS? A CASE STUDY

Pat was applying for a bank loan to start her new business, Nutrivite, a retail store selling nutritional supplements, vitamins, and herbal remedies. She described her concept to Kim, a loan officer at the bank.

Kim: How much money will you need to get started?

Pat: I estimate $80,000 for the beginning inventory, plus $36,000 for store signs, shelves, fixtures, counters, and cash registers, plus $24,000 working capital to cover operating expenses for about two months. That's a total of $140,000 for the startup.

Kim: How are you planning to finance the investment of the $140,000?

Pat: I can put in $100,000 from my savings, and I'd like to borrow the remaining $40,000 from the bank.

Kim: Suppose the bank lends you $40,000 on a one-year note, at 15% interest, secured by a lien on the inventory. Let's put together projected financial statements from the figures you gave me. Your beginning balance sheet would look like what you see on my computer screen:

Nutrivite

Projected Balance Sheet as of January 1, 200X

Assets		Liabilities and Equity	
Cash	$ 24,000	Bank loan	$ 40,000
Inventory	80,000		
Current assets	104,000	Current liabilities	40,000
Fixed assets:		Equity:	
Equipment	36,000	Owner capital	100,000
Total assets	$140,000	Liabilities and equity	$140,000

The left side shows Nutrivite's investment in assets. It classifies the assets into "current" (which means turning into cash in a year or less) and "noncurrent" (not turning into cash within a year). The right side shows how the assets are to be financed: partly by the bank loan and partly by your equity as the owner.

Pat: Now I see why it's called a "balance sheet." The money invested in assets must equal the financing available—its like the two sides of a coin. Also, I see why the assets and liabilities are classified as "current" and "noncurrent"—the bank wants to see if the assets turning into cash in a year or less will provide enough cash to repay the one-year bank loan. Well, in a year there should be cash of $104,000. That's enough cash to pay off more than twice the $40,000 amount of the loan. I guess that guarantees approval of my loan!

Kim: We're not quite there yet. We need some more information. First, tell me, how much do you expect your operating expenses will be?

Pat: For year 1, I estimate as follows:

Store rent	$36,000	
Phone and utilities	14,400	
Assistants' salaries	40,000	
Interest on the loan	6,000	(15% on $40,000)
Total	$96,400	

Kim: We also have to consider depreciation on the store equipment. It probably has a useful life of 10 years. So each year it depreciates by 10% of its cost of $36,000. That's $3,600 a year for depreciation. So operating expenses must be increased by $3,600 a year, from $96,400 to $100,000. Now, moving on, how much do you think your sales will be this year?

Pat: I'm confident that sales will be $720,000 or even a little better. The wholesale cost of the items sold will be $480,000, giving a markup of $240,000—which is 33⅓% on the projected sales of $720,000.

Kim: Excellent! Let's organize this information into a projected income statement. We start with the sales, then deduct the cost of the items sold to arrive at the gross profit. From the gross profit we deduct your operating expenses, giving us the income before taxes. Finally we deduct the income tax expense in order to get the famous "bottom line," which is the net income. Here is the projected income statement shown on my computer screen:

Nutrivite

***Projected Income Statement for the
Year Ending December 31, 200X***

Sales		$720,000
Less cost of goods sold		480,000
Gross profit		240,000
Less expenses		
Salaries	$ 40,000	
Rent	36,000	
Phone and utilities	14,400	
Depreciation	3,600	
Interest	6,000	100,000
Income before taxes		140,000
Income tax expense (40%)		56,000
Net income		$ 84,000

Pat, this looks very good for your first year in a new business. Many business startups find it difficult to earn income in their first year. They do well just to limit their losses and stay in business. Of course, I'll need to carefully review all your sales and expense projections with you, in order to make sure that they are realistic. But first, do you have any questions about the projected income statement?

Pat: I understand the general idea. But what does "gross profit" mean?

Kim: It's the usual accounting term for sales less the amount that your suppliers charged you for the goods that you sold to your customers. In other words, it represents your markup from the wholesale cost you paid for goods and the price for which you sold those goods to your customers. It is called "gross profit" because your operating expenses have to be deducted from it. In accounting, the word *gross* means "before deductions." For example "gross sales" means sales before deducting goods returned by customers. Sales after deducting goods returned by customers are referred to as "net sales." In accounting, the word *net* means "after deductions." So "gross profit" means income before deducting operating expenses. By the same token, "net income" means income after deducting operating expenses and income taxes. Now, moving along, we are ready to figure out your projected balance sheet at the end of your first year in business. But first I need to ask you how much cash you plan to draw out of the business as your compensation?

Pat: My present job pays $76,000 a year. I'd like to keep the same standard of compensation in my new business this coming year.

Kim: Let's see how that works out after we've completed the projected balance sheet at the end of year 1. Here it is on my computer screen:

Nutrivite

Projected Balance Sheet as of December 31, 200X

Assets			Liabilities and Equity	
Cash		$ 35,600	Bank loan	$ 40,000
Inventory		80,000		
Current assets		115,600	Current liabilities	40,000
Fixed assets:			Equity:	
Equipment	$36,000		Capital: Jan 1	100,000
Less depreciation	3,600		Add net income	84,000
Net equipment	$32,400	32,400	Less drawings	(76,000)
			Capital: Dec 31	108,000
Total assets		$148,000	Liabilities and equity	$148,000

Let's go over this balance sheet together, Pat. It has changed compared to the balance sheet as of January 1. On the Liabilities and Equity side of the balance sheet, the Net Income of $84,000 has increased Capital to $184,000 (because earning income adds to the owner's Capital), and deducting Drawings of $76,000 has reduced Capital to $108,000 (because Drawings take Capital out of the business). On the asset side, notice that the Equipment now has a year of depreciation deducted, which writes it down from the original $36,000 to a net (there's that word *net* again) $32,400 after depreciation. The Equipment had an expected useful life of 10 years, now reduced to a remaining life of 9 years. Last but not least, notice that the Cash has increased by $11,600 from $24,000 at the beginning of the year to $35,600 at year-end. This leads to a problem: The Bank Loan of $40,000 is due for repayment on December 31. But there is only $35,600 in Cash available on December 31. How can the Loan be paid off when there is not enough Cash to do so?

Pat: I see the problem. But I think it's bigger than just paying off the loan. The business will also need to keep about $25,000 cash on hand to cover two months operating expenses and income taxes. So, with $40,000 to repay the loan plus $25,000 for operating expenses, the cash requirements add up to $65,000. But there is only $35,600 cash on hand. This leaves a cash shortage of almost $30,000 ($65,000 less $35,600). Do you think that will force me to cut down my drawings by $30,000, from $76,000 to $45,000? Here I am opening my own business, and it looks as if I have to go back to what I was earning five years ago!

Kim: That's one way to do it. But here's another way that you might like better. After your suppliers get to know you and do business with you for a few months, you can ask them to open credit accounts for Nutrivite. If you get the customary 30-day credit terms, then your suppliers will be financing one month's inventory. That amounts to one-twelfth of your $480,000 annual cost of goods sold, or $40,000. This $40,000 will more than cover the cash shortage of $30,000.

Pat: That's a perfect solution! Now, can we see how the balance sheet would look in this case?

Kim: Sure. When you pay off the Bank Loan, it vanishes from the balance sheet. It is replaced by Accounts Payable of $40,000. Then the balance sheet looks like this:

Nutrivite

Projected Balance Sheet as of December 31, 200X

Assets			Liabilities and Equity	
Cash		$ 35,600	Accounts payable	$ 40,000
Inventory		80,000		
Current assets		115,600	Current liabilities	40,000
Fixed assets:			Equity:	
Equipment	$36,000		Capital: Jan 1	100,000
Less depreciation	3,600		Add net income	84,000
Net equipment	$32,400	32,400	Less drawings	(76,000)
			Capital: Dec 31	108,000
Total assets		$148,000	Liabilities and equity	$148,000

Now the cash position looks a lot better. But it hasn't been entirely solved: There is still a gap between the Accounts Payable of $40,000 and the Cash of $35,600. So you will need to cut your drawings by about $5,000 in year 1. But that's still much better than the cut of $30,000 that had seemed necessary before. In year 2 the Bank Loan will be gone, so the interest expense of $6,000 will be saved. Then you can use $5,000 of this saving to restore your drawings back up to $76,000 again.

Pat: That's good news. I'm beginning to see how useful projected financial statements are for business planning. Can we look at the revised projected balance sheet now?

Kim: Of course. Here it is:

Nutrivite

Projected Balance Sheet as of December 31, 200X

Assets			Liabilities and Equity	
Cash		$ 40,600	Accounts payable	$ 40,000
Inventory		80,000		
Current assets		120,600	Current liabilities	40,000
Fixed assets:			Equity:	
Equipment	$36,000		Capital: Jan 1	100,000
Less depreciation	3,600		Add net income	84,000
Net equipment	$32,400	32,400	Less drawings	(71,000)
			Capital: Dec 31	113,000
Total assets		$153,000	Liabilities and equity	$153,000

As you can see, Cash is increased by $5,000 to $40,600—which is sufficient to pay the Accounts Payable of $40,000. Drawings is decreased by $5,000 to $71,000, which provided the $5,000 increase in Cash.

Pat: Thanks. That makes sense. I really appreciate everything you've taught me about financial statements.

Kim: I'm happy to help. But there is one more financial statement to discuss. Besides the balance sheet and income statement, a full set of financial statements also includes a cash flow statement. Here is the projected cash flow statement:

Nutrivite

*Projected Cash Flow Statement for the
Year Ending December 31, 200X*

Sources of Cash			
From Operations:			
Net income		$ 84,000	
Add depreciation		3,600	
Add increase in current liabilities		40,000	
Total cash from operations	(a)	$ 127,600	
From Financing:			
Drawings		$ (71,000)	*Negative cash*
Bank loan repaid		(40,000)	*Negative cash*
Net cash from financing	(b)	(111,000)	*Negative cash*
Total sources of cash	(a + b)	$ 16,600	

Uses of Cash

Total uses of cash	0	
Total sources less total uses of cash	$ 16,600	Net cash increase
Add cash at beginning of year	24,000	
Cash at end of year	$ 40,600	

Pat, do you have any questions about this Cash Flow Statement?

Pat: Actually, it makes sense to me. I realize that there are only two sources that a business can tap in order to generate cash: internal (by earning income) and external (by obtaining cash from outside sources, such as bank loans). In our case the internal sources of cash are represented by the "Cash from Operations" section of the Cash Flow Statement, and the external sources are represented by the "Cash from Financing" section. It happens that the "Cash from Financing" is negative because no additional outside financing is received for the year 200X, but cash payments are incurred for Drawings and for repayment of the Bank Loan. I also understand that there are no "Uses of Cash" because no extra Equipment was acquired. In addition, I can see that the Total Sources of Cash less the Total Uses of Cash must equal the Increase in Cash, which in turn is the Cash at the end of the year less the Cash at the beginning of the year. But I am puzzled by the "Cash from Operations" section of the Cash Flow Statement. I can understand that earning income produces Cash. However why do we add back Depreciation to the Net Income in order to calculate Cash from Operations?

Kim: This can be confusing, so let me explain. Certainly Net Income increases Cash, but first an adjustment has to be made in order to convert Net Income to a cash basis. Depreciation was deducted as an expense in figuring Net Income. So adding back depreciation to Net Income just reverses the charge for depreciation expense. We back it out because depreciation is *not* a cash outflow. Remember that depreciation represents just one year's use of the Equipment. The cash outflow for purchasing the Equipment was incurred back when the Equipment was first acquired and amounted to $36,000. The Equipment cost of $36,000 is spread out over the 10-year life of the Equipment at the rate of $3,600 per year, which we call Depreciation expense. So it would be double counting to recognize the $36,000 cash outflow for the Equipment when it was originally acquired and then to recognize it a second time when it shows up as Depreciation expense. We do not write a check to pay for Depreciation each year, because it is not a cash outflow.

Pat: Thanks. Now I understand that Depreciation is not a cash outflow. But I don't see why we also added back the Increase in Current Liabilities to the Net Income to calculate Cash from Operations. Can you explain that?

Kim: Of course. The increase in Current Liabilities is caused by an increase in Accounts Payable. These Accounts Payable are amounts owed to our suppliers for our purchases of goods for resale in our business. Purchasing goods for resale from our suppliers on credit is not a cash outflow. The cash outflow only occurs when the goods are actually paid for by writing out checks to our suppliers. That is why we added back the Increase in Current Liabilities to the Net Income in order to calculate Cash from Operations. In the future, the Increase in Current Liabilities will, in fact, be paid in cash. But that will take place in the future and is not a cash outflow in this year. Going back to the Cash Flow Statement, notice that it ties in neatly with our balance sheet amount for Cash. It shows how the Cash at the beginning of the year plus the Net Cash Increase equals the Cash at the end of the year.

Pat: Now I get it. Am I right that you are going to review my projections and then I'll hear from you about my loan application?

Kim: Yes, I'll be back to you in a few days. By the way, would you like a print-out of the projected financial statements to take with you?

Pat: Yes, please. I really appreciate your putting them together and explaining them to me. I picked up some financial skills that will be very useful to me as an aspiring entrepreneur.

POINTS TO REMEMBER ABOUT FINANCIAL STATEMENTS

When Pat arrived home, she carefully reviewed the projected financial statements, then made notes about what she had learned.

1. The basic form of the balance sheet is Assets = Liabilities + Owner Equity.

2. Assets are the expenditures made for items, such as Inventory and Equipment, that are needed to operate the business. The Liabilities and Owner Equity reflect the funds that financed the expenditures for the Assets.

3. Balance sheets show the financial position of a business at a given moment in time.

4. Balance sheets change as transactions are recorded.

5. Every transaction is an exchange, and both sides of each transaction are recorded. For example, when a company obtains a bank loan, there is an increase in the asset cash that is matched by an increase in a liability entitled "Bank Loan." When the loan is repaid, there is a decrease in cash which is matched by a decrease in the Bank Loan liability. After every transaction, the balance sheet stays in balance.

6. Income increases Owner Equity, and Drawings decrease Owner Equity.

7. The income statement shows how income for the period was earned.

8. The basic form of the income statement is:

    a. Sales − Cost of Goods Sold = Gross Income.

    b. Gross Income − Expenses = Net Income.

9. The income statement is simply a detailed explanation of the increase in Owner Equity represented by Net Income. It shows how the Owner Equity increased from the beginning of the year to the end of the year because of the Net Income.

10. Net Income contributes to Cash from Operations after it has been adjusted to a cash basis.

11. Not all expenses are cash outflows—for instance, Depreciation.

12. Changes in Current Assets (except Cash) and Current Liabilities are not cash outflows nor inflows in the period under consideration. They represent future, not present, cash flows.

13. Cash can be generated internally by operations or externally from sources such as lenders or equity investors.

14. The Cash Flow Statement is simply a detailed explanation of how cash at the start developed into cash at the end by virtue of cash inflows, generated internally and externally, less cash outflows.

15. As previously noted:

    a. The Income Statement is an elaboration of the change in Owner Equity in the Balance Sheet caused by earning income.

    b. The Cash Flow Statement is an elaboration of the Balance-Sheet change in beginning and ending Cash.

    Therefore, all three financial statements are interrelated or, to use the technical term, "articulated." They are mutually consistent, and that is why they are referred to as a "set" of financial statements. The three-piece set consists of a balance sheet, income statement, and cash flow statement.

16. A set of financial statements can convey much valuable information about the enterprise to anyone who knows how to analyze them. This information goes to the core of the organization's business strategy and the effectiveness of its management.

While Pat was making her notes, Kim was carefully analyzing the Nutrivite projected financial statements in order to make her recommendation to the bank's loan committee about Nutrivite's loan application. She paid special attention to the Cash Flow Statement, keeping handy the bank's guidelines on cash flow analysis, which included the following issues:

- Is cash from operations positive? Is it growing over time? Is it keeping pace with growth in sales? If not, why not?

- Are cash withdrawals by owners only a small portion of cash from operations? If owners' cash withdrawals are a large share of cash from operations, then the business is conceivably being milked of cash and may not be able to finance its future growth.

- Of the total sources of cash, how much is being internally generated by operations versus obtained from outside sources? Normally wise businesses rely more on internally generated cash for growth than on external financing.
- Of the outside financing, how much is derived from equity investors and how much is borrowed? Normally, a business should rely more on equity than debt financing.
- What kind of assets is the company acquiring with the cash being expended? Are these asset expenditures likely to be profitable? How long will it take for these assets to repay their cost and then to earn a reasonable return?

Kim reflected carefully on these issues and then finalized her recommendation, which was to approve the loan. The bank's loan committee accepted Kim's recommendation and even went further. They authorized Kim to tell Pat that—if she met all her responsibilities in regard to the loan throughout the year—the bank would renew the loan at the end of the year and even increase the amount. Kim called Pat with the good news. Their conversation included the following dialogue:

Kim: To renew the loan, the bank will ask you for new projected financial statements for the subsequent year. Also, the loan agreement will require you to submit financial statements for the year just past—that is, not projected but actual financial statements. The bank will require that these actual financial statements be reviewed by an independent CPA before you submit them.

Pat: Let me be sure I understand: Projected financial statements are forward-looking, whereas actual financial statements are backward looking, is that correct?

Kim: Yes, that's right.

Pat: Next, what is an independent CPA?

Kim: As you probably know, a CPA is a certified public accountant, a professional trained in finance and accounting and licensed by the state. *Independent* means a CPA who is not an employee of yours or a relative. It means someone in public practice in a CPA firm, someone who will likely make an objective and unbiased evaluation of your financial statements.

Pat: And what does *reviewed* mean?

Kim: Good question. CPAs offer three levels of service relating to financial statements:

- An *audit* is a thorough, in-depth examination of the financial statements and test of the supporting records. The result is an audit report, which states whether the financial statements are free of material misstatements (whether caused by error or fraud). A "clean" audit report provides assurance that the financial statements are free of material misstatements. A "modified" report gives no such assurance and is cause for concern. Financial professionals always read the auditor's report first, even before looking at any financial statement, to see if the report is clean. The auditor is a watchdog, and this watchdog barks by issuing a modified audit report. By law all companies that have publicly traded securities must have their financial statements audited as a protection to investors, creditors, and other financial statement users. Private companies are not required by law to have audits, but sometimes particular investors or creditors demand them. An audit provides the highest level of assurance that a CPA can provide and is the most expensive level of service. Less expensive and less thorough levels of service include the following.

- A *review* is a less extensive and less expensive level of financial statement inspection by a CPA. It provides a lower level of assurance that the financial statements are free of material misstatements.

- Finally, the lowest level of service is called a *compilation,* where the outside CPA puts together the financial statements from the client company's books and records without examining them in much depth. A compilation provides the least assurance and is the least expensive level of service.

So the bank is asking you for the middle level of assurance when it requires a review by an independent CPA. Banks usually require a review from borrowers that are smaller private businesses.

Pat: Thanks. That makes it very clear.

We now leave Pat and Kim to their successful loan transaction and move on.

FINANCIAL STATEMENTS: WHO USES THEM AND WHY

Here is a brief list of who uses financial statements and why. This list gives only a few examples and is by no means complete.

1. Existing equity investors and lenders, to monitor their investments and to evaluate the performance of management.
2. Prospective equity investors and lenders, to decide whether or not to invest.
3. Investment analysts, money managers, and stockbrokers, to make buy/sell/hold recommendations to their clients.
4. Rating agencies (such as Moody's, Standard & Poor's, and Dun & Bradstreet), to assign credit ratings.
5. Major customers and suppliers, to evaluate the financial strength and staying power of the company as a dependable resource for their business.

6. Labor unions, to gauge how much of a pay increase a company is able to afford in upcoming labor negotiations.
7. Boards of directors, to review the performance of management.
8. Management, to assess its own performance.
9. Corporate raiders, to seek hidden value in companies with underpriced stock.
10. Competitors, to benchmark their own financial results.
11. Potential competitors, to assess how profitable it may be to enter an industry.
12. Government agencies responsible for taxing, regulating, or investigating the company.
13. Politicians, lobbyists, issue groups, consumer advocates, environmentalists, think tanks, foundations, media reporters, and others who are supporting or opposing any particular public issue the company's actions affect.
14. Actual or potential joint venture partners, franchisors or franchisees, and other business interests who need to know about the company and its financial situation.

This brief list shows how many people and institutions use financial statements for a large variety of business purposes and suggests how essential the ability to understand and analyze financial statements is to success in the business world.

FINANCIAL STATEMENT FORMAT

Financial statements have a standard format whether an enterprise is as small as Nutrivite or as large as a major corporation. For example, a recent set of financial statements for Microsoft Corporation can be summarized in millions of dollars as follows:

Income Statement

Years Ended June 30	XXX1	XXX2	XXX3
Revenue	$15,262	$19,747	$22,956
Cost of revenue	2,460	2,814	3,002
Research and development	2,601	2,970	3,775
Other expenses	3,787	4,035	5,242
Total expenses	$ 8,848	$ 9,819	$12,019
Operating income	$ 6,414	$ 9,928	$10,937
Investment income	703	1,963	3,338
Income before income taxes	7,117	11,891	14,275
Income taxes	2,627	4,106	4,854
Net income	$ 4,490	$ 7,785	$ 9,421

Cash Flow Statement

Years Ended June 30	XXX1	XXX2	XXX3
Operations			
Net income	$ 4,490	$ 7,785	$ 9,421
Adjustments to convert net income to cash basis	3,943	5,352	4,540
Cash from operations	$ 8,433	$ 13,137	$ 13,961
Financing			
Stock repurchased, net	$(1,509)	$ (1,600)	$ (2,651)
Stock warrants sold	538	766	472
Preferred stock dividends	(28)	(28)	(13)
Cash from financing	$ (999)	$ (862)	$ (2,192)
Investing			
Additions to property and equipment	$ (656)	$ (583)	$ (879)
Net additions to investments	(6,616)	(10,608)	(11,048)
Net cash invested	$(7,272)	$ (11,191)	$(11,927)
Net change in cash	162	1,084	(158)

Balance Sheet

Years Ended June 30	XXX2	XXX3
Current Assets		
Cash and equivalents	$ 4,975	$ 4,846
Short-term investments	12,261	18,952
Accounts receivable	2,245	3,250
Other	2,221	3,260
Total current assets	$21,702	$30,308
Property and equipment, net	$ 1,611	$ 1,903
Investments	15,312	19,939
Total fixed assets	$16,923	$21,842
Total assets	$38,625	$52,150
Current Liabilities		
Accounts payable	$ 874	$ 1,083
Other	7,928	8,672
Total current liabilities	8,802	9,755
Noncurrent liabilities	1,385	1,027
Total liabilities	$10,187	$10,782
Preferred stock	$ 980	
Common stock	13,844	$23,195
Retained earnings	13,614	18,173
Total equity	$28,438	$41,368
Total liabilities and equity	$38,625	$52,150

Note: There are only two years of balance sheets but three years of income statements and cash flow statements. This is because the Microsoft financial statements above were obtained from filings with the U.S. Securities and Exchange Commission (SEC), and the SEC requirements for corporate annual report filings are two years of balance sheets, plus three years of income statements and cash flow statements.

The Microsoft financial statements contain numbers very much greater than those for Nutrivite. But there is no difference in the general format of these two sets of financial statements.

HOW TO ANALYZE FINANCIAL STATEMENTS

Imagine that you are a nurse or a physician and you work in the emergency room of a busy hospital. Patients arrive with all kinds of serious injuries or illnesses, barely alive or perhaps even dead. Others arrive with less urgent injuries, minor complaints, or vaguely suspected ailments. Your training and experience have taught you to perform a quick triage, to prioritize the most endangered patients by their vital signs—respiration, pulse, blood pressure, temperature, and reflexes. A more detailed diagnosis follows based on more thorough medical tests.

We check the financial health of a company in much the same fashion by analyzing the financial statements. The vital signs are tested mostly by various financial ratios that are calculated from the financial statements. These vital signs can be classified into three main categories:

1. Short-term liquidity.
2. Long-term solvency.
3. Profitability.

We explain each of these three categories in turn.

SHORT-TERM LIQUIDITY

In the emergency room the first question is: Can this patient survive? Similarly, the first issue in analyzing financial statements is: Can this company survive? Business survival means being able to pay the bills, meet the payroll, and come up with the rent. In other words, is there enough liquidity to provide the cash needed to pay current financial commitments? "Yes" means survival. "No" means bankruptcy. The urgency of this question is why current assets (which are expected to turn into cash within a year) and current liabilities (which are expected to be paid in cash within a year) are shown separately on the balance sheet. Net current assets (current assets less current liabilities) is known as *working capital*. Because most businesses cannot operate without positive working capital, the question of whether current assets exceed current liabilities is crucial.

When current assets are greater than current liabilities, there is sufficient liquidity to enable the enterprise to survive. However, when current liabilities exceed current assets the enterprise may well be in immanent danger of bankruptcy. The financial ratio used to measure this risk is current assets divided by current liabilities, and is known as the *current ratio*. It is expressed as "2.5 to 1" or "2.5:1" or just "2.5." Keeping the current ratio from dropping below 1 is the bare minimum to indicate survival, but it lacks any margin of safety. A company must maintain a reasonable margin of safety, or cushion, because the current ratio, like all financial ratios, is only a rough approximation. For this reason, in most cases a current ratio of 2 or more just begins to provide credible evidence of liquidity.

An example of a current ratio can be found in the current sections of the balance sheets shown earlier in this chapter:

Nutrivite

Selected Sections of Projected Balance Sheet
as of December 31, 200X

Assets		Liabilities and Equity	
Cash	$ 40,600	Accounts payable	$40,000
Inventory	80,000		
Current assets	$120,600	Current liabilities	$40,000

The current ratio is 120,600/40,000, or 3. This is only a rough approximation for several reasons. First, a company can, quite legitimately, improve its current ratio. In the earlier case of Nutrivite, assume the business wanted its balance sheet to reflect a higher current ratio. One way to do so would be to pay off $20,000 on the bank loan on December 31. This would reduce current assets to $100,600 and current liabilities to $20,000. Then the current ratio is changed to $100,600/$20,000, or 5. By perfectly legitimate means, the current ratio has been improved from 3 to 5. This technique is widely used by companies that want to put their best foot forward in the balance sheet, and it always works provided that the current ratio was greater than 1 to start with.

Current assets usually include:

- Cash and Cash Equivalents.
- Securities expected to become liquid by maturing or being sold within a year.
- Accounts Receivable (which Nutrivite did not have, because it did not sell to its customers on credit).
- Inventory.

Current liabilities usually include:

- Accounts Payable.
- Other current payables, such as taxes, wages, or insurance.
- The current portion of long-term debt.

Some items included in Current Assets need a further explanation. These are:

- Cash Equivalents are near-cash securities such as U.S. Treasury bills maturing in three months or less.

- Accounts Receivable are amounts owed by customers and should be reported on the balance sheet at "realizable value," which means "the amount reasonably expected to be collected in cash." Any accounts whose collectibility is in doubt must be reduced to realizable value by deducting an allowance for doubtful debts.

- Inventories in some cases may not be liquid in a crisis (except at fire-sale prices). This condition is especially likely for goods of a perishable, seasonal, high-fashion, or trendy nature or items subject to technological obsolescence, such as computers. Since inventory can readily lose value, it must be reported on the balance sheet at the "lower of cost or market value," or what the inventory cost to acquire (including freight and insurance), or the cost of replacement, or the expected selling price less costs of sale—whichever is lowest.

  Despite these requirements designed to report inventory at a realistic amount, inventory is regarded as an asset subject to inherent liquidity risk, especially in difficult economic times and especially for items that are perishable, seasonal, high-fashion, trendy, or subject to obsolescence. For these reasons the current ratio is often modified by excluding inventory to get what is called the *quick ratio* or *acid test ratio:*

$$\text{Quick Ratio} = \left(\frac{\text{Current Assets} - \text{Inventory}}{\text{Current Liabilities}} \right)$$

- In the case of Nutrivite, the quick ratio as of December 31 is \$40,600/\$40,000, or 1. This indicates that Nutrivite has a barely adequate quick ratio, with no margin of safety at all. It is a red flag or warning signal.

The current ratio and the quick ratio deal with all or most of the current assets and current liabilities. There are also short-term liquidity ratios that focus more narrowly on individual components of current assets and current liabilities. These are the *turnover ratios,* which consist of:

- Accounts Receivable Turnover.
- Inventory Turnover.
- Accounts Payable Turnover.

Turnover, which means "making liquid," is a key factor in liquidity. Faster turnover allows a company to do more business without increasing assets. Increased turnover means that less cash is tied up in assets, and that improves liquidity. Moving to the other side of the balance sheet, slower turnover of liabilities conserves cash and thereby increases liquidity. Or more simply, achieving better turnover of working capital can significantly improve liquidity. Turnover ratios thus provide valuable information. The working capital turnover ratios are described next.

Accounts Receivable Turnover

The equation is:

$$\text{Accounts Receivable Turnover} = \frac{\text{Credit Sales}}{\text{Accounts Receivable}}$$

So, if Credit Sales are $120,000 and Accounts Receivable are $30,000, then

$$\text{Accounts Receivable Turnover} = \frac{\$120,000}{\$30,000} = 4$$

On average, Accounts Receivable turn over 4 times a year, or every 91 days.

The 91-day turnover period is found by dividing a year, 365 days, by the Accounts Receivable Turnover ratio of 4. This average of 91 days is how long it takes to collect Accounts Receivable. That is fine if our credit terms call for payment 90 days from invoice but not fine if credit terms are 60 days, and it is alarming if credit terms are 30 days.

Accounts Receivable, unlike vintage wines or antiques, do not improve with age. Accounts Receivable Turnover should be in line with credit terms; turnover sliding out of line with credit terms signals increasing danger to liquidity.

Inventory Turnover

Inventory turnover is computed as follows:

$$\text{Inventory Turnover} = \frac{\text{Cost of Goods Sold}}{\text{Inventory}}$$

If Cost of Goods Sold is $100,000 and Inventory is $20,000, then

$$\text{Inventory Turnover} = \frac{\$100,000}{\$20,000} = 5 \text{ times a year}$$

or about 70 days. Note that the numerator for calculating Accounts Receivable Turnover is Credit Sales but for Inventory Turnover is Cost of Goods Sold. The reason is that both Accounts Receivable and Sales are measured in terms of the selling price of the goods involved. That makes Accounts Receivable Turnover a consistent ratio, where the numerator and denominator are both expressed at selling prices in an "apples-to-apples" manner. Inventory Turnover is also an "apples-to-apples" comparison in that both numerator, Cost of Goods Sold, and denominator, Inventory, are expressed in terms of the cost, not the selling price, of the goods.

In our example, the Inventory Turnover was 5, or about 70 days. Whether this is good or bad depends on industry standards. Companies in the auto-retailing or the furniture-manufacturing industry would accept this ratio. In the supermarket business or in gasoline retailing, however, 5 would fall far below their norm of about 25 times a year, or roughly every 2 weeks. As with Accounts Receivable Turnover, an Inventory Turnover that is out of line is a red flag.

Accounts Payable Turnover

This measure's equation is:

$$\text{Accounts Payable Turnover} = \frac{\text{Cost of Goods Sold}}{\text{Accounts Payable}}$$

If Cost of Goods Sold is $100,000 and Accounts Payable is $16,600, then

$$\text{Accounts Payable Turnover} = \frac{\$100,000}{\$16,600}$$

which is about 6, or around 60 days. Again, note the consistency of the numerator and denominator, both stated at the cost of the goods purchased. Accounts Payable Turnover is evaluated by comparison with industry norms. An Accounts Payable Turnover that is appreciably faster than the industry norm is fine, if liquidity is satisfactory, because prompt payments to suppliers usually earn cash discounts, which in turn lower the Cost of Goods Sold and thus lead to higher income. However, such faster-than-normal Accounts Payable Turnover does diminish liquidity and is therefore unwise when liquidity is tight. Accounts Payable Turnover that is slower than the industry norm enhances liquidity and is therefore wise when liquidity is tight but inadvisable when liquidity is fine, because it sacrifices cash discounts from suppliers and thus reduces income.

This concludes our survey of the ratios relating to short-term liquidity—the current ratio; quick, or acid test, ratio; Accounts Receivable Turnover; Inventory Turnover; and Accounts Payable Turnover.

If these ratios are seriously deficient, our diagnosis may be complete. The subject business may be almost defunct, and even desperate measures may be insufficient to revive it. If these ratios are favorable, then short-term liquidity does not appear to be a threat and the financial doctor should proceed to the next set of tests, which measure long-term solvency.

It is worth noting, however, that there are some rare exceptions to these guidelines. For example, large gas and electric utilities typically have current ratios less than 1 and quick ratios less than 0.5. This is due to utilities' exceptional characteristics:

- They usually require deposits before providing service to customers, and they can shut off service to customers who do not pay on time. Customers are reluctant to go without necessities such as gas and electricity and therefore tend to pay their utility bills ahead of most other bills. These factors sharply reduce the risk of uncollectible accounts receivable for gas and electric utility companies.

- Inventories of gas and electric utility companies are not subject to much risk from changing fashion trends, deterioration, or obsolescence.
- Under regulation, gas and electric utility companies are stable, low-risk businesses, largely free from competition and consistently profitable.

This reduced risk and increased predictability of gas and electric utility companies make short-term liquidity and safety margins less crucial. In turn, the ratios indicating short-term liquidity become less important, because short-term survival is not a significant concern for these businesses.

LONG-TERM SOLVENCY

Long-term solvency focuses on a firm's ability to pay the interest and principal on its long-term debt. There are two commonly used ratios relating to servicing long-term debt. One measures ability to pay interest, the other the ability to repay the principal. The ratio for interest compares the amount of income available for paying interest with the amount of the interest expense. This ratio is called Interest Coverage or Times Interest Earned.

The amount of income available for paying interest is simply earnings before interest and before income taxes. (Business interest expense is deductible for income tax purposes; therefore, income taxes are based on earnings after interest, otherwise known as earnings before income taxes.) Earnings before interest and taxes is known as EBIT. The ratio for Interest Coverage or Times Interest Earned is EBIT/Interest Expense. For instance, assume that EBIT is $120,000 and interest expense is $60,000. Then:

$$\text{Interest Coverage or Times Interest Earned} = \frac{\$120,000}{\$60,000} = 2$$

This shows that the business has EBIT sufficient to cover 2 times its interest expense. The cushion, or margin of safety, is therefore quite substantial. Whether a given interest coverage ratio is acceptable depends on the industry. Different industries have different degrees of year-to-year fluctuations in EBIT. Interest coverage of 2 times may be satisfactory for a steady and mature firm in an industry with stable earnings, such as regulated gas and electricity supply. However, when the same industry experiences the uncertain forces of deregulation, earnings may become volatile, and interest coverage of 2 may prove to be inadequate. In more-turbulent industries, such as movie studios and Internet retailers, an interest coverage of 2 may be regarded as insufficient.

The long-term solvency ratio that reflects a firm's ability to repay principal on long-term debt is the "Debt to Equity" ratio. The long-term capital structure of a firm is made up principally of two types of financing: (1) long-term debt and (2) owner equity. Some hybrid forms of financing mix characteristics of debt and equity but usually can be classified as mainly debt or equity in nature. Therefore the distinction between debt and equity is normally clear.

If long-term debt is $150,000 and equity is $300,000, then the debt-equity relationship is usually measured as:

$$\text{Debt to Equity Ratio} = \frac{\text{Long-Term Debt}}{\text{Long-Term Debt} + \text{Equity}}$$

$$= \frac{\$150,000}{(\$150,000 + \$300,000)}$$

$$= 33 \tfrac{1}{3}\%$$

Long-term debt is frequently secured by liens on property and has priority on payment of periodic interest and repayment of principal. There is no priority for equity, however, for dividend payments or return of capital to owners. Holders of long-term debt thus have a high degree of security in receiving full and punctual payments of interest and principal. But, in good times or bad, whether income is high or low, long-term creditors are entitled to receive no more than these fixed amounts. They have reduced their risk of gain or loss in exchange for more certainty. By contrast, owners of equity enjoy no such certainty. They are entitled to nothing except dividends, if declared, and, in the case of bankruptcy, whatever funds might be left over after all obligations have been paid. Theirs is a totally at-risk investment. They prosper in good times and suffer in bad times. They accept these risks in the hope that in the long run gains will substantially exceed losses.

From the firm's point of view, long-term debt obligations are a burden that must be carried whether income is low, absent, or even negative. But long-term debt obligations are a blessing when income is lush since they receive no more than their fixed payments, even if incomes soar. The greater the proportion of long-term debt and smaller the proportion of equity in the capital structure, the more the incomes of the equity holders will fluctuate according to how good or bad times are. The proportion of long-term debt to equity is known as leverage. The greater the proportion of long-term debt to equity, the more leveraged the firm is considered to be. The more leveraged the firm is, the more equity holders prosper in good times and the worse they fare in bad times. Because increased leverage leads to increased volatility of incomes, increased leverage is regarded as an indicator of increased risk, though a moderate degree of leverage is thus considered desirable. The debt-to-equity ratio is evaluated according to industry standards and each industry's customary volatility of earnings. For example, a debt-to-equity ratio of 80% would be considered conservative in banking (where leverage is customarily above 80% and earnings are relatively stable) but would be regarded as extremely risky for toy manufacturing or designer apparel (where earnings are more volatile). The well-known junk bonds are an example of long-term debt securities where leverage is considered too high in relation to earnings volatility. The increased risk associated with junk bonds explains their higher interest yields. This illustrates the general financial principle that the greater the risk, the higher the expected return.

In summary, the ratios used to assess long-term solvency are Interest Coverage and Long-Term Debt to Equity.

Next, we consider the ratios for analyzing profitability.

PROFITABILITY

Profitability is the lifeblood of a business. Businesses that earn incomes can survive, grow, and prosper. Businesses that incur losses cannot stay in operation, and will last only until their cash runs out. Therefore, in order to assess business viability, it is important to analyze profitability.

When analyzing profitability, it is usually done in two phases, which are:

1. Profitability in relation to sales.
2. Profitability in relation to investment.

Profitability in Relation to Sales

The analysis of profitability in relation to sales recognizes the fact that:

$$Income = Sales - Expenses$$

or, rearranging terms:

$$Sales = Expenses + Income$$

Therefore, Expenses and Income are measured in relation to their sum, which is Sales. The expenses, in turn, may be broken down by line item. As an example, we use the Nutrivite Income Statement for the first three years of operation.

Income Statements for the Years Ending December 31

	Year 1	Year 2	Year 3
Sales	$720,000	$800,000	$900,000
Less cost of goods sold	480,000	530,000	600,000
Gross profit	$240,000	$270,000	$300,000
Less expenses			
Salaries	$ 40,000	$ 49,600	$ 69,000
Rent	36,000	49,400	54,400
Phone and utilities	14,400	19,400	26,000
Depreciation	3,600	3,600	3,600
Interest	6,000	6,000	6,000
Total expenses	$100,000	$128,000	$159,000
Income before taxes	$140,000	$142,000	$141,000
Income tax expense (40%)	56,000	56,800	56,400
Net income	$ 84,000	$ 85,200	$ 84,600

These income statements show a steady increase in Sales and Gross Profits each year. Despite this favorable result, the Net Income has remained virtually unchanged at about $84,000 for each year. To learn why this is the case, we need to convert expenses and income to percentages of sales. The income statements converted to percentages of sales are known as "common size" income statements and look like the following:

Common Size Income Statements for the Years Ending December 31

	Year 1	Year 2	Year 3	Change Years 1–3
Sales	100.0%	100.0%	100.0%	0.0%
Less cost of goods sold	66.7	66.2	66.7	0.0
Gross profit	33.3%	33.8%	33.3%	0.0%
Less expenses				
Salaries	5.6%	6.2%	7.7%	2.1%
Rent	5.0	6.2	6.0	1.0
Phone and utilities	2.0	2.4	2.9	0.9
Depreciation	0.5	0.4	0.4	−0.1
Interest	0.8	0.8	0.7	−0.1
Total expenses	13.9%	16.0%	17.7%	3.8%
Income before taxes	19.4%	17.8%	15.6%	−3.8%
Income tax expense (40%)	7.8	7.2	6.2	−1.6
Net income	11.6%	10.6%	9.4%	−2.2%

From the percentage figures above it is easy to see why the Net Income failed to increase, despite the substantial growth in Sales and Gross Profit. Total Expenses rose by 3.8 percentage points, from 13.9% of Sales in Year 1 to 17.7% of Sales in Year 3. In particular, the increase in Total Expenses relative to Sales was driven mainly by increases in Salaries (2.1 percentage points), Rent (1 percentage point) and Phone and Utilities (0.9 percentage point). As a result, Income before Taxes relative to Sales fell by 3.8 percentage points from Year 1 to Year 3. The good news is that the drop in Income before Taxes caused a reduction of Income Tax Expense relative to Sales of 1.6 percentage points from Year 1 to Year 3. The net effect was a drop in Net Income, relative to Sales, of 2.2 percentage points from Year 1 to Year 3.

This useful information shows that:

1. The profit stagnation is not related to Sales or Gross Profit.
2. It is entirely due to the disproportionate increase in Total Expenses.
3. Specific causes are the expenses for Salaries, Rent, and Phone and Utilities.
4. Action to correct the profit slump requires analyzing these particular expense categories.

The use of percent-of-sales ratios is a simple but powerful technique for analyzing profitability. Generally used ratios include:

- Gross Profit.
- Operating Expenses:
  a. In total.
  b. Individually.
- Selling, General, and Administrative Expenses (often called SG&A).
- Operating Income.
- Income before Taxes.
- Net Income.

The second category of profitability ratios is profitability in relation to investment.

Profitability in Relation to Investment

To earn profits, usually a firm must invest capital in items such as plant, equipment, inventory, and/or research and development. Up to this point we have analyzed profitability without considering invested capital. That was a useful simplification in the beginning, but, since profitability is highly dependent on the investment of capital, it is now time to bring invested capital into the analysis.

We start with the balance sheet. Recall that Working Capital is Current Assets less Current Liabilities. So we can simplify the balance sheet by including a single category for Working Capital in place of the separate categories for Current Assets and Current Liabilities. An example of a simplified balance sheet follows:

Example Company

Simplified Balance Sheet as of December 31, 200X

Assets		Liabilities and Equity	
Working capital	$ 40,000	Long-term debt	$ 30,000
Fixed assets, net	80,000	Equity	90,000
Total assets	$120,000	Liabilities and equity	$120,000

A simplified Income Statement for Example Company for the year 200X is summarized below:

Income before interest and taxes (EBIT)	$36,000
Less interest expense	3,000
Income before income taxes	33,000
Less income taxes (40%)	13,200
Net income	$19,800

The first ratio we will consider is EBIT (also known as Operating Profit) to Total Assets. This ratio is often referred to as Return on Total Assets (ROTA), and it can be expressed as either before tax (more usual) or after tax. From the Example Company, the calculations are as follows:

Return on Total Assets	Before Tax	After Tax
EBIT/total assets = $36,000/$120,000	30%	
EBIT/total assets = $21,600/$120,000		18%

This ratio indicates the raw (or basic) earning power of the business. Raw earning power is independent of whether assets are financed by equity or debt. This independence exists because:

1. The numerator (EBIT) is free of interest expense.
2. The denominator, Total Assets, is equal to total capital regardless of how much capital is equity and how much is debt.

Independence allows the ratio to be measured and compared:

- For any business, from one period to another.
- For any period, from one business to another.

These comparisons remain valid, even if the debt to equity ratio may vary from one period to the next and from one business to another.

Now that we have measured basic earning power regardless of the debt to equity ratio, our next step is to take the debt to equity ratio into consideration. First, it is important to note that long-term debt is normally a less expensive form of financing than equity because:

1. Whereas Dividends paid to stockholders are not a tax deduction for the paying company, Interest Expense paid on Long-Term Debt is. Therefore the net after-tax cost of Interest is reduced by the related tax deduction. This is not the case for Dividends, which are not deductible.
2. Debt is senior to equity, which means that debt obligations for interest and principal must be paid in full before making any payments on equity, such as dividends. This makes debt less risky than equity to the investors, and so debt holders are willing to accept a lower rate of return than holders of the riskier equity securities.

This contrast can be seen from the simplified financial statements of Example Company above. The interest of $3,000 on the Long-Term Debt of $30,000 is 10% before tax. But after the 40% tax deduction the interest after tax is only $1,800 ($3,000 – 40% tax on $3,000), and this $1,800 represents an after-tax interest rate of 6% on the Long-Term Debt of $30,000. For comparison let us turn to the rate of return on the Equity. The Net Income, $19,800, represents a 22% rate of return on the Equity of $90,000. This 22% rate of return is a financial ratio known as Return on Equity, sometimes abbreviated *ROE*. Return on Equity is an important and widely used financial ratio.

There is much more to be said about Return on Equity, but first it may be helpful to recap briefly the main points we have covered about profitability in relation to investment.

The EBIT of $36,000 represented a 30% return on total assets, before income tax, and this $36,000 was shared by three parties, as follows:

1. Long-Term Debt holders received Interest of $3,000, representing an interest cost of 10% before income tax, and 6% after income tax.
2. City, state, and/or federal governments were paid Income Taxes of $13,200.
3. Stockholder Equity increased by the Net Income of $19,800, which represented a 22% Return on Equity.

If there had been no Long-Term Debt, there would have been no Interest Expense. The EBIT of $36,000 less income tax at 40% would provide a Net Income of $21,600, which is larger than the prior Net Income of $19,800 by $1,800. This $1,800 equals the $3,000 amount of Interest before tax less the 40% tax, which is $1,200. In the absence of Long-Term Debt, the Total Assets would have been funded entirely by equity, which would have required equity to be $120,000. In turn, with Net Income of $21,600, the revised Return on Equity would be

$$\frac{\text{Net Income}}{\text{Equity}} = \frac{\$21,600}{\$120,000} = 18\%$$

The increase in the Return on Equity, from this 18% to 22% was attributable to the use of Long-Term Debt. The Long-Term Debt had a cost after taxes of only 6% versus the Return on Assets after tax of 18%. When a business earns 18% after tax, it is profitable to borrow at 6% after tax. This in turn improves the Return on Equity from 18% to 22%, which illustrates the advantage of leverage: A business earning 18% on assets can, with a little leverage, earn 22% on equity.

But what if EBIT is only $3,000? The entire $3,000 would be used up to pay the interest of $3,000 on the Long-Term Debt. The Net Income would be $0, resulting in a 0% Return on Equity. This illustrates the disadvantage of leverage. Without Long-Term Debt, the EBIT of $3,000 less 40% tax would result in Net Income of $1,800. Return on Equity would be $1,800 divided by equity of $120,000, which is 1.5%. A Return on Equity of 1.5% may not be impressive, but it is certainly better than the 0% that resulted with Long-Term Debt.

Leverage is a fair-weather friend: It boosts Return on Equity when earnings are robust but depresses ROE when earnings are poor. Leverage makes the good times better but the bad times worse. Therefore, it should be used in moderation and in businesses with stable earnings. In businesses with volatile earnings, leverage should be used sparingly and cautiously.

We have now described all of the main financial ratios, and they are summarized in Exhibit 1.1.

EXHIBIT 1.1   Summary of main financial ratios.

Ratio	Numerator	Denominator
Short-Term Liquidity		
Current ratio	Current assets	Current liabilities
Quick ratio (acid test)	Current assets (excluding inventory)	Current liabilities
Receivables turnover	Credit sales	Accounts receivable
Inventory turnover	Cost of sales	Inventory
Payables turnover	Cost of sales	Accounts payable
Long-Term Solvency		
Interest coverage	EBIT	Interest on L/T debt
Debt to capital	Long-term debt	L/T debt + equity
Profitability on Sales		
Gross profit ratio	Gross profit	Sales
Operating expense ratio	Operating expenses	Sales
SG&A expense ratio	SG&A expenses	Sales
EBIT ratio	EBIT	Sales
Pretax income ratio	Pretax income	Sales
Net income ratio	Net income	Sales
Profitability on Investment		
Return on total assets:		
Before tax	EBIT	Total assets[a]
After tax	EBIT times (1-tax rate)	Total assets[a]
Return on equity	Net income: Common[b]	Common equity

[a] Total Assets = Fixed Assets + Working Capital (Current Assets less Current Liabilities)
[b] Net Income less Preferred Dividends

USING FINANCIAL RATIOS

Some important points to keep in mind when using financial ratios are:

- Whereas all balance sheet numbers are end-of-period numbers, all income statement numbers relate to the entire period. For example, when calculating the ratio for Accounts Receivable Turnover, we use a numerator of Credit Sales, which is an entire-period number from the income statement, and a denominator of Accounts Receivable, which is an end-of-period number from the balance sheet. To make this an apples-to-apples ratio, the Accounts Receivable can be represented by an average of the beginning-of-year and end-of-year figures for Accounts Receivable. This average is closer to a mid-year estimate of Accounts Receivable and therefore is more comparable to the entire-period numerator, Credit Sales. Because using averages of the beginning-of-year and end-of-year figures for balance sheet numbers helps to make ratios more of an apples-to-apples comparison, averages should be used for all balance sheet numbers when calculating financial ratios.

- Financial ratios can be no more reliable than the data with which the ratios were calculated. The most reliable data is from audited financial statements, if the audit reports are clean and unqualified.
- Financial ratios cannot be fully considered without yardsticks of comparison. The simplest yardsticks are comparisons of an enterprise's current financial ratios with those from previous periods. Companies often provide this type of information in their financial reporting. For example, Apple Computer Inc., recently disclosed the following financial quarterly information, in millions of dollars:

Quarter	4	3	2	1
Net sales	$1,870	$1,825	$1,945	$2,343
Gross margin	$1,122	$1,016	$1,043	$1,377
Gross margin	25%	30%	28%	28%
Operating costs	$ 383	$ 375	$ 379	$ 409
Operating income	$ 64	$ 168	$ 170	$ 100
Operating income	4%	9%	9%	4%

This table compares four successive quarters of information, which makes it possible to see the latest trends in such important items as Sales, and Gross Margin and Operating Income percentages. Other types of comparisons of financial ratios include:

1. *Comparisons with competitors.* For example, the financial ratios of Apple Computer could be compared with those of Compaq, Dell, or Gateway.
2. *Comparisons with industry composites.* Industry composite ratios can be found from a number of sources, such as:
   a. The *Almanac of Business and Industrial Financial Ratios*, authored by Leo Troy and published annually by Prentice-Hall (Paramus, NJ). This publication uses Internal Revenue Service data for 4.6 million U.S. corporations, classified into 179 industries and divided into categories by firm size, and reporting 50 different financial ratios.
   b. Risk Management Associates: Annual Statement Studies. This is a database compiled by bank loan officers from the financial statements of more than 150,000 commercial borrowers, representing more than 600 industries, classified by business size, and reporting 16 different financial ratios. It is available on the Internet at www.rmahq.org.
   c. Financial ratios can also be obtained from other firms who specialize in financial information, such as Dun & Bradstreet, Moody's, and Standard & Poor's.

COMBINING FINANCIAL RATIOS

Up to this point we have considered financial ratios one at a time. However, there is a useful method for combining financial ratios known as Dupont[1] analysis. To explain it, we first need to define some financial ratios, together with their abbreviations, as follows:

Ratio	Calculation	Abbreviation
Profit margin[2]	Net income/sales	NI/S
Asset turnover	Sales/total assets	S/TA
Return on assets[3]	Net income/total assets	NI/TA
Leverage	Total assets/common equity	TA/CE
Return on equity	Net income/common equity	NI/CE

Now, these financial ratios can be combined in the following manner:

$$\text{Profit Margin} \times \text{Asset Turnover} = \text{Return on Assets}$$
$$\frac{\text{Net Income}}{\text{Sales}} \times \frac{\text{Sales}}{\text{Total Assets}} = \frac{\text{Net Income}}{\text{Total Assets}}$$

and

$$\text{Return on Assets} \times \text{Leverage} = \text{Return on Equity}$$
$$\frac{\text{Net Income}}{\text{Total Assets}} \times \frac{\text{Total Assets}}{\text{Common Equity}} = \frac{\text{Net Income}}{\text{Common Equity}}$$

In summary:

$$\frac{\text{NI}}{\text{S}} \times \frac{\text{S}}{\text{TA}} \times \frac{\text{TA}}{\text{CE}} = \frac{\text{NI}}{\text{CE}}$$

This equation says that Profit Margin × Asset Turnover × Leverage = Return on Equity.

Also, this equation provides a financial approach to business strategy. It recognizes that the ultimate goal of business strategy is to maximize stockholder value, that is, the market price of the common stock. This goal requires maximizing the return on common equity. The Dupont equation above breaks the return on common equity into its three component parts: Profit Margin (Net Income/Sales), Asset Turnover (Sales/Total Assets), and Leverage (Total Assets/Common Equity). If any one of these three ratios can be improved (without harm to either or both of the remaining two ratios), then the return on common equity will increase. A firm thus has specific strategic targets:

- Profit Margin improvement can be pursued in a number of ways. On the one hand, revenues might be increased or costs decreased by:

1. Raising prices perhaps by improving product quality or offering extra services. Makers of luxury cars have done this successfully by providing free roadside assistance and loaner cars when customer cars are being serviced.
2. Maintaining prices but reducing the quantity of product in the package. Candy bar manufacturers and other makers of packaged foods often use this method.
3. Initiating or increasing charges for ancillary goods or services. For example, banks have substantially increased their charges to stop checks and for checks written with insufficient funds. Distributors of computers and software have instituted fees for providing technical assistance on their help lines and for restocking returned items.
4. Improving the productivity and efficiency of operations.
5. Cutting costs in a variety of ways.

- Asset Turnover may be improved in ways such as:
  1. Speeding up the collection of accounts receivable.
  2. Increasing inventory turnover, perhaps by adopting "just in time" inventory methods.
  3. Slowing down payments to suppliers, thus increasing accounts payable.
  4. Reducing idle capacity of plant and equipment.

- Leverage may be increased, within prudent limits, by means such as:
  1. Using long-term debt rather than equity to fund additions to plant, property, and equipment.
  2. Repurchasing previously issued common stock in the open market.

The chief advantage of using the Dupont formula is to focus attention on specific initiatives that will improve return on equity by means of enhancing profit margins, increasing asset turnover, or employing greater financial leverage within prudent limits.

In addition to the Dupont formula, there is another way to combine financial ratios, one that serves another useful purpose—predicting solvency or bankruptcy for a given enterprise. It uses what is known as the z score.

THE Z SCORE

Financial ratios are useful not only to assess the past or present condition of an enterprise, but also to reliably predict its future solvency or bankruptcy. This type of information is of critical importance to present and potential creditors and investors. There are several different methods of analysis for obtaining this predictive information. The best-known and most time-tested is the z score, developed for publicly traded manufacturing firms by Professor

Edward Altman of New York University. Its reliability can be expressed in terms of the two types of errors to which all predictive methods are vulnerable, namely:

1. Type I error: predicting solvency when in fact a firm becomes bankrupt (a false positive).
2. Type II error: predicting bankruptcy when in fact a firm remains solvent (a false negative).

The predictive error rates for the Altman z score have been found to be as follows:

Years Prior to Bankruptcy	% False Positives	% False Negatives
1	6	3
2	18	6

Given the inherent difficulty of predicting future events, these error rates are relatively low, and therefore the Altman z score is generally regarded as a reasonably reliable bankruptcy predictor. The z score is calculated from financial ratios in the following manner:

$$z = 1.2 \times \frac{\text{Working Capital}}{\text{Total Assets}} + 1.4 \times \frac{\text{Retained Earnings}}{\text{Total Assets}} + 3.3 \times \frac{\text{EBIT}}{\text{Total Assets}}$$
$$+ 0.6 \times \frac{\text{Equity at Market Value}}{\text{Debt}} + 1.0 \times \frac{\text{Sales}}{\text{Total Assets}}$$

A z score above 2.99 predicts solvency; a z score below 1.81 predicts bankruptcy; z scores between 1.81 and 2.99 are in a gray area, with scores above 2.675 suggesting solvency and scores below 2.675 suggesting bankruptcy.

Since the z score uses equity at market value, it is not applicable to private firms, which do not issue marketable securities. A variation of the z score for private firms, known as the z' score, has been developed that uses the book value of equity rather than the market value. Because of this modification, the multipliers in the formula have changed from those in the original z score, as have the scores that indicate solvency, bankruptcy, or the gray area. For non-manufacturing service-sector firms, a further variation in the formula has been developed. It omits the variable for asset turnover and is known as the z'' score. Once again, the multipliers in the formula have changed from those in the z' score, and so have the scores that indicate solvency, bankruptcy, or the gray area.

Professor Altman later developed a bankruptcy predictor more refined than the z score and named it ZETA. ZETA uses financial ratios for times interest earned, return on assets (the average and the standard deviation), and debt to equity. Other details of ZETA have not been made public. ZETA is proprietary and is made available to users for a fee.

SUMMARY AND CONCLUSIONS

Financial statements contain critical business information and are used for many different purposes by many different parties inside and outside the business. Clearly all successful businesspeople should have a good basic understanding of financial statements and of the main financial ratios. For further information and explanations about financial statements, see the following chapters in this book:

Chapter 2: Analyzing Business Earnings
Chapter 6: Forecasts and Budgets
Chapter 15: The Board of Directors
Chapter 18: Business Valuation

INTERNET LINKS

Some useful Internet links on financial statements and financial ratios are:

www.aicpa.org	Web site for the American Institute of Certified Public Accountants.
www.freedgar.com	This site lets users download financial statements and other key financial information filed with the SEC and maintained in Edgar (the name of its database) for all corporations with securities that are publicly traded in the United States. This service is free of charge. Another Web site, Spredgar.com, displays financial ratios calculated from freedgar.com.
www.10k.com	Provides free downloads of annual reports (which include financial statements) filed with the SEC for all corporations with securities that are publicly traded in the United States.
www.rmahq.org	Web site of the Risk Management Association (RMA) that contains financial ratios classified by size of firm for more than 600 industries.
www.cpaclass.com	Information and instruction on many finance and accounting topics.
www.financeprofessor.com	Information and instruction on many finance and accounting topics.
www.smallbusiness.org	Information and instruction from public television on many finance and accounting topics.

www.wmw.com   The World Market Watch (wmw) provides business research information, including financial ratios, for many companies and 74 different industries.

FOR FURTHER READING

Anthony, Robert N., *Essentials of Accounting,* 6th ed. (Boston, MA: Addison-Wesley, 1996).

Brealey, Richard A., and Stewart C. Myers, *Fundamentals of Corporate Finance,* 3rd ed. (New York: McGraw-Hill, 2001).

Fridson, Martin S., *Financial Statement Analysis: A Practitioner's Guide,* 2nd ed. (New York: John Wiley, 1995).

Simini, Joseph P., *Balance Sheet Basics for Nonfinancial Managers* (New York: John Wiley, 1990).

Tracy, John A., *How to Read a Financial Report: Wringing Cash Flow and Other Vital Signs Out of the Numbers,* 4th ed. (New York: John Wiley, 1994).

Troy, Leo, *Almanac of Business and Industrial Financial Ratios* (Paramus, NJ: Prentice-Hall, Annual).

Financial Studies of the Small Business (Winter Haven, FL: Financial Research Associates, Annual).

Industry Norms and Key Business Ratios (New York: Dun & Bradstreet, Annual).

RMA Annual Statement Studies (Philadelphia, PA: Risk Management Association, Annual).

Standard and Poor's Industry Surveys (New York: Standard & Poor's, Quarterly).

NOTES

1. The name comes from its original use at the Dupont Corporation.
2. After income taxes.
3. Ibid.

2 ANALYZING BUSINESS EARNINGS

Eugene E. Comiskey

Charles W. Mulford

A special committee of the American Institute of Certified Public Accountants (AICPA) concluded the following about earnings and the needs of those who use financial statements:

> Users want information about the portion of a company's reported earnings that is stable or recurring and that provides a basis for estimating sustainable earnings.[1]

While users may want information about the stable or recurring portion of a company's earnings, firms are under no obligation to provide this earnings series. However, generally accepted accounting principles (GAAPs) require separate disclosure of selected nonrecurring revenues, gains, expenses, and losses on the face of the income statement or in notes to the financial statements. Further, the Securities and Exchange Commission (SEC) requires the disclosure of material nonrecurring items.

The prominence given the demand by users for information on nonrecurring items in the above AICPA report is, no doubt, driven in part by the explosive growth in nonrecurring items over the past decade. The acceleration of change together with a passion for downsizing, rightsizing, and reengineering have fueled this growth. The Financial Accounting Standards Board's (FASB) issuance of a number of new accounting statements that require recognition of previously unrecorded expenses and more timely recognition of declines in asset values has also contributed to the increase in nonrecurring items.

A limited number of firms do provide, on a voluntary basis, schedules that show their results with nonrecurring items removed. Mason Dixon Bancshares provides one such example. Exhibit 2.1 shows a Mason Dixon schedule that adjusts reported net income to a revised earnings measure from which nonrecurring revenues, gains, expenses, and losses have been removed. This is the type of information that the previously quoted statement of the AICPA's Special Committee calls for.

Notice the substantial number of nonrecurring items that Mason Dixon removed from reported net income in order to arrive at a closer measure of core or sustainable earnings. In spite of the number of nonrecurring items removed from reported net income, the revised earnings differ by only about 6% from the original reported net income.

Firms that record either a large nonrecurring gain or loss frequently attempt to offset its effect on net income by recording a number of offsetting items. In the case of Mason Dixon, the large gain on the sale of branches if not offset may raise earnings expectations to levels that are unattainable. Alternatively, the recording of offsetting charges may be seen as a way to relieve future earnings of their burden. We do not claim that this was done in the case of Mason Dixon Bancshares, but its results are consistent with this practice.

Though exceptions like the Mason Dixon Bancshares example do occur, the task of developing information on a firm's recurring or sustainable results normally falls to the statement user. Companies do provide, to varying degrees, the raw materials for this analysis; however, the formidable task of creating—an analysis comparable to that provided by Mason Dixon—is typically left to the user. The central goal of this chapter is to help users develop the background and skills to perform this critical aspect of earnings analysis. The chapter will discuss nonrecurring items and outline efficient approaches for locating them in financial statements and associated notes. As key background we will also discuss and illustrate income statement formats and other issues of classification. Throughout the chapter, we illustrate concepts using information drawn from

EXHIBIT 2.1   Core business net income: Mason Dixon Bancshares Inc., year ended December 31 (in thousands).

	1998
Reported net income	$10,811
Adjustments, add (deduct), for nonrecurring items:	
Gain on sale of branches	(6,717)
Special loan provision for loans with Year 2000 risk	918
Special loan provision for change in charge-off policy	2,000
Reorganization costs	465
Year 2000 costs	700
Impairment loss on mortgage sub-servicing rights	841
Income tax expense on the nonrecurring items above	1,128
Core (sustainable) net income	$10,146

SOURCE: Mason Dixon Bancshares Inc., annual report, December 1998. Information obtained from *Disclosure, Inc., Compact D/SEC: Corporate Information on Public Companies Filing with the SEC* (Bethesda, MD: Disclosure Inc., June 2000).

the financial statements of many companies. As a summary exercise, a comprehensive case is provided that removes all nonrecurring items from reported results to arrive at a sustainable earnings series.

THE NATURE OF NONRECURRING ITEMS

Defining *nonrecurring items* is difficult. Writers often begin with phrases like "unusual" or "infrequent in occurrence." Donald Keiso and Jerry Weygandt in their popular intermediate accounting text use the term *irregular* to describe what most statement users would consider nonrecurring items.[2] For our purposes, irregular or nonrecurring revenues, gains, expenses, and losses are not consistent contributors to results, in terms of either their presence or their amount. This is the manner in which we use the term *nonrecurring items* throughout this chapter.

From a security valuation perspective, nonrecurring items have a smaller impact on share price than recurring elements of earnings. Some items, such as restructuring charges, litigation settlements, flood losses, product recall costs, embezzlement losses, and insurance settlements, can easily be identified as nonrecurring. Other items may appear consistently in the income statement but vary widely in sign (revenue versus expense, gain versus loss) and amount. For example, the following gains on the disposition of flight equipment were reported over a number of years by Delta Air Lines:[3]

1992	$35 million
1993	65 million
1994	2 million
1995	0 million
1996	2 million

The gains averaged about $25 million over the 10 years ending in 1996 and ranged from a loss of $1 million (1988) to a gain of $65 million (1993). The more recent five years typify the variability in the amounts for the entire 10-year period. These gains did recur, but they are certainly irregular in amount.

There are at least three alternative ways to handle this line item in revising results to identify sustainable or recurring earnings. First, one could simply eliminate the line item based on its highly inconsistent contribution to results.[4] Second, one could include the line item at its average value ($25 million for the period 1987 to 1996) for some period of time. Third, one could attempt to acquire information on planned aircraft dispositions that would make possible a better prediction of the contribution of gains on aircraft dispositions to future results. While the last approach may appear to be the most appealing, it may prove to be difficult to implement because of lack of information, and it may also be less attractive when viewed from a cost-benefit perspective. In general, we would normally recommend either removing the gains or simply employing a fairly recent average value for the gains in making earnings projections.

After 1996, Delta Air Lines disclosed little in the way of nonrecurring gains on the sale of flight equipment. Its 2000 annual report, which covered the years from 1998 to 2000, did not disclose any gains or losses on the disposition of flight equipment.[5] With hindsight, the first option, which would remove all of the gains and losses on flight equipment, may have been the most appropriate alternative.

The Goodyear Tire and Rubber Company provides a timeless example of the impact of nonrecurring items on the evaluation of earnings performance. Exhibit 2.2 shows pretax results for Goodyear, with and without losses on foreign exchange.

As with Delta Air Lines, it may seem questionable to characterize as nonrecurring exchange losses that appear repeatedly. However, in line with the key characteristics of nonrecurring items given earlier, Goodyear's foreign exchange losses are both irregular in amount and unlikely to be consistent contributors to results in future years. Across the period 1993 to 1995 the reduction in foreign exchange losses contributed to Goodyear's pretax results by $35.5 million in 1994 and $60.2 million in 1995. That is, the entire $60.1 million increase in earnings for 1995 could be attributed to the $60.2 million decline in foreign exchange losses. The only way that the foreign exchange line could contribute a further $60.2 million to pretax earnings in 1996 would be for Goodyear to produce a foreign exchange gain of $42.8 million ($60.2 − $17.4).[6]

Other examples of irregular items of revenue, gain, expense, and loss abound. For example, there were temporary revenue increases and decreases associated with the Gulf War. ("Sales to the United States government increased substantially during the Persian Gulf War. However, sales returned to more normal levels in the second half of the year."[7]) Temporary revenue increases have been associated with expanded television sales due to World Cup

EXHIBIT 2.2   The Goodyear Tire and Rubber Company, results with and without foreign-exchange losses, years ended December 31 (in millions).

	1993	1994	1995
Income before income taxes, extraordinary item and cumulative effect of accounting change	$784.9	$865.7	$925.8
Add back foreign exchange losses	113.1	77.6	17.4
Income exclusive of foreign-exchange losses	$898.0	$943.3	$943.2
Percentage income increase:			
Income as reported		10.3%	6.9%
Income exclusive on foreign-exchange losses		5.0%	0.0%

SOURCE: The Goodyear Tire and Rubber Company, annual report, December 1995, 24.

soccer. Temporary increases or decreases in earnings have resulted from adjustments to loan loss provisions resulting from economic downturns and subsequent recoveries in the financial services industry. Most recently, there have been widely publicized problems with tires produced for sports utility vehicles that will surely create substantial nonrecurring increases in legal and warranty expenses.

Identifying nonrecurring or irregular items is not a mechanical process; it calls for the exercise of judgment and involves both line items and as the period-to-period behavior of individual income statement items.

THE PROCESS OF IDENTIFYING NONRECURRING ITEMS

Careful analysis of past financial performance aimed at removing the effects of nonrecurring items is a more formidable task than one might suspect. This task would be fairly simple if (1) there was general agreement on just what constitutes a nonrecurring item and (2) if most nonrecurring items were prominently displayed on the face of the income statement. However, neither is the case. Some research suggests that fewer than one-fourth of nonrecurring items are likely to be found separately disclosed in the income statement.[8] Providing guidance for locating the remaining three-fourths is a key goal of this chapter.

Identifying Nonrecurring Items:
An Efficient Search Procedure

The search sequence outlined in the following discussion locates a high cumulative percentage of material nonrecurring items and does so in a cost-effective manner. Search cost, mainly in time spent by the financial analyst, is an important consideration. Time devoted to this task is not available for another and, therefore, there is an *opportunity cost* to consider. The discussion and guidance that follows are organized around this recommended search sequence (see Exhibit 2.3). Following only the first five steps in this search sequence is likely to locate almost 60% of all nonrecurring items.[9] Continuing through steps six and seven will typically increase this location percentage. However, the 60% discovery rate is higher if the focus is only on *material* nonrecurring items. The nonrecurring items disclosed in other locations through steps 6 and 7 are fewer in number and normally less material than those initially found through the first five.

NONRECURRING ITEMS IN THE INCOME STATEMENT

An examination of the income statement, the first step in the search sequence, requires an understanding of the design and content of contemporary income statements. This knowledge will aid in the location and analysis of nonrecurring

EXHIBIT 2.3   Efficient search sequence for nonrecurring items.

Search Step	Search Location
1	Income statement.
2	Statement of cash flows—operating activities section only.
3	Inventory note, generally assuming that the firm employs the LIFO inventory method. However, even with non-LIFO firms, inventory notes may reveal inventory write-downs.
4	Income tax note, with attention focused on the tax-reconciliation schedule.
5	Other income (expense) note in cases where this balance is not detailed on the face of the income statement.
6	MD&A of Financial Condition and Results of Operations—a Securities and Exchange Commission requirement and therefore available only for public companies.
7	Other notes which often include nonrecurring items:

Note	Nonrecurring items revealed
a. Property and equipment	Gains and losses on asset sales
b. Long-term debt	Foreign currency and debt-retirement gains and losses.
c. Foreign currency	Foreign currency gains and losses
d. Restructuring	Current and prospective impact of of restructuring activities
e. Contingencies	Prospective revenues and expenses
f. Segment disclosures	Various nonrecurring items
g. Quarterly financial data	Various nonrecurring items

components of earnings. Generally accepted accounting principles (GAAPs) determine the structure and content of the income statement. Locating nonrecurring items in the income statement is a highly efficient and cost-effective process. Many nonrecurring items will be prominently displayed on separate lines in the statement. Further, leads to other nonrecurring items, disclosed elsewhere, may be discovered during this process. For example, a line item that summarizes items of other income and expense may include an associated note reference detailing its contents. These notes should always be reviewed—step 5 in the search sequence—because they will often reveal a wide range of nonrecurring items.

Alternative Income Statement Formats

Examples of the two principal income statement formats under current GAAPs are presented below. The income statement of Shaw Industries Inc., in Exhibit 2.4 is *single step* and that of Toys "R" Us Inc. in Exhibit 2.5 is *multistep*. An annual survey of financial statements conducted by the American Institute of Certified Public Accountants (AICPA) reveals that about one-third of the 600 companies in its survey use the single-step format and the other two-thirds the multistep.[10]

EXHIBIT 2.4   Consolidated single-step statements of income: Shaw Industries Inc. (in thousands).

	Year Ended		
	Jan. 3 1998	Jan. 2 1999	Jan. 1 2000
Net sales	$3,575,774	$3,542,202	$4,107,736
Cost of sales	$2,680,472	$2,642,453	$3,028,248
Selling, general and administrative	722,590	620,878	627,075
Charge to record loss on sale of residential retail operations, store closing costs and write-down of certain assets	—	132,303	4,061
Charge to record plant closing costs	—	—	1,834
Pre-opening expenses	3,953	—	—
Charge to record store closing costs	36,787	—	—
Write-down of U.K. assets	47,952	—	—
Interest, net	60,769	62,553	62,812
Loss on sale of equity securities	—	22,247	—
Other expense (income), net	(7,032)	4,676	1,319
Income before income taxes	30,283	57,092	382,387
Provision for income taxes	5,586	38,407	157,361
Income before equity in income of joint ventures	24,697	18,685	225,026
Equity in income of joint ventures	4,262	1,947	2,925
Net income	$ 28,959	$ 20,632	$ 227,951

Note: Per share amounts omitted.

SOURCE: Shaw Industries Inc., annual report, January 2000, 24.

The distinguishing feature of the multistep statement is that it provides intermediate earnings subtotals that are designed to measure pretax operating performance. In principle, operating income should be composed almost entirely of recurring items of revenue and expense, which result from the main operating activities of the firm. In practice, numerous material nonrecurring items are commonly included in operating income. For example, "restructuring" charges, one of the most common nonrecurring items of the past decade, is virtually always included in operating income.

Shaw Industries' single-step income statement does not partition results into intermediate subtotals. For example, there are no line items identified as either "gross profit" or "operating income." Rather, all revenues and expenses are separately listed and "income before income taxes" is computed in a single step as total expenses are deducted from total revenues. However, the Toys "R" Us multistep income statement provides both gross profit and operating income/(loss) subtotals.

Note that Shaw Industries has a number of different nonrecurring items in its income statements. While they vary in size, the following would normally be considered to be nonrecurring: charges related to residential retail operations,

EXHIBIT 2.5   Consolidated multi-step statements of earnings: Toys "R" Us Inc. (in millions).

	Year Ended		
	Jan. 31 1998	Jan. 30 1999	Jan. 29 2000
Net sales	$11,038	$11,170	$11,862
Cost of sales	7,710	8,191	8,321
Gross Profit	3,328	2,979	3,541
Selling, general and administrative expenses	2,231	2,443	2,743
Depreciation, amortization and asset write-offs	253	255	278
Restructuring charge	—	294	—
Total Operating Expenses	2,484	2,992	3,021
Operating Income/(Loss)	844	(13)	520
Interest expense	85	102	91
Interest and other income	(13)	(9)	(11)
Interest Expense, Net	72	93	80
Earnings/(loss) before income taxes	772	(106)	440
Income taxes	282	26	161
Net earnings/(loss)	$ 490	$ (132)	$ 279

Note: Per share amounts omitted.

SOURCE: Toys "R" Us Inc., annual report, January 2000, 25.

plant closing costs, record-store closing costs, write-down of U.K. assets, the loss on sale of equity investments, and the preopening expenses.

There will usually be other nonrecurring items lurking in other statements or footnotes. Note the approximately $12-million change in the Other expense (income) net balance for the year ending January 2, 1999, compared to the year ending January 3, 1998. Also, there must be something unusual about income taxes in the year ending January 3, 1998. The effective tax rate ($5,586,000 divided by $30,283,000) is only about 18%, well below the 35% statutory federal tax rate for large companies. By contrast, the effective tax rate ($38,407,000 divided by $57,092,000) for the year ending January 2, 1999, is about 67%.

Nonrecurring Items Located in Income from Continuing Operations

Whether a single- or multistep format is used, the composition of income from continuing operations is the same. It includes all items of revenue, gain, expense, and loss except those (1) identified with discontinued operations, (2) meeting the definition of extraordinary items, and (3) resulting from the cumulative effect of changes in accounting principles. Because income from continuing operations excludes only these three items, it follows that all other nonrecurring items of revenues or gains and expenses or losses are included in this key profit subtotal.

The Nature of Operating Income

Operating income is designed to reflect the revenues, gains, expenses, and losses that are related to the fundamental operating activities of the firm. Notice, however, that the Toys "R" Us operating loss for the year ending January 30, 1999, included two nonrecurring charges. These were the asset write-offs and a restructuring charge. While operating income or loss may include only operations-related items, some of these items may be nonrecurring. Hence, operating income is not the "sustainable" earnings measure called for in our opening quote from the AICPA Special Committee on Financial Reporting. Even at this early point in the operations section of the income statement, nonrecurring items have been introduced that will require adjustment in order to arrive at an earnings base "that provides a basis for estimating sustainable earnings."[11] Also be aware that "operating income" in a multistep format is an earlier subtotal than "income from continuing operations." Moreover, operating income is a pretax measure, whereas income from continuing operations is after tax. A more extensive sampling of items included in operating income is provided next.

Nonrecurring Items Included in Operating Income

Reviewing current annual reports reveals that corporations very often include nonrecurring revenues, gains, expenses, and losses in operating income. A sample of nonrecurring items included in the operating income section of multistep income statements is provided in Exhibit 2.6. As is typical, nonrecurring expenses and losses are more numerous than nonrecurring revenues and gains. This imbalance is due in part to GAAP, which require firms to recognize unrealized losses but not unrealized gains. Moreover, fundamental accounting conventions, such as the historical cost concept and conservatism, may also provide part of the explanation.

Many of the nonrecurring expense or loss items involve declines in the value of specific assets. Restructuring charges have been among the most common items in recent years in this section of the income statement. These charges involve asset write-downs and liability accruals that will be paid off in future years. Seldom is revenue or gain recorded as a result of writing up assets. Further, unlike the case of restructuring charges, the favorable future consequences of a management action would seldom support current accrual of revenue or gain.

There is substantial variety in the nonrecurring expenses and losses included in operating income. Many of the listed items appear closely linked to operations, and their classification seems appropriate. However, some appear to be at the fringes of normal operating items. Examples related to expenses and losses include the flood costs of Argosy Gaming, merger-related charges incurred by Brooktrout Technologies, the embezzlement loss of Osmonics, and the loss on the sale of Veeco Instruments' leak detection business. Among the gains, the Fairchild and H.J. Heinz gains on selling off businesses would seem to be candidates for inclusion further down the income statement.

EXHIBIT 2.6   Nonrecurring items of revenue, gain, expense, and loss included in operating income.

Company	Nonrecurring Item
Expenses and Losses	
Air T Inc. (2000)	Start-up/merger expense
Akorn Inc. (1999)	Relocation costs
Amazon.Com Inc. (1999)	Stock-based compensation
Argosy Gaming Company (1995)	Flood costs
Avado Brands Inc. (1999)	Asset revaluation charges
Brooktrout Technologies Inc. (1998)	Merger related charges
Burlington Resources Inc. (1999)	Impairment of oil and gas properties
Cisco Systems Inc. (1999)	Charges for purchased R&D
Colonial Commercial Corporation (1999)	Costs of an abandoned acquisition
Dean Foods Company (1999)	Plant closure costs
Delta Air Lines Inc. (2000)	Asset write-downs and other special charges
Detection Systems Inc. (2000)	Shareholder class action litigation charge
Escalon Medical Corporation (2000)	Write-down of patents and goodwill
Gerber Scientific Inc. (2000)	Write-downs of inventory and receivables
Holly Corporation (2000)	Voluntary early retirement costs
JLG Industries Inc. (2000)	Restructuring charges
Osmonics Inc. (1993)	Embezzlement loss
Saucony Inc. (1999)	Write-down of impaired real estate
Silicon Valley Group Inc. (1999)	Inventory write-downs
Veeco Instruments Inc. (1999)	Loss on sale of leak detection business
Wegener Corporation (1999)	Write-down of capitalized software
Revenues and Gains	
Alberto-Culver Company (2000)	Gain on sale of European trademark
The Fairchild Corporation (2000)	Gains on the sale of subsidiaries
H.J. Heinz Company (1995)	Gain on sale of confectionery business
Lufkin Industries Inc. (1999)	LIFO-liquidation benefit
National Steel Corporation (1999)	Benefit from property-tax settlement
Praxair Inc. (1999)	Hedge gain in Brazil and income-hedge gain
Tyco International Ltd. (2000)	Reversal of restructuring accrual

SOURCES: Companies' annual reports. The year following each company name designates the annual report from which each example was drawn.

Comparing the items included in operating income to those excluded reveals a reasonable degree of flexibility and judgment in the classification of many of these items. In any event, operating income may not be a very reliable measure of ongoing operating performance given the wide range of nonrecurring items that are included in its determination.

Nonrecurring Items Excluded from Operating Income

Unlike the multistep format, the single-step income statement omits a subtotal representing operating income. The task of identifying core or operating income is therefore more difficult. Nonrecurring items of revenue or gain and expense or loss are either presented as separate line items within the listing of revenues or gain and expense or loss, or are included in an "other income (expense)" line. A sampling of nonrecurring items found in the other-income-and-expense category of the multistep income statements of a number of companies is provided in Exhibit 2.7.

A comparison of the items in two exhibits reveals some potential for overlap in these two categories. The first, nonrecurring items in operating income, should be dominated by items closely linked to company operations. The nonrecurring items in the second category, below operating income, should fall outside the operations area of the firm. Notice that there is a litigation charge included in operating income (Exhibit 2.6, Detection Systems) as well as several excluded from operating income (Exhibit 2.7, Advanced Micro Devices, Cryomedical Sciences, and Trimark Holdings). Gains on the sale of investments are found far less frequently within operating income. Firms may avoid

EXHIBIT 2.7   Nonrecurring items of revenue or gain and expense or loss excluded from operating income.

Company	Nonrecurring Item
Expenses or Losses	
Advanced Micro Devices Inc. (1999)	Litigation settlement charge
Baltek Corporation (1997)	Foreign currency loss
Champion Enterprises (1995)	Environmental reserve
Cryomedical Sciences Inc. (1995)	Settlement of shareholder class action suit
Galey & Lord Inc. (1998)	Loss on foreign-currency hedges
Global Industries (1993)	Fire loss on marine vessel
Hollywood Casino Corporation (1992)	Write-off of deferred preacquisition costs
Imperial Holly Corporation (1994)	Workforce reduction charge
Trimark Holdings Inc. (1995)	Litigation settlement
Revenues or Gains	
Artistic Greetings Inc. (1995)	Unrealized gains on trading securities
Avado Brands Inc. (1999)	Gain on asset disposals
Colonial Commercial Corporation (1999)	Gain on land sale
Delta Air Lines Inc. (2000)	Gains from the sale of investments
The Fairchild Corporation (2000)	Gains on the sale of subsidiaries and affiliates
Freeport-McMoRan Inc. (1991)	Insurance settlement (tanker grounding)
Gerber Scientific Inc. (2000)	Litigation award
Imperial Sugar Company (1999)	Realized securities gains
Meredith Corporation (1994)	Sale of broadcast stations
National Steel Corporation (1999)	Gain on disposal of noncore assets
New England Business Service Inc. (1996)	Gain on sale of product line
Noble Drilling (1991)	Insurance on rig abandoned in Somalia
Pollo Tropical Inc. (1995)	Business-interruption insurance recovery
Raven Industries Inc. (2000)	Gain on sale of investment in affiliate
Saucony Inc. (1999)	Foreign currency gains

SOURCES: Companies' annual reports. The year following each company name designates the annual report from which each example was drawn.

classifying these nonrecurring gains within operating income to prevent share-holders' unrealistic expectations for earnings in subsequent periods. It is common to see foreign-currency gains and losses classified below operating income. This is somewhat difficult to rationalize because currency exposure is an integral part of operations when a firm does business with foreign customers and/or has foreign operations.

The operating income subtotal should measure the basic profitability of a firm's operations. It is far from a net earnings number because its location in the income statement is above a number of other nonoperating revenues, gains, expenses, and losses, as well as interest charges and income taxes. Clearly, the range and complexity of nonrecurring items create difficult judgment calls in implementing this concept of operating income. Management may use this flexibility to manage the operating income number. That is, the classification of items either inside or outside operating income could be influenced by the goal of maintaining stable growth in this key performance measure.

Some of the items in Exhibit 2.7 would seem to have been equally at home within the operating income section. An environmental reserve (Champion Enterprises) appears to be closely tied to operations, as are the workforce reduction charges, a common element of restructuring charges (Imperial Holly); the insurance settlement from the tanker grounding (Freeport-McMoRan); and business interruption insurance (Pollo Tropical).

Nonrecurring Items Located below Income from Continuing Operations

The region in the income statement below income from continuing operations has a standard organization and is the same for both the single- and multistep income statement. This format is outlined in Exhibit 2.8. The income statement of AK Steel Holding Corporation, shown in Exhibit 2.9, illustrates this format. Each of the special line items—that is, discontinued operations, extraordinary

EXHIBIT 2.8   Income statement format with special items.

Income from continuing operations	$000
Discontinued operations	000
Extraordinary items	000
Cumulative effect of changes in accounting principles	000
Net income	000
Other comprehensive income	000
Comprehensive income	$000

SOURCES: Key guidance is found in Accounting Principles Board Opinion No. 30, *Reporting the Results of Operations* (New York: AICPA, June 1973) and Statement of Financial Accounting Standards (SFAS), No. 130, *Reporting Comprehensive Income* (Norwalk, CT: FASB, June 1997).

EXHIBIT 2.9   Consolidated statements of income: AK Steel Holding Corp., years ended December 31 (in millions).

	1997	1998	1999
Net sales	$4,176.6	$4,029.7	$4,284.8
Cost of products sold	3,363.3	3,226.5	3,419.8
Selling, general and administrative expense	288.0	278.0	309.8
Depreciation	141.0	161.2	210.7
Special charge	—	—	99.7
Total operating costs	3,792.3	3,665.7	4,040.0
Operating profit	384.3	364.0	244.8
Interest expense	111.7	84.9	123.7
Other income	48.4	30.3	20.8
Income from continuing operations before income taxes and minority interest	321.0	309.4	141.9
Income tax provision	127.5	105.5	63.9
Minority interest	8.1	8.1	6.7
Income from continuing operations	185.4	195.8	71.3
Discontinued operations	1.6	—	7.5
Income before extraordinary item and cumulative effect of a change in accounting	187.0	195.8	78.8
Extraordinary loss on retirement of debt, net of tax	1.9	—	13.4
Cumulative effect of change in accounting, net of tax	—	133.9	—
Net income	185.1	329.7	65.4
Other comprehensive income, net of tax:			
Foreign currency translation adjustment	(1.4)	0.3	(1.4)
Unrealized gains (losses) on securities:			
Unrealized holding gains (losses) arising during the period	2.1	(0.5)	(1.2)
Less: reclassification for gains included in net income	(0.2)	(1.0)	(1.9)
Minimum pension liability adjustment	—	(2.6)	1.2
Comprehensive income	$ 185.6	$ 325.9	$ 62.1

Note: Note references as well as earnings-per-share data included in the AK Steel income statement were omitted from the above.

SOURCE: AK Steel Holdings Corp., annual report, December 1999, 20.

items, and changes in accounting principles—along with examples is discussed in the following sections. All of these items are presented in the income statement on an after-tax basis.

Discontinued Operations

The discontinued operations section is designed to enhance the interpretive value of the income statement by separating the results of continuing operations from those that have been or are being discontinued. Only the discontinuance of operations that constitute a separate and complete segment of the business have normally been reported in this special section. The current segment-reporting standard, SFAS 131, *Disclosures about Segments of an Enterprise and Related Information,* identifies the following as characteristics of a segment:

1. It engages in business activities from which it may earn revenues and incur expenses (including revenues and expenses relating to transactions with other components of the same enterprise).
2. Its operating results are regularly reviewed by the enterprise's chief operating decision maker to allocate resources to the segment and assess its performance.
3. Discrete financial information is available.[12]

Some examples of operations that have been viewed as segments and therefore classified as "discontinued operations" are provided in Exhibit 2.10. Most of the discontinued operations that are disclosed in Exhibit 2.10 appear to satisfy the traditional test of being separate and distinct segments of the business. The retail furniture business of insurance company Atlantic American is a good example. The case of Textron is a somewhat closer call. Textron reports its operations in four segments: Aircraft, Automotive, Industrial, and Finance. The disposition of Avco Financial Services could be seen as a product line within the Finance segment. However, it may very well qualify as a segment under the newer guidance of SFAS No. 131, *Disclosures about Segments of an Enterprise and Related Information,* previously presented. The treatment of vegetables as a separate segment of the food processor Dean Foods also suggests that there are judgment calls in deciding whether a disposition is a distinct segment or simply a product line and thus only part of a segment.

Extraordinary Items

Income statement items are considered extraordinary if they are *both* (1) unusual and (2) infrequent in occurrence.[13] Unusual items are not related to the typical activities or operations of the firm. Infrequency of occurrence simply implies that the item is not expected to recur in the foreseeable future.

In practice the joint requirement of "unusual and nonrecurring" results in very few items being reported as extraordinary. GAAPs identify two types of extraordinary transactions the gains or losses from which do not have to be both unusual and nonrecurring. These are (1) gains and losses from the extinguishment of debt[14] and (2) gains or losses resulting from "troubled debt restructurings."[15] Included in the latter type are either the settlement of obligations or their continuation with a modification of terms.

A tabulation of extraordinary items, based on an annual survey of 600 companies conducted by the American Institute of CPAs, is provided in

EXHIBIT 2.10 Examples of discontinued operations.

Company	Principal Business	Discontinued Operation
American Standard Companies Inc. (1999)	Air conditioning, bathroom fixtures, and electronics	Medical systems
Atlantic American Corporation (1999)	Insurance	Retail furniture
Bestfoods Inc. (1999)	Food preparations	Corn refining
Dean Foods Inc. (1999)	Food processor	Vegetables segment
Decorator Industries Inc. (1999)	Interior furnishing products	Manufacture and sale for the retail market
The Fairchild Corporation (2000)	Aerospace fasteners and aerospace parts distribution	Fairchild technologies business
Gleason Corporation (1995)	Gear machinery and equipment	Metal stamping and fabricating
Maxco Inc. (1996)	Manufacturing, distribution, and real estate	Automotive refinishing products
A.O. Smith Corporation (1999)	Motors and generators	Storage tank and fiberglass pipe markets
Standard Register Company (1999)	Document management and print production	Promotional direct mail operation
Textron Inc. (1999)	Aircraft engines, automotive parts, and finance	Avco Financial Services
Watts Industries Inc. (1999)	Valves for plumbing, heating and water quality industries	Industrial oil and gas businesses

SOURCES: Companies' annual reports. The year following each company name designates the annual report from which each example was drawn.

Exhibit 2.11. This summary highlights the rarity of extraordinary items under current reporting requirements. Debt extinguishments represent the largest portion of the disclosed extraordinary items. This leaves only from two to five discretionary extraordinary items per year among the 600 companies surveyed.

The small number of gains and losses classified as extraordinary is consistent with their definition. However, this rarity adds to the challenge of locating all nonrecurring items as part of a thorough earnings analysis. Few nonrecurring items will qualify for the prominent disclosure that results from display in one of the special sections, such as for extraordinary items, of the income statement. A sample of discretionary extraordinary items—that is, items not treated as extraordinary by a specific standard—is provided in Exhibit 2.12.

Natural disasters and civil unrest are some of the more typical causes of extraordinary items. The extraordinary gain of American Building Maintenance may appear to fail the criterion of *unusual* since small earthquakes are

EXHIBIT 2.11 Frequency and nature of extraordinary items.

	1996	1997	1998	1999
Debt extinguishments	60	62	73	56
Other	5	3	2	6
Total extraordinary items	65	65	75	62
Companies presenting extraordinary items	63	64	74	61
Companies not presenting extraordinary items	537	536	526	539
Total companies	600	600	600	600

SOURCE: American Institute of Certified Public Accountants, *Accounting Trends and Techniques* (New York: AICPA, 1999), 392.

EXHIBIT 2.12 Discretionary extraordinary items.

Company	Item or Event
American Building Maintenance Inc. (1989)	Gain on an insurance settlement for damage to a building from a San Francisco earthquake
Avoca Inc. (1995)	Insurance proceeds from the destruction of a building by a fire
BLC Financial Services Inc. (1998)	Settlement of a lawsuit
KeyCorp Ohio (1999)	Gain on the sale of residential mortgage loan-servicing operations
Noble Drilling Corporation (1991)	Insurance settlement due to deprivation of use of logistics and drilling equipment abandoned in Somalia due to civil unrest
NACCO Industries Inc. (1995)	Gain on a downward revision of an obligation to the United Mine Workers of America Combined Benefit Fund
NS Group Inc. (1992)	Loss from an accidental melting of radioactive substance in the steel-making operation
Phillips Petroleum Company (1990)	Gain from a settlement with the government of Iran over the expropriation of Phillips' oil production interests
SunTrust Banks Inc. (1999)	Gain on the sale of the Company's consumer credit portfolio
Weyerhaeuser Company (1980)	Losses from Mount St. Helens eruption

SOURCES: Companies' annual reports. The year following each company name designates the annual report from which each example was drawn.

frequent in the Bay Area. However, the magnitude of this quake, at about 7.0 on the Richter scale, was probably enough for it to qualify as *both* unusual and nonrecurring. Earthquakes of such magnitude have not occurred since the San Francisco quake of 1906. The Mount St. Helens eruption (Weyerhaeuser) was certainly enormous on the scale of volcanic eruptions.

The discretionary character of the definition of *extraordinary items* combined with the growing complexity of company operations results in considerable diversity in the classification of items as extraordinary. For example, Sun Company (not displayed in Exhibit 2.12) had a gain from an expropriation settlement with Iran. Unlike Phillips Petroleum, however, Sun did not classify the gain as extraordinary. Neither Exxon nor Union Carbide (also not in Exhibit 2.12) classified as extraordinary their substantial losses from what could be seen as accidents related to their operating activities.[16] The classifications as extraordinary of gains on the sale of servicing operations by KeyCorp and on a consumer credit portfolio by SunTrust are rather surprising. These two items would seem to fail the *unusual* part of the test for extraordinary items.

The task of locating all nonrecurring items of revenue or gain and expense or loss is aided only marginally by the presence of the extraordinary category in the income statement, because the extraordinary classification is employed so sparingly. Location of most nonrecurring items calls for careful review of other parts of the income statement, other statements, and notes to the financial statements.

Changes in Accounting Principles

The cumulative effects (catch-up adjustments) of changes in accounting principles are also reported below income from continuing operations (see Exhibit 2.8). Most changes in accounting principles result from the adoption of new standards issued by the Financial Accounting Standards Board (FASB).

The most common reporting treatment when a firm changes from one accepted accounting principle to another is to show the cumulative effect of the change on the results of prior years in the income statement for the year of the change. Less common is the retroactive restatement of the prior-year statements to the new accounting basis. Under this method, the effect of the change on the years prior to those presented in the annual report for the year of the change is treated as an adjustment to retained earnings of the earliest year presented.

As noted previously, in recent years accounting changes have been dominated by the requirement to adopt new generally accepted accounting principles (GAAPs). Discretionary changes in accounting principle are a distinct minority. Examples of discretionary changes would be a switch from accelerated to straight-line depreciation or from the LIFO to FIFO inventory method.

Information on accounting changes in both accounting principles and in estimates is provided in Exhibit 2.13. This information is drawn from an annual survey of the annual reports of 600 companies conducted by the American

EXHIBIT 2.13   Accounting changes.

Subject of the Change	Number of Companies			
	1996	1997	1998	1999
Software development costs (SOP 98-1)	—	1	37	66
Start-up costs (SOP 98-5)	—	2	29	39
Inventories	5	4	5	5
Revenue recognition (SAB 101)	—	—	—	5
Depreciable lives	3	3	4	4
Software revenue recognition	—	—	4	3
Derivatives and hedging activities	—	—	—	3
Market-value valuation of pension assets	—	—	—	3
Bankruptcy code reporting (SOP 90-7)	—	—	—	3
Recoverability of goodwill	—	—	—	2
Depreciation method	4	3	—	2
Business process reengineering (EITF 97-13)	—	28	10	2
Impairment of long-lived assets (SFAS 121)	134	39	3	—
Reporting entity	1	1	2	—
Other	28	57	13	10

SOURCE: American Institute of Certified Public Accountants, *Accounting Trends and Techniques* (New York: AICPA, 2000), 79.

Institute of Certified Public Accountants (AICPA). The distribution of adoption dates across several years, especially for SFAS 121, occurs because some firms adopt the new statement prior to its mandatory adoption date. In addition, the required adoption date for new standards is typically for years beginning after December 15 of the year specified. This means that firms whose fiscal year starts on January 1 are the first to be required to adopt the new standard. Other firms adopt throughout the following year.

Most recent changes in accounting principles have been reported on a cumulative-effect basis. The cumulative effect is reported net of tax in a separate section (see Exhibit 2.8) of the income statement. The cumulative effect is the impact of the change on the results of previous years. The impact of the change on the current year, that is, year of the change, is typically disclosed in a note describing the change and its impact. However, it is not disclosed separately on the face of the income statement. An example of the disclosure of both the cumulative effect of an accounting change and its effect on income from continuing operations is provided below:

Cumulative effect

Effective January 1, 1998, Armco changed its method of amortizing unrecognized net gains and losses related to its obligations for pensions and other postretirement benefits. In 1998, Armco recognized income of $237.5 million, or $2.20 per share of common stock, for the cumulative effect of this accounting change.

Effect on income from continuing operations for the year of change

Adoption of the new method increased 1998 income from continuing operations by approximately $3.0 million or $0.03 per share of common stock.[17]

In analyzing earnings, the effect of an accounting change on the results of previous years will be prominently displayed net of its tax effect on the face of the income statement. However, the effect on the current year's income from continuing operations appears only in the note describing the change. While not the case for the Armco example, the current-year effect of the change is often large and should be considered in interpreting the performance of the current year in relation to previous years.

Most of the entries in Exhibit 2.13 represent the mandatory adoption of new GAAP. Two statements of position (SOP), SOP 98-1 and 98-5, produced most of the accounting changes in 1998. Statements of position are issued by the AICPA and are considered part of the body of GAAP. The same is true for EITF 97-13. An EITF represents a consensus reached on a focused technical accounting and reporting issue by the Emerging Issues Task Force of FASB. The item listed as SAB 101 is a document issued by the SEC and will continue to cause changes in the timing of the recognition of income by many companies.[18] The single listed FASB statement, SFAS 121, illustrates the multiyear adoption pattern that reflects early adopters in 1995, followed by mandatory adopters in subsequent years.

Some of the items listed in Exhibit 2.13 represent changes in accounting estimates as opposed to accounting principles. Changes in depreciation method are changes in accounting principle, whereas changes in depreciable lives are changes in estimate. The accounting treatments of the two different types of changes are quite different. Changes in accounting estimates are discussed next.

Changes in Estimates

Whereas changes in accounting principles are handled on either a cumulative-effect (catch-up) or retroactive restatement basis, changes in accounting estimates are handled on a prospective basis only. The impact of a change is included only in current or future periods; retroactive restatements are not permitted. For example, effective January 1, 1999, Southwest Airlines changed the useful lives of its 737-300 and 737-500 aircraft. This is considered a change in estimate. Southwest's change in estimate was disclosed in the following note:

Change in Accounting Estimate

Effective January 1, 1999, the Company revised the estimated useful lives of its 737-300 and 737-500 aircraft from 20 years to 23 years. This change was the result of the Company's assessment of the remaining useful lives of the aircraft based on the manufacturer's design lives, the Company's increased average aircraft stage (trip) length, and the Company's previous experience. The effect of this change was to reduce depreciation expense approximately $25.7 million and increase net income $.03 per diluted share for the year ended December 31, 1999.[19]

The $25.7 million reduction in 1999 depreciation was not set out separately in Southwest's 1999 income statement, as would be the case if the depreciation reduction resulted from a change to straight-line from the accelerated method. Unlike the case of AK Steel (Exhibit 2.9), there is no cumulative-effect adjustment in the Southwest income statement.

Southwest reported pretax earnings of $774 million in 1999. Pretax earnings in 1998 were $705 million. On an as-reported basis, Southwest's pretax earnings grew by 10% in 1999. Without the $25.7 million benefit from the increase in aircraft useful lives, however, the pretax earnings increase in 1999 would have been only 6%. That is, on a consistent basis Southwest's improvement in operating results is sharply lower than the as-reported results would suggest. Locating the effect of this accounting change and determining its contribution to Southwest's 1999 net income is essential in any effort to judge its 1999 financial performance.

Identifying nonrecurring items in the income statement as outlined above is a key first step in earnings analysis; many such items will be located at other places in the annual report. The discussion that follows considers other locations where additional nonrecurring items may be located.

NONRECURRING ITEMS IN THE STATEMENT OF CASH FLOWS

After the income statement, the operating activities section of the statement of cash flows is an excellent secondary source to use in locating nonrecurring items (step 2 in the search sequence in Exhibit 2.3). The diagnostic value of this section of the statement of cash flows results from two factors. First, gains and losses on the sale of investments and fixed assets must be removed from net income in arriving at cash flow from operating activities. Second, noncash items of revenue or gain and expense or loss must also be removed from net income. All cash inflows associated with the sale of investments and fixed assets must be classified in the investing activities section of the statement of cash flows. This classification requires removal of the gains or losses typically nonrecurring in nature from net income in arriving at cash flow from operating activities. Similarly, because many nonrecurring expenses or losses do not involve a current-period cash outflow, such items must be adjusted out of net income in arriving at cash flow from operating activities. Such adjustments, if not simply combined in a miscellaneous balance, often highlight nonrecurring items.

The partial statement of cash flows of Escalon Medical Corporation in Exhibit 2.14 illustrates the disclosure of nonrecurring items in the operating-activities section of the statement of cash flows. The nonrecurring items would appear to be (1) the write-down of intangible assets, (2) the net gain on sale of the Betadine product line, (3) the net gain on the sale of the Silicone Oil product

EXHIBIT 2.14   Nonrecurring items disclosed in the statement of cash flows: Escalon Medical Corporation, partial consolidated statements of cash flows, years ended June 30.

	1998	1999	2000
Cash Flows from Operating Activities			
Net income (loss)	$ 171,472	$1,193,787	$ (862,652)
Adjustments to reconcile net income (loss) to net cash provided from (used in) operating activities:			
Depreciation and amortization	331,987	363,687	666,770
Equity in net loss of joint venture	—	—	33,382
Income from license of intellectual laser property	(75,000)	—	—
Write-down of intangible assets	—	24,805	—
Net gain on sale of Betadine product line	—	(879,159)	—
Net gain on sale of Silicone Oil product line	—	—	(1,863,915)
Write-down of patents and goodwill	—	—	417,849
Change in operating assets and liabilities:			
Accounts receivable	(353,113)	(48,451)	586,424
Inventory	115,740	(410,476)	162,862
Other current and long-term assets	(16,862)	(116,491)	(164,960)
Accounts payable and accrued expenses	(360,396)	519,764	(416,506)
Net cash provided from (used in) operating activities	$(186,172)	$647,466	$(1,440,746)

SOURCE: Escalon Medical Corporation, annual report, June 2000, F-6.

line, and (4) the write-down of patent costs and goodwill. The Escalon income statement also disclosed, on separate lines, each of the nonrecurring items revealed in the operating activities section, with the exception of the intangible assets write-down.

The asset write-downs, items (1) and (4) above, are added back to net income or loss because they are noncash. The gains on the product-line sales are deducted from net income or loss because all cash from such transactions, including the portion represented by the gain, must be classified in the investing activities section of the cash flow statement. As the gains are part of net income or loss, a failure to remove them would both overstate cash flows from operating activities and understate investing cash inflows.

Examples of nonrecurring items disclosed in the operating activities section of a number of different companies are presented in Exhibit 2.15. Frequently, nonrecurring items appear in both the income statement and operating activities section of the statement of cash flows. However, some nonrecurring items are disclosed in the statement of cash flows but not the income statement. Exhibit 2.15 provides examples of both types of disclosure.

EXHIBIT 2.15 Disclosure of nonrecurring items in both the income statement and operating activities section of the statement of cash flows.

Company	Nonrecurring Item
Separately disclosed in both the income statement and statement of cash flows	
Advanced Micro Devices Inc. (1999)	Gain on sale of Vantis
Air T Inc. (2000)	Loss on the sale of assets
AmSouth Bancorporation (1999)	Merger-related costs
Armstrong World Industries Inc. (1999)	Charge for asbestos liability
Baycorp Holdings Ltd. (1999)	Unrealized loss on energy trading contracts
Callon Petroleum Company (1999)	Impairment of oil and gas properties
Corning Inc. (1999)	Nonoperating gains
Delta Air Lines Inc. (2000)	Asset write-downs and other special charges
The Fairchild Corporation (2000)	Restructuring charges
Gerber Scientific Inc. (2000)	Nonrecurring special charges
Hercules Inc. (1999)	Charge for acquired in-process R&D
Raven Industries Inc. (2000)	Gain on sale of investment in affiliate
Separately disclosed only in the statement of cash flow	
Advanced Micro Devices Inc. (1999)	Charge for settlement of litigation
Brush Wellman Inc. (1999)	Impairment of fixed assets and related intangibles
Chiquita Brands International Inc. (1999)	Write-down of banana production assets, net
Dal-Tile International Inc. (1999)	Impairment of assets and foreign-currency gain
Evans & Sutherland Computer Corporation (1998)	Inventory write-downs
M.A. Hanna Company (1999)	Provision for loss on sale of assets
H.J. Heinz Company (1999)	Gain on sale of bakery products unit
JLG Industries Inc. (2000)	Restructuring charges
Kulicke & Soffa Industries Inc. (1999)	Provision for impairment of goodwill
Petroleum Helicopters Inc. (1999)	Gain on asset dispositions
Schnitzer Steel Industries Inc. (1999)	Environmental reserve reversal
Synthetech Inc. (2000)	Realized gain on sale of securities

SOURCES: Companies' annual reports. The year following each company name designates the annual report from which the example was drawn.

Interpreting Information in the Operating Activities Section

The statement of cash flows is an important additional source of information on nonrecurring items. It enables one to detect items that are not disclosed separately in the income statement but appear in the statement of cash flows because of either their noncash or nonoperating character. To realize the diagnostic value of the statement of cash flows, one must determine which items in the operating activities section of the statement of cash flows are nonrecurring. The appearance in the statement of cash flows as merely an addition to or deduction from net income or loss does not signify that the item is nonrecurring. Some entries in this section simply reflect the noncash character of certain items of revenue, gain, expense, and loss. For example, depreciation and amortization are added back to Escalon's net income or loss (Exhibit 2.14) because they are not cash expenses.[20] The two asset write-downs are likewise added back to net income or loss because of their noncash character. However, a separate judgment may also be made that, unlike depreciation, these two items are *both* noncash and nonrecurring.

Also notice that two different gains on sales of product lines are deducted in arriving at operating cash flow. It would be tempting to assume that these are noncash gains. However, the investing activities section of the Escalon statement of cash flows, a portion of which is included in Exhibit 2.16, reveals this not to be the case. Cash inflows of $2,059,835 and $2,117,180 from the sales of Betadine and Silicone Oil, respectively, are disclosed in cash flows from investing activities. The gains are fully backed by cash inflows, but they are deducted from net income because they are not considered a source of operating cash flow. Whatever the specific basis for deducting these gains from net income to arrive at cash flow from operating activities, the process of deduction simultaneously discloses these nonrecurring items.

Two other items in Escalon's operating activities section (Exhibit 2.14) require comment. First, the addition to the 2000 net loss of $33,382 for "equity in net loss of joint venture" is required because of the noncash nature of this loss. GAAPs require that a firm (the investor) with an ownership position that permits it to exercise significant influence over another company (the investee) short of control must recognize its share of the investee's results. This principle caused Escalon to recognize its share of its investee's loss in 2000. However, there is no cash outflow on Escalon's part associated with simply recognizing this loss in its income statement.[21] Therefore, the addition of the loss to net income simply reflects its noncash character. Determining whether the loss is nonrecurring would require an examination of the income statement of the underlying investee company.

The second item is the $75,000 of "income from license of intellectual laser property." This item is deducted from 1998 net income in arriving at

EXHIBIT 2.16   Investing cash flows: Escalon Medical Corporation, partial investing cash flows section, years ended June 30.

	1998	1999	2000
Cash Flows from Investing Activities:			
Purchase of investments	$(470,180)	$ (259,000)	$(7,043,061)
Proceeds from maturities of investments	375,164	589,016	7,043,061
Net change in cash and cash equivalents—restricted	—	(1,000,000)	1,000,000
Proceeds from the sale of Betadine product line	—	2,059,835	—
Proceeds from sales of Silicone Oil product line	—	—	2,117,180

SOURCE: Escalon Medical Corporation, annual report, June 2000, F-6.

operating cash flow. This deduction may indicate either that no cash was collected in connection with recording this income or that the income is not considered to be an operating cash-flow item. The absence of a cash inflow is the
more likely explanation. But should the $75,000 be seen as nonrecurring? If
this were a one-time licensing fee, then it should be treated as nonrecurring
in evaluating the $171,472 of 1998 net income. Escalon has a substantial
net-operating-loss carryforward, and its 1998 pretax and after-tax results are
the same. As a result, this $75,000 of income amounted to 44% of Escalon's
1998 net income. The absence of this item in the cash flows statement in either
1999 or 2000 gives the licensing fee the appearance of being nonrecurring.

NONRECURRING ITEMS IN THE INVENTORY
DISCLOSURES OF LIFO FIRMS

The carrying values of inventories maintained under the LIFO method are
sometimes significantly understated in relationship to their replacement cost.
For public companies, the difference between the LIFO carrying value and
replacement cost (frequently approximated by FIFO) is a required disclosure
under SEC regulations.[22] An example of a substantial difference between
LIFO and current replacement value is found in a summary of the inventory
disclosures of Handy and Harman Inc. in Exhibit 2.17.

   A reduction in the physical inventory quantities of a LIFO inventory is
called a LIFO liquidation. With a LIFO liquidation a portion of the firm's cost
of sales for the year will consist of the carrying values associated with the liquidated units. These costs are typically lower than current replacement costs,
resulting in increased profits or reduced losses.

   As with the differences between the LIFO cost and the replacement
value of the LIFO inventory, SEC regulations also call for disclosures of the effect of LIFO liquidations.[23] Handy and Harman had LIFO liquidations in both
1996 and 1997. In line with these SEC requirements, Handy and Harman provided the following disclosure of the effects of these inventory reductions:

   Included in continuing operations for 1996 and 1997 are profits before taxes of
   $33,630,000 and $6,408,000, respectively, from reduction in the quantities of

**EXHIBIT 2.17   LIFO inventory valuation differences: Handy and Harman
                 Inc. inventory footnote, years ended December 31
                 (in thousands).**

	1996	1997
Precious metals stated at LIFO cost	$24,763	$ 20,960
LIFO inventory—excess of year-end market value over LIFO cost	97,996	106,201

SOURCE: Data obtained from Disclosure Inc., *Compact D/SEC: Corporate Information on Public Companies Filing with the SEC* (Bethesda, MD: Disclosure Inc., June 1998).

precious metal inventories valued under the LIFO method. The after-tax effect on continuing operations for 1996 and 1997 amounted to $19,260,000 ($1.40 per basic share) and $3,717,000 ($.31 per basic share), respectively.[24]

The effect of the Handy and Harman LIFO liquidation is quite dramatic. Including the effects of the LIFO liquidations, Handy and Harman reported after-tax income from continuing operations of $33,773,000 in 1996 and $20,910,000 in 1997. Of the after-tax earnings from continuing operations 57% in 1996 and 18% in 1997 resulted from the LIFO liquidations. Handy and Harman reported benefits from LIFO liquidations for most years between 1991 and 1997.

Although Handy and Harman reported LIFO liquidations with some regularity, an analysis of sustainable earnings should consider the profit improvements from the liquidations to be nonrecurring. The LIFO-liquidation benefits result from reductions in the physical quantity of inventory. There are obvious limits on the ability to sustain these liquidations in future years; as a practical matter, the inventory cannot be reduced to zero.[25] Moreover, the variability in the size of the liquidation benefits argues for the nonrecurring classification. The profit improvements resulting from the LIFO liquidations simply represent the realization of an undervalued asset and are analogous to the gain associated with the disposition of an undervalued investment, piece of equipment, or plot of land.

A statement user cannot rely on the disclosure requirements of the SEC when reviewing the statements of nonpublic companies, especially where an outside accountant has performed only a review or compilation.[26] However, one can infer the possibility of a LIFO liquidation through the combination of a decline in the dollar amount of inventory across the year and an otherwise unexplainable improvement in gross margins. Details on the existence and impact of a LIFO liquidation could then be discussed with management.[27]

NONRECURRING ITEMS IN THE INCOME TAX NOTE

Income tax notes are among the more challenging of the disclosures found in annual reports. They can, however, be a rich source of information on nonrecurring items. Fortunately, our emphasis on the persistence of earnings requires a focus on a single key schedule found in the standard income tax note. The goal is simply to identify nonrecurring tax increases and decreases in this schedule.

The key source of information on nonrecurring increases and decreases in income taxes is a schedule that reconciles the actual tax expense or tax benefit with the amount that would have resulted if all pretax results had been taxed at the statutory federal rate. This disclosure for Archer Daniels Midland Company (ADM) is presented in Exhibit 2.18.

Notice that ADM's effective tax rate is reduced in 2000 by 17 percentage points as a result of redetermining taxes in prior years. This percentage reduction

EXHIBIT 2.18   Reconciliation of statutory and actual federal tax rates: Archer Daniels Midland Company, years ended June 30.

	1998	1999	2000
Statutory rate	35.0%	35.0%	35.0%
Prior years tax redetermination	—	—	(17.0)
Foreign sales corporation	(4.7)	(4.5)	(6.3)
State income taxes, net of federal benefit	2.4	2.2	2.7
Indefinitely invested foreign earnings	0.7	(1.8)	(0.3)
Litigation settlements and fines	1.4	—	—
Other	(1.0)	2.1	0.7
Effective rate	33.8%	33.0%	14.8%

SOURCE: Archer Daniels Midland Company, annual report, June 2000, 32.

is expressed in terms of the relationship of the tax reduction to income from continuing operations before taxes. ADM's 2000 pretax income from continuing operations is $353,237,000 and its total tax provision was $52,334,000. The 2000 effective tax rate, disclosed in Exhibit 2.18, is derived by dividing the total tax provision by income from continuing operations before taxes: $52,334,000 divided by $353,237,000 equals 14.8%.

The dollar, as opposed to percentage tax savings, is found by multiplying 17% times the 2000 pretax earnings: $353,237,000 × 0.17 = $60 million. ADM explained that "The decrease in income taxes for 2000 resulted primarily from a $60 million tax credit related to a redetermination of foreign sales corporation benefits and the resolution of various other tax issues."[28] ADM had a dispute with tax authorities over taxes for previous years, and it won. While there may be some ongoing benefit from this outcome, the $60 million should be viewed as nonrecurring in evaluating ADM's earnings performance. Ongoing tax savings from its foreign sales corporations will continue to be realized and will be reflected in the reduced level of the ADM effective tax rate.

ADM's 1998 effective tax rate was also increased by 1.4 percentage points as a result of fines and litigation settlements being deducted in arriving at pretax earnings. For income tax purposes, however, these amounts are not deductible, which means that unlike most other expenses these fines and settlements reduce after-tax earnings by the full amount of the expenses. There are no associated income tax savings, and the 1.4-percentage-point increase in the effective tax rate for 1998 is due to the nondeductible character of the litigation settlements and fines. The nonrecurring item in this case is simply the total of the fines and settlements. The tax benefit not realized because of the nondeductibility of the fines and settlements is not a separate nonrecurring item.

ADM's net income increased from about $266 million in 1999 to about $301 million in 2000. Without the $60 million nonrecurring tax benefit, ADM's 2000 net income would have declined to $241 million: $301 million − $60 million = $241 million. Identifying and adjusting 2000 earnings for this nonrecurring tax benefit results in a far different message: a decline in earnings in contrast to the reported increase.

The benefit from the tax redetermination is clearly a nonrecurring item. The tax reductions due to the foreign sales corporation feature of the tax law may or may not be sustainable. Any profit component that relies on a specific feature of the current tax law should be viewed as somewhat vulnerable. That is, its continuance requires that (1) this feature of the tax law be preserved and (2) that ADM continues to take the actions necessary to earn these tax benefits.

The ADM disclosures provide one example of a nonrecurring tax benefit plus at least one example of a benefit that may be somewhat more vulnerable than other sources of operating profit. Exhibit 2.19 provides a sampling of other nonrecurring tax benefits and tax charges that were found in recent company tax notes.

The tax benefits of both Biogen and Dana result from utilizing loss carryforwards whose benefits had not previously been recognized. The losses that produced the tax savings originated in earlier periods. Because the likelihood of their realization was not sufficiently high, the potential tax savings of the losses were not recognized in the income statements in the years in which these losses were incurred. The subsequent realization of these benefits occurs when the operating and capital loss carryforwards are used to shield operating earnings and capital gains, respectively, from taxation. These benefits should be treated as nonrecurring in analyzing earnings performance for the year in which the benefits are realized.

Gerber Scientific's effective tax rate was reduced as a result of its recognizing benefits from research and development tax credits. This feature of the tax law is designed to encourage R&D spending. As with all other tax credits, continuation of this source of tax reduction requires that the feature continue to be part of the tax law and that Gerber make the R&D expenditures necessary to earn future benefits.

The nonrecurring items of First Aviation Services and Micron Technology both result from adjustments of their tax valuation allowances. The allowance balances represent the portion of tax benefits that have been judged unlikely to be realized.[29] Increasing this balance will create a nonrecurring tax

EXHIBIT 2.19 Examples of nonrecurring income tax charges and benefits.

Company	Nonrecurring Charge or Benefit
Biogen Inc. (1999)	Benefits from net operating loss utilization
Dana Corporation (1999)	Capital loss utilization tax benefit
Detection Systems Inc. (2000)	Benefit from lower foreign tax rates
First Aviation Services Inc. (1999)	Benefit from valuation allowance decrease
The Fairchild Corporation (2000)	Benefit from revision of estimate for tax accruals
Gerber Scientific Inc. (2000)	Research and development tax credit
M.A. Hanna Company (1999)	Benefit from reversal of tax liability—tax settlement
Micron Technology Inc. (2000)	Charge for valuation allowance increase
Pall Corporation (2000)	Tax benefit of Puerto Rico operations

SOURCES: Companies' annual reports. The year following each company name designates the annual report from which the example was drawn.

charge; decreasing it, a benefit. The prospects for realization of the tax benefit must have declined for Micron Technology but improved for First Aviation Services.

Both the Fairchild Corporation and M.A. Hanna Company tax benefits were the result of reducing previously recorded tax obligations. Subsequent information indicated that the liabilities where overstated. The liability reduction was offset by a comparable reduction in the tax provision. This benefit should also be viewed as nonrecurring.

Pall Corporation has a tax reduction that is associated with operations located in Puerto Rico. In fact, most firms with operations in other countries produce such tax benefits. Foreign states offer these benefits to encourage companies, typically manufacturing companies, to locate within their borders. In many cases these benefits are for a limited period of time, though renewals are sometimes possible. As a result, while the benefits are real, there remains a possibility that they will cease at some point. In fact, Pall Corporation disclosed just such a change in its income tax note:

> The Company has two Puerto Rico subsidiaries that are organized as "possessions corporations" as defined in Section 936 of the Internal Revenue Code. The Small Business Job Protection Act of 1996 repealed Section 936 of the Internal Revenue Code, which provided a tax credit for U.S. companies with operations in certain U.S. possessions, including Puerto Rico. For companies with existing qualifying Puerto Rico operations, such as Pall, Section 936 will be phased out over a period of several years, with a decreasing credit being available through the last taxable year beginning before January 1, 2006.

This change in U.S. tax law means that previous tax benefits from the operations in Puerto Rico are not sustainable. When a company reports tax benefits because of operations in other countries, the possibility that the benefits might end or be reduced should be considered.

NONRECURRING ITEMS IN THE OTHER INCOME AND EXPENSE NOTE

An "other income (expense), net," or equivalent line item is commonly found in both the single- and multistep income statement. In the case of the multistep format, the composition of other income and expenses is sometimes detailed on the face of the income statement. In both the multi- and single-step formats, the most typical presentation is a single line item with a supporting note. Even though a note detailing the contents of other income and expense may exist, companies typically do not specify its location. Other income and expense notes tend to be listed close to the end of the notes to the financial statements.

The other income and expense note of The Sherwin-Williams Company is provided in Exhibit 2.20. The balance (income) of the Sherwin-Williams other income and expense note shows a modest increase between 1997 to 1998 and

EXHIBIT 2.20 Composition of an other income and expense note: The Sherwin-Williams Company, years ended December 31 (in thousands).

	1997	1998	1999
Dividend and royalty income	$(3,361)	$(3,069)	$(4,692)
Net expense of financing and investing activities	3,688	2,542	7,084
Provisions for environmental matters, net	107	695	15,402
Provisions for disposition and termination of operations	4,152	12,290	3,830
Foreign currency transaction losses	15,580	11,773	3,333
Miscellaneous	3,199	1,815	4,583
	$23,365	$26,046	$29,540

Note: Note references included in the Sherwin-Williams this schedule have been omitted.
SOURCE: The Sherwin-Williams Company, annual report, December 1999, 30.

1998 to 1999. In the absence of sharp changes in the balance over time, an analyst would be less inclined to look for a note detailing the makeup of the balance on the face of the income statement. However, some large nonrecurring items underlie this net balance.

Notice the very large increase in the provision for environmental matters. This increase is in turn offset in part by the sharp decline in the provision for disposition and termination of operations. Similarly, the foreign currency loss declined by about $12 million over the three years covered by the note. Some or all of the large 1999 increase in the provision for environmental matters should be considered to be nonrecurring. This would mean that results for 1999 would appear somewhat stronger with the provision added back to earnings. Some or all of the $12 million provision for disposition and termination of operations should also be added back to results for 1998.

Foreign currency gains and losses usually are not treated as nonrecurring. However, the case was made in Exhibit 2.2 (Goodyear Tire and Rubber Company) for treating them as nonrecurring when they are very irregular, either in terms of amount or sign (i.e., gain versus loss). The Sherwin-Williams foreign-currency loss declined by about $12 million between 1997 and 1999. Nonrecurring elements are included in at least three of the line items in the Sherwin-Williams other income and expense note. The net balance of the other income and expense line item has changed only modestly in the face of very substantial changes in the components of the net balance. The smooth and modest growth in this net balance contributes in turn to preserving the growth and stability of the bottom line, or net income. There is always the possibility that some of the offsetting balances in the Sherwin-Williams note were recorded for the purpose of producing smooth growth in this line item.

The location and careful analysis of the other income and expense note is especially important in the case of income statements with very little detail. In this regard, firm size and the level of detail in the income statement appear to

EXHIBIT 2.21 Composition of the other income and expense note: C.R. Bard Inc., years ended December 31 (in thousands).

	1997	1998	1999
Interest income	$(3,500)	$(6,000)	$(2,100)
Foreign exchange (gains) losses	—	(2,100)	(900)
Legal and patent settlements, net	2,000	(48,600)	—
Asset write-down	8,500	34,100	9,700
Restructuring	44,100	3,200	—
Gains from sale of product lines and other	(24,500)	—	—
Acquired R&D	—	6,400	—
Other, net	—	10,100	(200)
Total	$26,600	$(2,900)	$ 6,500

SOURCE: C.R. Bard Inc., annual report, December 1999, 27.

be inversely related. For example, excluding subtotals and the bottom line of the income statement, C.R. Bard had a total of only eight line items on its 1997 to 1999 income statements. However, its other income and expense note (Exhibit 2.21) includes numerous nonrecurring items.

A review only of C.R. Bard's 1997 to 1999 income statements would have yielded a single nonrecurring item. Depending on what is judged to be nonrecurring, Bard's other income and expense note yields an additional nine to eleven nonrecurring items. As with the Sherwin-Williams note, there is a tendency for nonrecurring items to offset each other. Notice that Bard booked a $24.5 million gain in 1997, when it also had a restructuring charge of $44.1 million. Also, an asset write-down of $34.1 million partially offset a $48.6 million gain from legal and patent settlements in 1998.[30]

Careful analysis of the composition of other income and expense line items is very important in locating nonrecurring items. As the disclosures of both Sherwin-Williams and C.R. Bard illustrate, this task is made far easier if a note is provided detailing the line item's composition. However, you should not expect to be guided to the note by a reference attached to this line item in the income statement.

NONRECURRING ITEMS IN MANAGEMENT'S DISCUSSION AND ANALYSIS (MD&A)

Management's Discussion and Analysis of Financial Condition and Results of Operations (MD&A) is an annual and a quarterly Securities and Exchange Commission reporting requirement. Provisions of this regulation have a direct bearing on the goal of locating nonrecurring items. As part of the MD&A, the SEC requires registrants to:

Describe any unusual or infrequent events or transactions or any significant economic changes that materially affected the amount of reported income from continuing operations and, in each case, indicate the extent to which income was so affected. In addition, describe any other significant components of revenues and expenses that, in the registrant's judgment, should be described in order to understand the registrant's results of operations.[31]

Complying with this regulation will require some firms to identify and discuss items that may have already been listed in other financial statements and notes. In reviewing the MD&A with a view to locating nonrecurring items, the analyst should focus on the section dealing with results of operations. Here management presents a comparison of results over the most recent three years; comparing, for example, 2001 with 2002 and 2002 with 2003 is standard.

Locating nonrecurring items in MD&A is somewhat more difficult than locating them in other places. Typically the nonrecurring items in MD&A are discussed in text and are not set out in schedules or statements. However, a small number of firms do summarize nonrecurring items in schedules within MD&A. These tend to be more comprehensive and user-friendly than piecemeal disclosures embedded in text.

The disclosure presented earlier in Exhibit 2.1 provided a restatement of the as-reported net income of Mason Dixon Bancshares. This restatement removed the effects of all items considered by Mason Dixon to be nonrecurring.[32] This disclosure was found in the MD&A of Mason Dixon. An additional example of the disclosure of nonrecurring items from the MD&A of Phillips Petroleum Company is presented in Exhibit 2.22. Unlike Mason Dixon, Phillips Petroleum's schedule simply presents a listing of their nonrecurring items.

Phillips Petroleum uses the term "special items" to describe the items in Exhibit 2.22. The reluctance to refer to these items as "nonrecurring" is understandable. Four of the seven line items include amounts in each of the three

EXHIBIT 2.22 Nonrecurring items included in MD&A of financial condition and results of operations: Phillips Petroleum Company, years ended December 31 (in millions).

	1997	1998	1999
Kenai tax settlement	$83	$115	—
Property impairments	(46)	(274)	$(34)
Tyonek prospect dry hole costs	—	(71)	—
Net gains on asset sales	16	21	73
Work force reduction charges	(3)	(60)	(3)
Pending claims and settlements	15	108	35
Other items	—	23	(10)
Total special items	$65	$(138)	$61

Note: The above numbers have been presented on an after-tax basis. Also, in a footnote to this schedule, not provided here, Phillips disclosed that the 1997 and 1998 numbers had been restated to exclude foreign-currency transaction gains and losses. That is, they were previously considered to be special (nonrecurring) items but now are not.

SOURCE: Phillips Petroleum Company, annual report, December 1999, 33.

years. This might seem inconsistent with the term *nonrecurring*. Phillips Petroleum provides the following explanation of the special items:

> Net income is affected by transactions defined by management and termed *special items,* which are not representative of the company's ongoing operations. These transactions can obscure the underlying operating results for a period and affect comparability of operating results between periods.[33]

While Phillips Petroleum uses *special* to describe what we have referred to as *nonrecurring*, the above description of its special items is consistent with earlier discussion in this chapter.

Phillips provided the following discussion of the effects of the information in Exhibit 2.22 on net income:

> Phillips's net income was $609 million in 1999, up 157 percent from net income of $237 million in 1998. Special items benefited 1999 net income by $61 million, while reducing net income in 1998 by $138 million. After excluding these items, net operating income for 1999 was $548 million, a 46 percent increase over $375 million in 1998.[34]

The above comments reveal a sharply lower growth in profit in 1999 after adjusting for the effects of the nonrecurring (special) items. A 157% increase in net income drops to 46% after adjustment for the nonrecurring items. Notice that the above discussion refers to the adjusted net income numbers as the "net operating income." This is consistent with the characterization of the special items as "not representative of the company's ongoing operations." Nevertheless, we will continue to use the term *sustainable* to refer to earnings that have been adjusted for nonrecurring items.

Presenting information on nonrecurring items in MD&A schedules is still a fairly limited practice but may be on the rise.[35] Though helpful in locating nonrecurring items, such schedules must be viewed as useful complements to but not substitutes for a complete search and restatement process. Textual discussion and disclosure of the effects on nonrecurring items on earnings is far more common than user-friendly schedules. The disclosures of C.R. Bard Inc. are illustrative:

> In 1999, Bard reported net income of $118.1 million or diluted earnings per share of $2.28. Excluding the impact of the after-tax gain on the sale of the cardiopulmonary business of $0.12 and the impact of the fourth quarter write-down of impaired assets of $0.11, diluted earnings per share was $2.27.[36]

Bard included information on revised results for each of the three years included in its 1999 annual report. The adjusted earnings-per-share series provides a better indicator of underlying trends in operating performance and is a more reliable base on which to develop projections of future earnings. The as-reported and revised earnings-per-share information is summarized in Exhibit 2.23. As is common, the adjusted earnings, from which the effects of nonrecurring items have been removed, are less volatile.

EXHIBIT 2.23   Reported and revised earnings per share: C.R. Bard Inc., years ended December 31.

Year	As-Reported Earnings per Share	Adjusted Earnings per Share
1997	$1.26	$1.67
1998	4.51	1.76
1999	2.28	2.27

SOURCE: C.R. Bard Inc., annual report, December 1999.

The discussion to this point has taken us through the first six steps in the nonrecurring-items search process outlined in Exhibit 2.3. The seventh and last step illustrates how additional nonrecurring items may sometimes be located in other selected notes to the financial statements.

NONRECURRING ITEMS IN OTHER SELECTED NOTES

Typically, most material nonrecurring items will have been located by proceeding through the first six steps of the search sequence in Exhibit 2.3. However, some additional nonrecurring items may be located in other notes. Nonrecurring items can surface in virtually any note to the financial statements. We will now discuss three selected notes that frequently contain other nonrecurring items: notes on foreign exchange, restructuring, and quarterly and segment financial data. Recall that inventory, income tax, and other income and expense notes have already been discussed in steps 3 to 5.

Foreign Exchange Notes

Foreign exchange gains and losses can result from both transaction and translation exposure. Transaction gains and losses result from either unhedged or partially hedged foreign-currency exposure.[37] This exposure is created by items such as accounts receivable and accounts payable resulting from sales and purchases denominated in foreign currencies. As foreign-currency exchange rates change, the value of the foreign-currency assets and liabilities will expand and contract. This results, in turn, in foreign currency transaction gains and losses. This is the essence of the concept of currency exposure.

Translation gains and losses result from either unhedged or partially hedged exposure associated with foreign subsidiaries. Translation exposure depends on the mix of assets and liabilities of the foreign subsidiary. In addition, the character of the operations of the foreign subsidiary and features of the foreign economy are also factors in determining both exposure and the translation method applied. There are two possible statement translation methods, and of the two only one results in translation gains or losses that appear as part of net income. With the other method, the translation adjustment will be reported as part of other comprehensive income.[38]

Foreign-currency gains and losses can also result from the use of various currency contracts, such as forwards, futures, options, and swaps, entered into for both hedging and speculation. It is not uncommon to observe foreign exchange gains and losses year after year in a company's income statement. The amounts of these items, however, as well as whether they are gains or losses are often very irregular, making them candidates for nonrecurring classification.

To illustrate, a portion of a note titled "foreign currency translation" from the 1993 annual report of Dibrell Brothers Inc. follows:

> Net gains and losses arising from transaction adjustments are accumulated on a net basis by entity and are included in the Statement of Consolidated Income, Other Income—Sundry for gains, Other Deductions—Sundry for losses. For 1993, the transaction adjustments netted to a gain of $4,180,000. The transaction adjustments were losses of $565,000 and $206,000 for 1992 and 1991, respectively, and were primarily related to the Company's Brazilian operations.[39]

The gains and losses disclosed above appeared as adjustments, reflecting either their noncash or nonoperating character, in the operating activities of Dibrell's statement of cash flows. The effect of the 1993 currency exchange gain is also referenced in Dibrell's MD&A as part of the comparison of earnings in 1993 to those in 1992.[40]

While appearing in each of the past three years, Dibrell's foreign-currency gains and losses were far from stable—two years of small losses followed by a year with a large gain. One way to gauge the significance of these exchange items is to compute their contribution to the growth in income before income taxes, extraordinary items, and cumulative effect of accounting changes. This computation is outlined for 1993 in Exhibit 2.24.

EXHIBIT 2.24 Contribution of foreign-currency gains to pretax income from continuing operations: Dibrell Brothers Inc., years ended December 31.

Pretax income from continuing operations	
1993	$58,259,560
1992	43,246,860
Increase	$15,012,700
Foreign-currency gains and losses	
1993 gain	$ 4,180,000
1992 loss	565,000
Improvement	$ 4,745,000
Contribution of the improvement in foreign currency results to 1993 pretax income from continuing operations:	
$4,745,000/$15,012,700	32%

Dibrell's currency gain made a major contribution to its profit growth in 1993. Hence, a separate note to the financial statements is devoted to its discussion and disclosure. Following the recommended search sequence, these items would be identified at step 2, the statement of cash flows, or step 6, MD&A. If search failures occur at these steps, then examination of the foreign exchange note would be a backup to ensure that the important information contained in this note is available in assessing Dibrell's 1993 performance.

Restructuring Notes

The past decade has been dominated by the corporate equivalent of a diet program. Call it streamlining, downsizing, rightsizing, redeploying, or strategic repositioning—the end result is that firms have been recording nonrecurring charges of a size and frequency that are unprecedented in our modern economic history. The size and scope of these activities ensure that they leave their tracks throughout the statements and notes. Notes on restructuring charges are among the most common transaction-specific notes. The Fairchild Corporation's restructuring note is provided in Exhibit 2.25.

A number of different items make up the Fairchild restructuring charge. Included are severance benefits, asset write-offs, and integration costs. Fairchild declares that the charges recorded in fiscal 2000 "were the direct result of formal plans to move equipment, close plants and to terminate employees." This point is made to counter criticism that some restructuring charges go well beyond restructuring activities to accrue unrelated costs plus costs that should properly be charged against future operations.

A tendency to overaccrue restructuring charges has a number of possible explanations. First, firms facing a poor year for profits may decide to take a "big

EXHIBIT 2.25 Sample restructuring note: The Fairchild Corporation, year ended June 30, 2000 (in thousands).

In fiscal 1999, we recorded $6,374 of restructuring charges. Of this amount, $500 was recorded at our corporate office for severance benefits and $348 was recorded at our aerospace distribution segment for the write-off of building improvements from premises vacated. The remaining $5,526 was recorded as a result of the Kaynar Technologies initial integration into our aerospace fasteners segment, i.e., for severance benefits ($3,932), for product integration costs incurred as of June 30, 1999 ($1,334) and for the write-down of fixed assets ($260). In fiscal 2000, we recorded $8,578 of restructuring charges as a result of the continued integration of Kaynar Technologies into our aerospace fasteners segment. All of the charges recorded during the current year were a direct result of product and plant integration costs incurred as of June 30, 2000. These costs were classified as restructuring and were the direct result of formal plans to move equipment, close plants and to terminate employees. Such costs are nonrecurring in nature. Other than a reduction in our existing cost structure, none of the restructuring charges resulted in future increases in earnings or represented an accrual of future costs. As of June 30, 2000, significantly all of our integration plans have been executed and our integration process is substantially complete.

SOURCE: The Fairchild Corporation, annual report, June 2000, F-27.

bath" and recognize excessive amounts of restructuring costs. The assumption is that simply increasing a current-period loss will not have additional negative consequences for share values. Moreover, by writing off costs currently, future profits are relieved of this burden and will therefore look stronger.

Restructuring charges have attracted the attention of the SEC. Arthur Levitt, chairman of the SEC, has registered strong objections against the use of overstated restructuring accruals to increase the earnings of subsequent periods.[41] The chairman refers to these excessive reserves as "cookie jar" reserves.[42]

There has also been some resistance to considering restructuring charges to be nonrecurring. The very need for restructuring charges indicates that earnings in previous periods were overstated. Moreover, restructuring charges commonly recur with some frequency. Note that the Fairchild disclosure in Exhibit 2.25 reveals a second charge following the initial charge for the restructuring of Kaynar Technologies. In some circles restructuring charges are referred to as "cockroach" charges—from the old saying that if you see one cockroach there are many more where that one came from.

Restructuring charges will continue to be common in income statements until the level of restructuring activity in the economy subsides. In the meantime, restructuring charges and associated reversals of charges should typically be treated as nonrecurring, even though they may appear with some repetition. At some point firms will complete the bulk of their restructuring activities, and the charges will either disappear or drop to immaterial levels.

The materiality of most restructuring charges is such that it would be difficult to miss them. In the case of The Fairchild Corporation (Exhibit 2.25), the restructuring charges were disclosed in at least five separate locations as follows:

1. On a separate line item within the operating income section of the income statement (step one in the nonrecurring items search sequence).
2. Within the operating activities section of the statement of cash flows, with the noncash portion of the charges added back to net earnings or loss (step 2 in the search sequence).
3. Disclosed in the section of the MD&A dealing with earnings (step 6 in the search sequence).
4. Disclosed in a separate note to the financial statements on restructuring charges (step 7[d]).
5. Disclosed in a note dealing with segment reporting (step 7[f] in the search sequence).

Quarterly and Segmental Financial Data

Quarterly and segmental financial disclosures frequently reveal nonrecurring items. In the case of segment disclosures, the goal is to aid in the evaluation of profitability trends by segments. The Fairchild Corporation discussion (Exhibit 2.25) disclosed its restructuring charges in the reports of segment results.

Quarterly financial data of Office Depot Inc. disclosed inventory write-downs of $56.1 million for the third quarter of 1999, a store closure and relocation charge of $46.4 million in the third quarter of 1999, and a $6.0 million reversal of the charge in the fourth quarter of 1999. Office Depot also disclosed merger and restructuring charges as part of the reporting for its segments.[43]

To complete this review of selected financial statement notes, we discuss one last item before illustrating the summarization of information on nonrecurring items and the development of the sustainable earnings series. This topic is the most recent standard-setting activity with a focus on the fundamental structure and content of the income statement.

EARNINGS ANALYSIS AND OTHER COMPREHENSIVE INCOME

The last section in the AK Steel Holdings income statement in Exhibit 2.9 is devoted to the reporting of *other comprehensive income.* This is a relatively new feature of the income statement and was introduced with the issuance by the FASB of SFAS No. 130, *Reporting Comprehensive Income.*[44] The goal of the standard is to expand the concept of income to included selected items of nonrecurring revenue, gain, expense and loss. Under the new standard, traditional net income is combined with a new component, "other comprehensive income," to produce a new bottom line, "comprehensive income."

The principal elements of other comprehensive income are listed in the other comprehensive income section of the AK Steel Holdings comprehensive income statement (Exhibit 2.9). They include:

1. Foreign currency translation adjustments.[45]
2. Unrealized gains and losses on certain securities.
3. Minimum pension liability adjustments.

Each one of these items was already recognized prior to the issuance of SFAS No. 130. However, they were reported not as part of net income but directly in shareholders' equity. The items made their way into the income statement only if they became realized gains or losses by, for example, selling securities. Notice that the AK Steel disclosures in Exhibit 2.9 list the reclassification of gains on securities that had previously been recognized in other comprehensive income. When these gains were realized they were reported in net income. However, since they had earlier been included in other comprehensive income, avoiding double counting them requires an adjustment to other comprehensive income in the year of sale.

SFAS No. 130 permitted other comprehensive income to be reported in three different ways. The preferred alternative was the income statement format of AK Steel, though reporting other comprehensive income in a separate income statement was also permitted. The third option permitted other comprehensive income to be reported directly in shareholders' equity. It should come as no surprise that most firms have elected this third option. Firms have an aversion to including items in the income statement that have the potential to increase the volatility of earnings. Hence, given the option, firms can and did choose to avoid the income statement.[46]

There is scant evidence at this time that statement users pay any attention to other comprehensive income. Companies do not include other comprehensive income in discussions of their earnings performance, nor does the financial press comment on it when earnings are announced. Earnings per share statistics do not incorporate other comprehensive income. Other comprehensive income is not currently part of earnings analysis. Hence, we consider it no further. Attitudes may change, however, about the usefulness of other comprehensive income as analysts and others become more familiar with these relatively new disclosures. It seems worthwhile to at least be made aware of these disclosures as part of a thorough treatment of income statement structure and content.

With the structure of the income statement and relevant GAAP now reviewed, the nature of nonrecurring items considered, and methods of locating nonrecurring items outlined and illustrated, we can turn to the task of developing the sustainable earnings series.

SUMMARIZING NONRECURRING ITEMS AND DETERMINING SUSTAINABLE EARNINGS

The work to this point has laid out important background but is not complete. Still required is a device to assist in summarizing information discovered on nonrecurring items so that new measures of sustainable earnings can be developed. We devote the balance of this chapter to introducing a worksheet specially designed to summarize nonrecurring items and illustrating its development and interpretation in a case study.[47]

THE SUSTAINABLE EARNINGS WORKSHEET

The sustainable earnings worksheet is shown in Exhibit 2.26. Detailed instructions on completing the worksheet follow:

1. Net income or loss is recorded on the top line of the worksheet.
2. All identified items of nonrecurring expense or loss, which were included in the income statement on a pretax basis, are recorded on the "add" lines provided. Where a prelabeled line is not listed in the worksheet, a descriptive phrase should be recorded on one of the "other" lines and the amounts recorded there. In practice, the process of locating nonrecurring items and recording them on the worksheet would take place at the same time. However, effective use of the worksheet calls for the background provided earlier in the chapter. This explains the separation of these steps in this chapter.

EXHIBIT 2.26   Adjustment worksheet for sustainable earnings base.

	Year	Year	Year
Reported net income or (loss)			
Add			
Pretax LIFO liquidation losses			
Losses on sales of fixed assets			
Losses on sales of investments			
Losses on sales of other asset			
Restructuring charges			
Investment write-downs			
Inventory write-downs			
Other asset write-downs			
Foreign currency losses			
Litigation charges			
Losses on patent infringement suits			
Exceptional bad-debt provisions			
Nonrecurring expense increases			
Temporary revenue reductions			
Other			
Other			
Other			
Subtotal			
Multiply by			
(1-combined federal, state tax rates)			
Tax-adjusted additions			
Add			
After-tax LIFO liquidation losses			
Increases in deferred tax valuation allowances			
Other nonrecurring tax charges			
Losses on discontinued operations			
Extraordinary losses			
Losses/cumulative-effect accounting changes			
Other			
Other			
Other			
Subtotal			
Total additions			
Deduct			
Pretax LIFO liquidation gains			
Gains on fixed asset sales			
Gains on sales of investments			
Gains on sales of other assets			
Reversals of restructuring accruals			
Investment write-ups (trading account)			
Foreign currency gains			
Litigation revenues			

(continued)

EXHIBIT 2.26 *(Continued)*

	Year	Year	Year
Gains on patent infringement suits	_____	_____	_____
Temporary expense decreases	_____	_____	_____
Temporary revenue increases	_____	_____	_____
Reversals of bad-debt allowances	_____	_____	_____
Other	_____	_____	_____
Other	_____	_____	_____
Other	_____	_____	_____
Subtotal	_____	_____	_____
Multiply by			
Times (1-combined federal, state tax rate)	_____	_____	_____
Tax-adjusted deductions	_____	_____	_____
After-tax LIFO liquidation gains	_____	_____	_____
Reductions in deferred tax valuation allowances	_____	_____	_____
Loss carryforward benefits from prior years	_____	_____	_____
Other nonrecurring tax benefits	_____	_____	_____
Gains on discontinued operations	_____	_____	_____
Extraordinary gains	_____	_____	_____
Gains/cumulative-effect accounting changes	_____	_____	_____
Other	_____	_____	_____
Other	_____	_____	_____
Other	_____	_____	_____
Subtotal	_____	_____	_____
Total deductions	_____	_____	_____
Sustainable earnings base	_____	_____	_____

3. When all pretax nonrecurring expenses and losses have been recorded, subtotals should be computed. These subtotals are then multiplied times 1 minus a representative combined federal, state, and foreign income-tax rate. This puts these items on an after-tax basis so that they are stated on the same basis as net income or net loss.

4. The results from step 3 should be recorded on the line titled "tax-adjusted additions."

5. All after-tax nonrecurring expenses or losses are next added separately. These items are either tax items or special income-statement items that are disclosed on an after-tax basis under GAAP, such as discontinued operations, extraordinary items, or the cumulative effect of accounting changes. The effects of LIFO liquidations are sometimes presented pretax and sometimes after-tax. Note that a line item is provided for the effect of LIFO liquidations in both the pretax and after-tax additions section of the worksheet.

6. Changes in deferred-tax-valuation allowances are recorded in the tax-adjusted additions (or deductions) section only if such changes affected net income or net loss for the period. Evidence of an income-statement impact will usually take the form of an entry in the income tax rate-reconciliation schedule.

7. The next step is to subtotal the entries for after-tax additions and then combine this subtotal with the amount labeled "tax adjusted additions." The result is then recorded on the "total additions" line at the bottom of the first page of the worksheet.

8. Completion of page 2 of the worksheet, for nonrecurring revenues and gains, follows exactly the same steps as those outlined for nonrecurring expense and loss.

9. With the completion of page 2, the sustainable earnings base for each year is computed by adding the "total additions" line item to net income (loss) and then deducting the "total deductions" line item.

ROLE OF THE SUSTAINABLE EARNINGS BASE

The sustainable earnings base provides earnings information from which the distorting effects of nonrecurring items have been removed. Some analysts refer to such revised numbers as representing "core" or "underlying" earnings. *Sustainable* is used here in the sense that earnings devoid of nonrecurring items of revenue, gain, expense, and loss are much more likely to be maintained in the future, other things equal. *Base* implies that sustainable earnings provide the most reliable foundation or starting point for projections of future results. The more reliable such forecasts become, the less the likelihood that earnings surprises will result. Again, Phillips Petroleum captures the essence of nonrecurring items in the following:

> Net income is affected by transactions defined by management and termed "special items," which are not representative of the company's ongoing operations. These transactions can obscure the underlying operating results for a period and affect comparability of operating results between periods.[48]

APPLICATION OF THE SUSTAINABLE EARNINGS BASE WORKSHEET: BAKER HUGHES INC.

This case example of using the SEB worksheet is based on the 1997 annual report of Baker Hughes Inc. and its results for 1995 to 1997. The income statement, statement of cash flows, management's discussion and analysis of results of operations (MD&A), and selected notes are in Exhibits 2.27 through 2.34. Further, to reinforce the objective of efficiency in financial analysis, we adhere to the search sequence outlined in Exhibit 2.3.

EXHIBIT 2.27 Consolidated statements of operations: Baker Hughes Inc., years ended September 30 (in millions).

	1995	1996	1997
Revenues:			
Sales	$1,805.1	$2,046.8	$2,466.7
Services and rentals	832.4	980.9	1,218.7
Total	$2,637.5	$3,027.7	$3,685.4
Costs and expenses:			
Costs of sales	$1,133.6	$1,278.1	$1,573.3
Costs of services and rentals	475.1	559.5	682.9
Selling, general, and administrative	743.0	814.2	966.9
Amortization of goodwill and other intangibles	29.9	29.6	32.3
Unusual charge		39.6	52.1
Acquired in-process research and development	—	—	118.0
Total	$2,381.6	$2,721.0	$3,425.5
Operating income	$ 255.9	$ 306.7	$ 259.9
Interest expense	(55.6)	(55.5)	(48.6)
Interest income	4.8	3.4	1.8
Gain on sale of Varco stock	—	44.3	—
Income before income taxes and cumulative effect of accounting changes	205.1	298.9	213.1
Income taxes	(85.1)	(122.5)	(104.0)
Income before cumulative effect of accounting changes	120.0	176.4	109.1
Cumulative effect of accounting changes:			
Impairment of long-lived assets to be disposed of (net of $6.0 income tax benefit)			(12.1)
Postemployment benefits (net of $7.9 income tax benefit)	(14.6)	—	—
Net income	$ 105.4	$ 176.4	$ 97.0

SOURCE: Baker Hughes Inc., annual report, September 1997, 37.

Most of the content of the Baker Hughes financial statements as well as relevant footnote and other textual information is provided. This is designed to make the exercise as realistic as possible.

THE BAKER HUGHES WORKSHEET ANALYSIS

The nonrecurring items located in the Baker Hughes annual report are enumerated in the completed SEB worksheet in Exhibit 2.35. Each of the nonrecurring items is recorded on the SEB worksheet. When an item is disclosed for the first, second, third, or fourth time, it is designated by a corresponding superscript

EXHIBIT 2.28   Consolidated statements of cash flows (operating activities only): Baker Hughes Inc., years ended September 30 (in millions).

	1995	1996	1997
Cash Flows from Operating Activities:			
Net income	$105.4	$176.4	$97.0
Adjustments to reconcile net income to net cash flows from operating activities:			
Depreciation and amortization of:			
Property	$114.2	$115.9	$143.9
Other assets and debt discount	40.4	39.9	42.1
Deferred income taxes	44.8	30.2	(6.8)
Noncash portion of unusual charge		25.3	32.7
Acquired in-process research and development			118.0
Gain on sale of Varco stock		(44.3)	
Gain on disposal of assets	(18.3)	(31.7)	(18.4)
Foreign currency translation (gain)/loss-net	1.9	8.9	(6.1)
Cumulative effect of accounting changes	14.6		12.1
Change in receivables	(94.7)	(84.1)	(129.8)
Change in inventories	(79.9)	(73.8)	(114.9)
Change in accounts payable	51.7	22.6	65.3
Changes in other assets and liabilities	(52.9)	9.4	(35.6)
Net cash flows from operating activities	$127.2	$194.7	$199.5

SOURCE: Baker Hughes Inc., annual report, September 1997, 40.

in a summary of the search process provided in Exhibit 2.36. For purposes of illustration, all nonrecurring items have been recorded on the SEB worksheet without regard to their materiality. We have followed this procedure because a materiality threshold would exclude a series of either immaterial gains or losses that could, in combination, distort a firm's apparent profitability. An effort is made to consider the possible effects of materiality in a report on the efficiency of the search process presented in Exhibit 2.37.

Without adjustment, Baker Hughes's income statement reports net income of $105.4 million in 1995, $176.4 million in 1996, and $97.0 million in 1997. The impression obtained is a company with a volatile earnings stream and no apparent growth. However, the complete adjustment for nonrecurring items conveys quite a different message. After restatement, sustainable earnings amount to $97.4 million in 1995, $158.6 million in 1996, and $241.3 million in 1997. This suggests that profits are in fact growing, though acquisitions have contributed to this result.

It should be clear that the number and magnitude of nonrecurring items identified in the Baker Hughes annual report caused its unanalyzed earnings data to be unreliable indicators of profit performance. Without the comprehensive identification of nonrecurring items and the development of the SEB

EXHIBIT 2.29 Income tax note: Baker Hughes Inc., years ended September 30 (in millions).

The geographical sources of income before income taxes and cumulative effect of accounting changes are as follows:

	1995	1996	1997
United States	$128.3	$116.4	$ 20.6
Foreign	76.8	182.5	192.5
Total	$205.1	$298.9	$213.1

The provision for income taxes is as follows:

	1995	1996	1997
Current:			
United States	$ 3.7	$ 40.1	$ 46.5
Foreign	36.6	52.2	64.3
Total current	40.3	92.3	110.8
Deferred:			
United States	42.1	20.7	(.2)
Foreign	2.7	9.5	(6.6)
Total deferred	44.8	30.2	(6.8)
Total provision for income taxes	$ 85.1	$122.5	$104.0

The provision for income taxes differs from the amount computed by applying the U.S. statutory income tax rate to income before income taxes and cumulative effect of accounting changes for the reasons set forth below:

	1995	1996	1997
Statutory income tax	$ 71.8	$104.6	$ 74.6
Nondeductible acquired in-process research and development charge			41.3
Incremental effect of foreign operations	24.8	12.5	(6.5)
1992 and 1993 IRS audit agreement			(11.4)
Nondeductible goodwill amortization	4.2	5.4	4.5
State income taxes, net of U.S. tax benefit	1.0	2.1	2.9
Operating loss and credit carryforwards	(13.1)	(3.3)	(4.2)
Other, net	(3.6)	1.2	2.8
Total provision for income taxes	$ 85.1	$122.5	$104.0

Deferred income taxes reflect the net tax effects of temporary differences between the carrying amounts of assets and liabilities for financial reporting purposes and the amounts used for income tax purposes, and operating loss and tax credit carryforwards. The tax effects of the Company's temporary differences and carryforwards are as follows:

EXHIBIT 2.29   *(Continued)*

	1996	1997
Deferred tax liabilities:		
Property	$ 62.3	$ 90.6
Other assets	57.7	147.5
Excess costs arising from acquisitions	64.0	67.6
Undistributed earnings of foreign subsidiaries	41.3	41.3
Other	37.4	36.5
Total	$262.7	$ 383.5
Deferred tax assets:		
Receivables	$ 4.1	$ 2.8
Inventory	72.4	72.4
Employee benefits	44.0	21.5
Other accrued expenses	20.2	40.6
Operating loss carryforwards	16.6	9.0
Tax credit carryforwards	30.8	15.9
Other	15.9	34.9
Subtotal	$204.0	$ 197.1
Valuation allowance	(13.1)	(5.7)
Total	190.9	191.4
Net deferred tax liability	$ 71.8	$ 192.1

A valuation allowance is recorded when it is more likely than not that some portion or all of the deferred tax assets will not be realized. The ultimate realization of the deferred tax assets depends on the ability to generate sufficient taxable income of the appropriate character in the future. The Company has reserved the operating loss carryforwards in certain non-U.S. jurisdictions where its operations have decreased, currently ceased or the Company has withdrawn entirely.

Provision has been made for U.S. and additional foreign taxes for the anticipated repatriation of certain earnings of foreign subsidiaries of the Company. The Company considers the undistributed earnings of its foreign subsidiaries above the amounts already provided for to be permanently reinvested. These additional foreign earnings could become subject to additional tax if remitted, or deemed remitted, as a dividend; however, the additional amount of taxes payable is not practicable to estimate.

SOURCE: Baker Hughes Inc., annual report, September 1997, 48–49.

EXHIBIT 2.30 Management's discussion and analysis (excerpts from results of operations section): Baker Hughes Inc., years ended September 30 (in millions).

Revenues

1997 versus 1996

Consolidated revenues for 1997 were $3,685.4 million, an increase of 22% over 1996 revenues of $3,027.7 million. Sales revenues were up $419.9 million, an increase of 21%, and services and rental revenues were up $237.8 million, an increase of 24%. Approximately 64% of the Company's 1997 consolidated revenues were derived from international activities. The three 1997 acquisitions contributed $192.1 million of the revenue improvement.

Oilfield Operations 1997 revenues were $2,862.6 million, an increase of 19.4% over 1996 revenues of $2,397.9 million. Excluding the Drilex acquisition, which accounted for $70.5 million of the revenue improvement, the revenue growth of 16.4% outpaced the 14.4% increase in the worldwide rig count. In particular, revenues in Venezuela increased 37.6%, or $58.6 million, as that country continues to work towards its stated goal of significantly increasing oil production.

Chemical revenues were $417.2 million in 1997, an increase of 68.5% over 1996 revenues of $247.6 million. The Petrolite acquisition was responsible for $91.6 million of the improvement. Revenue growth excluding the acquisition was 31.5% driven by the strong oilfield market and the impact of acquiring the remaining portion of a Venezuelan joint venture in 1997. This investment was accounted for on the equity method in 1996.

Process Equipment revenues for 1997 were $386.1 million, an increase of 9.4% over 1996 revenues of $352.8 million. Excluding revenues from 1997 acquisitions of $32.7 million, revenues were flat compared to the prior year due to weakness in the pulp and paper industry combined with delays in customers' capital spending.

1996 versus 1995

Consolidated revenues for 1996 increased $390.2 million, or 14.8%, over 1995. Sales revenues were up 13.4% and services and rentals revenues were up 17.8%. International revenues accounted for approximately 65% of 1996 consolidated revenues.

Oilfield Operations revenues increased $325.7 million or 15.7% over 1995 revenues of $2,072.2 million. Activity was particularly strong in several key oilfield regions of the world including the North Sea, Gulf of Mexico and Nigeria where revenues were up $93.4 million, $56.8 million and $30.1 million, respectively. Strong drilling activity drove a $35.5 million increase in Venezuelan revenues.

Chemical revenues rose $23.9 million, or 10.7% over 1995 revenues as its oilfield business benefited from increased production levels in the U.S.

Process Equipment revenues for 1996 increased 10.4% over 1995 revenues of $319.6 million. Excluding revenues from 1996 acquisitions of $21.5 million, revenues increased 3.7%. The growth in the minerals processing and pulp and paper industry slowed from the prior year.

Costs and Expenses Applicable to Revenues

Costs of sales and costs of services and rentals have increased in 1997 and 1996 from the prior years in line with the related revenue increases. Gross margin percentages, excluding the effect of a nonrecurring item in 1997, have increased from 39.0% in 1995 to 39.3% in 1996 and 39.4% in 1997. The nonrecurring item relates to finished goods inventory acquired in the Petrolite acquisition that was increased by $21.9 million to its estimated selling price. The Company sold the inventory in the fourth quarter of 1997 and, as such, the $21.9 million is included in cost of sales in 1997.

EXHIBIT 2.30 *(Continued)*

Selling, General, and Administrative

Selling, general and administrative ("SG&A") expense increased $152.7 million in 1997 from 1996 and $71.2 million in 1996 from 1995. The three 1997 acquisitions were responsible for $54.3 million of the 1997 increase. As a percent of consolidated revenues, SG&A was 26.2%, 26.9% and 28.2% in 1997, 1996 and 1995, respectively.

Excluding the impact of acquisitions, the Company added approximately 2,500 employees during 1997 to keep pace with the increased activity levels. As a result, employee training and development efforts increased in 1997 as compared to the previous two years. These increases were partially offset by $4.1 million of foreign exchange gains in 1997 compared to foreign exchange losses of $11.4 million in 1996 due to the devaluation of the Venezuelan Bolivar.

The three-year cumulative rate of inflation in Mexico exceeded 100% for the year ended December 31, 1996; therefore, Mexico is considered to be a highly inflationary economy. Effective December 31, 1996, the functional currency for the Company's investments in Mexico was changed from the Mexican Peso to the U.S. Dollar.

Amortization Expense

Amortization expense in 1997 increased $2.7 million from 1996 due to the Petrolite acquisition. Amortization expense in 1996 remained comparable to 1995 as no significant acquisitions or dispositions were made during those two years.

Unusual Charge

1997: During the fourth quarter of 1997, the Company recorded an unusual charge of $52.1 million. In connection with the acquisitions of Petrolite, accounted for as a purchase, and Drilex, accounted for as a pooling of interests, the Company recorded unusual charges of $35.5 million and $7.1 million, respectively, to combine the acquired operations with those of the Company. The charges include the cost of closing redundant facilities, eliminating or relocating personnel and equipment and rationalizing inventories that require disposal at amounts less than their cost. A $9.5 million charge was also recorded as a result of the decision to discontinue a low margin, oilfield product line in Latin America and to sell the Tracor Europa subsidiary, a computer peripherals operations, which resulted in a write-down of the investment to its net realizable value. Cash provisions of the unusual charge totaled $19.4 million. The Company spent $5.5 million in 1997 and expects to spend substantially all of the remaining $13.9 million in 1998. Such expenditures relate to specific plans and clearly defined actions and will be funded from operations and available credit facilities.

1996: During the third quarter of 1996, the Company recorded an unusual charge of $39.6 million. The charge consisted primarily of the write-off of $8.5 million of Oilfield Operations patents that no longer protected commercially significant technology, a $5.0 million impairment of a Latin America joint venture due to changing market conditions in the region in which it operates and restructuring charges totaling $24.1 million. The restructuring charges include the downsizing of Baker Hughes INTEQ's Singapore and Paris operations, a reorganization of EIMCO Process Equipment's Italian operations and the consolidation of certain Baker Oil Tools manufacturing operations. Noncash provisions of the charge totaled $25.3 million and consist primarily of the write-down of assets to net realizable value. The remaining $14.3 million of the charge represents future cash expenditures related to severance under existing benefit arrangements, the relocation of people and equipment and abandoned leases. The Company spent $4.2 million of the cash during 1996, $6.3 million in 1997 and expects to spend the remaining $3.8 million in 1998.

(continued)

EXHIBIT 2.30 *(Continued)*

Acquired In-Process Research and Development

In the Petrolite acquisition, the Company allocated $118.0 million of the purchase price to in-process research and development. In accordance with generally accepted accounting principles, the Company recorded the acquired in-process research and development as a charge to expense because its technological feasibility had not been established and it had no alternative future use at the date of acquisition.

Interest Expense

Interest expense in 1997 decreased $6.9 million from 1996 due to lower average debt levels, primarily as a result of the maturity of the 4.125% Swiss Franc Bonds in June 1996. Interest expense in 1996 remained comparable to 1995 as slightly higher average debt balances were offset by a slightly lower weighted average interest rate.

Gain on Sale of Varco Stock

In May 1996, the Company sold 6.3 million shares of Varco International, Inc. ("Varco") common stock, representing its entire investment in Varco. The Company received net proceeds of $95.5 million and recognized a pretax gain of $44.3 million. The Company's investment in Varco was accounted for using the equity method. Equity income included in the Consolidated Statements of Operations for 1996 and 1995 was $1.8 million and $3.2 million, respectively.

Income Taxes

During 1997, the Company reached an agreement with the Internal Revenue Service ("IRS") regarding the audit of its 1992 and 1993 U.S. consolidated income tax returns. The principal issue in the examination related to intercompany pricing on the transfer of goods and services between U.S. and non-U.S. subsidiary companies. As a result of the agreement, the Company recognized a tax benefit through the reversal of deferred income taxes previously provided of $11.4 million ($.08 per share) in the quarter ended June 30, 1997.

The effective income tax rate for 1997 was 48.8% as compared to 41.0% in 1996 and 41.5% in 1995. The increase in the rate for 1997 is due in large part to the nondeductible charge for the acquired in-process research and development related to the Petrolite acquisition offset by the IRS agreement as explained above. The effective rates differ from the federal statutory rate in all years due primarily to taxes on foreign operations and nondeductible goodwill amortization. The Company expects the effective income tax rate in 1998 to be between 38% and 39%.

SOURCE: Baker Hughes Inc., annual report, September 1997, 30–32.

EXHIBIT 2.31 Summary of significant accounting policies note (partial): Baker Hughes Inc., years ended September 30 (in millions).

Impairment of assets: The Company adopted Statement of Financial Accounting Standards ("SFAS") No. 121, *Accounting for the Impairment of Long-lived Assets and for Long-lived Assets to be Disposed Of,* effective October 1, 1996. The statement sets forth guidance as to when to recognize an impairment of long-lived assets, including goodwill, and how to measure such an impairment. The methodology set forth in SFAS No. 121 is not significantly different from the Company's prior policy and, therefore, the adoption of SFAS No. 121 did not have a significant impact on the consolidated financial statements as it relates to impairment of long-lived assets used in operations. However, SFAS No. 121 also addresses the accounting for long-lived assets to be disposed of and requires these assets to be carried at the lower of cost or fair market value, rather than the lower of cost or net realizable value, the method that was previously used by the Company. The Company recognized a charge to income of $12.1 million ($.08 per share), net of a tax benefit of $6.0 million, as the cumulative effect of a change in accounting in the first quarter of 1997.

SOURCE: Baker Hughes Inc., annual report, September 1997, 41.

EXHIBIT 2.32 Acquisitions and dispositions note: Baker Hughes Inc., years ended September 30 (in millions).

1997

Petrolite

In July 1997, the Company acquired Petrolite Corporation ("Petrolite") and Wm. S. Barnickel & Company ("Barnickel"), the holder of 47.1% of Petrolite's common stock, for 19.3 million shares of the Company's common stock having a value of $730.2 million in a three-way business combination accounted for using the purchase method of accounting. Additionally, the Company assumed Petrolite's outstanding vested and unvested employee stock options that were converted into the right to acquire 1.0 million shares of the Company's common stock. Such assumption of Petrolite options by the Company had a fair market value of $21.0 million resulting in total consideration in the acquisitions of $751.2 million. Petrolite, previously a publicly held company, is a manufacturer and marketer of specialty chemicals used in the petroleum and process industries. Barnickel was a privately held company that owned marketable securities, which were sold after the acquisition, in addition to its investment in Petrolite.

The purchase price has been allocated to the assets purchased and the liabilities assumed based on their estimated fair market values at the date of acquisition as follows (millions of dollars):

Working capital	$ 64.5
Property	170.1
Prepaid pension cost	80.3
Intangible assets	126.0
Other assets	89.6
In-process research and development	118.0
Goodwill	263.7
Debt	(31.7)
Deferred income taxes	(106.7)
Other liabilities	(22.6)
Total	$751.2

In accordance with generally accepted accounting principles, the amount allocated to in-process research and development, which was determined by an independent valuation, has been recorded as a charge to expense in the fourth quarter of 1997 because its technological feasibility had not been established and it had no alternative future use at the date of acquisition.

The Company incurred certain liabilities as part of the plan to combine the operations of Petrolite with those of the Company. These liabilities relate to the Petrolite operations and include severance of $13.8 million for redundant marketing, manufacturing and administrative personnel, relocation of $5.8 million for moving equipment and transferring marketing and technology personnel, primarily from St. Louis to Houston, and environmental remediation of $16.5 million for redundant properties and facilities that will be sold. Cash spent during the fourth quarter of 1997 totaled $7.7 million. The Company anticipates completing these activities in 1998, except for some environmental remediation that will occur in 1998 and 1999.

The operating results of Petrolite and Barnickel are included in the 1997 consolidated statement of operations from the acquisition date, July 2, 1997. The following unaudited pro forma information combines the results of operations of the Company, Petrolite and Barnickel assuming the acquisitions had occurred at the beginning of the periods presented. The pro forma summary does not necessarily reflect the results that would have occurred had the acquisitions been completed for the periods presented, nor do they purport to be indicative of the results that will be obtained in the future, and excludes certain nonrecurring charges related to the acquisition which have an after tax impact of $155.2 million.

(continued)

EXHIBIT 2.32   *(Continued)*

	(Millions of dollars, except per share amounts)	
	1996	**1997**
Revenues	$3,388.4	$3,944.0
Income before accounting change	189.3	283.9
Income per share before accounting change	1.16	1.69

In connection with the acquisition of Petrolite, the Company recorded an unusual charge of $35.5 million. See Note 5 of Notes to Consolidated Financial Statements.

Environmental Technology Division of Deutz AG

In July 1997, the Company acquired the Environmental Technology Division, a decanter centrifuge and dryer business, of Deutz AG ("ETD") for $53.0 million, subject to certain postclosing adjustments. This acquisition is now part of Bird Machine Company and has been accounted for using the purchase method of accounting. Accordingly, the cost of the acquisition has been allocated to assets acquired and liabilities assumed based on their estimated fair market values at the date of acquisition, July 7, 1997. The operating results of ETD are included in the 1997 consolidated statement of operations from the acquisition date. Pro forma results of the acquisition have not been presented as the pro forma revenue, income before accounting change and earnings per share would not be materially different from the Company's actual results. For its most recent fiscal year ended December 31, 1996, ETD had revenues of $103.0 million.

Drilex

In July 1997, the Company acquired Drilex International Inc. ("Drilex") a provider of products and services used in the directional and horizontal drilling and workover of oil and gas wells for 2.7 million shares of the Company's common stock. The acquisition was accounted for using the pooling of interests method of accounting. Under this method of accounting, the historical cost basis of the assets and liabilities of the Company and Drilex are combined at recorded amounts and the results of operations of the combined companies for 1997 are included in the 1997 consolidated statement of operations. The historical results of the separate companies for years prior to 1997 are not combined because the retained earnings and results of operations of Drilex are not material to the consolidated financial statements of the Company. In connection with the acquisition of Drilex, the Company recorded an unusual charge of $7.1 million for transaction and other one time costs associated with the acquisition. See Note 5 of Notes to Consolidated Financial Statements. For its fiscal year ended December 31, 1996 and 1995, Drilex had revenues of $76.1 million and $57.5 million, respectively.

1996

In April 1996, the Company purchased the assets and stock of a business operating as Vortoil Separation Systems, and certain related oil/water separation technology, for $18.8 million. In June 1996, the Company purchased the stock of KTM Process Equipment, Inc., a centrifuge company, for $14.1 million. These acquisitions are part of Baker Hughes Process Equipment Company and have been accounted for using the purchase method of accounting. Accordingly, the costs of the acquisitions have been allocated to assets acquired and liabilities assumed based on their estimated fair market values at the dates of acquisition. The operating results are included in the consolidated statements of operations from the respective acquisition dates.

In April 1996, the Company exchanged the 100,000 shares of Tuboscope Inc. ("Tuboscope") Series A convertible preferred stock held by the Company since October 1991, for 1.5 million shares of Tuboscope common stock and a warrant to purchase 1.25 million shares of Tuboscope common stock. The warrants are exercisable at $10 per share and expire on December 31, 2000.

SOURCE: Baker Hughes Inc., annual report, September 1997, 43–45.

EXHIBIT 2.33 Unusual charges note: Baker Hughes Inc., years ended September 30 (in millions).

1997

During the fourth quarter of 1997, the Company recognized a $52.1 million unusual charge consisting of the following (millions of dollars):

Baker Petrolite:	
Severance for 140 employees	$ 2.2
Relocation of people and equipment	3.4
Environmental	5.0
Abandoned leases	1.5
Integration costs	2.8
Inventory write-down	11.3
Write-down of other assets	9.3
Drilex:	
Write-down of property and other assets	4.1
Banking and legal fees	3.0
Discontinued product lines:	
Severance for 50 employees	1.5
Write-down of inventory, property and other assets	8.0
Total	$52.1

In connection with the acquisitions of Petrolite and Drilex, the Company recorded unusual charges of $35.5 million and $7.1 million, respectively, to combine the acquired operations with those of the Company. The charges include the cost of closing redundant facilities, eliminating or relocating personnel and equipment and rationalizing inventories that require disposal at amounts less than their cost. A $9.5 million charge was recorded as a result of the decision to discontinue a low margin, oilfield product line in Latin America and to sell the Tracor Europa subsidiary, a computer peripherals operation, which resulted in a write-down of the investment to net realizable value. Cash provisions of the unusual charge totaled $19.4 million. The Company spent $5.5 million in 1997 and expects to spend substantially all of the remaining $13.9 million in 1998.

1996

During the third quarter of 1996, the Company recognized a $39.6 million unusual charge consisting of the following (millions of dollars):

Patent write-off	$ 8.5
Impairment of joint venture	5.0
Restructurings:	
Severance for 360 employees	7.1
Relocation of people and equipment	2.3
Abandoned leases	2.8
Inventory write-down	1.5
Write-down of assets	10.4
Other	2.0
Total	$39.6

The Company has certain oilfield operations patents that no longer protect commercially significant technology resulting in the write-off of $8.5 million. A $5.0 million impairment of a Latin America joint venture was recorded due to changing market conditions in the region in which it operates. The Company recorded a $24.1 million restructuring charge including the downsizing of Baker Hughes INTEQ's Singapore and Paris operations, a reorganization of EIMCO Process Equipment's Italian operations and the consolidation of certain Baker Oil Tools manufacturing operations. Cash provisions of the charge totaled $14.3 million. The Company spent $4.2 million in 1996, $6.3 million in 1997 and expects to spend the remaining $3.8 million in 1998.

SOURCE: Baker Hughes Inc., annual report, September 1997, 45.

EXHIBIT 2.34   Segment and related information note: Baker Hughes Inc., years ended September 30 (in millions).

NOTE 10

Segment and Related Information

The Company adopted SFAS No. 131, *Disclosures about Segments of an Enterprise and Related Information,* in 1997 which changes the way the Company reports information about its operating segments. The information for 1996 and 1995 has been restated from the prior year's presentation in order to conform to the 1997 presentation.

The Company's nine business units have separate management teams and infrastructures that offer different products and services. The business units have been aggregated into three reportable segments (oilfield, chemicals and process equipment) since the long-term financial performance of these reportable segments is affected by similar economic conditions.

Oilfield: This segment consists of five business units—Baker Hughes INTEQ, Baker Oil Tools, Baker Hughes Solutions, Centrilift and Hughes Christensen—that manufacture and sell equipment and provide services and solutions used in the drilling, completion, production and maintenance of oil and gas wells. The principle markets for this segment include all major oil and gas producing regions of the world including North America, Latin America, Europe, Africa and the Far East. Customers include major multinational, independent and national or state-owned oil companies.

Chemicals: Baker Petrolite is the sole business unit reported in this segment. They manufacture specialty chemicals for inclusion in the sale of integrated chemical technology solutions for petroleum production, transportation and refining. The principle geographic markets for this segment include all major oil and gas producing regions of the world. This segment also provides chemical technology solutions to other industrial markets throughout the world including petrochemicals, steel, fuel additives, plastics, imaging and adhesives. Customers include major multinational, independent and national or state-owned oil companies as well as other industrial manufacturers.

Process Equipment: This segment consists of three business units—EIMCO Process Equipment, Bird Machine Company and Baker Hughes Process Systems—that manufacture and sell process equipment for separating solids from liquids and liquids from liquids through filtration, sedimentation, centrifugation and floatation processes. The principle markets for this segment include all regions of the world where there are significant industrial and municipal wastewater applications and base metals activity. Customers include municipalities, contractors, engineering companies and pulp and paper, minerals, industrial and oil and gas producers.

The accounting policies of the reportable segments are the same as those described in Note 1 of Notes to Consolidated Financial Statements. The Company evaluates the performance of its operating segments based on income before income taxes, accounting changes, nonrecurring items and interest income and expense. Intersegment sales and transfers are not significant.

Summarized financial information concerning the Company's reportable segments is shown in the following table. The "Other" column includes corporate related items, results of insignificant operations and, as it relates to segment profit (loss), income and expense not allocated to reportable segments (millions of dollars).

1997

Revenues	$2,862.6	$417.2	$386.1	$19.5	$3,685.4
Segment profit (loss)	416.8	41.9	36.3	(281.9)	213.1
Total assets	3,014.3	1,009.5	363.7	368.8	4,756.3
Capital expenditures	289.7	24.8	6.4	21.8	342.7
Depreciation and amortization	143.2	20.5	8.4	4.1	176.2

EXHIBIT 2.34 *(Continued)*

1996

Revenues	$2,397.9	$247.6	$352.8	$29.4	$3,027.7
Segment profit (loss)	329.1	23.3	31.2	(84.7)	298.9
Total assets	2,464.6	270.3	258.9	303.6	3,297.4
Capital expenditures	157.5	16.6	6.6	1.5	182.2
Depreciation and amortization	123.6	12.2	6.7	3.0	145.5

1995

Revenues	$2,072.2	$223.7	$319.6	$22.0	$2,637.5
Segment profit (loss)	249.6	17.8	29.7	(92.0)	205.1
Total assets	2,423.7	259.8	187.3	295.8	3,166.6
Capital expenditures	119.1	11.0	5.0	3.8	138.9
Depreciation and amortization	123.9	12.4	5.4	2.4	144.1

The following table presents the details of "Other" segment profit (loss).

	1995	1996	1997
Corporate expenses	$(39.7)	$(40.2)	$(44.3)
Interest expense-net	(50.8)	(52.1)	(46.8)
Unusual charge		(39.6)	(52.1)
Acquired in-process research and development			(118.0)
Nonrecurring charge to cost of sales for Petrolite inventories			(21.9)
Gain on sale of Varco stock		44.3	
Other	(1.5)	2.9	1.2
Total	$(92.0)	$(84.7)	$(281.9)

The following table presents revenues by country based on the location of the use of the product or service.

	1995	1996	1997
United States	$972.9	$1,047.2	$1,319.7
United Kingdom	207.6	277.9	288.0
Venezuela	122.7	160.0	244.2
Canada	157.5	165.1	204.5
Norway	104.2	145.6	175.0
Indonesia	54.5	92.7	128.0
Nigeria	33.5	64.1	83.5
Oman	45.7	56.8	77.2
Other (approximately 60 countries)	938.9	1,018.3	1,165.3
Total	$2,637.5	$3,027.7	$3,685.4

The following table presents property by country based on the location of the asset.

	1995	1996	1997
United States	$353.0	$359.9	$593.3
United Kingdom	67.6	77.7	145.3
Venezuela	19.0	25.1	33.3
Germany	18.4	19.3	21.4
Norway	11.3	10.9	20.0
Canada	8.0	9.1	16.9
Singapore	25.0	17.7	11.7
Other countries	72.8	79.3	141.0
Total	$575.1	$599.0	$982.9

SOURCE: Baker Hughes Inc., annual report, September 1997, 49–51.

EXHIBIT 2.35 Adjustment worksheet for sustainable earnings base: Baker Hughes Inc., years ended September 30 (in millions).

	1995	1996	1997
Reported net income or (loss)	$105.4	$176.4	$97.0
Add			
Pretax LIFO liquidation losses			
Losses on sales of fixed assets			
Losses on sales of investments			
Losses on sales of "other" assets			
Restructuring charges (unusual charge)		39.6	52.1
Investment write-downs			
Inventory write-downs (included in cost of sales)			21.9
Other asset write-downs			
Foreign currency losses	1.9	11.4	
Litigation charges			
Losses on patent infringement suits			
Exceptional bad debt provisions			
Temporary expense increases			
Temporary revenue reductions			
Other			
Other			
Other			
Subtotal	$1.9	$51.0	$74.0
Multiply by			
(1 – Combined federal and state tax rates)	58%	58%	58%
Tax-adjusted additions	$1.1	$29.6	$42.9
Add			
After-tax LIFO liquidation losses			
Increases in deferred tax valuation allowances			
Other nonrecurring tax charges			
Losses on discontinued operations			
Extraordinary losses			
Losses/cumulative-effect accounting changes	14.6		12.1
Other (acquired in-process R&D)			118.0
Other			
Other			
Subtotal	$14.6		$130.1
Total additions	$15.7	$29.6	$173.0

EXHIBIT 2.35   *(Continued)*

	1995	1996	1997
Deduct			
Pretax LIFO liquidation gains			
Gains on sales of fixed assets (disposal of assets)	18.3	31.7	18.4
Gains on sales of investments (Varco stock)		44.3	
Gains on sales of other assets			
Reversals of restructuring charges			
Investment write-ups (trading account)			
Foreign currency gains			4.1
Litigation revenues			
Gains on patent infringement suits			
Temporary expense decreases			
Temporary revenue increases			
Reversals of bad-debt allowances			
Other			
Other			
Other			
Subtotal	$18.3	$76.0	$22.5
Multiply by			
(1 – Combined federal and state tax rate)	58%	58%	58%
Tax-adjusted deductions	$10.6	$44.1	$13.1
Deduct			
After-tax LIFO liquidation gains			
Reductions in deferred tax valuation allowances			
Loss carryforward benefits—from prior periods	13.1	3.3	4.2
Other nonrecurring tax benefits			
(IRS audit agreement)			11.4
Gains on discontinued operations			
Extraordinary gains			
Gains/cumulative-effect accounting changes			
Other			
Other			
Other			
Subtotal	$13.1	$3.3	$15.6
Total deductions	$23.7	$47.4	$28.7
Sustainable earnings base	$97.4	$158.6	$241.3

EXHIBIT 2.36   Summary of nonrecurring items search process: Baker Hughes Inc.

Step and Search Location	Nonrecurring Item Revealed
1. Income statement	Unusual charge (1996-1997)[1]
	Acquired in-process research and development (1997)[1]
	Gain on sale of Varco stock (1996)[1]
	Cumulative effect of accounting changes (1995, 1997)[1]
2. Statement of cash flows	Acquired in-process research and development (1997)[2]
	Gain on sale of Varco stock (1996)[2]
	Gain on disposal of assets (1995–1997)[1]
	Foreign currency translation (gain)/loss, net (1995–1997)[1]
	Cumulative effect of accounting changes (1995, 1997)[2]
3. Inventory note	No nonrecurring items located
4. Income tax note	1992 and 1993 IRS audit agreement (1997)[1]
	Operating loss and credit carryforwards (1995–1997)[1]
5. Other income (expense) note	No note provided
6. MD&A	Petrolite inventory writedown in cost of sales (1997)[1]
	Unusual charge (1996-1997)[2]
	Acquired in-process research and development (1997)[3]
	Gain on sale of Varco stock (1996)[3]
	1992 and 1993 IRS audit agreement (1997)[2]
	Foreign currency translation (gain)/loss, net (1996–1997)[2]
7. Other notes revealing nonrecurring items:	
a. Significant accounting policies	Cumulative effect of accounting changes (1995, 1997)[3]
b. Acquisitions and dispositions	Acquired in-process research and development (1997)[4]
	Unusual charges (1996-1997)[3]
	Gain on sale of Varco stock (1996)[4]
c. Unusual charge	Unusual charges (1996-1997)[4]
d. Segment information	Unusual charges (1996-1997)[5]
	Acquired in-process research and development (1997)[5]
	Petrolite inventory writedown in cost of sales (1997)[2]
	Gain on sale of Varco stock (1996)[5]

Note: The superscripts 1, 2, 3, and so on indicate the number of times the nonrecurring item was found. For instance, "Gain on sale of Varco stock" was found in the income statement (first location); in the statement of cash flows (second location); in MD&A (third location); in the "Acquisitions and dispositions" note (fourth location); and in the "Segment and related information" note (fifth location).

EXHIBIT 2.37   Efficiency of nonrecurring items search process: Baker Hughes Inc.

Step and Search Location	Incremental Nonrecurring Items Discovered			
	(1) All Non-recurring Items	(2) Cumulative % Located	(3) All Material[a] Items	(4) Cumulative % Located
1. Income statement	6	35%	6	50%
2. Statement of cash flows	6	71	3	75
3. Inventory note	0	71	0	75
4. Income tax note	4	94	2	92
5. Other income (expense) note	0	94	0	92
6. MD&A	1	100	1	100
7a. Significant accounting policies note	0	100	0	100
7b. Acquisitions and dispositions note	0	100	0	100
7c. Unusual charge note	0	100	0	100
7d. Segment and related information note	0	100	0	100
Total nonrecurring items	17	100%	12	100%

[a] Five percent or more of the amount of the net income or net loss, on a tax-adjusted basis.

worksheet, the company's three-year operating performance is virtually impossible to discern.

The efficient search sequence for identifying nonrecurring items in Exhibit 2.3 was based on the experience of the authors supported by a large-scale study of nonrecurring items by H. Choi. While the recommended search sequence may not be equally effective in all cases, Exhibit 2.37 demonstrates that most of Baker Hughes's nonrecurring items could be located by employing only steps 1 to 5, a sequence that is very cost-effective. In fact, 92% of all *material* nonrecurring items were located through the first four steps of the search sequence. Further, locating these items requires reading very little text, and the nonrecurring items are generally set out prominently in either statements or schedules.

Exhibit 2.37 presents information on the efficiency of the search process. The meaning of each column in the exhibit is as follows:

Column 1:   The number of nonrecurring items located at each step in the search process. This is based on all 17 nonrecurring items without regard to their materiality.

Column 2:   The cumulative percentage of all nonrecurring items located through each step of the search process. Ninety four percent of the total nonrecurring items were located through the first five steps of the search process. All nonrecurring items were located by step 6.

Column 3:   Same as column 1 except only material nonrecurring items (those items exceeding 5% of net income on an after-tax basis).

Column 4:   Same as column 2 except that only material nonrecurring items were considered.

SOME FURTHER POINTS ON THE BAKER HUGHES WORKSHEET

The construction of an SEB worksheet always requires a judgment call. One could, of course, avoid all materiality judgments by simply recording all nonrecurring items without regard to their materiality. However, the classification of items as nonrecurring, as well as on occasion their measurement, calls for varying degrees of judgment. Some examples of Baker Hughes items that required the exercise of judgment, either in terms of classification or measurement, are discussed next.

The Petrolite Inventory Adjustment

A pretax addition was made in Exhibit 2.35 for the effect on 1997 earnings of inventory obtained with the Petrolite acquisition (see Exhibits 2.30 and 2.34). Accounting requirements for purchases call for adjusting acquired assets to their fair values. This adjustment required a $21.9 million increase in Petrolite inventories to change them from cost to selling price. This meant that there was no profit margin on the subsequent sale of this inventory in the fourth quarter of 1997. That is, cost of sales was equal to the sales amount. Baker Hughes labeled this $21.9 million acquisition adjustment "nonrecurring charge to cost of sales for Petrolite inventories" (see segment disclosures in Exhibit 2.34).

This Petrolite inventory charge raised the level of cost of sales in relationship to sales. However, this temporary increase in the cost-of-sales percentage (cost of sales divided by sales) was not expected to persist in the future. We concurred with the Baker Hughes judgment and treated this $21.9 million cost-of-sales component as a nonrecurring item in developing sustainable earnings.

Foreign Exchange Gains and Losses

Information on foreign exchange gains and losses was disclosed in the statement of cash flows (Exhibit 2.28) and in the MD&A (Exhibit 2.30). The statement of cash flows disclosed foreign-currency losses of $1.9 million in 1995 and $8.9 million in 1996. A $6.1 million gain was disclosed in 1997. However, the MD&A disclosed a foreign-currency loss of $11.4 million for 1996 and a gain of $4.1 million for 1997. The foreign-currency items in the statement of cash flows represent recognized but unrealized gains and losses. As such, there are no associated cash inflows and outflows. However, the disclosures in the MD&A represent all of the net foreign-exchange gains and losses, both realized and unrealized. These are the totals that would have been added or deducted in arriving at net income and also represent the nonrecurring foreign currency gains and losses.

For 1996 and 1997, the Baker Hughes worksheet includes the foreign currency gain and loss disclosed in the MD&A, a loss of $11.4 million for 1996 and a gain of $4.1 million for 1997. In the absence of a disclosure of any foreign currency gain or loss in the MD&A for 1995, the worksheet simply included the $1.9 million loss disclosed in the statement of cash flows. Adjusting the foreign-currency gains and losses out of net income is based on a judgment that comparative performance is better represented in the absence of these irregular items.

The Tax Rate Assumption and Acquired R&D

The tax rate used in the Baker Hughes worksheet was a combined (state, federal, and foreign) 42%. This is the three-year average effective tax rate for the company once nonrecurring tax items were removed from the tax provision. Two nonrecurring tax items stand out in the income tax disclosures in Exhibit 2.29. First is the increase in the tax provision because of the lack of tax deductibility of the $118 million of acquired in-process research and development in 1997.[49] The tax effect of this nonrecurring item, $41.3 million, pushed the effective rate up to 49% for 1997. Because of this lack of deductibility for tax purposes, the pretax and after-tax amounts of this charge are the same, $118 million. Therefore, we recorded the $118 million charge with the other tax and after-tax items in the bottom section of the SEB worksheet. Because this item is added back to net income on its after-tax basis, no additional adjustment was needed for the $41.3 million tax increase resulting from the lack of deductibility.

The second adjustment was for the $11.4 million nonrecurring tax reduction that resulted from an IRS audit agreement. The tax rate scales the numbers in the worksheet to their after-tax amounts. The goal should be a rate that is a reasonable representation of this combined rate. It is usually not cost beneficial to devote an inordinate amount of time to making this estimate.

Equity Earnings and Disposal of the Varco Investment

The MD&A included discussion of the gain on the sale of the Varco investment. This is a clear nonrecurring item, and it was adjusted from results in the Baker Hughes SEB worksheet. Baker Hughes accounted for its investment in Varco by using the equity method. This indicates that its ownership was sufficient to provide it with the capacity to exercise significant influence over Varco. Baker

Hughes disclosed that it recognized equity income from Varco of $3.2 million in 1995 and $1.8 million in 1996. However, the disposal of the Varco investment did not qualify as a discontinued operation. If it had been so classified, then the Baker Hughes share of earnings would have been removed from income from continuing operations of 1995 and 1996 and reported with discontinued operations—along with the gain on the disposition of the investment.

Clearly, a case could be made for treating the 1995 and 1996 equity earnings as nonrecurring and removing them from earnings in developing the SEB worksheet. This would not alter the message conveyed by the SEB worksheet in this particular case. However, if the effect were more material, then a judgment to treat as nonrecurring the equity earnings from the Varco investment would be in order.

Using the Summary Disclosures of Unusual Charges

In completing the worksheet, the summary totals from the unusual-charge disclosures (Exhibit 2.33) were used. Alternatively, the detail on the charges could have been recorded in appropriate lines in the worksheet. We saw this as offering no advantage here.

Having the detail on the makeup of the unusual charges is helpful in determining whether other additional nonrecurring items have already been included in these totals. Recall that the 1997 Petrolite inventory adjustment of $21.9 million was not included in the unusual charges total (it was included in cost of sales). Summaries for unusual charges, it should be noted, usually do not include all items that could reasonably be considered nonrecurring. In addition, care should be taken not to duplicate the recording of items already included in summary totals for unusual charges.

SUMMARY

An estimation of the sustainable portion of earnings should be the centerpiece of analyzing business earnings. This task has become a far greater challenge over the past decade as the number of nonrecurring items has increased dramatically. This explosion has been driven by corporate reorganizations and associated activities. Some of the labels attached to these producers of nonrecurring items are restructuring, rightsizing, downsizing, reengineering, redeployment, repositioning, reorganizing, rationalizing, and realignment. The following are some key points for the reader to consider:

- An earnings series from which nonrecurring items have been purged is essential in order to both evaluate current trends in operating performance and make projections of future results.
- The identification and measurement of nonrecurring items will typically require the exercise of judgment.

- There are no agreed-upon definitions of nonrecurring items as part of GAAP. Moreover, a variety of labels are used beyond the term *nonrecurring* and they include *special, unusual, nonoperating,* and *noncore.*
- It is common to treat items as nonrecurring even though they may appear with some regularity in the income statement. However, these items are usually very irregular in terms of their amount as well as whether they are revenues/gains or expenses/losses.
- The key question to pose in making the nonrecurring judgment is: Will underlying trends in operating performance be obscured if the item remains in earnings?
- Many material nonrecurring items will be separately disclosed on the face of the income statement. However, a substantial number will be disclosed in other statements and locations. It is typically necessary to extend the search for nonrecurring items well beyond the income statement.
- In response to reductions in the time available for a whole range of important activities, an efficient and abbreviated search sequence is presented in the chapter and illustrated with a comprehensive case example. While a comprehensive review of all financial reporting is the gold standard, reliable information on sustainable earnings can typically be developed while employing only a subset of reported financial information.

FOR FURTHER READING

Bernstein, L., and J. Wild, *Financial Statement Analysis: Theory, Application, and Interpretation,* 6th ed. (Homewood, IL: Irwin McGraw-Hill, 1998).

Comiskey, E., and C. Mulford, *Guide to Financial Reporting and Analysis* (New York: John Wiley, 2000).

Comiskey, E., C. Mulford, and H. Choi, "Analyzing the Persistence of Earnings: A Lender's Guide," *Commercial Lending Review* (winter 1994–1995).

White, G., A. Sondhi, and D. Fried, *The Analysis and Use of Financial Statements* (New York: John Wiley, 1997).

Mulford, C., and E. Comiskey, *Financial Warnings* (New York: John Wiley, 1996).

Special Committee on Financial Reporting of the American Institute of Certified Public Accountants, *Improving Business Reporting—A Customer Focus* (New York: AICPA, 1994).

INTERNET LINKS

www.fasb.org	This site provides updates on the agenda of the FASB. It also includes useful summaries of FASB statements and other information related to standard setting.
www.freeedgar.com	This site provides a very convenient alternative source of SEC filings.

www.sec.gov   A source for accessing company Securities and
                     Exchange Commission filings. This site also includes
                     Accounting and Auditing Enforcement Releases of the
                     SEC. These releases provide very useful examples of
                     the actions sometimes taken by companies to
                     misrepresent their financial performance or position.

ANNUAL REPORTS REFERENCED IN THE CHAPTER

Advanced Micro Devices Inc. (1999)
Air T Inc. (2000)
Akorn Inc. (1999)
AK Steel Holdings Corporation (1999)
Alberto-Culver Company (2000)
Amazon.Com Inc. (1999)
American Building Maintenance Inc. (1989)
American Standard Companies Inc. (1999)
AmSouth Bancorporation (1999)
Archer Daniels Midland Company (2000)
Argosy Gaming Company (1995)
Armco Inc. (1998)
Armstrong World Industries Inc. (1999)
Artistic Greetings Inc. (1995)
Atlantic American Corporation (1999)
Avado Brands Inc. (1999)
Avoca Inc. (1995)
Baker Hughes Inc. (1997)
Baltek Corporation (1997)
C.R. Bard Inc. (1999)
Baycorp Holdings Ltd. (1999)
Bestfoods Inc. (1999)
Biogen Inc. (1999)
BLC Financial Services Inc. (1998)
Brooktrout Technologies Inc. (1998)
Brush Wellman Inc. (1999)
Burlington Resources Inc. (1999)
Callon Petroleum Company (1999)
Champion Enterprises Inc. (1995)
Chiquita Brands International Inc. (1999)

Cisco Systems Inc. (1999)
Colonial Commercial Corporation (1999)
Corning Inc. (1999)
Cryomedical Sciences Inc. (1995)
Dal-Tile International Inc. (1999)
Dana Corporation (1999)
Dean Foods Company (1999)
Decorator Industries Inc. (1999)
Delta Air Lines Inc. (1996, 2000)
Detection Systems Inc. (2000)
Dibrell Brothers Inc. (1993)
Escalon Medical Corporation (2000)
Evans and Sutherland Computer Corporation (1998)
The Fairchild Corporation (2000)
First Aviation Services Inc. (1999)
Freeport-McMoRan Inc. (1991)
Galey & Lord Inc. (1998)
Geo. A. Hormel & Company (1993)
Gerber Scientific Inc. (2000)
Gleason Corporation (1995)
Goodyear Tire and Rubber Company (1995, 1998)
Handy and Harman Inc. (1997)
M.A. Hanna Company (1999)
Hercules Inc. (1999)
H.J. Heinz Company (1995)
Holly Corporation (2000)
Hollywood Casino Corporation (1992)
Imperial Holly Corporation (1994)
Imperial Sugar Company (1999)
JLG Industries Inc. (2000)
KeyCorp Ohio Inc. (1999)
Kulicke & Soffa Industries Inc. (1999)
Lufkin Industries Inc. (1999)
Mason Dixon Bancshares Inc. (1999)
Maxco Inc. (1996)
Meredith Corporation (1994)
Micron Technology Inc. (2000)
NACCO Industries Inc. (1995)
National Steel Corporation (1999)

New England Business Services Inc. (1996)

Noble Drilling Inc. (1991)

NS Group Inc. (1992)

Office Depot Inc. (1999)

Osmonics Inc. (1993)

Pall Corporation (2000)

Petroleum Helicopters Inc. (1999)

Phillips Petroleum Company (1990)

Pollo Tropical Inc. (1995)

Praxair Inc. (1999)

Raven Industries Inc. (2000)

Saucony Inc. (1999)

Schnitzer Steel Industries Inc. (1999)

Shaw Industries Inc. (1999)

The Sherwin-Williams Company (1999)

Silicon Valley Group Inc. (1999)

Southwest Airlines Inc. (1999)

Standard Register Company (1999)

SunTrust Banks Inc. (1999)

Synthetech Inc. (2000)

Textron Inc. (1999)

Toys "R" Us Inc. (1999)

Trimark Holdings Inc. (1995)

Tyco International Ltd. (2000)

Watts Industries Inc. (1999)

Wegener Corporation (1999)

NOTES

1. The American Institute of CPA's Special Committee on Financial Reporting, *Improving Business Reporting—A Customer Focus* (New York: AICPA, November 1993), 4.

2. Donald Kieso and Jerry Weygandt, *Intermediate Accounting*, 9th ed. (New York: John Wiley, 1998), 154–161.

3. Delta Air Lines, annual reports, June 1996, 50–51, and June 2000.

4. Some might also remove these gains because they do not represent operating items. However, the ongoing disposition of flight equipment is an inherent feature of being in the airline business. It is not what they are in the business to do, but it does come with the territory.

5. Delta Air Lines does disclose some proceeds from the sale of flight equipment in its 1998–2000 statements of cash flow. The gains and losses were probably too small

to receive separate disclosure. Delta Air Lines, annual report, June 2000, 36. Delta does disclose balances for deferred gains on sale and leaseback transactions. These balances declined by $50 million in 2000, suggesting that gains equal to this amount were included in earnings for 2000. They are treated as a reduction in lease expense and do not appear on a line item as gains on the disposition of flight equipment.

6. In fact, 1996 saw a loss of $7.4 million, followed by gains of $34.1 in 1997 and $2.6 million in 1998. Goodyear Tire and Rubber Company, annual report on Form 10-K to the Securities and Exchange Commission, December 1998, 32.

7. George A. Hormel & Company, annual report, 1993, 58.

8. H. Choi, *Analysis and Valuation Implications of Persistence and Cash-Content Dimensions of Earnings Components Based on Extent of Analyst Following*, unpublished PhD thesis, Georgia Institute of Technology, October 1994, 80.

9. Ibid. The authors of this chapter served as committee member and committee chair for Dr. Choi's thesis guidance committee.

10. AICPA, *Accounting Trends and Techniques* (New York: AICPA, 2000), 311.

11. AICPA's Special Committee on Financial Reporting, *Improving Business Reporting—A Customer Focus* (New York: AICPA, November 1993), 4

12. SFAS 131, *Disclosures about Segments of an Enterprise and Related Information* (Norwalk, CT: Financial Accounting Standards Board, June 1997), para. 10.

13. APB Opinion No. 30, *Reporting the Results of Operations* (New York: AICPA, July 1973), para. 20.

14. SFAS 4, *Reporting Gains and Losses from the Extinguishment of Debt* (Stamford, CT: FASB, March 1975).

15. SFAS 15, *Accounting by Debtors and Creditors for Troubled Debt Restructurings* (Stamford, CT: FASB, June 1977).

16. Exxon's accident took the form of a massive oil spill in Alaska, and Union Carbide's was a release of toxic fumes in India.

17. Armco Inc. annual report, December 1998. Information obtained from Disclosure Inc., *Compact D/SEC: Corporate Information on Public Companies Filing with the SEC* (Bethesda, MD: Disclosure Inc., June 2000).

18. Securities and Exchange Commission, *Staff Accounting Bulletin No. 101* (Washington, DC: SEC, 1999).

19. Southwest Airlines Inc., annual report, December 1999.

20. This statement needs some expansion. With the exception of barter transactions, almost all expenses involve a cash outflow at some point in time. In the case of depreciation, the cash outflow normally takes place when the depreciable assets are acquired. At that time, the cash outflow is classified as an *investing* cash outflow in the statement of cash flows. If the depreciation were not added back to net income in computing operating cash flow, then cash would appear to be reduced twice—once when the assets were purchased and a second time when depreciation is recorded, and with it net income is reduced.

21. To keep the books in balance, the recognition of the loss in the income statement is matched by a reduction in the carrying value of the investment in the balance sheet.

22. SEC Reg. S-X, Rule 5-02.6 (Washington, DC: SEC, 2001).

23. SEC, *Staff Accounting Bulletin No. 40* (Washington, DC: SEC, February 8, 1981).

24. Handy and Harman Inc., annual report, December 1997. Information obtained from Disclosure Inc., *Compact D/SEC: Corporate Information on Public Companies Filing with the SEC* (Bethesda, MD: Disclosure Inc., June 1998.

25. Even with great improvements in supply chain management, it is still difficult to get along without any inventories.

26. Reviews and compilations represent a level of outside accountant service well below that of an audit. Compilations typically provide only an income statement and balance sheet. Neither notes nor a statement of cash flows are part of the standard compilation disclosures.

27. Absent disclosures, the effect of a LIFO liquidation can be estimated. This requires the assumption that the observed increase in the gross margin is due largely to the LIFO liquidation. The pretax effect of the LIFO liquidation can then be approximated by multiplying sales for the period of the liquidation times the increase in the gross margin percentage.

28. Archer Daniels Midland Company, annual report, June 2000, 20.

29. Guidance in this area is found in SFAS No. 109, *Accounting for Income Taxes* (Norwalk, CT: FASB, February 1992).

30. The offsetting of gains and losses in the 1998 other income and expense note is swamped by a $329 million nonrecurring gain on the disposition of C.R. Bard's cardiology business.

31. Reg. S-K, Subpart 229.300, Item 303(a)(3)(i) (Washington, DC: SEC, 2001).

32. Mason Dixon Bancshares might take issue with this characterization. Financial firms tend to characterize these disclosures as designed to measure *core earnings.* However, our experience is that the end product is very similar to *sustainable earnings,* where the focus is on purging nonrecurring items from reported net income.

33. Phillips Petroleum, annual report, December 1999, 33.

34. Ibid., 33.

35. Other companies that have provided similar presentations in recent years include Amoco Corp., Carpenter Technology, Chevron Corp., Deere & Company Inc., Halliburton Co. Inc., Maxus Energy Corp., and Raychem Corp.

36. C. R. Bard Inc., annual report, December 1999, 17.

37. A hedge of foreign-currency exposure is achieved by creating an offsetting position to the financial statement exposure. The most common offsetting position is established by the use of a foreign-currency derivative. These issues are discussed more fully in Chapter 12.

38. These alternative translation methods are discussed and illustrated in Chapter 12.

39. Dibrell Brothers Inc., annual report, December 1993, 35.

40. Ibid., 14.

41. Arthur Levitt, *The Numbers Game,* speech given at the NYU Center for Law and Business, September 28, 1998 (available at: www.sec.gov/news/speeches /spch220.txt).

42. The earnings of a subsequent period are increased by reducing the previously accrued restructuring charge on the basis that the accrual was too large. The amount by which the liability is reduced is also included in the income statement as either an item of income or an expense reduction.

43.   Office Depot Inc., annual report, December 1999, 57, 56.

44.   SFAS No. 130, *Reporting Comprehensive Income* (Norwalk, CT: FASB, June 1997).

45.   Translation (remeasurement) gains and losses that result from the application of the temporal (remeasurement) method continue to be included in the income statement as part of conventional net income. Only translation adjustments that result from application of the all-current translation method are included in other comprehensive income. Recent changes in the accounting for financial derivatives also result in the inclusion of certain hedge gains and losses in other comprehensive income: SFAS No. 133, *Accounting for Derivative Instruments and Hedging Activities* (Norwalk, CT: FASB, November 1998).

46.   An annual survey conducted by the AICPA reveals the following pattern of adoption of the alternative reporting methods of SFAS No. 130 for 497 firms: (1) a combined statement of income and comprehensive income, 26 firms; (2) a separate statement of comprehensive income, 65 firms; and (3) reporting comprehensive income directly in shareholders' equity, 406 firms. AICPA, *Accounting Trends and Techniques* (New York: AICPA, 2000), 429.

47.   An earlier version of the Baker Hughes case study also appeared in E. Comiskey and C. Mulford, *Guide to Financial Reporting and Analysis* (New York: John Wiley, 2000), chapter 3.

48.   Phillips Petroleum, annual report, December 1999, 33.

49.   Research and development costs must be written off immediately—even if the in-process R&D is purchased from another firm. Whether this expense is deductible for tax purposes turns on the manner in which the acquisition is structured. Generally, the expense is deductible in transactions structured as asset acquisitions but not in the case of stock acquisitions.

3 COST-VOLUME-PROFIT ANALYSIS

William C. Lawler

Abigail Peabody was a very well-known nature photographer. Over the years she had had a number of best-sellers, and her books adorned the coffee tables of many households worldwide. On this particular day she was contemplating her golden years, which were fast approaching. In particular she was reviewing her year-end investment report and wondering why she was not better prepared. After all, she had been featured in the Sunday *New York Times* book section, had discussed her works with Martha Stewart, and had been the keynote speaker at the Audubon Society's annual fund-raiser. She knew it was not her investment advisers' fault. Their performance over the past years had been better than many of the market indixes. She wondered if she was just a poor businessperson.

The last thought struck a pleasant chord. She had a grandson who was a junior at a well-known business school just outside Boston. It was time, anyway, to catch up to his latest business idea. She dialed the number from memory.

He was as lively as usual. "Hi, Abbey, I was just going to call you. How's the new bird book coming?" [Of her many grandchildren, he had the most irresistible charm.] How she loved his ability to make her feel young—and his ability to remember never to call her anything that began with *Grand-*.

"Actually, Stephen, that's why I'm calling. I was just reviewing my retirement portfolio, and I think it's time for me to renegotiate my royalty structure with my publisher. I could use some help from a bright business mind."

"Love to help you. What's wrong with the current contract? Haven't you been with them since the beginning?"

"Yes I have, but things have changed. In the old days, they provided me with many services. They brainstormed projects with me, suggested different ideas such as the *Baskets of Nantucket* best-seller, and edited my work word-by-word and frame-by-frame. They worked hard for me and earned every penny they made on me. I was not the easiest artist to put up with."

Stephen was interested. "Go on."

"Well, now I barely talk with them. I am at the point where loyal readers suggest many of my projects. I design them myself, edit them myself, and even help my publisher prepare the promotion materials. They don't work so hard anymore. I think I have paid my dues. I want a bigger piece of the pie."

"That could be a problem, Abbey. I just finished a case study on that industry, and it is very competitive. There are many parts to the industry value system that ultimately ends with someone buying a book (see Exhibit 3.1). It starts with people like you who have the intellectual capital. The next piece of the system is the publisher, who manages the creativity process, supplies the editing, prints the book, and markets it. Wholesalers like Ingram add value to this system by buying books in large quantity from publishers, warehousing them, and selling in smaller quantities to bookstores. Of course, the last piece is the bookstore, where in-store promotion and the final sales process takes place. On, say, a $50 book, the bookstore buys it from the wholesaler for about $35, netting about $15 to cover its costs such as rent and salespeople. The wholesaler buys the book from the publisher in large lot sizes for about $30 a book, giving the wholesaler about $5 to cover its logistics costs. Of the $30 the publisher sells it for, 15% of the retail price, or $7.50 ($50 × 15%) is your royalty, and the rest covers printing, client development, returned books, administrative expenses, and a profit. The publisher really can't give you too much more since its margin is already very slim. Sorry to disappoint you but that's how it is."

Abbey was disappointed. "Stephen, for all that money your parents are paying, doesn't that business school teach creativity? You have to look at the world and think of what it could be, not what it is today."

Unembarrassed by Abbey's chastisement, Stephen, reacted positively. "How much risk do you want to take on this new project, Abbey?"

EXHIBIT 3.1 Publishing industry value system.

Competency:	Author	Publisher	Wholesaler	Bookstore	Customer
	Intellectual Capital	Development Editing Printing	Logistics Warehousing	Promotion Sales	
Revenue:	$7.50	$30.00	$35.00	$50.00	
Purchase cost:			30.00	35.00	
Gross margin:			$ 5.00	$15.00	

"That's more like it. For now, let's 'roll the bones'—I mean, assume risk is not an issue. What do you have in mind?"

"Well, this semester I have a Web-marketing course and I need a project. Are you familiar with the World Wide Web?"

"I spend a good part of the day corresponding with friends on it."

"Good. What you just said to me is that you don't see too many pieces of the publishing system adding value commensurate with the value they extract. How about setting up your own Web site and selling your latest project yourself? We would have to contract with others to provide the necessary parts of the chain, but selling the book through our Web site is possible. It could fail, and you would have one very unhappy publisher."

Abbey thought she was now getting somewhere. "As long as you are getting credit for it, why don't you develop this idea further. See if it's possible and what my risks would be. I might even give you a piece of the action."

COST STRUCTURE ANALYSIS

A month later Abbey met Stephen for lunch in Boston. He was excited.

"Abbey, this is what I have found so far. Setting up a Web site is very easy, but maintaining it and keeping it fresh and exciting so that people want to revisit it is the challenge. Neither you nor I want to do that, trust me. I have talked with a number of companies who offer this type of service. Many of them were excited when I showed them copies of your past books. To set up and maintain the site, the offers ran anywhere from a low of $25,000 a year to four times that. The high-end ones also charge a 5% fee on all revenues generated. I think we want a high-end site that is creative, custom designed, and exciting so I lean toward the more expensive ones. They are good."

Abbey liked how he used the word *we*. And being an artist, she too thought that her Web site should be exciting, creative, and different. "Go on."

"I also found a number of printers who specialize in small run sizes, typically less than 50 books in any one printing. Their technology is called print-on-demand, and they also work with photographs. I brought some samples of printed photos."

Abbey was impressed with the quality. It looked no different than her previous books. "What would they charge?"

"They said they could print your books on demand and guarantee the quality for about $35 each. Now, this is much more than what traditional printers charge, but they always run large volumes, a minimum of 5,000 copies in one printing, and want to be paid for every one of them even before we could sell them. Bottom line, we would be at risk if this doesn't work."

Abbey was disappointed that she was again making someone else rich, but moved on. "How would we do all the promotion and sales?"

"Two ways. Once your readers learn of your site, they will visit it. If the Web-design company delivers what they promise, we should be able to sell directly to them. Until that traffic happens, the Web designers will develop links with all the major sites that might be interested."

"How does that work?"

"Well, your newest project is a Florida bird book for all the retired baby boomers down there, right? So we develop what is called a link with the Audubon's Web site and maybe AARP and the Florida Tourism Bureau. When people see your book on those sites, they click on a link and get transferred to our site. If they buy the book, we pay the site a 10% royalty."

"Does that mean I spend all my days, assuming we are successful, mailing books all over the world? That doesn't interest me."

"No. I also talked with logistics companies like UPS and FedEx. They will do all of that. When we sell a book, we just notify them electronically. They work with the printer to obtain the book and with the credit card company to get paid, and they ship it. They even collect the money, pay everyone involved with the sale, and electronically deposit the remainder in your account. They would charge about $10 per book for all of this, assuming we can guarantee a certain minimal volume."

"Now that sounds like your parents are getting their money's worth. Have you summarized all of this?"

"Sure have. You're still thinking about a price of $80 for this book?"

"My others have sold for that, and I think the demand for this might even be greater. So $80 is a good assumption."

"Okay. First, all business models have only two types of costs, variable and fixed. Each is defined by the behavior of the *total* cost function. Variable costs are those that increase proportionately with volume—basically, the more books we sell the higher these *total* costs will be. They can be expressed either on a per-unit basis or as a percentage of the selling price. Notice we have both types. Our printing and logistics costs total $45 for each book sold—$35 printing plus $10 logistics. Our Web-site sales referral cost of 10% and Web-design cost of 5% for every dollar of revenue are examples of the latter kind of variable cost. For the targeted price of $80, these costs come to $12 for each book sold ($80 × 15%). Note this type of variable cost is a little more complicated than the simple $45 per book—here if we change selling price, the variable cost will change. Given the $80 selling price, the total variable cost per book is then $57 per unit ($45 + $12). Unlike these costs, the Web-site design cost is a mixed cost[1] and has to be broken into a variable and a fixed component. We have already treated the 5% variable cost component. There is also a fixed charge per year of about $100,000 if we go high-end. Note the difference in behavior of this cost. Here the *total* cost is not dependent on a volume factor such as "books sold." Fixed costs are often called period costs since they are time dependent. So in summary, we have a time-dependent fixed charge of $100,000 per year, which remains the same regardless of the number of books sold, and a variable cost, which is better understood on a per-unit or, in this case, per-book rate of $57. I made a graph of this—what businesspeople call cost structure (see Exhibit 3.2)."[2]

EXHIBIT 3.2   Web site cost structure.

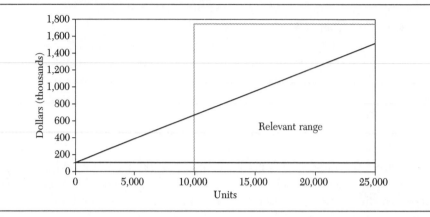

Abbey thought she understood. "So this structure will always be the same?"

"With one proviso," Stephen affirmed. "Although my chart looks the same from zero volume to an infinite amount sold, we really should only be talking about a smaller relevant range. Both the printer and the logistics company are assuming an annual volume of between 10,000 and 25,000 books—essentially what your past books sold. Outside this range, especially on the high side, the costs probably will change. I don't think the printer can do much more than 25,000 a year for us. Likewise, at greater than this volume, we would probably have to redesign the Web site. So the cost structure could change if we were to move outside the range."

"Okay. So now I think I do understand what the cost structure would be given our plans for the Web site. All that you said makes sense, and I'm sure my new book will sell in that range. So tell me why I shouldn't do this."

COST-VOLUME-PROFIT ANALYSIS

"If we add a revenue line to my first exhibit," said Stephen, "we will start to get a better picture of the answer to this question (see Exhibit 3.3). First, you must understand the concept of contribution margin. For us, it is simple. For every $80 book we sell, there is a variable cost to print, sell, and deliver that book of $57. This means that the net contribution of each book sold is $23. Does this make sense?"

"Sure does," Abbey answered, delighted. "This is wonderful. I was only making $12 with my publisher, and now I can make almost double that."

"Not quite. You forgot one thing. Contribution margin must first go toward covering the fixed costs before we can realize any profit. Each year we have to cover the Web-site designer's charge of $100,000. At a contribution margin of $23 per book, it will take about 4,350 books sold to do this (see

EXHIBIT 3.3   Web site CVP analysis.

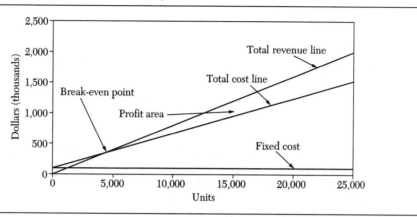

Exhibit 3.4). On my graph, this is the point where the revenue line intersects the total cost line and is called the break-even point. After that, you are correct. For any additional book we sell, the $23 contribution per book is all profit. So, as I see it, there is little risk since you are sure that we will sell at a minimum 10,000 copies per year."

Abbey became a bit uncomfortable. "Actually, I think this book will sell about 20,000 copies per year at a minimum. But isn't my alternative to stay with my publisher? And if so, shouldn't we be talking about whether I would be better off with the Web site?"

Stephen was suddenly not so cocky. Abbey thought that maybe some remedial work on those tuition dollars was needed. "I have some work to do. Why don't you get back to me on that, Stephen?"

Two nights later, after faxing her two charts, Stephen phoned Abbey. "I sent you a different type of chart, called a profit chart, which shows the two

EXHIBIT 3.4   Break-even calculations.

$$\text{Sales Revenue} = \text{Fixed Costs} + \text{Variable Costs}$$
$$\$80x = \$100,000 + \$57x$$

Solving for x,

$$\$80x - \$57x = \$100,000$$
$$\$23x = \$100,000$$
$$x = \frac{\$100,000}{23} = 4,348 \text{ books}$$

General Rule: Break-even point $= \dfrac{\text{Fixed Costs}}{\text{Contribution Margin}}$

EXHIBIT 3.5   Profit chart.

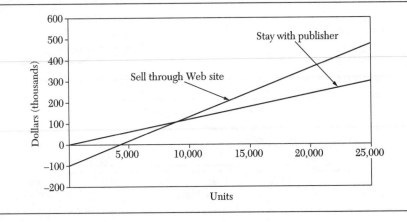

alternatives (see Exhibit 3.5). 'Stay with the publisher' shows that you make $12 for every book sold. 'Sell through the Web site' is a bit more involved in that it shows that you first must cover your fixed cost before making any profit. Note that they intersect at about 9,100 books sold, which means that you would be indifferent to which business model you chose at this volume of books sold.[3] But at less than the 9,100 you should stay with your publisher; at greater than that volume, build your own Web site. At the 20,000 books-per-year level you said you are sure this project will hit, you make $240,000 per year (20,000 × $12 royalty per book) if you stay with your publisher, and $360,000 with the Web site (20,000 × [$80 − $57] − $100,000 fixed costs). Another way to think about this is that if we set up our own Web site there is an additional variable cost for each book we sell—the $12 we could have made from the publisher (see Exhibit 3.6). This is called an *opportunity cost*. It is a relative measure—

EXHIBIT 3.6   Revised Web site CVP analysis.

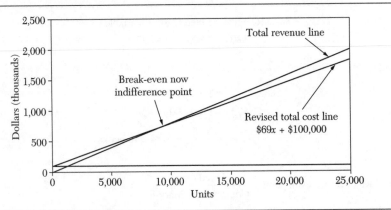

what is sacrificed when we choose one alternative, selling through the Web site, over the next best alternative, staying with the publisher. If we think this way, our contribution margin is now only $11 ($80 selling price less $57 variable costs less $12 royalty per book sacrificed). We do arrive at the same indifference point using this method—using the general rule:

$$\text{CVP Point} = \frac{\text{Fixed Costs}}{\text{Contribution Margin}}$$
$$= \frac{\$100,000}{\$11}$$
$$= 9,091 \text{ units}$$

I think this is the better way to think about the Web-site alternative. Note, using this method, at 20,000 books per year we make a total contribution of $220,000 (20,000 × $11), which covers our fixed costs and yields the $120,000 incremental profit—same as ($360,000 − $240,000).”

Abbey was becoming very interested in this business opportunity. She liked the 50% greater return ($120,000/$240,000). “How fast can we get this Web site up and running?”

“Let's talk a bit more. I also presented today in class what we have done so far. Many students liked the idea. The only criticism was that Web customers expect lower prices since they know the middle person has been eliminated. The class agreed that a 10% to 15% price decline would be very likely, resulting in a price closer to $70. This is not so good for us. Even though our variable cost will fall to $67.50 since part of it is price dependent ($35 printing + $10 logistics + $12 opportunity cost + [15% × $70]), our contribution margin would now only be $2.50 per book. Just to match what you could make with your publisher, we would have to sell about 40,000 books a year ($100,000/$2.50 per book). At the 20,000-book level, we would now be worse off by $50,000 ([20,000 × $2.50] − $100,000). Well, you asked about the risks and here they are. The price could even be lower, so there is a high probability we could wind up worse off.”

“So, you're my business partner, what do you suggest?” was Abbey's reply.

“That's a hard one,” was all Stephen could say.

CVP for Decision Making

The next day Abbey called Stephen for more advice. “Public Broadcasting System of Florida called me after our talk yesterday. They just began planning their end-of-year membership drive and heard about my book project. They want to offer a free copy of my book to any member who donates $250 or more.”

Stephen thought that was great.

“Unfortunately, since they are a public company they have constraints on their spending. They can give a gift equivalent to only 20% of the donation.

Fifty dollars a book for 5,000 books was their offer to me. Since we just went over the numbers, I said I couldn't possibly do this since our variable costs alone were greater than $50 a unit. This analysis we did does help with decision making. Last year I might have agreed to the deal. I am starting to feel like a businessperson."

Stephen asked whether the PBS group accepted her decision. When Abbey said that they were very persistent and would call back next week, Stephen suggested he and Abbey meet again for lunch. He needed to review some of his class notes on *relevant cost analysis,* specifically on something he remembered as "special orders."

At lunch Stephen explained some analysis he had done. "Abbey, this is called a special order situation. These types of business decisions are short-run decisions that have no long-term ramifications.[4] Assuming that we have the Web site up by that time, we have to be careful in identifying only those costs that are relevant to the decision. For instance, the $100,000 we will spend on our site per year is not relevant, since regardless of whether we accept this special order, those costs will still be there. The rule that we use is: A cost is relevant if and only if it will change due to the decision being analyzed, in this case our special order. Let's review the relevant costs. First, there's the $35 charge to print the books on demand. Since this is a 5,000-unit order the printer's costs to prepare the run, called set-up costs, will be spread over a much larger number of books. I talked with him, and he would be willing to do this run for $30 per book. Likewise, UPS or FedEx will ship these books all at once and not individually, so the $10 charge per book will be avoided. A one-time fixed charge of $250 for shipment of the 5,000-book order is closer to the correct number. Since this order was not sold through a

EXHIBIT 3.7   Relevant cost analysis of special order.

	Accept the Order, No Adjustments to Costs	Accept the Order, Adjusted Costs	Reject the Order	Difference
Number of books sold	5,000	5,000	0	5,000
Revenue	$250,000	$250,000	$ 0	$250,000
Relevant costs:				
Printing	$175,000	$150,000	$ 0	$150,000
Logistics	50,000	250	0	250
10% site referral	25,000	0	0	0
5% Web site expense	12,500	12,500	0	12,500
Total relevant costs	$262,500	$162,750	$ 0	$162,750
Nonrelevant costs				
Web site design	$100,000	$100,000	$100,000	$ 0
Profit from order				$ 87,250

site reference, the 10% commission can also be avoided. I looked into the Web-site contract, and I do think we will have to pay this charge of $2.50 per book (5% × $50). Summing up, the variable cost per book for this special order will be only $32.50 ($30 printing charge plus $2.50 Web-site fee)—less than the $50 PBS is willing to pay. The end result is a $17.50 contribution margin per book for this special order. There is an incremental fixed charge of $250 but we still will make just over $87,000 (5,000 × [$50 − $32.50] − $250 = $87,250). So we should think about reconsidering the offer" (see Exhibit 3.7).

Though Abbey was beginning to appreciate the complexity of this type of analysis, all the numbers did make sense. She had only one question: "What happens if customers I would have sold to anyway get their books this way? Don't I lose money?"

Stephen had done that analysis. "In the business world, we call that *cannibalization.* On every book sold through this special offer, you could potentially lose the $23 contribution margin per book sold through the regular Web site if these people would have bought anyway. To solve for the potential number of regular customers that would have to be cannibalized in order for us to lose money on this special order, follow this procedure:

$$23x = \$87,250$$

Solving for x, we get

$$x = \frac{\$87,250}{\$23}$$
$$= 3,793 \text{ customers}$$

This means that if about 3,800 of the 5,000 books sold by PBS go to customers that would have bought anyway, we are indifferent to accepting this order. If more than 3,800 would have bought anyway, we lose on this special order. Do you think 76% (3,800/5,000) of these people would buy from our Web site? I don't think it is anywhere near that. And, on the positive side, these 5,000 people would now be advertising our Web site with your book on their coffee tables all over Florida."

Abbey was searching for the PBS phone number before Stephen had finished the last sentence. She made a mental note to understand this "relevant cost" analysis a bit more.

Price Discrimination

In the above special order situation, there was a legitimate reason to offer PBS the lower price. As Exhibit 3.7 illustrates, the relevant cost analysis justified the lower price. When offering different prices to different customers, one must be aware of the laws regarding price discrimination. Under the federal Robinson-Patman Act and many state laws, it is illegal to price discriminate unless there are mitigating circumstances. One must be very careful to do a relevant cost analysis before granting any price concessions to customers on a selective basis.

CVP in a Multiple Product Situation

The special order was a great opportunity, but both Abbey and Stephen knew that the success of the Web site ultimately would depend on the regular, day-to-day business activity. The two of them were still worried about the potential Web discount resulting in a $70 price point. As an artist Abbey understood risk and had learned long ago to accept risk and figure a way to minimize it. She decided to talk with some of her artist friends.

In two weeks she and Stephen met again. Stephen was desperate to finish his project since semester end was right around the corner. Abbey walked in wearing a rather stylish straw hat.

"I think I have the solution, Stephen. I do not want to drop my price from $80. My other books sold at this price, and to drop the price on this one might send the wrong message to my loyal following. This book will not be in any manner inferior to my past works. But I do have an idea. We are going to expand our product offerings. I have a dear friend who makes these hats, and I think this would be a perfect complement to my bird book. After all, if you are going out bird-watching in Florida you need both to look good and to have sun protection. We are going to package the book with a hat and a *Peterson's Florida Bird Guide* at a very reasonable price for those that are more price conscious."

Stephen was stunned. "Whoa, do you want all this complexity in your business, Abbey?"

She smiled. "I, too, can do some field research. My friend will package the three items as orders come in. I don't have to do any more work than before. She was happy to build demand for her hats."

"So, how about the costs?"

"This is how I see it. We sell the hats for $50 by themselves; the books for $80 by themselves; and then offer the package for $140. A *Peterson's Guide* typically sells for $20, so this package price is a deal—you could say I'm selling my book for $70 as part of this package, although I would never admit to it. I coerced my friend to give us her hats for $24 each, and the book costs when included in this package will change a bit. I put your relevant cost technique to work here. My friend and I think we can assemble the package for a variable cost of about $100 (see Exhibit 3.8). Peterson will give us the guide for $10 to get the exposure, and since we are still shipping only one item, I'm hoping that the logistics charge will not change too much. I had some problems figuring out what we have to sell since there were now multiple items—hats, books, and packages. But I have faith in you."

As his laptop was booting Stephen began. "CVP analysis for multiple products is very common since few companies sell just one item. Instead of

EXHIBIT 3.8   Variable package cost estimates.

Hat	$ 24
Book printing	35
10% site referral fee	14
5% Web site commission	7
Peterson Guide	10
Package logistics	10
	$100

focusing on a contribution margin per unit, when we have multiple products we must base our calculations on the percentage contribution margin for each dollar of revenue."

"Sounds complicated."

"Not really, Abbey. It's probably easier, though, for me to show you how it works than to explain it. All I need is your estimate of the sales mix. For every book you sell individually, how many hats will you sell and how many packages will you sell? These estimates do not have to be exact—businesspeople typically talk about ballpark estimates."

"My friend and I did discuss this. We were not sure, so we came up with a range. We think that for every 100 books we sell individually, we will sell 50 packages. A surprisingly large number of people are active in this regard. They actually do enjoy seeking these birds out in the wild. And, of course, everyone knows you need a wide-brimmed hat in Florida. We guessed that we might also sell 20 hats individually for every 100 books sold. If things go really well, we might sell as many as 70 packages and 30 hats for every 100 books. On the pessimistic side, we could sell as few as 30 packages and 10 hats for the same 100 books. Is this okay?"

"Actually, that's even better. If you're sure of these ranges, then we can do a *sensitivity analysis* to see how our profits will change as the mix changes. We need to know how much our profit will vary with changes in the mix. Are you comfortable with these ranges?"

"Yes."

"To do this analysis we must first build a product mix analysis. Here, I'll show you."

Abbey was very impressed as Stephan built the analysis on his laptop (see Exhibit 3.9). "Just as we analyzed the unit costs before, we build a similar cost analysis. The only difference is that this time we build it for a composite unit defined by the mix. For your expected mix, 100 books plus 50 packages plus 20 hats, we see that for every $16,000 in sales you will have $11,180 in variable costs. This means that on a percentage basis your variable costs are 69.9% of sales as long as you sell in that mix. Note that we now have a percentage definition of contribution margin, not a unit definition—contribution margin

EXHIBIT 3.9   Mix contribution estimates.

	Books		Packages		Hats		Mix
	Per Unit	Total	Per Unit	Total	Per Unit	Total	Total
Low Mix		100		30		10	
Revenue	$80	$8,000	$140	$4,200	$50	$ 500	$12,700
Variable Cost	$57	$5,700	$100	$3,000	$24	$ 240	$ 8,940
Contribution	71.3%		71.4%		48.0%		70.4%
Expected Mix		100		50		20	
Revenue	$80	$8,000	$140	$7,000	$50	$1,000	$16,000
Variable Cost	$57	$5,700	$100	$5,000	$24	$ 480	$11,180
Contribution	71.3%		71.4%		48.0%		69.9%
High Mix		100		70		30	
Revenue	$80	$8,000	$140	$9,800	$50	$1,500	$19,300
Variable Cost	$57	$5,700	$100	$7,000	$24	$ 720	$13,420
Contribution	71.3%		71.4%		48.0%		69.5%

percentage of 30.1%. Our fixed costs are still $100,000 per year, so we now adjust the general rule for CVP point as follows:[5]

$$\text{Sales} - \text{Variable Costs} - \text{Fixed Costs} = 0$$
$$x - (69.9\%)x - \$100,000 = 0$$

Solving for x,

$$(30.1\%)x = \$100,000$$
$$x = \frac{\$100,000}{30.1\%}$$
$$= \$332,226 \text{ in sales revenue}$$

To test this model, assume that we have $332,226 in sales revenue and we did sell the planned mix. Our contribution margin will be 30.1%, which yields the $100,000 necessary to cover the fixed costs. We do, in fact, break even. The key, of course, is to be able to forecast the correct mix and then to attain it."

Abbey was quick to correct Stephen. "Don't forget, I still want to be at least as well off as if I chose to stay with my publisher—say the 20,000 books at my $12 royalty."

"Easy enough. We just revise the equation by adding a necessary profit requirement—this is why they call it cost-volume-*profit* analysis:

$$\text{Sales} - \text{Variable Costs} - \text{Fixed Costs} = \text{Profit}$$
$$x - (69.9\%)x - \$100,000 = \$240,000$$

Solving for x,

$$(30.1\%)x = \$340,000$$

$$x = \frac{\$340,000}{30.1\%}$$

$$= \$1,128,631 \text{ (with no rounding)}$$

We find that you must do about $1.130 million in sales to be as well-off."

"Hmm. I'm not sure what this means. So how much of what do I have to sell? That's what I want to know."

"What we do is take the total required sales of $1.130 million and split it by your revenue mix percentages. Given your expected mix estimates, half of your revenues will come from sales of books, or $564,315; seven-sixteenths from packages, or $493,776; and the other one-sixteenth from sales of hats, or $70,539. Dividing by the selling price of each item, we can also compute the necessary unit sales levels—7,054 books, 3,527 packages, and 1,411 hats. With our variable cost estimates, if you meet these targets we will indeed meet the targeted profit level (see Exhibit 3.10). In summary, we were worried that our 9,100-book target was too optimistic because price cuts were possible. With this mix we will have to sell 10,581 books—7,054 individually and 3,527 in packages—but one-third of them will essentially sell for around $70. This seems more realistic if the packages are marketed correctly."

"What does the sensitivity analysis tell us?"

"Since the contribution percentage for the package is about equal to an individual book, this solution is not very sensitive to variation in mix. If you do meet your 'optimistic' mix projection, your contribution percentage increases by less than 1%—30.1% to 30.5% (see Exhibit 3.11). As a result your

EXHIBIT 3.10 Required unit revenues and sales volumes expected mix.

	Books		Packages		Hats		Mix
	Per Unit	Total	Per Unit	Total	Per Unit	Total	Total
Expected mix		100		50		20	
Revenue	$80	$ 8,000	$140	$ 7,000	$50	$ 1,000	$ 16,000
Percentage of total		50.00%		43.75%		6.25%	100.00%
CVP target							$1,128,631
Mix % allocation		$564,315		$493,776		$70,539	$1,128,631
Variable cost	71.3%	402,075	71.4%	352,697	48.0%	33,859	
Contribution margin		$162,241		$141,079		$36,680	$ 340,000
Divide by unit price to find unit sales needed		Books 7,054		Packages 3,527		Hats 1,411	

EXHIBIT 3.11   Mix sensitivity analysis optimistic mix.

	Books		Packages		Hats		Mix
	Per Unit	Total	Per Unit	Total	Per Unit	Total	Total
Expected mix		100		70		30	
Revenue	$80	$ 8,000	$140	$ 9,800	$50	$ 1,500	$ 19,300
Percentage of total		41.45%		50.78%		7.77%	100.00%
CVP target							$1,115,986
Mix % allocation		$462,585		$566,667		$86,735	$1,115,986
Variable cost	71.3%	329,592	71.4%	404,762	48.0%	41,633	
Contribution margin		$132,993		$161,905		$45,102	$ 340,000
Divide by unit price to find unit sales needed		Books 5,782		Packages 4,048		Hats 1,735	

sales revenue target to meet your profitability goal will drop only a small amount—from about $1.130 million ($340,000/30.1%) to $1.120 million ($340,000/30.5%). Basically, we would have to sell only 9,830 books with 41% at discount. This would mean, though, that we would have to sell substantially more packages. All in all, our answer is not that sensitive to the mix."

Abbey now asked Stephen if he wanted to partner with her.

METHODS OF COST BEHAVIOR ESTIMATION

CVP analysis is a rough, first-pass analytic technique. Businesspeople use it to make some initial profitability estimates of potential opportunities and to cull those that show the most promise. More in-depth analysis would then follow.[6]

The key to CVP analysis is correctly identifying the cost structure of the business opportunity being analyzed. Without a proper knowledge of the cost behaviors—identification of the fixed period costs and the variable costs per unit or as a percentage of sales revenue—business planning cannot be done properly. There are four methods used to analyze cost behavior. Three are analytic approaches that require historical data, and the other is more judgmental.

Abbey's Web-site example discussed above is an example of the latter. Since the business was not yet operating, there was no database to study. Rather, the cost structure was estimated by analyzing the processes on which Abbey's business would be based. The data came from discussions with process partners such as the Web-site designer and the logistics company and from Abbey's firsthand knowledge of the book business. This procedure depends on correctly identifying all the necessary business processes and the experience and ability of those who provide accurate process cost estimates. Since Abbey's business model was relatively simple and many of the processes were outsourced to experienced third-party providers, the resulting cost structure estimates are probably relatively accurate. Given a more complex business opportunity that might require many internal process steps that are not yet well understood, this methodology might not yield such accurate results.

The three analytic approaches are techniques used when historical data is available. Unfortunately, many firms first develop this analysis *after* they have begun operations—an inopportune time. For instance, now that the bloom is off the Internet rose, there are many such firms scrambling to do this analysis after the fact. Investors are withholding later-round financing until these firms can develop the analysis we illustrated above.

Assume that Books "R" Us is one of those firms. Since it has not yet broken even, its investors want to better understand the cost structure and when, if ever, they can expect a return. The company has been in business for two years and over the past 12 months has shifted from building infrastructure to its primary focus, selling books.[7] All agree that these past 12 months would be a good basis on which to develop the analysis.[8] The relevant data are given in Exhibit 3.12.

There are many ways to analyze this data. They all assume the following first-order cost equation:

$$\text{Total Cost} = \text{Variable Cost} + \text{Fixed Cost}$$
$$= (\text{Variable Cost Percentage} \times \text{Sales Revenue}) + \text{Fixed Cost}$$

The first of the three databased techniques is simply to plot the data in an x-y coordinate system with costs on the y-axis and sales revenues on the x-axis. It

EXHIBIT 3.12 Books "R" Us data.

	Revenue $(000)	Total Costs $(000)	Profit $(000)
January	$ 12,250	$ 13,500	$ (1,250)
February	14,500	16,000	(1,500)
March	15,000	16,500	(1,500)
April	16,250	17,250	(1,000)
May	15,250	16,500	(1,250)
June	13,750	15,500	(1,750)
July	11,500	13,000	(1,500)
August	17,500	18,250	(750)
September	23,750	25,000	(1,250)
October	15,500	16,500	(1,000)
November	16,000	17,250	(1,250)
December	22,500	22,000	500
Total	$193,750	$207,250	$(13,500)

is called *visual fit* because one simply draws a straight line through the data that "best fits" the pattern (see Exhibit 3.13). The point where this line intersects the *y*-axis yields an estimate of the fixed cost component—those costs that exist even without any sales activity. The slope of the line drawn is defined mathematically as: rise over run or change in *y*-axis values divided by the change in *x*-axis values. Using business rather than mathematical terminology, how much the total costs change (the *y*-axis or rise) as the sales volume changes (the *x*-axis or run). As was discussed above, this is simply the variable cost expressed as a percentage of sales. For the Books "R" Us example, given the line I've drawn subjectively, the result would be:

Fixed Cost Estimate: line crosses *y*-axis at about $4 million dollars

Variable Cost Percentage of Sales Estimate = Slope: about 85.2%[9]

With today's computer software, this method is easy and time efficient. Unfortunately, it lacks verifiability. If 20 people were to analyze this same data set, you could end up with twenty different cost structure estimates.

The second method is called *high-low analysis*. It also is time efficient and has the added advantage of verifiability. Since it is rule based, all twenty people in this case would arrive at the same estimate. It has four steps:

1. On the *x*-axis, identify the high and the low points of the data set.
2. Identify the historical costs for each of those points.
3. Assume a straight line through these two points and calculate the variable cost component using the traditional slope equation:

$$\text{Slope} = \frac{\text{Change in } y\text{-Axis Values}}{\text{Change in } x\text{-Axis Values}}$$

4. For either the high or the low set of data points, plug the values into the cost equation and solve for the fixed cost component.

EXHIBIT 3.13   Books "R" Us scatter plot.

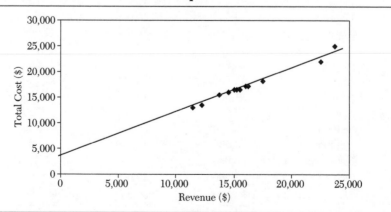

For the example and data set in Exhibit 3.12, the steps would be as follows:

1. High and low points = September sales or $23.75 million and July sales of $11.5 million.
2. Historical costs for each point = $25,000 (September) and $13,000 (July).
3. Slope = Rise/Run = ($25,000 − 13,000)/($23,750 − $11,500) = 98%.
4. Fixed component: Total Cost = Variable Cost + Fixed Cost.
    For high data points:

$$\$25,000 = 98\%\,(\$23,750) + \text{Fixed Cost}$$
$$\text{Fixed Cost} = \$25,000 - 98\%\,(\$23,750)$$
$$= \$1.725 \text{ million (rounded)}$$

For low data points:

$$\$13,000 = 98\%\,(\$11,500) + \text{Fixed Cost}$$
$$\text{Fixed Cost} = \$13,000 - 98\%\,(\$11,500)$$
$$= \$1.725 \text{ million (rounded)}$$

This method has two weaknesses. First, the high and low data points chosen are assumed to reflect the pattern of all data points. Often, however, either or both of these points may not be such, and the analysis is flawed.[10] The second weakness is an extension of the first. We had 12 data points but chose to analyze only two of them, ignoring the other 10. This method is data inefficient; if you have 12 data points, all 12 should be considered for the analysis.

The third databased technique is called *regression analysis*. Here a function is fit through all data points in a manner that minimizes the total squared error between each data point and the fitted line. The mathematics underlying this technique are beyond the scope of this chapter, but the method is widely used and preferred when the data set has problems such as a stepped fixed cost or variable costs based on multiple factors. All spreadsheet software packages have a function that performs simple regression analysis.[11] Exhibit 3.14 is an example of what the output would look like for a least-squares regression analysis using Excel. The estimate for the fixed cost is $2.73 million, and the variable cost is 90% per sales dollar. The adjusted R^2 of 98% means that 98% of the variance of the Total Cost data is explained by this equation. The drawback of this analysis is that it is not intuitive. One must trust the output from the statistical package. If the user does not understand the statistical technique and the assumptions of the software package, the output is often flawed.[12] This approach needs a sound grounding in statistical analysis.

In summary, for the data set being analyzed, the three databased techniques yield results that vary considerably (see Exhibit 3.15). The key to correctly using databased techniques, however, is not choosing the right technique but beginning with a data set that truly reflects the cost structure being

EXHIBIT 3.14 Least-squares regression output (Books "R" Us data).

SUMMARY OUTPUT

Regression Statistics

Multiple R	99.1%
R square	98.2%
Adjusted R square	98.0%
Standard error	471.36
Observations	12

ANOVA

	df	SS	MS	F	Significance F
Regression	1	119,835,495	119835495	539.363	4.956E-10
Residual	10	2,221,797	222179.69		
Total	11	122,057,292			

	Coefficients
Intercept	$2,733
X variable 1	90%

analyzed. To emphasize this, the cost function, Total Cost = (76%)Revenue + $5 million, was used to generate the data set in Exhibit 3.12. A randomized error term was then added to these data estimates, they were rounded to the nearest quarter million, and then the high and low data points, July and September, were purposely changed. For instance, assume September was a very busy month for Books "R" Us because of the many college-student book orders. This rush caused overtime and other disruptive cost behavior. Without the analyst first adjusting the data point for this aberrant behavior, the results are skewed. For databased techniques such as these, the adage "Garbage in, garbage out" holds true. Before employing any of these techniques first ensure that your data does truly reflect the cost structure being studied.

EXHIBIT 3.15 Databased cost structure estimates.

	Variable Cost Percentage	Fixed Cost (in millions)
Visual fit	85	$4.0
High-low	98	1.725
Least squares	90	2.733

THE ROLE OF PRICING IN CVP ANALYSIS

CVP analysis is often erroneously used to set prices. The *P* in *CVP* does not stand for "price"; it stands for "profit." A rule to remember: There is no such thing as "cost-based pricing." Prices are market driven. If a firm finds itself in a competitive market where competition among rivals is based on delivering comparable value to customers at the lowest cost, the market sets the price. As Adam Smith wrote centuries ago, only the most efficient firms will survive. To use CVP analysis in this situation, one starts with estimates of the market-driven price and then calculates the profitability given probable unit demand and the current cost structure. If the forecasted profit is not sufficient to satisfy investors, one must then focus on reducing costs, not raising prices.

Incumbent firm behavior in the U.S. health care industry after deregulation in the 1980s is a perfect example of incorrect use of this technique. New entrants into the lower, more profitable segments of this industry—for example, the walk-in clinics that have sprung up in metropolitan areas—gave patients (and insurance providers) a lower-cost option than traditional hospitals for minor health-care procedures. Large hospitals responded to this loss of segment revenue by spreading their costs (mostly fixed) over their remaining health-care offerings and raising prices. With those higher prices, the clinics were able to offer lower-priced alternatives for more complex procedures. With the loss of these revenues, the hospitals responded in the same manner. This is called the "doom loop," and it led to the closing of many such institutions. The proper move for the hospitals should have been to pare expenses on the noncompetitive offerings.

For firms that compete by differentiating themselves from rivals by offering additional value to customers at comparable cost, pricing should be based on value to the customer, not cost. Microsoft certainly does not price its products on the costs to develop and deliver them. Bill Gates long ago understood the value of an industry-standard PC operating system and has priced Microsoft's offerings accordingly. The key here, of course, is that the additional value must exceed the costs to create it. CVP analysis in this situation is basically no different than previous examples. Only here, one starts with estimates of the *value-based* price and then calculates the profitability given probable unit demand and the current cost structure. If the forecasted profit is not sufficient to satisfy investors, one must then focus not simply on raising prices but on reducing costs or increasing the willingness of consumers to pay more.

Predatory Pricing

In recent years a legal battle raged between two of the nation's largest tobacco companies.[13] The Brooke Group Inc. (previously known as Liggett Group Inc.) accused Brown & Williamson Tobacco Corporation of predatory pricing in the wholesale cigarette market. At trial in federal court the jury decided that Brown & Williamson had indeed engaged in predatory pricing against Brooke.

The jury awarded damages of $150 million to be paid to Brooke by Brown & Williamson. However, the presiding judge threw out this verdict. Brooke then filed an appeal, and the case continued.

Predatory pricing cases are not unusual, and damage awards as large as $150 million are not unheard of. *Predatory pricing*, as the name implies, is a tactic where the predator company slashes prices in order to force its competitors to follow suit. The purpose is to wage a price war and inflict upon the competition losses of such severity that they will be driven out of business. After destroying the competition, the predator company will be free to raise prices so that it can recover the losses it sustained in the price war and also rake in profits that will greatly exceed normal earnings at the competitive level. This final result is harmful to competition, and predatory pricing has therefore been made unlawful.

To determine whether a firm has engaged in predatory pricing, the courts need a test that will supply the correct answer. One of the usual tests is whether there is a sustained pattern of pricing below average variable cost. If the answer is yes, this indicates predatory pricing. Let us examine the logic underlying this widely used test.

First, recall that contribution is the margin between selling price and variable cost. Contribution goes toward paying fixed costs and providing a profit. If price is less than variable cost, contribution is negative. In that case, the firm cannot fully cover its fixed costs, and certainly it will suffer losses. Therefore, it makes no sense for the firm to charge a price that is below variable cost unless the firm is engaging in predatory pricing in order to destroy competing firms. That is why pricing below variable cost is considered to be consistent with predatory pricing.

We should bear in mind that the variable cost used in the test is that of the alleged predator, not of the alleged victim. The reason is that the alleged predator may be an efficient low-cost producer, whereas the alleged victim may be an inefficient high-cost producer. Therefore, a price below the alleged victim's variable cost may be above that of the alleged predator, in which case it could be a legitimate price and simply a reflection of the superior efficiency of the alleged predator. The antitrust laws are designed to protect competition, but not competitors (especially those competitors who are inefficient).

Of course, this is only one indicator of predatory pricing, and all of the relevant evidence must be considered. There should also be a pattern of sustained pricing below variable cost. Prices that are slashed only sporadically or occasionally are probably legitimate business tactics, such as loss-leader pricing to attract customers or clearance sales to get rid of obsolete goods.

Predatory pricing is an important topic and has been the subject of major lawsuits in a wide variety of industries. Because it is a common test for predatory pricing, variable cost is also a very important topic that all successful businesspeople will benefit from thoroughly understanding.

Predatory pricing is usually thought of in a regional sense, or perhaps on a national scale. But it can also occur on an international basis. In that case, it is known as dumping.

Dumping

If a foreign company is the predator, there is no inherent difference in the tactics or the goal of predatory pricing. Pricing below variable cost would still remain a valid test. However, U.S. law imposes a stricter test on foreign than on domestic companies. The legal test for dumping does not involve variable cost. Rather, it focuses on whether the foreign company is selling its product here at a price less than the price in its home market.

Dumping is simply predatory pricing by a foreign company. So the logic that supported using variable cost as a test for predatory pricing would also support using the same test for dumping. But the test actually used is the domestic selling price (usually higher than variable cost). This test makes it easier to prove dumping than to prove predatory pricing. It favors the domestic firms and is harder on the foreign company. This may be a matter of politics as well as one of economics.

Perhaps the best-known cases of dumping have involved the textile and steel industries. Another recent case of dumping concerned Japanese auto companies accused by U.S. competitors of dumping minivans in this country. Also, the Japanese makers of flat screens for laptop computers (active matrix liquid crystal displays) were alleged to have sold their products in the United States at prices below those in the home market.

It is not always easy to ascertain the home market selling price. Even if there are list prices or catalog prices in the home market, there may be discounts or rebates that are difficult to detect. Therefore, instead of using the home market selling price as the test, the production cost may be used instead. This is reasonable, because the production cost is likely to be below the home market selling price. Therefore a dumping price below production cost is virtually certain to be also below the home market selling price. But production cost includes both fixed and variable costs and is therefore above variable cost. Also, it may be arguable as to what should be included in production cost. For example, some may include interest expense on money borrowed to purchase manufacturing material inventories. Others may believe that interest is not part of production cost.

If it is determined that dumping has indeed taken place, then the U.S. International Trade Commission (ITC) will impose an import duty on the foreign product involved. This duty will be sufficiently high to boost the U.S. selling price to the same level as the home market price.

Dumping has a large potential impact on businesses and industries in our economy. By extension, production cost is also a subject that successful businesspeople will find profitable to understand.

FOR FURTHER READING

Garrison, Ray, and Eric Noreen, *Managerial Accounting,* 8th ed. (New York: McGraw-Hill, 1999).

Hilton, Ronald, *Managerial Accounting,* 4th ed. (New York: McGraw-Hill, 1998).

Horngren, Charles, *Cost Accounting: A Managerial Emphasis,* 9th ed. (Upper Saddle River, NJ: Prentice-Hall, 1998).

Zimmerman, Jerold, *Accounting for Decision Making and Control,* 3rd ed. (New York: McGraw-Hill, 1999).

NOTES

1.   *Mixed* simply means that it has both a variable- and a fixed-cost component. Mixed costs are very common—note your monthly phone bill or many car rental contracts.

2.   Economists argue that variable costs should not be represented by linear functions, since economies and diseconomies of scale do exist. For instance, price discounts are often given if one buys inputs such as paper for book printing in large quantities. They are better represented by quadratic functions. Most agree, however, that if we are analyzing a narrow enough range the assumption of linearity does not lead to material error.

3.   This can be expressed in an algebraic equation as follows. Since the indifference point is where the two alternatives are equal:

$$\$12x = \$23x - \$100,000$$

Solving for x yields:

$$\$11x = \$100,000$$
$$x = \frac{\$100,000}{\$11}$$
$$= 9,091 \text{ units}$$

4.   Defining the parameters of a "short-run" decision is often difficult. For this special offer, if accepted, will PBS assume that this will be the price in the future? Will other customers learn of this offer and expect the same terms? Short-run decisions often have hidden long-run effects—they should always be scrutinized.

5.   In this format, x represents required *dollar* sales volume, not required *unit* sales volume.

6.   ABC analysis, which is covered in the following chapter, is one such technique.

7.   When estimating cost structure from historical data the analyst must first ascertain that the structure has not changed during the period being analyzed. If Books "R" Us made major additions to its infrastructure, it would make little sense to aggregate the costs pre- and postaddition and consider them to be representative of a single cost structure.

8.   For this simple example we will assume that there are none of the seasonalities in the fixed cost one would expect, say, for heating costs during the winter in New England. Likewise, we will assume that the variable cost per dollar of revenue is the same for all types of books.

9.   To compute the slope, find a point that the line intersects and then measure the "rise-over-run" using the y-axis intercept and that point. For this calculation my line intersected the June data at point ($13,500, $15,500) so my rise was $11,500 ($4,000 to $15,500 in Total Cost) and my run was $13,500 ($0 to $13,500 in Revenue). The slope, therefore, was $11,500/$13,500 or 85.2%.

10.   To avoid this shortcoming, many analysts first plot the data and then select high and low data points that "best fit" the data set. This technique is a melding of the first two databased techniques discussed.

11.   For instance, Excel has a function that will perform a simple least-squares regression on a given data set. Other regression techniques that relax the linear fit assumption are also available on many statistical software packages.

12.   For instance, infrastructure may have been expanded over the period the data set covers. The regression software will assume a constant fixed cost rather than some type of step function unless otherwise told. This can be treated using dummy variables, but the user needs to have a working knowledge of the statistical technique.

13.   The final two sections of this chapter were written by John Leslie Livingstone for earlier editions of this book. They are reproduced here in their entirety.

4 ACTIVITY-BASED COSTING

William C. Lawler

Dave Roger, CEO of Electronic Transaction Network (ETN/W), sat stunned in his office. He had just come out of a preliminary third-round financing meeting with potential investors. Six months ago his CFO had assured him that third-round financing would not be a problem. Much had happened since that date. The Internet stocks had crashed. Money for the technology sector was now tight. In the two rounds before the crash, ETN/W had so many prospective investors, the company had to turn some away. Since then their business model had not changed; ETN/W had a solid revenue stream, and the forecast was for continued revenue growth—unlike many of the recently failed Internet companies, ETN/W had real customers who were happy with its services. Yet the meeting had concluded without closure on the third round for one simple reason. When Dave started talking about their "proven" business model the potential investors immediately asked for specific details—"Explain your business model in terms of how you will create wealth for us, your investors."

As he fumbled to explain how ETN/W would create shareholder wealth, they stopped him and suggested an approach with which they were all comfortable.

> If you were a manufacturer we would expect you to tell us how you will use our investment—some goes to infrastructure such as plant and equipment and some to working capital such as inventory and receivables. You would then tell us how much it would cost you to build your product, how much to market it, how much to service it, and what customers would be willing to pay for it. Our first two rounds of investment would have given you sufficient experience to gather this type of data. With this information, you could explain your business model— how you would create enough wealth to pay back our principal plus our required

return. Now, since you are a service provider rather than a manufacturer, explain your business model in like terms. What infrastructure is necessary for your business? What does it cost you to provide your service? How much does it cost to market these services? What are customers willing to pay for it?

As he sat there now, Dave wondered if the analogy the investors had used was appropriate. In a manufacturing environment these questions were more easily answered than in a service company like ETN/W. Yet after two rounds of investment and eighteen months in business he had fumbled the most important question in the meeting. In his hand he had the business card of a consultant suggested by his investors. They said this person had worked with a number of their clients and could help him develop the appropriate analysis. As much as he disliked being pushed by anyone to make decisions, he knew that 25 employees were counting on him. He lifted the phone to call Denise Pizzi.

PREPARING FOR DENISE

Denise was very professional on the phone. She was awaiting his call and suggested that he prepare some documentation for their first meeting: a brief history of the company, their customer value proposition (she called it CVP), a blueprint of the value system for their industry, and their strategy—what was it that ETN/W could offer clients that was distinct and value producing? Much of this had already been prepared.

ETN/W History

Three MBA classmates with extensive experience in electronic commerce had founded ETN/W in Dallas, Texas, 18 months ago. Two came from a Houston computer giant—Carol Kelly from the hardware side and Eric Rock, a senior software applications manager. The third, Dave Roger, came from a well-known Dallas IT consultancy, a company focused on the Internet and e-commerce. The idea had come from Dave. Many of his clients were in e-commerce, and all had the same problem—transaction processing. Although most people think online commerce is a relatively simple process—point and click—it is actually quite complicated (see Exhibit 4.1). Assume customer A buys an item at Books "R" Us. When the order comes in, the company must first ascertain A's creditworthiness. This means a credit check with a payment processor. If credit is okay, then Books "R" Us has to contact the book wholesaler it partners with to see if the book is in stock (this is called fulfillment). If the answer is in the affirmative, Books "R" Us gives the wholesaler the appropriate shipping information, gets the tracking information from the shipper, and contacts the payment processor once more to charge customer A. Books "R" Us then relays this information to A. This all has to be done in real time. Customer A does not want to wait and will quickly move to a competitor if not satisfied. In addition,

EXHIBIT 4.1   E-Commerce transaction detail.

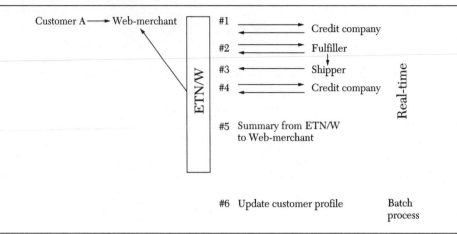

Books "R" Us will update Customer A's buying profile (or open a new one) in order to better serve that person in the future. Books "R" Us's focus is on retail sales and Web-site design; this is the key to its success. The transaction processing is a necessary evil. In order to do this, Web merchants typically, purchase three to four software systems—one each for credit and payment processing, inventory management and fulfillment, tracking, and customer-information storage and mining. All these systems must talk to one another, which means that interfaces must be maintained. This interfacing is a nightmare because updates for each of these software systems are constantly being brought to market, requiring all interfaces to be rewritten. IT personnel in this area are highly valued, and retention is a major issue, especially for the smaller Web merchants.

This nightmare blossomed into a business opportunity during a golf match. Carol was complaining about a new assignment—setting up a server farm.[1] She was given the task of transforming her company from a provider of "boxes" (servers) to a provider of the services embedded in the box. This meant that her company had to get closer to customers, understand their computing needs, and meet those needs with a bundle of services delivered by the "server farm" she would be running. Basically this was a hardware outsourcing service similar to an offering of one of Dave's sister divisions. Although he understood the move, and although servers were becoming commodified and margins were falling, he doubted that Carol could change the culture of her company. Maintaining customer relationships was expensive, much like the required maintenance on any hardware system; but unlike hardware maintenance they also required a unique set of people skills.

On the next hole it was Dave's turn to complain about his customers and how he had to hold their hands every time one of their transaction processing systems needed updating—every day the same thing only a different customer and a different software system. Eric laughed at this since he had much the same problems within his software applications group. Yet all three realized that this was how software companies made their money. Once they captured a customer with an installed software system, that client was treated as an annuity. Every update required an additional payment to move each installed customer to the new system. They all agreed that this would never change.

The golf round continued, as did the complaining about both work and golf. It was not until later, over libations in the 19th Hole, that they realized this could be a real opportunity. Dave was convinced that his customers would be more than willing to outsource their transaction-processing headaches. If a company could provide an integrated service that would perform all the tasks, it would be a winner. A customer value proposition (CVP) that said, "All your e-commerce transactions will be processed with the latest technology, and you will never have to worry about a customer waiting, updating your interfaces, or hiring and training another IT person," would be music to their ears. Eric insisted that most application service providers (ASPs), much like Carol's hardware company, were focused on selling their software packages, not on service. They were not capable of providing such a service. Carol agreed with both Eric and Dave—although she would try her hardest, her new assignment was like pushing a boulder uphill. All systems inside her company were focused on selling product; engineers designed the latest bells and whistles into their hardware and avoided customer contact whenever possible. All commission systems were based on dollar revenues; the top salespeople only sold what made them money, high priced items. They were not interested in selling low-commission service contracts.

Within a month the threesome was working almost full-time on developing the business model. Carol was focused on designing the necessary hardware infrastructure—N/T and UNIX servers, hubs and routers, firewalls, disk arrays, frame relays, and the like—and identifying the staffing requirements. Eric was researching the software offering for payment, fulfillment, tracking, and storage and attempting to identify which systems would likely become industry standards. Dave was running focus groups with a number of potential customers, trying to refine the CVP—exactly what should they offer these Web merchants?—and measure their willingness to pay.

The business plan came together rather quickly. As expected, Dave found that customers would highly value the ability to focus all their attention on their primary activity, Web-based marketing and selling, rather than transaction processes and the hiring and training of people involved in these processes. In addition, the avoidance of investment in this type of infrastructure was important since capital was becoming scarce for many Web-based merchants and obsolescence was always a problem. An additional value that potential customers asked about involved the nature of the charge: Was it to be a variable per-transaction charge or a fixed fee? For this type of business, scalability was always a problem. No one knew what size system to build, but to have a system crash due to excess demand was fatal. As a result, idle infrastructure charges were always a problem. Many customers were ready to sign on immediately if the charge was on a per-transaction basis.

Carol found that the infrastructure build-out would not be cheap. She estimated that it would cost approximately $8 million in the startup mode and require about a dozen people. She estimated that this would give them the capacity to process about 120,000 transactions per day, which would be about 10 average-sized customers in a peak demand period such as Christmas or Valentines Day.

Eric found that the software system would be cheaper. He also found some additional interesting information. Many ASPs such as Yantra, Oracle, and Cybersource offered to work with them in an alliance if they could advertise their applications, say, like the "Intel inside" model in the PC industry. He estimated that to build a totally integrated software platform would cost around $600,000 to $800,000.

In this manner ETN/W (Electronic Transaction Network) was started. Angel investors and alliance partners contributed $20 million, and the doors were open for business 18 months ago. Within a year they had nine customers and added another three in the following six months. Various pricing schemes were tried, but ETN/W seemed to be gravitating toward a market-based, purely per-transaction charge between $0.10 and $0.15. Although transaction volume had not met the projected 120,000-per-day level, they were currently in the process of identifying potential new customers.

ETN/W CVP

The group provided Denise the following from one of their marketing brochures:

> Web merchants should spend the majority of their time on their primary mission, creating value through innovative marketing and sales to customers and clients.[2] You should avoid spending both scarce managerial talent and investor capital on any activity that could best be performed by third-party partners such as ETN/W. Do investors see the value in your using their investment dollars and your creative energy to build transaction-processing systems that are suboptimal in scale and soon obsolete? In you spending your scarce time to hire and train high-cost personnel to manage and run these inefficient systems? The answer is clearly *no*.
>
> Join our network and get all these services seamlessly provided with state-of-the-art applications run by highly trained IT professionals. We will convert a difficult-to-manage fixed infrastructure cost into a totally scaleable variable cost that you pay only on a per-transaction basis. With us as your partner, you can spend your creative energies on tasks of value to your investors.

ETN/W Value System & Strategy

This part of preparing for their meeting with Denise was an interesting task for the threesome, one that they had not previously performed. After referring to some of their old MBA notes, they prepared the following:

Value System. ETN/W is an intermediary providing services to the Web merchant and its fulfillment, payment, and shipping partners. Although ETN/W charges the merchant for the service, who ultimately pays for the service could be left to negotiation amongst the parties (see Exhibit 4.2).

This exercise did open some interesting discussion regarding our narrowly defined CVP. We recalled Metcalf's Law: The value of a network is equal to the square of the number of nodes. Clearly, as our network expands, fulfillers such as Ingram, a $2 billion wholesaler of books, PCs, and home electronics, would see value in joining because it could provide fulfillment services to a number of the network's Web merchants. Likewise, UPS and FedEx would want to join ETN/W to offer their services if there was enough commerce going over the network. We did not have time to fully develop this thought, but discussion of an expanded scope for our CVP and potential pricing schemes is on the agenda for an upcoming meeting. This process might really be worth your fee.

Strategy. ETN/W will be the global cost leader in transaction processing for e-commerce providers. Exactly what is it that ETN/W offers that others cannot copy? A sustainable strategy is based on doing things differently or doing different things, not simply doing the same thing as other competitors only better. As noted above, it would be difficult for any of the hardware companies and ASPs to copy our model, since their culture and internal systems are so geared to selling hardware or software rather than servicing customers. Hewlett Packard coined the term *solution provider* almost thirty years ago but still struggles in making the requisite transition. We all feel that ETN/W can successfully compete with hardware providers and ASPs. The problem is the low barriers to entry: If all it takes is building an infrastructure with hardware and software technology that are readily available, what is to stop others from imitating our model? The only advantage we see is to be the first mover; once someone joins our network, why join another? We understand the urgency of building the network as quickly as possible to be recognized as the industry standard for transaction processing.

EXHIBIT 4.2   ETN/W value system.

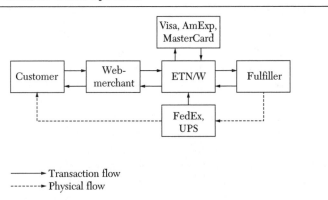

———→ Transaction flow
------→ Physical flow

THE FIRST MEETING

Denise was very happy with the work they had done. She had reviewed the materials and asked a few questions. Within an hour all felt comfortable that she understood ETN/W in sufficient detail to aid them in preparing an answer for the investment group. They then turned to this phase of the meeting.

Denise began.

> The value system analysis you did is a map at an aggregate level of the many firm-level value chains that together form this industry. It identifies all the processes that create value for an end customer or set of end customers and maps all the players and who adds what to the system. Our focus is on ETN/W, but we cannot lose sight of how it interacts with other members of the system. The next step is to add another layer of detail—what are the process steps that ETN/W performs, and do their values exceed the costs to perform them?

Dave, Carol, and Eric did not understand what she meant and asked for clarification.

"Simply stated," Denise replied, "what is it that you do? Map the value-producing processes you add to the system."

Carol was quick to answer: "We already told you—we process e-commerce transactions."

"Okay. So that is all you do? If I were to talk to any number of your people spread throughout this building, they would say, 'I process transactions'?"

Dave jumped in this time: "Well, not really. While most of us are involved in this in some form, we also have marketing and sales people."

"What do they do?"

This dialog went on for another hour, with Denise at a blackboard capturing their discussion. After many edits the group arrived at the following. The process map for ETN/W had three sequential steps:

1. *Customer Capture.*
2. *Customer Loading* onto the network.
3. *Transaction Processing.*

Denise then stated:

> The next phase of this analysis is critical. Although most accounting systems capture costs by function—for example, manufacturing costs such as direct material, labor, and overhead and operating costs such as sales, marketing, R&D, and administrative—we can understand and forecast them only if we identify their causes. This analysis is called activity-based costing, or ABC. Not everyone believes the cost of ABC is worth the benefit, but higher cost is, I believe, more often due to how it is implemented rather than to the approach itself. Too many firms have limited it to manufacturing situations, yet it is appropriate also for service companies such as yours. ABC is also often too narrowly applied—some now argue that ABC begins too late and ends too soon in many companies. We have to analyze costs across the value system since causal factors for one

company's costs often are found within another company in the value system. Although this may sound confusing, I will of course show you examples as we analyze your costs.

Let's start with what I think will be the easiest process—*customer capture.* Exactly what activities do you perform that result in a capture, which we defined as a signed contract?

Again, the discussion went on for at least an hour. Denise nearly drove the group crazy asking the most basic questions, "Why?" and "How?" By the end, all three agreed that the first activity was *customer identification.* This was accomplished either through cards filled out at trade shows or responses from their advertising campaign. The next activity was *customer qualification,* which entailed basic research on these companies to identify those with enough size and creditworthiness to pursue. And the final one was *customer sale,* where an inside salesperson first made contact with each customer to see if there still was interest. Few were ready to sign contracts at this point, and often multiple site visits were necessary before contracts were signed to assure the customer that ETN/W understood their business.

Denise then gave them a template to be filled in for the next meeting (see Exhibit 4.3).

What you have to do is reformat the way your costs are compiled. For external reporting your financial statements are sufficient, but for decision making and communicating your business model they are worthless. As I have drawn in the template, we need to build the total costs for each activity we identified above. To do this, some of my past clients estimated as best they could from historical data, and others, if they perform the activity frequently enough, develop the

EXHIBIT 4.3   Activity-based costing process.

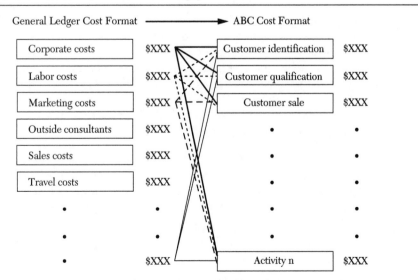

activity costs by studying their processes real time. I suggest you recreate from past data as best you can what you spent to capture the clients you already have on your system, since you're currently selling to only a few—a sample size too small to study real time. A detailed discussion with all those involved with the process typically is sufficient to develop a crude analysis. I can meet next week—Okay?

THE SECOND MEETING

Dave, Carol, and Eric did a lot of work that week. After many false starts they agreed to use the financial statement data from the past 12 months for the analysis. Discussions with a number of their employees resulted in some interesting analyses. Although unsure of a few of their assumptions, they walked in with deeper insight into customer identification, qualification, and sale.

The activities we initially agreed upon needed some refinement. The first, customer identification, was correct. There are actually three subactivities, trade show attendance, trade show preparation, and advertising, which lead to an identified customer. These activities are not mutually exclusive; often people respond to the advertising after seeing us at a trade show, or, vise versa, they come to our booth because they remember one of our advertising pieces. Using your template, we arrived at some interesting results. First, you were correct, customer identification does draw on many resources within the company. People from across ENT/W attend the trade shows: our sales and marketing people as you would expect; our corporate officers, who typically talk with the top management of potential customers; and our operations people, who demonstrate the system and answer the technical questions. In addition, for each show there is quite a bit of preparation: Collateral materials such as brochures have to be produced, booths have to be designed and built, and site contracts negotiated. Aside from the trade shows, we also spend a large amount on advertising in trade journals. In the last 12 months, we spent approximately $875,000 on these three subactivities, which resulted in 1,200 customer leads (potential customers). We arrived at this number by talking with just about everybody in the organization, checking travel itineraries, expense reports, ad agency vouchers, and the like. It's not an exact number, so we decided to round all our numbers to the nearest $5,000; but we think it's close. This comes out to about $730 per lead ($875,000/1,200, rounded). We think this is a reasonable number given some industry benchmarks. Is that OKAY?

Denise was excited; these could be good clients. "Yes, ABC analysis does sacrifice some accuracy for relevance. So, when you divided by the 1,200, you implicitly assumed that each of these leads were the same. Is this true?"

Dave answered since he had done most of this analysis. "Yes, each lead is about the same. When people show interest, either at a show or from answering an ad, we do about the same thing: talk with them, take down their information, and pass it on to the next step."

Denise thought it was now time to do a little process review. "Good, you have just concluded your first activity-based cost analysis. Let me review the steps. First, we drilled down from a high-level value system view to a process map and then ultimately into an activity and subactivity analysis. I have only one question: After identifying subactivities, why did you pool the costs together; why not analyze them separately?"

"We initially did it separately but then found that there was no additional value to this added work. Ultimately, we were concerned with what it cost us to generate a lead, and, since we found that the subactivities were not mutually exclusive, we think the $730 number is sufficient," Dave replied.

> Let that be you first lesson. ABC involves pooling costs from various functions within the company into homogeneous activity pools, as you have just done. The $875,000 reflects your best estimate of the total customer identification cost pool for the last 12 months. ABC analysis is often done at too fine a level of detail. You could have tried to identify the cost of identifying each customer by having your people keep a log and entering the exact time they spent with each customer—in essence, 1,200 cost pools. Would this additional level of accuracy be worth the effort? Certainly not. The first key to ABC is to find the correct level of disaggregation of cost information: too little and the system does not provide relevant information; too much and the system becomes too complex and hard to communicate. I once saw a system installed by a consulting group with over 6,000 cost pools. No one understood it but the consultants that designed it, and when they left no one was able to explain the information from it or update it. It died in less than six months. Okay, what was your next step?

Carol had done the customer qualification analysis. "This was an easy one. We outsource this function to a credit agency that gives us a report on each lead—credit history, sales history, and any other relevant information. We paid them about $210,000 for the 1,200 reports—about $175 per report, which is about the contract rate."

Denise thought, "Can I do one more lesson without overreaching? Why not try?"

> Note the difference between these two cost pools. This pool is very much a variable cost—the more customer reports, the greater the total cost pool. And the manner in which we apply the total costs to the object we wish to cost—a customer cost report—is obvious—the number of cost reports, since each is the same. ABC is a two-step process. First we identify the appropriate level of disaggregation—that is, the cost pools—and then we identify the appropriate "driver" for each pool. A driver is the method we use to take the total cost pool and trace it to the object we wish to cost. It's the causal factor for the cost pool. For customer qualification, the total pool of $210,000 was spread over its causal factor, the 1,200 cost reports, to arrive at the $175 per cost report. This is what it costs to qualify a customer, the cost object. ABC is nothing more than pools and drivers. Are you totally comfortable with our first two analyses?"

Dave answered: "We did argue about this. Now I think we are beginning to understand. The first activity we discussed, customer identification, is more a fixed cost pool—it doesn't vary with the number of customer leads. Once we agree on how many trade shows we will present at and what our budget is with the ad agency, this cost is relatively fixed. Maybe one person more or less might travel to the show, but the cost is budgeted. As a result, the cost per lead decreases as we become more successful in generating leads. We have already talked about ways of being more effective in this regard."

"Exactly," said Denise. "We will no doubt go more deeply into proper identification of drivers for fixed and variable cost pools. What you should understand, though, is that ABC is just a first stage in a long journey. Most people, as you did, move quickly into ABM—activity-based management. Once you make your cost system transparent, you then naturally seek to optimize it as you are doing with customer identification. So, our end objective of this 'long journey' is simply that, transparency of the cost system. And the final piece?"

Eric had this one.

> This was my responsibility and it was a lot more difficult than Carol's piece. The final activity, customer sale, also has subactivities. We review the consultant reports and identify those we want to pursue. Of the 1,200, we identified eighty as "high potential" and tried to sell to them. Although all the effort did not fall neatly into the 12-month window, essentially we went through the full process to a signed contract for the equivalent of 10 customers. The process included phone conversations and site visits. In total, we spent $410,000 to bring to contract these 10—many of the others went through part of the process before either they or we lost interest. As with the other two activities, the costs that loaded into this pool came from across the company. Often we had to fly out technicians to explain how the system works as well as salespeople. For larger clients, they expected a visit from a corporate officer for the formal signing. So in the end it cost us about $41,000 each to sign them to contracts."

Denise asked only one question: "Would you say this is a variable- or a fixed-cost pool?"

After a lengthy discussion, the consensus was that it clearly was both a variable and a fixed cost since more high-potential leads meant more resources dedicated to pursuing them. But it was not a pure variable cost since once you hire someone to do this work, they can handle a certain number of leads rather than just one. At the end, they agreed on the following: Unlike setting a budget for a year, this cost was a step function. Within certain steps, defined as the number of high potentials a sales person could pursue—say, eight at a time—the cost was fixed. In essence, the cost was step fixed in units of eight. They also agreed that this thinking should also be applied to the customer-identification cost analysis, but left that for later.

Denise then asked, "Is the $41,000 roughly the same for each potential customer sale?"

Eric was quick to respond, "Absolutely not. Some require a lot more work than others."

They were at the end of the agreed meeting time but Denise thought one more lesson would not hurt.

> When this happens, it is an indication that you have improperly identified the driver for the pool. You must drill down to a more detailed driver definition. As

we discussed last meeting, on one hand, you could keep an individual log on each customer to identify the cost to sell them, but this would be time-consuming and few people take the time to accurately enter this information. On the other hand, you could aggregate the cost and average it over the 10 customers sold. But it seems that this is also not appropriate. A reasonable midpoint is to identify a separate driver defined as your best-case and worst-case customer and see if this gives you the required amount of detail. Why don't you do that for next time and also develop a summary of the total cost to capture a customer.

THE THIRD MEETING

Denise watched as the group approached the room. They were arguing something in a manner that indicated they were enjoying themselves. This was a good sign.

Dave began:

It's amazing to us as an organization how much we didn't know we knew about our business. When we relayed your first assignment for this meeting to those that work with potential customers, they immediately began identifying characteristics that made some more expensive to sell than others. Large ones expect to meet our management team before signing a contract, whereas smaller ones do not. Flying one of us to these customers is expensive given our larger salaries and what it takes to backfill in our absence. Also, customers who do not really understand e-commerce and the complexity of transaction processing require on average twice as many trips as those who do. They want us to demonstrate what is wrong with their systems and to see how ours works better. Since we are not familiar with their systems, this takes a while. For the selling process, the best-case customer is a midsized company familiar with e-commerce and the headaches caused by transaction processing. We can sell them on the first trip. Unfortunately, of the 10 we signed to a contract in our sample, only 3 were of this type. The other 7 were worst-case customers—larger with less knowledge of the intricacies of e-commerce. In summary, when we trace the $410,000 using these driver definitions we estimate that the best-case customers cost about $18,300 each and the worst-case about $50,700 ($18,300 × 3 + $50,700 × 7 ≈ $410,000). What amazed us is that, once we asked these questions, our people had a number of good suggestions on how to reengineer this process. They knew these worst-case people were a problem, but never saw how much more they cost. Transparency does help.

The answer to your second assignment, to calculate the total cost to capture a customer, is also amazing. This *customer capture* process is like a funnel. Last time we said that the activity cost per lead of $730 was reasonable, as was the $175 for each research report. But when you recognize that the process ended with only 10 signed contracts, you get a different picture. The overall process cost us a total of $1.495 million ($875 for identification, $210 for qualification, and $410 for selling) or about $150,000 per signed contract ($1.495/10, rounded)—quite a bit less for best case and a bit more for worst case. Some of these costs are variable, some fixed, and some step fixed, but all of them can be better managed. Although our accountant classified these costs as expenses, they are really an investment, and, at this amount, we would have to do a lot of transactions just to recoup our investment in each customer. The key for us is to identify better-qualified customers in the first stage and then to convert a greater number of these to signed contracts.

Denise had only one question: "Why did you charge the costs of the 70 customers you failed to convert to the 10 that you sold?"

Dave answered, "Actually, initially we broke out the cost of the 70, but we felt that, as with any business process, you spoil some units in order to get good ones (see Exhibit 4.4). It really cost us only about $8,000 to sell each best-case customer and almost three times that for the worst-case one. But when you allocated the cost of the 70 customers dropped during the process, these costs increase dramatically. Don't you agree?"

The depth of the analysis impressed Denise. She thought she might even invest in this company. It was time for another summary.

There is no right answer, since we could argue over the correct way to allocate the dropped-customer costs. But that is not what is important here. You have to be careful with any reallocation procedure since this is a strategic analysis. You have already noted that your only advantage was being first to enter. By your actions, I am not sure you know what that means. Since all of your technology comes from third-party suppliers, the only way you will win in this industry is to become the low-cost provider. Your first-mover advantage means simply that you are first down the experience curve. Research has shown that as one repeats an activity, one can become more efficient and thus lower the cost of the activity. This, however, does not happen automatically; one must manage the learning process. Until we began the ABC analysis it seems that you had not leveraged your first-mover advantage. Do you agree? Remember saying, "As an organization, we were amazed at how much we didn't know we knew"?

None of the three were willing to argue with her.

The key number in your exhibit is the $8,000 cost to sell a best-case customer. If you were able to identify only those that understood your CVP and wanted to

EXHIBIT 4.4   Customer-sale activity analysis.

	Best-Case	Worst-Case	Dropped	Total
Number of customers	3	7	70	80
Estimated cost pool	$24,000	$154,000	$ 232,000	$410,000
Cost/customer	$ 8,000	$ 22,000	N/A	N/A
Reallocation°	$31,000	$201,000	$(232,000)	
Adjusted cost pool	$55,000	$355,000	—	$410,000
Full cost/customer	$18,300	$ 50,700		

° Dropped Cost total was allocated based on relative total cost/customer ratios:

$$3 \times \frac{\$8,000}{7} \times \$22,000 = \frac{\$24,000}{\$154,000} \cong \frac{\$31,000}{\$201,000}$$

buy, this would be the cost, not the average of $41,000 or the higher one for worst-case. Are you getting better? Is your cost of this activity decreasing? The research from the Chasm Group seems relevant here.[3] They found that new-technology buyers over the product life cycle fall into four segments. Each responds to a different CVP and requires a different selling approach. The first product life-cycle segment, called *early adopters,* is the smallest but the most important. They seek new technology, are risk takers, and are probably much like your three best-case customers. This customer group is important because you can use their results as validation of your new offering. The later life-cycle segments are larger, less technologically savvy, and more risk averse. They are skeptics and need to see validation before they buy. If you studied your seven worst-case data points they probably fall into this segment. If you learn to use the experiences of your first customers to sell to these more risk-averse segments, your cost should approach the $8,000, and you would have a true first-mover advantage.

Denise didn't like to further dampen their spirits but knew she had to. "We haven't finished yet. Don't forget you also have to load the customers on the network. What does this process cost?"

After a collective groan, the group got to work. The *customer loading* process involves the activities necessary to enter a Web merchant and its ful-filler(s) onto the ETN/W network. Although the activities are much different than for customer capture, the analysis is similar. The activities in this process are *customer business operations review, system design,* and *implementation and certification.* Over the past 12 months seven customers had been loaded. The analysis was a bit easier since there was no funnel effect; seven went through each activity.[4]

Business operations review was outsourced to a number of subcontractors that ETN/W used. Their report detailed the customer's IT systems and how transactions were treated. While most handled them real time, some batched the orders and dealt with these at the end of the business day, sending confirmation to customers on the next business day. For the seven customers loaded, ETN/W paid $25,000, or about $3,600 each. System design—writing the necessary software interfaces and configuring hardware linkages for the payment processing, fulfillment, and shipping systems—was done by ETN/W technical staff, as was implementation and certification. System design cost $35,000, and implementation and design, $160,000. Both the business operations review and system design activities were relatively homogeneous—they did not vary from customer to customer. The final activity, however, implementation and certification, was much like the customer sale activity. Depending upon the customer, the cost could vary greatly. From discussions with those involved with these activities, the threesome recognized this variability and did the necessary analysis. A best-case customer was one that understood the process, had compiled the necessary documentation, had their IT group prepared, and had only one or two fulfillers. As before, the worst-case was unprepared, unresponsive, and had numerous fulfillment agreements. Of the seven studied, three fell in the former

EXHIBIT 4.5 Customer-capture and customer-loading cost summary.

Activity	Average Cost	Ideal Cost
Customer identification	$ 87,500 [$875,000/10]	$ 730
Customer qualification	21,000 [$210,000/10]	175
Customer sale	41,000 [$410,000/10]	8,000
Business process review	3,600 [$ 25,000/7]	3,600
System design	5,000 [$ 35,000/7]	5,000
Implementation & certification	23,000 [$160,000/7]	13,000
Total (rounded)	$181,000	$30,500

group and four in the latter with the following result: best-case cost to load onto network approximately $13,000, and worst-case a bit, under $30,000 ($13,000 × 3 + $30,000 × 4 ≈ $160,000). Dave reported that this result necessitated adding a penalty clause to their standard contract to emphasize the importance of the customer prework for the implementation team.

Denise thought there was time for a quick summary. She went to the board and drew the following chart (see Exhibit 4.5). "As I see it there is a lot of room for improvement. Granted, you will never reach the ideal cost of $30,500, which is the total of the activity costs to capture and load a customer. But the transparency you now have given these activities means that, as an organization, you should make steady progress down the experience curve. Next time, let's tackle *transaction processing*."

TRANSACTION PROCESSING—MEETING 1

Since Carol was the hardware guru, she had taken the lead in this analysis.

> Our transaction-processing system has three front-end N/T systems that do the order entry, transaction-processing, and fulfillment inventory management. They sit on a UNIX backbone system that also runs the database. It made little sense to go back and compile the costs for these systems over the past 12 months, since we were expanding them continually. What we did was take the costs of the system for the last month and annualize it. The costs fall into two groupings—people and system depreciation.
>
> I have one systems manager and three shifts of two people—don't forget, we do provide service on a 365-by-24-by-7 basis. One person monitors the system and troubleshoots any transaction-related problems, and the other handles all hardware-related problems. Fully loaded, these seven people cost us approximately $750,000 per year.
>
> Ideally, we would have cost the N/T systems independently of the UNIX backbone. We didn't have that fine a separation of costs in this area, however, and we ultimately grouped all of them together. Since the UNIX system

represents the large majority of the cost, this probably doesn't cause us any material error. In total we estimate that at the current level our systems cost us about $1.35 million a year in depreciation of hardware and amortization of software. We are writing off the technology over a three-year life, which is reasonable. So we estimate that it will cost us in total about $2.1 million a year ($1.35 million in systems and 0.75 million in personnel) at our current level of operations. This pool is a fixed pool since both the people and systems costs are independent of volume—our people now are nowhere near capacity but you can't hire a half-person.

The driver for this cost pool is clearly the number of transactions processed, but arriving at the proper measure was difficult. For the order-entry and payment-processing systems a transaction is measured at the order level. But for the fulfillment and database systems, transactions are dependent on the line items in the order. Once that was understood we found that we were currently handling about 20,000 transactions per day on average, which annualizes to about 7.3 million per year ($20,000 \times 365$). Dividing this total into the cost to run the system—people and systems—we estimate that it costs us just under $0.30 for each transaction that is processed by our system ($[\$750 + 1,350]/7,300 \approx \$0.29$). This cost is far above our target price of between $0.10 and $0.15 per transaction.

"How do you plan to become more competitive?" Denise asked.

"We were hoping you could help us," was the answer.

Denise had a number of questions. "Okay, first, a lesson. Driver identification is different for variable- and fixed-cost pools. For variable pools, drivers are usage based—for ETN/W, the customer-qualification cost pool driver was the number of reports outsourced; for materials cost pools in car manufacturing, it is cars produced; and for fuel cost pools in freight hauling, it is miles driven. But for fixed-cost pools, the causal factor is capacity, not usage—the $2.1 million gives you the capacity to handle a given number of transactions; the number that you do deal with is not meaningful other than as an indication of the capacity utilized. And when we talk about capacity, we have to be aware of the distinction between *used* and *useful.* You said that you are processing about 20,000 transactions per day. Is every day the same?

"Absolutely not," Dave shot back. "Christmas and special holidays such as Mother's Day are our busy time."

Denise then asked Carol, "How does this impact your area?"

Carol thought she understood. "When I planned the system, I had to use our peak demand forecasts as the long-run target for the capacity. Unfortunately, just as you can't build an apartment complex apartment by apartment to meet demand, you cannot build a system such as ours in small increments. Right now our system is larger than what is needed, and it is built to meet a projected peak demand, not today's average demand."

Denise asked, "Do you have that data?"

"No, but I can get it within the week. Why don't you let us build this into our model, and we will have a "version 2.0" transaction processing cost for you next week?"

Denise said she could meet then and added one more piece of advice. "When you do your cost estimates, do them from the customer's viewpoint. Assume that your system is fully transparent to your customer and that they must see the value of anything you charge to them."

TRANSACTION PROCESSING—MEETING 2

The group started by explaining their transaction-processing chart (see Exhibit 4.6).

"Right now," said Carol, "the data discussed last time, 20,000 transactions per day on average, is correct, but our current peak demand is closer to 80,000. Our system today can process close to 120,000 transactions per day, so we do have excess capacity because of the cost of acquiring technology in certain sizes. Likewise, the 80,000 peak demand represents about 50% of the capacity of our personnel because of the decision we made in hiring and training the six people in anticipation of future demand. As we said last week, using part-time people may have been cheaper in the short run, but we decided to fully staff for the future.

"So, we have developed the following analysis (see Exhibit 4.7). For the personnel costs, we took 50% of them and charged it to an idle-capacity account. Clearly, the other $375,000 is, to our customers, value added.

"Likewise, we have some idle capacity in our hardware and software systems. From a customer point of view, we feel that the amount they should see as value added is our peak capacity of 80,000. Although they only average 20,000 transactions per day, when they have their peaks they need us to be ready, so this is value added and not excess. Only 40,000 currently is idle (120,000 capacity less the 80,000 peak). This means that $450,000 of the systems costs ($1.35 million × [40,000/120,000]) is not adding value to our current customers. So we feel that currently about $825,000 ($375,000 personnel and $450,000 systems) is idle and not chargeable to our customers. The other

EXHIBIT 4.6 Transaction-processing volume.

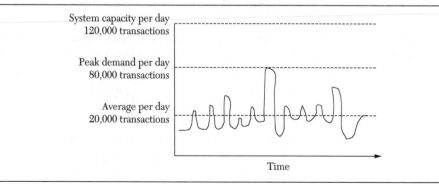

EXHIBIT 4.7 Transaction-processing cost summary.

	Value Add Portion	Idle Portion	Total	Value Add Portion	
Personnel	$ 375,000	$375,000	$ 750,000	$0.051	[$375/7,300]
H/W & S/W	900,000	450,000	1,350,000	0.123	[$900/7,300]
	$1,275,000	$825,000	$2,100,000	$0.174	[$1,275/7,300]
System usage	20,000 × 365 days	7,300,000 transactions/day			
Useful capacity	80,000 × 365 days	29,200,000 transactions/day		$0.044	[$1,275/29,200]

$1.275 million ($375,000 in personnel and $900,000 in systems) is of value to our customers, and they should be willing to pay for this. Unfortunately, if we charge these costs to the current annual level of transactions, 7.2 million, we arrive at a cost per transaction of about $0.175 ($1.275 million/7.2 million transactions). Our research shows that the maximum we can charge is $0.15. The peak demand problem is killing us."

Denise agreed. "Your work is well thought out and your results seem correct. Your problem is a classic one for all systems operators. Electric utilities have studied this peak load problem for decades and have developed demand-management solutions such as off-peak discounts. Can you do anything like this?"

Dave answered this one. "Some of our current customers do not need their transactions dealt with on a real-time basis. They send us their orders at end of day in batches, and we treat them by the next business day. I'm sure that others would do this if given some type of incentive."

Denise asserted that this could be the key to their profitability. "If you were able to decrease the peak demands, your costs per transactions would decrease. In the extreme, assume that there was no peak loads and the 80,000 was utilized every day. Your analysis shows that when your $1.275 million system costs are spread over useful capacity of 29.2 transactions per year, this results in an ideal systems cost under $0.05 per transaction."

Eric then summarized: "This would mean that if we could sell it for $0.15, we could be very profitable. And given the growth rate forecasts for e-commerce, we could get rich."

Denise then tied it all together. "Let's see. Assume that with some management focus, you could get your costs to acquire and load a customer onto your network down to about, say, $35,000. If you make a nickel profit on a transaction, you would need 700,000 transactions to recoup your investment. Given that your average customer now does about 3,000 transactions per day (average demand of 20,000 per day/7 customers current on network), this means that you cover your investment in about 240 days (700,000/3,000) or eight months. After that, it's pure profit. For larger customers, this payback happens sooner, meaning you become profitable more quickly."

Denise concluded: "So, it looks like the keys to success for ETN/W are threefold. First, study your *customer capture* and *customer loading* processes and make them more efficient. Second, figure out a way to minimize your peak periods such that you run your transaction processing systems at capacity most of the time. And last, focus your business model on large-volume e-commerce retailers such that you recoup your front-end investment sooner. If you can address these three issues, your investors should grant your third-round request. Of course, we could not have come to these action steps until we achieved transparency of your cost systems through ABC analysis. Good luck.

A REVIEW OF THE ABC METHODOLOGY

There are a number of lessons to be taken from the ETN/W example.

ABC is a strategic model. The strategy literature states in various ways that a company will achieve a strategic advantage over rivals if it can deliver (1) additional value to customers at a cost comparable to rivals or (2) comparable value at a cost lower than rivals. This advantage is sustainable if and only if the company does this in a manner different than its rivals. The myth that all companies have a strategic cost model that provides the necessary information unfortunately, in today's world, does not hold true. Most cost systems mainly provide aggregated cost information for estimating inventory valuation and cost of goods sold—they focus on external financial reporting. ABC, if done correctly, can provide the necessary strategic information.

The earlier ABC is done in the strategic planning process, the more value it creates. In the mid-1980s, when ABC analysis was being touted as the key tool in making the United States more competitive on a global basis, some researchers focused their studies on Japanese companies. Their hypothesis was that, since the Japanese have dominated many key industries over the last two decades, they must have some type of ABC methodologies. These researchers found exactly the opposite; costing systems for Japanese companies had even more arbitrary cost allocations than their U.S. rivals. Further research, however, unveiled a key competitive advantage.[5] Japanese product development was very cost based. They employed a technique, called target costing, in which prices were first set for new products through extensive market research, then profitability targets based upon investor capital requirements for the new product were estimated, yielding cost targets which were set at the design stage. Techniques such as value engineering and experience-curve analysis were employed to ensure that when the production began, the product would meet its target cost. The Japanese understood that this type of activity-cost analysis was best done very early in the product development stage. An interesting additional insight was that these strategic cost systems were more often under the responsibility of the engineering rather than the finance department in Japanese companies.

When done after the strategy implementation stage, ABC becomes ABM. Much research has demonstrated that about 85% of costs for a new product are committed in the design stage. As a result, it can be argued that performing an ABC analysis after this point is of little value—once a system is in place, operational efficiency should be the goal.[6] The challenge is to maximize output given the constraints of the system.[7] Note that by optimizing output, the fixed costs are minimized on a per-unit basis leading to the lowest-cost situation and the best possible shareholder value position. Since pricing is not cost dependant, detailed cost information is not really necessary.[8] This is not quite correct since no business situation is static. Note in the ETN/W example, we did do an ABC analysis after the fact. But also note that the final result of the analysis was not an ABC model. The key to the analysis was the managerial decisions that were implemented to make ETN/W more competitive. When done after the fact, the focus of ABC is not costing—it is to gain transparency of the business model so that it can be reengineered to create additional shareholder value. When done after the fact ABC necessarily leads to ABM, activity-based management.

The value of ABC analysis is the "journey" rather than the final result. As was stated in the ETN/W example, the purpose of ABC is ultimately to gain business-wide transparency of your business model. It is important that every function within the organization understand the strategic logic of how your company is going to create shareholder value. This includes how it is positioned in the industry-level value system, how its processes link to those of upstream and downstream partners, as well as a detailed activity-by-activity understanding of internal processes. The steps are as follows.

1. Develop a cross-functional team to do the analysis and assign ownership of the final ABC system to one function within your organization. If an outside consulting group is used, its role should be facilitator rather than designer of the system. It is important that ownership of the ABC model be internal since it will have to be updated on a regular basis. Because this is a strategic tool, ownership need not reside in the finance function. Many companies have found that, since this analysis requires business-wide vision, the strategy function is a more appropriate owner.

2. Begin with a map of the industry-level value system that shows all participants in the value creation process. Before moving to the next step, ensure that each member of the team understands and agrees with the strategic positioning logic for your company. This is necessary because all members must agree upon the strategic underpinnings of the analysis. In addition, cost drivers for one company often

reside within another in the chain. For instance, the driver for the ETN/W customer sale cost pool was the technical sophistication of the potential customer. Those that did not understand the costs of transaction processing and what ETN/W could provide were much more difficult to sell, and more costly. Once ETN/W understood this, it developed a short video that explained the transaction processing side of e-commerce and the cost and complexity of performing this function internally. This video made the selling process much easier for those customers—and less costly.

3. Once the industry-level value system is understood, prepare a process map for your company. Identify what value pieces of the overall system your company contributes. Although most people assume that everyone "knows what we do," this is most often not the case. Like the Hindu parable of the blind men trying to describe an elephant by feeling only one piece—trunk, ear, leg—few managers within an organization truly understand how all processes are integrated across the firm.

4. Prepare a detailed activity analysis for each internal process—exactly what steps are taken, who does them, and with what resources. Since this will be the basis for determining your cost pools, activities must first be identified at a granular level—if you are too fine you always can aggregate them later.[9] Activity identification can be done from a historical perspective or by studying the activity real time. In either case this stage will require discussion with those people responsible for the process to identify the activity steps. Since these steps often are performed by many functions within an organization, it is sometimes necessary to gather all participants such that a true cross-functional activity map be drawn and agreed upon.

5. Estimate the cost pools for each activity and identify their behavior—variable or fixed. If an activity has both fixed and variable costs, use two pools for that activity. Often secondary support functions such as payroll and human resources are first "allocated" to primary ledger accounts such as manufacturing labor or sales salaries accounts before being traced to activities.[10] At the end of this step a reconciliation should be performed. All of the costs from the general ledger should be traced to activity pools using the activity map. Typically some costs such as corporate administration and R&D do not get traced to activity pools since they have little to do with current operations. This is acceptable, and the key parameter one looks at is what percentage of overall costs is ultimately charged to activity pools. Rather than being discouraged by the 10% to 20% of costs not traced to any activity pool, focus on the 80% to 90% of which you now have a better understanding. To reiterate, this analysis is a strategic one; the acceptable percentage of unknowns is dependent on how good your rivals' cost systems are.

6. Select drivers for each pool—that is, the method to be used to transfer the costs from the pool to the object we wish to cost. Note the different

"objects" we developed costs for in the ETN/W example—capturing and loading a customer onto the network and processing a transaction.

- For variable cost pools, drivers should be *usage based* since this is the causal factor for a variable cost. Note how we used Outsourced Credit Reports as a driver for the customer-qualification cost pool.
- For fixed-cost pools, the driver should be *capacity based* since this is the causal factor for a fixed cost. Capacity drivers are often more complex than usage drivers. Since fixed-cost pools are "chunkier" than variable ones that increase in a proportionate fashion,[11] idle costs are often a problem. Only that portion of the fixed cost pool that is "useful" to a cost object should be charged to it—note how peak demand was used to define that portion of the transaction-processing system that was deemed idle in the ETN/W example.

7. Develop the final cost estimates for your system. Understand that there are no right answers. Since this is a strategic analysis, the long-run value of your results is dependent upon actions of rivals. For ETN/W we found that the current cost for each transaction processed was $0.175. Can it make any money at this cost level? Probably there are a few customers who understand that their costs are higher than this and would be willing to pay ETN/W a price today that is in excess of the $0.175. But in the long run, rivals could enter and provide services at a lower price. Given that ETN/W set its pricing target in the $0.10 to $0.15 range, it understands that it currently has no sustainable advantage. By figuring out how to better manage the peak problem, it thinks it can attain that advantage. The main goal of an ABC analysis is a set of activity-based target costs that everyone in the organization may see. The message should be: "If we as an organization achieve these, we will be successful." Progress towards these goals is the key strategic performance indicator.

FOR FURTHER READING

Brimson, James, *Activity Accounting: An Activity-Based Costing Approach* (New York: John Wiley, 1997).

Cokins, Gary, *Activity-Based Cost Management: Making It Work: A Manager's Guide to Implementing and Sustaining an Effective ABC System* (Chicago: Irwin, 1996).

Forrest, Edward, *Activity-Based Management: A Comprehensive Implementation Guide* (New York: McGraw-Hill, 1996).

Kaplan, Robert, and Robin Cooper, *Cost and Effect: Using Integrated Cost Systems to Drive Profitability and Performance* (Cambridge, MA: Harvard Business School Press, 1997).

Player, Steve, and David Keys, *Activity-Based Management: Arthur Andersen's Lessons From the ABM Battlefield*, 2nd ed. (New York: John Wiley, 1999).

NOTES

1. A server farm is a new service-offering concept in the IT industry enabled by advances in optic fiber connectivity. NT- and UNIX-based IT computer systems (i.e., servers) are housed in a service facility, and customers are given the option of buying the service on a usage basis rather than buying the computer itself. Customers are then supplied this service through a fiber-optic telecommunication network.

2. Clients are also called fulfillers. An apt analogy in the non-ebusiness world is the role played by Wal-Mart for its suppliers ("fulfillers" in the e-commerce world), such as a Procter & Gamble.

3. See Geoffrey Moore, *Crossing the Chasm* (New York: HarperCollins, 1990) and *Inside the Tornado* (New York: HarperCollins, 1995).

4. As discussed previously, some of these had been started but not finished at the beginning of the period, and at the end some were still in process; but on average they estimated that the equivalent of seven customers were loaded onto the network during this period.

5. See Womack et al., *The Machine That Changed the World* (New York: Macmillan, 1990), chapter 5 particularly.

6. See Eli Goldratt, *Theory of Constraints* (Croton on Hudson: North River Press, 1990).

7. Where *output* is defined by any parameter—units produced for a manufacturing system, units sold for a sales infrastructure, customers serviced for a service infrastructure, and so on.

8. Economists argue that in a competitive market prices are set by the marketplace, and in a market where there is product differentiation, prices are value based—i.e., dependent on the perceived value to the customer, not on cost to produce.

9. Many companies today do not limit their analysis to within company walls. This type of activity analysis is often done across the value system to understand how much value is being developed as a whole and who is capturing the majority of it. This understanding can be very valuable when negotiating with partners. See Gadlesh & Gilbert, "How to Map Your Industry's Profit Pool," *Harvard Business Review,* May–June 1998, pp. 149–162.

10. Quotation marks are used here to emphasize that this analysis needs to have causal underpinnings. The key here is to allocate these costs using some type of a logical procedure; avoid doing it in an arbitrary manner. The simple rule is: If there is no logical manner in which to trace the cost, don't!

11. Note in the ETN/W example, the customer-qualification activity pool increased with each additional outsourced report while the customer-sale pool increased with each additional person hired. It increased in larger increments, thus the descriptor *chunky* is often used.

INFORMATION TECHNOLOGY AND YOU

5

Edward G. Cale Jr.

Amazing though it may seem, the personal computer has only been around for about 20 years. Before 1980 the world of computing belonged to highly trained technical people who worked their wizardry wearing white coats in hermetically sealed rooms. Today kindergarten students use personal computers to learn the alphabet, grade school students use the Internet to research term papers, and on-the-go executives are always in touch with their beepers, Web-enabled cell phones, cellular personal digital assistants (PDAs), and laptop computers. However, many people are not yet comfortable with these technologies. The range of people's acceptance and knowledge of information technology is wide, with the technical novice at one end of the continuum and the "techie" at the other end. Where you fall in this range will dictate what you gain from this chapter. If you are fortunate to fall near the techie side, skim this chapter for ideas which you might find interesting.

Technology has changed the way people conduct business. Computers have replaced pencil and paper in contemporary business life. In the past, when a new employee was hired, he or she was shown to a desk and given pen, pencil, paper, and a telephone. Today, the new hire is given a computer, usually attached to a network; a cellular phone; a beeper; and possibly a laptop computer for portable use. People's lives have been turned upside down as they learn to manage the latest technology. E-mail is replacing U.S. Mail. Secretaries are being replaced by personal productivity technology such as voice

149

mail and Internet-based calendaring. People question how much more productive they as workers can be. Technology will allow managers' and workers' productivity to reach the next plateau and enable them to find better and alternative modes for working and succeeding.

Information technology has changed not only the way people work but also in some cases the venue from which they perform their work. No longer are workers chained to their desks. The number of *telecommuters*—people who work from home via computer and telephone communications—is increasing dramatically. Business people who travel with their portable computers have become so prevalent that hotels have installed special hardware on their hotel room telephones that allows guests to plug their computers into the telephone system and communicate with their home offices. Sometimes people even connect their laptop computer modems to the airline telephones at their seats!

How much do you need to understand about the technology to become technologically enabled? The answer to this question will depend in part on the job you hold and the organization for which you work. However, at this time, when information technology is having a dramatic impact on the very definition of many industries, the material covered in this chapter and in Chapter 16 has to be considered essential.

HARDWARE

Computer hardware comes in several shapes and sizes. This chapter concentrates on personal computers (PCs). Over the past 15 years, Microsoft and Intel have become so dominant in the software and hardware ends of the PC business that they have, de facto, set the worldwide standard for PCs, which is referred to as the *Wintel standard,* short for Microsoft Windows and the Intel CPU chip. More than 90% of all personal computers use the Wintel standard, affecting both the hardware marketplace and the applications software that is developed. Currently, Dell and Compaq are the largest producers of personal computers, with Gateway, Hewlett-Packard, and IBM following closely.

Personal computers come in two basic shapes: desktop and laptop. Regardless of their shape, all PCs have the same basic components. When you buy a computer, you usually have a choice on the size, speed, or amount of any given component that will be a part of your system. The basic components with which users must concern themselves are the CPU, RAM, hard disk, CD ROM/DVD ROM, modem, various adapters, and the monitor. Most of the rest of this section deals with the basic options you will have to choose in selecting these components.

However, beyond personal computers, we are also seeing the emergence of a whole range of small digital products for supporting effective managers. These products as a group are called personal digital assistants, or PDAs, and will be discussed briefly.

Desktop Computers

Underneath their covers, most desktop computers are very similar. Many of the various manufacturers of desktop machines use parts from the same suppliers because there are only a handful of companies that manufacture hard disk drives and many other desktop components. Before buying a machine, compare the attributes and capabilities of many different ones. Also, check the warranty offered by the different manufacturers. Though one-year warranties are fairly typical, some computers come with two- or three-year warranties. Beware of hype advertising and read the fine print. Most advertised specials do not include the monitor, which will cost upward of $200 depending on the size and quality.

Laptop Computers

The laptop has become a mainstay for the traveling worker. It provides all the functionality and most of the power of most desktop units, in a package that weighs approximately six pounds. Laptops are powered by standard electricity or, for about two hours, by their self-contained batteries. Unlike desktop units, under the covers all laptops are not the same. While they all utilize either an Intel or Intel clone chip, the majority of the electronics are frequently custom designed. Consequently, servicing laptops is more complicated and more expensive, and laptop parts are not necessarily interchangeable.

The display screen is one of the most important features of the laptop computer. Display quality and size are rapidly approaching that of desktop machines.

Although laptops provide the luxury of portability, that is their *only* advantage over desktop machines. Desktops offer better displays, more memory, and higher speed—higher performance for far less money. A laptop computer will cost between twice and three times as much as a comparable desktop unit.

Personal Digital Assistants (PDAs)

PDAs are small digital devices that can be used to take notes, to manage tasks, to keep track of appointments and addresses, and even to send and receive e-mail. Similar to PCs, PDAs have CPUs, RAM, displays, and keyboards of sorts, and some even have modems. However, a PDA can typically fit easily into a pocket or purse. Today, the most popular PDA is made by Palm Inc. and has its own proprietary software. However, there are a number of competing PDAs, some of which use a stripped-down version of Windows software called Windows CE. As miniaturization continues to develop and as cellular and computer technologies continue to be woven together, we can expect a further blurring of the line between PDAs and PCs.

Probably the two most popular capabilities of PDAs are their ability to keep track of appointments and to store and retrieve contact information such as phone numbers and addresses. These same capabilities are also available on PCs, most typically in software products such as Microsoft Outlook, which also includes e-mail. Most PDAs come with the ability to transfer appointments and contact information bidirectionally between the PDA and a PC.

Computer Components

Exhibit 5.1 shows a schematic rendition of the components in a computer system. This section of Chapter 5 will explain the basic functioning of these components and present some of the tradeoffs that you will face in making an intelligent decision to buy a computer system.

CPU

All basic computers have a *central processing unit (CPU)*. The CPU is the basic logical unit that is the computer's "brain." As mentioned earlier, it is usually provided by Intel Corporation or one of the clone-chip manufacturers such as AMD. While Intel enjoys the lion's share of the market, the clones have recently made significant inroads by offering lower prices for comparable products. State-of-the-art CPUs manage to integrate onto one thumbnail sized silicon chip tens of millions of electronic components. CPUs such as the Pentium come in different speeds, expressed in megahertz or gigahertz (millions or billions of cycles per second). Speed represents how fast the CPU is capable of performing its various calculations and data manipulations. A typical CPU today operates at between 800 MHz and 1.5 GHz.

EXHIBIT 5.1   Layout of a personal computer.

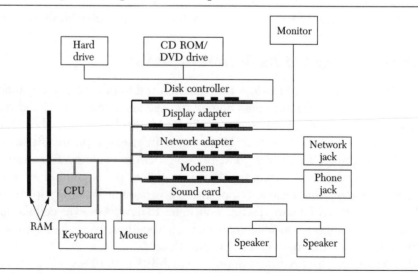

RAM

Random access memory (RAM) is the space that the computer uses to execute programs. The amount of RAM required is dictated by the number of applications that the computer is asked to run simultaneously as well as by the systems software in use (e.g., Windows 98, Windows XP). For most average users, 128 megabytes of RAM is an appropriate amount (a megabyte is 1,048,576 bytes of data). You can never have too much RAM, though, so the more, the better. While RAM prices fluctuate widely with supply and demand, you should plan on spending about a dollar per megabyte.

Hard Disk

All programs and data are stored on the *hard disk*. Disk technology has advanced greatly in the past five years. Recording density has enabled disk capacity to approach numbers previously unheard of except in large mainframe commercial systems. In 1992 the typical disk stored 80 megabytes. Today typical disk capacity on desktop machines ranges from 10 to 20 gigabytes. Although it seems unimaginable to fill up an entire 10-gigabyte disk, it happens faster than one might think. Typical office applications require 100 megabytes of storage for the application alone, not including any associated data. Multimedia applications (sound and video) are very data intensive and quickly consume disk space. For example, CD-quality music recordings consume roughly 10 megabytes per minute! Again, the more storage the better.

Reminder: Hard disk failures do occur. Always back up your data onto a removable disk or tape!

CD ROM/DVD ROM

Today an increasing amount of data and number of applications are being supplied on digital, compact disk (CD) technology. Using this technology, large amounts of data can be stored inexpensively. *CD ROMs*, which have the storage capacity for approximately 700 megabytes of data, are usually sold as "read only." Recently, however, inexpensive recordable CD drives have become popular, allowing people to store massive databases or record music on their own. Other than the speed at which they access and transfer data, all CD ROMs are very similar. Speed is expressed as a multiple of the speed of the original CD ROMs, which were produced in the early 1990s. Today, typical CD ROMs transfer data 32 or 48 times faster than the original CD ROMs and are referred to as 32X or 48X CD ROMs. Again, the faster, the better.

There are numerous information databases available on CD that would interest the accountant or finance executive. For example, most census data is available on CD. Also, historical data on stock and bond prices, copies of most trade articles, IRS regulations, state tax regulations, tax forms, recent court decisions, tax services, accounting standards (GAAP and GAAS), continuing education courses, and many other topics are available on CD.

Today, DVD ROMs, which have roughly ten times the capacity of CD ROMs, are becoming popular and in many cases replacing CD ROMs. DVD popularity is being driven at least in part by the fact that a single DVD can accommodate the massive amount of data necessary to digitally store the sound and pictures of a full-length feature movie. Recordable DVD drives are now becoming reasonably priced. With their ability to read both CDs and DVDs and their ability to record DVDs, one would expect that recordable DVD drives will soon replace CD drives in new computer systems.

Modems

Modems are devices that allow computers to communicate with each other using standard telephone lines. In the past few years, modem technology has increased the speed of data communications over standard telephone lines to speeds more than 10 times higher than in 1990. However, there is a practical limit to how fast computers can transmit data over ordinary telephone lines—currently about 56 KB (kilobit—a thousand bits) per second.

Because of the limitations of telephone lines, alternatives have been and are being developed. Cable modems, which use cable television wires, and DSL connections, which use regular telephone wires but with a new technology, both have the capability of transmitting data at rates higher than 1 MB (megabit) per second. While both technologies are spreading quickly, neither is yet available in all geographic locations. In addition, satellite data service, similar to satellite television service, is an available high-speed possibility for data communications.

Network Adapter

Whereas modems connect computers using phone lines, network adapters allow computers to directly communicate with each other over wires or cables that physically connect the computers. In most office environments, the various computers are interconnected through a local area network (LAN) so that they can share printers, data, access to the Internet, and other capabilities. Today, the dominant type of LAN is called an Ethernet network, and most network adapters are Ethernet adapters. In addition, Ethernet adapters are the most common form of hardware connection between PCs and cable modems or DSL connections. An Ethernet network adapter typically costs between $30 and $50.

Multimedia

By the latter half of the 1990s, most new personal computers came equipped for *multimedia,* the ability to seamlessly display text, audio, and full-motion video. To be capable of multimedia, a computer must be equipped with a high-resolution monitor and a CD or DVD drive and have audio capabilities. Because of the amount of storage that video requires, full-motion video is somewhat difficult to accomplish on a personal computer. For it to look smooth, video requires roughly 30 frames (pictures) per second, and each frame requires about 500,000 characters of information. In other words, one minute of smooth video could require as much as 900,000,000 characters of storage. In order to manage the large amount of storage that video processing requires, the video data is compressed. Data compression examines the data and, using an algorithm or formula, reduces the amount of storage space needed by eliminating redundancies in the data. Then, before the data is displayed, it is inflated back to its original form with little or no loss of picture quality.

Printers

Printer technology has stabilized in recent years, with two standards having emerged, *laser printers* and *inkjet printers.* Laser printers offer the best quality and speed. They are, for the most part, black-and-white and offer high print resolution. There are several speed and memory options, and models range in price from $400 for the individual user to several thousand dollars for a fast unit that offers printer sharing and color. Inkjet printers offer the lowest price. Models cost as little as $100. In higher-priced inkjet printers, print quality is excellent in black-and-white and color. Today many people are using high-end inkjet printers to print pictures taken with digital cameras. With high-end inkjet printers and digital cameras, the results can be virtually indistinguishable from prints produced from film cameras.

Laser printers are the clear choice for network sharing, whereas inkjets have become the mainstay of the individual user. In either case Hewlett-Packard is the market leader in the development of printers.

Monitors

The most common type of computer monitor is a cathode ray tube, or CRT, which physically resembles a television. In recent years, however, flat-panel or LCD (Liquid Crystal Display) have emerged. The major advantage of the flat-panel display is that it takes up much less space on a desktop than does the CRT. This advantage comes at a cost roughly three times as much as a comparably sized CRT. Whether CRT or flat panel, there are significant advantages to having a display that is as large as space and budget allow. Some of the real power of windowing software is the ability to view several windows of data at the same time. Small displays make such windowing much more difficult. A 17-inch display (the screen measured diagonally) is about the minimum acceptable size.

OPERATING SYSTEMS

The *operating system* is the basic software that makes the computer run. *Applications software* is the software that runs a particular user function. Some say that the operating system is the software closest to the machine, while the applications software is the software closest to the user.

Microsoft Windows is the predominant operating-system software for the personal computer. In the past 10 years, Microsoft has become the acknowledged leader in the development of both operating-system and office-automation software. The Windows operating system provides a graphical format for communicating between the computer and the user, while a pointing device, such as a mouse, is used to point to the icon of the folder or application that the user wishes to open.

APPLICATIONS SOFTWARE

Applications software is the personal computer's raison d'être. Although there are a multitude of applications available for the PC, this chapter focuses on the following personal-productivity programs:

- Word processing.
- Spreadsheets.
- Presentation graphics.
- Databases.
- Personal finance.
- Project management.

Most of the popular packages are available as application suites that include word processing, spreadsheets, graphics, and sometimes database management systems. Microsoft Office is one of the most widely used suites; it includes Word for Windows (word processing), Excel (spreadsheet), PowerPoint (presentation graphics), Access (database), as well as several other applications.

The original spreadsheet application was developed at the very beginning of the PC revolution and was called VisiCalc. It was later replaced by Lotus 1-2-3, which became the standard until the tremendous success of Microsoft Office and Excel.

Word Processing

One of the two most popular applications, word processing and spreadsheets, word processing has increased people's ability to communicate more effectively. With word processing software, the user can create, edit, and produce a high-quality document that appears as professional as that of any large organization. Thus, word processing has become the great business equalizer, making it difficult to decipher a small company or single practitioner from the large, Fortune 500 company with a dedicated media department.

Today's word processing is as powerful as most desktop publishing software, and it is so simple to use that any novice equipped with simple instructions can master the software. Not only can documents include text, but they can also contain spreadsheet tables, drawings, and pictures; be specially formatted; and be black-and-white or color. Most word processing applications come with clip art, which consists of drawings, cartoons, symbols, and/or caricatures that can be incorporated into the document for emphasis.

Spreadsheet Software

For the accounting and finance executive, spreadsheet software has had the greatest impact on productivity. Imagine a company controller who has been asked to prepare the budget for the coming year. The company manufactures in over a thousand products with special pricing depending on volume. The controller not only has to make assumptions about material costs, which might change over time, but also has a history of expense levels that must be factored into the analysis. Using pencil and paper (usually a columnar pad), the controller calculates and prepares all of the schedules necessary to produce the final page of the report, which contains the income statement and cash flow. Confident that all calculations are complete, the controller presents the findings to management, only to be asked to modify some of the underlying assumptions to reflect an unexpected change in the business. As a result, the controller must go back over all of the sheets, erasing and recalculating, then erasing and recalculating some more.

Computer spreadsheets rendered this painful process unnecessary. Spreadsheets allow the user to create the equivalent of those columnar sheets, but with embedded formulas. Consequently, any financial executive can create a financial simulation of a business. Thus, merely by changing any of a multitude of assumptions (formulas), one can immediately see the ramifications of those changes. Spreadsheets allow for quick and easy what-if analyses. What if the bank changes the interest rate on my loan by 1%? What impact will that have on my cash flow and income? In addition, most of the packages provide utilities for graphing results, which can be used independently or integrated into a word processing report or graphics presentation.

A spreadsheet is composed of a series of columns and rows. The intersection of a row and column is referred to as a *cell*. Columns have alphabetic letters, while rows have numbers. Cell reference "B23" indicates the cell in column B and row 23.

Exhibit 5.2 provides an example of a simple spreadsheet application. A company's pro forma income statement, the sample spreadsheet is a plan for what the company expects its performance to reflect. In this example, the company expects to earn $275,475 (cell H18) after tax on $774,000 (cell H3) of sales revenues. At the bottom of the exhibit, there is a series of assumptions

EXHIBIT 5.2 Pro forma income statement (in dollars).

Pro Forma Income Statement

	January	February	March	April	May	June	Year to Date
Sales	100,000	125,000	135,000	127,000	132,000	155,000	774,000
Cost of goods sold	32,750	40,938	44,213	41,593	43,230	50,763	253,485
Gross profit	67,250	84,063	90,788	85,408	88,770	104,238	520,515
Operating Expenses							
Salaries	22,800	28,500	30,780	28,956	30,096	35,340	176,472
Benefits	11,200	14,000	15,120	14,224	14,784	17,360	86,688
Rent	3,200	3,200	3,200	3,200	3,200	3,200	19,200
Utilities	4,300	4,750	3,790	4,100	3,100	2,800	22,840
Advertising	12,000	15,000	16,200	15,240	15,840	18,600	92,880
Supplies	1,300	1,400	1,270	1,500	1,550	1,600	8,620
Total operating expenses	54,800	66,850	70,360	67,220	68,570	78,900	406,700
Net profit before taxes	45,200	58,150	64,640	59,780	63,430	76,100	367,300
Income taxes	11,300	14,538	16,160	14,945	15,858	19,025	91,825
Net profit after taxes	33,900	43,613	48,480	44,835	47,573	57,075	275,475
Assumptions							
Costs of goods sold %	0.3275						
Salaries (% sales)	0.228						
Benefits (% sales)	0.112						
Advertising (% sales)	0.12						
Income taxes %	0.25						

that govern the way the calculations are performed in this spreadsheet. For example, cost of goods sold is always equal to 32.75% of sales, and advertising is always equal to 12% of sales. Likewise, the income tax rate for this company is set at 25%.

Looking behind the cells (Exhibit 5.3), you can see the spreadsheet's formula infrastructure. For example, cell B4, which calculates the cost of goods sold for the month of January, contains the formula that requires the spreadsheet to multiply the cost-of-goods-sold percentage that is shown in cell B21 by the sales shown in cell B3; the formula in cell B5, which calculates the gross profit, subtracts the cost of goods sold in cell B4 from the sales in cell B3; and cell H5, which calculates the total gross profit for the six months of January through June, contains the formula that adds the contents of cells B5 through G5.

The spreadsheet is set up so that, should the user wish to change any of the assumptions, such as the cost-of-goods-sold-percentage, the contents of cell B21 would be changed to a new desired value, and any other cell that was affected by this change would immediately assume its new value. As mentioned earlier, most spreadsheet packages provide excellent facilities for displaying

EXHIBIT 5.3 Spreadsheet formula infrastructure.

	Pro Forma Income Statement						
	January	February	March	April	May	June	Year to Date
Sales	100,000	125,000	135,000	127,000	132,000	155,000	=SUM(B3:G3)
Cost of goods sold	=$B21*B3	=$B21*C3	=$B21*D3	=$B21*E3	=$B21*F3	=$B21*G3	=SUM(B4:G4)
Gross profit	=B3-B4	=C3-C4	=D3-D4	=E3-E4	=F3-F4	=G3-G4	=SUM(B5:G5)
Operating Expenses							
Salaries	=$B22*B3	=$B22*C3	=$B22*D3	=$B22*E3	=$B22*F3	=$B22*G3	=SUM(B8:G8)
Benefits	=$B23*B3	=$B23*C3	=$B23*D3	=$B23*E3	=$B23*F3	=$B23*G3	=SUM(B9:G9)
Rent	=3,200	=3,200	=3,200	=3,200	=3,200	=3,200	=SUM(B10:G10)
Utilities	4,300	4,750	3,790	4,100	3,100	2,800	=SUM(B11:G11)
Advertising	=$B24*B3	=$B24*C3	=$B24*D3	=$B24*E3	=$B24*F3	=$B24*G3	=SUM(B12:G12)
Supplies	1,300	1,400	1,270	1,500	1,550	1,600	=SUM(B13:G13)
Total operating expenses	=SUM(B8:B13)	=SUM(C8:C13)	=SUM(D8:D13)	=SUM(E8:E13)	=SUM(F8:F13)	=SUM(G8:G13)	=SUM(B14:G14)
Net profit before taxes	=B3-B14	=C3-C14	=D3-D14	=E3-E14	=F3-F14	=G3-G14	=SUM(B16:G16)
Income taxes	=$B25*B16	=$B25*C16	=$B25*D16	=$B25*E16	=$B25*F16	=$B25*G16	=SUM(B17:G17)
Net profit after taxes	=B16-B17	=C16-C17	=D16-D17	=E16-E17	=F16-F17	=G16-G17	=SUM(B18:G18)
Assumptions							
Costs of goods sold %	0.3275						
Salaries (% sales)	0.228						
Benefits (% sales)	0.112						
Advertising (% sales)	0.12						
Income taxes %	0.25						

data in a graphical format. Exhibit 5.4 presents a graph of the information in our demonstration spreadsheet. It contrasts sales and net profit over the six months.

Presentation Graphics Software

Presentation graphics software is used to create slide presentations. These presentations can include a variety of media through which information can be presented to an audience, such as text, graphs, pictures, video, and sound. Special effects are also available, meaning animation can be incorporated as the system transitions from one slide to the next. Slides can be printed, in black-and-white and color, for use on overhead projectors. Alternatively, the computer can be directly connected to a system for projection onto a screen or a television monitor, allowing the presenter to utilize the software's animation and sound features. Most of the software comes equipped with various predeveloped background formats and clip art to help simplify the process of creating the presentation. Also, these software packages allow the user to import both graphs and text from other software packages, such as word processing and spreadsheets.

EXHIBIT 5.4   Pro forma sales and income.

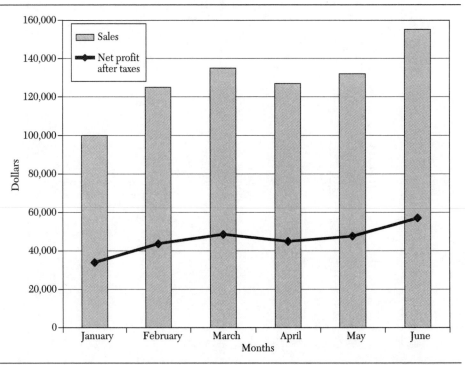

Database Software

A *database* is a collection of data stored in such a way that the user may create and identify relationships among data. For example, a mailing list of one's customers might contain information about each customer's purchases and everything about the sales transactions, including the prices the customer paid, who sold it to him, how she paid, and so forth. This information can be retrieved in a variety of ways usually specified by the user at the time of execution. The user might want a list of all customers that purchased a specific product between January and May or perhaps an aggregate list of all products a customer has ordered and purchased from a particular salesperson. The number of possible combinations and permutations and ways one may view the data is limited only by the collection of the data and the imagination of the user. Databases are discussed in more detail in Chapter 16, Information Technology and the Firm.

Personal Finance Software

There are several software packages that allow individuals or small businesses to manage finances, such as paying bills either electronically or by check, and monitor investments. The packages are fairly sophisticated in that they provide for secure communications for electronic bill paying and other online banking services such as account reconciliation, as well as the importing of current stock-market quotes. The most widely used package is Quicken and, for small businesses, Quickbooks. Microsoft Money is also a comparable and popular package.

Exhibit 5.5 displays a sample screen that is used to enter bills to be paid. As you can see, the user input metaphor is a check, the very same document the user would use if he or she were paying the bill manually. The difference using Quicken is that data is collected for a host of other purposes such as:

- Paying bills.
- Tracking paid bills by category for budgeting purposes.
- Tracking payments for tax purposes.
- Reconciling the checking account.

The system has the capability to keep track of more than one account and to make interaccount transfers.

Project Management Software

Often a manager or entrepreneur is faced with the challenge of managing the many details concerned with a project, be it constructing a building or pulling together a financial plan. With fairly simple projects, paper and pencil or a simple spreadsheet might be an adequate tool for coordinating the people and steps involved in a project. But, as the project gets complex, involving, say,

EXHIBIT 5.5 Personal financial software check-writing screen.

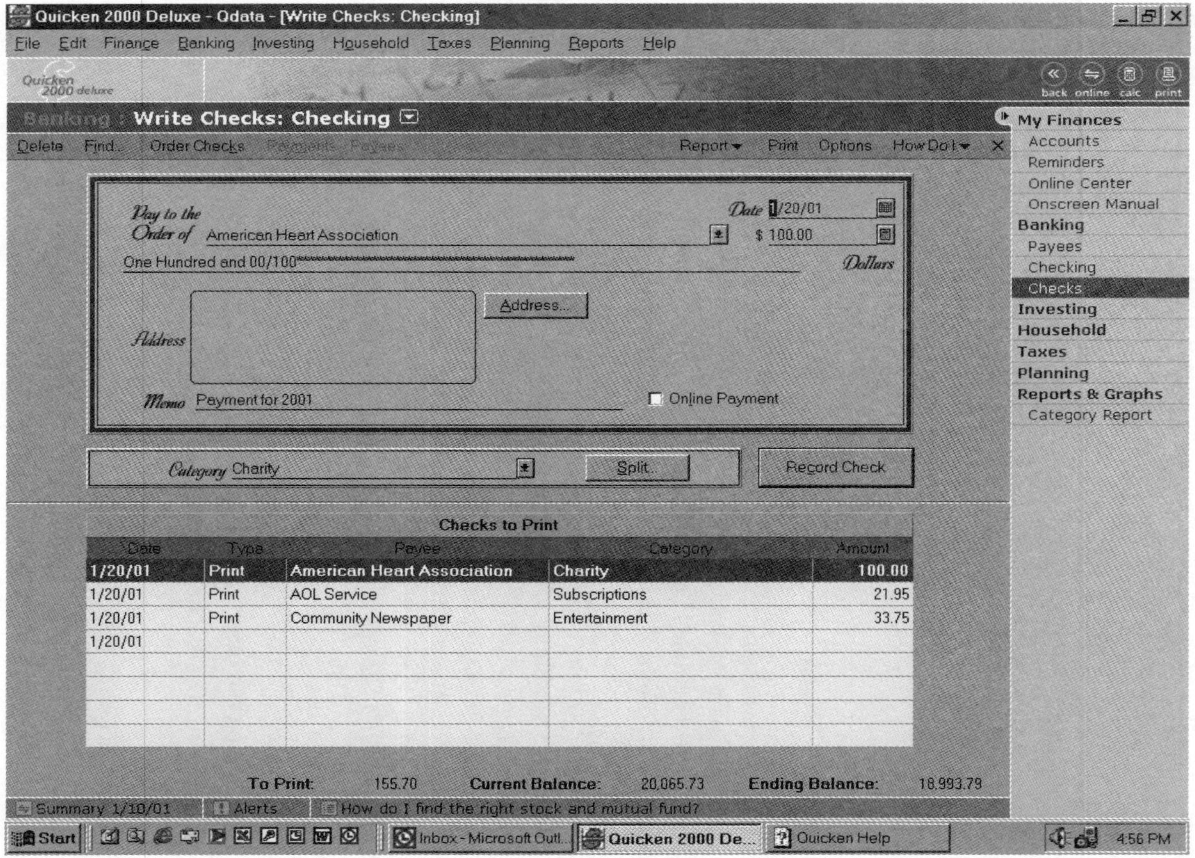

Screen shot printed with permission of Intuit.

EXHIBIT 5.6 Project management software screen.

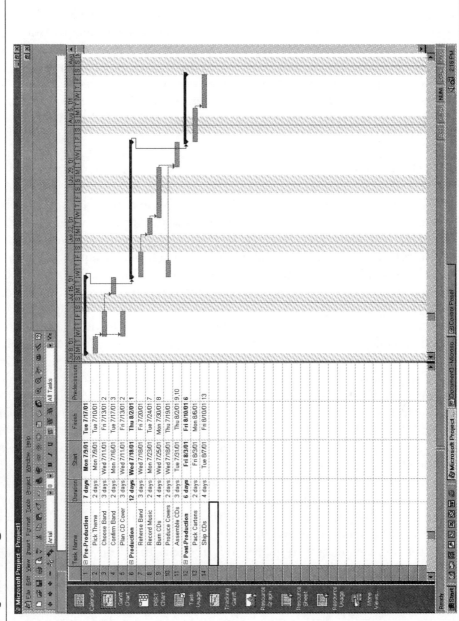

more than a few people and more than a few dozen steps, one should consider using project management software to help with the planning and control of the activities.

Project management software allows a manager to plan for and then control the steps in a project with an eye toward managing the people working and resources being spent on the project. Good project-management software can help a manager foresee bottlenecks or constraints in a plan and can help the manager bring the project to completion in the shortest possible time.

One popular tool for managing projects is Microsoft Project. Exhibit 5.6 shows a typical screen from Microsoft Project, which shows the steps in a project along with a graphical representation of those steps called a *GAANT chart.*

NETWORKING

Another electronic advent of the 1990s was extensive *networking,* or interconnecting, of computers, which has facilitated the sharing and exchanging of information. The interconnecting may be done through wires within a building; via the telephone system using modems; or through radio frequency transmissions between the computers using *wireless modems.* There are several different approaches, or types of *architecture,* for computer networks. In a small office environment with only a few computers, the computers might be connecting in what is referred to as a *peer-to-peer* network. Here all the computers function on the same level as peers or equals to each other. Peer-to-peer networking software comes built into Windows 98 and Windows Millennium Edition (ME), making it relatively easy to set up a peer-to-peer network between two or more PCs. All one needs is a network adapter card in each computer, the cables for connecting the computers, and a connecting piece of hardware called a *hub.*

However, in a larger networking environment (dozens, hundreds, or even thousands of computers hooked together), the situation is more complex. In this case, the most common network architecture is called a *client-server* network. To deal with the added complexity, in a client-server network there is a hierarchy of computers with a host or *file server* acting as the traffic policeman, storing common data and directing the network traffic. In this architecture, the user computer is frequently referred to as the *client* in the network. A picture of a typical client-server network appears in Exhibit 5.7.

As mentioned earlier, the file server is the centerpiece of the network, and the software that makes the network operate is called the *network operating system.* Novell's NetWare and Microsoft's Windows 2000 (formerly Windows NT) are two popular network operating systems. Within a business the typical network is called a *local area network,* or *LAN.* Clients are connected to the server, using wires or fiber-optic cables. Transmission speeds are generally either 10 or 100 megabytes per second. As with the peer-to-peer network, there is a hub that acts as a concentrator for all of the cabling. Again, each PC

EXHIBIT 5.7   Diagram of client-server network.

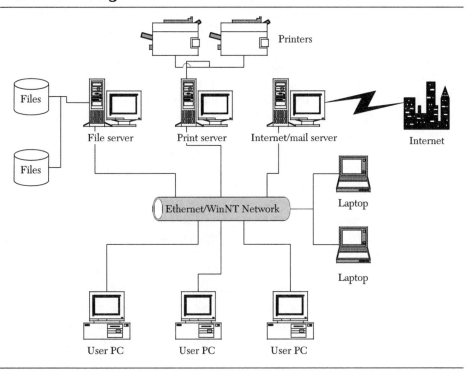

on the network must have a network interface card if it is connected to a LAN, or a modem if it is connected through telephone lines. When a series of LANs in different cities are interconnected, they form a *wide area network,* or *WAN.* Large businesses with facilities around the country or world network their users' personal computers together in a series of LANs that are further interconnected into a large WAN. The largest WAN, the Internet, connects together millions of computers of commercial companies, government agencies, schools, colleges and universities, and nonprofit agencies around the world.

Preventing unauthorized people from accessing confidential information is one of the biggest challenges posed by networks. To do so, people and organizations use special security software. One technique, a *fire wall,* allows outside users to obtain only that data which is outside the "fire wall" of the file server; subsequently, only people inside the company may access information inside the fire wall.

Electronic Mail (E-mail)

E-mail is the most popular network application because it has become the method of choice for communicating over both short distances (interoffice) and long distances. It allows you to send communications to any other person on your local network as well as to any other network within your WAN, including the Internet. E-mail has become so popular that U.S. Mail and overnight delivery services such as FedEx are being rendered obsolete for some types of communication.

Most e-mail software packages include a basic word-processing application with which you can generate your letters. In addition, these packages allow you to keep mailing lists and send a document to numerous people simultaneously. Once sent, a document can be received within seconds by people thousands of miles away. One of the more advantageous features of e-mail is that it allows you to attach another document—a spreadsheet, graphic presentation, another word processing report, a picture, or even a database—to your letter, much as you would do with a paper clip.

Imagine that you have used a spreadsheet package to prepare a budget for your division in Boston. You print out your letter and spreadsheet and mail or ship it overnight to the main office in Chicago. You may even include an electronic copy of your spreadsheet on a floppy disk, in case the individual in Chicago needs to further modify the numbers. Sometime within the next day or two, the recipient will receive the package. He or she will then read the information and may even use the floppy disk for additional reporting. Alternatively, using e-mail, you could draft your letter, electronically attach the spreadsheet file, and send it via e-mail to your recipient in Chicago. Within a matter of seconds or minutes, she or he will receive the electronic package, read your letter, and be able to extract your attachment and load it directly into a spreadsheet software package for any necessary additional processing.

Since colleges and universities have sites on the Internet, many college students use e-mail regularly to keep in contact with their friends both in the United States and around the world. Likewise, parents of college students have picked up the e-mail bug and use it to correspond with their children.

The Internet

The Internet is the worldwide WAN that has become the major growth area in technology and the business community. While the Internet has been around for decades, its popularity exploded with the development of the World Wide Web and the necessary software programs that made the "Web" very user-friendly to explore.

Accessing the Internet requires that the user establish a connection to it called a *node*. Large organizations have a dedicated data link to the Internet using very fast data telephone lines. Individual users connect to the Internet using third-party companies called *Internet Service Providers* (ISPs), such as America Online (AOL) and Microsoft Network (MSN). These ISPs allow users to dial into their computers, which are connected directly to the Internet. Recently, a number of ISPs have started providing high-speed or broadband connectivity between users and the Internet with the use of cable modems or DSL technology (as discussed previously). High-speed connectivity will typically cost $20 to $30 more than the normal $20 per month for modem speed (56K) access.

World Wide Web

Though the terms *Internet, World Wide Web, the Web,* and *the Net* have become synonymous, the Web is actually a subsystem of the Internet. One of the major attractions of the Web is that it is quite easy for the average person to access any of the millions of sites on the Web. All you need is a *Web browser* and a connection to the Internet. Web browsers are merely software programs that allow users to navigate the Web. The two most common browsers are Microsoft Explorer and Netscape Navigator. Internet Explorer comes free with Windows, and Netscape Navigator can be downloaded for free from Netscape's Web site.

Every site that appears on the Internet has an address composed of a company or organization name, called a domain name, and a domain type. For example, "www.GenRad.com" refers to the Web site of a commercial company named GenRad. These addresses are referred to as *universal resource locators,* or URLs. Some of the more common domain types are as follows:

.com	commercial organization
.org	not-for-profit organization
.gov	government organization
.mil	military group
.edu	educational institution

Each Web site displays its information using a series of Web pages. A Web page may contain text, drawings, pictures, even audio and video, as well as blue text called hypertext. Position your mouse pointer over one of these words, and the arrow changes to a drawing of a hand. Click the mouse, and the computer will automatically move to a new Web page. This move is called a *hypertext link.* Using these hypertext links, a user can move around the Internet, from page to page, company to company, state to state, country to country.

Internet e-mail addresses often consist of a username followed by the symbol "@," followed by the domain name, followed by the domain type. Thus, Bill Smith's e-mail address at GenRad might well be bsmith@genrad.com.

Many companies have put much of their literature on the Web, thereby using the Web as an electronic catalogue. Home pages are the first page of information that you encounter when you reach an organization's Web site. Companies use their Web sites for marketing and distributing information about their products. Instead of waiting on a telephone line for customer service, the user can go online to get expert help about frequently asked questions (FAQs), at any time of day, unattended. For example, the AICPA (American Institute of CPAs) has a Web site at www.aicpa.org. Available at that Web site are many of the AICPA services, including information on their membership, conferences, continuing education, publications, and IRS forms. The home page for the Financial Management Association, located at www.fma.org, is another interesting site for financial executives. This site provides information on all of the association's services with links to other pages.

Computer hardware and software companies use the Web as a device for distributing software to users. As software device drivers change, users can download the new software over the Net. The Net also provides a venue for people with common interests to "chat" electronically in "chat rooms."

Internet Search Engines

The Web has become so extensive with so much information available to the user that often one literally does not know where to look. Consequently, search engines were created to help users navigate the Web. Search engines like Yahoo, Alta Vista, Lycos, Google, and Northernlight constantly explore the Web, indexing each site. When presented with key words or a topic to be searched, they provide the user with a list and description of each site that contains the information requested in the search. The search results also display the hypertext links to the sites found, enabling the user to click on and immediately go to those sites that seem most promising.

Electronic Commerce

Electronic commerce, the ability to purchase goods and services over the Net, has grown geometrically in recent years. Before e-commerce can achieve its full potential, however, there are a number of hurdles that must be overcome successfully. First, as will be discussed in more detail in the following section, there are strong concerns over the security of credit card and other confidential data concerning sales transactions. Until consumers can be assured that their personal data are confidential and their financial transactions are secure, e-commerce will be under a cloud of suspicion. Second, shopping in cyberspace is different from shopping in physical space. When shopping in physical space, consumers see, touch, try on, test-drive, and buy physical products. In cyberspace, consumers shop on the Net by referring only to metaphors, two-dimensional representations of what they see when shopping in stores. Essentially, cyberspace consumers are supplied only secondhand information about products.

For electronic commerce to be successful, therefore, the mode and the metaphor for the cyberspace shopping experience must be improved. New mechanisms for Internet shopping will be developed, many of which will include experiments in virtual reality and the appearance of three-dimensional venues. Also, the shopping experience will be custom-tailored to you, the individual consumer. Many Internet sites already keep a profile on you when you visit their site. These profiles include information on what products you buy and what products you tend to look at, allowing the Internet sites to create shopping experiences specific to your needs. Along these lines, the mail-order and online shopping company Lands End now provides their customers with the opportunity to have a three-dimensional computer model built from laser scans of the customer's body. Once this model is built, the customer can "try on" clothing on their computer screen to see how the actual clothes will look on their computer-based body.

As electronic shopping becomes more effective, virtual malls, or group-ings of stores that share the same electronic Internet address, will spring up on the Internet, creating the feel of a physical mall. Both consumers and retailers will be able to benefit from one-stop shopping in cyberspace.

Privacy on the Internet

When using the Internet for e-mail, e-commerce, or other applications, you must remember that, like the radio spectrum, the Internet is a public network. With the right skill, anyone on the Internet has the ability to "listen in" on your electronic transaction. While the transaction will appear to be processed nor-mally, its confidentiality might well be compromised. Beware! Never send across the Net any confidential information that you would not want any other person or company to know.

However, Web browsers usually have the ability to encrypt data that is transmitted between a user and a Web site. Most organizations conducting business on the Web will, therefore, only send and receive confidential infor-mation using encryption technology, which should provide you with adequate protection. Generally, Web sites will notify you that they are using such a se-cure connection. In addition, whenever you are connected to a secure site, your Web browser will show a little icon of a closed padlock on the status bar at the bottom of your screen.

Beyond protecting data as it is transmitted, there is a significant privacy issue surrounding the use of data in your Internet activities. Whenever you sign onto a Web site, those sites can collect information about your activities, such as purchases, credit card number, address, and so on. At the moment, there is very little legislation either at the federal or state level preventing Internet sites from selling or sharing information about you with third parties. Various industry groups are trying to encourage self-regulation in the e-commerce industry, and many Web sites will post their privacy policy, usually as a link on the home page. However, at the moment there is little consistency or enforcement of pri-vacy policy. We can expect that there will be significant legislation on privacy issues in the future, but until such legislation is in place, beware!

In addition, some Internet sites place small files, called *cookies,* on your hard drive when you are in contact with the site. In most cases, these cookies are innocuous, allowing you to access the site without having to remember a password or providing you with your favorite screen. However, cookies can also be used to help track your Web actions and build a profile of you and your ac-tivities. Inexpensive or free software is available to help you manage or prevent cookies being placed on your computer, but blocking cookies may prevent you from being able to use certain Web sites.

Internet Multimedia

The Internet provides an amazing plethora of information, and not just in text or still-picture format. Video and audio *streaming media* is becoming increasingly available on the Internet. There are several sites on the Net where one can obtain audio clips, listen to music, or listen to radio shows. For example, NFL football games and commentaries are available on the National Football League's or National Public Radio's Web pages. In addition, many music companies are allowing consumers to listen to music in the comfort of their homes before buying the CDs. In addition, sites such as Napster have been created to allow users to share or swap music and other files. Some of this *sharing* comes dangerously close to violating copyright legislation. We have seen and can expect to continue to see the courts play a significant role in defining the boundary of propriety.

THE FUTURE—TODAY, TOMORROW, AND NEXT WEEK

Although the industrial revolution began in the United States toward the beginning of the nineteenth century, we are still feeling its effects today. Consider for a moment how our everyday lives have changed as a result of those innovations. The computer revolution began about 1950, and the microprocessor—the heart of the PC revolution—has been exploited only for the last 20 years. Now think about how our everyday lives have changed as a result of these innovations. Remember, the microprocessor is part of so many of our appliances, computers, automobiles, watches, and so forth. The impact of the computer revolution is just as large if not larger than its precursor, the industrial revolution, and has taken far less time. Moreover, the acceleration of change in our lives that results from the use of computer technology has been rapidly increasing. Technologists speak about the rapid changes in the development of the Internet and its allied products. They even joke that things are happening so fast that three months is equivalent to an "Internet year." Funny, but true.

One of the biggest trends in the last several years has been the merging of heretofore separate technologies. As we mix computer technology with communication technology and throw in a good measure of miniaturization, it is difficult to imagine the products we may soon see.

Mix together a PDA, a cell phone, and a global positioning satellite (GPS) receiver, miniaturize the result, and you have a product that will remind you as you drive past the supermarket where you were supposed to pick up a quart of milk on the way home! Walk in the door to the market, and your pocket wonder may tell you, based on your past love of Snickers candy bars, that they are on sale for half-price on aisle 5. As you move towards the checkout line, the clerk, who has never met you, may greet you by name because your pocket wonder has announced your arrival to her cash register. While this scenario may sound fanciful, *all* of the technologies exist today that could make this fancy real. How these technologies will be used in the future, and the tremendous entrepreneurial potential for new products and services, is wide open for the resourceful.

This section is titled "The Future—Today, Tomorrow, and Next Week," because the horizon for change in the world of technology is very short. Each year, major enhancements to both hardware and technology are released, rendering previous technology obsolete. Some people are paralyzed from buying computers because they are concerned that the technology will change very soon. How right they are! The promise of technology is that it is constantly changing. Today's worker must recognize that fact and learn to adapt to the changing methods. Those who are technologically comfortable will be the first to gain strategic advantage in the work environment and succeed. A word to the wise: Hold on to your hat, and enjoy the ride. Adapt and go with it.

FOR FURTHER READING

There are many excellent books on the personal use of computer systems. Topics run the spectrum from books about individual software packages to those that explain how to program a computer. Many of these books come equipped with a floppy disk or CD and include step-by-step examples and exercises. There are several popular series of these books. The following are but a few of the books you might consider. You would probably find it worth your while to browse through a number of books at your local store, searching for those that meet your needs for detail and appear to be aimed at your current level of understanding.

SYBEX has a series of books on Microsoft's Office software, including *Microsoft Office 2000: No Experience Required* by Courter and Marquis.

QUE has published many books on various software applications, including *Microsoft Office 2000 User Manual*.

Hungry Minds Inc. has a series of very noteworthy books, the *for Dummies* series, one book for nearly every software package (e.g., Excel: *Excel for Dummies*). See books on Office 2000, the Internet, and so on.

Microsoft Press also publishes numerous titles for users on both its operating-system and application software.

USEFUL WEB SITES

Search Engines

www.yahoo.com	A good search site which organizes the Web into a hierarchy of categories
www.northernlight.com	A very extensive search engine that organizes search findings by subject matter
www.google.com	A very extensive search site

Computer Information Sites

www.cnet.com	A site that provides product reviews and prices on a broad range of technology products
www.zdnet.com	Web site of a large technology publisher, with product reviews, software downloads, useful articles, and price comparisons

Accounting Sites

www.aicpa.org	Homepage of the American Institute of Certified Public Accountants, with lots of useful information and many links to other Web sites of interest to accountants
www.rutgers.edu /Accounting/raw/aaa	Homepage of the American Accounting Association

Financial Management Site

www.fma.org	Homepage of the Financial Management Association International, with lots of useful information and many links to other Web sites of interest to financial managers
finance.yahoo.com	Very useful homepage for personal financial management, with many links to other personal finance Web sites

6 FORECASTS AND BUDGETS

Robert Halsey

THE CONCEPT OF BUDGETING

Budgets serve a critical role in managing any business, from the smallest sole proprietor to the largest multinational corporation. Businesses cannot operate effectively without estimating the financial implications of their strategic plans and monitoring their progress throughout the year. During preparation, budgets require managers to make resource allocation decisions and, as a result, to reaffirm their core operating strategy by requiring each business unit to justify its part of the overall business plan. During the subsequent year, variances of actual results from expectations serve to direct management to the areas that may deserve a greater allocation of capital and those that may need adjustments to retain their viability.

A *budget* is a comprehensive formal plan, expressed in quantitative terms, describing the expected operations of an organization over some future time period. Thus, the characteristics of a budget are that it deals with a *specific entity*, covers a *specific future time* period, and is expressed in *quantitative terms*.

This chapter describes the essential features of a budget and includes a comprehensive example of the preparation of a monthly budget for a small business. Although the focus of this chapter is on budgeting from a business perspective, many of the principles are also applicable to individuals in the planning of their personal finances.

FUNCTIONS OF BUDGETING

The two basic functions of budgeting are planning and control. *Planning* encompasses the entire process of preparing the budget, from initial strategic direction through preparation of expected financial results. Planning is the process that most people think of when the term *budgeting* is mentioned. Most of the time and effort devoted to budgeting is expended in the planning stage. Careful planning provides the framework for the second function of budgeting, control.

Control involves comparing actual results with budgeted data, evaluating the differences, and taking corrective actions when necessary. The comparison of budget and actual data can occur only after the period is over and actual accounting data are available. For example, April manufacturing cost data are necessary to compare with the April production budget to measure the difference between planned and actual results for the month of April. The comparison of actual results with budget expectations is called performance reporting. The budget acts as a gauge against which managers compare actual financial results.

REASONS FOR BUDGETING

Budgeting is a time-consuming and costly process. Managers and employees are asked to contribute information and time in preparing the budget and in responding to performance reports and other control-phase budgeting activities. Is it all worth it? Do firms get their money's worth from their budgeting systems?

The answer to those questions cannot be generalized for all firms. Some firms receive far more value than other firms for the dollars they spend on budgeting. Budgets do, however, provide a wealth of value for many firms who effectively operate their budgeting systems. I now discuss some of the reasons for investing in formal budgeting systems. In the next section of this chapter I discuss issues that contribute to effective budgeting.

Budgets offer a variety of benefits to organizations. Some common benefits of budgeting include the following:

1. Requires periodic planning.
2. Fosters coordination, cooperation, and communication.
3. Forces quantification of proposals.
4. Provides a framework for performance evaluation.
5. Creates an awareness of business costs.
6. Satisfies legal and contractual requirements.
7. Orients a firm's activities toward organizational goals.

Periodic Planning

Virtually all organizations require some planning to ensure efficient and effective use of scarce resources. Some managers are compulsive planners who continuously update plans that have already been made and plan for new activities and functions. At the other extreme are people who do not like to plan at all and, therefore, find little or no time to get involved in the planning process. The budgeting process closes the gap between these two extremes by creating a formal planning framework that provides specific, uniform periodic deadlines for each phase of the planning process. People who are not attuned to this process must still meet budget deadlines. Of course, planning does not guarantee success. People must still execute the plans, but budgeting is an important prerequisite to the accomplishment of many activities.

Coordination, Cooperation, and Communication

Planning by individual managers does not ensure an optimum plan for the entire organization. The budgeting process, however, provides a vehicle for the exchange of ideas and objectives among people in an organization's various segments. The budget review process and other budget communication networks should minimize redundant and counterproductive programs by the time the final budget is approved.

Quantification

Because we live in a world of limited resources, virtually all individuals and organizations must ration their resources. The rationing process is easier for some than for others. Each person and each organization must compare the costs and benefits of each potential project or activity and choose those that result in the most efficient resource allocation.

Measuring costs and benefits requires some degree of quantification. Profit-oriented firms make dollar measurements for both costs and benefits. This is not always an easy task. For example, the benefits of an advertising campaign are increased sales and a better company image, but it is difficult to estimate precisely the additional sales revenue caused by a particular advertising campaign, and it is even more difficult to quantify the improvements in the company image. In nonprofit organizations such as government agencies, quantification of benefits can be even more difficult. For example, how does one quantify the benefits of better police protection, more music programs at the city park, or better fire protection, and how should the benefits be evaluated in allocating resources to each activity? Despite the difficulties, resource-allocation decisions necessitate some reasonable quantification of the costs and benefits of the various projects under consideration.

Performance Evaluation

Budgets serve as estimates of acceptable performance. Managerial effectiveness in each budgeting entity is appraised by comparing actual performance with budgeted projections. Most managers want to know what is expected of them so that they can monitor their own performance. Budgets help to provide that information. Of course, managers can also be evaluated on other criteria, but it is valuable to have some quantifiable measure of performance.

Cost Awareness

Accountants and financial managers are concerned daily about the cost implications of decisions and activities, but many other managers are not. Production supervisors focus on output, marketing managers on sales, and so forth. It is easy for people to overlook costs and cost-benefit relationships. At budgeting time, however, all managers with budget responsibility must convert their plans for projects and activities to costs and benefits. This cost awareness provides a common ground for communication among the various functional areas of the organization.

Legal and Contractual Requirements

Some organizations are required to budget. Local police departments, for example, cannot ignore budgeting even if it seems too much trouble, and the National Park Service would soon be out of funds if its management decided not to submit a budget this year. Some firms commit themselves to budgeting requirements when signing loan agreements or other operating agreements. For example, a bank may require a firm to submit an annual operating budget and monthly cash budgets throughout the life of a bank loan.

Goal Orientation

Resources should be allocated to projects and activities according to organizational goals and objectives. Logical as this may sound, relating general organizational goals to specific projects or activities is sometimes difficult. Many general goals are not operational, meaning that determining the impact of specific projects on the organization's general goals is difficult. For example, organizational goals may be stated as follows:

1. Earn a satisfactory profit.
2. Maintain sufficient funds for liquidity.
3. Provide high-quality products for customers.

These goals, which use terms such as *satisfactory, sufficient,* and *high-quality,* are not operational: the terms may be interpreted differently by each manager. To be effective, goals must be more specific and provide clear direction for managers. The previous goals can be made operational as follows:

1. Provide a minimum return on gross assets invested of 18%.
2. Maintain a minimum current ratio of 2 to 1 and a minimum quick ratio of 1.2 to 1.
3. Products must receive at least an 80% approval rating on customer satisfaction surveys.

EFFECTIVE BUDGETING

There are many reasons why some firms use budgeting more effectively than others, including the following:

1. Budgets should be oriented to help a firm accomplish its goals and objectives.
2. Budgets must be realistic plans of action rather than wishful thinking.
3. The control phase of budgeting must be used effectively to provide a framework for evaluating performance and improving budget planning.
4. Participative budgeting should be utilized to instill a sense of cooperation and team play.
5. Budgets should not be used as an excuse for denying appropriate employee resource requests.
6. Management should use the budgeting process as a vehicle for modifying the behavior of employees to achieve company goals.

Goal Orientation

Some firms have more resources than others, but it seems no firm has all the resources it needs to accomplish all its goals. Consequently, budgets should provide a means by which resources are allocated among projects, activities, and business units in accordance with the goals and objectives of the organization. As logical as this may sound, it is sometimes difficult to relate general, organization-wide goals to specific projects or activities. Many general goals are not operational, meaning the impact of specific projects on the achievement of the general goals of the organization is not readily measurable.

A prerequisite to goal-oriented budgeting is the development of a formal set of operational goals. Some organizations have no formally defined goals, and even those that do often have only general goals for the entire organization. Major operating units may function without written or clearly defined goals or objectives. A logical first step toward effective budgeting is to formalize the goals of the organization. Starting at the top, general organizational goals should be as specific as possible, and written. Next, each major unit of the organization should develop more specific operational goals. The process should continue down the organizational structure to the lowest level of budget responsibility. This goal development process requires management at all levels to resolve difficult issues, but it results in a budgeting framework that is much more likely to be effective since all business units proceed in a coordinated manner toward the achievement of a common objective. Even individuals need to understand their goals and objectives as they prepare budgets for their own activities.

Realistic Plan

Budgeting is not wishful thinking; it is a process designed to optimize the use of scarce resources in accordance with the goals of the company. Many firms have budgets that call for sales growth, higher profits, and improved market share, but to be effective such plans must be based on specific executable plans and on available resources and management talent that the company can bring to bear in meeting the budget. If the management of a firm wants to improve its level of operations, there must be a clearly defined path between the present and the future that the firm can travel.

The process begins with an analysis of the market and preparation of a SWOT (strengths, weaknesses, opportunities, and threats) analysis. Utilizing this background information, the company develops an overall strategy together with the operational tactics required to achieve it (the development of a business plan is discussed further in Chapter 9). The financial impact of this strategy is then assessed in the preparation of the budget. If the financial results are unfavorable, strategies and tactics must be revised until an acceptable outcome is achieved. Once the budget is finalized, strategies are implemented and the company's operations are subsequently monitored throughout the year in the control phase, as discussed next. Exhibit 6.1 presents an iterative model that embodies these concepts.

Participative Budgeting

Most behavioral experts believe that individuals work harder to achieve objectives that they have had a part in creating. Applied to budgeting, this concept states that employees will strive harder to achieve performance levels defined by budgets if the employees have had a part in creating the budget. Budgets imposed by top-level management, in contrast, may get little support from employees. The concept of building budgets from the bottom up with input from all employees and managers affected by the budget is called *participative budgeting*.

The Control Phase of Budgeting

The first and most time-consuming phase of budgeting is the planning process. The control phase of budgeting, however, may be the time when firms get the most value from their budgeting activities. Exhibit 6.2 is a budget-performance report for the first quarter of 2001. The difference between budgeted and

EXHIBIT 6.1   Comprehensive budgeting process.

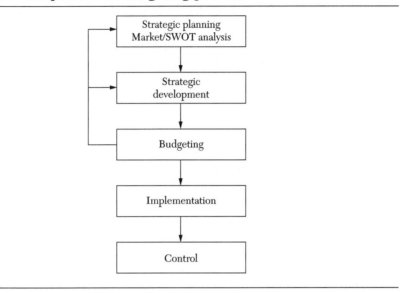

actual amount is called a budget variance. Budget variances are reported for both revenues and costs separately. In this case, revenues were $20,000 under budget and are, therefore, considered as an unfavorable budget variance (U). Expenses, though, were $30,000 less than expected, a favorable budget variance (F). The net result is a favorable, profit budget variance of $10,000.

Each category is then separately analyzed to uncover the source of the variance. Although total revenues are lower than expected, management is interested in the actual product lines causing this variance. Further analysis might reveal, for example, that all of the product lines are performing satisfactorily except for one that is performing more poorly than expected. On the expense side, a favorable budget variance may be due to positive effects of management actions to operate the company more efficiently. Or, positive variances may have occurred because costs necessary for long-term performance—such as maintenance of machinery, research and development, or advertising—were deferred to achieve short-term gains.

Management must thoroughly investigate the causes for budget discrepancies so that corrective action can be taken. Are markets as a whole performing

EXHIBIT 6.2   Budget variance report.

	Budgeted	**Actual**	**Variance**
Revenues	$800,000	$780,000	$(20,000)U
Expenses	(500,000)	(470,00)	30,000 F
Profit	300,000	310,000	10,000 F

better or worse than expected? Is the company's marketing support adequate? Has the competitive landscape changed? Are cost variances the result of management actions in response to competitive pressures or due to inadequate control? The answers to these questions may suggest changes in the company's strategic and tactical plans to compensate for the variances.

When actual prices and quantities are compared with expected prices and quantities, an additional level of analysis can be conducted. Exhibit 6.3 illustrates a more in-depth analysis of price and quantity variance. During the month, the firm realizes a positive variance of $6,000 relating to the cost of aluminum, one of its production inputs.

This $6,000 variance can then be further decomposed into a price variance and a quantity variance. The price variance is $21,000 favorable because of the lower than expected purchase price for aluminum. It is computed by multiplying the price variance per unit ($3 to $2.80) by the actual pounds utilized (105,000). The quantity variance is $15,000 unfavorable as a result of lower efficiency in the production process that led to more material usage than had been expected. This is computed by multiplying the quantity variance (105,000 to 100,000) by the expected price ($3). This analysis reveals that the manufacturing process was less efficient than planned in that it utilized more material to produce its products. This inefficiency was more than offset, however, by lower prices for direct materials than had been forecasted. The price variance, therefore, masks the production inefficiency, which would not be revealed without the additional level of analysis.

Comparing actual results with the budget, adjusting plans when necessary, and evaluating the performance of managers are essential elements of budget control. Many people, however, find the control phase difficult. When business results are less than expected it may be painful to evaluate the results. For some it is much easier to look ahead to future periods when things hopefully will be better. But frequently, realistic plans for future success can be made only when management learns from its past mistakes. The control phase of budgeting provides much of that learning process. Firms must be willing to evaluate performance carefully, adjusting plans and performance to stay on track toward achieving goals and objectives.

EXHIBIT 6.3 Price and quantity variance analysis.

	Budgeted	Actual	Variance
Production level in units	20,000	20,000	0
Lbs aluminum/unit	5.00	5.25	0.25 U
Aluminum cost/lb	$ 3.00	$ 2.80	$ 0.20 F
Total lbs aluminum	100,000	105,000	5,000 U
Total material cost	$300,000	$294,000	$ 6,000 F
Price variance	($3.00 − $2.80) × 105,000 =		$21,000 F
Quantity variance	(105,000 − 100,000) × $3.00 =		$15,000 U
	Total net variance		$ 6,000 F

Many companies have intricate budget performance reporting systems in place, but the firms achieve little control from their use. In order to provide effective control, a business must use the budget as an integral part of the company's reward system. That is, employees must understand that budget performance reports are a component of their performance evaluation. Rewards such as pay raises, bonuses, and promotions should be tied to budget performance.

Generally it is easy to determine if a company's budget performance reporting system is working effectively. If, on one hand, discussions with managers yield comments such as, "If we fail to achieve the budget, we just add more to it next period," the budget-control process is likely ineffective. If, on the other hand, employees say, "If we are over our budget by more than 2%, we will be called on the carpet and forced to explain the problem," then one knows the control process is having an effect.

Improper Use of Budgets

Sometimes managers use budgets as scapegoats for unpopular decisions. For example, rather than telling a department head that his or her budget request for three additional employees is not convincing when compared with all of the other budget requests, the vice president says, "The budget just would not allow any new employees this year." In another case, the director of the marketing department requests travel funds to send all of his staff to an overseas education program. The vice president believes the program is a waste of money. Instead of giving the marketing director his opinion, the vice president says, "We would really like to send your staff to the program, but the budget is just too tight this year." Of course, the truth in this situation is that the trip is not a good use of business resources, regardless of the condition of the budget. The marketing director is left with the impression that the real problem is the state of the budget, when in fact the benefits of his travel proposal did not outweigh the cost. Management should be careful not to undermine the budgeting process by assigning to it adverse characteristics.

Behavioral Issues in Budgeting

Many of the internal accounting reports firms prepare are intended to influence managers and employees to behave in a particular way. For example, many manufacturing cost reports are intended to enable and motivate employees to reduce costs or keep them at an acceptable level. Similarly, reports that compare the performance of one division with those of other divisions are used to evaluate the performance of division managers and encourage better results for each division.

Budgets and budget performance reports are among the more useful internal accounting reports businesses use to influence employee performance in a positive manner. Budget control is based on the principle that managers be held responsible for activities they manage. Performance reports reflect the degree of achievement of plans embodied in the budget. To minimize adverse behavioral problems, managers should take care to develop and administer budgets appropriately. Budgets should not be used as a hammer to demand unattainable performance from employees. The best safeguard against unrealistic budgets is participative budgeting.

DEVELOPING A BUDGET

Budgets are useful, and in most cases essential, to the success of virtually all organizations whether they are for-profit or not-for-profit organizations. The larger and more complex the organization, the more time, energy, and resources are needed to prepare and implement the budget.

The Structure of Budgets

Regardless of the size or type of organization, most budgets can be divided into two categories: the operating budget and the financial budget. The operating budget consists of plans for all those activities that make up the normal operations of the firm. For a manufacturing business, the operating budget includes plans for sales, production, marketing, distribution, administration, and any other activities that the firm carries on in its normal course of business. For a merchandising firm, the operating budget includes plans for sales, merchandise purchases, marketing, distribution, advertising, personnel, administration, and any other normal activities of the merchandising firm. The financial budget includes all of the plans for financing the activities described in the operating budget plus any plans for major new projects, such as a new production plant or plant expansion. Both the operating and financial budgets are described later in more detail.

The Master Budget

The master budget is the total budget package for an organization; it is the end product of the budget preparation process. The master budget consists of all the individual budgets for each part of the organization combined into one overall budget for the entire organization. The exact composition of the master budget depends on the type and size of the business. However, all master budgets represent the organization's overall plan for a specific budget period. Exhibit 6.4 lists the common components of a master budget for a manufacturing business.

The components of the master budget form the firm's detailed operating plan for the coming year. As noted earlier, the master budget is divided into the operating budget and the financial budget. The operating budget includes revenues, product costs, operating expenses, and other components of the income statement. The financial budget includes the budgeted balance sheet, capital expenditure budget, and other budgets used in financial management. A large part of the financial budget is determined by the operating budget and the beginning balance sheet.

EXHIBIT 6.4 A manufacturing firm's master budget.

Operating Budget

Sales budget
Budget of ending inventories
Production budget
    Materials budget
    Direct labor budget
    Manufacturing overhead budget
Administrative expense budget
Budgeted non-operating items
Budgeted net income

Financial Budget

Capital expenditure budget
Budgeted statement of financial position (balance sheet)
Budgeted statement of cash flows

Exhibit 6.5 is a simplified budget for C&G's Gift Shop. It is prepared on a monthly basis. The number preceding each heading refers to the applicable line in the budget.

Sales Budget (1–3)

The sales budget, or revenue budget, is the first to be prepared. It is usually the most important budget because so many other budgets are directly related to sales and therefore largely derived from the sales budget. Inventory budgets, production budgets, personnel budgets, marketing budgets, administrative budgets, and other budget areas are all affected significantly by the overall sales volume expected.

For C&G's Gift Shop, expected sales in units are reported on line 1. Note that the business is highly seasonal, with most of the sales and profits realized during the months of November and December. To keep the budget simple, we assume an average sales price of $100 per unit. In practice, the business would forecast unit sales by individual product lines.

Budgeted Cost of Goods Sold (4)

C&G assumes a cost of goods sold of 65% of sales revenues. This results in a gross profit of 35%. For a retailing company, cost of goods sold represents the purchase cost of inventories sold during the period. It is computed as

$$\text{Cost of Goods Sold} = \text{Beginning Inventory} + \text{Purchases during the Period} - \text{Ending Inventory}$$

where all inventories and purchases are computed at the purchase price to the company.

EXHIBIT 6.5 C&G's Gift Shop: 2000 cash budget.

Line		Assumptions	Nov-99	Dec-99	Jan	Feb	Mar
1	Total sales—units		5000	6430	3680	3530	2760
2	Selling price		100	100	100	100	100
3	TOTAL GROSS SALES		500000	643000	368000	353000	276000
4	TOTAL COST OF SALES	65%	325000	417950	239200	229450	179400
5	GROSS MARGIN	35%	175000	225050	128800	123550	96600
6							
7	Selling expense	15%	75000	96450	55200	52950	41400
8	Administration (fixed)		23000	23000	23000	23000	23000
9	Administration (variable)	10%	50000	64300	36800	35300	27600
10	Depreciation expense	15yr sl amort	3472	3472	3472	3472	3472
11	TOTAL OPERATING EXPENSE		151472	187222	118472	114722	95472
12							
13	OPERATING PROFIT		23528	37828	10328	8828	1128
14	Interest income		0	0	0	0	354
15	Interest expense		−1956	−2872	−1989	−441	0
16	PROFIT BEFORE TAX		21572	34956	8339	8387	1482
17	Taxes at 35%		7550	12235	2918	2936	519
18	PROFIT AFTER TAX		14022	22721	5420	5452	963
19	Cumulative profit				5420	10872	11835
20	BALANCE SHEET						
21	Cash			25000	25000	95836	160060
22	Accounts and interest receivable	65%,30/35%,60		637000	412050	300800	218904
23	Inventory	Next month sales		239200	229450	179400	170950
24	TOTAL CURRENT ASSETS			901200	666500	576036	549914
25							
26	Property, plant, & equipment (gross)			625000	625000	625000	625000
27	Accumulated depreciation	15yr sl amort		−41667	−45139	−48611	−52083
28	Property, plant, & equipment (net)			583333	579861	576389	572917
29							
30	TOTAL ASSETS			1484533	1246361	1152425	1122831
31							
32	Bank loan (line of credit)			198949	44056	0	0
33	Accounts payable			239200	229450	179400	170950
34	Accrued expenses			198857	119908	114626	92519
35	TOTAL CURRENT LIABILITIES			637006	393414	294026	263469
36							
37	Common stock			800000	800000	800000	800000
38	Retained earnings			47527	52947	58399	59362
39	TOTAL SHAREHOLDERS' EQUITY			847527	852947	858399	859362
40							
41	TOTAL LIAB. + S/H EQUITY			1484533	1246361	1152425	1122831
42	STATEMENT OF CASH FLOWS (INDIRECT METHOD)						
43	Net income				5420	5452	963
44	Depreciation				3472	3472	3472
45	Change in current assets (other than cash)				234700	161300	90346
46	Change in current liabilities (other than notes payable)				−88699	−55332	−30557
47	Net cash flow from operations				154893	114892	64224
48							
49	Net cash flow from investing activities				0	0	0
50							
51	Net cash flow from financing activities				−154893	−44056	0
52							
53	Net change in cash				0	70836	64224
54	Beginning cash					25000	95836
55	Ending cash					95836	160060

	Apr	May	Jun	Jul	Aug	Sep	Oct	Nov	Dec	Jan
	2630	2580	2600	2650	2780	2990	4370	5220	7200	4220
	100	100	100	100	100	100	100	100	100	100
	263000	258000	260000	265000	278000	299000	437000	522000	720000	422000
	170950	167700	169000	172250	180700	194350	284050	339300	468000	274300
	92050	90300	91000	92750	97300	104650	152950	182700	252000	
	39450	38700	39000	39750	41700	44850	65550	78300	108000	
	23000	23000	23000	23000	23000	23000	23000	23000	23000	
	26300	25800	26000	26500	27800	29900	43700	52200	72000	
	3472	3472	3472	3472	3472	3472	3472	3472	3472	
	92222	90972	91472	92722	95972	101222	135722	156972	206472	
	−172	−672	−472	28	1328	3428	17228	25728	45528	
	675	874	932	953	952	921	855	401	0	
	0	0	0	0	0	0	0	0	−80	
	503	202	460	981	2280	4349	18083	26129	45448	
	176	71	161	343	798	1522	6329	9145	15907	
	327	132	299	637	1482	2827	11754	16984	29541	
	12162	12294	12593	13231	14713	17540	29294	46278	75819	
	199895	211494	215548	215369	209279	196033	105282	25000	25000	
	179275	169924	170232	175953	190702	216221	361505	494351	721700	
	167700	169000	172250	180700	194350	284050	339300	468000	274300	
	546871	550419	558031	572022	594331	696304	806087	987351	1021000	
	625000	625000	625000	625000	625000	625000	625000	625000	625000	
	−55555	−59027	−62499	−65971	−69443	−72915	−76387	−79859	−83331	
	569445	565973	562501	559029	555557	552085	548613	545141	541669	
	1116316	1116392	1120532	1131051	1149888	1248389	1354700	1532492	1562669	
	0	0	0	0	0	0	0	8042	146036	
	167700	169000	172250	180700	194350	284050	339300	468000	274300	
	88926	87571	88161	89593	93298	99272	138579	162645	218987	
	256626	256571	260411	270293	287648	383322	477879	638687	639323	
	800000	800000	800000	800000	800000	800000	800000	800000	800000	
	59689	59821	60120	60758	62240	65067	76821	93805	123346	
	859689	859821	860120	860758	862240	865067	876821	893805	923346	
	1116316	1116392	1120532	1131051	1149888	1248389	1354700	1532492	1562669	
	327	132	299	637	1482	2827	11754	16984	29541	
	3472	3472	3472	3472	3472	3472	3472	3472	3472	
	42879	8051	−3558	−14170	−28399	−115220	−200534	−261546	−33649	
	−6843	−55	3840	9882	17355	95674	94557	152766	−137358	
	39835	11599	4054	−179	−6091	−13246	−90751	−88324	−137994	
	0	0	0	0	0	0	0	0	0	
	0	0	0	0	0	0	0	8042	137994	
	39835	11599	4054	−179	−6091	−13246	−90751	−80282	0	
	160060	199895	211494	215548	215369	209279	196033	105282	25000	
	199895	211494	215548	215369	209279	196033	105282	25000	25000	

For a manufacturing company, cost of goods sold is computed similarly, but in place of purchases we have the cost of the raw materials together with the labor and overhead incurred in the manufacturing process. Beginning and ending inventories consist of raw materials, work-in-process, and finished goods.

Administrative Expense Budget (7–10)

The expected administrative costs for an organization are presented in the administrative expense budget. This budget may contain many fixed costs, some of which may be avoidable if subsequent operations indicate some cost cuts are necessary. These avoidable costs, sometimes called discretionary fixed costs, include such items as research and development, employee education and training programs, and portions of the personnel budget. Fixed costs that cannot be avoided during the period are called committed fixed costs. Mortgage payments, bond interest payments, and property taxes are classified as committed costs. Variable administrative costs may include some personnel costs, a portion of the utility costs, computer service bureau costs, and supplies costs. Fixed and variable costs and the application of these concepts to the budget process is discussed in detail in Chapters 3 and 7.

C&G's Gift Shop budgets selling expenses at 15% of sales. These are variable costs since they change in proportion to changes in sales. You might think of these as commissions paid to the sales personnel as a percent of the sales made during the period. The fixed portion of administration expense is budgeted as $23,000 per month. These expenses might be rent, salaries of administrative personnel, and so forth. The administrative expense also contains a variable component, budgeted at 10% of sales. Finally, depreciation is computed on a straight-line basis over 15 years and is a fixed expense budgeted at $3,472 per month.

Budgeted Income Statement (3–18)

The budgeted income statement shows the expected revenues and expenses from operations during the budget period. Budgeted income is a key figure in the firm's profit plan and reflects a commitment of most of the firm's talent, time, and resources for the period.

A firm may have budgeted nonoperating items such as interest on investments or gains or losses on the sale of fixed assets. Usually they are relatively small, although in large firms the dollar amounts can be sizable. If nonoperating items are expected, they should be included in the firm's budgeted income statement. Income taxes are levied on actual, not budgeted, net income, but the budget should include expected taxes; therefore, the last figure in the budgeted income statement is budgeted after-tax net income.

Nonoperating items in C&G's income statement include interest income and interest expense. Amounts borrowed carry an interest rate of 12% (1% per month), and cash in excess of the $25,000 required for daily transactions is invested in marketable securities earning an investment return of 6% per annum (0.5% per month). Finally, taxes are levied at the rate of 35% on pre-tax income.

The Financial Budget

The financial budget presents the plans for financing the operating activities of the firm. The financial budget is made up of the budgeted balance sheet and the budgeted statement of cash flows, each providing essential financial information.

Budgeted Balance Sheet (20–41)

The budgeted balance sheet for the coming accounting period is derived from the *actual* balance sheet at the beginning of the current budget period and the *expected* changes in the account balances of the operating, capital-expenditure, and cash budgets.

The budgeted balance sheet is more than a collection of residual balances resulting from other budget estimates. Undesirable projected balances and account relationships may cause management to change the operating plan. For instance, if a lending institution requires a firm to maintain a certain relationship between current assets and current liabilities, the budget must reflect these requirements. If it does not, the operating plan must be changed until the agreed requirements are met.

Budgeted Accounts Receivable (22)

Budgeted accounts receivable are a function of expected sales on open account and the period of time that the receivables are expected to be outstanding. For C&G's Gift Shop, all sales are assumed to be on open account to other businesses. The company expects that 65% of the sales during the period will be collected in the following month, and 35% will be collected in the next month. For this exercise, we have assumed that all of the accounts are collectible. If not, the company would have to build in a provision for uncollectible accounts that would reduce expected collections and be reflected in the income statement as bad debt expense.

Budget of Ending Inventories (23)

Inventories comprise a major portion of the current assets of many manufacturing firms. Separate decisions about inventory levels must be made for raw materials, work-in-process, and finished goods. Raw material scarcities, management's attitude about inventory levels, inventory carrying costs, inventory ordering costs, and other variables may all affect inventory-level decisions.

C&G's Gift Shop has a policy to maintain inventory on hand equal to the next month's expected cost of goods sold.

Capital Expenditure Budget (26)

The capital expenditure budget is one of the components of the financial budget. Each of the components has its own unique contribution to make toward the effective planning and control of business operations. Some components, however, are particularly crucial in the effective management of businesses, such as the cash and capital expenditure budgets.

Capital budgeting is the process of identifying, evaluating, planning, and financing an organization's major investment projects. Decisions to expand production facilities, acquire new production machinery, buy a new computer, or remodel the office building are all examples of capital-expenditure decisions. Capital-budgeting decisions made now determine to a large degree how successful an organization will be in achieving its goals and objectives in the years ahead. Capital budgeting plays an important role in the long-range success of many organizations because of several characteristics that differentiate it from most other elements of the master budget.

First, most capital budgeting projects require relatively large commitments of resources. Major projects, such as plant expansion or equipment replacement, may involve resource outlays in excess of annual net income. Relatively insignificant purchases are not treated as capital budgeting projects even if the items purchased have long lives. For example, the purchase of 100 calculators at $15 each for use in the office would be treated as a period expense by most firms, even though the calculators may have a useful life of several years.

Second, most capital expenditure decisions are long-term commitments. The projects last more than 1 year, with many extending over 5, 10, or even 20 years. The longer the life of the project, the more difficult it is to predict revenues, expenses, and cost savings. Capital-budgeting decisions are long-term policy decisions and should reflect clearly an organization's policies on growth, marketing, industry share, social responsibility, and other goals. This is discussed in greater depth in Chapter 10.

For purposes of this exercise, we have assumed that C&G's Gift Shop will not be making any capital expenditures in the upcoming year. As a result, property, plant, and equipment (PP&E; line 26) remains constant. Net PP&E (line 28), however, is reduced each period by the addition of depreciation expense to accumulated depreciation.

Budgeted Accounts Payable (33)

Accounts payable represent amounts owed to other businesses for the purchase of goods and services. These are usually non-interest bearing. We have assumed that all the inventories are purchased on open account and that the terms of credit require payment in full in the following month. As a result, accounts payable are equal to the cost of inventories in this example.

Budgeted Accrued Expenses (34)

Expenses are recognized in the income statement when incurred, regardless of the period in which they are paid. For this example, we assume that all of the operating expenses incurred and recognized during the month are paid in the following month. These expenses include selling expenses, administrative expenses other than depreciation, interest expense, and taxes.

Bank Loan (Line of Credit) (32)

Businesses require cash to cover the portion of inventories and accounts receivable that are not financed by trade accounts payable and accrued expenses. This is very pronounced in seasonable businesses. For example, C&G's Gift Shop must purchase inventories one month in advance of sales. And when these inventories are sold, 65% of the proceeds are collected in the subsequent month and 35% in the month thereafter. As a result, C&G has a considerable amount of cash invested in the business that is not recouped for at least two months.

Typically, short-term cash needs such as the needs of seasonal businesses are met with a bank line of credit that allows the company to borrow funds up to a predetermined maximum and to repay those loans at a later date. In this case, funds are borrowed to finance the purchase of inventories and these amounts are repaid when the receivables are collected.

Stockholders' Equity (37–39)

No sales of common stock are budgeted. Since no dividends are projected, retained earnings (38) increase by the amount of profit for the month.

Cash Budget

Of all the components of the master budget, none is more important than the cash budget. Of the two major goals of most profit-seeking firms—to earn a satisfactory profit and to remain liquid—liquidity is more important. Many companies lose money for many years, but with adequate financing they are able to remain in business until they can become profitable. Firms that cannot remain liquid, in contrast, are unable to pay their bills as they come due. In such cases, creditors can and often do force firms out of business. Even government and nonprofit organizations such as churches and charities must pay their bills and other obligations on time.

Meeting cash obligations as they come due is not as simple as it may appear. Profitability and liquidity do not necessarily go hand-in-hand. Some firms experience their most critical liquidity problems when they go from a break-even position to profitability. At that time growing receivables, increased inventories, and growing capacity requirements may create cash shortages.

The cash budget is a very useful tool in cash management. Managers estimate all expected cash flows for the budget period. The typical starting point is cash from operations, which is net income adjusted for non-cash items, such as depreciation, and required investment in net working capital (accounts receivable and inventories less accounts payable). All nonoperating cash items are also included. Purchase of land and equipment, sales of bonds and common stock, and the acquisition of treasury stock are a few examples of nonoperating items affecting the cash budget. The net income figure for an accounting period usually is very different from the cash flow for the period because of nonoperating cash flow items or changes in working capital.

Often, cash budgets are prepared much more frequently than other budgets. For example, a company may prepare quarterly budgets for all of its operating budget components such as sales and production and also for its other financial budget components such as capital expenditures. For its cash budget, however, the firm prepares weekly budgets to ensure that it has cash available to meet its obligations each week and that any excess cash is properly invested. In companies with very critical cash problems, even daily cash budgets may be necessary to meet management's information requirements. The frequency of cash budgets depends on management's planning needs and the potential for cash management problems.

Cash management is intended to optimize cash balances; this means having enough cash to meet liquidity needs but not so much that profitability is sacrificed. Excess cash should be invested in earning assets and should not be allowed to lie idly in the cash account. Cash budgeting is useful in dealing with both types of cash problems.

Budgeted Statement of Cash Flows— Indirect Method (42–55)

The final element of the master budget package is the statement of cash flows. The increased emphasis by management in recent years on cash and the sources and uses of cash has made this an ever more useful management tool. This statement is usually prepared from data in the budgeted income statement and changes between the estimated balance sheet at the beginning of the budget period and that at the end of the budget period.

The statement of cash flows consists of three sections, net cash flows from operations, net cash flows from investing activities, and net cash flows from financing activities. Net cash flows from operations are equal to net income plus depreciation expense plus or minus changes in current assets (other than cash) and current liabilities (other than bank loans). Increases (decreases) in current assets are treated as cash outflows (inflows), and increases (decreases) in current liabilities are treated as cash inflows (outflows).

Net cash flows from investing activities consist of changes in long-term assets. Since we do not project any capital expenditures, net cash flows from investing activities are equal to zero in all months.

Net cash flows from financing activities consist of changes in borrowed funds (short and long term), changes in other long-term liabilities, changes in common stock, and dividends paid. The only financing activities in this example are increases (decreases) in bank loans outstanding. The bank line of credit is the buffer that keeps assets equal to liabilities and stockholders' equity. As assets grow with increases in inventories and accounts receivable, bank loans increase as well to finance this growth. And as the inventories are sold and the receivables collected during slower periods, the excess cash is used to repay the amounts borrowed. Banks typically require that the line of credit be paid in full at some point during the year. Any excess funds generated after repayment of the bank loans are invested in short-term marketable securities until required again to finance seasonal growth in assets.

FORECASTING

Sales budgets are influenced by a wide variety of factors, including general economic conditions, pricing decisions, competitor actions, industry conditions, and marketing programs. Often the sales budget starts with individual sales representatives or sales managers predicting sales in their particular areas. The basic sales data are aggregated to arrive at a raw sales forecast that is then modified to reflect many of the variables mentioned previously. The resulting sales budget is expressed in dollars and must include sufficient detail on product mix and sales patterns to support decisions about changes in inventory levels and production quantities.

In addition to the input from sales personnel, companies frequently utilize a number of statistical techniques to estimate future sales. For example, Exhibit 6.6 is a graph of the quarterly sales of Kellogg Company from 1990 to 2000.

The sales appear to demonstrate some variation around an upward trend. How would one forecast sales for the next 12 quarters? Projecting from the most recent sales level might overstate the estimates if the last quarter was unusually high because of, say, the effects of a major advertising campaign or new-product introduction, or seasonal increases. An alternative is to estimate the underlying trend in quarterly sales. Exhibit 6.7 presents such a graph.

In Exhibit 6.7, I have estimated a trend line for Kellogg's quarterly sales using a statistical technique called regression analysis. This line was estimated with a statistical software package called *Minitab*, but the analysis is also available in Microsoft Excel and many other software programs. The equation for the trend line is

$$\text{Sales}_t = \$1,475,002 + \$8,357.73 \times t$$

where Sales_t is the sales for time t ($t = 41$ for the first quarter estimated, since our data ended at quarter number 40). Our forecasts for the next 12 quarters

EXHIBIT 6.6   Kellogg company's quarterly sales (1990–2000).

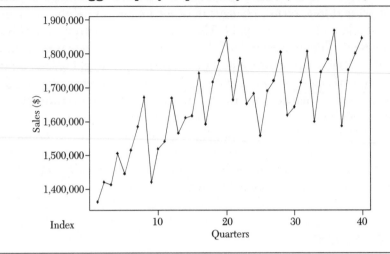

extend linearly with a continuation of the same slope that was estimated in the trend line fit through the data.

A potential problem with fitting a trend line through the data with regression analysis is that each observation is treated the same way. That is, we are not weighting the information contained in the latest set of observations more heavily than those that occurred 30 quarters ago. Other statistical techniques are available to address this concern. One of these is exponential smoothing. Exhibit 6.8 presents the same quarterly sales data with a trend line that has been exponentially smoothed.

EXHIBIT 6.7   Trend analysis for Kellogg company's quarterly sales (1990–2000).

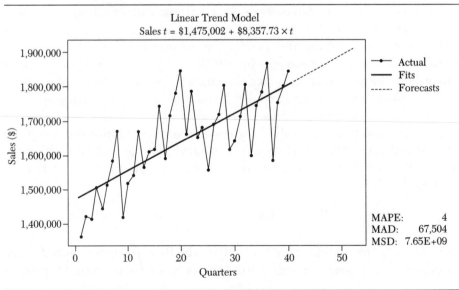

EXHIBIT 6.8   Double exponential smoothing of Kellogg company's quarterly sales (1990–2000).

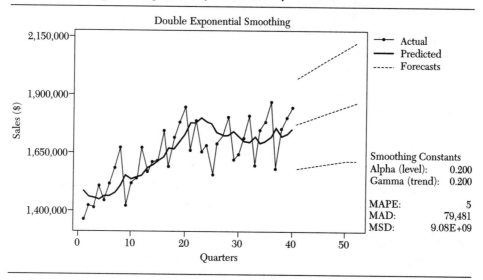

Double Exponential Smoothing

Smoothing Constants
Alpha (level):   0.200
Gamma (trend):   0.200

MAPE: 5
MAD: 79,481
MSD: 9.08E+09

Notice how the estimated trend line reacts to changes in quarterly sales. This technique weights recent observations more heavily than those in the distant past. The result is a trend line whose slope changes over time to reflect changes in sales growth. Our projections for the next 12 quarters, then, begin from the last estimate of the underlying trend and at the most recent slope indicated by the data.

Many other statistical techniques can also be brought to bear on this problem. These provide an objective estimate of future sales from the data itself. Their advantage is that they are not prone to biases from wishful thinking or undue pessimism. Their drawback is that they cannot take into account all of the variables witnessed by our sales personnel and therefore, do not have as much of a "feel" for the market. Companies must utilize a variety of inputs into the projection process, and they derive some level of comfort when several different approaches yield similar results.

Projection is a critical part of the budgeting process. It follows from our SWOT analysis and the resulting strategic and tactical plan. Once these are formulated, sales projections and the subsequent budgeting process outlined above provide an evaluation of the effectiveness of the business plan.

FIXED VERSUS FLEXIBLE BUDGETS

Many organizations operate in an environment where they can predict with great accuracy the volume of business they will experience during the upcoming budget period. In such cases, budgets prepared for a single level of activity typically are very useful in planning and controlling business activities. Budgets prepared for a single level of activity are called *fixed budgets*.

Organizations that have trouble predicting accurately the volume of activity they will experience during the budget period often find that a budget prepared for only one level of activity is not very helpful in planning and controlling their business activities. These organizations can operate better with a budget prepared for several levels of activity covering a range of possible levels of activity. This type of budget is called a *flexible budget.*

Fixed Budgets

A fixed budget, or *static budget,* contains budget data for only one specific volume of activity. Because fixed budgets use only one volume of activity in determining all budgeted data, the fact that some costs are fixed and some costs are variable has no impact on the budgeted figures. The budget data used in preparing the budget for the planning phase of the process are also used in budget performance reports during the control phase of the budget process regardless of whether the volume of activity is actually achieved.

The planning and control framework provided by a budgeting system is an essential element of effective management. In many organizations, fixed budgets are tools that offer managers the ability to plan and control operations and to evaluate performance. If, however, the actual volume of activity achieved by a firm is sufficiently different from the volume planned in the fixed budget, the fixed budget may be a very poor measure on which to base the performance of employees.

Flexible Budgets

A flexible budget, also called a *dynamic budget,* is prepared for more than one level of activity. For example, a firm may prepare budgets for 10,000, 11,000, and 12,000 units produced. The purpose of preparing budgets for multiple activity levels is to provide managers with information about a range of activity in case the actual volume of activity differs from the expected level. For planning material acquisitions, labor needs, and other resource requirements, managers continue to rely heavily on the budget based on the expected level of activity, but the flexible budget provides additional information useful in modifying plans if operating data indicate that some other level of activity will occur. When performance reports are prepared, actual results are compared with a budget based specifically on the level of activity actually achieved.

Actual activity may differ significantly from budgeted activity because of an unexpected strike, cancellation of a large order, an unexpected new contract, or other factors. In a business that frequently experiences variations in its volume of activity, a flexible budget may be more useful than a fixed budget. Flexible budgets provide managers with more useful information for planning and a better basis for comparing performance when activity levels fluctuate than is available from a fixed budget. Flexible budgets are discussed in more detail in Chapter 7.

The Profit Plan

Though the term *profit plan* is sometimes used to refer to a master budget, it probably best describes the operating part of the master budget of a for-profit firm. It can be argued, however, that the entire master budget of such firms is the total profit plan for the firm. The operating budget shows details of budgeted net income, but the financial budgets, such as cash and capital expenditure budgets, are also an integral part of the overall profit planning of the firm.

Naturally, the term *profit plan* is not suitable for public-sector firms. Organizations such as a fire department do not generate a net income. For public-sector organizations, *master budget* is the more logical term for the total budget package. Because we are concerned with both public- and private-sector organizations, we use *master budget* predominantly. However, be aware of *profit plan* because it is used occasionally in practice.

THE BUDGET REVIEW PROCESS

The budget plan determines the allocation of resources within the organization. Typically, the resources available are less than the demand for the resources. Consequently, there should be some systematic process for evaluating all proposals relating to the budget. The process of systematically evaluating budget proposals is referred to as the budget review process.

In the early planning stages, budget review may not be a formal process. Sometimes a few people (or even a single individual) make the budgeting decisions. For example, production-line supervisors may determine resource allocations within their department. Next, a plant budget committee may evaluate budget proposals for all production supervisors. The budget proposals for the entire plant go to a division budget committee, and the final budget review is made by a budget committee of the controller and corporate vice presidents.

The budget review process varies among organizations. Even within a single firm, different budget review processes may be used in various segments of the firm, and at various levels of responsibility. However, the basic review process is fairly standard.

Accountants and financial managers participate in the preparation and implementation of the budget, but all business managers, including marketing managers, production supervisors, purchasing officers, and other nonfinancial managers are interested in developing budgets for their particular part of the business. In addition, each functional manager must be keenly interested in selling her or his budget to higher-level management. Selling the budget means convincing the budget review committee that a particular budget proposal should be accepted. For some managers, selling the budget is the single most important activity in their job, because if they fail at this task, even a tremendous management effort cannot obtain desired results.

With such an awesome description of the importance of selling the budget, one might conclude that it is an exceedingly difficult process. Not so. Actually, the process requires a mixture of logic and diligence. There is no precise formula for success, but some common suggestions are:

1. Know your audience.
2. Make a professional presentation.
3. Quantify the material.
4. Avoid surprises.
5. Set priorities.

Know Your Audience

A large part of a budget-selling strategy may depend on the budget review audience, whether it is one person or a group of people. Information that may prove essential to the successful budget approval effort includes: Strategies that have succeeded or failed in the past; pet peeves or special likes of review members; and a variety of other committee characteristics.

Make a Professional Presentation

A professional presentation is critical to gaining acceptance of the proposal. This typically includes:

- An enthusiastic and polished presentation.
- A neat, concise, and understandable budget proposal.
- Ample supporting documentation.
- A willingness and ability to answer relevant questions.

Quantify the Material

Because most resource allocation decisions are in some way affected by their cost-benefit relationships, it is necessary to quantify both the costs and benefits of virtually all budget proposals. Cost estimation is seldom easy, but it is usually far easier than the measurement of benefits. Even in the private sector, benefits are not always easy to measure in terms of the corporate goals of profitability and liquidity. In the nonprofit sector, benefit measurement is even more difficult. For example, how does one measure the benefits of 20 new park rangers, 10 new police cars, or a decorative fountain in the city park? Obviously the quantification process would be different for each of these, and direct comparisons could be inconclusive. Yet, such comparisons may be necessary in arriving at final budget allocations.

It is easy to dismiss the value of quantification when the resulting numbers are hard to compare with other budget proposals or the numbers are hard to verify. Nevertheless, some quantitative support typically is better than just general statements about the desirability of the budget proposal. Budget sales-manship should be approached with the same ingenuity that is found in the external marketing effort. If certain budget proposals have benefits that are difficult to quantify directly, various types of statistics might support the projects in an indirect way. For example, if a police department wants to justify 10 new police officers, it might offer supporting statistics on rising population in the community, rising crime rates, or relatively low per-capita police cost ratios. Although none of the suggested statistics measures direct benefits, they may be more useful in swaying a budget review committee than some vague statement about the value of more officers. Statistics that are not direct measures of benefits are used widely in both the public and private sectors when supporting budget proposals.

Avoid Surprises

Avoid surprising either review committee or those who present the budget. New proposals and information are hard to sell to a budget review committee and should be introduced and developed long before the final review process.

Surprises to managers presenting the budgets most often occur during the questioning process or when a budget proposal is more detailed than prior budgets. To minimize this problem, budget presentations should be carefully rehearsed. The rehearsal might include a realistic or even pessimistic mock review committee. The mock review should ask pointed and difficult questions. Sometimes knowing the answer to a relatively immaterial question is enough to secure a favorable opinion.

Set Priorities

Few managers receive a totally favorable response to all budget requests. In a world of limited resources, wants exceed available resources, and managers should be prepared for a budget allocation that is somewhat different from the initial request. Typically, all proposed budget items are not equally desirable. Some projects and activities are essential; others are highly desirable. Some would be nice but are really not essential.

Priority systems established by the managers of each budgeting entity before the review process starts aid in structuring the budget proposal so that important items are funded first. Setting priorities avoids embarrassing questions and last-minute decision crises that affect the quality of a professional presentation.

FOR FURTHER READING

Brownell, P., "Participation in Budgeting, Locus of Control, and Organizational Effectiveness," *The Accounting Review*, 56, no. 4 (Oct. 1981): 844–861.

Carruth, Paul J., and Thurrel O. McClendon, "How Supervisors React to Meeting the Budget Pressure," *Management Accounting,* 66 (Nov. 1984): 50.

Chandler, John S., and Thomas N. Trone, "Bottom Up Budgeting and Control," *Management Accounting,* 63 (Feb. 1982): 37.

Chandler, Susan, "Land's End Looks for Terra Firma," *Business Week,* July 8, 1996, 130–131.

Collins, Frank, Paul Munter, and Don W. Finn, "The Budgeting Games People Play," *The Accounting Review,* 62 (Jan. 1987): 29.

Leitch, Robert A., John B. Barrack, and Sue H. McKinley, "Controlling Your Cash Resources," *Management Accounting,* 62 (Oct. 1980): 58.

Merchant, Kenneth A., "The Design of the Corporate Budgeting System: Influences on Managerial Behavior and Performance," *The Accounting Review,* 56 (Oct. 1981): 813.

―――― and J. Manzoni, "The Achievability of Budget Targets in Profit Centers: A Field Study," *The Accounting Review,* 64, no. 3 (July 1989): 539–558.

Merewitz, Leonard, and Stephen H. Sosnick, *The Budget's New Clothes* (Chicago: Markham Publishing Company, 1973).

Penne, Mark, "Accounting Systems, Participation in Budgeting, and Performance Evaluation," *The Accounting Review,* 65, no. 2 (April 1990): 303–314.

"Tenneco CEO Mike Walsh's Fight of His Life," *Business Week,* September 20, 1993, 62.

Trapani, Cosmo S., "Six Critical Areas in the Budgeting Process," *Management Accounting,* 64 (Nov. 1982): 52.

Wildavsky, Aaron, *The Politics of the Budgetary Process,* 2nd ed. (Boston: Little, Brown, 1974).

7 MEASURING PRODUCTIVITY

Michael F. van Breda

"Control is what we need. Cost control. And urgently," said owner-manager Dana Jackson emphatically to her management team. "Just a glance at these reports tells me that our costs are going up faster than our revenues. We won't survive much longer on that basis."

"Well, we could try using cheaper inks and lower quality paper," said Tom Dodge, production manager of Jackson Printing, half-facetiously.

"That's not the answer," exclaimed marketing manager Ahmad Grande. "We're having a hard enough time as it is selling in this competitive market. If we start to produce an inferior product, our sales will tumble even further. Nobody is going to pay our prices and take cheaper quality."

"Ahmad's right," said Dana. "Our aim should not be to reduce costs so much as to control them. Remember that we have a goal to meet in this organization—to produce the best-quality products that we can. If we don't keep our eyes on that goal we won't be effective as an organization.

"What I'm really after is efficiency. I want to see us produce quality products as cheaply as possible—but I don't want us to produce cheap products. We must improve productivity.

"To get the ball rolling, I want Tom to draw up a set of standards for production. Our attorney has been explaining the new system they have installed in their office to control their billable hours. We could do something similar in our business."

As eyes rolled, Dana explained what their law firm had done. "I was telling their senior partner about our concerns and he related to me his own

199

conversation with one of his associates. She was expected to bill approximately 500 hours each quarter to clients. She had actually reported 570 hours, which pleased him, but she had only brought in $70,500 when he would have expected $85,500 based on her standard billing rate of $150 per billable hour. That was $15,000 below his expectations.

"She explained to him that on the Prescot case the partner that she was assisting had asked her to do some library research on an alternative theory of liability. She spent 80 hours working on this research, but in the end the partner decided not to adopt that alternative theory. The partner instructed her not to charge those 80 hours out, so, at her hourly billing rate of $150, that was $12,000 of the total shortfall.

"As for the other $3,000, she explained that on the Klinger case the client felt that the $150 per hour was an excessive rate to charge for an inexperienced lawyer like her. The partner in charge of this case agreed to cut her hourly rate to $125. She spent 120 hours on that case, so, at $25 per hour not billed, there was the other $3,000. He summarized her results for me like this:

$$\text{Actual Billings} = \$70,500 = 490 \text{ billable hours} \times \$143.88 \text{ per hour}$$
$$\text{Budgeted Billings} = \$75,000 = 500 \text{ billable hours} \times \$150.00 \text{ per hour}$$
$$\text{Total Variance} = \$70,500 - \$75,000 \text{ billable hours} = \$4,500 \text{ unfavorable}$$

"In other words, as he explained it, she actually put in only 490 billable hours, even though she worked 570 hours, as opposed to the expected 500 hours. She charged an average $143.88 instead of the expected $150. They use these numbers to break their total variance into two parts: a *volume* variance and a *rate* variance computed as follows:

$$\text{Volume Variance} = (500 - 490) \text{ hours} \times \$150.00 = \$1,500$$
$$\text{Rate Variance} = \$(150.00 - 143.88) \times 490 \text{ hours} = \$3,000$$

"They like to do this in percentage or index terms, too.

$$\text{Volume Index} = \frac{490}{500} = 0.98 \text{ or a 2\% drop}$$
$$\text{Rate Index} = \frac{143.88}{150} = 0.96 \text{ or a 4\% drop}$$

"So they know not only the total amount that their actual costs differed from the budget but also causes of this difference, namely the drop in 10 hours and the drop in the rate of $6.12, and they can identify the effect of each cause on their costs in dollars and percentage terms. That way they can pinpoint the areas that need particular investigation. Things that don't need attention can be safely neglected, leaving time to more carefully manage the exceptions.

"The percentage approach also enables them to introduce two other indices, that of the hours billed to the hours actually worked, namely 490/570 or 86%, and the hours actually worked to those budgeted, 570/500 or 114%. In other words, this associate worked 14% more than she should have but actually billed only 86% of those hours. As he noted, that suggests a serious problem, especially when one compares her with the firm average.

"Their firm," continued Dana, "does this for every one of their associates. They can thereby track the actual revenues of their firm and compare it with the budgeted revenues. They can see whether any shortfalls or overages are due to charging out more or fewer billable hours than expected, or to charging clients more or less than the standard rate, or to some combination of the two. It gives them an excellent tool to see how their firm is doing. They can also analyze productivity in the firm: in total, month by month, as well as by departments within the law firm, such as trust and estate, corporate, litigation, family law, and so on, right down to individual lawyers in the firm. And knowing what has happened in the past, they have an excellent tool for beginning to plan for the future. I think we should be doing something similar!

"If we do, we'll have an idea whether the production staff is working efficiently. If we have those standards in hand, then we can check how much our product should be costing us. And, we'll be able to compare that figure with actual product cost. Checking the difference between actual and budget will tell us where our big problems are. With that information in hand, we should be able to get our costs much more under control and our productivity up."

"Agreed," responded Ahmad. "People will pay for a quality product if it is competitively priced. We've just got to make sure that we're working as efficiently as our competition, and we'll be fine. That means, when we draw up a price quote, we need to be able to come in at or below the quotes of our competitors."

"That's all very well for you to say," said Tom, feeling a little aggrieved. "You're not the one who has to draw up these productivity standards. I've tried doing this before and it's not easy, let me tell you. For starters everyone seems to want perfection."

"The other thing that I think we need to be aware of," added Ahmad, "is that variance analysis is just a start. We need a range of performance measures that capture not only our productivity but also the value that we are adding to our customers. For instance, we know from the newspapers that the firm saved the Prescots tens of thousands of dollars. That was a very successful case for them, and that needs noting. What we really need is a *balanced scorecard* that adds a customer perspective to our more internal focus."[1]

With that the meeting broke up. Tom went back to his office, realizing that he was not quite sure where to begin. For one thing, he hadn't shared the fact that he had not succeeded in his last attempt to install a standard cost system. What chance did he have this time? A call to a friend of his, Jane Halverson, who had just completed her MBA, seemed in order.

BUDGETARY CONTROL

"Jane, I need your help badly," Tom pleaded. "My boss is after a set of production standards and I don't know what to do or where to begin!"

Defining Standards

That evening Tom went over to Jane's home, and she pulled out her cost accounting textbook. "Tell me everything you think I need to know about standard costs," Tom said.

"Okay. First, Tom, let's get straight what we mean by a *standard* and why we're calculating it. A standard is a basis of comparison; it's a norm, if you will, or a yardstick. Some like to compare it to a gauge—a gauge to measure efficiency.

"But a standard is more than that really because it is also the basis for control. Standards enable management to keep score. The difference between standards and actuals directs management's attention to areas requiring their efforts. In that sense, standards are attention getters. They form the heart of what is known as *management by exception,* the concept that one does not watch everything all the time; instead one focuses one's attention on the exceptions, the events that are unexpected."

Tom smiled knowingly. "I've experienced this and it's terrible. My boss at my last job never noticed the good job that I did every day. But, when something went wrong, he was down like a shot to bawl me out!"

"That's one of the traps of managing by exception," said Jane. "But you're smart enough as a manager to know that people need to be rewarded for their regular jobs. You also know that the exceptions are highlighted so that you can help them remedy things—not shout at them. Also, outstanding performance should be rewarded, and so, by means of management by exception, favorable results are highlighted, allowing high performers to receive praise."

Types of Standards

"Then you have to realize," Jane went on, "that there are different kinds of standards. First you have your *basic* standards. These are the one's that are unchanging over long periods of time. Many of these are captured in policy statements and may reflect things like the percentage of waste that is permitted or the amount of time one might be away from a workstation. Basic standards are not much use in forming costs, though, because the work environment tends to change too much.

"At the other extreme there are *theoretical* or *ideal* standards. These get set by engineers and are the ideals to which one is expected to strive. These are the standards that I think you feel are unrealistic."

"Hear! Hear!" broke in Tom. "My guys never would accept those standards—that's the perfection mentality I was telling you about."

"But," asked Jane, "aren't the Japanese always striving towards ideal standards?"

"True, but the difference between them and us is that their system of lifetime employment provides a more supportive atmosphere in which they can strive for perfection and not feel they are going to get fired if they don't quite make it this time around. It's not enough to look at standards in isolation. One must view them in the context of total management."

"Right," said Jane approvingly. "And that means that your best norms to develop are probably what are called *currently attainable* standards. These are standards that can be met but still represent a challenging goal. Let me read you a quote:

> Such standards provide definite goals, which employees can usually be expected to reach, and they also appear to be fair bases from which to measure deviations for which the employees are held responsible. A standard set at a level which is high yet still attainable with reasonably diligent effort and attention to the correct methods of doing the job may also be effective for stimulating efficiency.[2]

I think that's the kind of standard you are after."

"You're right. And, I tell you there are real advantages to standards set at this level. My guys find them very motivating. Also, when it comes time to costing jobs out for pricing purposes, we have a reasonable shot at making those standards. Of course, that wouldn't stop us from trying for perfection. It's just that we wouldn't have management breathing down our necks when we didn't make it."

Budgets

"Tell me one more thing, though," said Tom. Why do we have to go to all this bother to develop standards. Why can't top management just use last year's numbers? That will give them a base for comparison."

"True," said Jane. "But you've got to remember that last year's actuals reflect last year's circumstances. Things may have changed this year so much that last year is not a fair comparison. How would you like it if they didn't adjust your materials budget for inflation but expected you to produce as much this year as you did last?"

"Okay—you've made your point. But, why can't they just get our controller to draw up a budget at the start of the year. Why do I have to get involved?"

"Two reasons. One is that the controller can't draw up a budget without standards. Standard costs are the unit costs that go into a budget. The budget contains your standards multiplied by the expected volume of sales provided by the marketing department.

"The other reason you need to get involved is that the budget needs to be adjusted for volume. You want them to evaluate you on the basis of a *flexible* budget, as opposed to a *static* budget. The only way to be fair to people is to use a flexible budget. Look at these numbers for instance." Jane scribbled down the numbers appearing in Exhibit 7.1.

"Notice how the budget is drawn up in the first column: You estimate the volume for the year and multiply it by the estimated unit selling price or the

EXHIBIT 7.1   Static versus flexible budgets.

	Budget (Static)	Budget (Flexible)	Actual
Volume in reams	1,000	1,200	1,200
Revenues	$12,000	$14,400	$13,800
	at $12/ream	at $12/ream	at $11.50/ream
Variable costs	$7,000	$8,400	$7,500
	at $7.00/ream	at $7.00/ream	at $6.25/ream
Fixed costs	$4,000	$4,000	$4,680
Net income	$1,000	$2,000	$1,620

estimated unit cost, the standard cost. Fixed costs remain the same, of course, and are just inserted into the budget. The last column shows the actual revenues and actual costs: To get them you multiply the actual selling or the actual unit cost by the actual volume. The middle column shows the estimated selling price and the estimated unit costs multiplied by the actual volume.

"Note that the only difference between the flexible budget in column 2 and the static budget in column 1 lies in the volume being used. The static budget uses the expected volume while the flexible budget uses the actual volume. In other words, the difference between flexible and static may be attributed entirely to changing activity levels. The difference is, therefore, dubbed an *activity variance*.

"The unit price and cost terms for the actual revenues and costs in column 3 differ from the corresponding price and cost terms for the flexible budget in column 2; however, the activity level is the same: Both use the actual level of sales. In other words, the difference between actual and flexible may be attributed to changing selling and cost prices. These differences are dubbed the *price variances*. Let's summarize the definitions of these terms.

$$\text{Price Variance} = \text{Actual Results} - \text{Flexible Budget}$$

$$\text{Activity Variance} = \text{Flexible Budget} - \text{Static Budget}$$

$$\text{Price Index} = \frac{\text{Actual Results}}{\text{Flexible Budget}}$$

$$\text{Activity Index} = \frac{\text{Flexible Budget}}{\text{Static Budget}}$$

"Now look what happens if all you have is the budget from the beginning of the year. The variable costs, for which you are responsible, are $1,400 above budget. You could reasonably expect to have your boss down here chewing you out for not controlling your costs. But, if you know your standard costs, you can adjust the budget for volume and give him the number in the second column. That comparison shows that you actually got your costs down by $900. Let me show you what I mean in more depth."

With that Jane started to prepare Exhibit 7.2. First, to prepare Panel A she compared the actual results with the original budget, the static budget. She derived the percentage change by dividing the actual by the budget, subtracting one from the result, and multiplying the remainder by 100. For instance, in the case of revenue:

$$\text{Step 1.} \quad \frac{13,800}{12,000} \quad = 1.15$$

$$\text{Step 2.} \quad 1.15 - 1 \quad = 0.15$$

$$\text{Step 3.} \quad 0.15 \times 100 = 15\%$$

She did similar computations for the other lines and other panels.

EXHIBIT 7.2 Comparing the budgets.

Panel A
Actual versus Static Budget

	Static Budget	Actual	Indixes	Percentage Change
Revenue	$12,000	$13,800	1.15	15
Variable costs	7,000	7,500	1.07	7
Contribution	$ 5,000	$ 6,300	1.26	26
Fixed costs	4,000	4,680	1.17	17
Net income	$ 1,000	$ 1,620	1.62	62

Panel B
Actual versus Flexible Budget

	Flexible Budget	Actual	Indixes	Percentage Change
Revenue	$14,400	$13,800	0.96	(4)
Variable costs	8,400	7,500	0.89	(11)
Contribution	$ 6,000	$ 6,300	1.05	5
Fixed costs	4,000	4,680	1.17	17
Net income	$ 2,000	$ 1,620	0.81	(19)

Panel C
Static versus Flexible Budget

	Static Budget	Flexible Budget	Indixes	Percentage Change
Revenue	$12,000	$14,400	1.20	20
Variable costs	7,000	8,400	1.20	20
Contribution	$ 5,000	$ 6,000	1.20	20
Fixed costs	4,000	4,000	1.00	0
Net income	$ 1,000	$ 2,000	2.00	100

Price Indices

"If you only examine Panel A of Exhibit 7.2," Jane said, "you will think that net income leaped 62% and that the reason for the dramatic increase lies in the relatively sharp increase of 15% in revenue. This increase in revenue appears to have more than compensated for the apparent increase in variable costs of 7% and fixed costs of 17%. You might be tempted to attribute the increase in net income to the superior ability of the sales staff."

"The fallacy of this interpretation is apparent when you examine Panel B, which compares the actual results with the flexible budget. Now, after adjusting for sales volume, we find that instead of that dramatic increase of 62% in net income, there was a 19% drop in net income from budget. Using that same basis of comparison, revenue actually fell by 4% instead of our earlier increase of 15%. Now you can also see that, after adjusting for sales activity, variable costs actually showed a steep decline of 11% rather than the increase of 7% shown in Panel A. In other words, at the actual volume of 1,200 units as opposed to the budgeted volume of 1,000 units, you should have budgeted more for variable costs than at first expected. The $8,400 is, in retrospect, the more appropriate budget figure.

"The apparent rise in revenues shown in Panel A melts away in Panel B, as does the apparent rise in variable costs shown in Panel A. The result is a whole new story. Volume rose perhaps because of the efforts of the sales staff but more probably because of the fall in the selling price from $12 per unit to $11.50 per unit.

"Fortunately," Jane said with a broad grin on her face, "the loss was partially offset by the heroic efforts of the production staff in getting their per-unit costs down by 11%."

"I like that heroic part," said Tom approvingly.

"You should, because with the volume effect eliminated, all of the fall in variable costs must be attributed to a fall in unit variable costs. More precisely, standard variable costs were $7.00 but actual unit variable costs were just $6.25. Dividing the actual unit cost of $6.25 by the standard variable cost of $7.00 yields an index of 0.89, or precisely the 11% decrease in variable costs noted earlier."

Activity Indices

"Now look at Panel C," said Jane. "This compares the flexible budget with the static budget. The only factor that changes between the two is sales activity, so the percentages measure the change in the number of units sold. As there is only one measure of activity, it is not surprising that all the activity-based indices show an increase of 20%, that is, 200 units extra on a base of 1,000. Fixed costs, though, are independent of activity levels. Net income, which is a combination of activity-related and activity-independent numbers, shows an increase that reflects its mixed nature."

Market Effects

"The rise in volume may or may not be attributable to good management. One possibility is that it was driven by an increase in the total market. For instance, one can imagine the larger market to have an expected 8,000 units in sales. The company was expecting to get 12.5% of the market. If one now assumes that the market grew to 12,000 units, then the company's sales of 1,200 units actually represents a decrease in market share. Writing this out more formally:

$$\text{Sales Activity Index} = \frac{1,200}{1,000}$$
$$= \frac{(10\% \times 12,000)}{(12.5\% \times 8,000)}$$
$$= \left(\frac{10\%}{12.5\%}\right) \times \left(\frac{12.5\%}{8,000}\right)$$
$$= 0.80 \times 1.50$$

In other words, given this scenario, the sales staff really should be queried on why they had a decrease of 20% in market share in a market that increased 50%."

Summary

"Finally, let's try to summarize what we have learned to this point. First, note that Panel B confirms that the price index in any variance computation can be derived by dividing the actual figure by the flexible budget figure. Panel C demonstrates that the activity index can be derived by dividing the flexible figure by the static figure. In short, the relationship between the overall index of the change from budget to actual is given by:

$$\text{Overall Index} = \frac{\text{Actual}}{\text{Static}}$$
$$= \left(\frac{\text{Actual}}{\text{Flexible}}\right) \times \left(\frac{\text{Flexible}}{\text{Static}}\right)$$
$$= \text{Price Index} \times \text{Activity Index}$$

To summarize, then, in the example shown in Exhibits 7.1 and 7.2, one has the following relationships connecting the actual results back to the static, through the flexible budget:

$$\text{Overall Index} = \text{Price Index} \times \text{Activity Index}$$
$$\text{Revenue: } 1.15 = 0.96 \times 1.20$$
$$\text{Variable Cost: } 1.07 = 0.89 \times 1.20$$
$$\text{Fixed Cost: } 1.17 = 1.17 \times 1.00$$

So, as you can see, the pieces fit together quite logically. The points underlying these pieces can be summarized quite briefly:

1. First, we saw the need to distinguish between basic, ideal, and currently attainable standards.
2. Second, we saw the wisdom of distinguishing flexible from static budgets.
3. Third, we noted that our standards are the foundation stones on which these budgets are based.
4. We noted that all cost variances follow one simple formula: Actual Cost less Budgeted Cost equals Standard Cost Variance.
5. Activity Variances = Flexible Budget − Static Budget

   Price Variances = Actual Results − Flexible Budget

   $$\text{Activity Indices} = \frac{\text{Flexible Budget}}{\text{Static Budget}}$$

   $$\text{Price Indices} = \frac{\text{Actual Results}}{\text{Flexible Budget}}$$

6. Flexible budgets adjust variable cost and their variances for volume.
7. Volume has no effect on fixed costs or the variances derived from fixed costs.

VARIABLE COST BUDGETS

"That's fine, but what am I going to do with these variances?" Tom asked a little impatiently. "Everything that I've seen so far may help top management, but it's not much help to me."

"Good point, Tom. That's why we need to examine productivity, which is the relationship between inputs and outputs. We'll enhance your productivity and your control over costs if we can focus on the elements that go into your costs."

With that Jane began to explain how in a typical cost accounting system the variable cost of a product or service is a function of:

1. The hours of labor (both direct and indirect) that go into a product.
2. The units of material that are used.
3. The other components of overhead.
4. The unit cost of each of these items.

"Let's call the amount of input that goes into one unit of output the productivity rate. For instance, one might need 500 pages or sheets of paper and 16 minutes of labor to produce a ream of letterhead. The material productivity rate is 500 pages per ream; the labor productivity rate is 18 minutes or 0.30 hour per ream. When the expected cost of the inputs is attached to the expected productivity rates, a standard cost is said to result. The productivity rates themselves are also known as standards. They are typically established by engineers."

As before, Jane began sketching out a numerical illustration of the points that she was making. Her sketches appear in Exhibit 7.3. "These are the standards," she said, "that determine the variable portion of the budget for production. Note the assumption here that variable overhead is a function of machine hours, or how long the machine runs. Other assumptions are possible but we will stick with this one in our example.

"Fixed overhead is a little different because it does not really have a productivity rate. Let's just put down the fixed overhead on a budgeted and an actual basis, and we can come back and discuss the details later." From these standards she began to derive the standard variable cost of the product; also its actual variable cost:

$$\begin{aligned}
\text{Standard Cost} &= \text{Material Cost} + \text{Labor Cost} + \text{Variable Overhead Cost} \\
&= (500 \text{ pages} \times \$0.008 \text{ per page}) + (0.30 \text{ hours} \times \$5.00 \text{ per hour}) \\
&\quad + (0.10 \text{ hours} \times \$15.00 \text{ per hour}) \\
&= \$4.00 + \$1.50 + \$1.50 \\
&= \$7.00 \text{ per ream}
\end{aligned}$$

$$\begin{aligned}
\text{Actual Cost} &= \text{Material Cost} + \text{Labor Cost} + \text{Variable Overhead Cost} \\
&= (500 \text{ pages} \times \$0.007 \text{ per page}) + (0.25 \text{ hours} \times \$6.00 \text{ per hour}) \\
&\quad + (0.125 \text{ hours} \times \$10.00 \text{ per hour}) \\
&= \$3.50 + \$1.50 + \$1.25 \\
&= \$6.25 \text{ per ream}
\end{aligned}$$

EXHIBIT 7.3   Standards and actuals for letterhead paper.

	Budgeted	Actual
Material:		
Productivity rate (pages per ream)	500	500
Cost per unit of input (per page)	$0.008	$0.007
Cost per unit of output (per ream)	$4.00	$3.50
Labor:		
Productivity rate (labor hours per ream)	0.30	0.25
Wage per unit of input (per labor hour)	$5.00	$6.00
Wage per unit of output (per ream)	$1.50	$1.50
Variable Overhead:		
Productivity rate (machine hours per ream)	0.10	0.125
Cost per unit of input (per machine hour)	$15.00	$10.00
Cost per unit of output (per ream)	$1.50	$1.25

Jane then used these numbers to show how the budgeted and actual variable costs in Exhibit 7.1 were derived. For the static budget:

$$\text{Material Costs} = \$4.00 \text{ per ream} \times 1,000 \text{ reams} = \$4,000$$
$$\text{Labor Costs} = \$1.50 \text{ per ream} \times 1,000 \text{ reams} = \$1,500$$
$$\text{Variable OH} = \$1.50 \text{ per ream} \times 1,000 \text{ reams} = \$1,500$$

$$\text{Total Variable Costs} = \$7,000 \text{ as reported in Exhibit 7.1}$$

For the flexible budget:

$$\text{Material Costs} = \$4.00 \text{ per ream} \times 1,200 \text{ reams} = \$4,800$$
$$\text{Labor Costs} = \$1.50 \text{ per ream} \times 1,200 \text{ reams} = \$1,800$$
$$\text{Variable OH} = \$1.50 \text{ per ream} \times 1,200 \text{ reams} = \$1,800$$

$$\text{Total Variable Costs} = \$8,400 \text{ as reported in Exhibit 7.1}$$

For the actual costs:

$$\text{Material Costs} = \$3.50 \text{ per ream} \times 1,200 \text{ reams} = \$4,200$$
$$\text{Labor Costs} = \$1.50 \text{ per ream} \times 1,200 \text{ reams} = \$1,800$$
$$\text{Variable OH} = \$1.25 \text{ per ream} \times 1,200 \text{ reams} = \$1,500$$

$$\text{Total Variable Costs} = \$7,500 \text{ as reported in Exhibit 7.1}$$

Material Indices

Jane also used the standards in Exhibit 7.3 to show Tom how indices for each of the components of the variable costs could be determined and interpreted. Consider first the material costs:

$$
\begin{aligned}
\text{Material Index} &= \frac{\text{Actual Costs}}{\text{Flexible Budget}} \\
&= \frac{\$4,200}{\$4,800} \\
&= \frac{(\$0.007 \text{ per page} \times 500 \text{ pages per ream} \times 1,200 \text{ reams})}{(\$0.008 \text{ per page} \times 500 \text{ pages per ream} \times 1,200 \text{ reams})} \\
&= \left(\frac{0.007}{0.008}\right) \times \left(\frac{500}{500}\right) \times \left(\frac{1,200}{1,200}\right) \\
&= 0.875 \times 1.00 \times 1.00 \\
&= 0.875
\end{aligned}
$$

In words, the material portion of the variable cost fell 12.5% from the flexible budget to the actual because of the 12.5% decrease in the cost of paper from $0.008 per page to $0.007 per page. There were no efficiencies or inefficiencies in the use of the paper: The number of pages actually used per ream was equal to budget.

Labor Indices

Jane then performed an identical analysis for labor costs:

$$\text{Labor Index} = \frac{\text{Actual Costs}}{\text{Flexible Budget}}$$

$$= \frac{\$1,800}{\$1,800}$$

$$= \frac{(\$6.00 \text{ per hour} \times 0.25 \text{ hours per ream} \times 1,200 \text{ reams})}{(\$5.00 \text{ per hour} \times 0.30 \text{ hours per ream} \times 1,200 \text{ reams})}$$

$$= \frac{\$6.00}{\$5.00} \times \frac{0.25}{0.30} \times \frac{1,200}{1,200}$$

$$= 1.20 \times 0.833 \times 1.00$$

$$= 1.00$$

In words, the labor portion of the variable cost remained the same from flexible to actual because the rise of 20% in the hourly wage was exactly offset by the 16.67% decrease in the time to produce a ream of letterhead.

   "I've just realized that what we have here," said Tom, "is a great way to measure increases in productivity. Dana keeps on talking about how our productivity is falling. One way to counteract that is to check how efficiently people are working. Before one measures physical productivity, though, one has to eliminate the wage effect, which is just what you have shown me how to do here."

Variable Overhead Indices

"I think I can now do the variable overhead analysis myself," said Tom. "I just take the three components of the actual cost and divide that by the three components of the flexible budget. Check me if you will."

$$\text{Variable OH Index} = \frac{\text{Actual Costs}}{\text{Flexible Budget}}$$

$$= \frac{\$1,500}{\$1,800}$$

$$= \frac{(\$10.00 \times 0.125 \times 1,200)}{(\$15.00 \times 0.10 \times 1,200)}$$

$$= \frac{\$10.00}{\$15.00} \times \frac{0.125}{0.10} \times \frac{1,200}{1,200}$$

$$= 0.667 \times 1.25 \times 1.00$$

$$= 0.833$$

"I can even tell you what that means in words: The overhead portion of the variable cost declined 16.67% from the flexible budget because the hourly overhead rate fell by 33.33% while the overhead used per ream rose 25%. How do you like that explanation?"

Variance Analysis

"Another way, in fact the more traditional way, to think about this," said Jane, "is to focus on the numbers rather than the percentages. The cost of the paper fell 0.001 cents per page while the company used 600,000 pages (500 pages per ream × 1,200 reams.) This price drop saved $600; since this price variance is favorable, it's denoted by an F. The company used the amount of paper that was budgeted, so the usage variance is zero.

$$
\begin{aligned}
\text{Materials Variance} =& \left[\left(600,000 - 600,000\right) \text{ pages} \times \$0.008 \text{ per page}\right] \\
&+ \left[\$(0.007 - 0.008) \text{ per page} \times 600,000 \text{ pages}\right] \\
=& \$600 \ F
\end{aligned}
$$

"In the case of labor, the wage paid was $1.00 per hour more than planned, which over the 300 hours that were worked meant an unfavorable wage variance of $300 denoted by a U. Employees actually worked 300 hours (0.25 hours per ream × 1,200 reams), whereas the plan was for them to work 360 hours (0.30 × 1,200 reams). That saved 60 hours, which, at the standard wage rate of $5.00, saved $300. The wage variance and the use variance offset one another here.

$$
\begin{aligned}
\text{Labor Variance} =& \left[\left(300 - 360\right) \text{ hours} \times \$5.00 \text{ per hour}\right] \\
&+ \left[\$(6.00 - 5.00) \text{ per hour} \times 300 \text{ hours}\right] \\
=& \$0
\end{aligned}
$$

"Finally, the variable overhead rate was $5.00 per machine hour less than expected. This gives a favorable rate variance of $750 or $5.00 × 150 actual machine hours. The base on which variable overhead was applied, namely machine hours, increased by 30 hours since the budget called for just 120 machine hours. At the standard rate of $15.00 per hour this gives an unfavorable usage variance of $450 or $15.00 × 30 machine hours. This leaves a favorable difference of $300.

$$
\begin{aligned}
\text{Overhead Variance} =& \left[\left(150 - 120\right) \text{ hours} \times \$15.00 \text{ per hour}\right] \\
&+ \left[\$(10.00 - 15.00) \text{ per hour} \times 150 \text{ hours}\right] \\
=& \$300
\end{aligned}
$$

"All this is summarized in Exhibit 7.4."

EXHIBIT 7.4   Variance analysis.

	Rate Variance	Usage Variance	Total Variance
Materials	$600 F	$0	$600 F
Labor	300 U	300 F	0
Variable overhead	450 U	750 F	300 F

Review

"One last question, Jane: Where do these variable overhead rates come from?"

"That's another subject altogether," said Jane. "Do you want a cup of coffee? I'm bushed. But before we break, let's summarize what we've learned.

1. The cost of a product consists of material, labor, and overhead.
2. Each of these components is made up of a productivity rate multiplied by a unit cost for that component.
3. Standard Costs = Standard Productivity Rates × Standard Unit Costs
4. Actual Costs = Actual Productivity Rates × Actual Unit Costs
5. Price Indices = Actual Unit Costs/Standard Costs
6. Activity Indices = Actual Productivity Rate/Standard Productivity Rate."

COLLECTING STANDARDS

After their coffee break, Jane and Tom shifted their conversation to how to develop these standard costs. Jane reminded Tom that standard costs are made up of two parts:

1. A standard cost per unit times.
2. A standard usage, or quantity of units of input per unit of output.

She pointed out that he was responsible for defining the amount of material and labor that should go into the product. The purchasing department was responsible for determining the amount that should be paid for materials, the personnel department determined wages. There are, as she explained, several ways to determine the appropriate usage.

Engineering Studies

"First, one can do an engineering study. In other words, one can look at the specifications of the product. Many products that are designed by engineers have quite detailed and explicit instructions on what materials should go into them. These standards often include an allowance for waste, though this isn't necessary. Where they do not include such an allowance they border on the ideal.

"To take an obvious example, most automobiles have one battery, and an engineering statement would so state. A perfection standard would call for 1 battery per automobile. When it comes to actual production, however, it would not be unusual for one or more batteries to be damaged during installation. If 10,100 batteries are used in the manufacture of 10,000 cars, then it might appear as if each automobile actually had 1.01 batteries. One might, therefore, want to set as one's standard a currently attainable goal of 1.01 batteries on average, thus providing a 1% allowance for wastage."

Time and Motion Studies

"Time and motion studies are the usual way in which engineering standards are set for the labor component," Jane explained. "An engineer watches over laborers as they work and determines how much time it should take for each part of the production process. When doing this, it is vital that the engineer gain labor's cooperation. If not, disastrous results can occur. I love the following quotation:"

> You got to use your noodle while you're working and think your work out ahead as you go along! You got to add in movements you know you ain't going to make when you're running the job! Remember, if you don't screw them, they're going to screw you! . . . Every moment counts! . . .
>
> When the time-study man came around, I set the speed at 180. I knew damn well he would ask me to push it up, so I started low enough. He finally pushed me up to 445, and I ran the job later at 610. If I'd started out at 445, they'd have timed it at 610. Then I got him on the reaming, too. I ran the reamer for him at 130 speed and .025 feed. He asked me if I couldn't run the reamer any faster than that, and I told him I had to run the reamer slow to keep the hole size. I showed him two pieces with oversize holes that the day man ran. I picked them out for the occasion! But later on I ran the reamer at 610 speed and .018 feed, same as the drill. So I didn't have to change gears.[3]

Tom smiled appreciatively at the story. As an old floor hand, he understood the sentiments completely.

Motivation

"This raises a broader question, you know," said Tom. "Should we invite people to participate in setting the standards? Will it make them more motivated? I've pondered this from a variety of angles. What's interesting about it is that participation doesn't always work.

"What I have discovered from my reading around the topic is that many people prefer to be told what to do. This seems to be particularly true for people who find their jobs boring and for those with a more authoritarian personality. So one has to be really careful when inviting people to participate."

"You know more about this than I do," responded Jane. "How do you handle feedback, then. That's a sort of after-the-fact participation isn't it."

"Well, I don't know about after the fact, but everyone that I've read—and my own experience for that matter—indicates that timely feedback is essential and a good motivator. People really need to know, and know as soon as possible, how they have done. That's especially true when they've done a good job, because it really builds their self-esteem. And in some cases, it makes them want to participate more *before* the fact in the next round.

"Of course, I don't want to lead you to think that a little participation and a lot of feedback is all one needs. These are what the psychologists call *intrinsic* motivators. People need these, but they also need *extrinsic* motivators like better pay for doing a better job.

"And, the other problem that I've encountered is that the more you focus people's attention on one goal, the more they tend to ignore other goals. It's only human nature: Ask salespeople to increase their turnover, and they'll sell goods at a loss.

"That's one of the reasons why I have misgivings about calling in a bunch of engineers to set standards. It's much easier to time how long a job should take and reward people for quantity than to measure and to reward quality. I really rely upon the innate good sense of my staff to provide quality products. Too much emphasis on measurement can make my task of maintaining quality much more difficult."

Past Data

"Probably, then, an easier way," Jane said, "to get the data you need for your business is to go back over your past records to see how much time various jobs have taken and how much material was used in the past. Some of that will have to be adjusted for changes in machines, changes in personnel, different kinds of material, and so on. But you know all that better than I do."

"Enough!" Tom exclaimed. "Enough for now! I'll come over tomorrow night and we can talk some more. We still need to discuss fixed overheads as you promised."

FIXED COST BUDGETS

"Fixed costs," Jane started out the next night after the two had gathered again, "are both easier and more difficult to control than variable costs. They are easier because there are no components into which to break them. Their variance is simply:

$$\text{Actual Fixed Costs} - \text{Budgeted Fixed Costs}$$

Their index is simply:

$$\frac{\text{Actual Fixed Costs}}{\text{Budgeted Fixed Costs}}$$

In our case, the budgeted fixed costs were $4,000 and the actual fixed costs were $4,680. The variance was simply $680, which means a 17% increase.

"Fixed costs are more difficult to control than variable costs because one cannot create an illusion of control through the elaborate computation of price, mix, and usage variances or indices."

"How, then, does one control fixed costs?" asked Tom.

"First," Jane replied, "one must recognize that if costs are truly fixed, there is no reason to control them. Consider depreciation costs as an example. Once one has purchased an item, the total depreciation costs are set—unless one disposes of the machinery when a disposal cost will substitute for the depreciation cost. No control is possible here. The control in this case has to be exerted when the machinery is purchased. Thereafter, it is a sunk cost that cannot be controlled. In other words, controlling fixed costs is in the first place a matter of timing.

"Traditional variance analysis uses one cost driver only, the volume of production. More modern variance analysis, such as that in *activity based costing*, uses multiple cost drivers.[4] For example, setup costs may not vary with volume of production but might vary with the number of batches. What appears at first glance to be a fixed cost may just be variable with respect to some other driver. The analysis of variance proceeds exactly as before except that one changes the driver from units produced to number of batches. One converts the fixed cost into a quasi-variable cost by finding and using the appropriate cost driver.

"Controlling fixed costs is also a matter of scale. Consider the machine again. Assume one has just one machine with a capacity of 1,000 boxes of greeting cards per day. Its cost is certainly fixed within this range. However, if the analysis is being done in terms of tens of thousands of boxes, and if the corporation has a hundred of these machines, then it is possible to think of machine costs as being a variable. One can ask, in other words, what the cost would be to produce an additional 'unit' of 1,000 boxes.

"This last question points to the fact that most fixed costs are usually only fixed within the context of a particular analysis. Consider, for instance, the ink you use in production. Assume its price is reset by a cartel every three months. Assume also that its planned usage is reset at the same time. A budgetary control system that computed variances every month and set the budgeted price and quantity to those of the latest quarter might show a variance of zero each month. This might lead everyone to believe that they were dealing with a fixed cost. However, were the same analysis to be done on an annual basis, with prices and quantities set at the start of the year, a substantial variance could arise. The example points up the old truism that all costs are variable in the long run.

"The example above also points up the need to set your net large enough to catch the fish you want. Many fixed costs cannot be controlled by a monthly, or even annual, budget system because they change too slowly. One needs a coarser net, that is, an annual, triennial, or even longer budgetary system to capture their change. The reverse is also true. A net that is too fine can capture a great deal of random noise. Consider, for instance, a product whose price fluctuates randomly around a fixed mean. If all you want is to see the true exceptions, then you should set the net to capture only those fluctuations that are greater than a certain number of standard deviations away from the mean.

"In short, fixed costs are best controlled in the long run and at a more aggregate level. In other words, it is important in the budgetary control of fixed costs to establish appropriate time and space horizons for one's analysis."

"Those are all good points," said Tom, "and it's good to be reminded of them. What you haven't yet told me, though, is whether there is a fixed overhead rate like the variable overhead rate that you had in Exhibit 7.3 and how the fixed overhead rate fits into the whole picture."

"Well, fixed overhead does and doesn't have a rate," responded Jane. "The rate itself comes from knowing the total fixed overhead and dividing it by the volume; for example, the budgeted fixed overhead of $4,000 divided by the budgeted 1,000 units gives us a fixed overhead rate of $4.00. In a sense, fixed overhead rates are secondary—unlike variable overhead rates, which are primary, meaning that fixed overhead rates are computed by dividing the total overhead by volume. Total variable overhead, on the other hand, is computed by multiplying the variable overhead rate by the volume. In other words, fixed overhead computes just the other way round from variable overhead.

"Variable overhead rates are used in computing variances and indices. Fixed overhead rates are completely ignored in this context. Their main purpose is to give you an estimate of the total product cost. We computed earlier that the estimated variable cost of a ream of letterhead was $7.00. We can now add the $4.00 fixed cost in and say the estimated total cost of a ream is $11.00. So fixed overhead rates fit in when calculating unit product costs. It's just that they don't fit into the rest of the budgetary control systems. But let's talk about standard cost systems when all this might become clearer. Let's pick it up tomorrow when we are both fresher."

STANDARD COST ACCOUNTING SYSTEMS

"Companies rarely enter their budgets into their ledgers. Usually budgetary control takes place outside of the books of the company. In other words, the budget is typically drawn up using spreadsheets outside of the general ledger system. At the end of the period under investigation, the actual results are drawn out of the ledger and transferred to the spreadsheet where the comparisons are done. Two exceptions to this general rule occur."

Government Accounting

"The first exception does not affect private companies but does affect state and local governments. It is common practice in their accounting systems to enter a budgeted number in the ledgers in anticipation of an actual number. For instance, city governments will enter budgeted revenues as a debit on the left side of the ledger account. Then when the sales are actually made, they will enter the actual revenues as a credit on the right column of the ledger account. The effect is that at the end of the year, only variances are left in accounts. For instance, sales greater than expected would leave a credit variance."

Standard Variable Costs

"The second exception involves so-called standard cost systems. In a typical implementation, the standard cost of a product, not the actual cost incurred, is entered into the work-in-process account. The difference between the standard cost and the actual cost creates a variance—in the actual accounts. For example, in the case of paper used, the inventory account would be charged with the standard $4.00 for every ream used but only $3.50 would be paid to the supplier. The difference of $0.50 would be shown in a separate variance account in the books of the company.

"The existence of a credit variance in the accounts indicates that the budgeted unit cost exceeds the actual unit cost, that is, there is a favorable variance. Were the variance a debit, it would be unfavorable.

"By the end of the job, after they have produced 1,200 reams, they will show in their accounts a variance of $0.50 per ream on all their variable costs times 1,200 reams, or a credit of $600. This is the same favorable $600 variance that we saw in Exhibit 7.4 when we subtracted the actual cost from the flexible budget. Standard cost systems, in other words, track the flexible budget.

"Each of these variances is identical to the variances computed above; each can be stated in percentage terms to indicate their relative size, that is, material costs are down 12.5%, labor costs are even, and variable overhead costs are down 16.67%. The key point to realize is that variances generated by a standard cost system are identical to those generated by a budgetary control system—once one removes the volume effect."

Standard Fixed Costs

"The parallels between standard cost systems and budgetary control systems do not extend to fixed costs, unfortunately. The reason lies in the way fixed costs are applied to products. In a standard cost system, a fixed overhead rate is established at the start of a period by dividing the budgeted fixed overhead by the budgeted volume. In our case, the predetermined fixed overhead rate was $4,000 divided by 1,000 reams, which equals $4.00 per ream. The predetermined fixed overhead rate is therefore based on the static budget.

"Fixed overhead is then applied to goods as they are produced by multiplying the number of reams produced by this overhead rate. In this case, one charges $4.00 of fixed overhead to each of the 1,200 reams produced. The result is $4,800, which is known as the *applied* overhead. The problem is that this is neither actual nor budgeted. It is really a miscomputed number. If the number of actual reams had been known in advance, one should have divided the $4,000 by 1,200 reams, giving $3.33 per ream. In other words, one should have used the flexible budget. Using that rate would have led to the application of $4,000 of fixed overhead exactly. The difference between the budgeted amount of $4,000 and the amount actually applied, namely $800, is said to have been *over-applied*—one might say over-applied in error. A correcting entry is typically made in the accounting system to fix this error.

"The accounts of the company record that it actually had fixed overhead costs of $4,680 and applied overhead of $4,800. This generates a credit variance of $120 in the accounts. Regardless of what appears in the accounts, the spending variance that should be reported is an unfavorable $680—not a favorable $120. No matter the confusions in the ledger, the only variance that one is interested in is:

$$\text{Applied Overhead} - \text{Budgeted Overhead} = \$4,680 - \$4,000$$

"The difference between the variance produced by a standard cost system and the variance wanted for budgetary control purposes is:

$$\text{Budgeted Overhead} - \text{Applied Overhead} = \$4,000 - \$4,800$$
$$= (\$4 \times 1,000) - (\$4 \times 1,200)$$
$$= \$4 \times 200$$

"In short, the error in the fixed overhead variance appearing in a standard cost system is due to volume changing from 1,000 units to 1,200 units. The result is a variance in the standard cost system that is useless for control purposes.

"The budgeted overhead will be equal to the applied overhead only when the actual volume equals the budgeted volume, which rarely happens. More commonly, a fixed cost variance is found in the ledger, but this is of no interest for budgetary control. For control purposes, you should compute the spending variance directly and simply ignore the net overhead variance derived in the books."

"Now I see why you ignored the fixed overhead when doing the variances originally," said Tom. "Let's hope that my management understands this as well as you seem to do!"

BUDGETARY CONTROL REVISITED

"Budgetary control, as we noted at the outset," Jane continued, "consists of comparing actual results with budget estimates. When doing this one is advised to distinguish between revenues and costs that vary with volume and those that are fixed with respect to volume changes. A revised budget, adjusted for the actual volumes rather than the predicted volumes, yields a flexible budget as opposed to the original or static budget.

"Since the static and the flexible budgets for fixed costs are identical, the fixed-cost spending variance is simply the difference between the actual and the original budget. The spending index for fixed costs is their quotient.

"In the case of variable costs and revenues, a few simple rules emerge. The ratio between the flexible and the static budgets indicates the difference in the quantities expected and the quantities actually experienced. The ratio between the actual results and the flexible budget indicates the change in costs or revenues that can be attributed to changes in unit costs or selling prices.

"In the case of multiple outputs or multiple inputs, the quantity indices can be further refined. They break into at least two indices. The first reveals the effect of changing mixes of either outputs or inputs. The second reveals the effect of changing the overall volume. The mix variance may be computed directly or simply by dividing the quantity index by the volume index. In the case of variable costs, it is usually possible to draw out another index indicating the total yield, that is, the amount of input required to produce a given amount of output.

"All these indices can be computed using an accounting system that collects only actual costs and comparing these in a spreadsheet with the budgeted costs. Alternatively, they may be derived by keeping a standard cost system. The variances that emerge as one enters standard costs into work-in-process and credits the corresponding asset or liability account at actual are identical to those derived from a flexible budgeting control system. The one exception to this identity is fixed costs, but the difference here is easily reconciled.

"In short, budgetary control analysis provides one vehicle for controlling a business. The budget reflects, ideally, a company's strategies and objectives. As actual results emerge they are compared with the budget to see to what extent the enterprise has met its goals and productivity targets. Any difference encountered can be decomposed to determine whether it was due to a change in usage or a change in price. Where inputs or outputs are substitutable, one can also examine the changing mix for further insight into how one achieved one's goals.

"In each case, the index derived is neither good nor bad. It simply indicates a change. As noted earlier, the same rise in sales may be a matter for congratulation when markets are declining and a matter for concern when markets are expanding faster than one's sales. All that the index does is to point one to where still more information must be gathered."

FOR FURTHER READING

Anthony, Robert N., David F. Hawkins, and Kenneth A. Merchant, *Accounting: Text and Cases,* 10th ed. (New York: Irwin/McGraw-Hill, 1999), esp. chs. 19 and 20.

Davidson, Sidney, and Roman L. Weil, *Handbook of Cost Accounting* (New York: McGraw-Hill, 1978), esp. chs. 15 and 16.

Ferris, Kenneth R., and J. Leslie Livingstone, eds., *Management Planning and Control: The Behavioral Foundations* (Columbus, OH: Century VII, 1989), esp. chs. 3, 8, and 9.

Horngren, Charles T., Gary L. Sundem, and William O. Stratton, *Introduction to Management Accounting,* 11th ed. (Englewood Cliffs, NJ: Prentice-Hall, 1999), esp. chs. 7 and 8.

Kaplan, Robert S., and Anthony A. Atkinson, *Advanced Management Accounting,* 3rd ed. (Englewood Cliffs, NJ: Prentice-Hall, 1998), esp. chs. 9 and 10.

Maher, Michael W., Clyde Stickney, Roman L. Weil, and Sidney Davidson, *Managerial Accounting* (Fort Worth, TX: Harcourt College Publishers, 1999), esp. chs. 10 and 11.

Shank, J.K., and N.C. Churchill, "Variance Analysis: A Management-Oriented Approach," *The Accounting Review,* 52 (Oct. 1977): 950–957.

Welsch, Glenn A., Ronald W. Hilton, and Paul N. Gordon, *Budgeting: Profit Planning and Control,* 5th ed. (Englewood Cliffs, NJ: Prentice-Hall, 1988), esp. ch. 16.

INTERNET LINKS

Internet links and Web sites have an uncomfortable way of disappearing. The reader is advised, therefore, to do her or his own search under key words such as "variance analysis" and "standard costing." This will turn up sites such as Conoco's and Corn Products International's discussions of their results at www.conoco.com and www.cornproducts.com. Both make excellent use of variance analysis. The U.S. Army Cost and Economic Analysis Center at www.ceac.army.mil/web/default.html provides a good discussion of standards, while the Association of Accounting Technicians, at www.aat.co.uk, provides an excellent forum for questions and answers on this and many other accounting topics. The Institute of Management Accountants maintains a site at www .imanet.org that provides all kinds of managerial accounting resources. Finally, the reader is invited to visit my own site, at www.smu.edu/~mvanbred, with its many links and notes on both financial and managerial accounting.

NOTES

1. R. Kaplan and D. Norton, "The Balanced Scorecard—Measures That Drive Performance," *Harvard Business Review,* 70 (Jan.–Feb. 1992): 71–79.

2. National Association of Accountants, *Standard Costs and Variance Analysis* (New York: NAA, 1974): 9.

3. Whyte, W.F., ed., *Money and Motivation: An Analysis of Incentives in Industry* (New York: Harper & Row, 1955).

4. Cooper, Robin, and Robert S. Kaplan, "How Cost Accounting Distorts Product Costs," *Management Accounting,* 69 (Apr. 1988): 20–27.

PART TWO

PLANNING AND FORECASTING

8 CHOOSING A BUSINESS FORM

Richard P. Mandel

THE CONSULTING FIRM

Jennifer, Jean, and George had earned their graduate business degrees together and had paid their dues in middle management positions in various large corporations. Despite their different employers, the three had maintained their friendship and were now ready to realize their dream of starting a consulting practice. Their projections showed modest consulting revenue in the short term offset by expenditures for supplies, a secretary, a small library, personal computers, and similar necessities. Although each expected to clear no more than perhaps $25,000 for his or her efforts in their first year in business, they shared high hopes for future growth and success. Besides, it would be a great pleasure to run their own company and have sole charge of their respective fates.

THE SOFTWARE ENTREPRENEUR

At approximately the same time that Jennifer, Jean, and George were hatching their plans for entrepreneurial independence, Phil was cashing a seven-figure check for his share of the proceeds from the sale of the computer software firm he had founded seven years ago with four of his friends. Rather than rest on his laurels, however, Phil saw this as an opportunity to capitalize on a complex piece of software he had developed in college. Although Phil was convinced that there would be an extensive market for his software, there was much work to be done before it could be brought to market. The software had to be converted from a mainframe operating system to the various popular microcomputer systems. In addition, there was much marketing to be done prior to its release. Phil anticipated that he would probably spend over $300,000 on programmers and salespeople before the first dollar of royalties would appear. But he was prepared to make that investment himself, in anticipation of retaining all the eventual profit.

THE HOTEL VENTURE

Bruce and Erika were not nearly as interested in high technology. Directly following their graduation from business school, they were planning to construct and operate a resort hotel near a popular ski area. They had chosen as their location a beautiful parcel of land in Colorado owned by their third partner, Michael. Rich in ideas and enthusiasm, the three lacked funds. They were certain, however, that they could attract investors to their enterprise. The location, they were sure, would virtually sell itself.

THE PURPOSE OF THIS CHAPTER

Each of these three groups of entrepreneurs would soon be faced with what might well be the most important decision of the initial years of their businesses: which of the various legal business forms to choose for the operation of their enterprises. It is the purpose of this chapter to describe, compare, and contrast the most popular of these forms in the hope that the reader will then be able to make such choices intelligently and effectively. After discussing the various business forms, we will revisit our entrepreneurs and analyze their choices.

BUSINESS FORMS

Two of the most popular business forms could be described as the default forms because the law will deem a business to be operating under one of these forms unless it makes an affirmative choice otherwise. The first of these forms is the sole proprietorship. Unless he or she has actively chosen another form, the individual operating his or her own business is considered to be a sole proprietor. Two or more persons operating a business together are considered a partnership (or general partnership), unless they have elected otherwise. Both of these forms share the characteristic that for all intents and purposes they are not entities separate from their owners. Every act taken or obligation assumed as a sole proprietorship or partnership is an act taken or obligation assumed by the business owners as individuals.

Many of the rules applicable to the operation of partnerships are set forth in the Uniform Partnership Act, which has been adopted in one form or another by 49 states. That Act defines a partnership as "an association of two or more persons to carry on as co-owners a business for profit." Notice that the definition does not require that the individuals agree to be partners. Although most partnerships can point to an agreement between the partners (whether written or oral), the Act applies the rules of partnership to any group of two or more persons whose actions fulfill the definition. Thus, the U.S. Circuit Court of Appeals for the District of Columbia, in a rather extreme case, held, over the defendant's strenuous objections, that she was a partner in her husband's burglary "business" (for which she kept the books and upon whose proceeds she lived), even though she denied knowing what her husband was doing at nights. As a result of this status, she was held personally liable for damages to the wife of a burglary victim her husband had murdered during a botched theft.

In contrast, a corporation is a legal entity separate from the legal identities of its owners, the shareholders. In the words James Thurber used to describe a unicorn, the corporation "is a mythical beast," created by the state at the request of one or more business promoters upon the filing of a form and the payment of the requisite, modest fee. Thereupon, in the eyes of the law, the corporation becomes for most purposes a "person" with its own federal identification number! Of course, one cannot see, hear, or touch a corporation, so it must interact with the rest of the world through its agents, the corporation's officers and employees.

Corporations come in different varieties. The so-called professional corporation is available in most states for persons conducting professional practices, such as doctors, lawyers, architects, psychiatric social workers, and the like. A subchapter S corporation is a corporation that is the same as a regular business corporation in all respects other than taxation. These variations are discussed later.

A fourth common form of business organization is the limited partnership, which may best be described as a hybrid of the corporation and the general partnership. The limited partnership consists of one or more general partners—who manage the business much in the same way as do the partners in a general partnership—and one or more limited partners, who are essentially silent investors with no control over business operations. Like the general partnership, limited partnerships are governed in part by a statute, the Uniform Limited Partnership Act (or its successor, the Revised Uniform Limited Partnership Act), which has also been adopted in one form or another by 49 states.

The limited liability company (LLC), is now available to entrepreneurs in all 50 states. The LLC is a separate legal entity owned by "members" who may, but need not, appoint one or more "managers" (who may but need not be members) to operate the business. A few states require that there be more than one member, but the trend is toward allowing single-member LLCs. An LLC is formed by filing an application with the state government and paying the prescribed fee. The members then enter into an operating agreement setting forth their respective rights and obligations with respect to the business. Most states that have adopted the LLC have also authorized the limited liability partnership, which allows general partnerships to obtain limited liability for their partners by filing their intention to do so with the state. This form of business entity is normally used by professional associations that previously operated as general partnerships, such as law and accounting firms.

COMPARISON FACTORS

The usefulness of the five basic business forms could be compared on a virtually unlimited number of measures, but the most effective comparisons will likely result from employing the following eight:

1. *Complexity and cost of formation.* What steps must be taken before your business can exist in each of these forms?
2. *Barriers to operation across state lines.* What steps must be taken to move your business to other states? What additional cost may be involved?
3. *Recognition as a legal entity.* Who does the law recognize as the operative entity? Who owns the assets of the business? Who can sue and be sued?
4. *Continuity of life.* Does the legal entity outlive the owner? This may be especially important if the business wishes to attract investors or if the goal is an eventual sale of the business.
5. *Transferability of interest.* How does one go about selling or otherwise transferring one's ownership of the business?
6. *Control.* Who makes the decisions regarding the operation, financing, and eventual disposition of the business?
7. *Liability.* Who is responsible for the debts of the business? If the company cannot pay its creditors, must the owners satisfy these debts from their personal assets?
8. *Taxation.* How does the choice of business form determine the tax payable on the profits of the business and the income of its owners?

FORMATION OF SOLE PROPRIETORSHIPS

Reflecting its status as the default form for the individual entrepreneur, the sole proprietorship requires no affirmative act for its formation. One operates a sole proprietorship because one has not chosen to operate in any of the other forms. The only exception to this rule arises in certain states when the owner chooses to use a name other than his own as the name of his business. In such event, he may be required to file a so-called d/b/a certificate with the local authorities, stating that he is "doing business as" someone other than himself.

This allows creditors and those otherwise injured by the operation of the business to determine who is legally responsible.

FORMATION OF PARTNERSHIPS

Similarly, a general partnership requires no special act for its formation other than a d/b/a certificate if a name other than that of the partners will be used. If two or more people act in a way which fits the definition set forth in the Uniform Act, they will find themselves involved in a partnership. However, it is strongly recommended that prospective partners consciously enter an agreement (preferably in writing) setting forth their understandings on the many issues which will arise in such an arrangement. Principal among these are the investments each will make in the business, the allocation and distribution of profits (and losses), the method of decision making (i.e., majority or unanimous vote), any obligations to perform services for the business, the relative compensation of the partners, and so on. Regardless of the agreements that may exist among the partners, however, the partnership will be bound by the actions and agreements of each partner—as long as these actions are reasonably related to the partnership business, and even if they were not properly authorized by the other partners pursuant to the agreement. After all, third parties have no idea what the partners' internal agreement says and are in no way bound by it.

CORPORATIONS

In order to form a corporation, in contrast, one must pay the appropriate fee and must complete and file with the state a corporate charter (otherwise known as a Certificate of Incorporation, Articles of Incorporation, or similar name in the various states). The fee is payable both at the outset and annually thereafter (often approximately $200). A promoter may form a corporation under the laws of whichever state she wishes; she is not required to form the corporation under the laws of the state in which she intends to conduct most of her business. This partially explains the popularity of the Delaware corporation. Delaware spent most of the last century competing with other states for corporation filing fees by repeatedly amending its corporate law to make it increasingly favorable to management. By now, the Delaware corporation has taken on an aura of sophistication, so that many promoters form their companies in Delaware just to appear to know what they are doing! In addition, it is often less expensive under Delaware law to authorize large numbers of shares for future issuance than it would be in other states. Nevertheless, the statutory advantages of Delaware apply mostly to corporations with many stockholders (such as those which are publicly traded) and will rarely be significant to a small business such as those described at the beginning of this chapter. Also, formation in Delaware (or any state other than the site of the corporation's principal place of business) will subject the corporation to additional, unnecessary expense. It is thus usually advisable to incorporate in the company's home state.

The charter sets forth the corporation's name (which cannot be confusingly similar to the name of any other corporation operating in the state) as well as its principal address. The names of the initial directors and officers of the corporation are often listed. Most states also require a statement of corporate purpose. Years ago this purpose defined the permitted scope of the corporation's activities. A corporation which ventured beyond its purposes risked operating "ultra vires," resulting in liability of its directors and officers to its stockholders and creditors. Today virtually all states allow a corporation to define its purposes extremely broadly (e.g., "any activities which may be lawfully undertaken by a corporation in this state"), so that operation ultra vires is generally impossible. Still directors are occasionally plagued by lawsuits brought by stockholders asserting that the diversion of corporate profits to charitable or community activities runs afoul of the dominant corporate purpose, which is to generate profits for its stockholders. The debate over the responsibility of directors to so-called corporate "stakeholders" (employees, suppliers, customers, neighbors, and so forth) currently rages in many forms but is normally not a concern of the beginning entrepreneur.

Corporate charters also normally set forth the number and classes of equity securities that the corporation is authorized to issue. Here an analysis of a bit of jargon may be appropriate. The number of shares set forth in the charter is the number of shares authorized, that is, the number of shares that the directors may issue to stockholders at the directors' discretion. The number of shares issued is the number that the directors have in fact issued and is obviously either the same or smaller than the number authorized. In some cases, a corporation may have repurchased some of the shares previously issued by the directors. In that case, only the shares which remain in the hands of shareholders are outstanding (a number obviously either the same or lower than the number issued). Only the shares outstanding have voting rights, rights to receive dividends, and rights to receive distributions upon full or partial liquidation of the corporation. Normally, we would expect an entrepreneur to authorize the maximum number of shares allowable under the state's minimum incorporation fee (e.g., 200,000 shares for $200 in Massachusetts) and then issue only 10,000 or so, leaving the rest on the shelf for future financings, employee incentives, and so forth.

The charter also sets forth the par value of the authorized shares, another antiquated concept of interest mainly to accountants. The law requires only that the corporation not issue shares for less than the par value, but it can, and usually does, issue the shares for more. Thus, typical par values are $0.01 per share or even "no par value." Shares issued for less than par are watered stock, subjecting both the directors and holders of such stock to liability to other stockholders and creditors of the corporation.

Corporations also adopt bylaws, which are not filed with the state but are available for inspection by stockholders. These are usually fairly standard documents describing the internal governance of the corporation and setting forth such items as the officers' powers and notice periods for stockholders' meetings.

LIMITED PARTNERSHIPS

As you might expect, given the limited partnership's hybrid nature, the law requires both a written agreement among the various general and limited partners and a Certificate of Limited Partnership to be filed with the state, along with the appropriate initial and annual fees. The agreement sets forth the partners' understanding of the items discussed earlier regarding general partnerships. The certificate sets forth the name and address of the partnership, its purposes, and the names and addresses of its general partners. In states where the Revised Uniform Limited Partnership Act has been adopted, it is no longer necessary to reveal the names of the limited partners, just as the names of corporate stockholders do not appear on a corporation's incorporation documents.

LIMITED LIABILITY COMPANIES

The LLC is formed by filing a charter (e.g., a Certificate of Organization) with the state government and paying a fee (usually similar to that charged for the formation of a corporation). The charter normally sets forth the entity's name and address, its business purpose, and the names and addresses of its managers (or persons authorized to act for the entity vis-à-vis the state if no managers are appointed). The same broad description of the entity's business which is allowable for modern corporations is acceptable for LLCs. The members of the LLC are also required to enter into an operating agreement that sets forth their rights and obligations with regard to the business. These agreements are generally modeled after the agreements signed by the partners in a general or limited partnership.

OUT OF STATE OPERATION OF SOLE PROPRIETORSHIPS AND PARTNERSHIPS

Partly as a result of both the Commerce clause and Privileges and Immunities clause of the U.S. Constitution, states may not place limits or restrictions on the operations of out-of-state sole proprietors or general partnerships that are different from those placed on domestic businesses. Thus, a state cannot force registration of a general partnership simply because its principal office is located elsewhere, but it can require an out-of-state doctor to undergo the same licensing procedures it requires of its own residents.

OUT OF STATE OPERATION OF CORPORATIONS, LIMITED PARTNERSHIPS, AND LIMITED LIABILITY COMPANIES

Things are different, however, with corporations, limited partnerships, and LLCs. As creations of the individual states, they are not automatically entitled to recognition elsewhere. All states require (and routinely grant) qualification as a foreign corporation, limited partnership, or LLC to nondomestic entities doing business within their borders. This procedure normally requires the completion of a form very similar to a corporate charter, limited partnership certificate, or LLC charter, and the payment of an initial and annual fee similar in amount to the fees paid by domestic entities. This requirement, incidentally, is one reason not to form a corporation in Delaware if it will operate principally outside that state. Much litigation has occurred over what constitutes "doing business" within a state for the purpose of requiring qualification. Similar issues arise over the obligation to pay income tax, collect sales tax, or accept personal jurisdiction in the courts of a state. Generally these cases turn on the individualized facts of the particular situation, but courts generally look for offices or warehouses, company employees, widespread advertising, or negotiation and execution of contracts within the state.

Perhaps more interesting may be the penalty for failure to qualify. Most states will impose liability for back fees, taxes, interest, and penalties. More important, many states will bar a nonqualified foreign entity from access to its courts and, thus, from the ability to enforce obligations against its residents. In most of these cases, the entity can regain access to the courts merely by paying the state the back fees and penalties it owes, but in a few states access will then be granted only to enforce obligations incurred after qualification was achieved, leaving all prior obligations unenforceable.

RECOGNITION OF SOLE PROPRIETORSHIPS AS A LEGAL ENTITY

By now it probably goes without saying that the law does not recognize a sole proprietorship as a legal entity separate from its owner. If Phil, our computer entrepreneur, were to choose this form, he would own all the company's assets; he would be the plaintiff in any suits it brought, and he would be the defendant in any suits brought against it. There would be no difference between Phil, the individual, and Phil, the business.

RECOGNITION OF PARTNERSHIPS AS A LEGAL ENTITY

A general partnership raises more difficult issues. Although most states allow partnerships to bring suit, be sued, and own property in the partnership name, this does not mean that the partnership exists for most purposes separately from its partners. As will be seen, especially in the areas of liability and taxation, partnerships are very much collections of individuals, not separate entities.

Ownership of partnership property is a particularly problematic area. All partners own an interest in the partnership, which entitles them to distributions of profit, much like stock in a corporation. This interest is the separate property of each partner and is attachable by the individual creditors of a partner in the form of a "charging order." Each partner also owns the assets of the partnership jointly with his other partners. This form of ownership (similar to joint ownership of a family home by two spouses) is called tenancy in partnership. Each partner may use partnership assets only for the benefit of the partnership's business; such assets are exempt from attachment by the creditors of an individual partner, although not from the creditors of the partnership. Tenancy in partnership also implies that, in most cases of dissolution of a partnership, the ownership of partnership assets devolves to the remaining partners, to the exclusion of the partner who leaves in violation of the partnership agreement or dies. The former partner is left only with the right to a dissolution distribution in respect of her partnership interest.

RECOGNITION OF CORPORATIONS AND LIMITED LIABILITY COMPANIES AS LEGAL ENTITIES

The corporation and LLC are our first full-fledged separate legal entities. Ownership of business assets is vested solely in the corporation or LLC as a separate legal entity. The corporation or LLC itself is plaintiff or defendant in suits and is the legally contracting party in all its transactions. Stockholders and members own only their stock or membership interests and have no direct ownership rights in the business's assets.

RECOGNITION OF LIMITED PARTNERSHIPS AS A LEGAL ENTITY

The limited partnership, as a hybrid, is a little of both partnership and corporation. The general partners own the partnership's property as tenants in partnership operating in the same manner as partners in a general partnership. The limited partners, however, have only their partnership interests and no direct ownership of the partnership's property. This is logically consistent with their roles as silent investors. If they directly owned partnership property, they would have to be consulted with regard to its use.

CONTINUITY OF LIFE

The issue of continuity of life is one which should concern most entrepreneurs, because it can affect their ability to sell the business as a unit when it comes time to cash in on their efforts as founders and promoters. The survival of the business as a whole in the form of a separate entity must be distinguished from the survival of the business's individual assets and liabilities.

Sole Proprietorships

Although a sole proprietorship does not survive the death of its owner, its individual assets and liabilities do. In Phil's case, for example, to the extent that these assets consist of the computer program, filing cabinets, and the like, they would all be inherited by Phil's heirs, who could then choose to continue the business or liquidate the assets as they pleased. Should they decide to continue the business, they would then have the same choices of business form which confront any entrepreneur. However, if Phil's major asset were a government license, qualification as an approved government supplier, or a contract with a software publisher, the ability of the heirs to carry on the business might be entirely dependent upon the assignability of these items. If the publishing contract is not assignable, Phil's death may terminate the business's major asset. If the business had operated as a corporation, Phil's death would likely have been irrelevant (other than to him); the corporation, not Phil, would have been party to the contract.

Partnerships

Consistent with the general partnership's status as a collection of individuals, not an entity separate from its owners, a partnership is deemed dissolved upon the death, incapacity, bankruptcy, resignation, or expulsion of a partner. This is true even if a partner's resignation violates the express terms of the partnership agreement. Those assets of the partnership that may be assigned devolve to those partners who are entitled to ownership, pursuant to the rules of tenancy in partnership. These rules favor the remaining partners if the former partner has died, become incapacitated or bankrupt, been expelled, or resigned in violation of the partnership agreement. If the ex-partner resigned without violating the underlying agreement, she or he retains ownership rights under tenancy in partnership. Those who thus retain ownership may continue the business as a new partnership, corporation, or LLC with the same or new partners and investors or may liquidate the assets at their discretion. The sole right of any partner who has forfeited direct ownership rights is to be paid a dissolution distribution after the partnership's liabilities have been paid or provided for.

Corporations

Corporations, in contrast, normally enjoy perpetual life. Unless the charter contains a stated dissolution date (extremely rare), and as long as the corporation pays its annual fees to the state, it will go on until and unless it is voted out of existence by its stockholders. The death, incapacity, bankruptcy, resignation, or expulsion of any stockholder is entirely irrelevant to the corporation's existence. Such a stockholder's stock continues to be held by the stockholder, is inherited by his heirs, or is auctioned by creditors as the circumstances demand, with no direct effect on the corporation.

Limited Partnerships

As you may have guessed, the hybrid nature of the limited partnership dictates that the death, incapacity, bankruptcy, resignation, or expulsion of a limited partner will have no effect on the existence of the limited partnership. The limited partner's partnership interest is passed in the same way as that of a stockholder's. However, the death, incapacity, bankruptcy, resignation, or expulsion of a general partner does automatically dissolve the partnership in the same way as it would in the case of a general partnership. This automatic dissolution can be extremely inconvenient if the limited partnership is conducting a far-flung enterprise with many limited partners. Thus, in most cases the partners agree in advance in their limited partnership agreement that upon such a dissolution the limited partnership will continue under the management of a substitute general partner chosen by those general partners who remain. In such a case, the entity continues until it is voted out of existence by its partners, in accordance with their agreement, or until the arrival of a termination date specified in its certificate.

Limited Liability Companies

The laws of the several states generally impose dissolution on an LLC upon the occurrence of a list of events similar to those which result in the dissolution of a limited partnership. However, these laws usually allow the remaining members to vote to continue the LLC's existence notwithstanding an event of dissolution. Under such laws, the LLC may effectively have perpetual life in the same manner as corporations.

TRANSFERABILITY OF INTEREST

To a large extent, transferability of an owner's interest in the business is similar to the continuity of life issue.

Sole Proprietorships

A sole proprietor has no interest to transfer because he and the business are one and the same, and thus he must be content to transfer each of the assets of the business individually—an administrative nightmare at best and possibly impractical in the case of nonassignable contracts, licenses, and government approvals.

Partnerships

To discuss transferability in the context of a general partnership, one must keep in mind the difference between ownership of partnership assets as tenants in partnership and ownership of an individual's partnership interest. A partner has no right to transfer partnership assets except as may be authorized by vote in accordance with the partnership agreement and in furtherance of the partnership business. However, a partner may transfer her partnership interest, and it may be attached by individual creditors pursuant to a charging order. This transfer does not make the transferee a partner in the business, because partnerships can be created only by agreement of all parties. Rather, it sets up the rather awkward situation in which the original partner remains, but his or her economic interest is, at least temporarily, in the hands of another. In such cases, the Uniform Partnership Act gives the remaining partners the right to dissolve the partnership by expelling the transferor partner.

Corporations

No such complications attend the transfer of one's interest in a corporation. Stockholders simply sell or transfer their shares. Since stockholders (solely as stockholders) have no day-to-day involvement in the operation of the business, the transferee becomes a full-fledged stockholder upon the transfer. This means that if Bruce, Erika, and Michael decide to operate as a corporation, each risks waking up one day to find that he or she has a new "partner" if one of the three has sold his or her shares. To protect themselves against this eventuality, most closely-held corporations include restrictions on stock transfer in their charter, their bylaws, or in stockholder agreements. These restrictions set forth some variation of a right of first refusal either for the corporation or the other stockholders whenever a transfer is proposed. In addition, corporate stock, as well as most limited partnership interests and LLC membership interests, is a security under the federal and state securities laws, and because the securities of these entities will not initially be registered under any of these laws, their transfer is closely restricted.

Limited Partnerships

Just as with general partnerships, the partners of limited partnerships may transfer their partnership interests. The rules regarding the transfer of the interests of the general partners are similar to those governing general partnerships described earlier. Limited partners may usually transfer their interests (subject to securities laws restrictions) without fear of dissolution, but transferees normally do not become substituted limited partners without the consent of the general partners.

Limited Liability Companies

As previously mentioned, although a membership interest in an LLC may be freely transferable under applicable state law, most LLCs require the affirmative vote of at least a majority of the members or managers before a member's interest may be transferred. Furthermore, membership interests in an LLC will usually qualify as securities under relevant securities laws and will therefore be subject to the restrictions on transfer imposed by such laws.

CONTROL

Simply put, control in the context of a business entity means the power to make decisions regarding all aspects of its operations. But the implications of control extend to many levels. These include control of the equity or value of the business, control over distribution of profits, control over day-to-day and long-term policy making, and control over distribution of cash flow. Each of these is different from the others, and control over each can be allocated differently among the owners and other principals of the entity. This can be seen either as complexity or flexibility, depending upon one's perspective.

Sole Proprietorships

No such debate over allocation exists for the sole proprietorship. In that business form, control over all these factors belongs exclusively to the sole proprietor. Nothing could be simpler or more straightforward.

Partnerships

Things are not so simple in the context of general partnerships. It is essential to appreciate the difference between the partners' relationships with each other (internal relationships) and the partnership's relations with third parties (external relationships).

Internally, the partnership agreement governs the decision-making process and sets forth the agreed division of equity, profits, and cash flows. Decisions made in the ordinary course of business are normally made by a majority vote of the partners, whereas major decisions, such as changing the character of the partnership's business, may require a unanimous vote. Some partnerships may weight the voting in proportion to each partner's partnership interest, while others delegate much of the decision-making power to an executive committee or a managing partner. In the absence of an agreement, the Uniform Partnership Act prescribes a vote of the majority of partners for most issues and unanimity for certain major decisions.

External relationships are largely governed by the law of agency; that is, each partner is treated as an agent of the partnership and, derivatively, of the other partners. Any action that a partner appears to have authority to take will be binding upon the partnership and the other partners, regardless of whether such action has been internally authorized (see Exhibit 8.1).

Thus, if Jennifer purchases a subscription to the *Harvard Business Review* for the partnership, and such an action is perceived to be within the ordinary course of the partnership's business, that obligation can be enforced against the partnership, even if Jean and George had voted against it. Such would not be the case, however, if Jennifer had signed a purchase and sale agreement for an office building in the name of the partnership, because reasonable third parties would be expected to know that such a purchase was not in the ordinary course of business.

These rules extend to tort liability, as well. If Jean were wrongfully to induce a potential client to breach its consulting contract with a competitor, the partnership would be liable for interference with contractual relations, even if the other two partners were not aware of Jean's actions. Such might not be the case, however, if Jean decided to dynamite the competition's offices, because such an act could be judged to be outside the normal scope of her duties as a partner.

These obligations to third parties can even extend past the dissolution of the partnership if an individual partner has not given adequate notice that he or she is no longer associated with the others. Thus, a former partner can be held liable for legal fees incurred by the other former partners, if he has not notified the partnership's counsel about leaving the firm.

It should also be noted that agency law reaches into the internal relationships of partners. The law imposes upon partners the same obligations of fiduciary loyalty, noncompetition, and accountability as it does upon agents with respect to their principals.

Corporations

There can be much flexibility and complexity in the allocation of control in the partnership form, but not nearly so much as in the corporate form. Many

EXHIBIT 8.1   Principal and agent.

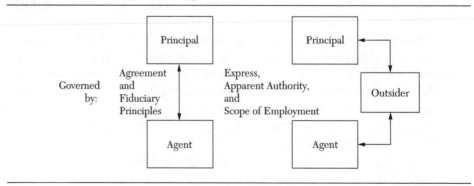

aspects of the corporate form have been designed specifically for the purpose of splitting off individual aspects of control and allocating them differently.

Stockholders

At its simplest, a corporation is controlled by its stockholders. Yet, except in those states which have specific (but rarely used) close corporation statutes governing corporations with very few stakeholders, the decision-making function of stockholders is exercised only derivatively. Under most corporate statutes, a stockholder vote is required only with respect to four basic types of decisions: an amendment to the charter, a sale of the company, a dissolution of the company, and an election of the board of directors.

Charter amendments may sound significant, until one remembers what information is normally included in the charter. A name change, a change in purpose (given the broad purpose of clauses now generally employed), and an increase in authorized shares (given the large amounts of stock normally left on the shelf) are neither frequent nor usually significant decisions. Certainly, a sale of the company is significant, but it normally can occur only after the recommendation of the board and will happen only once, if at all. The same can be said of the decision to dissolve. It is the board of directors that makes all the long-term policy decisions for the corporation. Thus, the right to elect the board is significant but indirectly so. Day-to-day operation of the corporation's business is accomplished by its officers, who are normally elected by the board, not the stockholders.

Even given the relative unimportance of voting power for stockholders, the corporation provides many opportunities to differentiate voting power from other aspects of control and allocate it differently. Assume Bruce and Erika (our hotel developers) were willing to give Michael a larger piece of the equity of their operation to reflect his contribution of the land but wished to divide their voting rights equally. They could authorize a class of nonvoting common stock and issue, for example, 1,000 shares of voting stock to each of themselves and an additional 1,000 shares of nonvoting stock to Michael. As a result, each would have one-third of the voting control, but Michael would have one-half of the equity interest.

Alternatively, Michael could be issued a block of preferred stock representing the value of the land. This would guarantee him a fair return on his investment before any dividends could be declared to the three of them as holders of the common stock. As a holder of preferred stock, Michael would also receive a liquidation preference upon dissolution or sale of the business, in the amount of the value of his investment, but any additional value created by the efforts of the group would be reflected in the increasing value of the common shares.

The previous information illustrates how one can separate and allocate decision-making control differently from that of the equity in the business, as well as from the distribution of profits. Distribution of cash flow can, of course, be accomplished totally separately from the ownership of securities, through salaries based upon the relative efforts of the parties, rent payments for assets leased to the entity by the principals, or interest on loans to the corporation.

Stockholders exercise what voting power they have at meetings of the stockholders, held at least annually but more frequently if necessary. Each stockholder of record, on a future date chosen by the party calling the meeting, is given a notice of the meeting containing the date, time, and purpose of the meeting. Such notice must be sent at least 7 to 10 days prior to the date of the meeting depending upon the individual state's corporate law, although the Securities and Exchange Commission requires 30 days' notice for publicly traded corporations. No action may be taken at a meeting unless a majority of voting shares is represented (known as a quorum). This results in the aggressive solicitation of proxy votes in most corporations with widespread stock ownership. Unless otherwise provided (as for a sale or dissolution of the company, for which most states require a two-thirds vote of all shares), a resolution is carried by a majority vote of those shares represented at the meeting.

The preceding rules require the conclusion that the board of directors will be elected by the holders of a majority of the voting shares. Thus, in the earlier scenario, even though Bruce and Erika may have given Michael one-third of the voting shares of common stock, as long as they continue to vote together, Bruce and Erika will be able to elect the entire board. To prevent this result, prior to investing Michael could insist upon a cumulative voting provision in the charter (under those states' corporate laws that allow it). Under this system, each share of stock is entitled to a number of votes equal to the number of directors to be elected. By using all their votes to support a single candidate, individuals with a significant minority interest can guarantee themselves representation on the board.

More directly (and in states which do not allow cumulative voting), Michael could insist upon two different classes of voting stock, differing only in voting rights. Bruce and Erika would each own 1,000 shares of class A stock and elect two directors. Michael, the sole owner of the 1,000 outstanding shares of class B stock, would elect a third director. Of course, the board also acts by majority, so Bruce and Erika's directors could dominate board decisions in any case, but at least Michael would have access to the deliberations.

In the absence of a meeting, stockholders may vote by unanimous written consent, where each stockholder indicates his approval of a written resolution by signing it. This eliminates the need for a meeting and is very effective in corporations with only a few stockholders (such as our hotel operation). Unlike the rules governing stockholders' meetings, however, in most states unanimity is required to adopt resolutions by written consent. This apparently reflects the belief that a minority stockholder is owed an opportunity to sway the majority with his arguments. A few states, notably Delaware, permit written consents of a majority, apparently reacting to the dominance of proxy voting at most meetings of large corporations, where the most eloquent of minority arguments would fall upon deaf ears (and proxy cards).

Directors

At the directors' level, absent a special provision in the corporation's charter, all decisions are made by majority vote. Typically, directors concentrate on long-term and significant decisions, leaving day-to-day management to the officers of the corporation. Decisions are made at regularly scheduled directors' meetings or at a special meeting if there is need to respond to a specific situation. Under most corporate laws, no notice need be given for regular meetings, and only very short notice need be given for special meetings (24 to 48 hours). The notice must be sent to all directors and must contain the date, time, and place of the meeting but, unlike stockholders' notices, need not contain the purpose of the meeting. It is assumed that directors are much more involved in the business of the corporation and do not need to be warned about possible agenda items or given long notice periods.

At the meeting itself, no business can be conducted in the absence of a quorum, which, unless increased by a charter or bylaw provision, is a majority of the directors then in office. Reflecting recent advances in technology, many corporate statutes allow directors to attend meetings by conference call or teleconference as long as all directors are able to hear and speak to each other at all times during the meeting. Individual telephone calls to each director will not suffice. Unlike stockholders, directors cannot vote by proxy, because each director owes to the corporation his or her individual judgment on items coming before the board. The board of directors can also act by written consent, but, even in Delaware, such consent must be unanimous, in recognition that the board is fundamentally a deliberative body.

Boards of directors, especially in publicly held corporations with larger boards, frequently delegate some of their powers to executive committees, or other committees formed for defined purposes. However, most corporate statutes prohibit boards from delegating certain fundamental powers, such as the declaration of dividends, the recommendation of charter amendments, or sale of the company. The executive committee can, however, be a powerful organizational tool to streamline board operations and increase efficiency and responsiveness.

Although directors are not agents of the corporation—in that they cannot bind the corporation to contract or tort liability through their individual actions—they are subject to many of the obligations of agents discussed in the context of partnerships, such as fiduciary loyalty. Directors are bound by the so-called corporate opportunity doctrine, which prohibits them from taking personal advantage of any business opportunity that may come their way, if the opportunity would reasonably be expected to interest the corporation. In such an event, the director must disclose the opportunity to the corporation, which normally must consider it and vote not to take advantage before the director may act on her or his own behalf.

Unlike stockholders, who under most circumstances can vote their shares totally in their own self-interest, directors must use their best business judgment and act in the corporation's best interest when making decisions for the corporation. At the very least, the director must keep informed regarding the corporation's operations, although he or she may in most circumstances rely on the input of experts hired by the corporation, such as its attorneys and accountants. Thus, when the widow of a corporation's founder accepted a seat on the board as a symbolic gesture of respect to her late husband, she found herself liable to minority stockholders for the misbehavior of her fellow board members. Nonparticipation in the misdeeds was not enough to exempt her from liability; she had failed to keep herself informed and exercise independent judgment.

Directors may also find themselves sued personally by minority stockholders or creditors of the corporation for declaration of dividends or other distributions to stockholders that render the corporation insolvent or for other decisions of the board that have injured the corporation. Notwithstanding such lawsuits, however, directors are not guarantors of the success of the corporation's endeavors; they are required only to have used their best independent "business judgment" in making their decisions. When individual directors cannot be totally disinterested (such as the corporate opportunity issue or when the corporation is being asked to contract with a director or an entity in which a director has an interest), the interested director is required to disclose her or his interest and is disqualified from voting. In many states, the director's presence will not even count for the maintenance of a quorum.

Apart from the question of the interested director, much of the modern debate on the role of the corporate director has focused around which constituencies a director may take into account when exercising his or her best business judgment. The traditional view has been that the director's only concern is to maximize return on the investment of the stockholders. More recently, especially in the context of hostile takeovers, directors have been allowed to take into account the effect of their decisions on other constituencies, such as suppliers, neighboring communities, customers, and employees.

In an early case on this subject, the board of directors of the corporation which owned Wrigley Field and the Chicago Cubs baseball team was judged to have appropriately considered the effect on its neighbors and on the game of baseball in voting to forgo the extra revenue that it would probably have earned if it had installed lights for night games.

When the stockholders believe the directors have not been exercising their best independent business judgment in a particular instance, the normal procedure is to make a demand on the directors to correct the decision either by reversing it or by reimbursing the corporation from their personal funds. Should the board refuse (as it most likely will), the stockholders then bring a derivative suit against the board on behalf of the corporation. They are, in effect, taking over the board's authority to decide whether such a suit should be brought in the corporation's name. The board's vote not to institute the suit is not likely to be upheld on the basis of the business judgment rule, since the board members are clearly interested in the outcome of the vote. As a result, the well-informed board will delegate the power to make such a decision to an independent litigation committee, usually composed of directors who were not involved in the original decision. The decision of such a committee is much more likely to be upheld in a court of law, although the decision is not immune from judicial review.

A more detailed discussion on the board of directors is contained in Chapter 15, "The Board of Directors."

Officers

The third level of decision making in the normal corporation is that of the officers, who take on the day-to-day operational responsibilities. Officers are elected by the board and consist, at a minimum, of a president, a treasurer, and a secretary or clerk (keeper of the corporate records). Many corporations elect additional officers such as vice presidents, assistant treasurers, CEOs, and the like.

Thus, the decision-making control of the corporation is exercised on three very different levels. Where each decision properly belongs may not be entirely obvious in every situation. The decision to go into a new line of business would normally be considered a board decision. Yet if by some chance the decision requires an amendment of the corporate charter, a vote of stockholders may be necessary. On the contrary, if the decision is merely to add a twelfth variety of relish to the corporation's already varied line of condiments, the decision may be properly left to a vice president of marketing.

Often persons who have been exposed to the preceding analysis of the corporate-control function conclude that the corporate form is too complex for any but the largest and most complicated publicly held companies. This is a gross overreaction. For example, if Phil, our software entrepreneur, should decide that the corporate form is appropriate for his business, it is very likely that he will be the corporation's 100% stockholder. As such, he will elect himself the sole director and his board will then elect him as the president, treasurer, and secretary of the corporation. Joint meetings of the stockholders and directors of the corporation may be held in the shower adjacent to Phil's bathroom on alternate Monday mornings.

Limited Partnerships

As you might expect, the allocation of control in a limited partnership reflects its origin as a hybrid of the general partnership and the corporation. Simply put, virtually all management authority is vested in the general partners. Like outside stockholders in a corporation, the limited partners normally have little or no authority. Third parties cannot rely on any apparent authority of a limited partner because that partner's name will not appear, as a general partner's name may, on the limited partnership's certificate on the public record.

General partners exercise their authority in the same way as they do in a general partnership. Voting control is allocated internally as set forth in the partnership agreement, but each general partner has the apparent authority to bind the partnership to unauthorized contracts and torts to the same extent as the partners in a general partnership.

Limited partners will normally have voting power over a very small list of fundamental business events, such as amending the partnership agreement and certificate, admitting new general partners, changing the basic business purposes of the partnership, or dissolving the partnership. These are similar to the decisions that must be put to a stockholders' vote in a corporation. The Revised Uniform Limited Partnership Act, now accepted by most states, has widened the range of decisions in which a limited partner may participate without losing his or her status as a limited partner. However, this range is still determined by the language of the agreement and certificate for each individual partnership.

Limited Liability Companies

An LLC which chooses not to appoint managers is operated much like a general partnership. The operating agreement sets forth the percentages of membership interests required to authorize various types of actions on the LLC's behalf, with the percentage normally varying according to the importance of the act. Although the LLC is a relatively new phenomenon, courts can be expected to deem members (in the absence of managers) to have apparent authority to bind the entity to contracts (regardless of whether they have been approved internally) and to expose the entity to tort liability for acts occurring within the scope of the entity's business.

An LLC that appoints managers is operated much like a limited partnership. The managers make most of the decisions on behalf of the entity, as do the general partners of a limited partnership. The members are treated much like limited partners and have voting rights only in rare circumstances involving very significant events. It can be expected that apparent authority to act for the entity will be reserved by the courts to the managers, as only their names will appear on the Certificate of Organization.

LIABILITY

Possibly the factor that most concerns the entrepreneur is personal liability. If the company encounters catastrophic tort liability, finds itself in breach of a significant contract, or just plain can't pay its bills, must the owner reach into her or his own personal assets to pay the remaining liability after the company's assets have been exhausted? If so, potential entrepreneurs may well believe that the risk of losing everything is not worth the possibility of success, and their innovative potential will be diminished or lost to society. Most entrepreneurs are willing to take significant risk, however, if the amount of that risk can be limited to the amount they have chosen to invest in the venture.

Sole Proprietorships

With the sole proprietorship, the owner has essentially traded off limitation of risk in favor of simplicity of operation. Since there is no difference between the entity and its owner, all the liabilities and obligations of the business are also liabilities and obligations of its owner. Thus, all the owner's personal assets are at risk. Failure of the business may well mean personal bankruptcy for the owner.

Partnerships

The result may be even worse within a general partnership. There, each owner is liable not only for personal mistakes but also for those of his or her partners. Each partner is jointly and severally liable for the debts of the partnership remaining after its assets have been exhausted. This means that a creditor may choose to sue any individual partner for 100% of any liability. The partner may have a right to sue the other partners for their share of the debt, as set forth in the partnership agreement, but that is of no concern to a third party. If the other partners are bankrupt or have fled the jurisdiction, the targeted partner may end up holding the entire bag.

If our three consultants operate as a partnership, Jennifer is 100% personally liable not only for any contracts she may enter into but also for any contracts entered into by either Jean or George. What's more, she is liable for those contracts, even if they were entered into in violation of the partnership agreement, because, as was demonstrated earlier, each partner has the apparent authority to bind the partnership to contracts in the ordinary course of the partnership's business, regardless of the partners' internal agreement. Worse, Jennifer is also 100% individually liable for any torts committed by either of her partners as long as they were committed within the scope of the partnership's business. The only good news in all this is that neither the partnership nor Jennifer is liable for any debts or obligations of Jean or George incurred in their personal affairs. If George has incurred heavy gambling debts in Las Vegas, his creditors can affect the partnership only by obtaining a charging order against George's partnership interest.

Corporations

Thus, we have the historical reason for the invention of the corporation. Unlike the sole proprietorship and partnership, the corporation is recognized as a legal entity separate from its owners. Its owners are thus not personally liable for its debts; they are granted limited liability. If the corporation's debts exhaust its assets, the stockholders have lost their investment, but they are not responsible for any further amounts. In practice, this may not be as attractive as it sounds, because sophisticated creditors, such as the corporation's bank, will likely demand personal guarantees from major stockholders.

But the stockholders will normally escape personal liability for trade debt and, most important, for torts.

This major benefit of incorporation does not come without some cost. Creditors may, on occasion, be able to "pierce the corporate veil" and assert personal liability against stockholders, using any one of three major arguments. First, to claim limited liability behind the corporate shield, stockholders must have adequately capitalized the corporation at or near its inception. There is no magic formula with which to calculate the amount necessary to achieve adequate capitalization, but the stockholders normally will be expected to invest enough money or property and obtain enough liability insurance to offset the kinds and amounts of liabilities normally encountered by a business in their industry. Thus, the owner of a fleet of taxicabs did not escape liability by canceling his liability insurance and forming a separate corporation for each cab. The court deemed each such corporation inadequately capitalized and, in a novel decision, pierced the corporate veil laterally by combining all the corporations into one for purposes of liability.

It is necessary to capitalize only for those liabilities normally encountered by corporations in the industry. The word *normally* is key because the corporation obviously need not have resources adequate to handle any circumstance no matter how unforeseeable. Also, adequate capitalization is necessary only at the outset. A corporation does not expose its stockholders to personal liability by incurring substantial losses and ultimately dissipating its initial capitalization.

A second argument used by creditors to reach stockholders for personal liability is failure to respect the corporate form. This may occur in many ways. The stockholders may fail to indicate that they are doing business in the corporate form by leaving the words "Inc." or "Corp." off their business cards and stationery, thus giving the impression that they are operating as a partnership. They may mingle the corporate assets in personal bank accounts or routinely use corporate assets for personal business. They may fail to respect corporate niceties such as holding annual meetings and filing the annual reports required by the state. After all, if the stockholders don't take the corporate form seriously, why should their creditors? Creditors are entitled to adequate notice that they may not rely on the personal assets of the stockholders. Even Phil, the software entrepreneur imagined earlier holding stockholder's and director's meetings in his shower, would be well advised to record the minutes in a corporate record book.

A third argument arises from a common mistake made by entrepreneurs. Fearful of the expense involved in forming a corporation, they wait until they are sure that the business will get off the ground before they spring for the attorneys' and filing fees. In the meantime, they may enter into contracts on behalf of the corporation and perhaps even commit a tort or two. Once the corporation is formed, they may even remember to have it expressly accept all liabilities incurred by the promoters on its behalf. Under simple agency law, however, one cannot act as an agent of a nonexistent principal. And a later assignment of one's liabilities to a newly formed corporation does not act to release the original obligor without the consent of the obligee. The best advice here is to form the corporation before incurring any liability on its behalf. Most entrepreneurs are surprised at how little it actually costs to get started.

Limited Partnerships

In keeping with its hybrid nature, a limited partnership borrows some of its aspects from the corporation and some from the general partnership. In summary, each general partner has unlimited joint and several liability for the debts and obligations of the limited partnership after exhaustion of the partnership's assets. In this respect, the rules are identical to those governing the partners in a general partnership. Limited partners are treated as stockholders in a corporation. They have risked their investment, but their personal assets are exempt from the creditors of the partnership.

As you might expect, however, things aren't quite as simple as they may initially appear. In limited partnerships, it is rather common for limited partners to make their investments in the form of a cash down payment and a promissory note for the rest, partly for reasons of cash flow and partly for purposes of tax planning. This arrangement is much less common in corporations because many corporate statutes do not permit it and because the tax advantages associated with this arrangement are generally not available in the corporate form. Should the limited partnership's business fail, limited partners will be expected, despite limited liability, to honor their commitments to make future contributions to capital.

In addition, it is fundamental to the status of limited partners that they have acquired limited liability in exchange for foregoing virtually all management authority over the business. The corollary to that rule is that a limited partner who excessively involves her- or himself in management may forfeit limited liability and be treated, for the purposes of creditors, as a general partner, with unlimited personal liability. Mitigating this somewhat harsh rule, the Revised Uniform Limited Partnership Act increased the categories of activities in which a limited partner may participate without crossing the line. Furthermore, and perhaps more fundamentally, in states that have adopted the Revised Act, the transgressing limited partner is now only personally liable to those creditors who were aware of the limited partner's activities and detrimentally relied upon his or her apparent status as a general partner.

Limited Liability Companies

One of the major benefits of employing the LLC form is that it shields all members and managers from personal liability for the debts of the business. However, even though the LLC is relatively new on the legal scene, courts can be expected to apply most of the same doctrines they use in piercing the corporate veil to pierce the veil of the LLC as well. Furthermore, it can be expected that the managers of an LLC will be held to the same fiduciary standards as corporate directors and general partners of limited partnerships, resulting in their potential personal liability to the members.

TAXATION

Entrepreneurs make a remarkable number of significant business decisions without first taking into account the tax consequences. Tax consequences should almost never be allowed to force an entrepreneur to take actions he or she otherwise would not have considered. But often tax considerations lead one to do what one wants in a different manner and to reap substantial savings as a consequence. Such is often the case in the organization of a business. The following discussion will be confined to the federal income tax, the tax with the largest and most direct effect upon organizational issues. Each entrepreneur would be well advised to consult a tax adviser regarding this tax as well as state income, estate, payroll, and other taxes to find out how they might impact a specific business.

Sole Proprietorships

Not surprisingly given the factors already discussed, a sole proprietorship is not a separate taxable entity for federal income tax purposes. The taxable income and deductible expenses of the business are set forth on Schedule C of the entrepreneur's Form 1040 and the net profit (loss) is carried back to page 1, where it is added to (or subtracted from) all the taxpayer's other income. The net effect of this is that the sole proprietor will pay tax on the income from this business at his highest marginal rate, possibly as high as 39.1% (in 2001), depending upon the amount of income received from this and other sources (see Exhibit 8.2).

In Phil's case, for example, if his software business netted $100,000 in 2001, that amount would be added to the substantial interest and dividend income from his other investments, so that he would likely owe the IRS $39,100 on this income. If Phil's business were run as a separate taxable corporation, the income generated from it would be taxed at the lowest levels of the tax-rate structure, because this corporate income would not be added to any other income. The first $50,000 of income would be taxed at only 15% and the next $25,000 at only 25% (see Exhibit 8.3).

This argument is turned on its head, however, if a business anticipates losses in the short term. Using Phil again as an example, if his business operated at a $100,000 loss and as a separate taxable entity, the business would pay no tax in its first year and would be able to net its early losses only against profits in future years and only if it ever realized such profits. At best, the value of this tax benefit is reduced by the time value of money: At worst, the loss may never yield a tax benefit if the business never does more than break

EXHIBIT 8.2   Individual federal income tax rates.

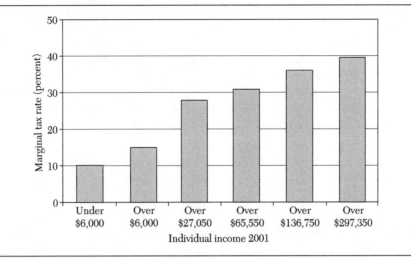

even. If Phil operated the business as a sole proprietorship, by contrast, the loss calculated on his Schedule C would be netted against the dividend and interest income generated by his investments, thus effectively rendering $100,000 of that income tax free. One can strongly argue, therefore, that the form in which one should operate one's business is dictated in part by the likelihood of its short-term success and the presence or absence of other income flowing to its owner.

EXHIBIT 8.3   Corporate federal income tax rates.

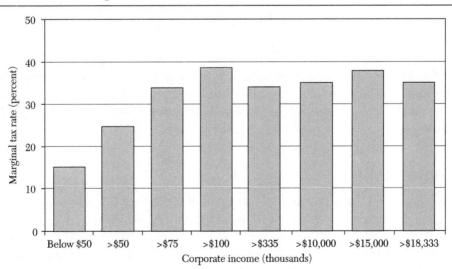

Partnerships

Partnerships are also not separate taxable entities for the purposes of the federal income tax, although, in most cases, they are required to file informational tax returns with the IRS. Any profits generated by a partnership appear on the federal income tax returns of the partners, generally in proportions indicated by the underlying partnership agreement. Thus, as with sole proprietorships, this profit is taxed at the individual partner's highest marginal tax rate, and the lower rates for the initial income of a separate taxable entity are forgone. In addition, each partner is taxed upon his or her proportion of the income of the partnership regardless of whether that income was actually distributed.

As an example, if Bruce and Erika, our hotel magnates, were to take $50,000 of a year's profits to add a deck to one of their properties, this expenditure would not lower the business's profits by that amount. As a capital expense it may be deducted over time only in the form of depreciation. Thus, assuming they were equal partners, even if Michael had objected to this expenditure, each of the three, including Michael, would be forced to pay a tax on $16,667 (minus that year's depreciation) despite having received no funds with which to make such a payment. The result would be the same in a sole proprietorship, but this obligation is considered less of a problem since it can be expected that the owner would manage cash flow in a way which would minimize this negative effect upon her- or himself.

As with a sole proprietorship, this negative result becomes a positive one if the partnership is losing money. The losses appear on the partners' individual tax returns in the proportions set forth in the partnership agreement and render an equal amount of otherwise taxable income tax free. In addition, not all losses suffered by businesses result from the dreaded negative cash flow. As illustrated earlier in the case of the deck, the next year the hotel business might well break even or show a small profit on a cash-flow basis, but the depreciation generated by the earlier addition of the deck might well result in a loss for tax purposes. Thus, with enough depreciation a partner might have the double benefit of a tax sheltering loss on his tax return and ownership of a growing, profitable business. This is especially true regarding real estate, such as the hotel itself. While generating a substantial depreciation loss each year, the value of the building may well be increasing, yielding the partners a current tax-sheltering loss while generating a long-term capital gain for a few years hence.

Corporations

Corporations are treated as separate entities for federal income tax purposes, consistent with their treatment for most other purposes. They have their own set of progressive tax rates, moving from 15% for the first $50,000 of income, through 25% for the next $25,000, to 34% and 35% for amounts above that. There are also 5% and 3% additional taxes at higher levels of income to compensate for the lower rates in the lower brackets. Certain "professional service corporations" have only a flat 35% rate at all levels of income. Also, losses currently generated by a corporation may be carried back as many as 2 years to generate a tax refund or carried forward as many as 20 years to shelter future income.

Although corporate rates may be attractive at lower levels of income, the common fear of using the corporate form is the potential for double taxation. Simply put, the corporation pays tax upon its profits and then distributes the remaining profit to its stockholders as nondeductible dividends. The stockholders then pay tax on the receipt of the dividends, thus amounting to two taxes on the same money. In 2001, for a corporation in the 34% bracket with stockholders in the 27.5% bracket, the net effect is a combined tax rate of 52.15%. Yet double taxation is rarely a concern for the small business. Such businesses generally manage compensation to their employees, who are usually their shareholders, in such a way that there is rarely much, if any, corporate profit remaining at the end of the year. Since compensation (as opposed to dividends) is deductible, the only level of taxation incurred by such businesses is at the stockholder level. Other opportunities for legitimate deductible payments to stockholders that have the effect of eliminating corporate profit include rental payments on assets leased by a stockholder to the corporation and interest on that portion of a stockholder's investment made in the form of debt.

Thus, the existence of the separate corporate entity with its own set of tax rates presents more of an opportunity for tax planning than a threat of double taxation. If the corporation intends to distribute all of its excess cash to its owners, it should manage compensation and other payments so as to show little profit and incur taxation only on the stockholder level. If the corporation intends to retain some of its earnings in the form of capital acquisitions (thus resulting in an unavoidable profit for tax purposes), it can take advantage of the lower corporate rates without subjecting its stockholders to taxation at their level. Contrast this to a partnership where the partners would be required to pay tax at their highest marginal rates on profits that they never received.

There are limits to the usefulness of these strategies. To begin with, one cannot pay salaries and bonuses to nonemployee stockholders who are not performing services for the corporation. Dividends may be the only way to give such shareholders a return on their investment. In addition, the Internal Revenue Service will not allow deductions for what it considers to be unreasonable compensation (as measured by compensation paid to comparable employees in the same industry). Thus, a highly profitable corporation might find some of its excessive salaries to employee-stockholders recharacterized as nondeductible dividends. Lastly, even profits retained at the corporate level will eventually be indirectly taxed at the stockholder level as increased capital gain when the stockholders sell their shares.

For most startup businesses, however, this corporate tax planning strategy will be useful, at least in the short term. In addition, entrepreneurs will find certain employee benefits are better offered in the corporate form because they are deductible to employers but excluded from income only for employees. Since a sole proprietor or partner is not considered an employee, the value of benefits such as group medical insurance, group life insurance, and disability insurance policies would be taxable income to them but tax free to the officers of a corporation.

Professional Corporations

There are two common variations of the corporate form. The first of these is the professional corporation. Taxation played a major part in its invention. Originally, limitations on the amounts of money that could be deducted as a contribution to a qualified retirement plan varied greatly depending upon whether the business maintaining the plan was a corporation, a partnership, or a sole proprietorship. The rules greatly favored the corporation. Partnerships and sole proprietorships were required to adopt Keogh plans with their substantially lower limits on deductibility. However, doctors, lawyers, architects, and other professionals, who often could afford large contributions to retirement plans, were not allowed to incorporate under applicable state laws. The states were offended by the notion that such professionals could be granted limited liability for the harms caused by their businesses.

Eventually, a compromise was struck and the "professional corporation" was formed. Using that form, professionals could incorporate their businesses, thus qualifying for the higher retirement plan deductions but giving up any claim to limited liability. As time went by, however, the Internal Revenue Code was amended to eliminate most of the differences between the deductions available to Keogh plans and those available to corporate pension and profit-sharing plans. Today, professional corporations are subject to virtually all the same rules as other corporations, with the exception that most are classified as professional service corporations and therefore taxed at a flat 35% rate on undistributed profit.

As the tax incentive for forming professional corporations has decreased, many states, perhaps with an eye toward maintaining the flow of fees from these corporations, have greatly liberalized the availability of limited liability for these corporations. Today in many states professional corporations now afford their stockholders protection from normal trade credit as well as tort liability arising from the actions of their employees or other stockholders. Of course, even under the normal business corporation form, a stockholder is personally liable for torts arising from his or her own actions.

Subchapter S Corporations

The second common variation is the subchapter S corporation, named for the sections of the Internal Revenue Code that govern it. Although indistinguishable from the normal (or subchapter C) corporation in all other ways, including limited liability for its stockholders, the subchapter S corporation has affirmatively elected to be taxed similarly to a partnership. Thus, like the partnership, it is not a separate taxable entity and files only an informational return. Profits appear on the tax returns of its stockholders in proportion to shares of stock owned, regardless of whether those profits were distributed to the stockholders or retained for operations. Losses appear on the returns of the stockholders and may potentially be used to shelter other income.

Although the subchapter S corporation is often referred to as a small business corporation, the size of the business has no bearing on whether this election is available. Any corporation that meets the following tests may, but need not, elect to be taxed as a subchapter S corporation:

1. It must have 75 or fewer stockholders.
2. It may have only one class of stock (although variations in voting rights are acceptable).
3. All stockholders must be individuals (or certain kinds of trusts).
4. No stockholder may be a nonresident alien.
5. With certain exceptions, it may not own or be owned by another corporation.

The subchapter S corporation is particularly suited to resolving problems presented by certain discrete situations. For example, if a corporation is concerned that its profits are likely to be too high to eliminate double taxation through compensation to its stockholders, the subchapter S election eliminates the worry over unreasonable compensation. Since there is no tax at the corporate level, it is not necessary to establish the right to a compensation deduction. Similarly, if a corporation has nonemployee stockholders who insist upon current distributions of profit, the subchapter S election would allow declaration of dividends without the worry of double taxation. This would undoubtedly be attractive to most publicly traded corporations were it not for the 75-stockholder limitation.

Many entrepreneurs have turned to the subchapter S election to eliminate the two layers of tax otherwise payable upon sale or dissolution of a corporation. The corporate tax otherwise payable upon the gain realized on the sale of corporate assets is eliminated by the use of the subchapter S election as long as the election has been in effect for 10 years or, if less, since the corporation's inception. Finally, many entrepreneurs elect subchapter S status for their corporations if they expect to show losses in the short term. These losses can then be passed through to their individual tax returns to act as a shelter for other income. When the corporation begins to show a profit, the election can be reversed.

Limited Partnerships

The tax treatment of limited partnerships is much the same as general partnerships. The profits and losses of the business are passed through to the partners in the proportions set forth in the partnership agreement. It must be emphasized that these profits and losses are passed through to all partners, including limited partners, even though one could argue that those profits and losses are derived entirely from the efforts of the general partners. It is this aspect of the limited partnership which made it the form of choice for tax-sheltered investments. The loss incurred by the business (much of which was created on paper through depreciation and the like) could be passed through to the limited partners, who typically had a considerable amount of other investment and compensation income to be sheltered.

Although the tax treatments of limited partnerships and subchapter S corporations are similar, there are some differences that drove the operators of tax shelters to use partnerships over the corporate form even at the risk of some unlimited liability. For one, although profits and losses must be allocated according to stock ownership in the subchapter S corporation, they are allocated by agreement in the limited partnership. Thus, in order to give the investors the high proportion of losses they demand, promoters did not necessarily have to give them an identically high proportion of the equity. The IRS will attack economically unrealistic allocations, but reasonable allocations will be respected. In addition, whereas the amount of loss the investor can use to shelter other income is limited to the tax basis in both types of entities, the tax basis in subchapter S stock is essentially limited to direct investment in the corporation, while in a limited partnership it is augmented by certain types of debt incurred by the entity itself.

Both types of entities are afflicted by the operation of the passive loss rules, added by the Tax Reform Act of 1986 in an attempt to eliminate the tax shelter. Thus, unless one materially participates in the operations of the entity (virtually impossible, by definition, for a limited partner), losses generated by those operations can normally be applied only against so-called passive income and not against active (salaries and bonuses) or portfolio (interest and dividend) income. Furthermore, owners of most tax pass-through real estate ventures are treated as subject to the passive loss rules, regardless of material participation.

Limited Liability Companies

LLCs are taxed in a manner substantially identical to limited partnerships. This combination of limited liability for all members (without the need to construct the unwieldy, double-entity, limited partnership with a corporate general partner) and a pass-through of all tax effects to the members' personal returns, makes the LLC the ideal vehicle for whatever tax shelter activity remains after the imposition of the passive-activity rules.

Technically, under recently adopted "check the box" regulations, LLCs, limited partnerships, and all other unincorporated business entities may choose to be taxed either as partnerships or as taxable corporations. Recognizing that the vast majority of these entities are formed to take advantage of the opportunity to have taxable income or loss pass through to the owners, these regulations provide that these entities will be taxed as partnerships unless the entity affirmatively chooses to be taxed as a corporation. Most corporations have already achieved that level of comfort through the availability of the subchapter S election.

Although the LLC would seem to have the advantage of affording tax pass-through treatment without the limitations of the subchapter S corporation rules, there are some disadvantages as well. Since the nonelecting LLC is not a corporation, it is not eligible for certain provisions the Internal Revenue Code grants only to the corporate entity. Among these privileges are the right to grant incentive stock options (ISOs) to employees and the right to take advantage of tax-free reorganizations when selling the company. LLCs must be converted to taxable entities well before relying on these provisions.

CHOICE OF ENTITY

The sole proprietorship, partnership, corporation (including the professional corporation and subchapter S corporation), the limited partnership, and the LLC are the most commonly used business forms. Other forms exist, such as the so-called Massachusetts business trust, in which the business is operated by trustees for the benefit of beneficiaries who hold transferable shares. But these are generally used for limited, specialized purposes. Armed with this knowledge and the comparative factors discussed previously, how should our budding entrepreneurs operate their businesses?

Consulting Firm

It will be obvious to Jennifer, Jean, and George that they can immediately eliminate the sole proprietorship and limited partnership as choices for their consulting business. The sole proprietorship, by definition, allows for only one owner, and there does not seem to be any need for the passive silent investors who would serve as limited partners. Certainly, none of the three would be willing to sacrifice the control and participation necessary to achieve limited partnership status.

The corporation gives the consultants the benefit of limited liability, not for their own mistakes but for the mistakes of each other and their employees. It also protects them from personal liability for trade debt. This protection, however, comes at the cost of additional complexity and expense, such as additional tax returns, annual reports to the state, and annual fees. Ease of transferability and enhanced continuity do not appear to be deciding factors, because a small consulting firm is often intensely personal and not likely to be transferable apart from its principals. Also, fear of double taxation does not appear to be a legitimate concern, since it is likely that the stockholders will be able to distribute any corporate profit to themselves in the form of compensation. In fact, to the extent that they may need to make some capital expenditures for word-processing equipment and office furniture, the corporate form would afford them access to the lower corporate tax brackets for small amounts of income (unless they were characterized as a personal service corporation). Furthermore, if the consultants earn enough money to purchase various employee benefits, such as group medical insurance and group life and disability, they will qualify as employees of the corporation and can exclude the value of such benefits from their taxable income, while the corporation deducts these amounts.

These positive aspects of choosing the corporate form argue strongly against making the subchapter S election. That election would eliminate the benefit of the low-end corporate tax bracket and put our consultants in the position of paying individual income tax on the capital purchases made. The election would also eliminate the opportunity to exclude the value of employee benefits from their personal income tax. The same problems argue against the choice of an LLC for this business.

The other possibility would be the general partnership. In essence, by choosing the partnership the consultants would be trading away limited liability for less complexity. The partnership would not be a separate taxable entity and would not be required to file annual reports and pay annual fees. From a tax point of view, the partnership presents the same disadvantages as the subchapter S corporation and LLC.

In summary, it appears that our consultants will be choosing between the subchapter C corporation and the partnership. The corporation adds complexity but grants limited liability. And it certainly is not necessary for a business to be large in order to be incorporated. One might question, however, how much liability exposure a consulting firm is likely to face. In addition, although the corporation affords them the tax benefits associated with employee benefits and capital expenditures, it is not likely that our consultants will be able to afford much in the way of employee benefits and capital expenditures in the short term. Further, these consultants will not likely have personal incomes placing them in tax brackets considerably higher than the corporation's. A strong case can be made for either the C corporation or the partnership in this situation. One can always incorporate the partnership in the future if the business grows to the point that some of the tax benefits become important.

It may also be interesting to speculate on the choice that would be made if our three consultants were lawyers or doctors. Then the choice would be between the partnership and the professional corporation. The comparisons would be the same except that, as a personal service corporation, the professional corporation does not have the benefit of the low-end corporate tax brackets.

Software Entrepreneur

Phil can easily eliminate the partnership and the limited partnership. Phil is clearly the sole owner of his enterprise and will not brook any other controlling persons. In addition, his plan to finance the enterprise with earnings from his last business eliminates the need for limited partner investors. Almost as easily, Phil can eliminate the sole proprietorship since it would seem highly undesirable to assume personal liability for whatever damage may be done by a product manufactured and distributed to thousands of potential plaintiffs. The corporation, therefore, appears to be Phil's obvious choice. It gives the benefit of limited liability, as well as the transferability and continuity essential to a business that seems likely to be an acquisition candidate in the future. Again, the lack of size is not a factor in this choice. Phil will likely act as sole director, president, treasurer, and secretary.

There remains, however, the choice between subchapters C and S. As may well be obvious by now, Phil's corporation fits the most common profile of the subchapter S candidate. For the first year or more, the corporation will suffer serious losses as Phil pays programmers and marketers to develop and presell his product. Subchapter S allows Phil to show these losses on his personal tax return, where they will shelter his considerable investment income. The passive loss limitations will not affect Phil's use of these losses, since he is clearly a material participant in his venture.

Phil could achieve much the same results by choosing an LLC, rather than a subchapter S corporation. Unfortunately, however, many states require that an LLC have two or more members, making Phil's business ineligible. In states which allow single-member LLCs, there would be little to recommend one choice over the other. Phil might feel more comfortable with an S corporation, however, if he fears that suppliers, customers, and potential employees might be put off by the relative novelty of the LLC. This might especially be true if he has any plans to eventually go public, as the LLC has not gained wide acceptance in the public markets. An S corporation can then usually revoke its S election without undue negative tax effect. Beginning as an S corporation would also eliminate the need to reincorporate as a corporation prior to selling the business in a potentially tax-free transaction.

Hotel Venture

The hotel venture contemplated by Bruce, Erika, and Michael presents the opportunity for some creative planning. One problem they may encounter in making their decision is the inherent conflict presented by Michael's insistence upon recognition and reasonable return for his contribution of the land. Also, Bruce and Erika fear being unduly diluted by Michael's share, in the face of their more than equal contribution to the ongoing work.

One might break this logjam by looking to one of the ways of separating cash flow from equity. Michael need not contribute the real estate to the business entity at all. Instead, the business could lease the land from Michael on a long-term (99-year) basis. This would give Michael his return in the form of rent without distorting the equity split among the three entrepreneurs. From a tax point of view, this plan also changes a nondepreciable asset (land) into deductible rent payments for the business. As their next move, the three may decide to form an entity to construct and own the hotel building, separate from the entity that manages the ongoing hotel business.

This plan would convert a rather confusing real estate/operating venture into a pure real estate investment opportunity for potential investors. The real estate entity would receive enough revenue from the management entity to cover its cash flow and would generate tax losses through depreciation, interest, and real estate taxes. These short-term losses would eventually yield long-term capital gains when the hotel is sold, so this entity would attract investors looking for short-term losses and long-term capital appreciation. For the short-term losses to be attractive, however, they must be usable by the investors on their personal returns and not trapped at the business entity level.

All these factors point inevitably to the use of either the limited partnership, LLC, or subchapter S corporation for the hotel building entity. All three entities allow the tax losses to pass through to the owners for use on their personal returns. Among these three choices, the limited partnership and LLC allow more flexibility in allocating losses to the investors, and away from Bruce, Erika, and Michael (who most likely do not need them), and they provide higher limits on the amounts of losses each investor may use.

In past years, our entrepreneurs would thus face the unenviable choice between losing the tax advantages of the limited partnership to preserve the limited liability offered by the subchapter S corporation or preserving the tax advantages (and the ability to attract investors) by either accepting personal liability as general partners or attempting to adequately capitalize a corporate general partner. This choice is no longer necessary with the advent of the LLC, which solves the problem by offering the tax advantages of the limited partnership and the liability protection of the subchapter S corporation. However, the passive loss limitations will still impact upon the usefulness of the losses for the members who do not have significant passive income, making this project (as is the case with most real estate investments in today's climate) more difficult to sell.

This leaves the entity which will operate the hotel business itself. The presence of our three principals immediately eliminates the sole proprietorship as a possibility. Because all the investment capital has already been raised for the real estate entity, there does not seem to be a need for further investors, thus eliminating the limited partnership as a possibility. The partnership seems inapplicable, since it is unlikely that any of the principals would wish to expose himself or herself to unlimited liability in such a consumer-oriented business.

Thus, the corporation and LLC with their limited liability, continuity, and transferability, seem to be the obvious choices for this potentially growing and successful business. As with Phil, it becomes necessary to decide whether to make the subchapter S election or choose an LLC to achieve tax pass-through. This decision will be made on the basis of the parties' projections. Are there likely to be serious losses in the short-term, which might be usable on their personal tax returns? Will there be a need for significant capital expenditures, thus indicating a need for the low-end corporate tax rates? Will the company offer a variety of employee benefits, which our principals would wish to exclude from their taxable income? Is the company likely to generate more profit than can be distributed in the form of "reasonable" compensation, thus calling for the elimination of the corporate-level tax. If these factors seem to favor a tax pass-through entity, the principals will likely analyze the choice between subchapter S and LLC in a manner similar to Phil. In addition, they may find the LLC's lack of eligibility rules attractive in the short run should they ever consider the possibility of corporate or foreign investors, or creative divisions of equity.

CONCLUSION

These and the many other factors described in this chapter deserve careful consideration by the thousands of entrepreneurs forming businesses every month. After the basic decision to start a new business itself, the choice of the appropriate form for the business may well be the most significant decision facing the entrepreneur in the short run.

FOR FURTHER READING

Bischoff, William, *Choosing the Right Business Entity* (New York: Harcourt Brace, 1997).

Burstiner, Irving, *The Small Business Handbook: A Comprehensive Guide to Starting and Running Your Own Business* (New Jersey: Fireside, 1997).

Diamond, Michael R., *How to Incorporate* (New York: John Wiley, 1996).

Pressment, Stanley, *Choice of Business Entity Answer Book* (Gaithersburg, MD: Aspen, 1998).

Shenkman, Martin M., *Starting a Limited Liability Company* (New York: John Wiley, 1996).

INTERNET LINKS

www.tannedfeet.com
  /choice_of_entity.htm   Entrepreneurs' Help Page
www.smallbiz.findlaw.com
  /book/su_structures/articles/01.html   Findlaw Small Business Center
www.lexspace.com/html   Lexspace-Business Entity
  /formation.html   Formation

9 THE BUSINESS PLAN

Andrew Zacharakis

The sole purpose of a business plan is to explore and answer questions—critical questions starting with whether the business idea is a viable opportunity. During the dot-com boom of the late 1990's, many entrepreneurs and venture capitalists questioned the importance of the business plan. Typical of this hyperstartup phase are stories like James Walker. He generated financing on a 10-day-old company based on "a bunch of bullet points on a piece of paper." He added, "It has to happen quick" in the hypercompetitive wireless-Internet-technology world. "There's a revolution every year and a half now," Mr. Walker said.[1]

Media stories abounded of the whiz kid college dropout who received venture capital, zoomed to IPO (initial public offering), and cashed out a multimillionaire in 18 months or less. The mythology of the dot-com entrepreneur was that he didn't have a business plan, only a couple of PowerPoint slides. That was all it took to identify the opportunity, secure venture backing, and go public. Why spend the 200 hours or so that a solid business plan often takes? The NASDAQ crash of March 2000 and the subsequent death of many dot-com high flyers provides the clearest answer. Many of these businesses didn't have the potential to make profits—not then, not now, and not anytime in the future. The easy money and quick returns of the late nineties have disappeared, and what we are left with is the fact that good opportunities need good execution in order to succeed and a rigorous business plan process can assist in the pursuit of entrepreneurial gold.

There is a common misperception that a business plan is primarily used for raising capital. Although a good business plan assists in raising capital, the

260

primary purpose of the process is to help the entrepreneur gain deep under-standing of the opportunity he or she is envisioning. A business plan tests the feasibility of an idea. Is it truly an opportunity? Many a would-be entrepreneur has doggedly pursued ideas that are not opportunities; the time invested in a business plan would save thousands of dollars and hours spent on such wild goose chases. For example, if a person makes $100,000 a year, spending 200 hours on a business plan equates to a $10,000 investment in time spent ($50/hour times 200 hours). However, the costs of launching a flawed business concept can quickly accelerate into the millions. Most entrepreneurial ventures raise enough money to survive two years even if the business ultimately fails. Assuming that the only expense is the time value of the lead entrepreneur, a two-year invest-ment equates to $200,000, not to mention the lost opportunity cost and the like-lihood that other employees were hired and paid and that other expenses were incurred. So do yourself a favor and spend the time and money up front.

The business plan process can not only prevent entrepreneurs from pur-suing a bad opportunity but also help them reshape their original visions into better opportunities. As we will explore in the remainder of this chapter, the business plan process involves raising a number of critical questions and then seeking answers. Part of that question-answering process involves talking to target customers and gauging what is their "pain." These conversations with customers as well as other trusted advisors can assist in better targeting the features and needs that customers most want in a good or service. This prestartup work saves untold effort and money otherwise spent trying to re-shape the product after the launch has occurred. This is not to say that new ventures don't adjust their offering based upon customer feedback, but the business plan process can anticipate some of these adjustments in advance of the initial launch.

Perhaps the greatest benefit of the business plan is that it allows the en-trepreneur to articulate the business opportunity to various stakeholders in the most effective manner. The plan provides the background to enable the entrepreneur to communicate the upside potential and attract equity invest-ment, and the validation needed to convince potential employees to leave their current jobs for the uncertain future of a new venture. It is also the instru-ment that can secure a strategic partner, key customer, or key supplier. In short, the business plan provides the entrepreneur the deep understanding he needs to answer the critical questions that various stakeholders will ask, even if the stakeholders don't actually read the written plan. Completing a well-founded business plan gives the entrepreneur credibility in the eyes of various stakeholders.

TYPES OF PLANS

A business plan can take a number of forms depending on its purpose. The pri-mary difference between business plan types is length. If outside capital is needed, a business plan geared towards equity investors or debt providers typically is 25 to 40 pages long. Professional equity investors such as venture capitalists and professional debt providers such as bankers will not read the entire plan from front to back. Recognizing this fact, the entrepreneur needs to produce the plan in a format that facilitates spot reading. We will investigate the major sections that comprise business plans throughout this chapter. My general rule of thumb is that less is more. For instance, I've seen a number of plans receive venture funding that were closer to 25 pages than 40 pages.

A second type of business plan, the operational plan, is primarily for the entrepreneur and his team to guide the development, launch, and initial growth of the venture. There really is no length specification for this type of plan; however, it is common for these plans to exceed 80 pages. The basic organization format between the two types of plans is the same, however the level of detail tends to be much greater in an operational plan. This effort is where the entrepreneur really gains the deep understanding important in discerning how to build and run the business.

The last type of plan is called a dehydrated business plan. This type is considerably shorter than the previous two, typically no more than 10 pages. Its purpose is to provide an initial conception of the business. As such, it can be used to test initial reaction to the entrepreneur's idea and can be shared with his confidants to obtain feedback before he invests significant time and effort on a longer business plan.

FROM GLIMMER TO ACTION: THE PROCESS

Perhaps the hardest part of writing any business plan is getting started. Compiling the data, shaping it into an articulate story, and producing the finished product can be a daunting task. The best way to attack a business plan, therefore, is in steps. First, write a four-to-five-page summary of your current vision. This provides a roadmap for you and others to follow as you complete the rest of the plan. Second, start attacking major sections of the plan. Although all of the sections interact and influence every other section, it is often easiest for entrepreneurs to write the product/service description first. This is usually the most concrete component of the entrepreneur's vision. Keep in mind, however, that writing a business plan isn't purely a sequential process. You will be filling in different parts of the plan simultaneously or in whatever order makes the most sense in your mind. Finally, after completing a first draft of all the major sections, come back and rewrite a shorter, more concise executive summary (one to two pages). Not too surprisingly, the executive summary will be quite different from the original summary because of all the learning and reshaping that the business plan process facilitates.

Common wisdom is that the business plan is a living document. Although your first draft will be polished, most business plans are obsolete the day they come off the presses. That means that entrepreneurs are continuously updating and revising their business plan. Again, the importance of the business plan isn't the final product but the learning that is gleaned from going through the process. The business plan is the story line of your vision. It articulates what you see in your mind and crystallizes that vision for you and your team. It also provides a history, a photo album, if you will, of the birth, growth, and maturity of your business. Each major revision should be kept and filed and occasionally looked back upon for the lessons you have learned. I find writing a business plan, although daunting, exciting and creative, especially if I am working on it with a founding team. Whether it is over a glass of wine, beer, or coffee, talking about your business concept with your founding team is invigorating, and the business plan is a critical outcome of these discussions. So now let us dig in and examine how to write effective business plans.

THE STORY MODEL

One of the major goals for business plans is to attract and convince various stakeholders of the potential of your business. You have to keep in mind, therefore, how these stakeholders will interpret your plan. The guiding principal is that you are writing a story. All good stories have a plot line, a unifying thread that ties the characters and events together. If you think about the most successful businesses in America, they all have well-publicized plot lines, more appropriately called taglines. When you hear these taglines, you immediately connect them to the business. For example, when you hear "absolutely, positively has to be there overnight," you probably connect that tagline to Federal Express and package delivery. Similarly, "Just do it" is intricately linked to Nike and the image of athletic proficiency (see Exhibit 9.1). A tagline is a sentence or fragment of a sentence that summarizes the pure essence of your business. It is the plot line that every sentence, paragraph, page, diagram, and other part of your business plan should correlate to. One useful tip that I share with every entrepreneur I work with is to put that tagline in a footer that runs on the bottom of every page. Most word-processing packages, such as Microsoft Word, enable you to insert a footer that you can see as you type. As you are writing, if the section doesn't build on, explain, or otherwise directly relate to the tagline, it most likely isn't a necessary component to the business plan. Rigorous adherence to the tagline facilitates writing a concise business plan.

EXHIBIT 9.1   Taglines.

Nike	*Just do it!*
Federal Express	*Absolutely, positively has to be there overnight.*
McDonalds	*We love to see you smile.*
Cisco Systems	*Discover all that's possible on the Internet.*
Microsoft	*Where do you want to go today.*

The key to beginning the story model is capturing the reader's attention. The tagline is the foundation, but in writing the plan you want to create a number of visual catch points. Too many business plans are dense, text-laden manifestos. Only the most diligent reader will wade through all that text to find the nuggets of value. Help the reader by highlighting different key points throughout the plan. How do you create these catch points? Some effective techniques include extensive use of headings and subheadings, strategically placed bullet-point lists, diagrams, charts, and the use of sidebars.[2] The point is to make the document not only content rich but visually attractive.

Now, let's take a look at the major sections of the plan (see Exhibit 9.2). Keep in mind that although there are some different variations, most plans have these components. It is important to keep your plan as close to this format as possible because many stakeholders are used to the format and it facilitates

EXHIBIT 9.2   Business plan outline.

I. Cover

II. Title Page

III. Executive Summary
   a. Hook—potential size of opportunity
   b. Business Concept—company and products
   c. Industry Overview
   d. Target Market
   e. Competitive Advantage
   f. Business Model
   g. Team
   h. Offering

IV. Industry, Customer, and Competitor Analysis
   a. Industry
      i. Overview—Market Demand, Market Size and Structure, and Margin Analysis
      ii. Trends
      iii. Market Space or Segment you will compete in
   b. Customer Analysis
   c. Competitor Analysis

V. Company and Product Description
   a. Company Description
   b. Product Description
   c. Competitive Advantage
   d. Entry Strategy
   e. Growth Strategy

VI. Marketing Plan
   a. Target Market Strategy
   b. Product/Service Strategy
   c. Pricing Strategy
   d. Distribution Strategy
   e. Advertising and Promotion Strategy
   f. Sales Strategy
   g. Sales and Marketing Forecasts

VII. Operations Plan
   a. Operations Strategy
   b. Scope of Operations
   c. Ongoing Operations

VIII. Development Plan
   a. Development Strategy
   b. Development Timeline

IX. Team
   a. Team Bios and Roles
   b. Advisory Boards, Board of Directors, Strategic Partners, External Members
   c. Compensation and Ownership

X. Critical Risks
   a. Market Interest and Growth Potential
   b. Competitor Actions and Retaliation
   c. Time and Cost of Development
   d. Operating Expenses
   e. Availability and Timing of Financing
   f. Other Risks

XI. Offering

XII. Financial Plan
   a. Description of Financial Assumptions
   b. Income Statement
   c. Cash Flow Statement
   d. Balance Sheet

XIII. Appendices

spot reading. So if you are seeking venture capital, for instance, you want to facilitate quick perusal because venture capitalists often spend, research shows, as little as five minutes on a plan before rejecting it or putting it aside for later study. If a venture capitalist becomes frustrated with an unfamiliar format, he will more likely reject it than try to pull out the pertinent information.

THE BUSINESS PLAN

We will progress through the sections in the order that they typically appear, but keep in mind that you can work on the sections in any order that you wish.

The Cover

The plan's cover should include the following information: company name, tagline, contact person and address, phone, fax, e-mail address, date, disclaimer, and copy number. Most of the information is self-explanatory, but I should point out a few things (see Exhibit 9.3). First, the contact person for a new venture should be the president or some other founding team member. I have seen some business plans that failed to have the contact person's name and phone on the cover. Imagine the frustration of an excited potential investor who can't find out how to contact the entrepreneur to gain more information; such plans usually end up in the rejected pile. Second, business plans should have a disclaimer along these lines:

> This business plan has been submitted on a confidential basis solely to selected, highly qualified investors. The recipient should not reproduce this plan nor distribute it to others without permission. Please return this copy if you do not wish to invest in the company.

Controlling distribution is particularly important when seeking investment capital, especially to comply with Regulation A of the Securities and Exchange Commission, which specifies that you must solicit qualified investors (high net-worth and income individuals).

The cover should also have a line specifying the copy number. You will often see on the bottom right portion of the cover a line that says something like "Copy 1 of 5 copies." Entrepreneurs should keep a log of who has copies so that they can control for unexpected distribution.

Finally, the cover should be eye-catching. If you have a product or prototype, a picture of it can draw the reader in. Likewise, a catchy tagline draws attention and encourages the reader to look further.

Table of Contents

Continuing the theme of making the document easy to read, a detailed table of contents is critical. It should list major sections, subsections, exhibits, and appendices. The table provides the reader a roadmap to your plan (see Exhibit 9.4).

EXHIBIT 9.3   Cover of PurePlay Golf business plan.

PurePlay Golf

Bringing Information to the Golfer's Palm

www.PurePlayGolf.com

Prepared by:

Amy Ball, Michael Bear, Christy Long,
Geoff Mall, and Hilary Tabor

Contact: Geoff Mall, gmall@PurePlayGolf.com
PurePlayGolf.com
Reynolds Center, Suite 1
Babson Park, MA 02457
(781) 555-5252
(781) 555-5253 (fax)

Draft: December 6, 2000

Note that the table of contents is customized to the specific business so that it doesn't perfectly correlate to the business plan outline presented in Exhibit 9.2. Nonetheless, a look at Exhibit 9.4 shows that the company's business plan includes most of the elements highlighted in the business outline and that the order of information is basically the same as well.

EXHIBIT 9.4 Sample table of contents.

Executive Summary (1–3 pages)

This section is the most important part of the business plan. If you don't capture readers' attention in the executive summary, it is unlikely that they will read any other parts of the plan. Therefore, you want to hit them with the most compelling aspects of your business opportunity right up front.

Hook the Reader

That means having the first sentence or paragraph highlight the potential of the opportunity. I have read too many plans that start with "Company XYZ, incorporated in the state of Delaware, will develop and sell widgets." Ho-hum. That doesn't excite me; but if, in contrast, the first sentence states, "The current market for widgets is $50 million and is growing at an annual rate of 20%. The emergence of the Internet is likely to accelerate this market's growth. Company XYZ is positioned to capture this wave with its proprietary technology—the secret formula VOOM." This creates the right tone. It tells me that the potential opportunity is huge and that company XYZ has some competitive advantage that enables it to become a big player in this market. I don't really care at this point whether the business is incorporated or that it is a Delaware corporation (aren't they all?).

Common subsections within the executive summary include: description of opportunity, business concept, industry overview, target market, competitive advantage, business model and economics, team, and offering. Remember that, since this is an executive summary, all these components are covered in the body of the plan. We will explore them in greater detail as we progress through the sections.

Since the executive summary is the most important part of the finished plan, it should be written after you have gained your deep learning by going through all the other sections.[3] The summary should be 1 to 3 pages, although I prefer executive summaries be no more than 2 pages.

Industry, Customer, and Competitor Analysis (3–6 pages)

Industry

The goal of this section is to illustrate the opportunity and how you are going to capture that opportunity. A useful framework for visualizing the opportunity is Timmons's model of opportunity recognition.[4] Using the "3Ms" helps quantify an idea and assess how strong an opportunity the idea is. First, examine Market demand. If the market is growing at 20% or better, the opportunity is more exciting. Second, we look at Market size and structure. A market that is currently $50 million with $1 billion potential is attractive. This often is the case in emerging markets, those that appear poised for rapid growth and have the potential to change how we live and work. For example, the PC, disk drive, and computer hardware markets of the eighties were very hot. Many new companies were born and rode the wave of the emerging technology, including Apple, Microsoft, and Intel. In the nineties, it was anything dealing with the Internet. As we enter the twenty-first century, it appears that wireless communications may be the next big market. Another market structure that tends to have promise is a fragmented market where many small, dispersed competitors compete on a regional basis. Many of the big names in retail revolutionized fragmented markets. For instance, category killers such as Wal-Mart, Staples, and Home Depot consolidated fragmented markets by providing quality products at lower prices. These firms replaced the dispersed regional and local discount, office-supply, and hardware stores. The final *M* is *M*argin analysis. Do firms in the industry enjoy high gross margins (revenues minus cost of goods sold) of 40% or greater? Higher margins allow for higher returns, which again leads to greater potential business.

The 3*M*s help distinguish opportunities and as such should be highlighted as early as possible in your plan. Describe your overall industry in terms of revenues, growth, and pertinent future trends. Avoid in this section discussing your concept, the proposed product or service you will offer. Instead, use dispassionate, arms-length analysis of the industry with the goal of highlighting a space or gap that is underserved. Thus, how is the industry segmented currently, and how will it be segmented in the future? After identifying the relevant industry segments, identify the segment that your product will target. Again, what are the important trends that will shape the segment in the future?

Customer

Once the plan has defined the market space it plans to enter, the target customer needs to be examined in detail. The entrepreneur needs to define who the customer is by using demographic and psychographic information. The better the entrepreneur can define his customer, the more apt he is to deliver a product that the customer truly wants. A venture capitalist recently told me that the most impressive entrepreneur is the one who not only identifies who the customer is in terms of demographics and psychographics but can also name who that customer is by address, phone number, and e-mail address. When you understand who your customer is, you can assess what compels them to buy, how your company can sell to them (direct sales, retail, Internet, direct mail, etc.), how much acquiring and retaining that customer will cost, and so forth. A schedule inserted into the text describing customers on these basic parameters communicates a lot of data quickly and can be very powerful.

Competition

The competition analysis follows directly from the customer analysis. You have just identified your market segment, described what the customer looks like, and what the customer wants. Now the key factor leading to competitive analysis is what the customer wants in a particular product. These product attributes form a basis of comparison against your direct and indirect competitors. A competitive profile matrix not only creates a powerful visual catch point, it conveys information regarding your competitive advantage and also the basis for your company's strategy (see Exhibit 9.5). The competitive profile matrix

EXHIBIT 9.5 Competitive profile matrix.

	VMC	Napster	Mp3.com	MYRadio	SonicNet	XM Radio
Have to be online to listen to music	No	No	No	No	Yes	No
Customized ads to individual users	Yes	N/A	No	N/A	No	No
Can purchase physical media on Web site	No	No	Yes	No	Yes	No
Can access personal music collection from remote location	Yes	No	No	No	No	No
Automatic play list generation	Yes	No	No	Yes	Yes	Yes
Offers a service without ads	Yes	N/A	No	No	No	Yes
Can choose to play specific songs on demand	Yes	Yes	No	No	No	No
Easy feedback for enhanced listening experience	Yes	No	No	No	Yes	No
Streams media	Yes	No	Yes	N/A	Yes	Yes
Download media	Yes	Yes	Yes	N/A	No	No
Can distribute user collections to other people	No	Yes	No	No	Yes	No
Offers portable device player option	Yes	Yes	Yes	Yes	No	Yes
Offers a free service	Yes	Yes	Yes	Yes	Yes	No
Offers service in telematics industry	Yes	No	No	No	No	Yes

should lead the section and be followed by text describing the analysis and its implications.

Finding information about your competition can be easy if the competing company is public, harder if it is private, and very difficult if it is operating in "stealth" mode (i.e., it hasn't yet announced itself to the world). Most libraries have access to databases that contain a mother lode of information about publicly traded companies (see Exhibit 9.6 for some sample sources), but privately held companies or stealth ventures represent a greater challenge. The best way for savvy entrepreneurs to gather this information is through their network and via trade shows. Who should be in the entrepreneur's network? First and foremost are the customers the entrepreneur hopes to sell to in the near future. Just as you are (or should be) talking to your potential customers, your existing competition is interacting with the customers every day, and your customers are likely aware of the stealth competition on the horizon. Although many entrepreneurs are fearful (verging sometimes on the brink of paranoia) that valuable information will fall in the wrong hands and lead to new competition that invalidates the current venture, the reality is that entrepreneurs who operate in a vacuum (don't talk to customers, attend tradeshows, etc.) fail far more often than those who are talking to everyone they can. Talking allows entrepreneurs to get invaluable feedback that enables them to reshape their product offering prior to launching a product that may or may not be accepted by the marketplace. So you should network not only to find out about your competition but also to improve your own venture concept.

EXHIBIT 9.6   Sample source for information on public/private companies.

Infotrac Index/abstracts of journals, general business and finance magazines; market overviews; and profiles of public and private firms.

Dow Jones Interactive Searchable index of articles from over 3,000 newspapers.

Lexis/Nexis Searchable index of articles.

Dun's Principal International Business International business directory.

Dun's One Million Dollar Premium Database of public and private firms with revenues greater than $1 million or more than eight employees.

Hoover's Online Profiles of private and public firms with links to Web sites, etc.

Corp Tech Profiles of high technology firms.

Bridge Information Services Detailed financial information on 1.4 million international securities that can be manipulated in tables and graphs.

RDS Bizsuite Linked databases providing data and full-text searching on firms.

Bloomberg Detailed financial data and analyst reports.

Company and Product Description (1–2 pages)

Completing the dispassionate analysis described in the previous section lays the foundation for describing your company and concept. In one paragraph identify the company name, where it is incorporated, and a brief overview of the company concept. Also highlight in this section what the company has achieved to date—what milestones have you accomplished that show progress.

More space should be used to describe the product. Again, graphic representations can be visually powerful (see Exhibit 9.7). Highlight how your product fits into the customer value proposition. What is incorporated in your product and what value do you add to the customer? This section should clearly and forcefully identify your venture's competitive advantage. Based upon your competitive analysis, why is your product better, cheaper, faster than what customers currently have? Your advantage may be a function of proprietary technology, patents, distribution. In fact, the most powerful competitive advantages are derived from a bundle of factors because this makes them more difficult to copy.

Entrepreneurs also need to identify their entry and growth strategies. Since most new ventures are resource constrained, especially in terms of available capital, it is crucial that the lead entrepreneur establish the most effective way to enter the market. Based upon analysis in the market and customer sections, entrepreneurs need to identify their primary target audience (PTA). Focusing on a particular subset of the overall market niche allows new ventures to utilize scarce resources to reach those customers and prove the viability of their concept.

EXHIBIT 9.7 Product/concept/description.

VMC Detailed Network Overview

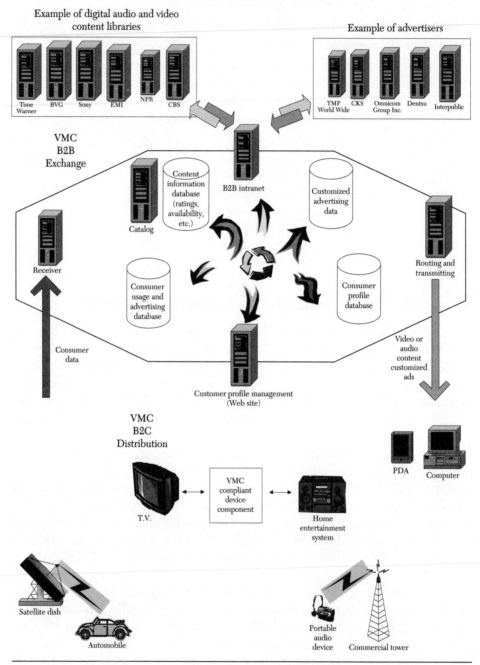

The business plan should also sell the entrepreneur's vision for growth because that vision indicates the business's true potential. Thus, a paragraph or two should be devoted to the firm's growth strategy. If the venture achieves success in its entry strategy, it will either generate internal cash flow that can be used to fuel the growth strategy or attract further equity financing at improved valuations. The growth strategy should talk about the secondary target audience and tertiary target audiences that the firm will pursue. For example, if I were starting a restaurant, my entry strategy might be to establish a presence in Wellesley, Massachusetts, geared toward college students and young professionals. Assuming that I achieved some success (e.g., generating sales and high table turns), my growth strategy might be to open up five more restaurants around the greater Boston area. If these restaurants also proved successful, I might franchise the concept nationwide to achieve rapid growth with less capital infusion than if I opened all company-owned restaurants. This in fact, appears to be the strategy that Joey Crugnale, the founder of Steve's Ice Cream, Bertucci's Brick Oven Pizza, and more recently the Naked Fish, is following. Crugnale opened the first Naked Fish in May 1999. After testing and refining the concept, he has opened another nine outlets (as of December 2000). The establishment of nine Naked Fish restaurants shows growth and success and enables Mr. Crugnale to attract further financing to grow the concept around Boston and beyond.

Marketing Plan (4–6 pages)

To this point, we have laid the stage for your company's potential to enter a market successfully and grow. Now we need to devise the strategy that will allow the company to reach its potential. The primary components of this section include a description of the target market strategy, product/service strategy, pricing strategy, distribution strategy, advertising and promotion, sales strategy, and sales and marketing forecasts. Let's take a look at each of these subsections in turn.

Target Market Strategy

Every marketing plan needs some guiding principals. Based on the knowledge gleaned from the target market analysis, entrepreneurs need to position their product. All product strategies fall somewhere on the continuum between "rational purchase" and "emotional purchase." As an example, when I buy a new car, the rational purchase might be a low-cost reliable car such as the Ford Aspire. However, there is an emotional element as well. I want the car to be an extension of my personality, so based on my economic means and self-perception, I will buy a BMW or Audi because of the emotional benefits I derive from owning a high-status car. Within every product space, there is room for products at different points along the continuum. Entrepreneurs need to decide where their product fits or where they would like to position it, because this position determines the other aspects of the marketing plan.

Product/Service Strategy

Building from the target market strategy, this section of the plan describes how your product is differentiated from the competition. Discuss why customers will switch to your product and how you will retain them so that they don't switch to your competition in the future. Using the attributes defined in your customer profile matrix, a powerful visual is a product attribute map showing how your firm compares to the competition. It is best to focus on the two most important attributes, one on the x-axis and the other on the y-axis. The map should show that your product is clearly distinguishable from your competition on desirable attributes (see Exhibit 9.8).

This section should also address how you will service the customer. What type of technical support will you provide? Will you offer warranties? What kind of product upgrades will be available and when? It is important to detail all these efforts and account for each in the pricing of the product. Entrepreneurs frequently underestimate the costs of these services, which leads to a drain on cash flow and can ultimately lead to bankruptcy.

Pricing Strategy

Determining how to price your product is always difficult. The two primary approaches are the "cost-plus" approach and the "market demand" approach. I advise entrepreneurs to avoid cost-plus pricing for a number of reasons. First, it is difficult to accurately determine your actual cost, especially if this is a new venture with a limited history. New ventures consistently underestimate the true cost of developing their products. For example, how much did it really

EXHIBIT 9.8   Competitive map for PurePlay Golf.

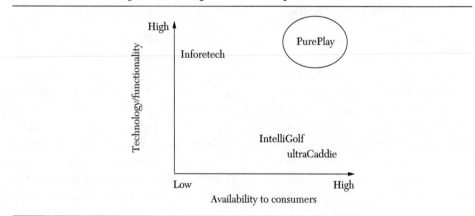

cost to write that software? The cost would include salaries and burden, computer and other assets, overhead contribution, and so forth. Since most entrepreneurs underestimate these costs, there is a tendency to underprice the product. Often entrepreneurs claim that they are offering a low price so that they can penetrate and gain market share rapidly. The problems with a low price are that it may be difficult to raise later, may create demand that overwhelms your ability to produce the product in sufficient volume, and may unnecessarily strain cash flow. Therefore, the better method is to canvass the market and determine an appropriate price based upon what the competition is currently offering and how your product is positioned. If you are offering a low-cost value product, price below market rates. If your product is of better quality and has lots of features (the more common case), it should be priced above market rates.

Distribution Strategy

This section identifies how you will reach the customer. For example, the e-commerce boom of the late 1990s assumed that the growth in Internet usage and purchases would create new demand for pure Internet companies. Yet the distribution strategy for many of these firms did not make sense. Pets.com and other online pet supply firms had a strategy where the pet owner would log on, order the product from the site, and then receive delivery via UPS or U.S. mail. In theory this works, but in practice the price the market would bear for this product didn't cover the exorbitant shipping costs of a forty-pound bag of dog food.

It is wise to examine how the customer currently acquires the product. If I buy my dog food at Wal-Mart, then you should probably use primarily traditional retail outlets to sell me a new brand of dog food. This is not to say that entrepreneurs might not develop a multichannel distribution strategy, but if they want to achieve maximum growth, at some point they will have to use common distribution techniques, or reeducate the customer on a new buying process (which can be very expensive).

If you determine that Wal-Mart is the best distribution channel, the next question becomes whether you can access it. As a new startup in dog food, it may be difficult to get shelf space at Wal-Mart. That may suggest an entry strategy of boutique pet stores to build brand recognition. The key here is to identify appropriate channels and then assess how costly it is to access them.

Advertising and Promotion

Communicating effectively to your customer requires advertising and promotion. Referring again to the dot-com boom of the late nineties, the soon to be defunct Computer.com made a classic mistake in its attempt to build brand recognition. It blew over half of the venture capital it raised on a series of expensive Super Bowl ads in January 2000 ($3 million of $5.8 million raised on three Super Bowl ads).[5] Resource-constrained entrepreneurs need to carefully select the appropriate strategies. What avenues most effectively reach your PTA (primary target audience)? If you can identify your PTA by names, then direct mail may be more effective. Try to utilize grassroots techniques such as public relations efforts geared toward mainstream media. Sheri Poe, founder of Ryka shoes, geared towards women, appeared on the Oprah Winfrey show touting shoes for women, designed by women. The response was overwhelming. In fact, she was so besieged by demand that she couldn't supply enough shoes.

As you develop a multipronged advertising and promotion strategy, create detailed schedules that show which avenues you will pursue and the associated costs (see Exhibits 9.9a and 9.9b). These types of schedules serve many purposes including providing accurate cost estimates that will help in assessing how much capital you need to raise. These schedules also build credibility in the eyes of potential investors since it shows that you understand the nuances of your industry.

Sales Strategy

This section provides the backbone that supports all of the above. Specifically, it illustrates what kind and level of human capital you will devote to the effort. How many salespeople, customer support staff, and the like do you need? Will these people be internal to the organization or outsourced? Again, this section builds credibility if the entrepreneur demonstrates an understanding of how the business should operate.

Sales and Marketing Forecasts

Gauging the impact of the above efforts is difficult. Nonetheless, to build a compelling story, entrepreneurs need to show projections of revenues well into the future. How do you derive these numbers? There are two methods, the comparable method and the buildup method. After detailed investigation of

EXHIBIT 9.9a   Advertising schedule.

Promotional Tools	Budget over 1 Year
Print advertising	$1,426,440
Television advertising	780,000
Sales promotions	100,000
Direct marketing	100,000
Public relations	93,560
Total	$2,500,000

EXHIBIT 9.9b   Magazine advertisement schedule.

Publication	Circulation	Ad Price	Cost per Thousand
Golf Digest	1,550,000	$35,820	$23.11
Sports Illustrated	3,150,000	57,600	18.29
Golf Magazine	1,400,000	26,000	18.57
Fortune	775,000	21,600	27.87
Money Magazine	1,400,000	34,900	24.93

the industry and market, entrepreneurs know the competitive players and have a good understanding of their history. The comparable method models sales forecasts after what other companies have achieved, adjusting for age of company, variances in product attributes, support services such as advertising and promotion, and so forth. In essence, the entrepreneur monitors a number of comparable competitors and then explains why her business varies from those models. The one thing we know for certain is that these forecasts will be wrong, but the question is the degree of error. Detailed investigation of comparable companies reduces that error. The smaller the error, the less likely the company will run out of cash. Also, rigorous comparable analysis builds credibility with your investors.

What happens when the market space you are entering doesn't have comparable companies because they are private or differ significantly on some other major parameter? In such situations, entrepreneurs may be able to identify similar business models in other industries, or what I call first-cousin companies. If that proves difficult, the other avenue is the buildup method. Starting with each revenue source, the entrepreneur estimates how much of that revenue type he can generate per day or some other small time period. For example, if Joey Crugnale was trying to estimate sales for his Naked Fish restaurant, he might identify the following revenue sources along with the average ticket price for each: bar, appetizers, entrees, and dessert. Then he might estimate the number of people to come through the restaurant on a daily basis and what percentage would purchase each revenue source. Those estimates can then be aggregated into larger blocks of time (say, months, quarters, or years) to generate rough estimates, which might be further adjusted based upon seasonality in the restaurant industry.

The buildup technique is an imprecise method for the new startup with limited operating history, but it is critically important to assess the viability of the opportunity—so important, in fact, that I advise entrepreneurs to use both the comparable and buildup techniques to assess how well they converge. If the two methods widely diverge, go back through and try to determine why. The deep knowledge you gain of your business model will greatly help you to articulate the opportunity to stakeholders as well as to manage the business when it is launched.

Operations Plan (2–3 pages)

The operations section of the plan has progressively shortened as more companies outsource nonvital aspects of their operation. The key in this section is to address how operations will add value to your customers and, furthermore, to detail the production cycle so that you can gauge the impact on working capital. For instance, when does the company pay for inputs? How long does it take to produce the product? When does the customer buy the product and, more importantly, when does the customer pay for the product? The time from the beginning of this process until the product is paid for will drain cash flow and has implications for financing. Counterintuitively, many rapidly growing new companies run out of cash, even though they have increasing sales, because they fail to properly finance the time that cash is tied up in the procurement, production, sales, and receivables cycle.

Operations Strategy

The first subsection provides a strategy overview. How does your business win/compare on the dimensions of cost, quality, timeliness, and flexibility? The emphasis should be on those aspects that provide your venture with a comparative advantage.

You should also discuss geographic location of production facilities and how this enhances the firm's competitive advantage. Discuss available labor, local regulations, transportation, infrastructure, proximity to suppliers, and so forth. The section should also provide a description of the facilities, how the facilities will be acquired (bought or leased), and how future growth will be handled (e.g., renting an adjoining building).

Scope of Operations

What is the production process for your product or service? A diagram powerfully illustrates how your company adds value to the various inputs (see Exhibit 9.10a). Constructing the diagram also facilitates the decision of which production aspects to keep in-house and which to outsource. Considering that cash flow is king and that resource-constrained new ventures typically should minimize fixed expenses on production facilities, the general rule is to outsource as much production as possible. However, there is a major caveat to that rule: Your venture should control aspects of production that are central to your competitive advantage. Thus, if you are producing a new component with hardwired proprietary technology, let's say a voice recognition security door entry, it is wise to internally produce that hardwired component. The locking mechanism, however, can be outsourced to your specifications. Outsourcing the aspects that aren't proprietary reduces fixed cost for production equipment and facility expenditures, which means that you have to raise less money and give up less equity.

EXHIBIT 9.10a   Operations flow diagram.

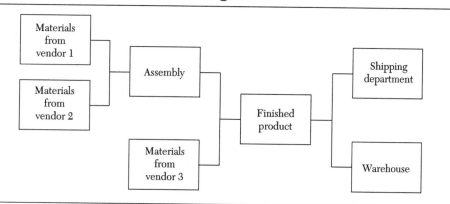

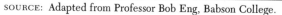

SOURCE: Adapted from Professor Bob Eng, Babson College.

The scope of operations should also discuss partnerships with vendors, suppliers, partners, and the like. Again, the diagram should illustrate the supplier and vendor relationships by category (or by name if the list isn't too long and you have already identified your suppliers). The diagram helps you visualize the various relationships and ways to better manage or eliminate them. The operations diagram also helps entrepreneurs identify personnel needs. For example, the diagram provides an indication of how many production workers might be needed depending on the hours of operations, number of shifts, and so forth.

Ongoing Operations

This section builds upon the scope of operations by providing details on day-to-day activities. For example, how many units will be produced in a day and what kind of inputs are necessary? An operating-cycle overview diagram graphically illustrates the impact of production on cash flow (see Exhibit 9.10b). As entrepreneurs complete this detail, they can start to establish performance parameters, which will help them monitor and modify the production process in the future. If this is an operational business plan the level of detail may include specific job descriptions, but for the typical business plan this level of detail would be much more than an investor, for example, would need or want to see in the initial evaluation phase.

Development Plan (2–3 pages)

The development plan highlights the development strategy and also provides a detailed development timeline. Many new ventures will require a significant level of effort and time to launch the product or service. This section tells how the business will be developed. For example, new software or hardware products

EXHIBIT 9.10b   Operating cycle overview diagram.

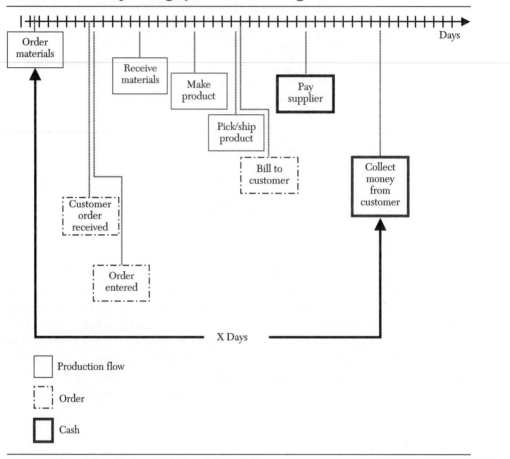

SOURCE: Adapted from Professor Bob Eng, Babson College.

often require months of development. Discuss what types of features you will develop and tie them to the firm's competitive advantage. This section should also talk about patent, trademark, or copyright efforts if applicable.

Development Strategy

What work remains to be completed? What factors need to come together for development to be successful? What risks to development does the firm face? For example, software development is notorious for taking longer and costing more than most companies originally imagined. Detailing the necessary work and the criteria for the work to be considered successful helps entrepreneurs to understand and manage the risks involved. After you have laid out these details, a development timeline is assembled.

Development Timeline

A development timeline is a schedule that highlights major milestones and can be used to monitor progress and make changes (see Exhibit 9.11). The timeline helps entrepreneurs track major events and to schedule activities to best execute on those events.

Team (2–3 pages)

Georges Doriot, the father of venture capital and founder of American Research and Development Corporation (the first modern venture capital firm), said that he would rather "back an 'A' entrepreneur with a 'B' idea than a 'B' entrepreneur with an 'A' idea." The team section of the business plan is often the section that professional investors read after the executive summary. Thus, it is critical that the plan depict the members responsible for key activities and convey that they are exceptionally skilled.

Team Bios and Roles

The best place to start is by identifying the key team members and their titles. Often, the lead entrepreneur assumes a CEO role. However, if you are young and have limited business experience, it is usually more productive to state that the company will seek a qualified CEO as it grows. The lead entrepreneur may then assume the role of chief technology officer (if he develops the technology) or vice president of business development. However, don't let these options confine you. The key is to convince investors that you have assembled the best team possible and that your team can execute on the brilliant concept you are proposing.

Once responsibilities and titles have been defined, names and a short bio should be filled in. The bios should demonstrate records of success. If you have previously started a business (even if it failed), highlight the company's accomplishments. If you have no previous entrepreneurial experience, discuss your achievements within your last job. For example, bios often contain a description of the number of people the entrepreneur previously managed and, more important, a measure of economic success, such as growing division sales by 20+%. The bio should demonstrate your leadership capabilities. To complement this description, resumes are often included as an appendix.

Advisory Boards, Board of Directors, Strategic Partners, External Members

To enhance the team's credentials, many entrepreneurs find that they are more attractive to investors if they have strong advisory boards. In building an advisory board, identify individuals with relevant experience within your industry.

EXHIBIT 9.11 Development timeline.

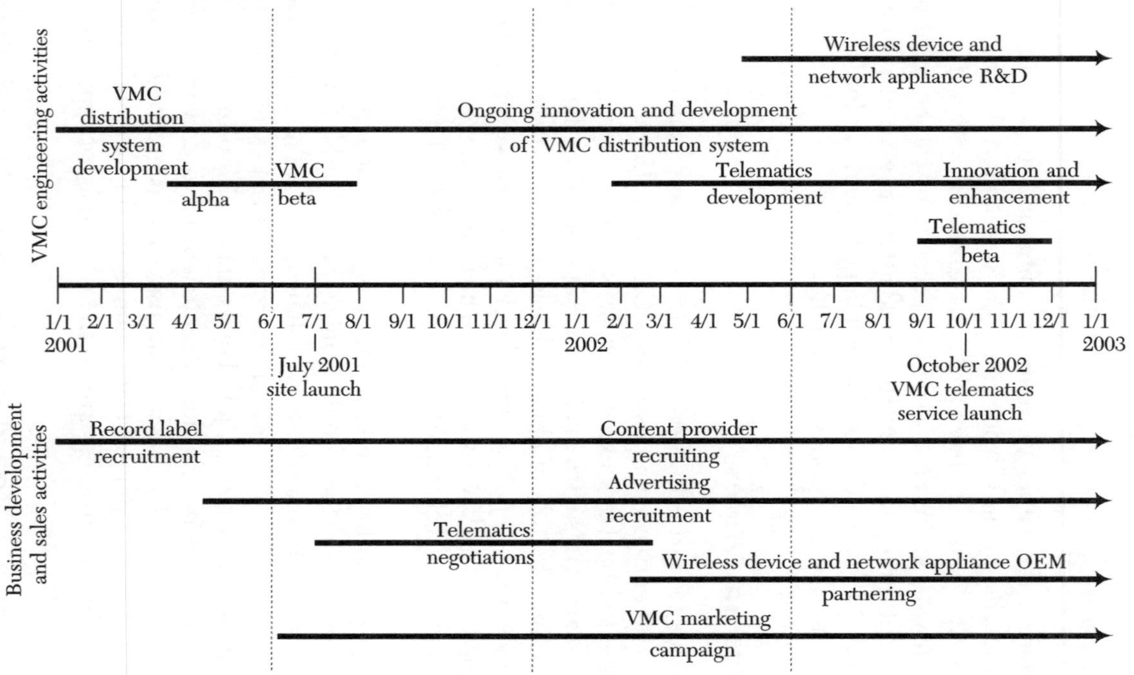

Industry experts provide legitimacy to your new business as well as strong technical advice. Other advisory board members may bring financial, legal, or management expertise. Thus, it is common to see lawyers, professors, accountants, and others who can assist the venture's growth on advisory boards. Moreover, if your firm has a strategic supplier or key customer, it may make sense to invite him or her onto your advisory board. Typically, these individuals are remunerated with a small equity stake and compensation for any organized meetings.

By law, most organization types require a board of directors. This is different than an advisory board (although these members can also provide needed expertise). The board's primary role is to oversee the company on behalf of the investors. Therefore, the business plan needs to briefly describe the size of the board, its role within the organization and any current board members. Most major investors, such as venture capitalists, will require one or more board seats. Usually, the lead entrepreneur and one or more inside company members (e.g., chief financial officers, vice presidents) will also have board seats.

Strategic partners, though not necessarily on your advisory board or board of directors, may still provide credibility to your venture. In such cases, it makes sense to highlight their involvement in your company's success. It is also common to list external team members, such as the law firm and accounting firm that your venture uses. The key in this section is to demonstrate that your firm can successfully execute the concept. A strong team provides the foundation on which your venture will implement the opportunity successfully.

Compensation and Ownership

The capstone to the team section should be a table containing key team members by role, compensation, and ownership equity. A brief description of the table should explain why the compensation is appropriate. Many entrepreneurs choose not to pay themselves in the early months. Although this strategy conserves cash flow, it would misrepresent the individual's worth to the organization. Therefore, the table should contain what salary the employee is due, and then, if necessary, that salary can be deferred until cash flow is strong. Another column that can be powerful shows what the person's current or most recent compensation was and what he will be paid in the new company. I am most impressed by highly qualified entrepreneurs taking a smaller salary than at their previous job. It suggests that the entrepreneur really believes in the upside payoff the company's growth will generate. Of course, the entrepreneur plans on increasing this salary as the venture grows and starts to thrive. As such, the description of the schedule should underscore the plan to increase salaries in the future. It is also a good idea to hold stock aside for future key hires and to establish a stock option pool for lower-level but critical employees, such as software engineers. Again, the plan should discuss such provisions.

Critical Risks (1–2 pages)

Every new venture faces a number of risks that may threaten its survival. Although the business plan, at this point, is creating a story of success, there are a number of threats that readers will identify and recognize. The plan needs to acknowledge these potential risks; otherwise, investors may believe that the entrepreneur is naïve or untrustworthy and therefore reject investment. How should you present these critical risks without scaring your investor? Identify the risk and then state your contingency plan (see Exhibit 9.12). Critical risks are critical assumptions, factors that need to happen if your venture is to succeed. The critical assumptions vary from one company to another, but some common categories are: market interest and growth potential, competitor actions and retaliation, time and cost of development, operating expenses, availability and timing of financing.

Market Interest and Growth Potential

The biggest risk any new venture faces is that once the product is developed, no one will buy it. Although there are a number of things that can be done to minimize this risk, such as market research, focus groups, beta sites, and others, it is difficult to gauge overall demand and growth of that demand until your product hits the market. This risk must be stated but tempered with the tactics and contingencies the company will undertake. For example, sales risk can be reduced by an effective advertising and marketing plan or identifying not only a primary target customer but secondary and tertiary target customers that the company will seek if the primary customer proves less interested.

Competitor Actions and Retaliation

Having worked with entrepreneurs and student entrepreneurs over the years, I have always been struck by the firmly held belief that direct competition either didn't exist or that it was sleepy and slow to react. There have been many cases

EXHIBIT 9.12   Sample critical risk.

6.2 Group's lack of experience in starting own company   Within our present team, we realize that we lack the real world experience in starting up a company, but we feel that this can be overcome in two different ways. First, we plan on hiring someone who has a background in managing a startup company and has a history in working with e-commerce businesses. Secondly, we will draw on family expertise within our group. William Smith's family has started a successful golf retail store that has been in operation for nearly 20 years and is just starting to utilize the Web to foster continued growth. Jim Meier's father is the managing partner of the largest public accounting firm in western Massachusetts. Mike Santana's uncle is an investment banker and has some good friends in the venture capital firm Canyon Partners in Beverly Hills. Pat Crown's father is the founder and president of Mathtech Corporation in Boston, Massachusetts. Mr. Crown's company develops math software.

where this is indeed true, but I caution against using it as a key assumption of your venture's success. Most entrepreneurs passionately believe that they are offering something new and wonderful that is clearly different from what is currently being offered. They are confident that existing competition won't attack their niche in the near future. The risk that this assessment is wrong should be acknowledged. One counter to this threat is that the venture has room in its gross margin and cash available to withstand and fight such attacks. You should also identify some strategies to protect and reposition yourself should an attack occur.

Time and Cost to Development

As mentioned in the development plan section, many factors can delay and add to the expense of developing your product. The business plan should identify the factors that may hinder development. For instance, during the extended high-tech boom of the late nineties and into the new century, there has been an acute shortage of skilled software engineers. One way to counter the resulting risk in hiring and retaining the most qualified professionals might be to outsource some development to the underemployed engineers in India. Compensation, equity participation, flexible hours, and other benefits that the firm could offer might also minimize the risk.

Operating Expenses

Operating expenses have a way of growing beyond expectations. Sales and administration, marketing, and interest expenses are some of the areas that the entrepreneur needs to monitor and manage. The business plan should highlight how these expenses were forecast (comparable companies and detailed analysis) but also discuss contingencies such as slowing the hiring of support personnel, especially if development or other key tasks take longer than expected.

Availability and Timing of Financing

I can't stress enough how important cash flow is to the survival and growth of a new venture. One major risk that most new ventures face is that they will have difficulty obtaining needed financing, both equity and debt. If the current business plan is meant to attract investors and is successful, that first capital infusion isn't a near-term risk, but most ventures will need multiple rounds of financing. If the firm fails to make progress (or meet key milestones), it may not be able to secure additional rounds of financing on favorable terms. To mitigate this risk, the firm could identify alternative sources that are viable or strategies to slow the "burn rate."[6]

There are a number of other risks that might apply to your business. Acknowledge them and discuss how you can overcome them. Doing so generates confidence in your investors.

Offering (½–1 page)

Based upon the entrepreneur's vision and estimates of the capital required to get there, the entrepreneur can develop a "sources and uses schedule" (see Exhibit 9.13). The sources section details how much capital the entrepreneur needs and the types of financing such as equity investment and debt infusions. The uses section details how the money will be spent. Typically, the entrepreneur should secure enough financing to last 12 to 18 months. Taking more capital means that the entrepreneur gives up more equity. Taking less means that the entrepreneur may run out of cash before reaching milestones that equate to higher valuations.

Financial Plan (4–8 pages)

If the preceding plan is your verbal description of the opportunity and how you will execute it, the financial plan is the mathematical equivalent. The growth in revenues speaks to the upside of your opportunity. The expenses illustrate what you need to execute on that opportunity. Cash flow statements serve as an early warning system to potential problems (or critical risks), and the balance sheet enables monitoring and adjusting the venture's progress. That being said, generating realistic financials is one of the most intimidating hurdles entrepreneurs face. I will highlight a dual strategy to building your model: comparable analysis and the buildup technique. Entrepreneurs should do both approaches; with work and skill the two approaches allow the entrepreneur to triangulate into a credible facsimile.

Entrepreneurs are notoriously overoptimistic in their projections. One phrase that entrepreneurs overuse in their business plan, especially the financial plan, is "conservative estimate." History proves that 99% of all entrepreneurs are amazingly aggressive in their projections. Professional investors recognize this problem and often discount financials up to 50% from the entrepreneur's projections. How do you prevent that from happening? Validate your projections by comparing your firm's pro forma financials to existing firm's actual performance. Obviously, no two firms are exactly alike, and if you were to launch an online bookstore, it would be unlikely that your firm would perfectly mirror Amazon.com. However, the comparable method doesn't mean that you substitute another firm's financials for your own; it means that you use

EXHIBIT 9.13 Sources and uses schedule.

Sources		Uses	
5,000,000	VC	1,688,750	Systems development
		1,652,000	Equipment
		1,125,000	Sales/business development
		534,250	Working capital
5,000,000	Total	5,000,000	

that comparable firm as a starting point. Entrepreneurs then need to articulate why their projections vary from the comparable firm, both in a positive and negative manner. Continuing the online bookstore example, I would be insane to believe that I could achieve the same rapid growth that Amazon.com experienced, because there is now more competition, especially from Amazon.com. On the flip side, I should be able to argue that my expenses won't be as stifling as Amazon's, because I have studied and learned from their excesses. I would also articulate how my fulfillment is more efficient than Amazon's. So the key in the comparable method is to use other firms and industry standards as a starting point and then adjust your projections based upon your strategy and other factors.

Industry averages also provide useful comparable information. The *Almanac of Business and Industrial Financial Ratios,* published by Prentice-Hall, or *Industry Norms and Key Business Ratios,* published by Dun and Bradstreet are excellent sources to use as starting points in building financial statements relevant to your industry. Specifically, these sources help entrepreneurs build income statements by providing industry averages for costs of goods sold, salary expenses, interest expenses, and the like. Again, your firm will differ from these industry averages, but you should be able to explain why your firm differs.

The second method is the buildup method. This approach derives from the scientific finding that people make better decisions by decomposing a problem into smaller parts. For financial pro forma construction, this is relatively easy. The place to start is the income statement. Identify all of your revenue sources (usually the various product offerings). Instead of visualizing what you will sell in a month or a year, break it down to the day. For example, if I am starting a new restaurant, I would estimate how many customers I might serve in a particular day and how much they would spend per visit based upon the types of meals and beverages they would buy. In essence, I am developing an average ticket price per customer. I then multiply that price by the number of days of operation in the year. Once I have the typical day, I can make adjustments for cyclical aspects of the business, such as slow days or slow months. If I were, say, to open up a chain of restaurants, I could then multiple my estimates by the number of restaurants. Once you have gone through a couple of iterations of each approach, you should be able to reconcile the differences.

One schedule that is particularly powerful in building up your cost estimates is a headcount schedule. This table should have time across the top and job categories down the side (see Exhibit 9.14). Next assign average salaries and burden to these employees and then funnel them into the appropriate income statement lines. Breaking down to this level of detail enables entrepreneurs to more accurately aggregate up to their real headcount expenses, which tend to be the major line item in most companies.

Going through the above exercises allows you to construct a realistic set of pro forma financials. The financial statements that must be included in your

EXHIBIT 9.14 Headcount chart.

	Month 1	Month 6	Month 12	Month 18	Month 24	Month 30	Month 36
Business development	1	2	3	3	3	3	3
Sales and administration	2	2	6	10	10	14	14
Software developers	3	3	3	18	18	23	26
Customer service	0	2	3	5	5	10	10
Total head count	6	9	15	36	36	50	53

plan are the income statement, cash flow statement, and balance sheet. I typically call for five years of financials, recognizing that the farther out one goes, the less accurate the forecasts are. The rationale behind five years is that the first two years show the firm surviving and the last three years show the upside growth potential. The majority of new ventures lose money for the first two years. Therefore, the income statement and cash flow statement should be month-to-month during the first two years to show how much cash is needed until the firm can become self-sustaining. Month-to-month analysis shows cash flow decreasing and provides an early warning system as to when the entrepreneur should seek the next round of financing. Years 3 through 5 need to be illustrated only on an annual basis, because these projections communicate your vision for growth but are likely to be less accurate because they are further out. The balance sheet can be on an annual basis for all five years since it is reporting a snapshot on the last day of a particular period.

Once the financial spreadsheets are completed, a two-to-three-page explanation of the financials should be written and it should precede the statements. Although you understand all the assumptions and comparisons that went into building the financial forecast, the reader needs the background spelled out. The explanation should have four subheadings: overview, income statement, cash flow, and balance sheet. The overview section should highlight the major assumptions that drive your revenue and expenses. This section should explain several of the critical risks you identified earlier. The income statement description goes into more detail as to some of the revenue and cost drivers that haven't been discussed in the overview section. The cash flow description talks about the timing of cash infusions, accounts payable, accounts receivable, and so forth. The balance sheet description illustrates how major ratios change as the firm grows.

Appendices (as many pages as necessary)

The appendices can include anything that you think further validates your concept but doesn't fit or is too large to insert in the main parts of the plan.

Common inclusions would be one-page resumes of key team members, articles that feature your venture, and technical specifications.

CONCLUSION

The business plan is more than just a document; it is a process. Although the finished product is often a written plan, the deep thinking that goes into that document provides the entrepreneur keen insight needed to marshal resources and direct growth. The whole process can be painful, but the returns on a solid effort almost always minimize the costs of starting a business, because the process allows the entrepreneur to better anticipate, instead of reacting to, the many issues the venture will face. More important, the business plan provides a talking point so that entrepreneurs can get feedback from a number of experts, including investors, vendors, and customers. Think of the business plan as one of your first steps on the journey to entrepreneurial success.

OTHER RESOURCES

A number of resources exist for those seeking help to write business plans. There are numerous software packages, but I find that generally the templates are too confining. The text boxes asking for information box writers into a dull, dispassionate tone. The best way to learn about business plans is digging out the supporting data, writing sections as you feel compelled, and circulating drafts among your mentors and advisors. I also think that the entrepreneur should read as many other articles, chapters, and books about writing business plans as possible. You will want to assimilate different perspectives so that you can find your own personal voice. To that end, I want to suggest a number of sources that you might want to check out.

FOR FURTHER READING

Timmons, J. A., *New Venture Creation,* 5th ed. (New York: Irwin/McGraw-Hill, 1999). Classic textbook on the venture creation process.

Tracy, J., *How to Read a Financial Report,* 5th ed. (New York: John Wiley, 1999). Classic book on how to create pro forma financial statements and how these statements tie together.

Sahlman, W., "How to Write a Great Business Plan," *Harvard Business Review* (July–Aug. 1997): 98–108.

Bhide, A., "The Questions Every Entrepreneur Should Ask," *Harvard Business Review* (Nov.–Dec. 1996): 120–130.

Kim, C., and R. Mauborgne, "Creating New Market Space," *Harvard Business Review* (Jan.–Feb. 1999): 83–93.

INTERNET LINKS

Business Plan Sites

www.pasware.com
www.brs-inc.com
www.jian.com

Other Useful Sites

www.entreworld.org
www.babson.edu/entrep

NOTES

1.   P. Thomas, "Rewriting the Rules: A New Generation of Entrepreneurs Find Themselves in the Perfect Time and Place to Chart Their Own Course," *Wall Street Journal,* May 22, 2000, R4.

2.   Running sidebar is a visual device that is positioned down the right hand side of the page that periodically highlights some of the key points in the plan. Don't overload the sidebar, but one or two items per page can draw attention to highlights that maintain reader interest.

3.   Don't confuse the executive summary included in the plan with the expanded executive summary that I suggested you write as the very first step of the business plan process. Again, the two summaries are likely to be significantly different since the later summary incorporates all the deep learning that you have gained throughout the process.

4.   J. Timmons, *New Venture Creation,* 5th ed. (New York: Irwin/McGraw-Hill, 1999).

5.   O. Sacirbey, "Private Companies Temper IPO Talk," *The IPO Reporter,* Dec. 18, 2000, 9.

6.   Burn rate is how much more cash the company is expending each month than earning in revenue.

10 PLANNING CAPITAL EXPENDITURE

Steven P. Feinstein

A beer company is considering building a new brewery. An airline is deciding whether to add flights to its schedule. An engineer at a high-tech company has designed a new microchip and hopes to encourage the company to manufacture and sell it. A small college contemplates buying a new photocopy machine. A nonprofit museum is toying with the idea of installing an education center for children. Newlyweds dream of buying a house. A retailer considers building a Web site and selling on the Internet.

What do these projects have in common? All of them entail a commitment of capital and managerial effort that may or may not be justified by later performance. A common set of tools can be applied to assess these seemingly very different propositions. The financial analysis used to assess such projects is known as "capital budgeting." How should a limited supply of capital and managerial talent be allocated among an unlimited number of possible projects and corporate initiatives?

THE OBJECTIVE: MAXIMIZE WEALTH

Capital budgeting decisions cut to the heart of the most fundamental questions in business. What is the purpose of the firm? Is it to create wealth for investors? To serve the needs of customers? To provide jobs for employees? To better the community? These questions are fodder for endless debate. Ultimately, however, project decisions have to be made, and so we must adopt a

291

decision rule. The perspective of financial analysis is that capital investment belongs to the investors. The goal of the firm is to maximize investors' wealth. Other factors are important and should be considered, but this is the primary objective. In the case of nonprofit organizations, wealth and return on investment need not be measured in dollars and cents but rather can be measured in terms of benefits to society. But in the case of for-profit companies, wealth is monetary.

A project creates wealth if it generates cash flows over time that are worth more in present-value terms than the initial setup cost. For example, suppose a brewery costs $10 million to build, but once built it generates a stream of cash flows that is worth $11 million. Building the brewery would create $1 million of new wealth. If there were no other proposed projects that would create more wealth than this, then the beer company would be well advised to build the new brewery.

This example illustrates the "net present value" rule. Net present value (NPV) is the difference between the setup cost of a project and the value of the project once it is set up. If that difference is positive, then the NPV is positive and the project creates wealth. If a firm must choose from several proposed projects, the one with the highest NPV will create the most wealth, and so it should be the one adopted. For example, suppose the beer company can either build the new brewery or, alternatively, can introduce a new product—a light beer, for example. There is not enough managerial talent to oversee more than one new project, or maybe there are not enough funds to start both. Let us assume that both projects create wealth: The NPV of the new brewery is $1 million, and the NPV of the new-product project is $500,000. If it could, the beer company should undertake both projects; but since it has to choose, building the new brewery would be the right option because it has the higher NPV.

COMPUTING NPV: PROJECTING CASH FLOWS

The first step in calculating a project's NPV is to forecast the project's future cash flows. Cash is king. It is cash flow, not profit, that investors really care about. If a company never generates cash flow, there can be no return to investors. Also, profit can be manipulated by discretionary accounting treatments such as depreciation method or inventory valuation. Regardless of accounting choices, however, cash flow either materializes or does not. For these reasons, cash flow is the most important variable to investors. A project's value derives from the cash flow it creates, and NPV is the value of the future cash flows net of the initial cash outflow.

We can illustrate the method of forecasting cash flows with an example. Let us continue to explore the brewery project. Suppose project engineers inform you that the construction costs for the brewery would be $8 million. The expected life of the new brewery is 10 years. The brewery will be depreciated to zero over its 10-year life using a straight-line depreciation schedule. Land for the brewery can be purchased for $1 million. Additional inventory to stock the new brewery would cost $1 million. The brewery would be fully operational within a year. If the project is undertaken, increased sales for the beer company would be $7 million per year. Cost of goods sold for this beer would be $2 million per year; and selling, administrative, and general expenses associated with the new brewery would be $1 million per year. Perhaps advertising would have to increase by $500,000 per year. After 10 years, the land can be sold for $1 million, or it can be used for another project. After 10 years the salvage value of the plant is expected to be $1.5 million. The increase in accounts receivable would exactly equal the increase in accounts payable, at $400,000, so these components of net working capital would offset one another and generate no net cash flow.

No one expects these forecasts to be perfect. Paraphrasing the famous words of baseball player Yogi Berra, making predictions is very difficult, especially when they are about the future! However, when investors choose among various investments, they too must make predictions. As a financial analyst, you want the quality of your forecasts to be on a par with the quality of the forecasts made by investors. Essentially, the job of the financial analyst is to estimate how investors will value the project, because the value of the firm will rise if investors decide that the new project creates wealth and will fall if investors conclude that the project destroys wealth. If the investors have reason to believe that sales will be $7 million per year, then that would be the correct forecast to use in the capital budgeting analysis. Investors have to cope with uncertainty in their forecasts. Similarly, the financial analyst conducting a capital budgeting analysis must tolerate the same level of uncertainty.

Note that cash flow projections require an integrated team effort across the entire firm. Operations and engineering personnel estimate the cost of building and operating the new plant. The human resources department contributes the labor data. Marketing people tell you what advertising budget is needed and forecast revenue. The accounting department estimates taxes, accounts payable, and accounts receivable and tabulates the financial data. The job of the financial analyst is to put the pieces together and recommend that the project be adopted or abandoned.

Initial Cash Outflow

The initial cash outflow required by the project is the sum of the construction cost ($8 million), the land cost ($1 million), and the required new inventory ($1 million). Thus, this project requires an investment of $10 million to launch. If accounts receivable did not equal accounts payable, then the new accounts receivable would add to the initial cash outflow, and the new accounts payable would be subtracted. These cash flows are tabulated in Exhibit 10.1.

EXHIBIT 10.1   Initial year cash flow for brewery project ($1,000s).

	Year 0
Construction	$ (8,000)
Land	(1,000)
Inventory	(1,000)
Account receivable	(400)
Accounts payable	400
Total cash flow	$(10,000)

Cash Flows in Later Years

We find cash flow in years 1 through 10 by applying the following formula:

Cash Flow = Sales – Cost of goods sold
- Selling, administrative, and general expenses
- Advertising
- Income tax
+ Decrease in inventory (or – increase)
+ Decrease in accounts receivable (or – increase)
- Decrease in accounts payable (or + increase)
+ Salvage
- Windfall tax on salvage

Notice that we already have most of the data needed for the cash-flow formula, but we are missing the forecasts for income tax and windfall tax. Before we can finalize the cash flow computation, we have to forecast taxes.

Income tax equals earnings before taxes (EBT) times the income tax rate. EBT is computed using the following formula:

Earnings before Taxes = Sales – Cost of goods sold
- Selling, administrative, and general expenses
- Advertising
- Depreciation

The formula for EBT is similar to the formula for cash-flow, with a few important exceptions. The cash-flow calculation does not subtract out depreciation, whereas the EBT calculation does. This is because depreciation is not a cash flow; the firm never has to write a check payable to "depreciation." Depreciation does reduce taxable income, however, because the government allows this deduction for tax purposes. So depreciation influences cash flow via its impact on income tax, but it is not a cash flow itself. The greater the allowable depreciation is in a given year, the lower taxes will be, and the greater the resulting cash flow to the firm.

Treatment of Net Working Capital

Changes in inventory, accounts receivable, and accounts payable are included in the cash-flow calculation but not in EBT. Changes in the components of working capital directly impact cash flow, but they are not deductible for tax purposes. When a firm buys inventory, it has essentially swapped one asset, (cash) for another asset (inventory). Though this is a negative cash flow, it is not considered a deductible expenditure for tax purposes.

Similarly, a rise in accounts receivable means that cash that otherwise would have been in the company coffers is now owed to the company instead. Thus, an increase in accounts receivable effectively sucks cash out of the company and must be treated as a cash outflow. Increasing accounts payable has the opposite effect.

One way to gain perspective on the impact of accounts payable and accounts receivable on a company's cash flow is to think of them as adjustments to sales and costs of goods sold. If a company makes a sale but the customer has not yet paid, clearly there is no cash flow generated from the sale. Though the sales variable will increase, the increase in accounts receivable will exactly offset that increase in the cash flow computation. Similarly, if the company incurs expenses in the manufacture of the goods sold but has not yet paid its suppliers for the raw materials, the costs of goods sold will be offset by the increase in accounts payable.

Depreciation

According to a straight-line depreciation schedule, depreciation in each year is the initial cost of the plant or equipment divided by the number of years over which the asset will be depreciated. So, the $8 million plant depreciated over 10 years generates depreciation of $800,000 each year. Land is generally not depreciated. Straight-line depreciation is but one acceptable method for determining depreciation of plant and equipment. The tax authorities often sanction other methods and schedules.

Windfall Profit and Windfall Tax

In order to compute windfall profit and windfall tax, we must be able to track an asset's book value over its life. Book value is the initial value minus all previous depreciation. For example, the brewery initially has a book value of $8 million, but that value falls $800,000 per year due to depreciation. At the end of the first year, book value falls to $7.2 million. By the end of the second year, following another $800,000 of depreciation, the book value will be $6.4 million. By the end of the tenth year, when the brewery is fully depreciated, the book value will be zero.

Windfall profit is the difference between the salvage value and book value. We are told the beer company will be able to sell the old brewery for

$1.5 million at the end of 10 years. By then, however, the book value of the brewery will be zero. Thus, the beer company will realize a windfall profit of $1.5 million. The government will want its share of that windfall profit. Multiplying the windfall profit by the tax rate determines the windfall tax. In this particular case, with a windfall profit of $1.5 million and a tax rate of 40%, the windfall tax would equal $600 thousand (= $1.5 million × 40%).

Taxable Income and Income Tax

Exhibit 10.2 shows how taxable income and income tax are computed for the brewery example. Income tax equals EBT times the company's income tax rate. In each of years 1 through 10, EBT is $2.7 million, so income tax is $1,080,000 (= $2.7 million × 40%).

Interest Expense

Notice that the calculation of taxable income and income tax in Exhibit 10.2 does not deduct any interest expense. This is not an oversight. Even if the company intends to finance the new project by selling bonds or borrowing from a bank, we should not deduct any anticipated interest expense from our taxable income, and we should not subtract interest payments in the cash flow computation. We will take the tax shield of debt financing into account later when we compute the company's cost of capital. The reason for omitting interest expense at this stage cuts to the core of the purpose of capital budgeting. We are trying to forecast how much cash is required from investors to start this project and then how much cash this project will generate for the investors once the project is up and running. Interest expense is a distribution of cash to one class of investors—the debt holders. If we want the bottom line of our cash-flow computation to reflect how much cash will be available to all investors, we must not subtract out cash flow going to one class of investors before we get to that bottom line.

EXHIBIT 10.2   Income tax forecasts for brewery project (thousands).

	Years 1–10
Sales	$ 7,000
Cost of goods sold	(2,000)
Selling, administrative, and general expenses	(1,000)
Advertising	(500)
Depreciation	(800)
Earnings before taxes	$ 2,700
Income tax (40%)	$(1,080)

Putting the Pieces Together to Forecast Cash Flow

We now have all the puzzle pieces to construct our capital budgeting cash-flow projection. These pieces and the resulting cash-flow projection are presented in Exhibit 10.3. Cash flows in years 1 through 9 are forecast to be $2.42 million, and the cash flow in year 10 is expected to be $5.32 million. Year 10 has a greater cash flow because of the recovery of the inventory and the assumed sale of the land and plant.

GUIDING PRINCIPLES FOR FORECASTING CASH FLOWS

The brewery example is one illustration of how cash flows are forecast. Every project is different, however, and the financial analyst must be keen to identify all sources of cash flow. The following three principles can serve as a guide: (1) Focus on cash flow, not on raw accounting data, (2) use expected values, and (3) focus on the incremental.

Principle No. 1: Focus on Cash Flow

NPV analysis focuses on cash flows—that is, actual cash payments and receipts flowing into or out of the firm. Recall that accounting profit is not the same thing as cash flow. Accounting profit often mixes variables whose timings differ. A sale made today may show up in today's profits, but since the cash receipt for the sale may be deferred, the corresponding cash flow takes place

EXHIBIT 10.3   Cash flow projections for brewery project (thousands).

Year:	0	1–9	10
Construction	$ (8,000)		
Land	(1,000)		$1,000
Inventory	(1,000)		1,000
Account receivable	(400)		400
Accounts payable	400		(400)
Sales		$7,000	7,000
Cost of goods sold		(2,000)	(2,000)
Selling, admin., and general		(1,000)	(1,000)
Advertising		(500)	(500)
Income tax		(1,080)	(1,080)
Salvage			1,500
Windfall tax			(600)
Total cash flow	$(10,000)	$2,420	$5,320

later. Since the cash flow is deferred, the true value of that sale to the firm is somewhat diminished.

By focusing on cash flows and when they occur, NPV reflects the true value of increased revenues and costs. Consequently, NPV analysis requires that accounting data be unraveled to reveal the underlying cash flows. That is why changes in net working capital must be accounted for and why depreciation does not show up directly.

Principle No. 2: Use Expected Values

There is always going to be some uncertainty over future cash flows. Future costs and revenues cannot be known for sure. The analyst must gather as much information as possible and assemble it to construct expected values of the input variables. Although expected values are not perfect, these best guesses have to be good enough. What is the alternative? The uncertainty in forecasting the inputs is accounted for in the discount rate that is later used to discount the expected cash flows.

Principle No. 3: Focus on the Incremental

NPV analysis is done in terms of "incremental" cash flows—that is, the change in cash flow generated by the decision to undertake the project. Incremental cash flow is the difference between what the cash flow would be with the project and what the firm's cash flow would be without the project. Any sales or savings that would have happened without the project and are unaffected by doing the project are irrelevant and should be ignored. Similarly, any costs that would have been incurred anyway are irrelevant. It is often difficult yet nonetheless important to focus on the incremental when calculating how cash flows are impacted by opportunity costs, sunk costs, and overhead. These troublesome areas will be elaborated on next.

Opportunity Costs

Opportunity costs are opportunities for cash inflows that must be sacrificed in order to undertake the project. No check is written to pay for opportunity costs, but they represent changes in the firm's cash flows caused by the project and must, therefore, be treated as actual costs of doing the project. For example, suppose the firm owns a parking lot, and a proposed project requires use of that land. Is the land free since the firm already owns it? No; if the project were not undertaken then the company could sell or rent out the land. Use of the company's land is, therefore, not free. There is an opportunity cost. Money that could have been earned if the project were rejected will not be earned if the project is started. In order to reflect fully the incremental impact of the proposed project, the incremental cash flows used in NPV analysis must incorporate opportunity costs.

Sunk Costs

Sunk costs are expenses that have already been paid or have already been committed to. Past research and development are examples. Since sunk costs are not incremental to the proposed project, NPV analysis must ignore them. NPV analysis is always forward-looking. The past cannot be changed and so should not enter into the choice of a future course of action. If research was undertaken last year, the effects of that research might bear on future cash flows, but the cost of that research is already water under the bridge and so is not relevant in the decision to continue the project. The project decision must be made on the basis of whether the project increases or decreases wealth from the present into the future. The past is irrelevant.

Overhead

The treatment of overhead often gives project managers a headache. Overhead comprises expenditures made by the firm for resources that are shared by many projects or departments. Heat and maintenance for common facilities are examples. Management resources and shared support staff are other examples. Overhead represents resources required for the firm to provide an environment in which projects can be undertaken. Different firms use different formulas for charging overhead expenses to various projects and departments. If overhead charges accurately reflect the shared resources used by a project, then they should be treated as incremental costs of operating the project. If the project were not undertaken, those shared resources would benefit another moneymaking project, or perhaps the firm could possibly cut some of the shared overhead expenditures. Thus, to the extent that overhead does represent resources used by the project, it should be included in calculating incremental cash flows. If, on the other hand, overhead expense is unaffected by the decision to undertake the new project, and no other proposed project could use those shared resources, then overhead should be ignored in the NPV analysis. Sometimes the formulas used to calculate overhead for budgeting purposes are unrealistic and overcharge projects for their use of shared resources. If the financial analyst does not correct this unrepresentative allocation of costs, some worthwhile projects might incorrectly appear undesirable.

COMPUTING NPV: THE TIME VALUE OF MONEY

In deciding whether a project is worthwhile, one needs to know more than *whether* it will make money. One must also know *when* it will make money. Time is money! Project decisions involve cash flows spread out over several periods. As we shall see, cash flows in different periods are distinct products in the financial marketplace—as different as apples and oranges. To make decisions affecting many future periods, we must know how to convert the different periods' cash flows into a common currency.

The concept that future cash flows have a lower present value and the set of tools used to discount future cash flows to their present values are collectively known as "time value of money" (TVOM) analysis. I have always thought this to be a misnomer; the name should be the "money value of time." But there is no use bucking the trend, so we will adopt the standard nomenclature.

You probably already have an intuitive grasp of the fundamentals of TVOM analysis, as your likely answer to the following question illustrates: Would you rather have $100 today or $100 next year? Why?

The answer to this question is the essence of TVOM. You no doubt answered that you would rather have the money today. Money today is worth more than money to be delivered in the future. Even if there were perfect certainty that the future money would be received, we prefer to have money in hand today. There are many reasons for this. Having money in hand allows greater flexibility for planning. You might choose to spend it before the future money would be delivered. If you choose not to spend the money during the course of the year, you can earn interest on it by investing it. Understanding TVOM allows you to quantify exactly how much more early cash flows are worth than deferred cash flows. An example will illuminate the concept.

Suppose you and a friend have dinner together in a restaurant. You order an inexpensive sandwich. Your friend orders a large steak, a bottle of wine, and several desserts. The bill arrives and your friend's share is $100. Unfortunately, your friend forgot his wallet and asks to borrow the $100 from you. You agree and pay. A year passes before your friend remembers to pay you back the money. "Here is the $100," he finally says one day. Such events test a friendship, especially if you had to carry a $100 balance on your credit card over the course of the year on which interest accrued at a rate of 18%. Is the $100 that your friend is offering you now worth the same as the $100 that he borrowed a year earlier? Actually, no; a $100 cash flow today is not worth $100 next year. The same nominal amount has different values depending on when it is paid. If the interest rate is 18%, a $100 cash flow today is worth $118 next year and is worth $139.24 the year after because of compound interest. The present value of $118 to be received next year is exactly $100 today. Your friend should pay you $118 if he borrowed $100 from you a year earlier.

The formula for converting a future value to a present value is:

$$PV = \frac{FV}{(1+r)^n}$$

where PV stands for present value, FV is future value, n is the number of periods in the future that the future cash flow is paid, and r is the appropriate interest rate or discount rate.

Discounting Cash Flows

Suppose in the brewery example that the appropriate discount rate for translating future values to present values was 20%. Recall that the brewery project was forecast to generate $2.42 million of cash in year 1. The present value of that cash flow, as of year 0, is $2,016,670, computed as follows:

$$PV = \frac{\$2,420,000}{(1.20)^1} = \$2,016,670$$

Similarly, the year-2 cash flow was forecast to be $2.42 million also. The present value of that second-year cash flow is only $1,680,560:

$$PV = \frac{\$2,420,000}{(1.20)^2} = \$1,680,560$$

The longer the time over which a cash flow is discounted, the lower is its present value. Exhibit 10.4 presents the forecasted cash flows and their discounted present values for the brewery project.

Summing the Discounted Cash Flows to Arrive at NPV

Finally, we can calculate the NPV. The NPV is the sum of all discounted cash flows, which in the brewery example equals $614,000. To understand precisely what this means, observe that the sum of the discounted cash flows from years 1 through 10 is $10,614,000. This means that the project generates future cash flows that are worth $10,614,000 today. The initial cost of the project is $10,000,000 today. Thus, the project is worth $10,614,000 but costs only $10,000,000 and therefore creates $614,000 of new wealth. The managers of the beer company would be well advised to adopt this project, because it has a positive NPV and therefore creates wealth.

EXHIBIT 10.4   Discounted cash flows for brewery project (thousands).

Year	Cash Flow	Discounted Cash Flow
0	$(10,000)	$(10,000)
1	2,420	2,017
2	2,420	1,681
3	2,420	1,400
4	2,420	1,167
5	2,420	973
6	2,420	810
7	2,420	675
8	2,420	563
9	2,420	469
10	5,320	859

MORE NPV EXAMPLES

Consider two alternative projects, A and B. They both cost $1,000,000 to set up. Project A returns $800,000 per year for two years starting one year after setup. Project B also returns $800,000 per year for two years, but the cash flows begin two years after setup. The firm uses a discount rate of 20%. Which is the better project, A or B?

Like project A, project C also costs $1,000,000 to set up, and it will pay back $1,600,000. For both A and C, the firm will earn $800,000 per year for two years starting one year after setup. However, C costs $500,000 initially and the other $500,000 need only be paid at the termination of the project (it may be a cleanup cost, for example). Project A requires the initial outlay all at once at the outset. Which is the better project, A or C? Of projects A, B, and C, which project(s) should be undertaken?

We should make the project decision only after analyzing each project's NPV. Exhibit 10.5 tabulates each project's cash flows, discounted cash flows, and NPVs. The NPVs of Projects A, B, and C, are, respectively, $222,222, −$151,235, and $375,000. Project C has the highest NPV. Therefore, if only one project can be selected, it should be project C. If more than one project can be undertaken, then both A and C should be selected since they both have positive NPVs. Project B should be rejected since it has a negative NPV and would therefore destroy wealth.

It makes sense that project C should have the highest NPV, since its cash outflows are deferred relative to the other projects, and its cash inflows are early. Project B, alternatively has all costs up front, but its cash inflows are deferred.

Suppose a project has positive NPV, but the NPV is small, say, only a few hundred dollars. The firm should nevertheless undertake that project if there are no alternative projects with higher NPV. The reason is that a firm's value is increased every time it undertakes a positive-NPV project. The firm's value increases by the amount of the project NPV. A small NPV, as long as it is positive, is net of all input costs and financing costs. So, even if the NPV is low,

EXHIBIT 10.5   Cash flows and discounted cash flows for three alternative projects (thousands).

Year	Project A Cash Flow	Project A Discounted Cash Flow	Project B Cash Flow	Project B Discounted Cash Flow	Project C Cash Flow	Project C Discounted Cash Flow
0	$(1,000,000)	$(1,000,000)	$(1,000,000)	$(1,000,000)	$(500,000)	$(500,000)
1	800,000	666,667	0	0	800,000	666,667
2	800,000	555,556	0	0	300,000	208,333
3	0	0	800,000	462,963	0	0
4	0	0	800,000	385,802	0	0
NPV =		$ 222,222		$ (151,235)		$ 375,000

the project covers all its costs and provides additional returns. If accepting the small-NPV project does not preclude the undertaking of a higher-NPV project, then it is the best thing to do. A firm that rejects a positive-NPV project is rejecting wealth.

Of course, this does not mean a firm should jump headlong into any project that at the moment appears likely to provide positive NPV. Future potential projects should be considered as well, and they should be evaluated as potential alternatives. The projects, current or future, that have the highest NPV should be the projects accepted. For maximum wealth-creation efficiency, the firm's managerial resources should be committed toward undertaking maximum NPV projects.

THE DISCOUNT RATE

At what rate should cash flows be discounted to compute net present values? In most cases, the appropriate rate is the firm's cost of funds for the project. That is, if the firm secures financing for the project by borrowing from a bank, the after-tax interest rate should be used to discount cash flows. If the firm obtains funds by selling stock, then an equity financing rate should be applied. If the financing combines debt and equity, then the appropriate discount rate would be an average of the debt rate and the equity rate.

Cost of Debt Financing

The after-tax interest rate is the interest rate paid on a firm's debt less the impact of the tax break they get from issuing debt. For example, suppose that a firm pays 10% interest on its debt and the firm's income tax rate is 40%. If the firm issues $100,000 of debt, then the annual interest expense will be $10,000 (10% × $100,000). But this $10,000 of interest expense is tax deductible, so the firm would save $4,000 in taxes (40% × the $10,000 interest). Thus, net of the tax break, this firm would be paying $6,000 to service a $100,000 debt. Its after-tax interest rate is 6% ($6,000/$100,000 principal).

The formula for after-tax interest rate $(R_{D, \text{after-tax}})$ is:

$$R_{D, \text{after-tax}} = R_D(1 - \tau)$$

where R_D is the firm's pretax interest rate, and τ is the firm's income tax rate.

Borrowing from a bank or selling bonds to raise funds is known as "debt financing." Issuing stock to raise funds is known as "equity financing." Equity financing is an alternative to debt financing, but it is not free. When a firm sells equity, it sells ownership in the firm. The return earned by the new shareholders is a cost to the old shareholders. The rate of return earned by equity investors is found by adding dividends to the change in the stock price and then dividing by the initial stock price:

$$R_E = \frac{D + P_1 - P_0}{P_0}$$

where R_E is the return on the stock and also the cost of equity financing, D is the dollar amount of annual dividends per share paid by the firm to stockholders, P_0 is the stock price at the beginning of the year, and P_1 is the stock price at the end of the year. For example, suppose the stock price is $100 per share at the beginning of the year and $112 at the end of the year, and the dividend is $8 per share. The stockholders would have earned a return of 20%, and this 20% is also the cost of equity financing:

$$R_E = \frac{\$8 + \$112 - \$100}{\$100} = 20\%$$

The capital asset pricing model (CAPM) is often used to estimate a firm's cost of equity financing. The idea behind the CAPM is that the rate of return demanded by equity investors will be a function of the risk of the equity, where risk is measured by a variable *beta* (β). According to the CAPM, β and cost of equity financing are related by the following equation:

$$R_E = R_F + \beta(R_M - R_F)$$

where R_F is a risk-free interest rate, such as a Treasury bill rate, and R_M is the expected return for the stock market as a whole. For example, suppose the expected annual return to the overall stock market is 12%, and the Treasury bill rate is 4%. If a stock has a β of 2, then its cost of equity financing would be 20%, computed as follows:

$$R_E = 4\% + \left[2 \times (12\% - 4\%)\right] = 20\%$$

Analysts often use the Standard & Poor's 500 stock portfolio as a proxy for the entire stock market when estimating the expected market return. The βs for publicly traded firms are available from a variety of sources, such as Bloomberg, Standard & Poor's, or the many companies that provide equity research reports. How β is computed and the theory behind the CAPM are beyond the scope of this chapter, but the textbooks listed in the bibliography to this chapter provide excellent coverage.

Weighted Average Cost of Capital

Most firms use a combination of both equity and debt financing to raise money for new projects. When financing comes from two sources, the appropriate discount rate is an average of the two financing rates. If most of the financing is debt, then debt should have greater weight in the average. Similarly, the weight given to equity should reflect how much of the financing is from equity. The resulting number, the "weighted average cost of capital" (WACC), reflects the firm's true cost of raising funds for the project:

$$WACC = W_E R_E + W_D\left[R_D(1-\tau)\right]$$

where W_E is the proportion of the financing that is equity, W_D is the proportion of the financing that is debt, R_E is the cost of equity financing, R_D is the pretax cost of debt financing, and τ is the tax rate.

For example, suppose a firm acquires 70% of the funds needed for a project by selling stock. The remaining 30% of financing comes from borrowing. The cost of equity financing is 20%, the pretax cost of debt financing is 10%, and the tax rate is 40%. The weighted average cost of capital would then be 15.8%, computed as follows:

$$WACC = (0.7 \times 20\%) + 0.3 \times \left[10\% \times (1-40\%)\right] = 15.8\%$$

This 15.8% rate should then be used for discounting the project cash flows.

Most often the choice of the discount rate is beyond the authority of the project manager. Top management will determine some threshold discount rate and dictate that it is the rate that must be used to assess all projects. When this is the policy, the rate is usually the firm's WACC with an additional margin added to compensate for the natural optimism of project proponents. A higher WACC makes NPV lower, and this biases management toward rejecting projects.

The Effects of Leverage

Leverage refers to the amount of debt financing used: the greater the ratio of debt to equity in the financing mix, the greater the leverage. The following example illustrates how leverage impacts the returns generated by a project. Suppose we have two companies that both manufacture scooters. One company is called NoDebt Inc., and the other is called SomeDebt Inc. As you might guess from its name, NoDebt never carries debt. SomeDebt is financed with equal parts of debt and equity. Neither company knows whether the economy will be good or bad next year, but they can make projections contingent on the state of the economy. Exhibit 10.6 presents balance-sheet and income-statement data for the two companies for each possible business environment.

Each company has $1 million of assets. Therefore, the value of NoDebt's equity is $1 million, since debt plus equity must equal assets—the balance-sheet equality. Since SomeDebt is financed with an equal mix of debt and equity, its debt must be worth $500,000, and its equity must also be worth $500,000. Aside from capital structure—that is, the mix of debt and equity used to finance the companies—the two firms are identical. In good times both companies make $1 million in sales. In bad times sales fall to $200,000. Cost of goods sold is always 50% of sales. Selling, administrative, and general expenses are a constant $50,000. For simplicity we assume there is no depreciation.

EXHIBIT 10.6   Performance of NoDebt Inc. and SomeDebt Inc.

Net Earnings	NoDebt Inc. (thousands)		SomeDebt Inc. (thousands)	
	Good Times	Bad Times	Good Times	Bad Times
Assets	$1,000	$1,000	$1,000	$1,000
Debt	0	0	500	500
Equity	$1,000	$1,000	$ 500	$ 500
Revenue	$1,000	$ 200	$1,000	$ 200
COGS	500	100	500	100
SAG	50	50	50	50
EBIT	450	50	450	50
Interest	0	0	50	50
EBT	450	50	400	0
Tax (40%)	180	20	160	0
Net Earnings	$ 270	$ 30	$ 240	$ 0
ROA	45.0%	5.0%	45.0%	5.0%
ROE	27.0%	3.0%	48.0%	0.0%

Earnings before interest and taxes (EBIT) is thus $450,000 for both companies in good times, and $50,000 for both in bad times. So far, this example illustrates an important lesson about leverage: Leverage has no impact on EBIT. If we define return on assets (ROA)[1] as EBIT divided by assets, then leverage has no impact on ROA.

If the pre-tax interest rate is 10%, however, then SomeDebt must pay $50,000 of interest on its outstanding $500,000 of debt, regardless of whether business is good or bad. NoDebt, of course, pays no interest. Because this is a standard income statement, not a capital budgeting cash-flow computation, we must account for interest. EBT (earnings before taxes, which is the same thing as taxable income) for NoDebt is the same as its EBIT: $450,000 in good times and $50,000 in bad times. For SomeDebt, however, EBT will be $50,000 less in both states: $400,000 in good times and zero in bad times. Income tax is 40% of EBT, so it must be $180,000 for NoDebt in good times, $20,000 for NoDebt in bad times, $160,000 for SomeDebt in good times, and zero for SomeDebt in bad times. Here we see the second important lesson about leverage: Leverage reduces taxes.

Net earnings is EBT minus taxes. For NoDebt, net earnings is $270,000 in good times and $30,000 in bad times. For SomeDebt, net earnings is $240,000 in good times and zero in bad times. Return on equity (ROE) equals net earnings divided by equity. ROE is the profit earned by the equity investors as a function of their equity investment. If, as in this example, there is no depreciation, no changes in net working capital, and no capital expenditures, then net earnings would equal the cash flow received by equity investors, and ROE would be that year's cash return on their equity investment. Notice that ROE for NoDebt is 27% in good times and 3% in bad times. ROE for SomeDebt is much more volatile: 48% in good times and 0% in bad times. This is the third and most important lesson to be learned about leverage from this example: For the equity investors, leverage makes the good times better and the bad times worse. One student of mine, upon hearing this, exclaimed, "Leverage is a lot like beer!"

Because leverage increases the riskiness of the cash flows to equity investors, leverage increases the cost of equity capital. But for moderate amounts of leverage, the impact of the tax shield on the cost of debt financing overwhelms the rising cost of equity financing, and leverage reduces the WACC. Economists Franco Modigliani and Merton Miller were each awarded the Nobel Prize in economics (in 1985 and 1990, respectively) for work that included research on this very issue. Modigliani and Miller proved that in a world where there are no taxes and no bankruptcy costs the WACC is unaffected by leverage. What about the real world in which taxes and bankruptcy exist? What we learn from their result, known as the Modigliani-Miller irrelevance theorem, is that as leverage is increased WACC falls because of the tax savings, but eventually WACC starts to rise again due to the rising probability of bankruptcy costs. The choice of debt versus equity financing must balance these countervailing concerns, and the optimal mix of debt and equity depends on the specific details of the proposed project.

Divisional versus Firm Cost of Capital

Suppose the beer company is thinking about opening a restaurant. The risk inherent in the restaurant business is much greater than the risk of the beer brewing business. Suppose the WACC for the brewery has historically been 20%, but the WACC for stand-alone restaurants is 30%. What discount rate should be used for the proposed restaurant project?

Considerable research, both theoretical and empirical, has been applied to this question, and the consensus is that the 30% restaurant WACC should be used. A discount rate must be appropriate for the risk and characteristics of the project, not the risk and characteristics of the parent company. The reason for this surprising result is that the volatility of the project's cash flows and their correlation with other risky cash flows are the paramount risk factors in determining cost of capital, not simply the likelihood of default on the company's obligations. The financial analyst should estimate the project's cost of capital as if it were a new restaurant company, not an extension of the beer company. The analyst should examine other restaurant companies to determine the appropriate β, cost of equity capital, cost of debt financing, financing mix, and WACC.

OTHER DECISION RULES

Some firms do not use the NPV decision rule as the criterion for deciding whether a project should be accepted or rejected. At least three alternative decision rules are commonly used. As we shall see, however, the alternative rules are flawed. If the objective of the firm is to maximize investors' wealth, the alternative rules sometimes fail to identify projects that further this end and in fact sometimes lead to acceptance of projects that destroy wealth. We will examine the payback period rule, the discounted payback rule, and the internal rate of return rule.

The Payback Period

The payback period rule stipulates that cash flows must completely repay the initial outlay prior to some cutoff payback period. For example, if the payback cutoff were three years, the payback rule would require that all projects return the initial outlay within three years. Projects that satisfy the rule would be accepted; projects that do not satisfy the rule would be rejected.

For example, suppose a project initially costs $100,000 to set up. Suppose the cash flows in the first three years were $34,000 each. The sum of the first three years' cash flows is $102,000. This is greater than the initial $100,000 outlay, and so this project would be accepted under the payback period rule.

There are two major problems with the payback period rule. First, it does not take into account the time value of money. Second, it ignores what happens after the payback. Because of these two failings, the payback rule sometimes accepts projects that should be rejected and rejects projects that should be accepted. A project that costs $100,000 to set up and returns $34,000 for three years would have a negative NPV at a 10% discount rate, since the $102,000 in deferred cash flows are worth less than the initial $100,000 outlay. Yet, the project would be adopted under the payback rule criterion.

Consider a project that costs $100,000 to set up, returns nothing for three years, and then returns $10 million in year 4. This project would have a positive NPV at any reasonable discount rate, yet would be rejected by the payback rule. The rejection stems from the fact that the payback rule is myopic, that is, it fails to take into account what happens after the payback period. Empirical studies have shown that, contrary to popular perceptions, stockholders do reward firms that take the longer view, NPV approach to project analysis.

The Discounted Payback Period

An improved, though still flawed, variant of the payback period rule is the discounted payback period rule. The discounted payback rule stipulates that the discounted cash flows from a project over some payback horizon must exceed the initial outlay. If the horizon were three years, the rule would require that the discounted present value of a project's first three years of cash flows be greater than the initial outlay. Although this rule explicitly takes into account the time value of money, it still ignores what might happen after the payback horizon. A project may be rejected even if the expected cash flows from the fourth year and beyond are very large, as might be the case in a research and development project. A project might be accepted even if there is a large cleanup cost that would have to be paid after the payback horizon. Although the rule incorporates the time value of money, it is still shortsighted. One might conjecture that the payback and discounted payback rules are popular since they are easy to apply. Yet, this ease is paid for in lost opportunities for creating wealth and occasional misallocation of resources into wasteful projects.

Internal Rate of Return

A project's internal rate of return (IRR) is the interest rate that the project essentially pays out. It is the interest rate that a bank would have to pay so that the project's cash outflows would exactly finance its cash inflows. Instead of investing money in the project, one could invest money in a bank paying a rate of interest equal to the project's IRR and receive the same cash flows. One can think of the IRR as an interest rate that a project pays to its investors. For example, a project that costs $100,000 to set up but then returns $10,000 every year forever has an IRR of 10%. If a project costs $100,000 to set up and then ends the following year when it pays back $105,000, that project would have an IRR of 5%. The IRR is the rate of return generated by the project.

Most financial calculators and spreadsheet programs have functions that find IRR using cash flows supplied by the user. For example, consider a project that requires a cash outflow of $100 in year 0 and produces cash inflows of $40 for each of four years. To find the IRR using a financial calculator one must specify that the present value equals −$100, annual payments equal +$40, and *n*, the number of years, equals 4. The present value and the annuity payments must have opposite signs in order to indicate to the calculator that the direction of cash flows has changed. The last step is to issue the instruction for the calculator to find the interest rate that allows these cash flows to make sense. The answer is the IRR, which in this example is 21.9%. For the beer brewery cash flows specified in Exhibit 10.4, the IRR is 21.7%.

Most TOVM problems involve specifying an interest rate and some of the cash flows and then instructing the calculator to find the missing cash flow variable—either present value, future value, or annual payment. IRR calculations involve specifying all of the cash flows and instructing the calculator to find the missing interest rate.

The IRR also happens to be the discount rate at which the project's cash flows have an NPV of zero. This relationship can be used to verify that an IRR is correct. First calculate NPV at a guessed IRR. If the resulting NPV is zero, the guessed IRR is in fact correct. If not, guess again. The IRR eventually can be found by trial and error.

For example, consider again the case in which the initial cash outflow is $100, followed by four annual cash inflows of $40. To use the trial and error method, one should calculate the NPV at a guessed discount rate. When we find the discount rate at which the NPV is zero, we will have identified the IRR. If we guess 10%, the NPV is $26.79. Apparently, the guessed discount rate is too low. A higher discount rate will give a lower NPV. So guess again, maybe 30% this time. At 30%, the NPV is −$13.35. Apparently, 30% is too high. The next guess should be lower. Following this algorithm, the IRR of 21.9% will eventually be located.

The IRR rule stipulates that a project should be accepted if its IRR is greater than some agreed-on threshold, and rejected otherwise. That is, to be accepted a project must produce percentage returns higher than some company-mandated minimum. Often the minimum threshold is set equal to the firm's cost of capital. If the IRR beats the WACC, then the project is accepted. If the IRR is less than the WACC, the project is rejected.

For example, suppose a project costs $1,000 to set up, and then produces a one-time cash inflow of $1,100 one year later. The IRR of this project is 10%. If the company imposes a minimum threshold of 20%, this project will be rejected. If the company's threshold is 8%, this project will be accepted. We saw previously that the brewery project IRR was 21.7%. If the agreed threshold is the brewery's 20% WACC, then the IRR rule would indicate that the project should be accepted.

The IRR rule is appealing in that it *usually* gives the same guidance as the NPV rule when the threshold equals the company's cost of capital. If a project's IRR exceeds the firm's cost of capital, the project must be creating wealth for the firm. The project would produce returns greater than the firm's financing costs, and the spread would be adding wealth for the investors. Unfortunately, the IRR rule frequently breaks down and gives misleading advice.

The IRR rule suffers from two flaws. First, it ignores the relative sizes of alternative projects. For example, suppose a firm had to choose between two projects, each of which lasts one year. The first project costs $10,000 to set up but then pays back $16,000 one year later. The second project costs $100,000 to set up but pays back $120,000 one year later. Clearly the IRR of the first project is 60%, and the IRR of the second project is 20%. On the basis of IRR the first project seems to be superior. However, if the firm's cost of capital is 10%, the first project has an NPV of $4,454, whereas the second project has an NPV of $9,091. Clearly the second project creates more wealth. The first project has a higher rate of return but on a smaller investment. The second project's lower return on a larger scale is a better use of the firm's scarce managerial resources.

The second flaw in the IRR rule stems from the fact that a given project may have multiple IRRs. IRR is not always a single, unique value. Consider a two-year project. Initially the project costs $1,000 to set up. In the first year it returns $3,000. In the second year there is a cleanup costing $2,000. It is easy to verify that 0% is one correct value for the firm's IRR: Discounting at 0% and adding up all the discounted cash flows gives an NPV of zero. Notice, however, that 100% is another correct value for the IRR: Discounting all cash flows at 100% per year also gives an NPV of zero. If the firm's cost of capital is 10%, should this project be accepted or rejected? Ten percent is greater than 0%, but less than 100%. Only by computing the NPV at the discount rate of 10% do we find out that this project has a positive NPV of $74 and so should be accepted. When a project has two or more IRRs, the analyst would have no way of knowing which was the correct one to use if he or she did not also compute the NPV and apply the NPV rule. If the analyst only computed the IRR of 100%, then she or he would reject this valuable project.

It turns out that a project will have one IRR for every change in sign in its cash flows. If a project has an initial outlay and then subsequently all cash flows are positive inflows, there will be one unique IRR. If a project has an initial outlay, a string of positive inflows, and then a cleanup cost at the end, there will be two IRRs since the direction of cash flow changed twice. If there were an initial outlay, a positive inflow, another net outflow during a retooling year, followed by a positive inflow, the three sign changes would produce three different IRRs. The IRR rule would provide little guidance in such a scenario and could possibly lead to an incorrect judgment of the project's worth.

In situations where its two fatal flaws are not an issue, the IRR rule gives the same result as the NPV rule. If the project's cash flows change sign only once, there is no problem of multiple IRRs. If all competing projects are of the same magnitude or if there is only one project under consideration, the size issue will not be a problem either. In such a situation, the firm would be justified in selecting the project on the basis of IRR.

One circumstance in which alternative projects are of equal size and cash flows only change direction once is in the analysis of alternative mortgage plans. These days, a person financing a home may choose from a multitude of mortgage plans. A variety of payment schedules are available and some plans charge points in exchange for lower monthly payments. Since all mortgages considered by the homebuyer finance the same house, the size issue is not a concern. Also, the typical home mortgage involves a cash inflow at the beginning and then only cash outflows over the period when the borrower must pay back the loan. Thus, there is only one sign change among the cash flows. A borrower can thus compare mortgages on the basis of their IRRs. The borrower should calculate the cash flows over the horizon during which he or she expects to pay back the mortgage, and should then choose the lowest IRR mortgage from among those whose monthly payments are affordable. The annual percentage rate (APR) quoted by mortgage companies is the IRR of the mortgage calculated after factoring in points and origination fees and assuming the mortgage will not be prepaid.

RECENT INNOVATIONS IN CAPITAL BUDGETING

Recent years have seen the introduction of two new capital budgeting paradigms. The fact that new approaches are still being invented tells us that NPV is not the last word in capital budgeting. Analysts and investors are constantly looking for better tools for making long-range capital decisions. One new approach, known as economic value added (EVA), was introduced by the consulting firm Stern Stewart & Company, which owns the term as a registered trademark. The second new paradigm we will briefly examine is known as "real options."

Economic Value Added

Economic value added (EVA™) is an accounting metric that aims to capture how much wealth a company creates in a given year. EVA is the amount of invested capital multiplied by the spread between the company's return on invested capital and its cost of capital. EVA aims to measure wealth creation in a given year rather than over the life of a project. EVA's advocates advise managers to adopt projects that maximize EVA and manage projects so as to maximize EVA each year. Managers should monitor projects and make modifications, award incentives, and impose penalties to continuously boost EVA.

Real Options

The real options paradigm seeks to measure not only the value of a project's forecasted cash flows but also the value of strategic flexibility that a project creates for a company. For example, suppose a company is contemplating an initiative to market its wares on the Internet. The forecast cash flows may be weak, but establishing a presence on the Internet may be valuable in that it wards off potential competition and creates opportunities that can later be exploited. The option to expand or the flexibility to later pursue a wide range of initiatives is captured using the real option paradigm, whereas the value of these options is usually missed completely in the standard NPV approach. The real options paradigm entails identifying the strategic options inherent in a proposed project and then valuing them using modern mathematical option-pricing formulas. If the value of a proposed project complete with its real options is greater than the cost of initiating the project, then the project should be given the go-ahead.

SUMMARY AND CONCLUSIONS

Capital budgeting is the process by which a firm chooses which projects to adopt and which to reject. It is an extremely important endeavor because it ultimately shapes the firm and the economy as a whole. The fundamental principal underlying capital budgeting is that a firm should adopt the projects that create the most wealth. Net present value (NPV) measures how much wealth a project creates. NPV is computed by forecasting a project's cash flows, discounting those cash flows at the project's weighted average cost of capital (WACC), and then summing the discounted cash flows. The cost of capital used to discount the cash flows is a function of the riskiness of the project and the financing mix selected.

Measures such as payback period, discounted payback period, and internal rate of return (IRR) give rise to alternative project decision rules. These rules, however, are flawed and can potentially lead a company to adopt an inferior project or reject an optimal one. Economic value added is a new tool recently introduced to help managers choose among projects and then manage the projects once started. The real options paradigm is another recent innovation that aims to capture the value of strategic flexibility created by projects. The tools of capital budgeting can be applied to large-scale corporate decisions, such as whether or not to build a new plant, but they can also be applied to smaller personal decisions, such as which home mortgage program to choose or whether to invest in new office equipment. Learning the language and tools of capital budgeting can help entrepreneurs better pitch their projects to investors or to the top executives at their own firms. Whether the decision is large or small, the fundamental principle is the same: A good project is ultimately worth more than it costs to set up and thereby generates wealth.

FOR FURTHER READING

Amram, Martha, and Nalin Kulatilaka, *Real Options: Managing Strategic Investment in an Uncertain World* (Boston: Harvard Business School Press, 1999).

Bodie, Zvi, and Robert C. Merton, *Finance* (Upper Saddle River, NJ: Prentice-Hall, 2000).

Brealey, Richard A., and Stewart C. Myers, *Principles of Corporate Finance* (New York: Irwin/McGraw-Hill, 2000).

Brigham, Eugene F., Michael C. Ehrhardt, and Louis C. Gapenski, *Financial Management: Theory and Practice* (New York: Dryden Press, 1999).

Dixit, Avinash K., and Robert S. Pindyck, "The Options Approach to Capital Investment," *Harvard Business Review,* 73(3) (May/June 1995): 105–115.

Emery, Douglas R., and John D. Finnerty, *Corporate Financial Management* (Upper Saddle River, NJ: Prentice-Hall, 1997).

Higgins, Robert C., *Analysis for Financial Management* (New York: Irwin/McGraw-Hill, 2001).

Ross, Stephen A., Randolph W. Westerfield, and Jeffrey Jaffe, *Corporate Finance* (New York: Irwin/McGraw-Hill, 1999).

Trigeorgis, Lenos, *Real Options: Managerial Flexibility and Strategy in Resource Allocation* (Cambridge, MA: MIT Press, 1997).

NOTE

1.   This is one definition of ROA; another definition is net earnings divided by total assets. Given the second definition, ROA would be affected by leverage.

11 TAXES AND BUSINESS DECISIONS

Richard P. Mandel

It is not possible to fully describe the federal taxation system in the space of one book chapter. It may not even be realistic to attempt to describe federal taxation in a full volume. After all, a purchaser of the Internal Revenue Code (the Code) can expect to carry home at least two volumes consisting of more than 6,000 pages, ranging from Section 1 through Section 9,722, if one includes the estate and gift tax and administrative provisions. And this does not even begin to address the myriad Regulations, Revenue Rulings, Revenue Procedures, Technical Advice Memoranda, private letter rulings, court decisions, and other sources of federal tax law that have proliferated over the better part of the twentieth century.

Fortunately, most people who enroll in a federal tax course during their progression toward an MBA have no intention of becoming professional tax advisers. An effective tax course, therefore, rather than attempting to impart encyclopedic knowledge of the Code, instead presents taxation as another strategic management tool, available to the manager or entrepreneur in his or her quest to reach business goals in a more efficient and cost-effective manner. After completing such a course, the businessperson should always be conscious that failure to consider tax consequences when structuring a transaction may result in needless tax expense.

It is thus the purpose of this chapter to illustrate the necessity of taking taxation into account when structuring most business transactions, and of consulting tax professionals early in the process, not just when it is time to file the return. This purpose will be attempted by describing various problems and opportunities encountered by a fictitious business owner as he progresses from early successes, through the acquisition of a related business, to intergenerational succession problems.

THE BUSINESS

We first encounter our sample business when it has been turning a reasonable profit for the past few years under the wise stewardship of its founder and sole stockholder, Morris. The success of his wholesale horticultural supply business (Plant Supply Inc.) has been a source of great satisfaction to Morris, as has the recent entry into the business of his daughter, Lisa. Morris paid Lisa's business school tuition, hoping to groom her to take over the family business, and his investment seems to be paying off as Lisa has become more and more valuable to her father. Morris (rightly or wrongly) does not feel the same way about his only other offspring, his son, Victor, the violinist, who appears to have no interest whatsoever in the business except for its potential to subsidize his attempts to break into the concert world.

At this time, Morris was about to score another coup: Plant Supply purchased a plastics molding business so it could fabricate its own trays, pots, and other planting containers instead of purchasing such items from others. Morris considered himself fortunate to secure the services of Brad (the plant manager of the molding company) because neither he nor Lisa knew very much about the molding business. He was confident that negotiations then underway would bring Brad aboard with a satisfactory compensation package. Thus, Morris could afford to turn his attention to the pleasant problem of distributing the wealth generated by his successful business.

UNREASONABLE COMPENSATION

Most entrepreneurs long for the day when their most pressing problem is figuring out what to do with all the money their business is generating. Yet this very condition was now occupying Morris's mind. Brad did not present any problems in this context. His compensation package would be dealt with through ongoing negotiations, and, of course, he was not family. But Morris was responsible for supporting his wife and two children. Despite what Morris perceived as the unproductive nature of Victor's pursuits, Morris was determined to maintain a standard of living for Victor befitting the son of a captain of industry. Of course, Lisa was also entitled to an affluent lifestyle, but surely she was additionally entitled to extra compensation for her long hours at work.

The simple and natural reaction to this set of circumstances would be to pay Lisa and Morris a reasonable salary for their work and have the corporation pay the remaining distributable profit (after retaining whatever was necessary for operations) to Morris. Morris could then take care of his wife and Victor as he saw fit. Yet such a natural reaction would ignore serious tax complications.

The distribution to Morris beyond his reasonable salary would likely be characterized by the IRS as a dividend to the corporation's sole stockholder. Since dividends cannot be deducted by the corporation as an expense, both the corporation and Morris would pay tax on these monies (the well-known bugaboo of corporate double taxation). A dollar of profit could easily be reduced to as little as $0.40 of after-tax money in Morris's pocket (Exhibit 11.1).

Knowing this, one might argue that the distribution to Morris should be characterized as a year-end bonus. Since compensation is tax deductible to the corporation, the corporate level of taxation would be removed. Unfortunately, Congress has long since limited the compensation deduction to a "reasonable" amount. The IRS judges the reasonableness of a payment by comparing it to the salaries paid to other employees performing similar services in similar businesses. It also examines whether such amount is paid as regular salary or as a year-end lump sum when profit levels are known. The scooping up by Morris of whatever money was not nailed down at the end of the year would surely come under attack by an IRS auditor. Why not then put Victor on the payroll directly, thus reducing the amount that Morris must take out of the company for his family? Again, such a payment would run afoul of the reasonableness standard. If Morris would come under attack despite his significant efforts for the company, imagine attempting to defend payments made to an "employee" who expends no such efforts.

Subchapter S

The solution to the unreasonable compensation problem may lie in a relatively well-known tax strategy known as the subchapter S election. A corporation making this election remains a standard business corporation for all purposes other than taxation (retaining its ability to grant limited liability to its stockholders, for example). The corporation elects to forgo taxation at the corporate level and to be taxed similarly to a partnership. This means that a corporation that has elected subchapter S status will escape any taxation on the corporate level, but its stockholders will be taxed on their pro rata share of the corporation's profits, regardless of whether these profits are distributed to them. Under this election, Morris's corporation would pay no corporate tax, but Morris would pay income tax on all the corporation's profits, even those retained for operations.

EXHIBIT 11.1   Double taxation.

$1.00	Earned
−0.34	Corporate tax at 34%
0.66	Dividend
−0.25	Individual tax at 39.1%*
0.41	Remains

* Highest federal income tax rate in 2001.

This election is recommended in a number of circumstances. One example is the corporation that expects to incur losses, at least in its start-up phase. In the absence of a subchapter S election, such losses would simply collect at the corporate level, awaiting a time in the future when they could be "carried forward" to offset future profits (should there ever be any). If the election is made, the losses would pass through to the stockholders in the current year and might offset other income of these stockholders such as interest, dividends from investments, and salaries.

Another such circumstance is when a corporation expects to sell substantially all its assets sometime in the future in an acquisition transaction. Since the repeal of the so-called General Utilities doctrine, such a corporation would incur a substantial capital gain tax on the growth in the value of its assets from their acquisition to the time of sale, in addition to the capital gain tax incurred by its stockholders when the proceeds of such sale are distributed to them. The subchapter S election (if made early enough), again eliminates tax at the corporate level, leaving only the tax on the stockholders.

The circumstance most relevant to Morris is the corporation with too much profit to distribute as reasonable salary and bonuses. Instead of fighting the battle of reasonableness with the IRS, Morris could elect subchapter S status, thus rendering the controversy moot. It will not matter that the amount paid to him is too large to be anything but a nondeductible dividend, because it is no longer necessary to be concerned about the corporation's ability to deduct the expense. Not all corporations are eligible to elect subchapter S status. However, contrary to a common misconception, eligibility has nothing to do with being a "small business." In simplified form, to qualify for a subchapter S election, the corporation must have 75 or fewer stockholders holding only one class of stock, all of whom must be individuals who are either U.S. citizens or resident aliens. Plant Supply qualifies on all these counts.

Alternatively, many companies have accomplished the same tax results, while avoiding the eligibility limitations of subchapter S, by operating as limited liability companies (LLCs). Unfortunately for Morris, however, a few states require LLCs to have more than one owner.

Under subchapter S, Morris can pay himself and Lisa a reasonable salary and then take the rest of the money either as salary or dividend without fear of challenge. He can then distribute that additional money between Lisa and Victor, to support their individual lifestyles. Thus, it appears that the effective use of a strategic taxation tool has solved an otherwise costly problem.

Gift Tax

Unfortunately, like most tax strategies, the preceding solution may not be cost free. It is always necessary to consider whether the solution of one tax problem may create others, sometimes emanating from taxes other than the income tax. To begin with, Morris needs to be aware that under any strategy he adopts, the gifts of surplus cash he makes to his children may subject him to a federal gift tax. This gift tax supplements the federal estate tax, which imposes a tax on the transfer of assets from one generation to the next. Lifetime gifts to the next generation would, in the absence of a gift tax, frustrate estate tax policy. Fortunately, to accommodate the tendency of individuals to make gifts for reasons unrelated to estate planning, the gift tax exempts gifts by a donor of up to $10,000 per year to each of his or her donees. That amount will be adjusted for inflation as years go by. Furthermore it is doubled if the donor's spouse consents to the use of her or his $10,000 allotment to cover the excess. Thus, Morris could distribute up to $20,000 in excess cash each year to each of his two children if his wife consented.

In addition, the federal gift tax does not take hold until the combined total of taxable lifetime gifts in excess of the annual exclusion amount exceeds $675,000 in 2001. This amount will increase to $1 million in 2002. Thus, Morris can exceed the annual $20,000 amount by quite a bit before the government will get its share.

These rules may suggest an alternate strategy to Morris under which he may transfer some portion of his stock to each of his children and then have the corporation distribute dividends to him and to them directly each year. The gift tax would be implicated to the extent of the value of the stock in the year it is given, but, from then on, no gifts would be necessary. Such a strategy, in fact, describes a fourth circumstance in which the subchapter S election is recommended: when the company wishes to distribute profits to nonemployee stockholders for whom salary or bonus in any amount would be considered excessive. In such a case, like that of Victor, the owner of the company can choose subchapter S status for it, make a gift to the nonemployee of stock, and adopt a policy of distributing annual dividends from profits, thus avoiding any challenge to a corporate deduction based on unreasonable compensation.

MAKING THE SUBCHAPTER S ELECTION

Before Morris rushes off to make his election, however, he should be aware of a few additional complications. Congress has historically been aware of the potential for corporations to avoid corporate-level taxation on profits and capital gains earned prior to the subchapter S election but not realized until afterward. Thus, for example, if Morris's corporation has been accounting for its inventory on a last in, first out (LIFO) basis in an inflationary era (such as virtually any time during the past 50 years), taxable profits have been depressed by the use of higher cost inventory as the basis for calculation. Earlier lower-cost inventory has been left on the shelf (from an accounting point of view), waiting for later sales. However, if those later sales will now come during a time when the corporation is avoiding tax under subchapter S, those higher taxable profits will never be taxed at the corporate level. Thus, for the year just preceding the election, the Code requires recalculation of the corporation's profits on a first in, first out (FIFO) inventory basis to capture the amount that was postponed. If Morris has been using the LIFO method, his subchapter S election will carry some cost.

Similarly, if Morris's corporation has been reporting to the IRS on a cash accounting basis, it has been recognizing income only when collected, regardless of when a sale was actually made. The subchapter S election, therefore, affords the possibility that many sales made near the end of the final year of corporate taxation will never be taxed at the corporate level, because these receivables will not be collected until after the election is in effect. As a result, the IRS requires all accounts receivable of a cash-basis taxpayer to be taxed as if collected in the last year of corporate taxation, thus adding to the cost of Morris's subchapter S conversion.

Of course, the greatest source of untapped corporate tax potential lies in corporate assets that have appreciated in value while the corporation was subject to corporate tax but are not sold by the corporation until after the subchapter S election is in place. In the worst nightmares of the IRS, corporations that are about to sell all their assets in a corporate acquisition first elect subchapter S treatment and then immediately sell out, avoiding millions of dollars of tax liability.

Fortunately for the IRS, Congress has addressed this problem by imposing taxation on the corporate level of all so-called built-in gain realized by a converted S corporation within the first 10 years after its conversion. Built-in gain is the untaxed appreciation that existed at the time of the subchapter S election. It is taxed not only upon a sale of all the corporation's assets, but any time the corporation disposes of an asset it owned at the time of its election. This makes it advisable to have an appraisal done for all the corporation's assets as of the first day of subchapter S status, so that there is some objective basis for the calculation of built-in gain upon sale somewhere down the line. This appraisal will further deplete Morris's coffers if he adopts the subchapter S strategy. Despite these complications, however, it is still likely that Morris will find the subchapter S election to be an attractive solution to his family and compensation problems.

Pass-Through Entity

Consider how a subchapter S corporation might operate were the corporation to experience a period during which it were not so successful. Subchapter S corporations (as well as most LLCs, partnerships, and limited partnerships) are known as pass-through entities because they pass through their tax attributes to their owners. This feature not only operates to pass through profits to the tax returns of the owners (whether or not accompanied by cash) but also results in the pass-through of losses. As discussed earlier, these losses can then be used by the owners to offset income from other sources rather than having the losses frozen on the corporate level, waiting for future profit.

The Code, not surprisingly, places limits on the amount of loss which can be passed through to an owner's tax return. In a subchapter S corporation, the amount of loss is limited by a stockholder's basis in his investment in the corporation. Basis includes the amount invested as equity plus any amount the stockholder has advanced to the corporation as loans. As the corporation operates, the basis is raised by the stockholder's pro rata share of any profit made by the corporation and lowered by his pro rata share of loss and any distributions received by him.

These rules might turn Morris's traditional financing strategy on its head the next time he sits down with the corporation's bank loan officer to negotiate an extension of the corporation's financing. In the past, Morris has always attempted to induce the loan officer to lend directly to the corporation. This way Morris hoped to escape personal liability for the loan (although, in the beginning he was forced to give the bank a personal guarantee). In addition, the corporation could pay back the bank directly, getting a tax deduction for the interest. If the loan were made to Morris, he would have to turn the money over to the corporation and then depend upon the corporation to generate enough profit so it could distribute monies to him to cover his personal debt service. He might try to characterize those distributions to him as repayment of a loan he made to the corporation, but, given the amount he had already advanced to the corporation in its earlier years, the IRS would probably object to the debt to equity ratio and recharacterize the payment as a nondeductible dividend fully taxable to Morris. We have already discussed why Morris would prefer to avoid characterizing the payment as additional compensation: His level of compensation was already at the outer edge of reasonableness.

Under the subchapter S election, however, Morris no longer has to be concerned about characterizing cash flow from the corporation to himself in a manner that would be deductible by the corporation. Moreover, if the loan is made to the corporation, it does not increase Morris's basis in his investment (even if he has given a personal guarantee). This fact limits his ability to pass losses through to his return. Thus, the subchapter S election may result in the unseemly spectacle of Morris begging his banker to lend the corporation's money directly to him, so that he may in turn advance the money to the corporation and increase his basis. This would not be necessary in an LLC, since most loans advanced to this form of business entity increase the basis of its owners.

Passive Losses

No discussion of pass-through entities should proceed without at least touching on what may have been the most creative set of changes made to the Code in recent times. Prior to 1987, an entire industry had arisen to create and market business enterprises whose main purpose was to generate losses to pass through to their wealthy investor/owners. These losses, it was hoped, would normally be generated by depreciation, amortization, and depletion. These would be mere paper losses, incurred while the business itself was breaking even or possibly generating positive cash flow. They would be followed some years in the future by a healthy long-term capital gain. Thus, an investor with high taxable income could be offered short-term pass-through tax losses with a nice long-term gain waiting in the wings. In those days, long-term capital gain was taxed at only 40% of the rate of ordinary income, so the tax was not only deferred but substantially reduced. These businesses were known as tax shelters.

The 1986 Act substantially reduced the effectiveness of the tax shelter by classifying taxable income and loss in three major categories: active, portfolio, and passive. Active income consists mainly of wages, salaries, and bonuses; portfolio income is mainly interest and dividends; while passive income and loss consist of distributions from the so-called pass-through entities, such as LLCs, limited partnerships, and subchapter S corporations. In their simplest terms, the passive activity loss rules add to the limits set by the earlier described basis limitations (and the similar so-called at-risk rules), making it impossible to use passive losses to offset active or portfolio income. Thus, tax shelter losses can no longer be used to shelter salaries or investment proceeds; they must wait for the taxpayer's passive activities to generate the anticipated end-of-the-line gains or be used when the taxpayer disposes of a passive activity in a taxable transaction (see Exhibit 11.2).

Fortunately for Morris, the passive activity loss rules are unlikely to affect his thinking for at least two reasons. First, the Code defines a passive activity as the conduct of any trade or business "in which the taxpayer does not materially participate." Material participation is further defined in a series of Code sections and Temporary Regulations (which mock the concept of tax simplification but let Morris off the hook) to include any taxpayer who participates in the business for more than 500 hours per year. Morris is clearly materially participating in his business despite his status as a stockholder of a subchapter S corporation, and thus the passive loss rules do not apply to him.

EXHIBIT 11.2   Passive activity losses.

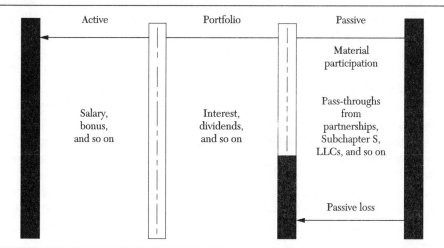

The second reason Morris is not concerned is that he does not anticipate any losses from this business; historically, it is very profitable. Therefore, let us depart from this detour into unprofitability and consider Morris's acquisition of the plastics plant.

ACQUISITION

Morris might well believe that the hard part of accomplishing a successful acquisition is locating an appropriate target and integrating it into his existing operation. Yet, once again, he would be well advised to pay some attention to the various tax strategies and results available to him when structuring the acquisition transaction.

To begin with, Morris has a number of choices available to him in acquiring the target business. Simply put, these choices boil down to a choice among acquiring the stock of the owners of the business, merging the target corporation into Plant Supply, or purchasing the assets and liabilities of the target. The choice of method will depend on a number of factors, many of which are not tax related. For example, acquisition by merger will force Plant Supply to acquire all the liabilities of the target, even those of which neither it nor the target may be aware. Acquisition of the stock of the target by Plant Supply also results in acquisition of all liabilities but isolates them in a separate corporation, which becomes a subsidiary. (The same result would be achieved by merging the target into a newly formed subsidiary of Plant Supply—the so-called triangular merger.) Acquisition of the assets and liabilities normally results only in exposure to the liabilities Morris chooses to acquire and is thus an attractive choice to the acquirer (Exhibit 11.3).

Yet tax factors normally play a large part in structuring an acquisition. For example, if the target corporation has a history of losses and thus boasts a tax-loss carryforward, Morris may wish to apply such losses to its future profitable operations. This application would be impossible if he acquired the assets and liabilities of the target for cash since the target corporation would still exist after the transaction, keeping its tax characteristics to itself. Cash mergers are treated as asset acquisitions for tax purposes. However, if the acquirer obtains the stock of the target, the acquirer has taken control of the taxable entity itself, thus obtaining its tax characteristics for future use. This result inspired a lively traffic in tax-loss carryforwards in years past, where failed corporations were marketed to profitable corporations seeking tax relief.

Congress has put a damper on such activity by limiting the use of a tax-loss carryforward in each of the years following an ownership change of more than 50% of a company's stock. The amount of that limit is the product of the value of the business at acquisition (normally its selling price) times an interest rate linked to the market for federal treasury obligations. This amount of tax-loss carryforward is available each year, until the losses expire (15 to 20 years

EXHIBIT 11.3   Acquisition strategies.

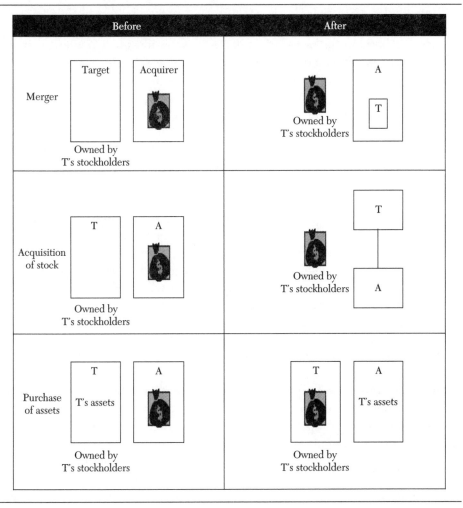

after they were incurred). Since a corporation with significant losses would normally be valued at a relatively low amount, the yearly available loss is likely to be relatively trivial.

Acquisition of the corporation's assets and liabilities for cash or through a cash merger eliminates any use by the acquirer of the target's tax-loss carryforward, leaving it available for use by the target's shell. This may be quite useful to the target because, as discussed earlier, if it has not elected subchapter S status for the past 10 years (or for the full term of its existence, if shorter), it is likely to have incurred a significant gain upon the sale of its assets. This gain would be taxable at the corporate level before the remaining portion of the purchase price could be distributed to the target's shareholders (where it will be taxed again).

The acquirer may have lost any carryforwards otherwise available, but it does obtain the right to carry the acquired assets on its books at the price paid (rather than the amount carried on the target's books). This is an attractive proposition because the owner of assets used in business may deduct an annual amount corresponding to the depreciation of those assets, subject only to the requirement that it lower the basis of those assets by an equal amount. The amount of depreciation available corresponds to the purchase price of the asset. This is even more attractive because Congress has adopted available depreciation schedules that normally exceed the rate at which assets actually depreciate. Thus, these assets likely have a low basis in the hands of the target (resulting in even more taxable gain to the target upon sale). If the acquirer were forced to begin its depreciation at the point at which the target left off (as in a purchase of stock), little depreciation would likely result. All things being equal (and especially if the target has enough tax-loss carryforward to absorb any conceivable gain), Morris would likely wish to structure his acquisition as an asset purchase and allocate all the purchase price among the depreciable assets acquired.

This last point is significant because Congress does not recognize all assets as depreciable. Generally speaking, an asset will be depreciable only if it has a demonstrable "useful life." Assets that will last forever or whose lifetime is not predictable are not depreciable, and the price paid for them will not result in future tax deductions. The most obvious example of this type of asset is land. Unlike buildings, land has an unlimited useful life and is not depreciable. This distinction has spawned some very creative theories, including one enterprising individual who purchased a plot of land containing a deep depression that he intended to use as a garbage dump. The taxpayer allocated a significant amount of his purchase price to the depression and took depreciation deductions as the hole filled up.

Congress has recognized that the above rules give acquirers incentive to allocate most of their purchase price to depreciable assets like buildings and equipment and very little of the price to nondepreciable assets such as land. Additional opportunities include allocating high prices to acquired inventory so that it generates little taxable profit when sold. This practice has been limited by legislation requiring the acquirer to allocate the purchase price in accordance with the fair market value of the individual assets, applying the rest to goodwill (which may now be depreciated over 15 years).

Although this legislation will limit Morris's options significantly, if he chooses to proceed with an asset purchase, he should not overlook the opportunity to divert some of the purchase price to consulting contracts for the previous owners. Such payments will be deductible by Plant Supply over the life of the agreements and are, therefore, just as useful as depreciation. However, the taxability of such payments to the previous owners cannot be absorbed by the target's tax-loss carryforward. And the amount of such deductions will be limited by the now familiar "unreasonable compensation" doctrine. Payments for agreements not to compete are treated as a form of goodwill and are deductible over 15 years regardless of the length of such agreements.

EXECUTIVE COMPENSATION

Brad's compensation package raises a number of interesting tax issues that may not be readily apparent but deserve careful consideration in crafting an offer to him. Any offer of compensation to an executive of his caliber will include, at the very least, a significant salary and bonus package. These will not normally raise any sophisticated tax problems; the corporation will deduct these payments, and Brad will be required to include them in his taxable income. The IRS is not likely to challenge the deductibility of even a very generous salary, since Brad is not a stockholder or family member and, thus, there is little likelihood of an attempt to disguise a dividend.

Business Expenses

However, even in the area of salary, there are opportunities for the use of tax strategies. For example, Brad's duties may include the entertainment of clients or travel to suppliers and other business destinations. Brad could conceivably fund these activities out of his own pocket on the theory that such amounts have been figured into his salary. Such a procedure avoids the need for the bookkeeping associated with expense accounts. If his salary reflects these expectations, Brad may not mind declaring the extra amount as taxable income, since he will be entitled to an offsetting deduction for these business expenses.

Unfortunately, however, Brad would be in for an unpleasant surprise under these circumstances. First of all, these expenses may not all be deductible in full. Meals and entertainment expenses are deductible, if at all, only to the extent they are not "lavish and extravagant," and even then they are deductible only for a portion of the amount expended. In addition, Brad's business expenses as an employee are considered "miscellaneous deductions"; they are deductible only to the extent that they and other similarly classified deductions exceed 2% of Brad's adjusted gross income. Thus, if Brad's adjusted gross income is $150,000, the first $3,000 of miscellaneous deductions will not be deductible.

Moreover, as itemized deductions, these deductions are valuable only to the extent that they along with all other itemized deductions available to Brad exceed the "standard deduction," an amount Congress allows each taxpayer to deduct, if all itemized deductions are foregone. Furthermore, until 2010, itemized deductions that survive the above cuts are further limited for taxpayers whose incomes are over $132,950 (the 2001 inflation-adjusted amount). The deductibility of Brad's business expenses is, therefore, greatly in doubt.

Knowing all this, Brad would be well advised to request that Morris revise his compensation package. Brad should request a cut in pay by the amount of his anticipated business expenses, along with a commitment that the corporation will reimburse him for such expenses or pay them directly. In that case, Brad will be in the same economic position, since his salary is lowered only by the amount he would have spent anyway. In fact, his economic position is enhanced, since he pays no taxes on the salary he does not receive and escapes from the limitations on deductibility described previously.

The corporation pays out no more money this way than it would have if the entire amount were salary. From a tax standpoint, the corporation is only slightly worse off, since the amount it would have previously deducted as salary can now still be deducted as ordinary and necessary business expenses (with the sole exception of the limit on meals and entertainment). In fact, were Brad's salary below the Social Security contribution limit (FICA), both Brad and the corporation would be better off because what was formerly salary (and thus subject to additional 7.65% contributions to FICA by both employer and employee) would now be merely business expenses and exempt from FICA.

Before Brad and Morris adopt this strategy, however, they should be aware that in recent years, Congress has turned a sympathetic ear to the frustration the IRS has expressed about expense accounts. Legislation has conditioned the exclusion of amounts paid to an employee as expense reimbursements upon the submission by the employee to the employer of reliable documentation of such expenses. Brad should get into the habit of keeping a diary of such expenses for tax purposes.

Deferred Compensation

Often, a high-level executive will negotiate a salary and bonus that far exceed her current needs. In such a case, the executive might consider deferring some of that compensation until future years. Brad may feel, for example, that he would be well advised to provide for a steady income during his retirement years, derived from his earnings while an executive of Plant Supply. He may be concerned that he would simply waste the excess compensation and consider a deferred package as a form of forced savings. Or, he may wish to defer receipt of the excess money to a time (such as retirement) when he believes he will be in a lower tax bracket. This latter consideration was more common when the federal income tax law encompassed a large number of tax brackets and the highest rate was 70%.

Whatever Brad's reasons for considering a deferral of some of his salary, he should be aware that deferred compensation packages are generally classified as one of two varieties for federal income tax purposes. The first such category is the qualified deferred compensation plan, such as the pension, profit-sharing, or stock bonus plan. All these plans share a number of characteristics. First and foremost, they afford taxpayers the best of all possible worlds by granting the employer a deduction for monies contributed to the plan each year, allowing those contributions to be invested and to earn additional monies without the payment of current taxes, and taxing the employee only upon withdrawal of funds in the future. However, in order to qualify for such favorable treatment, these plans must conform to a bewildering array of conditions imposed by both the Code and the Employee Retirement Income Security Act (ERISA). Among these requirements is the necessity to treat all employees of the corporation on a nondiscriminatory basis with respect to the plan, thus rendering qualified plans a poor technique for supplementing a compensation package for a highly paid executive.

The second category is nonqualified plans. These come in as many varieties as there are employees with imaginations, but they all share the same disfavored tax treatment. The employer is entitled to its deduction only when the employee pays tax on the money, and if money is contributed to such a plan the earnings are taxed currently. Thus, if Morris were to design a plan under which the corporation receives a current deduction for its contributions, Brad will pay tax now on money he will not receive until the future. Since this is the exact opposite of what Brad (and most employees) have in mind, Brad will most likely have to settle for his employer's unfunded promise to pay him the deferred amount in the future.

Assuming Brad is interested in deferring some of his compensation, he and Morris might well devise a plan which gives them as much flexibility as possible. For example, Morris might agree that the day before the end of each pay period, Brad could notify the corporation of the amount of salary, if any, he wished to defer for that period. Any amount thus deferred would be carried on the books of the corporation as a liability to be paid, per their agreement, with interest after Brad's retirement. Unfortunately, such an arrangement would be frustrated by the "constructive receipt" doctrine. Using this potent weapon, the IRS will impose a tax (allowing a corresponding employer deduction) on any compensation that the employee has earned and might have chosen to receive, regardless of whether he so chooses. The taxpayer may not turn his back upon income otherwise unconditionally available to him.

Taking this theory to its logical conclusion, one might argue that deferred compensation is taxable to the employee because he might have received it if he had simply negotiated a different compensation package. After all, the impetus for deferral in this case comes exclusively from Brad; Morris would have been happy to pay the full amount when earned. But the constructive receipt doctrine does not have so extensive a reach. The IRS can tax only monies the taxpayer was legally entitled to receive, not monies he might have received if he had negotiated differently. In fact, the IRS will even recognize elective deferrals if the taxpayer must make the deferral election sufficiently long before the monies are legally earned. Brad might, therefore, be allowed to choose deferral of a portion of his salary if the choice must be made at least six months before the pay period involved.

Frankly, however, if Brad is convinced of the advisability of deferring a portion of his compensation, he is likely to be concerned less about the irrevocability of such election than about ensuring that the money will be available to him when it is eventually due. Thus, a mere unfunded promise to pay in the future may result in years of nightmares over a possible declaration of bankruptcy by his employer. Again, left to their own devices, Brad and Morris might well devise a plan under which Morris contributes the deferred compensation to a trust for Brad's benefit, payable to its beneficiary upon his retirement. Yet such an arrangement would be disastrous to Brad, since the IRS would currently assess income tax to Brad on such an arrangement, using the much criticized "economic benefit" doctrine. Under this theory, monies irrevocably set aside for Brad grant him an economic benefit (presumably by improving his net worth or otherwise improving his creditworthiness) upon which he must pay tax.

If Brad were aware of this risk, he might choose another method to protect his eventual payout by requiring the corporation to secure its promise to pay with such devices as a letter of credit or a mortgage or security interest in its assets. All of these devices, however, have been successfully taxed by the IRS under the same economic benefit doctrine. Very few devices have survived this attack. However, the personal guarantee of Morris himself (merely another unsecured promise) would not be considered an economic benefit by the IRS.

Another successful strategy is the so-called rabbi trust, a device first used by a rabbi who feared his deferred compensation might be revoked by a future hostile congregation. This device works similarly to the trust described earlier except that Brad would not be the only beneficiary of the money contributed. Under the terms of the trust, were the corporation to experience financial reverses, the trust property would be available to the corporation's creditors. Since the monies are thus not irrevocably committed to Brad, the economic benefit doctrine is not invoked. This device does not protect Brad from the scenario of his bankruptcy nightmares, but it does protect him from a corporate change of heart regarding his eventual payout. From Morris's point of view, he may not object to contributing to a rabbi trust, since he was willing to pay all the money to Brad as salary, but he should be aware that since Brad escapes current taxation the corporation will not receive a deduction for these expenses until the money is paid out of the trust in the future.

Interest-Free Loans

As a further enticement to agree to work for the new ownership of the plant, Morris might additionally offer to lend Brad a significant amount of money to be used, for example, to purchase a new home or acquire an investment portfolio. Significant up-front money is often part of an executive compensation package. While this money could be paid as a bonus, Morris might well want some future repayment (perhaps as a way to encourage Brad to stay in his new position). Brad might wish to avoid the income tax bite on such a bonus so he can retain the full amount of the payment for his preferred use. Morris and Brad might well agree to an interest rate well below the market or even no interest at all to further entice Brad to take his new position. Economically, this would give Brad free use of the money for a period of time during which it could earn him additional income with no offsetting expense. In a sense, he would be receiving his salary in advance while not paying any income tax until he earned it. Morris might well formalize the arrangement by reserving the right to offset loan repayments against future salary. The term of the loan might even be accelerated should Brad leave the corporation's employ.

This remarkable arrangement was fairly common until fairly recently. Under current tax law, however, despite the fact that little or no interest passes between Brad and the corporation, the IRS deems full market interest payments to have been made and further deems that said amount is returned to Brad by his employer. Thus, each year, Brad is deemed to have made an interest payment to the corporation for which he is entitled to no deduction. Then, when the corporation is deemed to have returned the money to him, he realizes additional compensation on which he must pay tax. The corporation realizes additional interest income but gets a compensating deduction for additional compensation paid (assuming it is not excessive when added to Brad's other compensation).

Moreover, the IRS has not reserved this treatment for employers and employees only. The same treatment is given to loans between corporations and their shareholders and loans between family members. In the latter situation, although there is no interest deduction for the donee, the deemed return of the interest is a gift and is thus excluded from income. The donor receives interest income and has no compensating deduction for the return gift. In fact, if the interest amount is large enough, he may have incurred an additional gift tax on the returned interest. The amount of income created for the donor, however, is limited to the donee's investment income except in very large loans. In the corporation/stockholder situation, the lender incurs interest income and has no compensating deduction as its deemed return of the interest is characterized as a dividend. Thus the IRS gets increased tax from both parties unless the corporation has elected subchapter S (see Exhibit 11.4).

All may not be lost in this situation, however. Brad's additional income tax arises from the fact that there is no deduction allowable for interest paid on unsecured personal loans. Interest remains deductible, however, in limited amounts on loans secured by a mortgage on either of the taxpayer's principal or

EXHIBIT 11.4   Taxable interest.

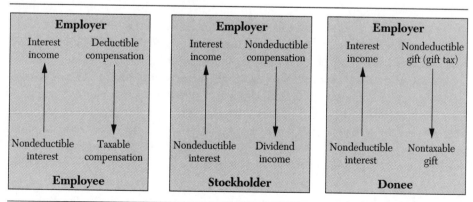

secondary residence. If Brad grants Plant Supply a mortgage on his home to secure the repayment of his no- or low-interest loan, his deemed payment of market interest may become deductible mortgage interest and may thus offset his additional deemed compensation from the imaginary return of this interest. Before jumping into this transaction, however, Brad will have to consider the limited utility of itemized deductions described earlier as well as certain limits on the deductibility of mortgage interest.

SHARING THE EQUITY

If Brad is as sophisticated and valuable an executive employee as Morris believes he is, Brad is likely to ask for more than just a compensation package, deferred or otherwise. Such a prospective employee often demands a "piece of the action," or a share in the equity of the business so that he may directly share in the growth and success he expects to create. Morris may even welcome such a demand because an equity share (if not so large as to threaten Morris's control) may serve as a form of golden handcuffs giving Brad additional reason to stay with the company for the long term.

Assuming Morris is receptive to the idea, there are a number of different ways to grant Brad a share of the business. The most direct way would be to grant him shares of the corporation's stock. These could be given to Brad without charge, for a discount from fair market value or for their full value, depending upon the type of incentive Morris wishes to design. In addition, given the privately held nature of Morris's corporation, the shares would probably carry restrictions designed to keep the shares from ending up in the hands of persons who are not associated with the company. Thus, the corporation would retain the right to repurchase the shares should Brad ever leave the corporation's employ or want to sell or transfer the shares to a third party. Finally, in order to encourage Brad to stay with the company, the corporation would probably reserve the right to repurchase the shares from Brad at cost should Brad's employment end before a specified time. As an example, all the shares (called restricted stock) would be subject to forfeiture at cost (regardless of their then actual value) should Brad leave before one year; two-thirds would be forfeited if he left before two years; and one-third if he left before three years. The shares not forfeited (called vested shares) would be purchased by the corporation at their full value should Brad ever leave or attempt to sell them.

One step back from restricted stock is the stock option. This is a right granted to the employee to purchase a particular number of shares for a fixed price over a defined period of time. Because the price of the stock does not change, the employee has effectively been given the ability to share in whatever growth the company experiences during the life of the option, without paying for the privilege. If the stock increases in value, the employee will exercise the option near the end of the option term. If the stock value does not grow, the employee will allow the option to expire, having lost nothing. The stock option is a handy device when the employee objects to paying for his piece of the action (after all, he is expecting compensation, not expense) but the employer objects to giving the employee stock whose current value represents growth from the period before the employee's arrival. Again, the exercise price can be more than, equal to, or less than the fair market value of the stock at the time of the grant, depending upon the extent of the incentive the employer wishes to give. Also, the exercisability of the option will likely vest in stages over time.

Often, however, the founding entrepreneur cannot bring herself to give an employee a current or potential portion of the corporation's stock. Although she has been assured that the block of stock going to the employee is too small to have any effect on her control over the company, the objection may be psychological and impossible to overcome. Or, in the case of a subchapter S corporation operating in numerous states, the employee may not want to have to file state income tax returns in all those jurisdictions. The founder seeks a device which can grant the employee a growth potential similar to that granted by stock ownership but without the stock. Such devices are often referred to as phantom stock or stock appreciation rights (SARs). In a phantom stock plan, the employee is promised that he may, at any time during a defined period so long as he remains employed by the corporation, demand payment equal to the then value of a certain number of shares of the corporation's stock. As the corporation grows, so does the amount available to the employee just as would be the case if he actually owned some stock. SARs are very similar except that the amount available to the employee is limited to the growth, if any, that the given number of shares has experienced since the date of grant.

Tax Effects of Phantom Stock and SARs

Having described these devices to Morris and Brad, it is, of course, important to discuss their varying tax impacts upon employer and employee. If Brad has been paying attention, he might immediately object to the phantom stock and SARs as vulnerable to the constructive receipt rule. After all, if he may claim the current value of these devices at any time he chooses, might not the IRS insist that he include each year's growth in his taxable income as if he had claimed it? Although the corporation's accountants will require that these devices be accounted for in that way on the corporation's financial statements, the IRS has failed in its attempts to require inclusion of these amounts in taxable income because the monies are not unconditionally available to the taxpayer. In order to receive the money, one must give up any right to continue to share in the growth represented by one's phantom stock or SAR. If the right is not exercisable without cost, the income is not constructively received.

However, there is another good reason for Brad to object to phantom stock and SARs from a tax point of view. Unlike stock and stock options, both of which represent a recognized form of intangible capital asset, phantom stock and SARs are really no different from a mere promise by the corporation to pay a bonus based upon a certain formula. Since these devices are not recognized as capital assets, they are not eligible to be taxed as long-term capital gains when redeemed. This difference is quite meaningful since the maximum tax rate on ordinary income in 2001 is 39.1% and on long-term capital gains is 20%. Thus, Brad may have good reason to reject phantom stock and SARs and insist on the real thing.

Taxability of Stock Options

If Morris and Brad resolve their negotiations through the use of stock options, careful tax analysis is again necessary. The Code treats stock options in three ways depending on the circumstances, and some of these circumstances are well within the control of the parties (see Exhibit 11.5).

If a stock option has a "readily ascertainable value," the IRS will expect the employee to include in his taxable income the difference between the value of the option and the amount paid for it (the amount paid is normally zero). Measured in that way, the value of an option might be quite small, especially if the exercise price is close or equal to the then fair market value of the underlying stock. After all, the value of a right to buy $10 of stock for $10 is only the speculative value of having that right when the underlying value has increased. That amount is then taxed as ordinary compensation income, and the employer receives a compensating deduction for compensation paid. When the employee exercises the option, the Code imposes no tax, nor does the employer receive any further deduction. Finally, should the employee sell the stock, the difference between, on the one hand, the price received and on the other the total of the previously taxed income and the amounts paid for the option and the stock is included in his income as a capital gain. No deduction is then granted to the employer since the employee's decision to sell his stock is not deemed to be related to the employer's compensation policy.

This taxation scenario is normally quite attractive to the employee because she is taxed upon a rather small amount at first, escapes tax entirely upon

EXHIBIT 11.5   Taxation of stock options.

	Grant	Exercise	Sale
Readily Ascertainable Value			
Employee	Tax of value	No tax	Capital gain
Employer	Deduction	No deduction	No deduction
No Readily Ascertainable Value			
Employee	No tax	Tax on spread	Capital gain
Employer	No deduction	Deduction	No deduction
ISOP			
Employee	No tax	No tax	Capital gain
Employer	No deduction	No deduction	No deduction

exercise, and then pays tax on the growth at a time when she has realized cash with which to pay the tax at a lower long-term capital gain rate. Although the employer receives little benefit, it has cost the employer nothing in hard assets, so any benefit would have been a windfall.

Because this tax scenario is seen as very favorable to the employee, the IRS has been loathe to allow it in most cases. Generally, the IRS will not recognize an option as having a readily ascertainable value unless the option is traded on a recognized exchange. Short of that, a case has occasionally been made when the underlying stock is publicly traded, such that its value is readily ascertainable. But the IRS has drawn the line at options on privately held stock and at all options that are not themselves transferable. Since Morris's corporation is privately held and since he will not tolerate Brad's reserving the right to transfer the option to a third party, there is no chance of Brad's taking advantage of this beneficial tax treatment.

The second tax scenario attaches to stock options which do not have a readily ascertainable value. Since, by definition, one cannot include their value in income on the date of grant (it is unknown), the Code allows the grant to escape taxation. However, upon exercise, the taxpayer must include in income the difference between the then fair market value of the stock purchased and the total paid for the option and stock. When the purchased stock is later sold, the further growth is taxed at the applicable rate for capital gain. The employer receives a compensation deduction at the time of exercise and no deduction at the time of sale. Although the employee receives a deferral of taxation from grant to exercise in this scenario, this method of taxation is generally seen as less advantageous to the employee, since a larger amount of income is exposed to ordinary income rates, and this taxation occurs at a time when the taxpayer has still not received any cash from the transaction with which to pay the tax.

Recognizing the harshness of this result, Congress invented a third taxation scenario which attaches to incentive stock options (ISOs). The recipient of such an option escapes tax upon grant of the option and again upon exercise. Upon sale of the underlying stock, the employee includes in taxable income the difference between the price received and the total paid for the stock and option and pays tax on that amount at long-term capital gain rates. This scenario is extremely attractive to the employee who defers all tax until the last moment and pays at a lower rate. Under this scenario, the employer receives no deduction at all, but since the transaction costs him nothing, that is normally not a major concern. Lest you believe that ISOs are the perfect compensation device, however, be aware that, although the employee escapes income taxation upon exercise of the option, the exercise may be deemed taxable under the alternative minimum tax described later in this chapter.

The Code imposes many conditions upon the grant of an incentive stock option. Among these are that the options must be granted pursuant to a written plan setting forth the maximum number of shares available and the class of employees eligible; only employees are eligible recipients; the options cannot be transferable; no more than $100,000 of underlying stock may be initially exercisable in any one year by any one employee; the exercise price of the options must be no less than the fair market value of the stock on the date of grant; and the options must expire substantially simultaneously with the termination of the employee's employment. Perhaps most important, the underlying stock may not be sold by the employee prior to the expiration of two years from the option grant date or one year from the exercise date, whichever is later.

This latter requirement has led to what was probably an unexpected consequence. Assume that Plant Supply has granted an incentive stock option to Brad. Assume further that Brad has recently exercised the option and has plans to sell the stock he received. It may occur to Brad that by waiting a year to resell, he will be risking the vagaries of the market for a tax savings which cannot exceed 19.1% (the difference between the maximum income-tax rate of 39.1% and the maximum capital-gain rate of 20%). By selling early, Brad will lose the chance to treat the option as an incentive stock option but will pay, at worst, only a marginally higher amount at a time when he does have the money to pay it. Furthermore, by disqualifying the options, he will be giving his employer a tax deduction at the time of exercise. An enterprising employee might go so far as to offer to sell early in exchange for a split of the employer's tax savings.

Tax Impact on Restricted Stock

The taxation of restricted stock is not markedly different from the taxation of nonqualified stock options without a readily ascertainable value (see Exhibit 11.6). Restricted stock is defined as stock that is subject to a condition that affects its value to the holder and which will lapse upon the happening of an event or the passage of time. The Code refers to this as "a substantial risk of forfeiture." Since the value of the stock to the employee is initially speculative, the receipt of the stock is not considered a taxable event. In other words, since Brad may have to forfeit whatever increased value his stock may acquire, if he leaves the employ of the corporation prior to the agreed time, Congress has allowed him not to pay the tax until he knows for certain whether he will be able to retain that value. When the stock is no longer restricted (when it "vests"),

EXHIBIT 11.6 Restricted stock tax impact.

	Grant	Restriction Removed	Sale
Restricted Stock			
Employee	No tax	Tax based on current value	Capital gain
Employer	No Deduction	Deduction	No deduction
Restricted Stock 83(b) Election			
Employee	Tax based on value without restriction	No tax	Capital gain
Employer	Deduction	No deduction	No deduction

the tax is payable. Of course, Congress is not being entirely altruistic in this case; the amount taxed when the stock vests is not the difference between what the employee pays for it and its value when first received by the employee but the difference between the employee's cost and the stock's value at the vesting date. If the value of the stock has increased, as everyone involved has hoped, the IRS receives a windfall. Of course, the employer receives a compensating deduction at the time of taxation, and further growth between the vesting date and the date of sale is taxed upon sale at appropriate capital gain rates. No deduction is then available to the employer.

Recognizing that allowing the employee to pay a higher tax at a later time is not an unmixed blessing, Congress has provided that an employee who receives restricted stock may, nonetheless, elect to pay ordinary income tax on the difference between its value at grant and the amount paid for it, if the employee files notice of that election within 30 days of the grant date (the so-called 83b election). Thus, the employee can choose for herself which gamble to accept.

This scenario can result in disaster for the unaware employee. Assume that Morris and Brad resolve their differences by allowing Brad to have an equity stake in the corporation, if he is willing to pay for it. Thus, Brad purchases 5% of the corporation for its full value on the date he joins the corporation, say, $5.00 per share. Since this arrangement still provides incentive in the form of a share of growth, Morris insists that Brad sell the stock back to the corporation for $5.00 per share should he leave the corporation before he has been employed for three years. Brad correctly believes that since he has bought $5.00 shares for $5.00 he has no taxable income, and he reports nothing on his income tax return that year.

Brad has failed to realize that despite his paying full price, he has received restricted stock. As a result, Congress has done him the favor of imposing no tax until the restrictions lapse. Three years from now, when the shares may have tripled in value and have finally vested, Brad will discover to his horror that he must include $10.00 per share in his taxable income for that year. Despite the fact that he had no income to declare in the year of grant, Brad must elect to include that nullity in his taxable income for that year by filing such an election with the IRS within 30 days of his purchase of the stock.

In situations in which there is little difference between the value of stock and the amount an employee will pay for it (e.g., in start-up companies when stock has little initial value), a grant of restricted stock accompanied by an 83b election may be preferable to the grant of an ISO, since it avoids the alternative minimum tax which may be imposed upon exercise of an ISO.

VACATION HOME

Morris had much reason to congratulate himself on successfully acquiring the plastics-molding operation as well as securing the services of Brad through an effective executive compensation package. In fact, the only real disappointment for Morris was that the closing of the deal was scheduled to take place during the week in which he normally took his annual vacation.

Some years ago, Morris had purchased a country home for use by himself and his wife as a weekend getaway and vacation spot. With the press of business, however, Morris and his wife had been able to use the home only on occasional weekends and for his two-week summer vacation each year. Morris always took the same two weeks for his vacation so he could indulge his love of golf. Each year, during those two weeks, the professional golfers would come to town for their annual tournament. Hotels were always booked far in advance, and Morris felt lucky to be able to walk from his home to the first tee and enjoy his favorite sport played by some of the world's best.

Some of Morris's friends had suggested that Morris rent his place during the weeks that he and his wife didn't use it. Even if such rentals would not generate much cash during these off-season periods, it might allow Morris to deduct some of the expenses of keeping the home, such as real estate taxes, mortgage payments, maintenance, and depreciation. Morris could see the benefit in that, since the latter two expenses were deductible only in a business context. Although taxes and mortgage interest were deductible as personal expenses (assuming, in the case of mortgage interest, that Morris was deducting such payments only with respect to this and his principal residence and no other home), the previously mentioned limits on the use of itemized deductions made the usefulness of these deductions questionable.

However, in addition to the inconvenience of renting one's vacation home, Morris had discovered a few unfortunate tax rules which had dissuaded him from following his friends' advice. First, the rental of a home is treated by the Code in a fashion similar to the conduct of a business. Thus, Morris would generate deductions only to the extent that his expenses exceeded his rental income. In addition, to the extent he could generate such a loss, the rental of real estate is deemed to be a passive activity under the Code, regardless of how much effort one puts into the process. Thus, in the absence of any relief provision, these losses would be deductible only against other passive income and would not be usable against salary, bonus, or investment income.

Such a relief provision does exist, however, for rental activities in which the taxpayer is "actively" involved. In such a case, the taxpayer may deduct up to $25,000 of losses against active or portfolio income, unless his total income (before any such deduction) exceeds $100,000. The amount of loss which may be used by such taxpayer, free of the passive activity limitations, is then lowered by $1 for every $2 of additional income, disappearing entirely at $150,000. Given his success in business, the usefulness of rental losses, in the absence of passive income, seemed problematic to Morris, at best.

Another tax rule appeared to Morris to limit the usefulness of losses even further. Under the Code, a parcel of real estate falls into one of three categories: personal use, rental use, or mixed use. A personal use property is one which is rented 14 days or less in a year and otherwise used by the taxpayer and his family. No expenses are deductible for such a facility except taxes and mortgage interest. A rental use property is used by the taxpayer and his family for less than 15 days (or 10% of the number of rental days) and otherwise offered for rental. All the expenses of such an activity are deductible, subject to the passive loss limitations. A mixed use facility is one that falls within neither of the other two categories.

If Morris were to engage in a serious rental effort of his property, his occasional weekend use combined with his two-week stay around the golf tournament would surely result in his home falling into the mixed use category. This would negatively impact him in two ways. The expenses that are deductible only for a rental facility (such as maintenance and depreciation) would be deductible only on a pro rata basis for the total number of rental days. Worse yet, the expenses of the rental business would be deductible only to the extent of the income, not beyond. Expenses which would be deductible anyway (taxes and mortgage interest) are counted first in this calculation, and only then are the remaining expenses allowed. The result of all this is that it would be impossible for Morris to generate a deductible loss, even were it possible to use such a loss in the face of the passive loss limitations.

Naturally, therefore, Morris had long since decided not to bother with attempting to rent his country getaway when he was unable to use it. However, the scheduling of the closing this year presents a unique tax opportunity of which he may be unaware. In a rare stroke of fairness, the Code, though denying any deduction of not otherwise deductible expenses in connection with a home rented for 14 days or less, reciprocates by allowing taxpayers to exclude any rental income should they take advantage of the 14-day rental window. Normally, such an opportunity is of limited utility, but with the tournament coming to town and the hotels full Morris is in a position to make a killing by renting his home to a golfer or spectator during this time at inflated rental rates. All that rental income would be entirely tax-free. Just be sure the tenants don't stay beyond two weeks.

LIKE-KIND EXCHANGES

Having acquired the desired new business and secured the services of the individual he needed to run it, Morris turned his attention to consolidating his two operations so that they might function more efficiently. After some time, he realized that the factory building acquired with the plastics business was not contributing to increased efficiency because of its age and, more important, because of its distance from Morris's home office. Morris located a more modern facility near his main location that could accommodate both operations and allow him to eliminate some amount of duplicative management.

Naturally, Morris put the molding facility on the market and planned to purchase the new facility with the proceeds of the old one plus some additional capital. Such a strategy will result in a tax on the sale of the older facility equal to the difference between the sale price and Plant Supply's basis in the building. If Morris purchased the molding company by merging or purchasing its assets for cash, then the capital gain to be taxed here may be minimal because it would consist only of the growth in value since this purchase plus any amount depreciated after the acquisition. If, however, Morris acquired the molding company through a purchase of stock, his basis would be the old company's preacquisition basis, and the capital gain may be considerable. Either way, it would surely be desirable to avoid taxation on this capital gain.

The Code affords Morris the opportunity to avoid this taxation if, instead of selling his old facility and buying a new one, he can arrange a trade of the old for the new so that no cash falls into his hands. Under Section 1031 of the Code, if properties of "like kind" used in a trade or business are exchanged, no taxable event has occurred. The gain on the disposition of the older facility is merely deferred until the eventual disposition of the newer facility. This deferral is accomplished by calculating the basis in the newer facility, starting with its fair market value on the date of acquisition, and subtracting from that amount the gain not recognized on the sale of the older facility. That process builds the unrecognized gain into the basis of the newer building so that it will be recognized (along with any future gain) upon its later sale. There has been considerable confusion and debate over what constitutes like-kind property outside of real estate, but there is no doubt that a trade of real estate used in business for other real estate to be used in business will qualify under Section 1031.

Although undoubtedly attracted by this possibility, Morris would quickly point out that such an exchange would be extremely rare since it is highly unlikely that he would be able to find a new facility which is worth exactly the same amount as his old facility, and thus any such exchange would have to involve a payment of cash as well as an exchange of buildings. Fortunately, however, Section 1031 recognizes that reality by providing that the exchange is still nontaxable to Morris so long as he does not receive any non-like-kind property (i.e., cash). Such non-like-kind property received is known as boot, and would include, besides cash, any liability of Morris's (such as his mortgage debt) assumed by the exchange partner. The facility he is purchasing is more expensive than the one he is selling, so Morris would have to add some cash, not receive it. Thus, the transaction does not involve the receipt of boot and still qualifies for tax deferral. Moreover, even if Morris did receive boot in the transaction, he would recognize gain only to the extent of the boot received, so he might still be in a position to defer a portion of the gain involved. Of course, if he received more boot than the gain in the transaction, he would recognize only the amount of the gain, not the full amount of the boot.

But Morris has an even more compelling, practical objection to this plan. How often will the person who wants to purchase your facility own the exact facility you wish to purchase? Not very often, he would surmise. In fact, the proposed buyer of his old facility is totally unrelated to the current owner of the facility Morris wishes to buy. How then can one structure this as an exchange of the two parcels of real estate? It would seem that a taxable sale of the one followed by a purchase of the other will be necessary in almost every case.

Practitioners have, however, devised a technique to overcome this problem, known as the three-corner exchange. In a nutshell, the transaction is structured by having the proposed buyer of Morris's old facility use his purchase money (plus some additional money contributed by Morris) to acquire the facility Morris wants to buy, instead of giving that money to Morris. Having thus acquired the new facility, he then trades it to Morris for Morris's old facility. When the dust settles, everyone is in the same position he would have occupied in the absence of an exchange. The former owner of the new facility has his cash; the proposed buyer of Morris's old facility now owns that facility and has spent only the amount he proposed to spend; and Morris has traded the old facility plus some cash for the new one. The only party adversely affected is the IRS, which now must wait to tax the gain in Morris's old facility until he sells the new one.

This technique appears so attractive that when practitioners first began to use it, they attempted to employ the technique even when the seller of the old facility had not yet found a new facility to buy. They merely had the buyer of the old facility place the purchase price in escrow and promise to use it to buy a new facility for the old owner as soon as she picked one out. Congress has since limited the use of these so-called delayed like-kind exchanges by requiring the seller of the old facility to identify the new facility to be purchased within 45 days of the transfer of the old one and by further requiring that the exchange be completed within six months of the first transfer.

DIVIDENDS

Some time after Morris engineered the acquisition of the molding facility, the hiring of Brad to run it, and the consolidation of his company's operations through the like-kind exchange, Plant Supply was running smoothly and profitably enough for Morris's thoughts to turn to retirement. Morris intended to have a comfortable retirement funded by the fruits of his lifelong efforts on behalf of the company, so it was not unreasonable for him to consider funding his retirement through dividends on what would still be his considerable holdings of the company's stock. Although Brad already held some stock and Morris expected that Lisa and Victor would hold some at that time, he still expected to have a majority position and thus sufficient control of the board of directors to ensure such distributions.

Morris also knew enough about tax law, however, to understand that such distributions would cause considerable havoc from a tax viewpoint. We have already discussed how characterizing such distributions as salary or bonus would avoid double taxation, but with Morris no longer working for the company such characterization would be unreasonable. These payments would be deemed dividends on his stock. They would be nondeductible to the corporation (if it were not a subchapter S corporation at the time) and would be fully taxable to him. But Morris had another idea. He would embark on a strategy of turning in small amounts of his stock on a regular basis in exchange for the stock's value. Although not a perfect solution, the distributions to him would no longer be dividends but payments in redemption of stock. Thus, they would be taxable only to the extent they exceeded his basis in the stock and, even then, only at long-term capital gain rates (not as ordinary income). Best of all, if such redemptions were small enough, he would retain his control over the company for as long as he retained over 50% of its outstanding stock.

However, the benefits of this type of plan have attracted the attention of Congress and the IRS over the years. If an individual can draw monies out of a corporation, without affecting the control he asserts through the ownership of his stock, is he really redeeming his stock or simply engaging in a disguised dividend? Congress has answered this question with a series of Code sections purporting to define a redemption.

Substantially Disproportionate Distributions

Most relevant to Morris is Section 302(b)(2), which provides that a distribution in respect of stock is a redemption (and thus taxable as a capital gain after subtraction of basis), only if it is substantially disproportionate. This is further defined by requiring that the stockholder hold, after the distribution, less than half of the total combined voting power of all classes of stock and less than 80% of the percentage of the company's total stock that he owned prior to the distribution.

Thus, if Morris intended to redeem 5 shares of the company's stock at a time when he owned 85 of the company's outstanding 100 shares, he would be required to report the entire distribution as a dividend. His percentage of ownership would still be 50% or more (80 of 95, or 84%), which in itself dooms the transaction. In addition, his percentage of ownership will still be 80% or more than his percentage before the distribution (dropping only from 85% to 84%—99% of his percentage prior to the distribution).

To qualify, Morris would have to redeem 71 shares, since only that amount would drop his control percentage below 50% (14 of 29, or 48%). And since his percentage of control would have dropped from 85% to 48%, he would retain only 56% of the percentage he previously had (less than 80%).

Yet, even such a draconian sell-off as thus described would not be sufficient for the Code. Congress has taken the position that the stock ownership of persons other than oneself must be taken into account in determining one's control of a corporation. Under these so-called attribution rules, a stockholder is deemed to control stock owned not only by himself but also by his spouse, children, grandchildren, and parents. Furthermore, stock owned by partnerships, estates, trusts, and corporations affiliated with the stockholder may also be attributed to him. Thus, assuming that Lisa and Victor owned 10 of the remaining 15 shares of stock (with Brad owning the rest), Morris begins with

95% of the control and can qualify for a stock redemption only by selling all his shares to the corporation.

Complete Termination of Interest

Carried to its logical conclusion, even a complete redemption would not qualify for favorable tax treatment, since Lisa and Victor's stock would still be attributed to Morris, leaving him in control of 67% of the corporation's stock. Fortunately, however, Code Section 302(b)(3) provides for a distribution to be treated as a redemption if the stockholder's interest in the corporation is completely terminated. The attribution rules still apply under this section, but they may be waived if the stockholder files a written agreement with the IRS requesting such a waiver. In such an agreement, Morris would be required to divest himself of any relationship with the corporation other than as a creditor and agree not to acquire any interest in the corporation for a period of 10 years.

In addition to the two safe harbors described in Sections 302(b)(2) and (3), the Code, in Section 302(b)(1), grants redemption treatment to distributions which are "not essentially equivalent to a dividend." Unlike the previous two sections, however, the Code does not spell out a mechanical test for this concept, leaving it to the facts and circumstances of the case. Given the obvious purpose of this transaction to transfer corporate assets to a stockholder on favorable terms, it is unlikely that the IRS under this section would recognize any explanation other than that of a dividend.

Thus, Morris's plan to turn in his stock and receive a tax-favored distribution for his retirement will not work out as planned unless he allows the redemption of all his stock; resigns as a director, officer, employee, consultant, and so forth; and agrees to stay away for a period of 10 years. He may, however, accept a promissory note for all or part of the redemption proceeds and thereby become a creditor of the corporation. Worse yet, if Lisa obtained her shares from Morris within the 10 years preceding his retirement, even this plan will not work unless the IRS can be persuaded that her acquisition of the shares was for reasons other than tax avoidance. It may be advisable to ensure that she acquires her shares from the corporation rather than from Morris, although one can expect, given the extent of Morris's control over the corporation, that the IRS would fail to appreciate the difference.

Employee Stock Ownership Plans

Although Morris should be relatively happy with the knowledge that he may be able to arrange a complete redemption of his stock to fund his retirement and avoid being taxed as if he had received a dividend, he may still believe that the tax and economic effects of such a redemption are not ideal. Following such a plan to its logical conclusion, the corporation would borrow the money to pay for Morris's stock. Its repayments would be deductible only to the extent of the interest. At the same time, Morris would be paying a substantial capital gain tax to the government. Before settling for this result, Morris might well wish to explore ways to increase the corporation's deduction and decrease his own tax liability.

Such a result can be achieved through the use of an employee stock ownership plan (ESOP), a form of qualified deferred compensation plan as discussed earlier in the context of Brad's compensation package. Such a plan consists of a trust to which the corporation makes deductible contributions of either shares of its own stock or cash to be used to purchase such stock. Contributions are divided among the accounts of the corporation's employees (normally in proportion to their compensation for that year), and distributions are made to the employees at their retirement or earlier separation from the company (if the plan so allows). ESOPs have been seen as a relatively noncontroversial way for U.S. employees to gain more control over their employers, and they have been granted a number of tax advantages not available to other qualified plans, such as pension or profit-sharing plans. One advantage is illustrated by the fact that a corporation can manufacture a deduction out of thin air by issuing new stock to a plan (at no cost to the corporation) and deducting the fair market value of the shares.

A number of attractive tax benefits would flow from Morris's willingness to sell his shares to an ESOP established by his corporation rather than to the corporation itself. Yet, before he could appreciate those benefits, Morris would have to be satisfied that some obvious objections would not make such a transaction inadvisable.

To begin with, the ESOP would have to borrow the money from a bank in the same way the corporation would; yet the ESOP has no credit record or assets to pledge as collateral. This is normally overcome, however, by the corporation's giving the bank a secured guarantee of the ESOP's obligation. Thus, the corporation ends up in the same economic position it would have enjoyed under a direct redemption.

Morris might also object to the level of control an ESOP might give to lower-level employees of Plant Supply. After all, his intent is to leave the corporation under the control of Lisa and Brad, but qualified plans must be operated on a nondiscriminatory basis. This objection can be addressed in a number of ways. First, the allocation of shares in proportion to compensation, along with standard vesting and forfeiture provisions, will tilt these allocations toward highly compensated, long-term employees, such as Lisa and Brad. Second, the shares are not allocated to the employees' accounts until they are paid for. While the bank is still being paid, an amount proportional to the remaining balance of the loan would be controlled by the plan trustees (chosen by management). Third, even after shares are allocated to employee accounts, in a closely held company, employees are allowed to vote those shares only on questions which require a two-thirds vote of the stockholders, such as a sale or merger of the corporation. On all other more routine questions (such as election of the board) the trustees still vote the shares. Fourth, upon an employee's retirement and before distribution of his shares, a closely held corporation

EXHIBIT 11.7   Corporate redemption versus ESOP purchase.

Corporate Redemption	ESOP Purchase
Only interest deductible	Principal and interest deductible
Capital gain	Gain deferred if proceeds rolled over

must offer to buy back the distributed shares at fair market value. As a practical matter, most employees will accept such an offer rather than moving into retirement with illiquid, closely held company stock.

If Morris accepts these arguments and opts for an ESOP buyout, the following benefits accrue. Rather than being able to deduct only the interest portion of its payments to the bank, the corporation may now contribute the full amount of such payment to the plan as a fully deductible contribution to a qualified plan. The plan then forwards it to the bank as a payment of its obligation.

Furthermore, the Code allows an individual who sells stock of a corporation to the corporation's ESOP to defer paying any tax on the proceeds of such sale, if the proceeds are rolled over into purchases of securities. No tax is then paid until the purchased securities are ultimately resold. Thus, if Morris takes the money received from the ESOP and invests it in the stock market, he pays no tax until and unless he sells any of these securities, and then only on those sold. In fact, if Morris purchases such securities and holds them until his death (assuming he dies prior to 2010), his estate will receive a step-up in basis for such securities and thus will avoid income tax on the proceeds of his company stock entirely (see Exhibit 11.7).

ESTATE PLANNING

Should Morris rebel at the thought of retiring from the company, his thoughts may naturally turn to the tax consequences of his remaining employed by the company in some capacity until his death. Morris's lifelong efforts have made him a rather wealthy man, and he knows that the government will be looking to reap a rather large harvest from those efforts upon his death. He would no doubt be rather disheartened to learn that after a $675,000 exemption (which increases to as much as $3.5 million in 2009), the federal government will receive 37% to anywhere from 45% to 55% of the excess upon his death, depending upon the year in which he dies. Proper estate planning can double the amount of that grace amount by using the exemptions of both Morris and his wife, but the amount above the exemptions appears to be at significant risk. It should further be noted that the federal estate tax is currently scheduled for repeal in 2010, but, under current law, will be reinstated in 2011.

Redemptions to Pay Death Taxes and Administrative Expenses

Since much of the money to fund this estate tax liability would come from redemption of company stock, if Morris had not previously cashed it in, Morris might well fear the combined effect of dividend treatment and estate taxation. Of course, if Morris's estate turned in all his stock for redemption at death, dividend treatment would appear to have been avoided and redemption treatment under Section 302(b)(3) would appear to be available, since this would amount to a complete termination of his interest in the company and death would appear to cut off Morris's relationship with the company rather convincingly. However, if the effect of Morris's death on the company or of other circumstances made a wholesale redemption inadvisable or impossible, Morris's estate could be faced with paying both ordinary income and estate tax rates on the full amount of the proceeds.

Fortunately for those faced with this problem, Code Section 303 allows capital gain treatment for a stock redemption if the proceeds of the redemption do not exceed the amount necessary to pay the estate's taxes and those further expenses allowable as administrative expenses on the estate's tax return. To qualify for this treatment, the company's stock must equal or exceed 35% of the value of the estate's total assets. Since Morris's holdings of company stock will most likely exceed 35% of his total assets, if his estate finds itself in this uncomfortable position, it will at least be able to account for this distribution as a stock redemption instead of a dividend. This is much more important than it may first appear and much more important than it would have been were Morris still alive. The effect, of course, is to allow payment at long-term capital gain rates (rather than ordinary income tax rates) for only the amount received in excess of the taxpayer's basis in the stock (rather than the entire amount of the distribution). Given that the death of the taxpayer prior to 2010 increases his basis to the value at date of death, the effect of Section 303 is to eliminate all but that amount of gain occurring after death, thus eliminating virtually all income tax on the distribution. This step-up of basis will be significantly less generous for taxpayer's dying after 2009.

Of course, assuring sufficient liquidity to pay taxes due upon death is one thing; controlling the amount of tax actually due is another. Valuation of a majority interest in a closely held corporation is far from an exact science, and the last thing an entrepreneur wishes is to have his or her spouse and other heirs engage in a valuation controversy with the IRS after his or her death. As a result, a number of techniques have evolved over the years which may have the effect of lowering the value of the stock to be included in the estate or, at least, making such value more certain for planning purposes.

Family Limited Partnerships

One such technique that has recently gained in popularity is the so-called family limited partnership. This strategy allows an individual to decrease the size of his taxable estate through gifts to his intended beneficiaries both faster and at less tax cost than would otherwise be possible, while at the same time retaining effective control over the assets given away. Were Morris interested in implementing this strategy, he would form a limited partnership, designating himself as the general partner and retaining all but a minimal amount of the limited partnership interests for himself. He would then transfer to the partnership a significant portion of his assets, such as stock in the company, real estate, or marketable securities. Even though he would have transferred these interests out of his name, he would be assured of continued control over these assets in his role as general partner. The general partner of a limited partnership exercises all management functions; limited partners sacrifice all control in exchange for limited liability.

Morris would then embark on a course of gifting portions of the limited partnership interests to Lisa, Victor, and perhaps even Brad. You will remember that in each calendar year, Morris and his wife can combine to give no more than $20,000 to each beneficiary before eating into their lifetime gift tax exemption. The advantage of the family limited partnership, besides retaining control over the assets given away, is that the amounts which may be given each year are effectively increased. For example, were Morris and his wife to give $20,000 of marketable securities to Lisa in any given year, that would use up their entire annual gift tax exclusion. However, were they instead to give Lisa a portion of the limited partnership interest to which those marketable securities had been contributed, it can be argued that the gift should be valued at a much lower amount. After all, while there was a ready market for the securities, there is no market for the limited partnership interests; and while Lisa would have had control over the securities if they had been given to her, she has no control of them through her limited partnership interest. These discounts for lack of marketability and control can be substantial, freeing up more room under the annual exclusion for further gifting. In proper circumstances, one might use this technique when owning a rapidly appreciating asset (such as a pre-IPO stock) to give away more than $20,000 in a year, using up all or part of the lifetime exclusion, to remove the asset from your estate at a discount from its present value, rather than having to pay estate tax in the future on a highly inflated value.

Of course, the IRS has challenged these arrangements when there was no apparent business purpose other than tax savings or when the transfer occurred just before the death of the transferor. And you can expect the IRS to challenge an overly aggressive valuation discount. But if Morris is careful in his valuations, he might find this arrangement attractive, asserting the business purpose of centralizing management while facilitating the grant of equity incentives to his executive employees.

Buy-Sell Agreements

Short of establishing a family limited partnership, Morris might be interested in a more traditional arrangement requiring the corporation or its stockholders to purchase whatever stock he may still hold at his death. Such an arrangement can be helpful with regard to both of Morris's estate-planning goals: setting a value for his stock that would not be challenged by the IRS and assuring sufficient liquidity to pay whatever estate taxes may ultimately be owed.

There are two basic variations of these agreements. Under the most common, Morris would agree with the corporation that it would redeem his shares upon his death for a price derived from an agreed formula. The second variation would require one or more of the other stockholders of the corporation (e.g., Lisa) to make such a purchase. In both cases, in order for the IRS to respect the valuation placed upon the shares, Morris will need to agree that he will not dispose of the shares during his lifetime without first offering them to the other party to his agreement at the formula price. Under such an arrangement, the shares will never be worth more to Morris than the formula price, so it can be argued that whatever higher price the IRS may calculate is irrelevant to him and his estate.

This argument led some stockholders in the past to agree to formulas that artificially depressed the value of their shares when the parties succeeding to power in the corporation were also the main beneficiaries of the stockholders' estates. Since any value forgone would end up in the hands of the intended beneficiary anyway, only the tax collector would be hurt. Although the IRS long challenged this practice, this strategy has been put to a formal end by legislation requiring that the formula used result in a close approximation to fair market value.

Which of the two variations of the buy-sell agreement should Morris choose? If we assume for the moment that Morris owns 80 of the 100 outstanding shares and Lisa and Brad each own 10, a corporate redemption agreement leaves Lisa and Brad each owning half of the 20 outstanding shares remaining. If, however, Morris chooses a cross-purchase agreement with Lisa and Brad, each would purchase 40 of his shares upon his death, leaving them as owners of 50 shares each. Both agreements leave the corporation owned by Lisa and Brad in equal shares, so there does not appear to be any difference between them.

Once again, however, significant differences lie slightly below the surface. To begin with, many such agreements are funded by the purchase of a life insurance policy on the life of the stockholder involved. If the corporation were to purchase this policy, the premiums would be nondeductible, resulting in additional taxable profit for the corporation. In a subchapter S corporation, such profit would pass through to the stockholders in proportion to their shares of stock in the corporation. In a C corporation, the additional profit would result in additional corporate tax. If, instead, Lisa and Brad bought policies covering their halves of the obligation to Morris's estate, they would be paying the premiums with after-tax dollars. Thus, a redemption agreement will cause Morris to share in the cost of the arrangement, whereas a cross-purchase agreement puts the entire onus on Lisa and Brad. This burden can, of course, be rationalized by arguing that they will ultimately reap the benefit of the arrangement by succeeding to the ownership of the corporation. Or, their compensation could be adjusted to cover the additional cost.

If the corporation is not an S corporation, however, there is an additional consideration that must not be overlooked. Upon Morris's death, the receipt of the insurance proceeds by the beneficiary of the life insurance will be excluded from taxable income. However, a C corporation (other than certain small businesses) is also subject to the alternative minimum tax. Simply described, that tax guards against individuals and profitable corporations paying little or no tax by "overuse" of certain deductions and tax credits otherwise available. To calculate the tax, the taxpayer adds to its otherwise taxable income, certain "tax preferences" and then subtracts from that amount an exemption amount ($40,000 for most corporations). The result is taxed at 20% for corporations (26% and 28% for individuals). If that tax amount exceeds the income tax otherwise payable, the higher amount is paid. The result of this is additional tax for those taxpayers with substantial tax preferences.

Among those tax preferences for C corporations is a concept known as adjusted current earnings. This concept adds as a tax preference, three-quarters of the difference between the corporation's earnings for financial reporting purposes and the earnings otherwise reportable for tax purposes. A major source of such a difference would be the receipt of nontaxable income. And the receipt of life insurance proceeds is just such an event. Therefore, the receipt of a life insurance payout of sufficient size would ultimately be taxed, at least in part, to a C corporation, whereas it would be completely tax free to an S corporation or the remaining stockholders.

An additional factor pointing to the stockholder cross-purchase agreement rather than a corporate redemption is the effect this choice would have on the taxability of a later sale of the corporation after Morris's death. If the corporation were to redeem Morris's stock, Lisa and Brad would each own one-half of the corporation through their ownership of 10 shares each. If they then sold the company, they would be subject to tax on capital gain measured by the difference between the proceeds of the sale and their original basis in their shares. However, if Lisa and Brad purchased Morris's stock at his death, they would each own one-half of the corporation through their ownership of 50 shares each. Upon a later sale of the company, their capital gain would be measured by the difference between the sale proceeds and their original basis in their shares plus the amount paid for Morris's shares. Every dollar paid to Morris lowers the taxable income received upon later sale. In a redemption agreement, these dollars are lost (see Exhibit 11.8).

SPIN-OFFS AND SPLIT-UPS

Morris's pleasant reverie caused by thoughts of well-funded retirement strategies and clever estate plans was brought to a sudden halt a mere two years after the acquisition of the molding operation, when it became clear

EXHIBIT 11.8   Corporate redemption versus cross-purchase agreement.

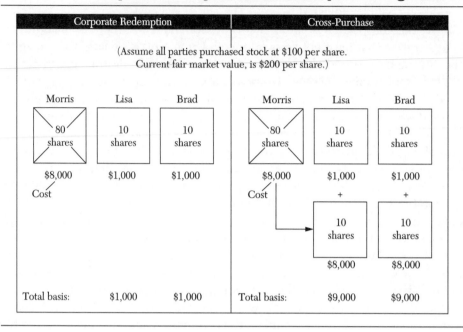

that the internecine jealousies between Brad and Lisa were becoming un-
manageable. Ruefully, Morris conceded that it was not unforeseeable that the
manager of a significant part of his business would resent the presence of a
rival who would be perceived as having attained her present position simply
by dint of her relationship to the owner. This jealousy was, of course, in-
flamed by the thought that Lisa might succeed to Morris's stock upon his
death and become Brad's boss.

After some months of attempting to mediate the many disputes between
Lisa and Brad, which were merely symptoms of this underlying disease, Morris
came to the conclusion that the corporation could not survive with both of
them vying for power and influence. He determined that the only workable solution would be to break the two businesses apart once again, leaving the two
rivals in charge of their individual empires, with no future binding ties.

Experienced in corporate transactions by this time, Morris gave the problem some significant thought and devised two alternate scenarios to accomplish his goal. Both scenarios began with the establishment of a subsidiary
corporation wholly owned by the currently existing company. The assets, liabilities, and all other attributes of the molding operation would then be transferred to this new subsidiary in exchange for its stock. At that point in the first
scenario (known as a spin-off), the parent corporation would declare a dividend of all such stock to its current stockholders. Thus, Morris, Lisa, and Brad

would own the former subsidiary in the same proportions in which they owned the parent. Morris, as the majority owner of the new corporation, could then give further shares to Brad, enter into a buy-sell agreement with him, or sell him some shares. In any case, upon Morris's death, Brad would succeed to unquestioned leadership in this corporation. Lisa would stay as a minority stockholder or, if she wished, sell her shares to Morris while he was alive. Lisa would gain control of the former parent corporation upon Morris's death.

In the second scenario (known as a split-off), after the formation of the subsidiary, Brad would sell his shares of Plant Supply to that parent corporation in exchange for stock affording him control of the subsidiary. Lisa would remain the only minority stockholder of the parent corporation (Brad's interest having been removed) and would succeed to full ownership upon Morris's death through one of the mechanisms discussed earlier.

Unfortunately, when Morris brought his ideas to his professional advisers, he was faced with a serious tax objection. In both scenarios, he was told, the IRS would likely take the position that the issuance of the subsidiary's stock to its eventual holder (Morris in the spin-off and Brad in the split-off) was a taxable transaction, characterized as a dividend. After all, this plan could be used as another device to cash out the earnings and profits of a corporation at favorable rates and terms. Instead of declaring a dividend of these profits, a corporation could spin off assets, with the fair market value of these profits, to a subsidiary. The shares of the subsidiary could then be distributed to its stockholders as a nontaxable stock dividend, and the stockholders could sell these shares and treat their profits as capital gain. The second scenario allows Brad to receive the subsidiary's shares and then make a similar sale of these shares at favorable rates and terms.

As a result, the Code characterizes the distribution of the subsidiary's shares to the parent's stockholders as a dividend, taxable to the extent of the parent's earnings and profits at the time of the distribution. This would certainly inhibit Morris if he were the owner of a profitable C corporation. It would be less of a concern if his corporation were operating as an S corporation, although even then he would have to be concerned about undistributed earnings and profits dating from before the S election.

Recognizing that not all transactions of this type are entered into to disguise the declaration of a dividend, the Code does allow spin-offs and split-offs to take place tax-free, under the limited circumstances described in Section 355. These circumstances track the scenarios concocted by Morris, but are limited to circumstances in which both the parent and subsidiary will be conducting an active trade or business after the transaction. Moreover, each trade or business must have been conducted for a period exceeding five years prior to the distribution and cannot have been acquired in a taxable transaction during such time. Since Morris's corporation acquired the molding business only two years previously and such transaction was not tax free, the benefits of Section 355 are not available now. Short of another solution, it would appear that Morris will have to live with the bickering of Brad and Lisa for another three years.

SALE OF THE CORPORATION

Fortunately for Morris, another solution was not long in coming. Within months of the failure of his proposal to split up the company, Morris was approached by the president of a company in a related field, interested in purchasing Plant Supply. Such a transaction was very intriguing to Morris. He had worked very hard for many years and would not be adverse to an early retirement. A purchase such as this would relieve him of all his concerns over adequate liquidity for his estate and strategies for funding his retirement. He could take care of both Lisa and Victor with the cash he would receive, and both Lisa and Brad would be free to deal with the acquirer about remaining employed and collecting on their equity.

However, Morris knew better than to get too excited over this prospect before consulting with his tax advisers. His hesitance turned out to be justified. Unless a deal was appropriately structured, Morris was staring at a significant tax bite, both on the corporate and the stockholder levels.

Morris knew from his experience with the molding plant that a corporate acquisition can be structured in three basic ways: a merger, a sale of stock, and a purchase of assets. In a merger, the target corporation disappears into the acquirer by operation of law, and the former stockholders of the target receive consideration from the acquirer. In the sale of stock, the stockholders sell their shares directly to the acquiring corporation. In a sale of assets, the target sells its assets (and most of its liabilities) to the acquirer, and the proceeds of the sale are then distributed to the target's stockholders through the liquidation of the target. A major theme of all three of these scenarios involves the acquirer forming a subsidiary corporation to act as the acquirer in the transaction.

In each case, the difference between the proceeds received by the target's stockholders and their basis in the target's stock would be taxable as capital gain. Morris was further informed that this tax at the stockholder level could be avoided if these transactions qualified under the complex rules that define tax-free reorganizations. In each case, one of the requirements would be that the target stockholders receive largely stock of the acquirer rather than cash. Since the acquirer in this case was closely held and there was no market for its stock, Morris was determined to insist upon cash. He thus accepted the idea of paying tax on the stockholder level.

Morris was quite surprised, however, to learn that he might also be exposed to corporate tax on the growth in the corporation's assets over its basis in them if they were deemed to have been sold as a result of the acquisition transaction. For one thing, he had been under the impression that a corporation was exempt from such tax if it sold its assets as part of the liquidation process. He was disappointed to learn that this exemption was another victim of the repeal of the General Utilities doctrine. He was further disappointed when reminded that even subchapter S corporations recognize all built-in gain that existed at the time of their subchapter S election, if their assets are sold within 10 years after their change of tax status.

As a result of the previous considerations, Morris was determined to avoid structuring the sale of his corporation as a sale of its assets and liabilities, to avoid any tax on the corporate level. He was already determined not to structure it as a sale of stock by the target stockholders, because he was not entirely sure Brad could be trusted to sell his shares. If he could structure the transaction at the corporate level, he would not need Brad's minority vote to accomplish it. Thus, after intensive negotiations, he was pleased that the acquiring corporation had agreed to structure the acquisition as a merger between Plant Supply and a subsidiary of the acquirer (to be formed for the purpose of the transaction). All stockholders of Plant Supply would receive a cash down payment and a five-year promissory note from the parent acquirer in exchange for their stock.

Yet even this careful preparation and negotiation leaves Morris, Lisa, and Brad in jeopardy of unexpected tax exposure. To begin with, if the transaction remains as negotiated, the IRS will likely take the position that the assets of the target corporation have been sold to the acquirer, thus triggering tax at the corporate level. In addition, the target's stockholders will have to recognize as proceeds of the sale of their stock both the cash and the fair market value of the promissory notes in the year of the transaction, even though they will receive payments on the notes over a period of five years.

Under the General Utilities doctrine, a corporation that was selling substantially all its assets needed to adopt a "plan of liquidation" prior to entering into the sale agreement to avoid taxation at the corporate level. The repeal of the doctrine may have left the impression that the adoption of such a liquidation plan is unnecessary because the sale will be taxed at the corporate level in any event. Yet, the Code still requires such a liquidation plan if the stockholders wish to recognize notes received upon the dissolution of the target corporation on the installment basis. Moreover, the liquidation of the corporation must be completed within 12 months of adoption of the liquidation plan.

Thus, Morris's best efforts may still have led to disaster. Fortunately, a small adjustment to the negotiated transaction can cure most of these problems. Through an example of corporate magic known as the reverse triangular merger, the newly formed subsidiary of the acquirer may disappear into Morris's target corporation, but the target's stockholders can still be jettisoned for cash, leaving the acquirer as the parent. In such a transaction, the assets of the target have not been sold; they remain owned by the original corporation. Only the target's stockholders have changed. In effect, the parties have sold stock without the necessity of getting Brad's approval. Because the assets have not changed hands, there is no tax at the corporate level. In addition, since the target corporation has not liquidated, no plan of liquidation is required, and the target stockholders may elect installment treatment as if they had sold their shares directly (see Exhibit 11.9).

EXHIBIT 11.9 Reverse triangle merger.

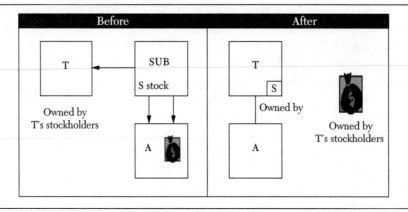

CONCLUSION

Perhaps no taxpayer will encounter quite as many cataclysmic tax decisions in as short a time as did Morris and Plant Supply. Yet, Morris's experience serves to illustrate that tax issues lurk in almost every major business decision made by a corporation's management. Many transactions can be structured to avoid unnecessary tax expense if proper attention is paid to tax implications. To be unaware of these issues is to play the game without knowing the rules.

FOR FURTHER READING

Gevurtz, Franklin A., *Business Planning* (New York: Foundation Press, 1995).

Jones, Sally M., *Federal Taxes and Management Decisions* (New York: Irwin/McGraw-Hill, 1998).

Painter, William H., *Problems and Materials in Business Planning*, 3rd ed. (Connecticut: West/Wadsworth, 1994).

Scholes, Myron S. et al., *Taxes and Business Strategy* (Upper Saddle River, NJ: Prentice-Hall, 2001).

INTERNET LINKS

http://smallbiz.biz.findlaw.com   FindLaw for Business
/sections/fn_taxes/articles.html

http://www.dtonline.com   Deloitte and Touche Tax Planning Guide
/taxguide99/cover.htm

http://www.smartmoney.com/tax   Smart Money.com tax guide

12 GLOBAL FINANCE

Eugene E. Comiskey
Charles W. Mulford

MANAGERIAL AND FINANCIAL REPORTING ISSUES AT SUCCESSIVE STAGES IN THE FIRM'S LIFE CYCLE

Fashionhouse Furniture started as a small southern retailer of furniture purchased mainly in bordering southeastern states. With a growing level of both competition and affluence in its major market areas, Fashionhouse decided that its future lay in a niche strategy involving specialization in a high quality line of Scandinavian furniture. Its suppliers were mainly located in Denmark, and they followed the practice of billing Fashionhouse in the Danish krone. Title would typically pass to Fashionhouse when the goods were dropped on the dock in Copenhagen. Payment for the goods was required within periods ranging from 30 to 90 days. As its business expanded and prospered, Fashionhouse became convinced that it needed to exercise greater control over its furniture supply. This control was accomplished through the purchase of its principal Danish supplier. Because this supplier also had a network of retail units in Denmark, the manufacturing operations in Denmark supplied both the local Danish market as well as the U.S. requirements of Fashionhouse.

More recently, Fashionhouse has been searching for ways to increase manufacturing efficiency and lower product costs. It is contemplating a relocation of part of its manufacturing activity to a country with an ample and low-cost supply of labor. However, Fashionhouse has noted that many such countries experience very high levels of inflation and other potentially disruptive economic and political conditions. It has also become aware that in some of the countries under consideration business practices are occasionally employed that could be a source of concern to Fashionhouse management. In some cases, the practices raise issues that extend beyond simply ethical considerations. Fashionhouse could become involved in activities that could place it in violation, not of local laws, but of U.S. laws. Fashionhouse management is still attempting to determine how to evaluate and deal with some of the identified managerial and financial issues associated with this contemplated move.

Each of the new stages in the evolution of the Fashionhouse strategy creates new challenges that have important implications for both management and financial reporting. The evolution from a strictly domestic operation to one involving the purchase of goods abroad thrusts Fashionhouse into the global marketplace, with its attendant risks and rewards. It is common for U.S. firms with foreign activities to enumerate some of these risks. These disclosures are normally made, at least in part, to comply with disclosure requirements of the Securities and Exchange Commission (SEC). As an example, consider the disclosures made by Western Digital Corporation of risk factors associated with its foreign manufacturing operations:

- Obtaining requisite U.S. and foreign governmental permits and approvals.
- Currency exchange-rate fluctuations or restrictions.
- Political instability and civil unrest.
- Transportation delays or higher freight fees.
- Labor problems.
- Trade restrictions or higher tariffs.
- Exchange, currency, and tax controls and reallocations.
- Loss or nonrenewal of favorable tax treatment under agreements or treaties with foreign tax authorities.[1]

While not listed above as a specific concern, there is the risk that a foreign government will expropriate the assets of a foreign operation. There were major expropriations of U.S. assets, for instance, located in Cuba when Fidel Castro came to power. There were also expropriations by Iran surrounding the hostage taking at the U.S. embassy in Tehran. Moreover there has been turmoil in Ecuador in recent years. Baltek, a New Jersey corporation with most of its operations in Ecuador, disclosed that it had taken out expropriation insurance to deal with this risk:

> All of the Company's balsa and shrimp are produced in Ecuador. The dependence on foreign countries for raw materials represents some inherent risks. However, the Company, or its predecessors, has operated without interruption in Ecuador since 1940. Operating in Ecuador has enabled the Company to produce raw materials at a reasonable cost in an atmosphere that has been favorable to exporters such as the Company. To mitigate the risk of operating in Ecuador, in 1999 the Company obtained a five-year expropriation insurance policy. This policy provides the Company coverage for its assets in Ecuador

against expropriatory conduct (as defined in the policy) by the government of Ecuador.[2]

Some of the important issues implicit in the Fashionhouse scenario outlined above are identified below and are discussed and illustrated in the balance of this chapter:

1. Fashionhouse incurs a foreign-currency obligation when it begins to acquire furniture from its Danish suppliers. A decrease in the value of the dollar between purchase and payment date increases the dollars required to discharge the Danish krone obligation and results in a foreign-currency transaction loss.

   Financial reporting issue: How are the foreign-currency obligations initially recorded and subsequently accounted for in the Fashionhouse books, which are maintained in U.S. dollars?

   Management issue: What methods are available to avoid the currency risk associated with purchasing goods abroad and also being invoiced in the foreign currency, and should they be employed?

2. The purchase of one of its Danish suppliers requires that this firm henceforth be consolidated into the financial statements of Fashionhouse and its U.S. operations.

   Financial reporting issues: (a) How are the Danish statements converted from the krone in order to consolidate them with the U.S. dollar statements of Fashionhouse? (b) What differences in accounting practices, if any, exist between Denmark and the United States and what must be done about such differences?

   Management issues: (a) Is there currency risk associated with the Danish subsidiary comparable to that described previously with the foreign purchase transactions? Are there methods available to avoid the currency risk associated with ownership of a foreign subsidiary and should they be employed? (b) How will the financial aspects of the management of the Danish subsidiary be evaluated in view of (1) the availability of two different sets of financial statements, those expressed in krone and those in U.S. dollars, and (2) the fact that most of its sales are to Fashionhouse, its U.S. parent?

3. Fashionhouse relocates its manufacturing to a high-inflation and low-labor cost country.

   Financial reporting issues: How will inflation affect the local-country financial statements and their usefulness in evaluating the performance of the company and its management?

   Management issues: (a) Are their special risks associated with locating in a highly inflationary country and how can they be managed? (b) What are the restrictions on U.S. business practices related to dealing with business and governmental entities in other countries?

For clarification and to indicate their order of treatment in the subsequent discussion, the issues raised above are enumerated below, without distinction between those that are mainly financial reporting as opposed to managerial issues:

1. Financial reporting of foreign-currency denominated transactions.
2. Risk management alternatives for foreign-currency denominated transactions.
3. Translation of the financial statements of foreign subsidiaries.
4. Managing the currency risk of foreign subsidiaries.
5. Dealing with differences between U.S. and foreign accounting policies.
6. Evaluation of the performance of foreign subsidiaries and their management.
7. Assessing the effects of inflation on the financial performance of foreign subsidiaries.
8. Complying with U.S. restrictions on business practices associated with foreign subsidiaries and governments.

FINANCIAL REPORTING OF FOREIGN-CURRENCY DENOMINATED TRANSACTIONS

When a U.S. company buys from or sells to a foreign firm, a key issue is the currency in which the transaction is to be denominated.[3] In the case of Fashionhouse, its purchases from Danish suppliers were invoiced to Fashionhouse in the Danish krone. This creates a risk, which is born by Fashionhouse and not its Danish supplier, of a *foreign exchange transaction loss* should the dollar fall in value. Alternatively, a gain would result should the dollar increase between the time the furniture is dropped on the dock in Copenhagen and the required payment date. With a fall in the value of the dollar, the Fashionhouse *dollar* cost for the furniture will be more than the dollar obligation it originally recorded. Fashionhouse is said to have *liability exposure* in the Danish krone. If, instead, Fashionhouse had been invoiced in the U.S. dollar, then it would have had no currency risk. Rather, its Danish supplier would bear the currency risk associated with a claim to U.S. dollars, in the form of a U.S. dollar account receivable. If the dollar were to decrease in value, the Danish supplier would incur a foreign exchange transaction loss, or a gain should the dollar increase in value. The Danish firm would have asset exposure in a U.S. dollar account receivable.

The essence of foreign-currency exposure or currency risk is that existing account balances or prospective cash flows can expand or contract simply as a result of changes in the values of currencies. A summary of foreign exchange gains and losses, by type of exposure, due to exchange rate movements is provided in Exhibit 12.1. To illustrate some of the computational aspects of the

EXHIBIT 12.1   Type of foreign currency exposure.

Change in Foreign Currency Value	Exposure	
	Asset	Liability
Appreciates	Gain	Loss
Depreciates	Loss	Gain

patterns of gains and losses in Exhibit 12.1, and the nature of exchange rates, assume that Fashionhouse recorded a 100,000 krone purchase when the exchange rate for the krone was $0.1180. That is, it takes 11.8 cents to purchase one krone. This expression of the exchange rate, dollars per unit of the foreign currency, is referred to as the *direct rate*. Alternatively, expressing the rate in terms of kroner per dollar is referred to as the *indirect rate*. In this case, the indirect rate is 1/0.1180, or K8.475. It requires 8.475 kroner to purchase one dollar. Both the direct and indirect rates are typically provided in the tables of exchange rates found in the financial press. The rates at which currencies are currently trading are called the *spot rates*.

When Fashionhouse records the invoice received from its Danish supplier, it must do so in its U.S. dollar equivalent. With the direct rate at $0.1180, the dollar equivalent of K100,000 is $0.1180 × K100,000, or $11,800. That is, Fashionhouse records an addition to inventory and an offsetting account payable for $11,800. Assume that Fashionhouse pays this obligation when the dollar has fallen to $0.1190. It will now take $11,900 dollars to acquire the K100,000 needed to pay off the account payable. The combination of liability exposure and a decline in the value of the dollar results in a foreign-currency transaction loss. This result is summarized below:

The exchange rate is $0.1190 when the account payable from the purchase is paid.

Dollar amount of obligation at payment date, 100,000 × $0.1190	$11,900
Dollar amount of obligation at purchase date, 100,000 × $0.1180	11,800
Foreign exchange transaction loss	$ 100

The dollar depreciated against the krone during the time when Fashionhouse had liability exposure in the krone. As a result, it took $100 more to discharge the account payable than the amount at which the liability was originally recorded by Fashionhouse.

If the foreign exchange losses incurred were significant, it might prove difficult to pass on this increased cost to Fashionhouse customers, and it could cause its furniture to be somewhat less competitive than that offered by other U.S. retailers with domestic suppliers. Fashionhouse might attempt to avoid the currency risk by convincing its Danish suppliers to invoice it in the dollar. However, this means that the Danish suppliers would bear the currency risk.

Experience indicates that such suppliers would expect to be compensated for bearing this risk and would charge more for their products.[4] An alternative approach, the use of various hedging procedures, is the more common method employed to manage the risk of foreign-currency exposure.

RISK MANAGEMENT ALTERNATIVES FOR FOREIGN-CURRENCY DENOMINATED TRANSACTIONS

Hedging is designed to protect the dollar value of a foreign-currency asset position or to hold constant the dollar burden of a foreign-currency liability.[5] At the same time, the volatility of a firm's cash flow or earnings stream is also reduced. This reduction is accomplished by maintaining an offsetting position that produces gains when the asset or liability position is creating losses, and vice versa. These offsetting positions may be created as a result of arrangements involving internal offsetting balances created through operational activities, or they may entail specialized external transactions with financial firms or markets.

Hedging with Internal Offsetting Balances or Cash Flows

Firms generally attempt to close out as much foreign-currency exposure as possible by relying upon their own operations. These arrangements are often referred to as *natural hedges*. As an example, consider the following commentary about currency exposure from the 1999 annual report of Air Canada:

> Foreign exchange exposure on interest obligations in Swiss francs and Deutsche marks *is fully covered* by surplus cash flows in European currencies, while yen-denominated cash flow surpluses provide a *natural hedge* to fully cover yen interest expense.[6]

Air Canada is able to prevent net exposure in the identified foreign currencies by having offsetting cash flows in the same currencies or in currencies whose values move in parallel to the currencies in which Air Canada has interest obligations. With the full transition to the Euro in 2002, Air Canada's currency exposure should be markedly reduced because most of the European Community countries will share the Euro as their currency.[7] This will not, of course, alter their exposure in the case of Asian currencies.

A sampling of other arrangements that could be characterized as *natural hedges* is provided in Exhibit 12.2. Virtually all of these examples illustrate the offsetting of exposure through the results of normal operations. In the cases of Baldwin Technologies and Interface, the hedges could be seen to be *seminatural* if they result from a conscious action to create offsetting exposure. That is, does Baldwin Technology determine the cash balances to maintain after first

EXHIBIT 12.2 Natural foreign currency hedges.

Company	Natural Hedge
Adobe Systems Inc. (1999)	We currently do not use financial instruments to hedge local currency denominated operating expenses in Europe. Instead, we believe that a *natural hedge* exists, in that local currency revenue from product upgrades substantially offsets the local currency denominated operating expenses.
Armstrong World Industries Inc. (1999)	Armstrong's global manufacturing and sales provide a *natural hedge* of foreign currency exchange-rate movements as foreign currency revenues are offset by foreign currency expenses.
Baldwin Technology Company Inc. (1999)	The Company also maintains certain levels of cash denominated in various currencies which acts as a *natural hedge.*
Baltek Corporation (1998)	During 1997, the Company began borrowing in Ecuador in local currency (sucre) denominated loans as a *natural hedge* of the net investments in Ecuador.
Interface Inc. (1999)	During 1998, the Company restructured its borrowing facilities which provided for multi-currency loan agreements resulting in the Company's ability to borrow funds in the countries in which the funds are expected to be utilized. Further, the advent of the Euro has provided additional currency stability with the Company's European markets. As such, these events have provided the Company *natural hedges* of currency fluctuations.
Pall Corporation (2000)	About one quarter of Pall's sales are in countries tied to the Euro. At current exchange rates, this could reduce our sales by close to 4%. Fortunately, many of our costs in Europe are also reduced by a weak Euro. The weak British Pound also reduces our exposure as most Pall sales to Europe are manufactured in England. This provides a natural hedge and helps preserve profitability.
Teleflex Inc. (1999)	Approximately 65% of the company's total borrowings of $345 million are denominated in currencies other than the US dollar, principally Euro, providing a *natural hedge* against fluctuations in the value of non-domestic assets.

SOURCES: Companies' annual reports. The year following each company name designates the annual report from which each example is drawn.

determining the extent of their liability exposure? Similarly, does Interface make decisions about the currency in which to borrow depending upon its existing asset exposure?[8]

Being the product of calculation and design does not make the seminatural hedges any less effective or desirable. In fact, their existence prompts management to be proactive in identifying hedging opportunities that do not require, for example, the use of either exchange-traded or over-the-counter derivative instruments.

While somewhat less contemporary, there are other examples of using a firm's own operations and activities to offset foreign-currency exposure. For example, California First Bank (now part of Union Bank) had a Swiss franc borrowing in the amount of Sfr20 million.[9] As this represented *liability exposure* to California First, Exhibit 12.1 shows that an increase in the value of the Swiss franc results in a foreign-currency transaction loss. The goal of the hedge would be to create a gain in this circumstance to offset the loss on the Swiss franc borrowing. Again, Exhibit 12.1 reveals that a gain would be produced from asset exposure in the Swiss franc in the case where the Swiss franc appreciated in value.

California First Bank sought an opportunity to establish an asset position in the Swiss franc for the same amount and term as the existing Swiss franc obligation. It created this offsetting position by making a loan and denominating the loan in the Swiss franc. This apparently met the borrower's needs and also served the hedging objective of California First Bank.

In an even more creative arrangement, Federal Express created a natural hedge of a term loan that was denominated in the Japanese yen.[10] This was accomplished by a special structuring of transactions with its own customers. As Federal Express explained:

> To minimize foreign exchange risk on the term loan, the Company has commitments from certain Japanese customers to purchase a minimum level of freight services through 1993.

Federal Express needed Japanese yen to make periodic repayments on the term loan. The arrangements with its Japanese customers ensured that yen would be available to pay down the term loan. If the yen appreciates against the dollar, the dollar burden of the Federal Express yen debt increases and results in a transaction loss. However, this loss is offset in turn by the increase in the dollar value of the stream of yen receipts from the freight-service contracts.[11] If instead the yen depreciates, a gain on the debt will be offset by losses on the service contracts. A summary of the operation of this hedge is provided in Exhibit 12.3.

California First and Federal Express both employed arrangements with their customers in order to create hedges. In addition, purely natural hedges

EXHIBIT 12.3 Offsetting gains and losses produced by Federal Express hedge.

Change in the value of Foreign Currency	Change in Dollar Value of the Loan (Liability)	Change in Dollar Value of the Revenue (Asset)
Appreciates	Increases (loss)	Increases (gain)
Depreciates	Decreases (gain)	Decreases (loss)

may exist due to offsetting balances that result from ordinary business transactions with no special arrangements being required. Several hedges that appear to be of this nature were presented in Exhibit 12.2, for example, Adobe Systems and Armstrong World Industries. Two other examples that appear to be totally natural are the cases of Lyle Shipping and Australian mining companies.

Lyle Shipping, a Scottish firm, had borrowings in the U.S. dollar. An increase in the value of the dollar would increase the pounds required to repay Lyle's dollar debt and result in a transaction loss. However, because Lyle's ships were chartered out at fixed rates in U.S. dollars, there would be an offsetting increase in the pound value of future lease receipts—a transaction gain.[12] A similar *natural* hedge is generally held to exist for Australian mining companies whose product is priced in U.S. dollars. Should the U.S. dollar depreciate, the exposure to shrinkage in the Australian dollar value of U.S. receipts (asset exposure) is offset by similar shrinkage in the Australian dollar value of their U.S. dollar debt (liability exposure).[13]

Fashionhouse would probably find it difficult to duplicate the hedging techniques used above by California First and Federal Express. Circumstances giving rise to a natural hedge, as in the case of Lyle Shipping, may not exist. It might have some capacity to hedge by applying the method of *leading and lagging*. This method involves matching the cash flows associated with foreign-currency payables and receivables by speeding up or slowing down their payment or receipt. Moreover, once Fashionhouse has operations in Denmark, it may be able to create at least a partial hedge of its asset exposure by funding operations with Danish krone debt. If natural hedging opportunities are not available, then Fashionhouse has the full range of both exchange-traded and privately negotiated currency derivatives that it can use as a hedging instrument to hedge currency risks.

The hedging requirements of the European operations of Fashionhouse should be reduced by the introduction of the Euro. Even though Denmark is not one of the original 11 members of the European Monetary Union (EMU), its European exposure with the 11 countries will be reduced to a single currency, the Euro.

Hedging with Foreign-Currency Derivatives

Foreign-currency derivatives are financial instruments that derive their value from an underlying foreign-currency exchange rate. Some of the more common currency derivatives include *forward contracts* to buy or sell currencies in the future at fixed exchange rates, foreign-currency *swaps*, foreign-currency *futures*, and *options*. The forward contracts and over-the-counter options have the advantage of making it possible to tailor hedges to meet individual requirements in terms of amounts and dates. The exchange-traded futures and options have liquidity and a ready market, but a limited number of dates and contract sizes. Examples of the use of both types of instruments, privately negotiated and exchange traded, are discussed next.

Forward Exchange Contracts

A forward contract is an agreement to exchange currencies at some future date at an agreed exchange rate. The exchange rate in a contract for either the purchase or sale of a foreign currency is referred to as the *forward rate*. Forward contracts are among the most popular of the foreign-currency derivatives, followed by privately negotiated (over-the-counter) currency options.[14] These privately negotiated contracts can be tailored to meet the user's needs in term of both the amount of currency and maturity of the contract. Exchange-traded currency derivatives, such as options and futures, come in standard amounts of currency and a limited number of relatively short maturities.

Forward-Contract Hedging Example   An example may help to illustrate the application of a forward contract to hedging currency exposure. Near the end of 2000, the forward contract rate for the British pound sterling (£), with a term of one month, was about $1.45. The $1.45 is the direct exchange rate because it expresses the price of the foreign currency in terms of dollars. The comparable indirect rate is found by simply taking the reciprocal of $1.45: 1/$1.45 equals 0.69. The dollar is worth 0.69 pounds.

If a U.S. firm had an account payable of 100,000 pounds due in 30 days, a hedge of this liability exposure could be effected by entering into a forward contract to buy £100,000 for delivery in 30 days. Buying the currency through the forward contract is necessary because the firm needs the pound in 30 days to satisfy its account payable. If the dollar were to decline to $1.48 against the pound over this 30-day period, then the dollar value of the account payable would increase, creating a foreign-currency transaction loss. That is, it would take more dollars to purchase the £100,000. However, offsetting this loss would be a gain from an increase in the value of the forward contract. The right to buy £100,000 at the fixed forward rate of $1.45 increases in value as the value of the pound increases to $1.48. The effects of this foreign-currency exposure and associated forward-contract hedge are summarized in Exhibit 12.4. For the

EXHIBIT 12.4   Hedge of foreign-currency liability exposure with a forward contract.

Item hedged: account payable of £100,000	
Value of the account payable at payment date, £100,000 × $1.48 =	$148,000
Value of the account payable when initially recorded, £100,000 × $1.45 =	145,000
Foreign currency transaction loss	$ 3,000
Hedging instrument: forward contract to buy £100,000 @ $1.45, 30 days	
Value of the forward contract at maturity, £100,000 × ($1.48 − $1.45) =	$ 3,000
Value of the forward contract at inception, £100,000 × ($1.45 − $1.45) =	0
Gain on forward contract	$ 3,000

sake of simplicity, we are assuming that the spot value of the pound is equal to the forward rate at the inception of the forward contract.[15]

The gains and losses would be reversed if the U.S. firm in the above example had a pound sterling accounting receivable. Moreover, the creation of a hedge of this asset exposure in the pound sterling would call for the sale and not the purchase of the pound sterling through the forward contract. Appreciation of the pound sterling to $1.48 produces a transaction gain on the account receivable for the U.S. firm. This would in turn be offset by a loss on the forward contract. The value of the forward contract declines when the spot value of the pound sterling, $1.48, is greater than the rate to be received through the forward contract, $1.45.

Beckman Coulter Inc. provides a useful description of the offsetting gains and losses created by hedges:

> When we use foreign-currency contracts and the dollar strengthens against foreign currencies, the decline in the value of the future foreign-currency cash flows is partially offset by the recognition of gains in the value of the foreign-currency contracts designated as hedges of the transactions. Conversely, when the dollar weakens, the increase in the value of the future foreign-currency cash flows is reduced by . . . the recognition of any loss in the value of the forward contracts designated as hedges of the transactions.[16]

Notice that Beckman Coulter talks of its future foreign-currency cash flows. This constitutes asset exposure to Beckman Coulter in the foreign currency. If the dollar strengthens, then it follows that the foreign currency declines in value. The dollar value of the steam of foreign cash flow decreases. Because Beckman Coulter is long the cash flow, it would hedge this exposure by selling (taking a short position) the foreign currency through the forward contract.

Examples of Forward-Contract Hedging from Annual Reports   A sampling of firms that disclosed the use of forward contracts, and the types of exposure they are hedging, is provided in Exhibit 12.5. There are a substantial number of different hedge targets in this small set of companies. They include:

- Inter-company loans.
- Cash flows associated with anticipated transactions.
- Bonds payable.
- Accounts payable.
- Accounts receivable.
- Net investments in foreign subsidiaries.
- Expected acquisition transaction.

Over-the-counter currency options are a close second in popularity as a hedging instrument and their nature and use are discussed next.

EXHIBIT 12.5 Hedging with forward contracts.

Company	Hedging Targets
Armstrong World Industries Inc. (1999)	Armstrong also uses *foreign currency forward exchange contracts* to hedge inter-company loans.
Arvin Industries Inc. (1999)	Arvin manages the foreign currency risk of anticipated transactions by forecasting such cash flows at the operating entity level, compiling the total Company exposure and entering into *forward foreign exchange contracts* to lessen foreign exchange exposures deemed excessive.
Dow Chemical Company (1999)	The Company enters into *foreign exchange forward contracts* and options to hedge various currency exposures or create desired exposures. Exposures primarily relate to assets and liabilities and bonds denominated in foreign currencies, as well as economic exposure, which is derived from the risk that the currency fluctuations could affect the dollar value of future cash flows related to operating activities.
Tenneco Inc. (1999)	Tenneco enters into *foreign currency forward purchase and sales contracts* to mitigate its exposure to changes in exchange rates on inter-company and third party trade receivables and payables. Tenneco has from time to time also entered into forward contracts to hedge its net investments in foreign subsidiaries.
UAL Inc. (1999)	United enters into Japanese yen *forward exchange contracts* to minimize gains and losses on the revaluation of short-term yen-denominated liabilities. The yen forwards typically have short-term maturities and are marked to fair value at the end of each accounting period.
Vishay Intertechnology Inc. (1999)	In connection with the Company's acquisition of all the common stock of TEMIC Semiconductor GmbH and 80.4% of the common stock of Siliconix, Inc., the Company entered into a forward exchange contract in December 1997 to protect against fluctuations in the exchange rate between the U.S. dollar and the Deutsche mark since the purchase price was denominated in Deutsche marks and payable in U.S. dollars. At December 31, 1997, the Company had an unrealized loss on this contract of $5,295,000, which resulted from marking the contract to market value. On March 2, 1998, the forward contract was settled and the Company recognized an additional loss of $6,269,000.

SOURCES: Companies' annual reports. The year following each company name designates the annual report from which each example is drawn.

Currency Option Contracts

A common feature of option contracts is that they provide the right, but not the obligation, to either acquire or to sell the contracted items at an agreed price. The agreed price is called the *strike price*. In addition, options are considered to be *in the money* or *out of the money* based upon the relationship between the strike price and the current price. The prices in the case of currency options are currency exchange rates. For example, a currency option contract is out of the money if the option provides the right to buy the Irish Punt at $1.12 when its spot price is $1.10. Conversely, an option is in the money if it provides the right to sell the German Mark at $0.45 when its spot value is $0.43.

An option contract that gives the holder the right to sell a currency at an agreed rate, the strike price, is called a *put option*. The contract that provides the right to purchase the currency at an agreed rate is termed a *call option*. The cost of acquiring an option is termed the option premium. The option premium is a function of a number of variables. These include the strike price, the spot value of the currency, the time remaining to expiration of the option and the volatility of currency and interest-rate levels. Option values are estimated using methodologies such as the widely used Black-Scholes option-pricing model.

Options Contrasted with Forwards   Options are frequently characterized as one-sided arrangements. Consider the case of a firm that wishes to hedge exposure resulting from an Euro account receivable. The Euro amount of the receivable is E62,500. Because the firm wishes to protect the dollar value of an asset position (exposure) in the Euro, it would invest in a Euro put option, with a maturity that is consistent with the collection date for the receivable. A single exchange-traded option is acquired and the option premium is $1,000. The spot value of the Euro is $0.88, resulting in a dollar valuation for the Euro receivable of $55,000 ($0.88 × 62,500 = $55,000). The strike price is also $0.88, meaning that the option contract is at the money, that is, the strike price and spot value of the currency are the same.[17] We will assume that at the expiration date for the option contract the spot value of the Euro is, alternatively, $0.84 and $0.92. The effects of these two different outcomes are summarized in Exhibit 12.6.

Unlike the option contract, a forward contract does not permit the holder to decline to fulfill the obligation simply because the hedged currency did not move in an *unfavorable* direction. The forward contract is a symmetrical arrangement. If a forward contract had been used to hedge the Euro exposure in Exhibit 12.6, then there would be offsetting gains and losses on both the Euro accounts receivable and on the forward contract, whether the Euro appreciated or depreciated in value.

One-Sided Nature a Hedge with a Currency Option   An option contract is simply permitted to expire unexercised if an option contract is out of the

EXHIBIT 12.6   The operation of a currency option.

Expiration-date spot value of $0.84

Notional amount of the put-option contract, in Euros	62,500	
Strike price of the Euro put option	$0.88	
Spot value of the Euro	0.84	
Amount by which option is in the money	.04	0.04
Contract gain		$ 2,500

Initial dollar value of the Euro receivables

Accounts receivable in Euros	62,500	
Times spot exchange rate	$0.88	
		$55,000

Final dollar value of the Euro receivables

Accounts receivable in Euros	62,500	
Times spot exchange rate	$0.84	52,500
Transaction loss on accounts receivable		$ 2,500

Expiration-date spot value of $0.92

Strike price of the Euro put option	$0.88
Spot value of the Euro	$0.92

The option is permitted to expire without being exercised. The contract provides the opportunity to sell the Euro for $0.88 when its value in the spot market is $0.92. It has no value upon its expiration.

Initial dollar value of the Euro receivables

Accounts receivable in Euros	62,500	
Times spot exchange rate	$0.88	
		$55,000

Final dollar value of the Euro receivables

Accounts receivable in Euros	62,500	
Times spot exchange rate	$0.92	57,500
Transaction gain on accounts receivable		$ 2,500

money at its maturity. The option contract is designed to protect the holder against possible shrinkage in the dollar value of the Euro account receivable that would result from a decline in the value of the Euro. In the first case, where the spot value of the Euro did decline, then the option is exercised and a gain of $2,500 is produced to offset the transaction loss of $2,500 on the Euro account receivable. However, in the second case, where the spot value of the Euro rose, the option is permitted to expire unexercised. After all, it permits the sale of the Euro at $0.88 when the spot value of the Euro is $0.92. The option contract expires without value.

Hedging a Euro receivable with a forward contract will result in a gain on the forward contract when the Euro declines in value and a loss when the Euro increases in value. These gains and losses will in turn offset the loss on the account receivable that results when the Euro declines in value and the gain that results when the Euro increases in value. The behavior of a hedge using a forward contract versus an option is summarized in Exhibit 12.7.

The symmetrical behavior of the forward contract in its hedging application is evident in Exhibit 12.7. In each of the four combinations of exposure and exchange rate movement the gains and losses on the balance sheet exposure are offset in turn by the losses and gains on the forward contracts. However, the option contracts produce offsetting gains and losses only in those cases where the unfavorable exchange rate change takes place.[18] Notice that a gain is produced on the option contract to offset the loss on the balance sheet asset exposure when the foreign currency depreciated. Currency depreciation when the firm has asset exposure is an unfavorable rate movement. In the case of liability exposure, notice that a gain is produced by the option contact when the foreign currency appreciated. The corollary of appreciation of the foreign currency is depreciation of the dollar. This is an unfavorable rate movement because it causes the dollar value of the liability to increase. In the other two cases, where the option contracts expire without value, the currency movements are favorable: (a) asset exposure and the foreign currency appreciated and (b) liability exposure and the foreign currency depreciated.

The positions taken in the forward and option contracts differ based upon the nature of the foreign-currency exposure. With the forward contract, the foreign currency is purchased in the case of liability exposure and sold in the

EXHIBIT 12.7 Behavior of hedge gains and losses with a forward versus an option.

Type of Exposure Hedged	Derivative Contract	
Asset	**Forward Contract**	**Put Option**
Foreign currency appreciates		
Gain on asset exposure	Loss on the forward contract	Contract expires with neither gain nor loss; option holder loses initial option premium paid
Foreign currency depreciates		
Loss on the asset exposure	Gain on the forward contract	Contract expires with a gain
Liability	**Forward Contract**	**Call Option**
Foreign currency appreciates		
Loss on the liability exposure	Gain on the forward contract	Contract expires with a gain
Foreign currency depreciates		
Gain on the liability exposure	Loss on the forward contract	Contract expires with neither gain nor loss; option holder loses initial option premium paid

case of asset exposure. With the option contract, a call option is acquired in the case of liability exposure and a put option in the case of asset exposure.

Some relevant commentary, in relation to the above discussion, on the effects of hedging with currency options, is provided by the disclosures of Analog Devices Inc.:

> When the dollar strengthens significantly against the foreign currencies, the decline in value of the future currency cash flows is partially offset by the gains in value of the purchased currency options designated as hedges. Conversely, when the dollar weakens, the increase in value of the future foreign-currency cash flows is reduced only by the premium paid to acquire the options.[19]

The Analog commentary highlights the one-directional nature of a hedge that employs a currency option as opposed to a forward contract. The corollary of the decline in the dollar is a weakening of the foreign currency. This is the unfavorable outcome that the hedge is designed to offset. Indeed, the above comments indicate that a *gain on the option contract is produced to offset the decline in future cash flows that result from a strengthening of the dollar.* However, when the dollar instead weakens, there is no offsetting loss, beyond "the premium paid to acquire the options." The corollary of the weakening of the dollar is the strengthening of the foreign currency. A strengthening of the foreign currency is not the unfavorable currency movement that the currency option was intended to protect against.

As with the forward contracts, a sampling of disclosures by companies that are using currency options for hedging purposes is provided in Exhibit 12.8. Currency options are used less frequently than forward contracts. Most of the options used are over-the-counter (OTC) as opposed to exchange-traded options. Given the OTC character of these currency options, they share the tailoring feature of the forward contracts. That is, unlike exchange traded options that come in standard amounts of currency and limited maturities, both forward contracts and options can be tailored in terms of currency amount and maturity. However, unlike forward contracts, the currency options do require an initial investment—the option premium. Little or no initial investment is required in the case of the forward contract.

Forwards and options are the most popular currency derivatives, and it is very common, as both Exhibits 12.5 and 12.8 reveal, for firms to use both instruments. The last currency derivative that is only briefly reviewed is the futures contract. The futures contract shares the symmetrical gain and loss feature of the forward contract.

Currency Futures

Currency futures are exchange-traded instruments. Entering into a futures contract requires a margin deposit and a round-trip commission must also be paid. As is true of exchange-traded currency options, futures contracts come in fixed currency amounts and for a limited set of maturities. Futures contracts

EXHIBIT 12.8 Hedging with option contracts.

Company	Hedging Targets
Analog Devices Inc. (1999)	The Company may periodically enter into *foreign currency option contracts* to offset certain probable anticipated, but no firmly committed, foreign exchange transactions related to the sale of product during the ensuing nine months.
Arch Chemicals Inc. (1999)	The Company enters into forward sales and purchases and *currency options* to manage currency risk resulting from purchase and sale commitments denominated in foreign currencies (principally Euro, Canadian dollar, and Japanese yen) relating to anticipated but not yet committed purchases and sales expected to be denominated in those currencies.
Olin Corporation (1999)	The Company enters into forward sales and purchase contracts and *currency options* to manage currency risk resulting from purchase and sale commitments denominated in foreign currencies (principally Australian dollar and Canadian dollar) and relating to particular anticipated but not yet committed purchases and sales expected to be denominated in those currencies.
Polaroid Corporation (1999)	The Company has limited flexibility to increase prices in local currency to offset the adverse impact of foreign exchange. As a result, the Company primarily purchases *U.S. dollar call/foreign currency put options* which allows it to protect a portion of its expected foreign currency denominated revenues from adverse currency exchange movement.
Quaker Oats Company (1999)	The Company uses foreign *currency options* and forward contracts to manage the impact of foreign currency fluctuations recognized in the Company's operating results.
York International Corporation (1999)	To reduce this risk, the Company hedges its foreign currency transaction exposure with forward contracts and *purchased options.*

SOURCES: Companies' annual reports. The year following each company name designates the annual report from which each example is drawn.

also have the high level of liquidity that is characteristic of other exchange-traded derivatives. They also share the symmetrical character of the forward contract. That is, gains and losses will be produced by the futures contract to offset losses and gains, respectively, on hedged positions. Currency futures are used rather infrequently in the hedging of foreign-currency exposures.

Summary of Currency Exposure and Hedging Positions

It is common for firms to first attempt to reduce currency exposure by using their own operating activities and other internal actions. This point is made in the following comments from the disclosures of JLG Industries: "The Company manages its exposure to these risks (interest and foreign-currency rates) principally through its regular operating and financing activities."[20] These approaches to reducing currency exposure are usually referred to as *natural* hedges. A number of examples of natural hedges were provided in Exhibit 12.2. When natural hedges do not close out sufficient currency exposure, it is common for firms to turn to currency derivatives to reduce exposure still further. Based upon the previous discussion of selected currency derivatives, the positions to be taken in the face of asset versus liability exposure are summarized in Exhibit 12.9.

The information in Exhibit 12.9 indicates how a number of different instruments can be used to hedge currency risk. However, management must decide whether, and to what extent, to hedge such risk. Some of the factors that bear on the hedging decision are discussed next.

Influences on the Hedging Decision

The first hedging decision is whether or not to hedge currency exposure at all. The decision of whether or not to hedge currency exposure is influenced, at least in part, by the attitude of management towards the risk associated with foreign-currency exposure. Other things equal, a highly risk-averse management will be more inclined to hedge some or all currency-related risk. Moreover, not all currency exposure is seen to be equal. Firms have different demands for hedging based upon whether the exposure has the potential to affect cash flows and earnings, or simply the balance sheet. Finally, the materiality of currency exposure as well as expected movement in exchange rates will also influence the demand for hedging.

Is Currency Exposure Material?

A common disclosure made by firms with currency exposure is the effect that a 10% change in exchange rates would have on results. For example, Titan International, Inc. has currency exposure from its net investment in foreign subsidiaries. Titan discloses the potential loss associated with an adverse movement in the exchange rates of these subsidiaries:

> The Company's net investment in foreign subsidiaries translated into U.S. dollars at December 31, 1999, is $55.4 million. The hypothetical potential loss in

EXHIBIT 12.9 Foreign currency exposure and hedging decisions: Forwards, options, and futures.

Hedging Instrument	Exposure	
	Asset	Liability
Forward contract	Sell foreign currency	Buy foreign currency
Option	Buy put options	Buy call options
Futures	Sell futures contract	Buy futures contracts

value of the Company's investment in foreign subsidiaries resulting from a 10% adverse change in foreign-currency exchange rates at December 31, 1999 would amount to $5.5 million.[21]

Titan International disclosed no currency hedging activities. This is not surprising given that the $5.5 million loss in investment value amounts to only about 2% of its total shareholders' equity at the end of 1999. Beyond this, as we will see in the subsequent discussion of the translation of the statements of foreign subsidiaries, the potential reduction in Titan's investment value does not affect either earnings or cash flow.[22] This, combined with the immaterial size of the potential loss in value, can easily explain the absence of hedging activity.

What Are Hedging Motivations and Objectives?

Much information on hedging motivation is implicit in the information provided in Exhibits 12.5 and 12.8. Recurrent themes are those of protecting earnings and cash flow from the potential volatility produced by exchange rate fluctuations. Information on the ranking of alternative hedging objectives, from a survey conducted at the Wharton Business School, is provided in Exhibit 12.10. The dominance of the desire to protect cash flows and earnings is clearly the dominant motivator for hedging. However, as will be discussed in the section on translation of the statements of foreign subsidiaries, there is some level of hedging of balance-sheet exposure.

How Much Exposure Is Hedged?

The extent to which currency exposure is hedged ranges from zero to 100%. It is common for firms to announce that they simply do not use currency derivatives to hedge against currency risk. However, such firms may have already reduced currency risk to tolerable levels through natural hedges. Again, the appetite of management for bearing currency risk will in large measure determine the extent of the hedging. The cost and availability of hedging instruments is

EXHIBIT 12.10   Rankings of alternative hedging objectives.

Hedging Objective	Percent of Respondents Ranking the Objective as Most Important
1. To manage volatility in cash flows	49%
2. To manage volatility in accounting earnings	41
3. To manage market value of the firm	8
4. To manage balance sheet accounts or ratios	2
	100%

SOURCE: G. Bodnar, G. Hayt, and R. Marston, "The Wharton Survey of Derivatives Usage by U.S. Non-Financial Firms," *Financial Management*, 25 (Winter 1996), 114–115.

also a factor. As with insurance generally, closing out fully the possibility of loss is more expensive.

Some firms provide information on the extent of their hedging through schedules of net exposure. E.I. DuPont de Nemours & Company (DuPont) provides such a schedule. A slightly abridged version is presented in Exhibit 12.11. DuPont also declares the following about the objective of its hedging program:

> The primary business objective of this hedging program is to maintain an approximately balanced position in foreign currencies so that exchange gains and losses resulting from exchange rate changes, net of related tax effects, are minimized.[23]

Exhibit 12.11 reveals that DuPont has hedged almost all of its exposure. The extent of their hedging means that their earnings and cash flows will not be affected in a material way from the hedged exposures. This is reinforced by the following disclosure:

> Given the company's balanced foreign exchange position, a 10 per cent adverse change in foreign exchange rates upon which these contracts are based would result in exchange losses from these contracts that, net of tax, would, in all material respects be fully offset by exchange gains on the underlying net monetary exposures for which the contracts are designated as hedges.[24]

Other firms disclose more limited hedging activity. For example, The Quaker Oats Company reported that about 60% of its net investment in foreign subsidiaries was hedged. This disclosure is presented in Exhibit 12.12.[25]

Other Hedging Considerations

Discussed above are a number of factors that bear on the hedging decision, such as whether or not to hedge, what to hedge, how to hedge, and how much to hedge. Some other issues center on the cost and term or duration of hedging arrangements. A sampling of company references to these issues is provided in Exhibit 12.13.

EXHIBIT 12.11 Net currency exposure: E.I. DuPont de Nemours & Company, December 31, 1999 (in millions).

Currency	After-Tax Net Monetary Asset/(Liability) Exposure	After-Tax Open Contracts to Buy/(Sell) Foreign Currency	Net After-Tax Exposure Asset/(Liability)
Brazilian real	$ 109	$(101)	$ 7
British pound	(337)	334	(3)
Canadian dollar	514	(509)	5
Japanese yen	76	(71)	5
Taiwan dollar	(136)	136	—

SOURCE: E.I. DuPont de Nemours & Company, annual report, December 1999, 37.

EXHIBIT 12.12 Disclosure of net investment hedge: The Quaker Oats Company, December 31, 1999 (in millions).

Currency	Net Investment	Net Hedge	Net Exposure
Dutch guilders	$15.1	$ 9.1	$6.0
German marks	18.3	11.9	6.4

SOURCE: The Quaker Oats Company, annual report, December 1999, 56.

EXHIBIT 12.13 Company references to hedging cost and the terms of currency derivatives.

Company	Reference
Hedging Costs	
Baxter International Inc. (1999)	The Company's hedging policy attempts to manage these risks to an acceptable level based on management's judgment of the appropriate trade-off between risk, opportunity, and *costs.* As part of the strategy to manage risk while *minimizing hedging costs,* the Company utilizes sold call options in conjunction with purchased put options to create collars.
Compaq Computer Corporation (1999)	The Company also sells foreign exchange option contracts, in order *to partially finance* (reduce their cost) the purchase of these foreign exchange option contracts.
Interface Inc. (1999)	The Euro may reduce the exposure to changes in foreign exchange rates, due to the netting effects of having assets and liabilities denominated in a single currency. As a result, the Company's foreign exchange *hedging activity and related costs may be reduced* in the future.
Derivative Maturities	
Blyth Industries Inc. (2000)	The foreign exchange contracts outstanding at January 31, 2000 have maturity dates ranging from February 2000 through June 2000.
Compaq Computer Corporation (1999)	The term of the Company's foreign exchange hedging instruments currently does not extend beyond six months.
Johnson & Johnson (1999)	The Company enters into forward foreign exchange contracts maturing within five years to protect the value of existing foreign currency assets and liabilities.
Pall Corporation (2000)	The Company enters into forward exchange contracts, generally with terms of 90 days or less.
Polaroid Corporation (1999)	The term of these contracts (forward exchange contracts) typically does not exceed six months.
Tenneco Inc. (1998)	Tenneco uses derivative financial instruments, principally foreign currency forward purchase and sale contracts, with terms of less than one year.

SOURCES: Companies' annual reports. The year following each company name designates the annual report from which each example is drawn.

Hedging Costs   There is little discussion in company reports about the cost of hedging. In some cases cost issues surely underlie decisions of firms not to hedge currency risk, but the consideration of cost is not reported. Also, the act of using internal operations to reduce currency exposure can be seen as designed to reduce the exposure that may then be hedged with currency derivatives—thus reducing hedging costs. Clear efforts to reduce hedging costs are represented by the activities of Baxter International and Compaq Computer. Each sells (is a writer of the option) currency option contracts from which it receives an option premium. They then use these amounts to reduce the cost of currency options used for hedging and where, as the holder of the option, they are paying an option premium.

Many firms report that they expect to be able to reduce hedging activity and hedging costs as a result of the introduction of the Euro. This will result from the replacement of 11 European currencies with the Euro. Transactions can take place by one Euro country with up to 10 others without incurring any currency exposure.

Terms of Currency Derivatives   The terms of derivative contracts are kept relatively short, usually less than one year. This partly reflects the fact that the maturity of the underlying item being hedged, an account payable or account receivable, for example, is also quite short. Moreover, the typical maturity of exchange traded derivatives are short. Also, the cost to acquire currency through either a forward or option contract also increases with the maturity. For example, the forward rate (rate at which the foreign currency can be purchased for future delivery) for the British pound sterling was the following at the end of 2000:

Contract Term	Forward Rate
One month	$1.4574
Three months	$1.4588
Six months	$1.4606

The prices of currencies in both futures and option contracts display the same increasing cost as maturity lengthens.

The discussion to this point has focused on currency risk and actions that management can take to reduce the effect of fluctuations in currency values on the volatility of earnings and cash flow. The examples have centered on what are normally termed transaction exposures. Examples of transaction exposure include accounts payable, accounts receivable and bonds payable that are denominated in foreign currencies. If left unhedged, increases and decreases in exchange rates cause these balances to expand and contract. This expansion and contraction produces transactional gains and losses.

Transaction gains and losses are also produced by the combination of (1) positions in currency derivatives and (2) increases and decreases in exchange rates. Offsetting losses and gains result when the derivatives are used for hedging purposes. Holding a derivative contract for other than hedging purposes is normally termed a speculation. It is common for companies to declare that they do not hold derivatives for speculative purposes: "The Company does not use financial instruments for speculative or trading purposes, nor is the Company a party to leveraged derivatives."[26] The disclaimer on the use of currency derivatives, as well as leveraged derivatives, is the legacy of huge losses incurred on certain derivative transactions in the late eighties and early nineties.

Attention now turns to translation currency risk. Here, currency exposure results from having foreign subsidiaries or investments in foreign firms that are accounted for using the equity method.[27]

TRANSLATION OF THE STATEMENTS OF FOREIGN SUBSIDIARIES

A number of new financial and managerial issues were added to the Fashionhouse agenda when it purchased its former Danish supplier. *Transactional* issues continue to the extent that (1) Fashionhouse continues to make some of its purchases from foreign suppliers and (2) the foreign suppliers continue to invoice Fashionhouse in the foreign currency. In addition, the Danish subsidiary may also have its own transactional exposure. However, with the emergence of the euro, the Danish subsidiary's currency exposure should be limited to the extent that it deals mainly with countries that have adopted the Euro.[28]

Since the Danish company is a wholly owned subsidiary, U.S. GAAP will call for its consolidation. However, the financial statements of the Danish subsidiary are in the Danish krone. This introduces a *translational* issue; the Danish subsidiary statements must be restated into dollars before their consolidation with its parent, Fashionhouse, can take place. To the extent that the accounting practices used in preparing a subsidiary's statements differ from those of their parent, the subsidiary's statements would need to be restated to conform to the accounting practices of the parent.[29] This would, of course, be the case with Fashionhouse and its Danish subsidiary. International GAAP differences are discussed in a subsequent section of this chapter.

FINANCIAL STATEMENT TRANSLATION

Translation means that the foreign-currency balances in the financial statements of a foreign subsidiary are restated into U.S. dollars. There is no conversion of currencies, which means that one currency is exchanged for another. Translation is accomplished by simply multiplying the foreign-currency statement balances by an exchange rate. Translation would be a nonevent if every balance in the statements of the foreign subsidiary were multiplied by the same exchange rate. Translation would simply amount to a scaling of the statements of the foreign subsidiary.

However, each of the translation alternatives requires the translation of some balances at different exchange rates. In accounting parlance, this throws the books out of balance. The amount by which the books are thrown out of balance by translation is termed the translation adjustment or remeasurement gain or loss, depending upon the translation process being applied. In the process of illustrating statement translation, the creation and interpretation of these translation balances will be discussed.

TRANSLATION ALTERNATIVES

There are two different translation methods under current GAAP. However, the second method is technically a remeasurement method as opposed to a translation method. As translation methods, the two alternatives are called the (1) all-current and (2) temporal methods, respectively. The key features of these two methods are summarized in Exhibit 12.14.

Examples of accounting policy notes describing the use of each of these translation policies are provided below:

The all-current translation method: H.J. Heinz Company (1999)

For all significant foreign operations, the functional currency is the local currency. Assets and liabilities of these operations are translated at the exchange rate in effect at each year-end. Income statement accounts are translated at the average rate of exchange prevailing during the year. Translation adjustments arising from the use of differing exchange rates from period to period are included as a component of shareholders' equity.

The temporal remeasurement (translation) method:
Storage Technology Corp. (1999)

The functional currency for StorageTek's foreign subsidiaries is the U.S. dollar, reflecting the significant volume of intercompany transactions and associated cash flows that result from the fact that the majority of the Company's storage products sold worldwide are manufactured in the United States. Accordingly, monetary assets and liabilities are translated at year-end exchange rates, while non-monetary items are translated at historical exchange rates. Revenue and expenses are translated at the average exchange rates in effect during the year, except for cost of revenue, depreciation, and amortization that are translated at historical exchange rates.

The key to the determination of the use of the all-current translation method by H.J. Heinz is its statement that the *functional currency is the local currency* for its foreign subsidiaries. That is, these subsidiaries conduct their operations in their local currency. The company does not identify its translation method as all current, but the combination of (1) the use of year-end, or current,

EXHIBIT 12.14   Alternative translation methods.

All-Current Translation Method

The all-current translation method is the standard procedure applied to foreign subsidiaries whose operations are conducted in the local foreign currency. That is, the local currency is the subsidiary's *functional currency.* The local foreign currency is expected to be the functional currency when the foreign subsidiary's operations are "relatively self-contained and integrated within a particular country." A further requirement for use of the all-current method is that the subsidiary not be located in a country that has experienced cumulative inflation over the previous three-year period of 100% or more. The logic is that meaningful results cannot be produced under these conditions by simply multiplying the foreign currency balances by current exchange rates.

- All asset and liability balances are translated at the current or end-of-period exchange rate.
- Paid-in capital is translated at the exchange rate when the funds were raised.
- Revenues and expenses are translated at the average exchange rate for the current period.
- The translation adjustment is included in other comprehensive income.

Temporal (Remeasurement) Translation Method

This method is applied in those cases where the local foreign currency is not the functional currency of the subsidiary. The functional currency is defined as "the currency of the primary economic environment in which the entity operates; normally, that is the currency of the environment in which the entity generates and spends cash." Moreover, as noted above, "A currency in a highly inflationary environment is not considered stable enough to serve as a functional currency and the more stable currency of the reporting parent is to be used instead."

- All monetary assets and liabilities are remeasured at current exchange rates.
- All nonmonetary assets, liabilities, and equity balances are remeasured at historical exchange rates.
- Revenues and expenses are remeasured at average exchange rates for the period. However, cost of sales and depreciation are remeasured at the same rates used to remeasure the related inventory and fixed assets, respectively.
- The remeasurement gain or loss is included in realized net income.

exchange rates and (2) the inclusion of translation adjustments in shareholders' equity marks it as using the all-current translation method.

Unlike H.J. Heinz, Storage Technology declares that the *functional currency* of its foreign subsidiaries *is the U.S. dollar,* not the local foreign currency. The explanation for this condition is found it its reference to significant volume of inter-company transactions and the manufacture of most of its products in the United States. As with H.J. Heinz, Storage Technology does not identify the translation method it is using. However, the fact that the U.S. dollar is the functional currency of its foreign subsidiaries determines that it must be the temporal method. Moreover, it describes its method as translating monetary assets and liabilities at year-end exchange rates and nonmonetary items at historical exchange rates. These procedures are followed when translation (remeasurement) follows the temporal method.

Translation under the all-current method and remeasurement under the temporal method are illustrated next.

The All-Current Translation Method Illustrated

Following the guidance in Exhibit 12.14, the all-current translation method is illustrated using the data below:

1. Foreign Sub is formed on January 1, 2002 with an initial funding from a stock issue that raised FC1,000 (FC = Foreign current units).
2. Selected exchange rates for 2002:

	Direct Exchange Rates
At January 1, 2002	$0.58
Average for 2002	0.62
At December 31, 2002	0.66

The above rates indicate the amount of U.S. currency required to equal (buy) a single unit of the foreign currency. The increase in the rate across the year means that the dollar has lost value and that the foreign currency has appreciated.

3. The trial balance of Foreign Sub, both in FC and in U.S. dollars and translated following the all-current rule, is given in Exhibit 12.15. Those accounts that would have debit balances, assets and expenses, are

EXHIBIT 12.15   Trial Balance in FC and translated US$ at December 31, 2002.

Accounts	FC	Exchange Rates	U.S.$
Cash	$ 200	$0.66	$ 132
Accounts receivable	100	0.66	66
Inventory	300	0.66	198
Property and equipment	2,000	0.66	1,320
Cost of sales	600	0.62	372
SG&A expense	100	0.62	62
Tax provision	120	0.62	74
Totals	$3,420		$2,224
Accounts payable	$ 400	0.66	$ 264
Notes payable	1,020	0.66	673
Common stock	1,000	0.58	580
Retained earnings	0		0
Translation adjustment	0		87
Sales	1,000	0.62	620
Totals	$3,420		$2,224

grouped first, and those with credit balances, liabilities, equities, and revenues, are grouped second.

The totals of the two groupings of account balances must be equal, that is, in balance. Notice that this is only achieved in the U.S. dollar trial balance through introduction of a translation adjustment account, with a balance just sufficient to establish this equality. Without the addition of the $87 translation adjustment account balance, the total of the *translated* assets and expenses, $2,224, exceeds the total of the *translated* liabilities, shareholders' equity and sales accounts by $87. This translation adjustment can also be directly calculated as shown next:

Beginning net assets (assets minus liabilities)	FC1,000	
times change in exchange rate from 1/1/02 to 12/31/02 (0.66 − 0.58)	0.08	$80
Net income	FC180	
times difference between end of year and average exchange rates (0.66 − 0.62)	0.04	7
Translation adjustment		$87

The $80 component represents the growth in the beginning net assets due to appreciation in the value of Sub's foreign currency. The $7 component is the additional net assets due to the translation of the income statement balances at the average rate for the year of $0.62 and balance sheet amounts at the end of year rate of $0.66. There is no retained earnings balance in the above trial balance because 2002 is the first year of operation and the net income for the year is added to retained earnings through a later process of closing the books.

The translated balance sheet and income statements are presented in Exhibits 12.16 and 12.17. They can be constructed from the translated data above. The translation of the FC data is presented again in these statements simply to reinforce the nature of the translation process.

EXHIBIT 12.16 Translated income statement, year ending December 31, 2002.

Income Statement	FC	Exchange Rates	U.S.$
Sales	$1,000	$0.62	$620
Less cost of sales	600	0.62	372
Gross margin	400		248
Less SG&A	100	0.62	62
Pretax profit	300		186
Less tax provision	120	0.62	74
Net income	$ 180		$112
Other comprehensive income			87
Comprehensive income			$199

EXHIBIT 12.17 Translated balance sheet, December 31, 2002.

Balance Sheet	FC	Exchange Rates	U.S.$
Cash	$ 200	$0.66	$ 132
Accounts receivable	100	0.66	66
Inventory	300	0.66	198
Property and equipment	2,000	0.66	1,320
Total assets	$2,600		$1,716
Accounts payable	$ 400	0.66	$ 264
Notes payable	1,020	0.66	673
Common stock	1,000	0.58	580
Accumulated OCI°			87
Retained earnings	180		112
Total liabilities and equity	$2,600		$1,716

° OCI = Other comprehensive income.

In the absence of dividends, the retained earnings in the balance sheet are simply the net income for the year. The translation adjustment of $87 is included in consolidated shareholders' equity as *accumulated other comprehensive income.* The net assets of Foreign Sub are in a currency that appreciated across the year. This growth in net assets is captured in the process of translation and represented, again, by the translation adjustment balance. It is common for the translation adjustment in this case to be referred to as a translation gain. It resulted because the U.S. parent has a net investment (assets minus liabilities) in a country whose currency appreciated against the U.S. dollar.

If, instead, the FC had depreciated, then the translation adjustment would represent a negative balance in the initial accumulated other comprehensive income for 2002. Also, in this circumstance it is common to see the translation adjustment referred to as a translation loss. With the translation completed, the above statements in Exhibit 12.16 and 12.17 would now be ready for consolidation with those of the U.S. parent.[30]

The Remeasurement of Statements (Temporal Translation) Illustrated

This illustration of the remeasurement of the statements of a foreign subsidiary uses the same data as used in the illustration of the all-current translation method.[31] However, some additional information is required:

1. Property and equipment were acquired when the exchange rate was $0.58.
2. Depreciation on this property and equipment of FC60 was included in SG&A expense.

3. The ending inventory was acquired at the average exchange rate of $0.62, and cost of sales is also made up of goods that were acquired when the exchange rate averaged $0.62.

The previous trial balance is remeasured into the U.S. dollar as shown in Exhibit 12.18. The income statement and balance sheet, prepared with the remeasured trial balance data, are presented in Exhibits 12.19 and 12.20.[32]

Notice how application of the remeasurement method sharply changes comprehensive income. Comprehensive income was $199 with translation under the all-current method but only $27 with the temporal method of remeasurement. This difference of $85 is explained as follows:

All-current method comprehensive income		$199
Reduction in depreciation under temporal method:		
FC60 (.62 – .58)		2[*]
Translation gain under the all-current method	$(87)	
Deduct remeasurement loss under temporal method	87	
		(174)
Temporal method net income		$ 27

[*]Depreciation was translated at $0.62 as part of SG&A under the all-current method. However, because the fixed assets, which give rise to the depreciation expense, are translated at their historical exchange rate of $0.58, the depreciation component of SG&A is reduced by $2 with remeasurement under the temporal method.

EXHIBIT 12.18 Remeasured trial balance, December 31, 2002.

Accounts	FC	Exchange Rates	U.S.$
Cash	$ 200	$0.66	$ 132
Accounts receivable	100	0.66	66
Inventory	300	0.62	186
Property and equipment	2,000	0.58	1,160
Cost of sales	600	0.62	372
SG&A expense	40	0.62	25
Depreciation	60	0.58	35
Tax provision	120	0.62	74
Remeasurement loss			87
Totals	$3,420		$2,137
Accounts payable	$ 400	0.66	$ 264
Notes payable	1,020	0.66	673
Common stock	1,000	0.58	580
Retained earnings	0		0
Sales	1,000	0.62	620
Totals	$3,420		$2,137

EXHIBIT 12.19 Remeasured income statement, year ended December 31, 2002.

Accounts	FC	Exchange Rates	U.S.$
Sales	$1,000	$0.62	$620
Less Cost of sales	600	0.62	372
Gross margin	400		248
Less: SG&A	40	0.62	25
Depreciation	60	0.58	35
Remeasurement loss		(Exhibit 12.18)	87
Pretax profit	300		101
Less: tax provision	120	0.62	74
Net income	$ 180		$ 27
Other comprehensive income			—
Comprehensive income			$ 27

The explanation for the *remeasurement* loss of $87 is that balance-sheet exposure changed from net asset under the all-current method to net a liability position under the temporal (remeasurement) method. Asset exposure in an appreciating foreign currency results in a gain. However, liability exposure in the same circumstance results in a loss. In the all-current example, all assets and liabilities are translated using the current rate. *Asset exposure existed* under the all-current method because assets exceeded liabilities. As a result, the appreciation of the foreign currency resulted in a growth (gain) in net assets. This gain of $87 was reported as other comprehensive income.

Under the temporal method of remeasurement, balance sheet exposure is the net of monetary assets and liabilities. These balance sheet accounts are

EXHIBIT 12.20 Remeasured balance sheet, December 31, 2002.

Balance sheet	FC	Exchange Rates	U.S.$
Cash	$ 200	$0.66	$ 132
Accounts receivable	100	0.66	66
Inventory	300	0.62	186
Property and equipment	2,000	0.58	1,160
Total assets	$2,600		$1,544
Accounts payable$	$ 400	0.66	$ 264
Notes payable	1,020	0.66	673
Common stock	1,000	0.58	580
Retained earnings	180	(income statement)	27
Total liabilities and equity	$2,600		$1,544

remeasured at the ever-changing current rate. However, none of the other non-monetary balance-sheet accounts creates exposure because their dollar value is frozen at fixed, historical exchange rates.

In the above example, monetary liabilities (accounts payable of FC400 plus notes payable of FC1,020) are well in excess of monetary assets (cash of FC200 plus accounts receivable of FC100) and *net liability exposure results.* Appreciation of the foreign currency increased the dollar valuation of this net liability exposure and produced a remeasurement loss of $87. This remeasurement loss is included in computing conventional net income, and not in other comprehensive income as is the case under the all-current translation method.

Beyond these separately reported income statement effects of translation gains and losses, the translated financial statements are affected in some other less obvious ways. These are discussed next.

Other Effects of Statement Translation and Remeasurement

The most noticeable effects of the statement translation and remeasurement are (1) the translation adjustment that is part of other comprehensive income under all-current translation and (2) the remeasurement gain or loss that is included in realized net income with statement remeasurement under the temporal method.

Statement Relationships under Translation versus Remeasurement

Significant differences in earnings resulted in the above example with translation under the all-current method versus remeasurement under the temporal method. These results are due to (1) differences in currency exposure under the two methods and (2) differences in the location of translation-related gains and losses in the financial statements under the two methods. Translation adjustments go to other comprehensive income under all-current translation, but remeasurement gains and losses are included in net income with remeasurement under the temporal method.

Key statement relationships are affected by translation versus remeasurement. For example, both the current ratio (ratio of current assets to current liabilities) and the debt to equity ratios differ between the two methods. It is also common for gross margins to differ between the two methods. However, the simple nature of this constructed example results in the same gross margins under each translation/remeasurement method. These measures are presented in Exhibit 12.21.

Noticeable in Exhibit 12.21 is the fact that the values of each of the measures from the foreign-currency statements are preserved with translation under the all-current method. However, both the working capital and debt to equity measures differ from these values in the case of remeasurement under

EXHIBIT 12.21   Key statement relationships under translation versus remeasurement.

Measurement	In the FC Statements	Translation	Remeasurement
Working capital ratio[a]	1.50/1	1.50/1	1.45/1
Gross margin	40%	40%	40%
Debt to equity[b]	.86/1	.86/1	1.11/1

[a] Only the accounts payable are included in current liabilities.
[b] Debt includes only the notes payable. Equity under the all-current method includes accumulated other comprehensive income.

the temporal method. The working capital ratio differs because inventory is translated at a rate of only $0.62 under remeasurement, but at $0.65 with translation under the all-current method. The debt-to-equity ratio is higher with the remeasured statements because of the remeasurement loss under the temporal method, but a translation gain under the all-current method. Preserving the relationships of the foreign-currency statements in the translated statements is seen to be a desirable feature of translation under the all-current method.

Effects of Exchange Rate Changes not Captured by Translation and Remeasurement

It is common for firms to comment on the effects of exchange-rate changes on key financial statement items. In particular, the effects of exchange-rate changes on the growth or decline in sales are frequently commented upon in Management's Discussion and Analysis (MD&A).

The processes of translation and remeasurement summarize the joint effects of currency exposure and exchange rate changes in a single summary statistic. However, there are other effects associated with changing exchange rates that are not set out separately in any financial statement. For example, assume that the physical volume of sales and local-currency sales prices are unchanged for a foreign subsidiary. If the currency of the country in which the subsidiary is located depreciates in value, then the translated amount of sales revenue will decline. If the product being sold is manufactured in the foreign country, then there should also be a partially offsetting decline in cost of sales.[33]

The disclosures in Exhibit 12.22 attempt to identify the effect of changing exchange rates on sales and profits. Galey & Lord's disclosure identifies a common concern about the dollar appreciating in value: it makes U.S. goods more expensive in the export market. This point is echoed by Illinois Tool Works and its disclosure that its operating revenues were reduced each of the last three years because of the strengthening of the U.S. dollar. Revenue reductions associated with a strengthened dollar normally come from a combination of (1) foreign sales

EXHIBIT 12.22   Exchange rate effects on sales and profit growth.

Galey & Lord Inc. (1999)
In addition to the direct effects of changes in exchange rates, which are a changed dollar value of the resulting sales and related expenses, changes in exchange rates also affect the volume of sales or the foreign currency sales price as competitors products become more or less attractive.

Illinois Tool Works Inc. (1999)
The strengthening of the U.S. dollar against foreign currencies in 1999, 1998 and 1997 resulted in decreased operating revenues of $59 million in 1999, $122 million in 1998 and $166 million in 1997 and decreased net income by approximately 1 cent per diluted share in 1999 and 4 cents per diluted share in 1998 and 1997.

Philip Morris Companies Inc. (1999)
Currency movements decreased operating revenues by $782 million ($517 million, after excluding excise taxes) and operating companies income by $46 million during 1999. Declines in operating revenues and operating companies income arising from the strength of the U.S. dollar against Western European and Latin American currencies were partially mitigated by currency favorabilities recorded against the Japanese yen and other Asian currencies.

Praxair Inc. (1999)
The sales decrease of 4% in 1999 as compared to 1998 was due primarily to unfavorable currency translation effects in South America. Excluding the impact of currency, sales grew by 2%.

The productivity improvements and currency translation impacts resulted in an $18 million decrease in selling, general, and administrative expenses despite the increase due to acquisitions.

Sales for 1998 were flat when compared to 1997, primarily because sales volume growth of 4% and price increases of 2% were offset by negative currency translation effects.

SOURCES: Companies' annual reports. The year following each company name designates the annual report from which each example is drawn.

simply translating into fewer dollars as well as (2) declines in the volume of foreign sales due to the weakening of the foreign currency.

The Philip Morris disclosures highlight the value of diversification in foreign sales by currency. Whereas revenues and profits were reduced by the depreciation of Western European and Latin American currencies, the Japanese yen appreciated and offset, but not fully, these negative effects. Notice that Philip Morris identifies the net effect of the appreciation and depreciation of foreign currencies on both revenues and income.

Praxair provides sufficient detail to reconcile its actual percentage growth or decline in sales to the results in the absence of changes in exchange rates. Notice that Praxair's sales declined by 4% in 1999, and that the decline was largely explained by currency depreciation in South America. However, explaining the behavior of sales in 1998 is more involved. The information disclosed by Praxair for 1998 is summarized here:

Disclosed sales growth	0%
Breakdown of Sales-Change Components	
Volume	+5%
Price changes	+2%
Currency depreciation	−7%
Sales growth	0%

The Praxair zero change in sales revenue in 1998 could be interpreted in a manner that is too negative. After all, in the face of the zero growth in actual dollar sales revenue, Praxair was able to increase prices and still improve sales volume by 5%. Disclosure of quantitative details on the effects of the three elements, volume, price and currency makes it possible to develop a much better understanding of Praxair's 1998 business performance.

In the case of positive revenue growth, increases from volume or price adjustments should be preferred to growth resulting from favorable exchange-rate movements. Revenue growth driven by changes in exchange rates may prove to be only temporary. Sustained revenue growth, in the absence of volume growth and/or price increases, would require ongoing strengthening of foreign currencies—not a very likely prospect.

The effects of changes in exchange rates on sales and profits can be controlled to some extent by management. As with most foreign-currency exposure, management can elect to control or hedge this risk through operational arrangements and currency derivatives. Much discussion of these matters has already been provided. However, the focus of the next section is on the management of currency risks associated with foreign subsidiaries.

MANAGING THE CURRENCY RISK OF FOREIGN SUBSIDIARIES

It is a common view that translation-related currency risk associated with the statements of foreign subsidiaries is quite different from currency risk associated with foreign-currency transactions. Transactional exposure has the clear potential to expand or contract the cash flows associated with foreign-currency asset and liability balances. If a U.S. firm holds a Japanese yen account receivable and the yen falls in value, then there is a loss of cash inflow. If a Japanese firm has an account payable in the U.S. dollar and the yen strengthens, then a smaller cash outflow is required to discharge this liability.

There are no identifiable cash inflows or outflows in the case of translation gains or losses that result from either statement translation or remeasurement. A study of both U.S. and U.K. multinationals found that "it was generally agreed that translation exposure management was a lesser concern" (less than transaction exposure management).[34] The Wharton survey results on hedging (Exhibit 12.10) found the management of the volatility of cash flows as the major objective of hedging. However, it is very common for disclosures of transaction-related currency hedging to cite the goal of protecting cash flows.

The reduced level of currency risk-management in the case of translation exposure is explained largely by the absence of direct cash flow and earnings risk. There is a somewhat greater effort to manage remeasurement-related risk because, unlike under the all-current method, remeasurement gains and losses are included in net income. Some companies do hedge translation exposure even though the translation adjustments are only included in other comprehensive income, with this element generally going straight to shareholders' equity. However, the absence of an impact on earnings under all-current translation makes it less likely that this exposure will be hedged.

Prior to the issuance of SFAS No. 52, *Foreign Currency Translation,* SFAS No. 8, *Accounting for the Translation of Foreign Currency Transactions and Foreign Financial Statements,* required all firms to use the temporal method and to include all translation gains and losses in the computation of net income.[35] As a result, one would expect the hedging of translation exposure to have declined after the issuance of Statement No. 52. Under SFAS No. 52, most translation is by the current-rate method and translation adjustments are omitted from conventional net income. Available evidence supports this view. For example, Houston and Mueller note: "In particular, firms that must no longer include all translation gains or losses arising from their foreign operations in their income statements are more likely to have stopped or reduced hedging translation exposure."[36]

To gain some insight into translation hedging practices, disclosures of translation-hedging policies by a number of firms are presented in Exhibit 12.23. The examples in Exhibit 12.23 are selective and do not represent the relative frequency with which translation exposure is hedged. Rather, the disclosures are simply designed to present some of the matters that appear to influence decisions on the hedging of translation exposure.

Notice that AGCO does not hedge its translation exposure. However, it attempts to achieve what could be called a natural hedge by the device of financing its foreign operations with local borrowings. Increasing local-currency borrowings reduces the net investment in the subsidiary—assets minus liabilities—and with it translation exposure. This example suggests a potential for misinterpretation of company statements about their translation hedging. AGCO apparently means that it does not use currency derivatives to hedge translation exposure. However, it does attempt to reduce exposure by other means.

Becton Coulter indicates occasional hedging of translation exposure. Note the reference to the hedge of the market (exchange rate) risk of a subsidiary's net-asset position. Again, in the case of translation with the all-current method, exposure is approximated by a subsidiary's net-asset position, that is, assets minus liabilities. Becton Coulter must be making reference to subsidiaries translated using the all-current method because it indicates that any gains or losses on hedges of translation exposure are included in accumulated other comprehensive income. This is also the location of the translation gains and losses that result from the all-current translation method. The gains and losses on the hedges of this translation exposure are included in other comprehensive income and offset, respectively, translation losses and gains.

EXHIBIT 12.23 Hedging of translation exposure: Selected company policies.

Company	Hedging Policy
AGCO Corporation (1999)	The Company's translation exposure resulting from translating the financial statements of foreign subsidiaries into U.S. dollars is not hedged. When practical, this translation impact is reduced by financing local operations with local borrowings.
Becton Coulter Inc. (1999)	We occasionally use foreign currency contracts to hedge the market risk of a subsidiary's net asset position. Market value gains and losses on foreign currency contracts used to hedge the market risk of a subsidiary's net asset position are recognized in "Accumulated Other Comprehensive Income" as translation gains and losses.
Becton, Dickenson & Company (1999)	The Company does not generally hedge these translation exposures since such amounts are recorded as cumulative currency translation adjustments, a separate component of shareholders' equity, and do not affect earnings or current cash flows.
DaimlerChyrsler AG (1999)	The net assets of the Group which are invested abroad in subsidiaries and affiliated companies are not included in the management of currencies.
The Quaker Oats Company (1999)	The Company uses foreign currency forward and option contracts and currency swap agreements to manage foreign currency rate risk related to certain cash flows from foreign entities and net investments in foreign subsidiaries.
Henry Schein Inc. (1998)	The Company considers its investments in foreign operations to be both long-term and strategic. As a result, the Company does not hedge the long-term translation exposure in its balance sheet.
Titan International (1999)	The Company views its investments in foreign subsidiaries as long-term commitments and does not hedge foreign currency transaction or translation exposures.

SOURCES: Companies' annual reports. The year following each company name designates the annual report from which each example is drawn.

The Becton Dickenson statement is the clearest statement of the case for not hedging translation exposure. The key elements of the Becton Dickenson position are that: (1) translation adjustments are included in shareholders' equity; (2) translation adjustments do not affect conventional net income; and (3) translation adjustments do not affect cash flow.

The DaimlerChyrsler reference to the net assets of subsidiaries located abroad not being included in the management of currencies means that they are not hedged. The Quaker Oats Company does do some hedging of net investments in foreign subsidiaries. Both Henry Schein and Titan International emphasize the long-term nature of the investments in foreign subsidiaries in explaining the decision not to hedge this exposure.

There is some hedging of translation, but the hedging of translation exposure is clearly less common than the hedging of transaction exposure. Hedging practice, based upon cited surveys and our own study of hundreds of company reports, suggests the following ordering of management demand for hedging, from high to low:

1. To protect cash flow and earnings, both level and stability.
2. To protect earnings, both level and stability.
3. To protect shareholders' equity, both level and stability.

In continuing to observe hedging motivated by both two and three above, it is important to consider the significance of earnings and equity amounts without regard to the issue of cash flows. For example, there is a tremendous current focus on whether or not earnings meet the consensus forecasts of Wall Street. The penalty for missing the forecast, sometimes by pennies, can be dramatic reductions in share value. Of the two translation methods, only the temporal (remeasurement) method includes the remeasurement gains or losses in the computation of net income. There is no evidence that a failure to meet the Wall Street consensus will be forgiven if it results from unhedged remeasurement exposure.

Management compensation is often based, directly or indirectly, upon reported earnings. This provides an incentive for management to hedge in order to avoid earnings reductions from remeasurement losses.

Finally, it is common for debt and credit agreements to include financial covenants that require the maintenance of minimum amounts of shareholders' equity or minimum ratios of debt to equity. Unhedged translation exposure, under either the all-current or temporal (remeasurement) methods, may reduce shareholders' equity and cause these covenants to be violated.

Differences in hedging practices are explained in part by different attitudes towards bearing currency risk as well as the cost and capacity to hedge exposures in different countries. In addition, firms will differ in their capacity to minimize currency exposure through various operational, organizational and business arrangements.

As a final topic in this coverage of currency risk and hedging, an overview of the current requirements in the accounting for currency derivatives is provided.

ACCOUNTING FOR HEDGES: CURRENT GAAP REQUIREMENTS

Important changes in the accounting for currency derivatives were introduced with the issuance of SFAS No. 133, *Accounting for Derivative Instruments and Hedging.*[37] Initial required application of the standard begins with the first fiscal quarter of the first fiscal year beginning after June 15, 2000.

One of the most important requirements of the new standard is that all derivative instruments must be recognized on the balance sheet and carried at their fair values. Whether or not these changes in fair value go immediately into the computation of net income will depend upon (1) whether or not the derivative is used for hedging purposes and (2) the nature of the hedge applications.

The accounting for changes in the fair value of a foreign-currency derivative depend upon its intended use. Possibilities include (1) the hedging of exposure to changes in the fair value of a recognized asset, liability or an unrecognized firm commitment, (2) the hedging of exposure to variable cash flows of a forecasted transaction, and (3) the hedging of a net investment in a foreign operation. These three hedging applications are referred to as fair value, cash flow and net-investment hedges, respectively.

Changes in the fair values of currency derivatives will either be reported in the income statement as these changes take place or they will initially be reported in other comprehensive income (OCI). The gains and losses that are initially included in OCI will subsequently be included in the income statement when the hedged transaction affects net income.

Fair Value Hedges

A firm purchase commitment in a foreign currency is an example of a transaction that could be a fair-value hedge candidate. Normally, there is no initial recording on the books of the firm commitment. However, there is currency risk and subsequent increases and decreases in the value of the foreign currency give rise to losses and gains, respectively. To illustrate how a hedge would be accounted for in this case, assume a purchase commitment made for 100 million yen when the yen rate was $0.008976. By the end of the accounting period the yen has appreciated to $0.009000. This increase in the yen of $0.000024 ($0.009000 − $0.008976) creates a loss on the purchase commitment of $2,400 ($0.000024 × 100 million yen). Also assume that the firm had entered into a forward contract to buy 100 million yen as a hedge of the firm commitment. We will assume that the forward contract (the currency derivative) also increased in value by $2,400.

Under SFAS No. 133, the $2,400 increase in the cost of the purchase commitment would be recorded as a loss on the commitment. In addition, the forward contract would also be marked to market value, creating an offsetting gain of $2,400. Each of these items would be reported in the income statement where they will offset each other.

The special feature of the above accounting (i.e., *hedge accounting*), is the recognition of the loss on the purchase commitment. Prior to SFAS No. 133, it would have been common not to recognize the loss on the purchase commitment, but to recognize and defer the gain on the forward contract. Then the loss on the purchase commitment would not be recognized until the purchase was made. At this time, the deferred gain on the currency derivative would be deducted from the cost of the purchase. SFAS No. 133 basically eliminates this type of gain or loss deferral on financial derivatives.

Many of the hedging examples disclosed in Exhibits 12.5 and 12.8 involved balances that were already recorded on the balance sheet of the hedging firms. The use of hedges in these cases *requires no special hedge accounting.* For example, consider the case of a one million pound sterling account receivable recorded when the sterling rate was $1.50. By the end of the year, but before the pound receivable was collected, the pound depreciated to $1.45. Assume that the U.S. firm hedged the full amount of the pound sterling account receivable by entering a forward contract to sell the one million pounds at the expected collection date.

Under current GAAP, the pound receivable must be revalued to the new rate of $1.45, and a foreign currency transaction loss of $50,000 would be recognized. Moreover, the currency derivative would be marked to its new market value, which is assumed to be $50,000, a perfect hedge.[38] This activity is summarized below:

£ *Account Receivable*		
Initial value of £1,000,000 at $1.50 equals	$1,500,000	
Value at year-end: £1,000,000 at $1.45 equals	1,450,000	
Foreign-currency transaction loss		50,000
Currency Derivative		
End-of-period value of the currency derivative	$ 50,000	
Initial value of the forward contract	0	
Gain on the currency derivative		(50,000)
Net effect on earnings		$ 0

No special hedge accounting is required in the above case to cause the loss on the receivable and the gain on the currency derivative to offset each other in the income statement.

Cash Flow Hedges

Hedges of forecasted transactions, *cash flow hedges,* are distinguished from hedges of firm commitments, which are classified as *fair value hedges.* As an example, a forecasted transaction might involve the future receipt of royalty payments in a foreign currency. There is currency exposure here because a decline in the value of the foreign currency will reduce the dollar value of the royalty, a cash flow, when it is received. A hedge of this exposure could be achieved by selling a futures contract, investing in a put option, or selling the foreign currency through a forward contract.

In order to illustrate hedge accounting for a cash-flow hedge, assume that a firm forecasts the receipt of one million German marks (DM) from royalties. A currency derivative is acquired to hedge all of this exposure. At the date that the derivative contract is entered into, the DM rate is $0.45. At the end of the accounting period, but before the royalties are received, the DM depreciates to $0.43. The value of the derivative contract increases by $20,000. SFAS No. 133 requires that a gain from the increase in the fair value of a derivative contract be recognized as it occurs. However, GAAP does not permit recognition of the loss from the decline in the dollar value of the forecasted DM cash flow.

Recognition of the $20,000 gain on the currency derivative as part of earnings would present a problem. There would be no offsetting loss in the income statement from the decline of the dollar value in the DM royalties. Hedge accounting deals with this problem by providing that the $20,000 gain on the derivative be included in other comprehensive income and not net income. Then, when the DM royalties are received, the $20,000 gain is reclassified out of accumulated other comprehensive income and in to net income.

To illustrate the above fully, assume that the one million DM of royalties are received, and that the value of the DM has not changed in value from its previous year-end rate of $0.43. The hedge accounting is summarized in Exhibit 12.24.

Notice that the total income recognized in the income statement in the period in which the royalty is received is $450,000. This is equal to the original value of the expected royalty cash flow. However, the $450,000 is made up of only $430,000 in royalty value and the remainder is the product of the cash flow hedge.

Hedges of Net Investments in Foreign Operations

Earlier discussion of statement translation revealed far less hedging of translation as opposed to transaction exposure. Most translation of the net investments in foreign operations, typically foreign subsidiaries, employs the all-current method. Under this translation procedure, all translation adjustments (translation gains and losses) are recorded in other comprehensive income. These translation adjustments are only included in the computation of net income if all or a significant portion of the foreign operation is sold or otherwise disposed of.

Some firms do hedge their translation exposure. Consistent with the translation adjustments being included in other comprehensive income, offsetting gains and losses on currency derivatives used to hedge translation exposure are

EXHIBIT 12.24   Hedge accounting for expected cash flow.

	Initial Period	Period of Receipt of Royalties
Included in net income		
Gain on currency derivative	0	$ 20,000
Royalty cash inflow	0	430,000
		$450,000
Included in other comprehensive income:		
Gain on currency derivative	$20,000	$ (20,000)

also recorded in other comprehensive income (see Becton Coulter Inc. in Exhibit 12.23 for an example of this treatment).

The review of current accounting requirements has not explored a number of technical points related to hedging. These matters go beyond the goals of this chapter. However, many of these items are included in more technical and comprehensive treatments of hedging and derivative instruments.[39]

U.S. AND INTERNATIONAL GAAP DIFFERENCES

A variety of new financial, accounting, tax, and managerial issues faced Fashionhouse when it acquired a Danish subsidiary. The issues of statement translation and currency risk-management were discussed above. Recall that the requirement to consolidate the Danish subsidiary into the dollar-based statements of Fashionhouse, the parent, requires translation. In addition, to the extent that Danish accounting practices differ from those in the U.S., adjustments must be made so that the subsidiary's statements conform to U.S. GAAP.

International GAAP Differences and the IASC

A review of the statements of companies located in different countries will reveal cases of both agreement and disagreement between foreign and U.S. GAAP. In order to address the high level of international disagreement found in accounting practices, the International Accounting Standards Committee (IASC) was formed in 1973. The IASC, which was comprised initially of representatives from the leading professional accounting bodies of Australia, Canada, France, Germany, Japan, Mexico, the Netherlands, the United Kingdom, Ireland, and the United States, began working toward the harmonization of accounting standards internationally. Today, the IASC represents accounting bodies from over 70 countries. Each member body has agreed to work towards the compliance of accounting standards in their home countries with the standards issued by the IASC. In fact, a number of countries, such as India, Kuwait, Malaysia, Singapore, and Zimbabwe, either adopt IASC standards as their own generally accepted accounting principles or place heavy reliance on them in developing their own accounting standards.

To date, 39 international accounting standards and several exposure drafts have been issued. The IASC has also issued a document that both identifies major differences in international accounting practices and categorizes them in terms of their being, (1) the required or preferred treatment, (2) the allowed alternative treatment, or (3) the treatment eliminated.[40] The immediate goal of the proposal is to eliminate most of the choices in accounting treatment now available in standards issued by the IASC. The IASC enumerated the expected benefits of this harmonization in financial reporting as follows:[41]

1. Improve the quality of financial reporting.
2. Make easier the comparison of the financial position, performance and changes in financial position of enterprises in different countries.
3. Reduce the costs borne by multinational enterprises that presently have to comply with different national standards.
4. Facilitate the mutual recognition of prospectuses for multinational securities offerings.

A subsequent statement has reported responses to this initial document and outlined plans for implementation of some of the initial proposals and additional study for others.[42] The major approach to implementation of the IASC proposals is to incorporate those proposals on which agreement has been reached into revised International Accounting Standards.

Examples of some of the accounting treatments that would be *eliminated* under the IASC proposals follow:

1. Completed contract method for the recognition of revenue on construction contracts.
2. Deferral of exchange gains and losses on long-term monetary items.
3. Translation of statements of subsidiaries operating in hyperinflationary economies, without first applying price-level adjustments.
4. Use of the closing (end of period) exchange rate to translate income statement balances.
5. Maintenance of investment properties on the books without depreciation
6. Immediate deduction of goodwill against shareholders' equity.

Examples of U.S. and international GAAP differences are provided in the next section along with an illustration of how international firms mitigate the impact of differences for U.S. statement users.[43]

U.S. and International GAAP Differences

In spite of the harmonizing efforts of the IASC, there remain numerous differences between the GAAP applied in countries around the world. A sampling of some areas of current or previous differences between U.S. GAAP and GAAP in selected other countries is provided in Exhibit 12.25.

As GAAP in different countries are constantly changing, as well as the specific methods selected by firms within countries, some of the GAAP differences in Exhibit 12.25 may no longer be current. However, they remain illustrative of areas in which major GAAP differences are found between U.S. GAAP and those employed in other countries. Fortunately, in the United States the Securities and Exchange Commission requires that listed foreign firms provide disclosures of differences between the GAAP on which their statements are prepared and U.S. GAAP.

EXHIBIT 12.25 Examples of U.S. and international GAAP differences.

Accounting Policy	Country/Company	GAAP Difference
Software costs	England/Reuters Holdings	Reuters expenses all software costs; a portion of such cost would normally be capitalized under U.S. GAAP.
Tax accounting	Malaysia/United Malacca Rubber Estates	Deferred taxes are not booked if temporary differences are deferred indefinitely; deferred taxes are booked on all temporary differences under U.S. GAAP.
Investments	Australia/BHP Limited	Equity accounting is not applied to investments in excess of 20% of voting shares; U.S. GAAP generally requires application of the equity method.
Property	Hong Kong/Hong Kong Telecommunications	Tangible fixed assets and property may be restated on the basis of appraised values; upward revaluations are not permitted under U.S. GAAP.
Sale/leaseback gains	Netherlands/PolyGram	Gains on sale/leaseback transactions are recognized in the year of sale; such gains are normally deferred and amortized into future earnings under U.S. GAAP.
Construction interest	Sweden/Pharmacia	Interest related to the construction of assets is expensed; U.S. GAAP requires capitalization and amortization.
Foreign exchange gains and losses (on loans to acquire aircraft)	England/British Airways	Foreign exchange gains and losses are deducted from or added to the cost of aircraft; included in income as incurred under U.S. GAAP.
Unrealized foreign exchange gains and losses	Germany/Continental Aktiengesellschaft	Losses are deducted from income but gains are not recorded; U.S. GAAP recognizes both in earnings.

SEC Requirements for Disclosing the Effects of GAAP Differences

With the continuing globalization of financial markets, international firms have become more sensitive to the analytical burdens that result from differences between foreign and domestic GAAP. Further, the U.S. Securities and Exchange Commission requires that some foreign firms file reports that include schedules reconciling earnings under U.S. and foreign GAAP (the 20-F Report). An example of such disclosure is provided below from the 20-F report of the Portuguese firm, Electricidade de Portugal SA (EP). As is required, EP provides a reconciliation of Portuguese to U.S. GAAP for both net income (Exhibit 12.26) and shareholders' equity (Exhibit 12.27). A selection of the principal differences between U.S. and Portuguese GAAP underlying these statements are discussed below:

1. EP writes up the value of its fixed assets. It in turn records depreciation on these revalued amounts. This causes depreciation in the Portuguese-GAAP statements to be greater than it would be under U.S. GAAP, where such revaluations are not permitted. This higher depreciation caused the EP earnings to be reduced below their level under U.S. GAAP. This explains the addition to net income made for "depreciation of revaluation of fixed assets" in the Exhibit 12.26 reconciliation of Portuguese GAAP to U.S. GAAP net income. Also notice that the cumulative effect of this GAAP difference results in a reduction in Portuguese GAAP shareholders'

EXHIBIT 12.26   Reconciliation of net income under Portuguese GAAP to income under U.S. GAAP: Electricidade de Portugal, year ended December 31, 1998 (in thousands except for per-share amounts and shares outstanding).

	Escudos	U.S.$
Net income as reported under Portuguese GAAP	104,808,918	539,307
U.S. GAAP adjustments increase (decrease) due to:		
a. Depreciation of revaluation of fixed assets	48,045,972	247,226
b. Capitalized overheads	(949,690)	(4,887)
c. Depreciation of exchange differences	5,121,052	26,351
d. Deferred costs	(1,537,691)	(7,912)
e. Hydrological correction adjustments	—	—
f. Distribution to management and employees	(3,845,532)	(19,788)
g. Pension and other post-retirement benefits	—	—
h. Self-insurance	—	—
i. Employee termination benefits	19,969,334	102,755
j. Accounts receivable—municipalities	(10,429,115)	(53,664)
k. Power purchase agreements	(343,236)	(1,766)
m. Income taxes	(19,642,655)	(101,074)
Net adjustments	36,388,439	187,241
Approximate net income in accordance with U.S. GAAP	141,197,357	726,548
Net income per share	235	1.21
Number of shares outstanding	600,000,000	600,000,000

SOURCE: Electricidade de Portugal SA, annual report, December 1998. Information obtained from Disclosure Inc., *Compact D/SEC: Corporate Information on Public Companies Filing with the SEC* (Bethesda, MD: Disclosure Inc., June 2000).

EXHIBIT 12.27   **Reconciliation of shareholders' equity under Portuguese GAAP to income under U.S. GAAP: Electricidade de Portugal, year ended December 31, 1998 (in thousands).**

	Escudos	U.S. $
Shareholders' equity as reported under Portuguese GAAP	1,228,414,979	6,320,958
U.S. GAAP adjustments increase (decrease) due to:		
a. Revaluation of fixed assets	(476,437,696)	(2,451,568)
b. Overheads capitalized	(139,891,196)	(719,287)
c. Exchange differences capitalized	(82,191,222)	(422,925)
d. Deferred costs	(4,906,140)	(25,245)
e. Hydrological correction account	77,688,063	399,213
f. Distribution to management and employees	(3,736,760)	(19,228)
g. Pension and other post-retirement benefits	21,868,807	112,529
h. Self-insurance	—	—
i. Employee termination benefits	25,844,334	132,985
j. Accounts receivable—municipalities	(10,429,115)	(53,664)
k. Power purchase agreements	2,317,186	11,923
l. Investments	12,659,000	65,139
m. Income taxes	183,082,286	942,072
Net adjustments	(394,132,453)	(2,028,056)
Approximate shareholders' equity in accordance with U.S. GAAP	834,282,526	4,292,902

SOURCE: Electricidade de Portugal SA, annual report, December 1998. Information obtained from Disclosure Inc., *Compact D/SEC: Corporate Information on Public Companies Filing with the SEC* (Bethesda, MD: Disclosure Inc., June 2000).

equity in the Exhibit 12.27 reconciliation of shareholders' equity. Writing up its fixed assets increased EP's shareholders' equity.

2. EP capitalized a portion of general and administrative overhead that would not be permitted under U.S. GAAP. This called for a reduction in both Portuguese GAAP net income and in shareholders' equity. These adjustments follow the same pattern as those required by the revaluation of fixed assets.

3. EP capitalized and amortized foreign exchange gains and losses. Under U.S. GAAP, the capitalization of these items is not permitted. EP's disclosures indicate that this practice is not followed for new exchange gains and losses after 1995. The adjustment in Exhibit 12.26 required an addition to Portuguese GAAP income of $26,351,000. This is the amount by which Portuguese GAAP earnings were understated in 1998. The adjustment of $422,925,000 in Exhibit 12.27 represents the remaining cumulative overstatement of shareholders equity that resulted from the capitalization of net foreign exchange losses under Portuguese GAAP.

4. Among costs deferred by EP were research and development. These costs must be expensed as incurred under U.S. GAAP.

5. The line item for "Pension and other post-retirement benefits" highlights the current consistency between Portuguese and U.S. GAAP in recognizing the associated expense. However, the adjustment in Exhibit 12.27, shareholders' equity reconciliation, reveals a continuing difference in the recognition of the associated benefit liability. EP had recognized a larger liability, and charged this amount against shareholders' equity, than would be required under U.S. GAAP. This explains the increase in shareholders' equity in Exhibit 12.27.

6. Prior to 1995, EP reduced income in recording an accrual for self-insurance that was not permitted under U.S. GAAP.

7. Termination benefits were accrued by EP in 1997 that would not have been accrued in that year under U.S. GAAP. The necessary adjustments are a $102,755,000 increase in Portuguese GAAP net income and a $132,985,000 increase in shareholders equity.

8. EP's policy of recognizing bad debts on accounts receivable results in their being recorded at a later point in time than would be true under U.S. GAAP.

9. EP records income taxes based upon the amount of taxes currently payable as determined by government tax regulations. U.S. GAAP requires that income taxes be recorded on the basis of earnings reported in the shareholder income statement as opposed to earnings in the income tax return. This results in an overstatement of the Portuguese-GAAP net income for 1998 and a cumulative understatement of shareholders' equity at the end of 1998.[44]

The differences between Portuguese GAAP net income and shareholders' equity are fairly substantial, but differences between foreign and U.S. GAAP in other countries may be far greater. EP's 1998 net income would have been about 35% *higher* under U.S. GAAP. However, shareholders' equity would have been about 32% *lower*.

This difference between the effects on net income and shareholders' equity result from the overstatement of assets (overstates depreciation and understates current earnings) and understated liabilities (understates expenses and overstates earnings). For a single year, an asset overstatement may understate net income because a portion of the asset overstatement is amortized as an additional expense in the income statement. Shareholders' equity remains overstated because asset net overstatements remain on the balance sheet.

Domestic users of foreign financial statements need to be aware of the differences in financial reporting practices, and also have some information on the effect of these differences on such key financial statistics as earnings-per-share and shareholders' equity. For example, security analysts use ratios of market price to earnings-per-share (the price/earnings or P/E ratio) as one way to judge whether a stock might be either over or undervalued. Electricidade de Portugal's P/E ratio is higher under Portuguese GAAP because its earnings per share are lower than they would be under U.S. GAAP. Under Portuguese GAAP Electricidade de Portugal would appear to be more conservatively valued than under U.S. GAAP. Similarly, bankers use the relationship of total debt to stockholders' equity to judge the capacity of firms to handle service and repay their borrowed funds. By this statistic, Electricidade de Portugal will appear to be less highly leveraged because its stockholders' equity is much higher under Portuguese GAAP.

The differences between U.S. and Portuguese GAAP, revealed in Exhibits 12.26 and 12.27, are multiplied if one adds to the types of companies and numbers of countries. As the markets for securities become more global, some claim that there is the absence of a level playing field because of these GAAP differences. If the efforts of the International Accounting Standards Committee (IASC) are fruitful, then the playing field should become much more level in the future. However, in the meantime there remains a great deal of international diversity in GAAP.

GAAP Differences and the Level Playing Field

Some argue that international competitiveness can be impaired if earnings and financial position under local GAAP appear weaker than they would under the GAAP of major competitor countries. That is, the playing field will not be level. As an example, concern has been expressed about international GAAP differences that deal with acquisition (of other companies) accounting. A typical acquisition will include the payment of a premium, in some cases involving billions of dollars, for what is collectively termed *goodwill.* This amount consists of the difference between the purchase price and the current value of the net assets acquired, as in the following example:

Purchase price	$1,000
Current fair value of net assets acquired (Assets – Liabilities)	700
Goodwill	$ 300

It has been a common practice in some countries to deduct immediately the goodwill recorded in an acquisition from shareholders' equity. (This is one of the practices that the IASC hopes to see eliminated under its harmonization project discussed earlier.) U.S. GAAP has for several decades required that goodwill be amortized through the income statement. This causes the post-acquisition earnings of a U.S. firm to appear weaker than a comparable firm in a country that permits the immediate write-off of goodwill.

If a foreign firm, located in a country where the immediate write-off of goodwill is permitted, and a U.S. firm were both bidding for the same company, the foreign firm would forecast a stronger post-acquisition earnings picture. This results because the foreign firm would deduct the goodwill immediately, whereas the U.S. firm would take the charge through its future income statements.[45]

It could be argued that the profit differences that result from the disparity in accounting for goodwill are purely cosmetic, and that they should not cause a U.S. bidder to be at a disadvantage in the acquisitions market. That is, the impact of the acquisition on the bidder's future cash flow should be the central issue. Differences in accounting policy should not have a direct impact on future cash flow. However, it is well to remember that, cash flow aside, the reported numbers take on a significance in their own right to the extent they are (1) a factor in determining managerial compensation or (2) are used by lenders to monitor compliance with debt agreements.

The U.S. GAAP requirements for goodwill accounting appear to be on the verge of major changes in 2001. The requirement to amortize goodwill would be eliminated in favor of a policy that would require goodwill write-offs only in cases where the goodwill is considered to be impaired:

> From the date of issuance, all goodwill would be accounted for using an impairment approach. Under that approach, goodwill would be reviewed for impairment, that is written down and expensed against earnings, only in the periods in which the recorded value of goodwill is more than its fair value.[46]

Some countries may criticize this change in goodwill accounting as contributing to international GAAP diversity. The change will also be seen as roughing up and not smoothing out the playing field.

The issue of international competitiveness was also raised with respect to the FASB statement on postretirement benefits accounting, SFAS No. 106, *Employers' Accounting for Postretirement Benefits Other Than Pensions*.[47] The Statement requires companies to apply accrual accounting to what are termed other postretirement benefits, mainly health and life insurance. When proposed, there was fierce lobbying against issuing the statement. Some excerpts from a statement to the FASB by the then Chief Financial Officer of Chrysler Corporation make the key points:[48]

> This higher cost recognition will depress reported profitability, and thereby ultimately discourage capital formation in job-creating enterprises in the U.S. There will be a powerful incentive to move our employment base to Canada, Europe and Third World countries.
>
> Foreign based companies will not be forced to adopt your new rules—all other things being equal, a European or Japanese company will report a billion dollars more profit doing the same business as Chrysler. In that environment, we will simply be unable to compete fairly for investor capital. Ultimately, I believe you will have added to the trend of foreign ownership of our U.S. industrial base.

One can only hope for the success of the IASC program to increase international harmony in reporting practices, if the arguments concerning the anticompetitive potential of diversity in international GAAP are meritorious.

EVALUATING THE PERFORMANCE OF FOREIGN SUBSIDIARIES AND THEIR MANAGEMENT

With the acquisition of its Danish subsidiary, Fashionhouse is faced with the need to report and evaluate the performance of the subsidiary as an economic entity, as well as the performance of the subsidiary's management. The discussion here will focus only on those differences that result from the foreign character of the subsidiary. Aside from this, performance evaluation should be fundamentally the same as for a domestic firm. The fact that, after the translation process, financial statements are available in both the domestic currency (krone in the case of Fashionhouse) and the U.S. dollar is an important difference. Should performance of the subsidiary and its management be judged on the basis of the krone or dollars results? Moreover, the earnings performance of the Fashionhouse subsidiary will be affected each year by (1) the movement of the krone against the dollar and (2) prices set (a transfer price) on the goods sold to Fashionhouse in the United States.

Impact of Exchange Rate Movements on Performance Evaluation

A number of years ago, an issue arose concerning the incentive compensation of the manager of a Netherlands subsidiary of a major U.S. heavy equipment manufacturer. A strong profit performance was produced in the European currency, but the translated results were a loss (note: translation followed the temporal and not the all current method). After lengthy consideration by senior management, a decision was made that no incentive compensation was to be awarded. Management held that failure of the Netherlands subsidiary to earn a profit in dollars resulted in its making no contribution to the parent, whose goal was to maximize the dollar earnings of the consolidated entity. The manager of the Netherlands subsidiary was not pleased.

A central precept of performance evaluation is that managers should only be held responsible for results that incorporate variables over which they exercise some reasonable control. Depending upon the circumstances, this might mean that in judging the performance of a department foreman, the quantity of material used is considered controllable but not its price. For performance evaluation purposes, the material used would be priced at some prearranged standard and not its actual cost. On the other hand, the vice president of manufacturing might well be held responsible for actual material cost on the basis that he or she has been assigned responsibility for the price of material used, as well as its quantity.

Applied to evaluating the performance of the management of foreign subsidiary, the concept of a *controllable* performance indicator would call for either (1) using the profit results from the foreign-currency statements or (2) using the translated dollar earnings, after adjustments designed to remove

EXHIBIT 12.28 Year 1 income statement (in foreign currency and dollars).

	FC	Exchange Rates	U.S.
Sales	1,000	$0.62	$620
Less cost of sales	600	0.62	372
Gross margin	400		248
Less SG&A	100	0.62	62
Pretax profit	300		186
Less tax provision	120	0.62	74
Net income	180		$112

the effects of changes in the value of the dollar, that is, the price of the dollar. As (1) involves no unique adjustments related to foreign subsidiary status, only (2) will be considered further.

Consider the income statements in Exhibit 12.28 in foreign currency (FC) and the U.S. dollar. Assume that in the following year, domestic results are as given in Exhibit 12.28 and that the foreign currency has depreciated to an average rate of $0.50 for the year (recall that income statement amounts are translated at the average rate under the all-current method). The new translation would now be as outlined in Exhibit 12.29.

Net income in year two, in the foreign currency, increased by 65% over Year 1 (from FC180 to FC 297). However, the income improvement on a translated dollar basis was less than half this amount, only 32% ($112 to $148). The impact of the change in exchange rates needs to be removed if the translated income statement is to be used to evaluate performance of the subsidiary's management—on the assumption that management has no control over exchange rates. Net income can be adjusted as follows:

Year 2 net income in the foreign currency	FC297
Translate at year 1 exchange rate	× 0.62
Year 2 net income at constant exchange rate	$184

EXHIBIT 12.29 Year 2 income statement (in foreign currency and dollars).

	FC	Exchange Rates	U.S.
Sales	1,200	$0.50	$600
Less cost of sales	660	0.50	330
Gross margin	540		270
Less SG&A	115	0.50	58
Pretax profit	425		212
Less tax provision	128	0.50	64
Net income	297		$148

The previous adjustment holds constant the value of the foreign currency in measuring net income for purposes of performance evaluation. In judging the subsidiary itself as an economic unit, translation at the depreciated value of the foreign currency may still be appropriate. The dollar value of the net income produced is indeed lower because of the currency depreciation in the subsidiary's country.[49]

An alternative approach that is sometimes used is to evaluate the performance of management is to use budgeted foreign exchange rates. This is similar to the above in that it holds the exchange rate constant. However, the constant rate is a budgeted exchange rate and not simply the rate from the previous year.

There is ample evidence in U.S. annual reports of adjustments to control for the impact of foreign-exchange changes on performance. It is standard for the Management's Discussion and Analysis of Operations section, an SEC requirement, to include commentary on the impact of exchange rate changes on revenues, though far less frequently on earnings. However, Philip Morris does identify the effect of exchange-rate changes on both revenues and the income of operating companies. Three recent examples follow:

Johnson & Johnson Inc. (1999)

Sales by international companies were $12.09 billion in 1999, $11.15 billion in 1998 and $10.93 billion in 1997. This represents an increase of 8.4% in 1999, 1.9% in 1998 and 1.5% in 1997. Excluding the impact of foreign currency fluctuations over the past three years, international company sales increased 12.4% in 1999, 7.1% in 1998 and 9.6% in 1997.

Philip Morris Companies Inc. (1999)

Currency movements decreased operating revenues by $782 million ($517 million, after excluding excise taxes) and operating companies income by $46 million during 1999.

Praxair Inc. (1999)

The sales decrease of 4% in 1999 as compared to 1998 is due primarily to unfavorable currency translation effects in South America. Excluding the impact of currency, sales grew 2%.

Changes in exchange rates present a clear challenge in evaluating the performance of both the economic units, such as the foreign subsidiaries, as well as the management of these organizations. The emphasis on foreign operations is on results in the domestic and not the foreign currency. This can create obvious problems in the evaluation of the management of foreign subsidiaries because their results in the foreign currency may improve or decline while their performance expressed in the domestic (parent's) currency declines or improves.

If foreign entity managers have little control over their results in the parent's currency, then judging their performance in that currency presents clear problems. Performance evaluation in the domestic versus the foreign currency should require that unit management have currency risk management as part of their responsibilities. At least in the case of transactional exposure, Black & Decker managers have in the past had this as part of their duties. However, this would still leave open the effect of translation exposure on results and performance evaluation. As Black & Decker reports:

> Foreign currency transaction and commitment exposures generally are the responsibility of the Corporation's individual operating units to manage as an integral part of their business. Management responds to foreign exchange movements through many alternative means, such as pricing actions, changes in cost structure, and changes in hedging strategies.[50]

The goal of the above discussion is to highlight how the evaluation of foreign subsidiaries and their management represents a special challenge because of the ways in which exchange rate movements can affect measures of financial performance. Another factor that also affects such performance evaluation is the issue of transfer pricing. These are the prices charged when goods are transferred between related foreign and domestic firms. The issue of *transfer pricing* is discussed next.

Transfer Pricing and the Multinational Firm

The prices at which goods or services are transferred between related entities, such as parents and subsidiaries and divisions of the same firm, are referred to as transfer prices. Transfer prices could be a major factor in determining the profits of the Fashionhouse Danish subsidiary because much of its product is shipped to its U.S. parent. As in the previous case, the discussion here will focus on the dimensions of transfer pricing that are influenced by the foreign status of the subsidiary. The general topic of transfer pricing has been hotly debated over many years. The setting of transfer prices, to both encourage optimal decision-making and to facilitate performance evaluation, is not yet a settled matter.

Transfer prices are generally based upon cost, cost plus some markup, or some approximation of market. Firms with international operations typically disclose their method of pricing transfers of goods and services among different taxing jurisdictions—typically countries. Some recent examples of transfer pricing policies are presented in Exhibit 12.30.

The levels at which transfer prices are set is influenced by a wide range of sometimes conflicting objectives. These include maximizing worldwide profits *after taxes*, maintaining flexibility in the repatriation of profits, encouraging optimal decision making by profit center management, providing profit data that are reliable indicators of managerial performance and entity profitability, building market share, and maintaining competitiveness in foreign markets.[51]

There is some variation in the transfer pricing policies used by U.S. firms, with the key distinction being market value versus cost-based transfer prices. Moreover, these policies can have a major impact on measures of financial performance of the foreign subsidiary. They become another factor, in addition to changing exchange rates, that must be considered in evaluating financial performance of a foreign subsidiary and its management.

EXHIBIT 12.30 Alternative transfer-pricing policies.

Company	Transfer-Pricing Policy
Arch Chemicals Inc. (1999)	**Prevailing market prices** Transfers between geographic areas are priced generally at prevailing market prices.
Conoco Inc. (1999)	**Estimated market values** Transfers between segments are on the basis of estimated market values.
Dow Chemical Company (1999)	**Cost and market-based prices** Transfers between operating segments are generally valued at cost. Transfers of products to the Agricultural Products segment from the other segments, however, are generally valued at market-based prices.
Pall Corporation (2000)	**Cost plus a markup on cost** Transfers between geographic areas are generally priced on the basis of a markup of manufacturing costs to achieve an appropriate sharing of profit between the parties.
Tenneco Inc. (1998)	**Market value** Products are transferred between segments and geographic areas on a basis intended to reflect as nearly as possible the *market value* of the products.

SOURCES: Companies' annual reports. The year following each company name designates the annual report from which each example is drawn.

Taxes and Transfer Pricing

A major issue surrounding transfer prices in the international arena is their effect upon the total tax burden of parent firms. The levels of income taxes and tariffs vary considerably across countries. Corporate income tax rates range from the middle teens up to 50% in some countries. This presents the possibility that transfer prices may be set in part to minimize a firm's worldwide tax bill. Establishing the reasonableness of international transfer prices is the principal defense against a charge of transfer price manipulation.

Ignoring other factors bearing on the setting of transfer prices, assume that the objective is to minimize worldwide income taxes. Assume that the income tax rate of the parent is 40% and that of the foreign subsidiary is 30%. Further, the parent is the manufacturer and transfers are made to the foreign subsidiary. The total cost of the product is $100 per unit and it can be sold by the foreign subsidiary at insignificant additional cost for an amount equal to $150. Therefore, the total worldwide pretax profit to be recognized is $50.

While the parent would not have unlimited flexibility in setting the transfer price, tax minimization would call for recognizing as much of the profit as possible in the earnings of the subsidiary. This is because the subsidiary's tax rate is only 30% while the parents is 40%. Tax minimization is accomplished by setting a relatively low transfer price as illustrated in Exhibit 12.31.

EXHIBIT 12.31 International transfer pricing and tax minimization.

	Low Transfer Price		High Transfer Price	
Parent revenue	$110		$140	
Cost	100		100	
Pretax profit	10		40	
Income tax (40%)	4	$ 4	16	$16
Subsidiary revenue	150		150	
Cost (transfer price)	110		140	
Pretax profit	40		10	
Income tax (30%)	12	12	3	3
Worldwide tax		$16		$19
Composite tax rate		32%		38%

The tax authorities of countries are well aware that multinationals have strong incentives to shift profits into low-rate counties. Recent years have seen governments increasingly willing to challenge tax computations that they believe are based upon the use of unreasonable transfer prices. Therefore, the example above simply shows how total tax payments can be influenced by alternative transfer prices. The degree of flexibility shown above may or may not be available.

Notice, in the above example that no change in policy would result if the foreign country also had an ad valorem tariff. Worldwide taxes would still be minimized by a low transfer price because this would also minimize the tariff. However, circumstances would differ if the parent's income tax rate were less than that of the subsidiary. Setting a high transfer price would cause more of the profit to be taxed at the lower income tax rate of the parent. But, this benefit is offset to some extent by the higher tariff in the subsidiary's country. The analysis would need to be extended to include tariffs in the total taxes to be minimized.

Other Influences on Transfer Pricing Policy and Potential Conflicts

Factors other than tax minimization also bear on the establishment of transfer prices. An effort to build market share or to respond to severe price competition might call for low transfer prices. However, this could be in conflict with a tax minimization objective if income tax rates in the country receiving the transferred goods (transferee country) were higher than the income tax rates of the country from which the transfer was made (transferor country).

Transfer pricing policy may sometimes be employed to circumvent restrictions on the repatriation of profits by charging high transfer prices. This effectively involves taking out profits in the form of payments for the goods shipped. There are, of course, some potential offsetting disadvantages from this practice:

1. Charging higher transfer prices will increase ad valorem tariffs.
2. Charging higher transfer prices will lower profits of the transferee firm and potentially present problems in evaluating the profit performance of the unit and its management.
3. Charging higher transfer prices might impair the competitive position of the transferee firm.
4. Charging higher transfer prices lowers profits of the transferee firm and could reduce its apparent financial strength in the eyes of lenders and other users of its financial statements.

This enumeration of factors bearing on the setting of transfer prices is not exhaustive. However, it should be sufficient to highlight the inherent complexity of setting transfer prices. This complexity is magnified as the global reach of multinational firms extends into a greater numbers of countries with wide variations in taxes, competitive conditions, business practices, types of governmental control, variability in exchange rates, and rates of inflation. This last factor, rates of inflation, is discussed next in terms of its impact on measuring the financial performance of domestic firms as well as foreign subsidiaries.

IMPLICATIONS OF INFLATION FOR FINANCIAL PERFORMANCE

As Fashionhouse continued its evolution as a global firm, it considered locating manufacturing capacity in countries with low labor costs. However, in many cases high rates of inflation were linked to low labor costs. Judging performance in highly inflationary environments presents special problems. At some point, financial statements prepared from unadjusted (historical) cost data lose their ability to provide reasonable indicators of either the financial performance or status of firms. Several different approaches have been developed to adjust historical cost financial statements. The principal methods can be classified as involving either (1) general price level or (2) current cost adjustments. These two methods are illustrated below and contrasted with historical-cost statements as the baseline. To provide some useful background, current management commentary on the impact of inflation on financial performance is presented.

Management Commentary on the Impact of and Response to Inflation

Management's Discussion and Analysis, a section of the annual report required by the SEC, often includes commentary on the implications of inflation for financial performance. This commentary provides useful insight into management's assessment of inflation's effects, as well as any company circumstances or actions taken which mitigate the negative effects of inflation. A series of these comments are presented in Exhibit 12.32.

The examples in Exhibit 12.32 are representative of over 100 such disclosures that were examined. A recurrent theme is that inflation has been low in

---

EXHIBIT 12.32   Management commentary on the effects of inflation.

Low inflation and cost recovery contracts: Air T Inc. (2000)
The Company believes that due to the current low levels of inflation the impact of inflation and changing prices on its revenues and net earnings will not have a material effect on its manufacturing operations, or on its air cargo business. This is because the major cost components of its operations, consisting principally of fuel, crew and certain maintenance costs are reimbursed, without markup, under current contract terms.

Inflation and fixed-price contracts may create problems: American Pacific Corporation (1999)
Inflation may have an effect on gross profit in the future as certain of the Company's agreements with AP and sodium azide customers require fixed prices, although certain such agreements contain escalation features that should somewhat mitigate the risks associated with inflation.

Inflation leaves assets undervalued, but depreciation understated: Hartmarx Corporation (1999)
Considering the impact of inflation, the current value of net assets would be higher than the Company's $189 million book value after reflecting the Company's use of the LIFO inventory method and increases in the value of properties since acquisition. Earnings would be lower than reported, assuming higher depreciation expense without a corresponding reduction in taxes.

Cost reduction programs, productivity improvements, and periodic price increases maintain profit margins: Johnson & Johnson Inc. (1999)
Inflation rates, even though moderate in many parts of the world during 1999, continue to have an effect on worldwide economies and, consequently, on the way companies operate. In the face of increasing costs, the Company strives to maintain its profit margins through cost reduction programs, productivity improvements and periodic price increases.

Inflation impact affected by ability to pass on cost increases to customers: Pegasus Systems Inc. (1999)
Substantial increases in cost and expenses could have a significant impact on results of operations to the extent such increases are not passed along to customers.

Pricing strategy and efficiency improvements offset inflation: Polaroid Corporation (1999)
Inflation continues to be a factor in many countries in which the Company does business. The Company's pricing strategy and continuing efficiency improvements have offset to a considerable degree inflation and normal cost increases. The overall inflationary impact on the Company's earnings has not been material.

Inflation increases borrowing costs: Silgan Holdings Inc. (1999)
Historically, inflation has not had a material effect on the Company, other than to increase its cost of borrowing. In general, the Company has been able to increase the sales prices of its products to reflect any increases in the prices of raw materials.

SOURCES: Companies' annual reports. The year following each company name designates the annual report from which each example is drawn.

recent years and, therefore, inflation has not been a significant issue. However, other firms with substantial international activity point out that inflation remains a significant issue in a number of countries where they are located or in which they do business.

The disclosed measures taken to mitigate the effects of inflation were very consistent and included:

- Selective price increases.
- Productivity improvements.
- Cost-containment efforts.
- Cost reimbursement.
- Price escalation agreements.

Some of the disclosures indicated protection from inflationary cost increases because of the presence of fixed-price contracts and escalation features in business agreements. Concern is frequently expressed about the ability to pass on the effects of inflationary cost increases in the form of higher product prices. Some protection from cost inflation of *commodities* is often achieved through the use of the same types of hedging vehicles employed to avoid cost increases created by exchange rate movements. For example, airlines and public transit systems routinely hedge the cost of fuel in order to avoid the erosion of profits from increases in petroleum prices.

A traditional concern, highlighted by the Hartmarx commentary in Exhibit 12.32, is the overstatement of profits in periods of significant inflation. The LIFO inventory method has traditionally been viewed as a method that reduces such profit overstatements. LIFO ensures that cost of sales approximates replacement cost. Profit overstatement is also avoided in cases where most depreciable assets are relatively new. In this circumstance depreciation is closer to replacement cost than if depreciation were based principally on the lower costs of older assets. The use of accelerated depreciation, especially for income tax purposes, is also seen to offset some of the potential profit overstatement associated with inflation.

The revision of traditional cost-based statements to reflect the effects of either general inflation or specific cost increases is a more comprehensive approach to assessing the effects of inflation upon measures of financial performance. The approach is illustrated next.

Adjusting Financial Statements for the Effects of Inflation

The use of LIFO and the reliance upon relatively new depreciable assets or accelerated depreciation to cause expenses to approximate current (replacement) costs is only a partial adjustment for the impact of inflation. Historically, the comprehensive restatement of results for the effects of general as well as specific price increases has been emphasized. In fact, in 1979 the FASB issued a statement that called for the disclosure of supplemental information on price-level adjusted earnings.[52] A subsequent statement, issued in 1986, held that these price-level adjusted disclosures, while still recommended, would no longer be required.[53] There was opposition by the business community to the requirements of SFAS No. 33, and efforts to demonstrate that the new disclosures were either used or useful were not successful. While principally of historical interest in this period of very modest inflation, some of the disclosures required by SFAS No. 33 are discussed and presented.[54]

SFAS No. 33, Price-Level Adjusted Disclosures

Beginning in 1979, certain large U.S. firms were required to provide supplemental information on the effect of inflation on financial performance. The disclosures included new information on earnings computed on both a constant-dollar and a current-cost basis. The *constant-dollar* method retains historical cost as the basis of financial measurement. However, it does make selected restatements so that all financial statement balances are presented in units of the same purchasing power, that is, expressed in the same price index. The *current-cost* method replaces historical cost balances with current (replacement) costs as the basis for financial statement measurement. Exhibit 12.33 provides an example of disclosures of price-level adjusted results under the requirements of SFAS No. 33.[55]

A very different message about profitability is conveyed by the adjusted information in Exhibit 12.33. A significant level of historical-cost profits is almost eliminated when current-cost adjustments are applied, and profit turns into loss under the constant-dollar alternative. The purchasing power of the resources invested in producing the 1980 results, as represented by the constant-dollar amount of expenses, exceeded Tiger's constant-dollar revenues. Closer

EXHIBIT 12.33   Income statements adjusted for changing prices: Tiger International Inc., December 31, 1980 (in thousands).

	Historical Financials	Current Cost	Constant Dollar
Revenues	$1,562,270	$1,562,270	$1,562,270
Cost and Expenses			
Cost of operations	1,104,672	1,108,673	1,109,324
Selling, general, and administrative	139,462	139,462	139,462
Depreciation and amortization	118,332	151,924	171,096
Interest, net	140,929	140,929	140,929
Income tax provision	16,500	16,500	16,500
	1,519,895	1,557,488	1,577,311
Net income (loss)	$ 42,375	$ 4,782	$ (15,041)

SOURCE: Tiger International Inc., annual report, December 1980, 39.

study of these data is necessary to understand the reasons behind these quite different messages.

The revenues in each of the three income statements are measured in the average price level for the year based upon the *Consumer Price Index for All Urban Consumers*. Tiger's revenues are earned fairly evenly across the year, and therefore, the revenues in the historical-cost income statement are already expressed in average prices for the year. Accordingly, the same revenue amount can be used in both the constant-dollar and current-cost statements. The same applies to the amounts for selling, general and administrative; interest, net; and the income tax provision.

Modest adjustments were made to cost of operations to convert them to constant dollars and current costs, respectively. The constant-dollar adjustment requires multiplying the historical cost of operations by a ratio of price indices. The index in the numerator is average price index for the current year, and in the denominator, is the value of the index at the date closest to the date on which the expense was incurred. To illustrate, assume that a $1,000 expense was recorded on January 1, 2002, when the price index was 100; the average price index for 2002 was 110. Adjustment to constant dollars is:

$$\$1,000 \times \left(\frac{110}{100} \right) = \$1,100$$

The same methodology is applied in adjusting historical cost of operations to current-cost amounts. The difference is that specific indices of replacement cost, or alternative measures of replacement cost, are used in place of a general price index.

Tiger reported that increases in inventory costs, included in cost of operations, accounted for the adjustments to historical cost of operations. In general, adjustments to the historical cost of sales will be small if the LIFO inventory valuation method is used; the LIFO cost flow ensures that cost of sales already approximates current costs. Adjustments will generally be greater where the FIFO or average cost methods are in use.

Impact of Differences in General and Specific Price Index Movements

The major Tiger cost adjustments were to depreciation and amortization. Depreciation and amortization represent the conversion to expense of asset balances. In many cases these balances were recorded years earlier when the price indices were far lower. Notice that the percentage increase in the current-cost and constant-dollar depreciation and amortization over the historical-cost amount is 28% and 45%, respectively. Tiger's disclosures explain the reason for the differences: "Depreciation expense is greater when adjusted for general inflation than when adjusted for changes in specific prices. The difference reflects the Consumer Price Index (general inflation) rising faster than the increase of costs over the last several years of the type of property, plant and equipment used in the Company's various businesses."[56]

Impact of Monetary Balances on Adjusted Results

In addition to the above two inflation-adjusted income presentations, Tiger provided additional income data because it did not feel that the required disclosures, adjusting mainly depreciation and cost of sales, were adequate. These adjustments, in Exhibit 12.34, expand upon the information in Exhibit 12.33.

The final adjusted net incomes above tell a totally different story from the initial display in Exhibit 12.33. Both measures of adjusted profits are sharply higher than the unadjusted historical-cost results. The new income element results from the impact of changes in the general price level on the purchasing power of monetary assets and liabilities. Tiger explains the impact of price changes on monetary balances as follows:

> A monetary asset represents money or a claim to receive money without reference to future changes in prices. Similarly, a monetary liability represents an obligation to pay a sum of money that is fixed or determinable without reference to changes in future prices. Holding a monetary asset during periods of inflation results in a decline in the value of the asset since the dollar loses purchasing power when it is held. Conversely, holders of monetary liabilities benefit during inflationary periods because less purchasing power is required to satisfy future obligations when they can be paid with less valuable dollars.[57]

Under the above reasoning, Tiger earned an unrealized purchasing-power gain because its monetary liabilities exceeded its monetary assets. This gain represents the reduction in the purchasing power that Tiger would need to expend to discharge its net monetary-liability position. The impact of both inflation and deflation on purchasing-power gains, under conditions of both monetary assets exceeding monetary liabilities (net asset exposure) and

EXHIBIT 12.34   Earnings adjusted for purchasing power gains from monetary position: Tiger International Inc., (in thousands).

	Historical Financials	Current Cost	Constant Dollar
Net income	$42,375	$ 4,782	$(15,041)
Decrease in depreciation and interest expense from the decline in the purchasing power of the net liabilities	—	82,195	82,195
Net income adjusted for the decrease in depreciation and interest expense	$42,375	$86,977	$ 67,154

SOURCE: Tiger International Inc., annual report, December 1980, 39.

EXHIBIT 12.35   Purchasing power gains and losses and net monetary position.

Price Movement	Net Monetary Position	
	Asset	Liability
Inflation	Loss	Gain
Deflation	Gain	Loss

monetary liabilities exceeding monetary assets (net liability exposure), are summarized in Exhibit 12.35.

Tiger treated the purchasing power gain as an adjustment to depreciation and interest expense based upon the following reasoning: "Because Tiger finances substantially all of its fixed assets with long-term debt, it effectively hedges against the impact of inflation on depreciation and interest expense." Tiger's liability exposure serves as a hedge because it produces a gain under inflationary conditions, to offset increases in the cost of asset replacement and interest expense, which go hand in hand with inflation.[58]

The price-level adjusted reporting illustrated above proved to be a very controversial requirement. It proved difficult to document that the price-level adjusted data were used by either creditors or investors, or that they aided analysis and decision making in any significant way. In 1986, SFAS No. 89: *Financial Reporting and Changing Prices* was issued, which eliminated mandatory disclosure of price-level adjusted data.[59] The Statement did encourage continued disclosure on a voluntary basis. U.S. firms have, however, not responded to this encouragement and the price-level adjusted disclosures have not been continued.

U.S. GOVERNMENT RESTRICTIONS ON BUSINESS PRACTICES ASSOCIATED WITH FOREIGN SUBSIDIARIES AND GOVERNMENT[60]

The last issue raised in the opening Fashionhouse scenario dealt with U.S. governmental restrictions on business practices associated with overseas operations. Recall that in reviewing the possible relocation of manufacturing to a high inflation/low labor-cost country, Fashionhouse management became aware of potential ethical and legal issues.

Over the years the U.S. government became concerned with the practices sometimes followed by U.S. firms doing business overseas. Of special concern were payments to foreign governmental officials made to obtain business. From hearings over a number of years, which focused on such incidents, a recurring theme emerged: Even though such payments did take place, key members of management were often unaware that the payments were being made.

The U.S. Congress addressed the issue of controlling what they saw to be improper activities, by passing the *Foreign Corrupt Practices Act of 1977*. The key features of this law were:

1. The prohibition of bribery of foreign governmental or political officials in order to promote business.
2. The requirement that firms (a) keep accurate and detailed records of the company financial activities and (b) maintain a system of internal accounting controls sufficient to provide reasonable assurance that transactions are properly authorized, recorded, and accounted for.

The above requirements are incorporated as amendments to Section 13(b) of the *Securities Exchange Act of 1934,* and apply to all publicly held companies. The record-keeping and internal control features of the *Act* were a response to claims that companies had been unaware of bribery payments, because their internal control systems had failed to detect or prevent them.

In a report addressed to the SEC, the National Commission on Fraudulent Financial Reporting, made the following recommendation:

> All public companies should be required by SEC rule to include in their annual reports to stockholders management reports signed by the chief executive officer

EXHIBIT 12.36 Report of management: Delta Air Lines Inc., year ended June 30, 2000.

The integrity and objectivity of the information presented in this Annual Report are the responsibility of Delta management. The financial statements contained in this report have been audited by Arthur Andersen LLP, independent public accountants, whose report appears below.

Delta maintains a system of internal financial controls that are independently assessed on an ongoing basis through a program of internal audits. These controls include the selection and training of Delta's managers, organizational arrangements that provide a division of responsibilities, and communication programs explaining our policies and standards. We believe that this system provides reasonable assurance that transactions are executed in accordance with management's authorization; that transactions are appropriately recorded to permit preparation of financial statements that, in all material respects, are presented in conformity with accounting principles generally accepted in the United States; and that assets are properly accounted for and safeguarded against loss from unauthorized use.

The Board of Directors pursues its responsibilities for these financial statements through its Audit Committee, which consists solely of directors who are neither officers nor employees of Delta. The Audit Committee meets periodically with the independent public accountants, the internal auditors and representatives of management to discuss internal control, accounting, auditing and financial reporting matters.

M. Michele Burns
Executive Vice President and
Chief Financial Officer

Leo F. Mullin
Chairman and
Chief Executive Officer

SOURCE: Delta Air Lines Inc., annual report, June 2000, 53.

and the chief accounting officer and/or the chief financial officer. The management report should acknowledge management's responsibilities for the financial statements and internal control, discuss how these responsibilities were fulfilled, and provide management's assessment of the effectiveness of the company's internal controls.[61]

While the SEC has not adopted the Commission's recommendation, many companies have elected to provide voluntarily a report of management's responsibilities. While the precise title of the report may vary, representative titles include, Report of Management Responsibility for Financial Statements and Internal Control and Financial Reporting Responsibility. Although the precise language of the report differs from company to company, Exhibit 12.36 provides a representative example from the 2000 annual report of Delta Air Lines.

The precise meaning of the provisions of the *Foreign Corrupt Practices Act* continues to evolve. However, in considering expansion into a country, where improper payments have a long and durable tradition, Fashionhouse must pay special attention to the existence and requirements of the Act.

SUMMARY

The evolution of Fashionhouse from a purely domestic firm to a truly global entity continues to confront it with new and increasingly complex problems of accounting, finance, and management. This chapter has followed Fashionhouse through this evolution and attempted to help the reader become aware of the problems faced and how they might be addressed. The range of issues addressed is broad and can become quite complex. It has not been possible, nor would it have been appropriate in a chapter such as this, to deal with all aspects of every issue raised. The reader should consult the books and articles cited throughout the chapter and in the list of "additional readings" for additional background.

The following are some key points for the reader to consider:

- International business and international operations raise challenges that transcend those of a strictly domestic operation.
- Exposure to potentially adverse movements of foreign-currency exchange rates is a key challenge for firms that engage in international business. This currency risk can arise from both transactional and translational exposure.
- Both transactional and translational currency risk can be managed or hedged to some extent by relying on aspects of a firm's own operations. This is normally referred to as employing natural hedges.
- Beyond the use of natural hedges, it is common for firms to use a variety of foreign-currency derivatives. Forward contracts and currency options are currently the most popular.

- Most hedging activity centers around efforts to protect cash flows and earnings from the volatility that would be produced by the combination of unhedged currency exposure and fluctuations in exchange rates. Translation exposure, which does not pose the same threat to cash flows and earnings, is hedged far less frequently than transaction exposure.

- Note all of the effects of changes in exchange rates are reflected in transaction and translation gains and losses. The strength of the U.S. dollar in recent years has both reduced the dollar value of foreign sales as well as the competitiveness of U.S. products.

- The emergence of the Euro has the potential to reduce both the cost and complexity of hedging because many European currencies are replaced by a single currency, the Euro. However, some companies express concern about possible adverse competitive effects associated with the pricing transparency that results from a common currency.

- Substantial differences continue to exist between GAAP in the U.S. and that in other countries. However, the International Accounting Standards Committee (IASC) continues its efforts to create more harmony in GAAP across the world. These GAAP differences create substantial challenges when analyzing the financial performance of foreign firms.

- The evaluation of the performance of foreign subsidiaries and their management can be affected by exchange-rate changes. A common response is to remove the effects of exchange rate changes from key performance indicators. Another approach is to evaluate performance using budgeted exchange rates. The extent to which the responsibility for hedging currency exposure is delegated to management of these entities should affect decisions about how to deal with the effects of exchange-rate changes. Removing the effects of exchange rate changes is consistent with an absence of responsibility for the hedging of currency risk.

- Recent changes in the accounting for derivative instruments and hedging activities call for the recording of all foreign-currency derivatives at their fair values. In some cases, gains and losses from the revaluation of currency derivatives will initially be included in other comprehensive income. However, these gains and losses will subsequently be included in net income when the related hedged transaction is included in earnings. The deferral of foreign-currency gains and losses on the balance sheet is no longer permitted.

- Transfer pricing policies between U.S. parents and their foreign subsidiaries create challenges in terms of both performance evaluation and worldwide tax minimization.

- Modest levels of inflation in the U.S. in recent years has meant that increases in the general price level have not been a major management issue. However, inflation continues to present issues for global firms because of substantial inflation in some of their foreign markets.

- The international expansion of business activities can create potential problems because of different business and cultural norms. Practices that may be common in some countries may be in direct conflict with U.S. law. Firms should be certain that they are familiar with and in compliance with the provisions of the *Foreign Corrupt Practices Act of 1977.*

FOR ADDITIONAL READING

Beaver, W., and W. Landsman, *Incremental Information Content of Statement 33 Disclosures* (Stamford, CT: FASB, 1983).

Choi, F., ed., *Handbook of International Accounting* (New York: John Wiley, 1991).

Comiskey, E., and C. Mulford, *Guide to Financial Reporting and Analysis* (New York: John Wiley, 2000).

Epstein, B., and A. Mirza, *Interpretation and Application of International Accounting Standards 2001* (New York: John Wiley, 1997).

SFAS No. 133, *Accounting for Derivative Instruments and Hedging Activities* (Norwalk, CT: FASB, June, 1998).

Financial Accounting Standards Board, *The IASC-U.S. Comparison Project: A Report on the Similarities and Differences between IASC Standards and U.S. GAAP* (Norwalk, CT: FASB, November, 1996).

———, *Financial Reporting in North America—Highlights of a Joint Study* (Norwalk, CT: FASB, December, 1994).

Frishkoff, P., *Financial Reporting and Changing Prices: A Review of Empirical Research* (Stamford, CT: FASB, 1982).

Goodwin, J., S. Goldberg, and C. Tritschler, "Understanding Foreign Currency Derivative Measurements as FASB Moves Toward Fair Value Reporting," *The Journal of Corporate Accounting and Finance,* 7, (spring 1996): 75–84.

Goldberg, S., and J. Godwin, "Foreign Corrupt Practices Act: Some Pitfalls and How to Avoid Them," *The Journal of Corporate Accounting and Finance ,* 7, (winter 1995–1996): 35–43.

Haskins, M., K. Ferris, and T. Selling, *International Financial Reporting and Analysis* (Chicago: Richard D. Irwin, 1996).

Kim, H., *Fundamental Analysis Worldwide* (New York: John Wiley, 1996).

Mulford, C., and E. Comiskey, *Financial Warnings* (New York: John Wiley, 1996).

Radebaugh, L., and S. Gray, *International Accounting for Multinational Enterprises,* 3rd ed. (New York: John Wiley, 1993).

Shapiro, A., *Multinational Financial Management,* 5th ed. (Upper Saddle River, NJ: Prentice-Hall, 1996).

ANNUAL REPORTS REFERENCED IN THE CHAPTER

Adobe Systems Inc. (1999)

AGCO Corporation (1999)

Air Canada (1999)

Air T Inc. (2000)

American Pacific Corporation (1999)

Analog Devices Inc. (1999)

Arch Chemicals Inc. (1999)

Armstrong World Industries Inc. (1999)

Arvin Industries Inc. (1999)

Baldwin Technology Company (1999)

Baltek Corporation (1999)

Baxter International Inc. (1999)

Beckman Coulter Inc. (1999)

Becton, Dickenson & Company (1999)

Black and Decker Inc. (1995)

Blyth Industries Inc. (2000)

California First Bank (1987)

Compaq Computer Corporation (1999)

Conoco Inc. (1999)

DaimlerChrysler AG (1999)

Delta Air Lines Inc. (2000)

Dow Chemical Company (1999)

E.I. DuPont de Nemours & Company (1999)

Electricidade de Portugal SA (1998)

Federal Express Inc. (1989)

Galey & Lord Inc. (1999)

Hartmarx Corporation (1999)

H.J. Heinz Co. (1999)

Henry Schein Inc. (1998)

Illinois Tool Works Inc. (1999)

Interface Inc. (1999)

JLG Industries Inc. (2000)

Johnson & Johnson, Inc. (1999)

Olin Corporation (1999)

Pall Corporation (2000)

Pegasus Systems Inc. (1999)

Philip Morris Companies Inc. (1999)

Polaroid Corporation (1999)

Praxair Inc. (1999)

Quaker Oats Company (1999)

Silgan Holdings Inc. (1999)

Storage Technology Corporation (1999)

Teleflex Inc. (1999)

Tenneco Inc. (1999)

Tiger International Inc. (1980)

Titan International Inc. (1999)

UAL Inc. (1999)

Vishay Intertechnology Inc. (1999)

Western Digital Corporation (2000)

York International Corporation (1999)

NOTES

1.   Western Digital Corporation, annual report, June 2000, 25–26.

2.   Baltek Corporation, annual report on Form 10-K to the Securities and Exchange Commission, December 1999, 3.

3.   It is unlikely that either side of the transaction would be indifferent to this matter. Insisting upon being invoiced by a foreign supplier in your own currency means that the supplier must bear the currency risk. The supplier will have a foreign-currency receivable. It is reasonable to expect the foreign supplier to attempt to be compensated for bearing this currency risk by charging a higher price for its product.

4.   A U.S. electronics company recently attempted to eliminate currency risk by having its Japanese supplier invoice them in the U.S. dollar. The Japanese supplier agreed to do this and introduced a new schedule of prices in dollars. The U.S. company deemed the increases to be so high that they decided to continue to be invoiced in the Japanese yen and to manage the associated exchange risk.

5.   Each of the actual case examples discussed in this section are treated in more detail, including income tax and cash-flow issues, in E. Comiskey and C. Mulford, "Risks of Foreign Currency Transactions: A Guide for Loan Officers," *Commercial Lending Review* (summer 1990), pp. 44–60.

6.   Air Canada, annual report, December 1999 (emphasis added). Information obtained from Disclosure, Inc., *Compact D/SEC: Corporation Information on Public Companies Filing with the SEC* (Bethesda, MD: Disclosure Inc., June 2000).

7.   On January 1, 1999, 11 of the 15 member countries of the European Union adopted the Euro as their common legal currency and established fixed conversion rates between their sovereign currencies and the Euro.

8.   Holding foreign currency cash, that is, an asset balance, would be consistent with the need to offset existing liability exposure in these foreign currencies. Alternatively, borrowing in foreign currencies to produce a hedge implies existing asset exposure in these foreign currencies.

9.   California First Bank, annual report, December 1987, 20.

10.   Federal Express Inc., annual report, December 1989, 35.

11.   The accounting treatment to insure that the offsetting gains and losses are included in the income statements at the same time was described by Federal

Express. It reported that "Exchange-rate gains and losses on the term loan are deferred and amortized over the remaining life of the loan as an adjustment to the related hedge (service) revenue." Federal Express Inc., annual report, December 1989, 36.

12.   This example is discussed in "FX Translation—Lyle Shipping's Losses," *Accountancy*, 110 (December 1984): 50. Lyle has an *economic* hedge of its dollar exposure.

13.   See P. Maloney, "Managing Currency Exposure: The Case of Western Mining," *Journal of Applied Corporate Finance*, 2 (winter 1990): 29–34, for an analysis of the effectiveness of this natural hedge during the eighties.

14.   Survey data support this view. See G. Bodnar, G. Hayt, and R. Marston, "The Wharton Survey of Derivatives Usage by U.S. Non-Financial Firms," *Financial Management*, 25 (winter 1996): 113–133.

15.   Spot and forward exchange rates normally differ. These rate differences are determined primarily by differences in interest rates in the respective countries of the domestic and foreign currency.

16.   Beckman Coulter Inc., annual report, December 1999, 47.

17.   An option that is acquired when the spot value for the currency and the strike price in the option contract are equal is said to have no *intrinsic value*. However, such contracts routinely have positive values. The value of an at-the-money option contract is normally referred to as time value.

18.   A currency option is similar to flight insurance. The option contract (insurance) only pays off if the plane crashes and the policyholder is injured or dies. That is, there is a gain only if the unfavorable event takes place. However, if the plane does not crash, the favorable outcome, the policyholder is simply out the amount of the insurance (option) premium.

19.   Analog Devices Inc., annual report, December 1999. Information obtained from Disclosure Inc.

20.   JLG Industries Inc., annual report, July 2000, 23.

21.   Titan International Inc., annual report, December 1999. Information obtained from Disclosure Inc.

22.   To be technically correct, a gain or loss from the translation of the statements of a foreign subsidiary does affect other comprehensive income. However, it does not affect net income, which continues to be the number which both company management and other users of financial statements emphasize.

23.   E.I. DuPont de Nemours & Company, annual report, December 1999, 37.

24.   Ibid., 37.

25.   However, this hedging by Quaker Oats is not aimed at protecting either earnings or cash flow. Gains and losses from net-investment hedges, along with their offsetting translation losses and gains, are reported in shareholders' equity.

26.   Arch Chemicals Inc., annual report, December 1999, 34.

27.   The equity method is usually employed when a voting stock interest of 20% or more is held in another company. The investor company recognizes its share of the investee company earnings or loss, without regard to whether any dividends are received. The receipt of dividends is treated as a reduction in the carrying value of the investment, and not as dividend income.

28.   Denmark has not yet (early 2001) adopted the Euro. Its currency exposure will be limited to the Euro to the extent that it trades mainly with Euro countries.

29.   Information on Danish GAAP can be found in E. Comiskey and C. Mulford, "Comparing Danish Accounting and Reporting Practices with International Accounting Standards," in *Advances in International Accounting,* ed. Kenneth S. Most (Greenwich, CT: JAI Press, 1991), 123–142.

30.   If there were differences between generally accepted accounting principles in the country of the foreign subsidiary and those in the U.S., then the statements would first have be adjusted to conform to U.S. GAAP before consolidation could take place.

31.   Statement No. 52, *Foreign Currency Translation,* refers to this alternative procedure as remeasurement and not translation. However, in the vast majority of cases, the remeasurement is from the foreign currency to the U.S. dollar. Therefore, remeasurement produces statements in the U.S. dollar that are ready to be consolidated with the statements of their U.S. parent. Remeasurement is tantamount to translation.

32.   It is simply coincidental that a translation gain of $87 resulted under the all-current translation and a remeasurement loss of $87 resulted from remeasurement under the temporal method.

33.   From this example, a fairly obvious case can be made for, other things equal, locating manufacturing in the same country where sales are made.

34.   P. Collier, E. Davis, J. Coates and S. Longden, "The Management of Currency Risk: Case Studies of US and UK Multinationals," *Accounting and Business Research,* 24 (summer 1990): 208.

35.   SFAS No. 8, *Accounting for the Translation of Foreign Currency Transactions and Foreign Financial Statements* (Stamford, CT: FASB, October 1975).

36.   C. Houston and G. Mueller, "Foreign Exchange Rate Hedging and SFAS No. 52—Relatives or Strangers?," *Accounting Horizons,* 2 (December 1988): 57.

37.   SFAS No. 133, *Accounting for Derivative Instruments and Hedging* (Norwalk, CT: FASB, June 1998).

38.   A common feature of derivatives is that they have little or no initial value. This would not be true in the case of some option contracts where an option premium is paid, even in the case of at or out-of-the-money options.

39.   For a reference on these matters, see E. Comiskey and C. Mulford, *Guide to Financial Reporting and Analysis* (New York: John Wiley, 2000), chapters 6 and 7.

40.   International Accounting Standards Committee, Exposure Draft 32, *Comparability of Financial Statements* (January 11, 1989).

41.   Ibid., paragraph 6.

42.   International Accounting Standards Committee, Statement of Intent, *Comparability of Financial Statements* (July 1990).

43.   For a standard-by-standard analysis of the differences between current U.S. GAAP and IASC standards, see *The IASC-U.S. Comparison Project: A Report on the Similarities and Differences between IASC Standards and U.S. GAAP* (Norwalk, CT: FASB, November, 1996).

44.   To examine the complete reconciliation disclosures of Electricidade de Portugal, go to the SEC Web site (www.sec.gov) and search for the Electricidade filings. The current reconciliation will be found in the most recent 20-F filing for the company.

45. A further negative for a U.S. firm has been the fact that goodwill amortization was not deductible for tax purposes, whereas it was in some other countries. A 1993 change in the tax law, Internal Revenue Code, section 197, now makes it possible to amortize goodwill in the tax return for qualifying acquisitions.

46. FASB, News Release, *Financial Accounting Standards Board Announces Additional Decisions Relating to the Treatment of Goodwill* (Norwalk, CT: FASB, December 20, 2000).

47. SFAS No. 106, *Employers' Accounting for Postretirement Benefits Other Than Pensions* (Norwalk, CT: FASB, December 1990).

48. From a statement made by R. S. Miller Jr., executive vice president and chief financial officer of Chrysler Corporation, to the Financial Accounting Standards Board, Washington, DC, November 3, 1989, 3.

49. Removing the effects of exchange rate changes in cases where the subsidiary is using the temporal (remeasurement) translation method, as opposed to the all-current method, is a greater challenge and beyond the scope of this chapter.

50. Black and Decker Inc., annual report, December 1995, 35.

51. The following two references were of great assistance in preparing this discussion of transfer pricing: Frederick D. S. Choi and Gerhard G. Mueller, *An Introduction to Multinational Accounting* (Englewood Cliffs, NJ: Prentice-Hall, 1978), chapter 9; and Jeffrey S. Arpan and Lee H. Radebaugh, *International Accounting and Multinational Enterprises* (New York: Warren, Gorham & Lamont, 1981), chapter 10.

52. SFAS No. 33, *Financial Reporting and Changing Prices* (amended and partially superseded) (Stamford, CT: FASB, September 1979).

53. SFAS No. 89, *Financial Reporting and Changing Prices* (Stamford, CT: FASB, December 1986).

54. Helpful in preparing this section was J. Largay and L. Livingstone, *Accounting for Changing Prices: Replacement Cost and General Price Level Adjustments* (Santa Barbara, CA: John Wiley/Hamilton, 1976). This is an excellent and comprehensive treatment of this subject area that is recommended for readers interested in a more expansive treatment of the subject.

55. Tiger International Inc., annual report, December 1980, 39.

56. Ibid., 39.

57. Ibid., 40.

58. Incorporating gain and losses on the net monetary position into the computation of restated results was not part of the SFAS No. 33 requirements.

59. SFAS No. 89, *Financial Reporting and Changing Prices* (Stamford, CT: FASB, 1986).

60. For further background on this topic see: K. Skousen, *An Introduction to the SEC,* 4th ed. (Cincinnati: South-Western, 1987), 32–35.

61. *Report of the National Commission on Fraudulent Financial Reporting* (Washington, DC, 1987), 44.

13 FINANCIAL MANAGEMENT OF RISKS

Steven P. Feinstein

For better or worse, the business environment is fraught with risks. Uncertainty is a fact of life. Profits are never certain, input and output prices change, competitors emerge and disappear, customers' tastes constantly evolve, technological progress creates instability, interest rates and foreign-currency values and asset prices fluctuate. Nonetheless, managers must continue to make decisions. Businesses must cope with risk in order to operate. Managers and firms are often evaluated on overall performance, even though performance may be affected by risky factors beyond their control. The goal of risk management is to maximize the value of the firm by reducing the negative potential impact of forces beyond the control of management.

There are essentially four basic approaches to risk management: risk avoidance, risk retention, loss prevention and control, and risk transfer.[1] Suppose after a firm has analyzed a risky business venture and weighed both the costs and benefits of exposure to risk, management chooses not to embark on the project. They determine that the potential rewards are not worth the risks. Such a strategy would be an example of risk avoidance. *Risk avoidance* means choosing not to engage in a risky activity because of the risks. Choosing not to fly in a commercial airliner because of the risk that the plane might crash is an example of risk avoidance.

Risk retention is another simple strategy, in which the firm chooses to engage in the project and do nothing about the identified risks. After weighing the costs and benefits, the firm chooses to proceed. It is the "damn the torpedoes" approach to risk management. For many firms, risk retention is the optimal strategy for all risks. Investors expect the company's stock to be risky, and they do not reward managers for reducing risks. Investors cope with business

423

risks by diversifying their holdings within their portfolios, and so they do not want business managers to devote resources to managing risks within the firm.

Loss prevention and control involves embarking on a risky project, yet taking steps to reduce the likelihood and severity of any losses potentially resulting from uncontrollable factors. In the flying example, loss prevention and control would be the response of the airline passenger who chooses to fly, but also selects the safest airline, listens to the preflight safety instructions, sits near the emergency exit, and perhaps brings his or her own parachute. The passenger in this example has no control over how many airplanes crash in a given year, but he or she takes steps to make sure not to be on one of them, and if so, to be a survivor.

Risk transfer involves shifting the negative consequences of a risky factor to another person, firm, or party. For example, buying flight insurance shifts some of the negative financial consequences of a crash to an insurance company and away from the passenger's family. Should the airplane crash, the insurance company suffers a financial loss, and the passenger's family is financially compensated. Forcing foreign customers to pay for finished goods in your home currency rather than in their local currency is another example of risk transfer, whereby you transfer the risk of currency fluctuations to your customers. If the value of the foreign currency drops, the customers must still pay you an agreed upon number of dollars, for example, even though it costs them more to do so in terms of their home currency.

No one risk management approach is ideal for all situations. Sometimes risk avoidance is optimal; sometimes risk retention is the desired strategy. Recent developments in the financial marketplace, however, have made risk transfer much more feasible than in the past. More and more often now, especially when financial risks are involved, it is the most desirable alternative.

In recent years there has been revolutionary change in the financial marketplace. The very same marketplace that traditionally facilitated the transfer of funds from investors to firms, has brought forth numerous derivative instruments that facilitate the transfer of risk. Just as the financial marketplace has been innovative in engineering various types of investment contracts, such as stocks, bonds, preferred stock, and convertible bonds, the financial marketplace now engineers risk transfer instruments, such as forwards, futures, options, swaps, and a multitude of variants of these derivatives.

Reading stories about derivatives in the popular press might lead one to believe that derivative instruments are dangerous and destabilizing—evil creatures that emerged from the dark recesses of the financial marketplace. The cover of the April 11, 1994, *Time* magazine introduced derivatives with the caption "High-tech supernerds are playing dangerous games with your money." The use of derivatives has been implicated in most of the financial calamities of the past decade: Barings Bank, Procter & Gamble, Metallgesellschaft, Askin Capital Management, Orange County, Union Bank of Switzerland, and Long-Term Capital Management, to name a few. In each of the cases, vast sums of money quickly vanished, and derivatives seemed to be to blame.

WHAT WENT WRONG: CASE STUDIES OF DERIVATIVES DEBACLES

Derivatives were not responsible for the financial calamities of the 1990s. Greed, speculation, and probably incompetence were. But just as derivatives facilitate risk management, they facilitate greed and accelerate the consequences of speculation and incompetence. For example, consider the following case histories and then draw your own conclusions.

Barings Bank

On February 26, 1995, Baring PLC, Britain's oldest merchant bank and one of the most venerable financial institutions in the world collapsed. Did this failure follow years of poor management and bad investments. Hardly. All of the bank's $615 million of capital had been wiped out in less than four months, by one employee, half way around the world from London. It seems that a Barings derivatives trader named Nicholas Leeson, stationed in Singapore, had taken huge positions in futures and options on Japanese stocks. Leeson's job was supposed to be *index arbitrage,* meaning that he was supposed to take low risk positions exploiting discrepancies between the prices of futures contracts traded in both Singapore and Osaka. Leeson's job was to buy whichever contract was cheaper and sell the one that was more dear. The difference would be profit for Barings. When he was long in Japanese stock futures in Osaka, he was supposed to be short in Japanese stock futures in Singapore, and vice versa. Such positions are inherently hedged. If the Singapore futures lost money, the Japanese futures would make money, and so little money, if any, could be lost.

Apparently, Leeson grew impatient taking hedged positions. He began to take unhedged bets, selling both call options and put options on Japanese stocks. Such a strategy, consisting of written call options and written put options is called a *straddle.* If the underlying stock price stays the same or does not move much, the writer keeps all the option premium, and profits handsomely. If, on the other hand, the underlying stock price either rises or falls substantially, the writer is vulnerable to large losses. Leeson bet and lost. Japanese stocks plummeted, and the straddles became a huge liability. Like a panicked gambler, Leeson tried to win back his losses by going long in Japanese stock futures. This position was a stark naked speculative bet. Leeson lost again. Japanese stocks continued to fall. Leeson lost more than $1 billion, and Barings had lost all of its capital. The bank was put into receivership.

Procter & Gamble

Procter & Gamble, the well-known manufacturer of soap and household products, had a long history of negotiating low interest rates to finance operations.

Toward this end, Procter & Gamble entered an interest rate swap with Bankers Trust in November of 1993. The swap agreement was far from plain-vanilla. It most certainly fit the description of an exotic derivative. The swap's cash flows were determined by a formula that involved short-term, medium-term, and long-term interest rates. Essentially, the deal would allow Procter & Gamble to reduce its financing rate by four-tenths of 1% on $200 million of debt, if interest rates remained stable until May 1994. If, on the other hand, interest rates spiked upward, or if the spread between 5-year and 30-year rates narrowed, Procter & Gamble would lose money and have to pay a higher rate on its debt.

Even in the rarefied world of derivatives, one cannot expect something for nothing. In order to achieve a cheaper financing rate, Procter & Gamble had to give up or sell something. In this case, implicit in the swap, they sold interest rate insurance. The swap contained an embedded option, sold by Procter & Gamble. If the interest rate environment remained calm, Procter & Gamble would keep a modest premium, thereby lowering its financing costs. If interest rates became turbulent, Procter & Gamble would have to make big payments. Most economists in 1993 were forecasting calm. The bet seemed safe. But it was a bet, nevertheless. This was not a hedge, this was speculation. And they lost.

The Federal Reserve unexpectedly raised interest rates on February 4, 1994. Procter & Gamble suddenly found themselves with a $100 million loss. Rather than lower their financing rate by four-tenths of 1%, they would have to pay an additional 14%!

Rather than lick its wounds and retire from swaps, Procter & Gamble went back for more—with prodding, of course, from Bankers Trust. As losses mounted on the first deal, Procter & Gamble entered a second swap, this one tied to German interest rates. German medium-term interest rates are remarkably stable, and so this bet seemed even safer than the first one. Guess what happened. Another $50 million of losses mounted before Procter & Gamble finally liquidated its positions. Losses totaled $157 million. Procter & Gamble sued Bankers Trust, alleging deception, mispricing, and violation of fiduciary responsibilities. Procter & Gamble claimed that they did not fully understand the risks of the swap agreements, nor how to calculate their value. Bankers Trust settled with Procter & Gamble, just as they settled with Gibson Greeting Cards, Air Products and Chemicals, and other companies that lost money in similar swaps.

Metallgesellschaft

Experts are still divided over what went wrong in the case of Metall-gesellschaft, one of Germany's largest industrial concerns. This much is certain: In 1993, Metallgesellschaft had assets of $10 billion, sales exceeding $16 billion, and equity capital of $50 million. By the end of the year, this industrial giant was nearly bankrupt, having lost $1.3 billion in oil futures.

What makes the Metallgesellschaft case so intriguing, is that the company seemed to be using derivatives for all the right reasons. An American subsidiary of Metallgesellschaft, MG Refining and Marketing (MGRM) had embarked on an ingenious marketing plan. The subsidiary was in the business of selling gasoline and heating oil to distributors and retailers. To promote sales, the company offered contracts that would lock in prices for a period of 10 years. A variety of different contract types was offered, and the contracts had various provisions, deferments, and contingencies built in, but the important feature was a long-term price cap. The contracts were essentially forwards. The forward contracts were very popular and MGRM was quite successful at selling them.

MGRM understood that the forward contracts subjected the company to oil price risk. MGRM now had a short position in oil. If oil prices rose, the company would experience losses, as it would have to buy oil at higher prices and sell it at the lower contracted prices to the customers. To offset this risk, MGRM went long in exchange-traded oil futures. The long position in futures should have hedged the short position in forwards. Unfortunately, things did not work out so nicely.

Oil prices fell in 1993. As oil prices fell, Metallgesellschaft lost money on its long futures, and had to make cash payments as the futures were marked to market. The forwards, however, provided little immediate cash, and their appreciation in value would not be fully realized until they matured in 10 years. Thus, Metallgesellschaft was caught in a cash crunch. Some economists argue that if Metallgesellschaft had held on to its positions and continued to make margin payments the strategy would have worked eventually. But time ran out. The parent company took control over the subsidiary and liquidated its positions, thereby realizing a loss of $1.3 billion.

Other economists argue that Metallgesellschaft was not an innocent victim of unforeseeable circumstances. They argue that MGRM had designed the entire marketing and hedging strategy, just so they could profit by speculating that historical patterns in oil prices would persist. Traditionally, oil futures prices are lower than spot prices, so the general trend in oil futures prices is upward as they near expiration. MGRM's hedging plan was to repeatedly buy short-term oil futures, holding them until just before expiration, at which point they would roll over into new short-term futures. If the historical pattern had repeated itself, MGRM would have profited many times from the rollover strategy. It has been alleged that the futures was the planned source of profits, while the forward contracts with customers was the hedge against oil prices dropping.

Regardless of MGRM management's intent, the case teaches at least two lessons. First, it is important to consider cash flow and timing when constructing a hedge position. Second, when a hedge is working effectively, it will appear to be losing money when the position it is designed to offset is showing profits. Accounting for hedges should not be independent of the position being hedged.

Askin Capital Management

Between February and April 1994, David Askin lost all $600 million that he managed on behalf of the investors in his Granite Hedge Funds. Imagine the surprise of the investors. Not only had they earned over 22% the previous year, but the fund was invested in mortgage-backed securities—instruments guaranteed by the U.S. government not to default. The lesson from the Askin experience, is that in the age of derivatives, investments with innocuous names might not be as safe and secure as they sound.

The particular type of mortgage-backed securities that Askin purchased were *collateralized mortgage obligations* (CMOs), which are bonds whose cash flows to investors are determined by a formula. The formula is a function of mortgage interest rates and also of the prepayment behavior of home buyers. Since the cash flow to CMOs is a function of some other economic variable, interest rates in this case, these instruments are categorized as derivatives. Some CMOs rise in value as interest rates rise, others fall. Askin's CMOs were very sensitive to interest rates. Askin's portfolio rose in value as interest rates fell in 1993. When interest rates began to rise again in February 1994, his portfolio suffered. Interest rate increases alone, however, were not the sole cause of Askin's losses. As interest rates rose and CMO prices fell, CMO investors everywhere got scared and sold. CMO prices were doubly battered as the demand dried up. It was a classic panic. Prices fell far more than the theoretical pricing models predicted. Eventually, calm returned to the market, investors trickled back, and prices rebounded. But it was too late for Askin. He had bought on margin, and his creditors had liquidated his fund at the market's bottom.

Orange County, California

Robert Citron, treasurer of Orange County, California, in 1994, fell into the same trap that snared Procter & Gamble and David Askin. He speculated that interest rates would remain low. The best economic forecasts at the time supported this outlook. Derivatives allowed speculators to bet on the most likely scenario. Small bets provided modest returns. Big bets promised sizable returns. What these speculators did was akin to selling earthquake insurance in New York City. The likelihood of an earthquake there is very small, so insurers would almost certainly get to keep the modest premiums without having to pay out any claims. If an earthquake did hit New York, however, the losses to the insurers would be enormous.

Citron bet and lost. The earthquake that toppled his portfolio was the unexpected interest rate hikes beginning in February 1994. Citron had borrowed against the bonds Orange County owned, and he invested the proceeds in derivative bonds called inverse-floaters, whose cash flow formulas made them extra sensitive to interest rate increases. Citron lost about $2 billion of the $7.7 billion he managed, and Orange County filed for bankruptcy in December 1994.

Union Bank of Switzerland

What happened at Union Bank of Switzerland (UBS) in 1997 would be funny if it weren't so sad. Imagine a bakery that sells cakes and cookies for less than the cost of the ingredients. Business would no doubt be brisk, but eventually the bakers would discover that they were not turning a profit. This is essentially what happened to UBS. UBS manufactured and sold derivatives to corporate customers. Unfortunately, there was an error in their pricing model, and they were selling the derivatives for too low a price. By the time they found the mistake, they had managed to lose over $200 million. Swiss banking officials concluded that losses sustained by the Global Equity Derivatives Business arm of UBS amounted to 625 million Swiss francs (about $428 million), but these losses stemmed not only from the pricing model error, but also from unlucky trading, an unexpected change in British tax laws, and market volatility. Some speculate that these losses forced the merger of UBS with Swiss Bank Corporation, a merger that was arranged exactly when the derivatives losses were discovered.

Long-Term Capital Management

The most surprising of the derivatives debacles is also one of the most recent. It is the saga of Long-Term Capital Management (LTCM). LTCM was a company founded by John Meriwether, and joined by Myron Scholes and Robert Merton. Meriwether had a reputation for being one of the savviest traders on Wall Street. Scholes and Merton are Nobel prize laureates, famous for inventing the Black-Scholes option pricing model.[2] Unlike the folks at Procter & Gamble, these individuals cannot plead ignorance. They were without a doubt among the smartest players in the financial marketplace. Paradoxically, it may have been their intellectual superiority that did them in. Their overconfidence engendered a false sense of security that seduced investors, lenders, and the portfolio managers themselves into taking enormous positions. The story of LTCM is a classic Greek tragedy set on modern Wall Street.

LTCM was organized as a "hedge fund." A hedge fund is a limited partnership, that in exchange for limiting the number and type of investors who can buy in, is not required to register with the Securities and Exchange Commission, and is not bound by the same regulations and reporting standards imposed on traditional mutual funds. Investors must be rich. A hedge fund can accept investments from no more than 500 investors who each have net worth of at least $5 million, or no more than 99 investors if they each have net worth of at least $1 million. A hedge fund is essentially a private investment club, unfettered by the rules designed to protect the general public.

Ironically, hedge funds are generally unhedged. Most hedge funds speculate, aiming to capture profits by taking risks. LTCM was a little different, and for them the moniker "hedge fund" appeared to fit. Capitalizing on their brainpower, LTCM sought to exploit market inefficiencies. That is, with an understanding of what the prices of various financial instruments *should* be, LTCM would identify instruments that were priced too high or too low. Once such an opportunity was identified, they would buy or sell accordingly, hedging long positions with matching shorts. As the prices in the financial marketplace trended toward the fair equilibrium dictated by the financial models, the prices of the assets held long would rise, and the prices of the instruments sold short would fall, thereby delivering to LTCM a handsome profit. LTCM's deals were generally not naked speculation, but hedged exploitation of arbitrage opportunities. With price risk thought to be hedged out, LTCM and their investors felt comfortable borrowing heavily to lever up the impact of the trades on profits. The creditors, banks and brokerages mostly, happily obliged.

LTCM opened its doors in 1994, with an initial equity investment of $150 million from the founding partners, and an investment pool of $1.25 billion in client accounts. Success was immediate and pronounced. They thrived in the tumultuous market of the mid-1990s. Apparently, as some of the institutions described above lost fortunes during this period, it was LTCM that managed to be on the receiving end. The fund booked a 28% return in 1994, a whopping 59% in 1995, followed by another 57% return in 1996. Word of this success spread, and new investors were clamoring to get into LTCM.[3]

LTCM could be picky when it came to choosing investors. This was not a fund for your typical dentist or millionaire next door. Former students of mine who have gone on to jobs at some of the world's largest banks and investment companies have confided to me that their firms subcontracted sizable portions of their portfolios to LTCM. By the end of 1995, bolstered by reinvested profits and by newly invested funds, LTCM managed $3.6 billion of invested funds. However, the portfolio was levered 28 to 1. For every $1 a client invested, the fund was able to borrow $28 from banks and brokerage houses. Consequently, LTCM managed positions worth over $100 billion. Moreover, because of the natural leverage inherent in the derivatives they bought, these positions were comparable to investments of a much larger magnitude, estimated to be in the $650 billion range.

By 1997, however, when the fund's capital base peaked at $7 billion, managers realized that profitable arbitrage opportunities were growing scarce. The easy pickings of the early days were over. The partners began to intentionally shrink the fund by returning money to investors, essentially forcing them out. Performance was sound in 1997, a 25% return, but with the payout of capital, the fund's capital base fell to $4.7 billion.

Things unraveled disastrously in 1998. Each of LTCM's major investment strategies failed. Based on sophisticated models and historical data, LTCM gambled that (1) stock market volatility would stay the same or fall, (2) swap spreads—a variable used to determine who pays whom how much in interest rate swaps, would narrow, (3) the spread of the interest rate on medium-term bonds over long-term bonds would flatten out, (4) the credit spread—the interest rate differential between risky bonds and high-grade bonds, would narrow, and (5) calm would return to the financial markets of Russia and other emerging markets. However, in each case the opposite happened. Equity volatility increased. Swap spreads widened. The yield curve retained its hump. Credit spreads grew. Emerging markets deteriorated.

Though LTCM had spread its bets over a wide variety of positions, they seemed to gain no diversification benefit. Everything went wrong at once. Recent research has shown that diversification does not protect speculative positions when markets behave erratically. Markets tend to go awry in tandem.

In August 1998 alone, the fund suffered losses of $1.9 billion. Losses for the year so far were 52%. Fund managers were confident that their strategies were sound, and that time would both prove them right and reward their prescience. But time is not a friend to a levered fund losing money. Banks and brokerages itched for their loans back. How ironic, Long-Term Capital Management faced a short-term liquidity crunch.

Leverage amplified LTCM's remaining $2.28 billion of equity into managed assets of $125 billion. If the market continued to move against them, LTCM would be wiped out in short order, and that is essentially what happened. On September 10, LTCM lost $145 million. The next day, they lost $120 million. The following three trading days brought losses of $55 million, $87 million, and $122 million, respectively. On one day alone, Monday, September 21, 1998, LTCM lost $553 million. By now traders at other firms could guess what LTCM's positions were, and by anticipating what LTCM would have to eventually sell, they could gauge which securities were good bets to short. This selling pressure added to LTCM's losses and woes.

At this point, in September 1998, any of several banks could bankrupt LTCM by calling in its loans. The Federal Reserve, which is the central bank of the United States, and is responsible for guarantying the stability of the American banking system, monitored the predicament. Though LTCM's equity was shrinking precipitously, on account of their borrowed funds and the inherent leverage of their derivatives positions, the notional principal of their positions was about $1.4 trillion. To put this quantity into perspective, the gross national product of the United States was about $8.8 trillion in 1998. Total bank assets in the United States stood at $4.3 trillion. It was feared that if LTCM went bankrupt, they would probably default on their derivative positions, triggering a domino effect of defaults and bankruptcies throughout the world's financial markets. It was decided, that LTCM was too big too fail.

The Federal Reserve orchestrated a plan for LTCM's creditors to buy the company's portfolio. Each of 14 banks ponied up money in exchange for a slice of the portfolio. The $3.65 billion paid by the bank syndicate for the portfolio was clearly greater than the value of the portfolio by then, but this infusion of capital prevented defaults that would have cost the banks much more. The money was used to pay off debts and shore up the trading accounts so that existing positions would perform without default. Very little was left over for the original partners who were required to run the fund until it was ultimately liquidated in 1999. The bottom line is that LTCM had lost $4.5 billion since the start of 1998. These losses included the personal fortunes amassed so quickly by the founding partners, which totaled $1.9 billion at one point but were completely wiped out by the end.

Moral of the Story

The lesson from these case studies should now be obvious. Risk management is not the art of picking good bets. Bets no matter how good are speculation. Speculation increases risk, and subjects corporations, investors, and even municipalities to potential losses. Derivatives are powerful tools to shed risk, but they can also be used to take on risk. The root causes of the debacles described in these cases are greed, speculation, and in some cases incompetence, not derivatives. But just as derivatives facilitate risk management, they facilitate greed and speculation. Anything that can be done with derivatives, can be done slower the old fashioned way with positions in traditional financial instruments. Speculators have always managed to lose large sums. With the aid of derivatives they now can lose larger sums faster.

Superior intellect and sophistication cannot protect the speculator. As the Long-Term Capital Management story illustrates, when you are smarter than the market, you can go broke waiting for the market to wise up.

Government regulation is not the answer either. The benefits of regulation must be weighed against the costs. Derivatives, properly used, are too important in the modern financial marketplace to be severely restricted. Abuse by a few does not warrant constraints on all users. A better solution to prevent repetition of the past debacles is full information disclosure by firms, portfolio managers, and municipalities. Investors and citizens should demand to know how derivatives are being used when their money is at stake. Better information and oversight is the most promising approach to prevent misuse of derivatives while retaining the benefits.

Derivatives can be dangerous, but they can also be tremendously useful. Dynamite is an appropriate analogy. Misused, it is destructive; handled with care, it is a powerful and constructive tool.

Derivatives are tools that facilitate the transfer of risk. Interest rate derivatives enable managers to shed business exposure to interest rate fluctuations, for example. But when one party sheds risk, another party necessarily must take on that very exposure. And therein lies the danger of derivatives. The same instrument that serves as a hedge to one firm, might be a destabilizing speculative instrument to another. Without a proper understanding of derivatives, a manager who intends to reduce risk, might inadvertently increase it. This chapter aims to provide the reader with a basic understanding of derivatives so that they can be used appropriately to manage financial risks. This understanding should help the reader avoid the common pitfalls that have proved disastrous to less informed managers.

SIZE OF THE DERIVATIVE MARKET
AND WIDESPREAD USE

A derivative is a financial instrument whose value or contingent cash flows depend on the value of some other underlying asset. For example, the value of a stock option depends on the value of the underlying stock. Derivatives as a class comprise forwards, futures, options, and swaps. Numerous hybrid instruments, combining the features of these basic building blocks have also been engineered. The first thing the interested manager must understand about derivatives is that the business in these instruments is now huge, and their use is pervasive. Since the initiation of trading in the first stock index futures contract in December of 1982—the Standard & Poor's 500 futures contract—the daily volume of stock index futures has grown so that it now rivals the daily volume in all trading on the New York Stock Exchange. (Volume of futures is measured in terms of *notional principal*, which is a measure of exposure.) On just one typical day in the 1990s, Tuesday, January 21, 1996, the notional volume of the Standard & Poor's 500 futures contract was just shy of $40 billion. The volume on the NYSE that same day was approximately $23 billion. On that day, therefore, just one specific futures contract was greater than the entire Big Board stock market in terms of trading volume. More recently, however, the tables have turned, and the New York Stock Exchange daily trading volume once again regularly beats that of the S&P 500 futures contract. Still the magnitudes are comparable, and futures trading is firmly established as a significant segment of financial market activity.

Similarly, the swaps market has revolutionized banking and finance. The notional principal of outstanding swaps today, is greater than the sum total of all assets in banks worldwide. The Bank for International Settlements reports that the sum total of all assets in banks around the world was approximately $12 trillion in June 2000. At that same time, according to the same source, the notional principal of outstanding swaps was over $50 trillion. Measured this way, the swaps business is now bigger than traditional banking.

The volume of the derivatives market reflects how widespread derivatives use has become in business. Almost all major corporations now use them in one form or another. Some use derivatives to hedge commodity price risks. Some use them to speculate on price movements. Some firms reduce their exposures to volatile interest rates and foreign exchange. Other firms take on exposures via derivatives in order to potentially increase profits. Some firms use derivatives to secure cheaper financing. Many corporations use derivatives to reduce the transaction costs associated with managing a pension fund, borrowing money, or budgeting cash. Some firms implement derivative strategies to reduce their tax burdens. Many companies offer stock options, a derivative, as employee compensation. Some investment funds enhance returns by replacing traditional portfolios with what are called synthetic portfolios—portfolios composed in part of derivatives. Some investment funds buy derivatives that act as insurance contracts, protecting portfolio value. Since their emergence in the early 1980s, derivatives have touched every aspect of corporate finance, banking, the investments industry, and arguably business in general.

THE INSTRUMENTS

The major derivative instruments are forwards, futures, options, and swaps. Also available today are hybrid instruments, exotics, and structured or engineered instruments. The hybrids, exotics, and engineered instruments are contracts that combine features of the basic building blocks: the options, futures, forwards, and swaps. Consequently, familiarity with the basic building blocks goes a long way toward understanding the whole mélange of derivative instruments available today. We will begin with forwards.

Forwards

Imagine the following nearly idyllic scenario. It is late summer. You are a wheat farmer in Kansas. The hard work of sowing and tending your acreage is about to pay off. You expect a bumper crop this year, and the harvest is just a few weeks away. The weather is expected to remain favorable. The crops have been sprayed to protect them from pests. In fact, you may even have purchased crop insurance to protect against crop damage.

Still, you cannot relax. One major uncertainty is keeping you awake at night. You figure that if you are expecting a bumper crop, the likelihood that your neighbors are also expecting a bumper crop is high. If the market is flooded with wheat, prices will plummet. If prices drop, you will receive little revenue for your harvest, and perhaps you will show a loss for the year. A worse case scenario might be that prices fall so low, that you cannot make the mortgage payments on your land or the machinery you bought. You very well might lose the farm—and through no fault of your own. You farmed well, but if prices fall, you will fail nevertheless.

Meanwhile, at the same time, another group of businesspeople is feeling similar anxiety. A baked goods company has recently built a new cookie bakery. The company identified its market niche as a provider of inexpensive, mass produced, medium quality cookies. The project analysis that led to the go-ahead for the new bakery assumed that wheat prices would stay fixed at their current levels. If wheat prices should rise, it is altogether possible that the firm will not be able to sell its cookies for a profit. The new bakery will appear to be a failure.

In these scenarios, both the farmers and the bakers are exposed to wheat price risk. The farmers worry that wheat prices will fall. The bakers worry that prices will rise. A forward contract is the obvious solution for both parties.

The farmers and bakers can negotiate a deferred wheat transaction. The farmers will deliver wheat to the bakers, one month from now, for a price currently agreed upon. Such a contract for a deferred transaction is a forward contract. A forward contract specifies an underlying asset to be delivered, a price to be paid, and the date of delivery. The specified transaction price is called the forward price. The party that will be selling wheat (the farmer) is known as the "short" party; the party that will be buying wheat (the baker) is known as the "long" party. In the jargon of the derivatives market, the long party is said to "buy" the forward, and the short party "sells" the forward. Note, however, that when the deal is initially struck, no money changes hands and no one has yet bought or sold anything. The "buyer" and "seller" have agreed to a deferred transaction.

Notice that the wheat forward reduces risk for both the farmers and the bakers. In this transaction, both parties are hedgers—that is, they are using the forward to reduce risk. Forward contracts are "over-the-counter" instruments, meaning that they are negotiated between two parties and custom-tailored, rather than traded on exchanges.

Suppose after one month, when the forward expires and the wheat is delivered, the current, or spot, price of wheat has risen dramatically. The farmer may have some regret that he entered into the contract. Had he not sold forward, he would have been able to receive more for his wheat by selling on the spot market. He may feel like a loser. The bakers, on the other hand, will feel like winners. By contracting forward they insulated themselves from the rising wheat price. When spot prices rise, the long party wins while the short party loses. A little reflection, however, will convince the farmer that although he lost some money relative to what he could have gotten on the spot market, going short in the forward was indeed a worthwhile strategy. He had piece of mind over the one month. He was guaranteed a fair price, and he did not have to fear losing the farm. Though there was an opportunity loss, he benefited by shedding risk. The farmer probably never regrets that he has never collected on his life insurance either. He similarly should not regret that the forward contract represents an opportunity loss. He would be well advised to go short again next year.

The wheat forward contract can be used by speculators as well as hedgers. An agent who anticipates a rise in wheat prices can profit from that foresight by going long in the forward contract. By going long in the contract, the speculator agrees to buy wheat at the fixed forward price. Upon expiration of the contract, the speculator takes delivery of the wheat, pays the forward price, and then sells the wheat on the spot market for the higher spot price. The profit is the difference between the spot and forward prices. Of course, if the speculator's forecast is wrong, and the wheat price falls, the speculator would suffer losses equal to the difference between the forward and spot price. For example, suppose the initial spot price is $3 per bushel, and the forward price is $3.50 per bushel. If the spot price upon expiration is $4.50 per bushel, the long speculator would earn a profit of $1 per bushel. The profit is the terminal spot of $4.50 minus the $3.50 initial forward price. If, alternatively, the terminal spot price is $3.25, the speculator would *lose* 25 cents per bushel—that is, $3.25 minus $3.50. Notice that the $3 initial spot price is irrelevant in both cases.

Speculators play important roles in the derivatives markets. For one, speculators provide liquidity. If farmers wish to short forward contracts but there are no bakers around who want to go long, speculators will step in and offer to take the long side when the forward price is bid down low enough. Similarly, they will take the short side when the forward price is bid up high enough. Speculators also bring information to the marketplace. The existence of derivatives contracts and the promise of speculative profits make it worthwhile for speculators to devote resources to forecasting weather conditions, crop yields, and other factors that impact prices. Their forecasts are made known to the public as they buy or sell futures and forwards.

Futures

Futures contracts are closely related to forward contracts. Like forwards, futures are contracts that spell out deferred transactions. The long party commits to buying some underlying asset, and the short party commits to sell. The differences between futures and forwards are mainly technical and logistical. Forward contracts are custom-tailored, over-the-counter agreements, struck between two parties via negotiation. *Futures,* alternatively, are standardized contracts that are traded on exchanges, between parties who probably do not know each other. The exact quantity, quality, and delivery location can be negotiated in a forward contract, but in a futures contract the terms are dictated by the exchange. Because of their standardization and how they are traded, futures are very liquid, and their associated transaction costs are very low.

Another feature differentiating futures from forwards is the process of marking-to-market. All day and every day, futures traders meet in trading pits at the exchanges and cry out orders to buy and sell futures on behalf of clients. The forces of supply and demand determine whether futures prices rise or fall. Marking-to-market is the process by which at the end of each day, losers pay winners an amount equal to the movement of the futures price that day. For example, if the wheat futures price at Monday's close is $4.00 per bushel, and the price rises to $4.10 by the close on Tuesday, the short party must pay the long party 10 cents per bushel after trading ends on Tuesday. If the price had fallen 10 cents, then long would pay short 10 cents per bushel. Both long and short parties have trading accounts at the exchange clearinghouse, and the transfer of funds is automatic. The purpose of marking-to-market is to reduce the chance of default by a party who has lost substantially on a futures position. When futures are marked-to-market, the greatest possible loss due to a default would be an amount equal to one day's price movement.

Futures are marked-to-market every day. When the contract expires, the last marking-to-market is based on the spot price. For example, suppose two days prior to expiration the futures price is $4.10 per bushel. On the second to last day the futures price has risen to $4.30. Short pays long 20 cents per bushel. Suppose at the end of the next day, the last day of trading, the spot price is recorded at $4.55. The last mark-to-market payment is from short to long for 25 cents per bushel, equal to the difference between the spot price upon expiration and the previous day's futures price.

Upon expiration, the futures contract might stipulate that the short party now deliver to the long party the specified quantity of wheat. The long party must now pay the short party the *spot price* for this wheat. Yes, the spot price, not the original futures price! The difference between the terminal spot price and the original futures price has already been paid via marking-to-market. A numerical example will make the mechanics of futures clearer, and show how similar futures are to forwards.

Suppose with five days remaining until expiration, the wheat futures price is $4.00 per bushel. A baker "buys" a futures contract in order to lock in a purchase price of $4.00. Suppose the futures prices on the next four days are $4.10, $3.90, $4.00, and $4.25. The spot price on the fifth day, the expiration day, is $4.30. Given those price movements, short pays the long baker 10 cents the first day. The long baker pays short 20 cents on the second day. On the third day, short pays long 10 cents, followed by a payment from short to long of 25 cents on the fourth day, and a payment from short to long of 5 cents on the last day. On net, over those five days, short has paid long 30 cents. When long now pays the spot price of $4.30 to short for delivery of the wheat, long indeed is paying $4.00 per bushel, net of the 30 cents profit on the futures contract. Recall that $4.00 was the original futures price. Thus, the futures contract did effectively lock in a fixed purchase price for the wheat.

A contract that stipulates a spot transaction in which the underlying commodity is actually delivered at expiration, is called a "physical delivery" contract. Many futures contracts do not stipulate such a final spot transaction with actual delivery of the underlying asset. After the last marking-to-market, the game is over. No assets are delivered. Contracts that stipulate no terminal spot transaction are called "cash settled." It should make little difference to traders whether a contract is cash settled or physical delivery. A cash settled contract can be turned into a physical delivery deal simply by choosing to make a spot transaction at the end. Likewise, a physical delivery contract can be turned into a cash settled deal by either making an offsetting spot transaction at the end, or by exiting the futures contract just before it expires.

Examples of the Use of Forwards and Futures in Risk Management

A wide variety of underlying assets is covered by futures and forwards contracts these days. For example, exchange-traded futures contracts are available on stocks, bonds, interest rates, foreign currencies, oil, gasoline, grains, livestock, metals, cocoa, coffee, sugar, and even orange juice. Consequently, these instruments are versatile risk management tools in a wide variety of situations. The most actively traded futures, however, are those that cover financial risks. Consider the following examples.

A Foreign Currency Hedge

Suppose an American electronics manufacturer has just delivered a large shipment of finished products to a customer in France. The French buyer has agreed to pay 1 million French francs in exactly 30 days. The manufacturer is worried that the French franc may be devalued relative to the American dollar during that interval. If the franc is devalued, the dollar value of the promised payment will fall and the American manufacturer will suffer losses. The American manufacturer can shed this foreign currency exposure by going short in a franc forward contract or a franc future. The contract will specify a quantity of francs to be exchanged for dollars, at a fixed exchange rate, 30 days in the future. The contract locks in the terms at which the deferred franc revenue can be converted to dollars. No matter what happens to the franc-dollar exchange rate, the American manufacturer now knows exactly how many dollars he will receive.

A Short-Term Interest Rate Hedge

Suppose a manufacturer of automotive parts has just delivered a shipment of finished products to a client. Business has been growing, and the company has approved plans to expand capacity next year. The manufacturer expects to receive payment from the customer in 60 days, but will need to use those funds for the planned capital expenditure 90 days after that. The plan is to invest the revenue in three-month Treasury bills as soon as the revenue is received. Interest rates are currently high. Managers worry that by the time the receivables are collected from the customer, however, interest rates will fall, resulting in less interest earned on the invested funds. The company can hedge against this risk by buying a Treasury bill futures contract, which essentially locks in the price and yield of Treasury bills to be purchased 60 days hence.

Longer-Term Interest Rate Hedge

A manufacturer of speed boats notices that when interest rates rise, sales fall, and the value of the firm's stock gets battered. The correlation is easy to understand. Customers buy boats on credit, and so when rates rise, the boats effectively become more expensive to buy. In order to insulate the company's fortunes from the vicissitudes of interest rates, the company could enter a contract that pays money when rates rise. A short position in a Treasury bond futures contract would pay off when rates rise and could thus be a desirable hedge. Each time the futures contract expires, the company can roll over into a new contract. The size of the position in the futures should be geared to the fluctuation in sales resulting from changes in interest rates. The Treasury bond hedge can reduce the volatility in the firm's net income, and the volatility of the firm's equity value.

Synthetic Cash

A company's pension fund is invested primarily in the stocks of the Standard & Poor's 500. The pension fund manager worries that there may be a downturn in the stock market sometime over the next six months. She considers selling all of the stock and investing the funds in Treasury bills. An alternate hedge strategy that will save considerable transaction costs would be to short S&P 500 futures contracts. By establishing a short futures position, she locks in the price at which the stocks will be sold six months hence. The fund is now insulated from any fluctuations in stock prices. Since the fund is now essentially risk free, it will earn the risk-free interest rate. Selling futures while holding the underlying spot instrument is a strategy known as "synthetic cash." The strategy essentially turns stock into cash. The fund performs as if it were invested in Treasury bills.

Synthetic Stock

A company's pension fund is invested primarily in Treasury bills. The stock market has been rising rapidly in recent weeks, and the pension fund manager wishes to participate in the boom. One strategy would be to sell the T-bills and invest the proceeds in equities. A more economical strategy would be to leave the value parked in T-bills, and gain exposure to the stock market by going long in stock futures. When the market rises, the futures will pay off. Should the market fall, the fund will suffer losses. The fund will thus behave as if it were invested in stocks. Ergo the name, "synthetic stock."

Market Timing

A manager wishes to be exposed to the stock market when he anticipates a market rise, and be out of stocks and into T-bills when he anticipates a drop. Buying and selling stocks to achieve this purpose is very expensive in terms of commissions. But entering and exiting the market via futures is very cheap. The manager should keep all his funds invested in T-bills. When he feels the market will rise, he should go long in stock index futures, such as S&P 500 futures. When he feels the market will drop, he should sell those futures, unwinding the position. If alternatively he wished to assemble a diversified portfolio such as the S&P 500 the old fashion way—a portfolio consisting of actual stocks and no derivatives—he would have to buy each of the 500 stock issues while selling his Treasury bills. This positioning would involve 501 separate transactions. Turning the actual stock portfolio back into T-bills would similarly require 501 transactions. Turning T-bills effectively into stocks via long futures contracts, on the other hand, involves just one futures trade. Unwinding the futures position would also be just one single trade. Market timing is much more economically executed with futures contracts than with actual equity trades.

A Cross-Hedge

A manufacturer of plastic water pistols wishes to hedge against increases in raw plastic pellet prices. Unfortunately, there are no futures contracts covering plastic prices. There is, however, a contract on oil prices, and the price of plastic is highly correlated with the price of oil. By going long in an oil contract, the manufacturer will be paid money when oil prices rise, which will likely be also when plastic prices rise. Hedging an exposure with a contract tied to a correlated underlying instrument is called a cross-hedge.

A Common Pitfall

The ease with which futures facilitate hedging sometimes coaxes managers to occasionally take speculative positions. A photographic film manufacturer, for example, might become experienced and comfortable hedging silver prices by going long in silver futures. Managers at the firm might come to believe that no one is better able to forecast silver prices than they are. A time may come when they wholeheartedly believe that silver prices will fall. Not only might they choose not to enter a long silver future hedge at this time, but they may choose to go short in silver futures so as to capitalize on the falling price. If silver prices fall they will not only benefit from a cheaper raw input, but the short silver futures will pay off as well. The danger here is that the manufacturer has lost sight of the fact that it is in the film manufacturing business, and not the business of speculating on commodity prices. Although silver prices might be expected to fall, there is always the possibility that they will rise instead. The probability of a rise might be small, but the consequences would be catastrophic. Not only will the firm's raw material price rise, but the firm will suffer additionally as it loses on the futures contract. The lesson here is that firms should stay clearly focused on what their business line is, and what role the use of futures plays in their business. Futures use should generally be authorized only for hedging and not for speculation. Auditing systems should be in place to oversee that futures are used appropriately.

Futures and Forwards Summary

As the above examples illustrate, futures and forwards are useful tools for hedging a wide variety of business and financial risks. Futures and forward contracts essentially commit the two parties to a deferred transaction. No money changes hands initially. As prices subsequently change, however, one party wins at the other's expense. Futures and forwards thus enable businesses to shed or take on exposure to changing prices. When used to offset an exposure the firm faces naturally, futures and forwards reduce risk.

Options

Options are another breed of derivatives. They share some similarities with futures and forwards, but they also differ in many important respects. Like futures and forwards, option prices are a function of the value of an underlying asset, thus they satisfy the definition of derivative. Unlike futures and forwards, however, options are assets that must be paid for initially. Recall that no money changes hands initially as parties enter into forwards and futures. Options, though, are an asset that has to be bought for a price at the outset.

There are two kinds of options, call and puts. A call option is an asset that gives the owner the right but not the obligation to buy some other underlying asset, for a set price, on or up to a set date. For example, consider a call option on Disney stock, that gives the owner the right to purchase one share of Disney stock for $70 per share, on or up to next June 15. (Actually, options are usually sold in blocks covering 100 shares. For expository purposes, however, we will describe an option on only one single share.) The underlying asset would be one share of Disney stock. The prespecified price, known as the "strike price," would be $70 per share. The expiration date would be June 15. The Disney option might cost $3 initially.

If on the expiration date, June 15, the market price of Disney stock stood at $75, the call option owner would exercise the option, allowing him to buy a share of Disney stock for $70. He could then turn around and sell the share for $75 in the marketplace, realizing a terminal payoff from the option of $5. The terminal payoff is $5, so the profit net of the $3 initial option price is $2.

Suppose, alternatively, that the market price of Disney stock on June 15 were $69. It would not be profitable to exercise the call option and thereby purchase for $70 what is elsewhere available for $69. In such a case, the option owner would choose not to exercise, and the call would expire worthless. It is the right not to execute the transaction that is the major difference between options and forwards. The long party in a forward contract must buy the goods upon expiration whether it is advantageous to do so or not. By contrast, a call option owner does not have to buy the underlying asset if he chooses not to. At expiration, a call option should be exercised if and only if the market price exceeds the strike price. When the market price is above the strike price, the call option is said to be "in the money." When the market price is less than the strike price, the call is "out of the money." When the market price equals the strike price, the option is "at the money." An option that is out of the money, or even at the money, at expiration, will expire unexercised and worthless.

An option's payoff is defined as the maximum amount of money the option owner would receive at expiration, if she totally liquidated her position. If the option expires out of the money, the payoff is zero. If the option expires in the money, the payoff is the amount of money received from exercising the call option, and then selling the stock in the open market. For example, if the strike price is $70 and the terminal stock price is $60, the payoff would be zero, since the option would be out of the money and should not be exercised. If the terminal stock price were $80, the payoff would be $10, since the option should be exercised, allowing the owner to buy the stock for $70, and then sell that stock for $80 in the open market. Mathematically, the payoff is the maximum of zero or the stock price minus the strike price.

The payoff ignores the initial price that was paid for the option. Payoff treats the initial price as a sunk cost, and measures only what the option owner might subsequently receive. The payoff minus the initial price is known as the option profit. The option payoff is the same for all owners of the option, regardless of what they each initially paid for it. Profit, however, depends on what was initially paid and therefore differs from one investor to another.

A payoff diagram is a valuable analytical device for understanding options. A payoff diagram graphs the payoff of an option as a function of the underlying asset's spot price at expiration. Exhibit 13.1 depicts the payoff diagram for the Disney call option with a strike price of $70. The payoff diagram is a picture of the option. It tells you when you will receive money and when you will not. It helps to visualize how the contract will perform, and whether or not the option is appropriate for any particular application.

The payoff diagram is flat and equal to zero in the entire range where the option is out of the money—that is, where the stock price is less than the strike price. This means that someone who buys an option might lose his entire investment in that option. You may pay $3 for the option, and lose 100% of that $3 by the expiration date. On the brighter side, the payoff diagram confirms that the most you can lose in an option is the initial premium, the $3 you paid for it. Unlike, futures or forwards, you will never be called on to make additional payments at a later date. Initially, you pay for the option, perhaps $3. From then on you can only receive cash inflows.

Note that the payoff diagram begins to rise at the point where the stock price equals the strike price. The payoff is dollar for dollar greater than zero for every dollar that the stock price exceeds the strike price. Thus we see that a call option rises in value as the underlying asset rises in price. For this reason, some people refer to call options as "bullish" instruments.

EXHIBIT 13.1   Call option payoff diagram.

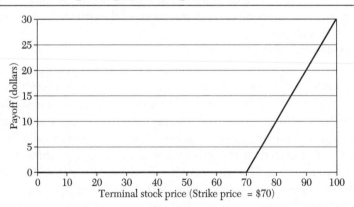

Hedging with a Call Option

Consider the trucking company whose rates are regulated yet costs fluctuate with market prices. The chief raw material purchased by the company is diesel fuel. If fuel prices rise, the trucking company will suffer losses, and may in fact be put out of business. As we saw above, the company can guarantee a fixed price for fuel by going long in a future or forward. Another strategy would be to buy a diesel fuel call option contract. The strike price of the call option would lock in the *highest* price that the company will have to pay for fuel. If fuel prices should drop below the strike price, the company would be under no obligation to exercise the option. It would simply buy fuel at the low market price. If, however, fuel prices rise above the strike price, the company would exercise the option and buy fuel at the relatively low strike price.

The added flexibility of the option over the futures strategy comes at a cost. When the company buys the call option it must pay a price or "premium." The call option is essentially an oil price insurance contract for the firm, insuring that fuel prices will not exceed the strike price. If fuel prices remain low, below the strike price, the company will not collect on this insurance policy, and the initial premiums will be lost.

Pricing Options

At this point the reader may wonder how the initial price of an option is determined. Option pricing is no trivial exercise, and a thorough treatment of option pricing is beyond the scope of this chapter. Some basic principles, however, can be explained here. First, an option's "intrinsic value" prior to expiration is equal to its payoff. That is, if an option is out of the money, its intrinsic value is zero. If a call option is in the money, for example, if the strike price is $70 and the current stock price is $80, then the intrinsic value equals the stock price minus the strike price, $10.

The value of an option, however, exceeds its intrinsic value. An out-of-the-money option is worth more than zero, and the in-the-money option described above is worth more than $10. This extra value is due to the fact that the downside losses are capped off, but the upside potential is unlimited. As long as there is still time remaining in the option's life, it is possible that an out-of-the-money option can go in-the-money. An in-the-money option can go further in the money, and has more upside potential than downside.

A call option's value is a function of the underlying stock price, the strike price, the amount of time remaining to expiration, the interest rate, the stock's dividend rate, and the volatility of the underlying asset price. As the underlying stock price rises, so will the call option's value. Holding the other variables constant, a call option's value will be greater when there is a higher stock price, lower strike price, longer time to expiration, higher interest rate, lower dividend rate, and more volatility in the underlying asset. Researchers have succeeded in formalizing an equation that prices options as a function of these input variables. The formula is known as the Black-Scholes option pricing formula. It is widely available on programmed computer software and in many option theory textbooks.

A Written Call Option

In the case of life insurance or automobile insurance, when the insured party collects another party must pay. It is a zero sum game. So it is with options. The party that sells the option is liable for the future payoff. "Writing" an option, and "shorting" an option are synonymous with selling an option. The payoff diagram for a written call option position is the mirror image of the long or bought call option position. As shown in Exhibit 13.2, the x-axis is the reflecting surface.

Note that once the call option writer has received the initial premium, all subsequent cash flows will be outflows. The best the writer can hope for is that the call will expire out of the money. Note that the potential liability of the written option position is unlimited. Notice as well, that the amount of money the buyer of the option might receive at expiration is the exact amount that writer will have to pay. Thus, when the media report that a particular company has lost millions of dollars in options, the reader should realize that this means some other party has made millions. The newspapers tend to focus on the losers.

Strategies Using Written Call Options

Why would anybody wish to sell a call option if doing so subjects them to the possibility of unlimited future liabilities? One answer is that speculators sometimes deem the risks worthwhile in light of the expected reward. They may be confident that the underlying asset price will not rise and the option will expire worthless.

EXHIBIT 13.2   Payoff diagram for a written call option position.

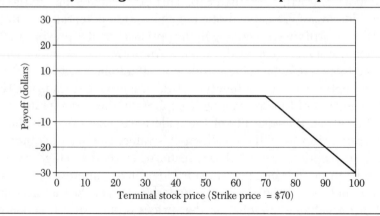

Written call options can also be used to hedge in certain circumstances. Consider oil exporting nations such as Mexico and Venezuela. When oil prices are low they are hungry for funds, funds that are much needed for national development projects. When oil prices are high, they have plenty of excess revenue. A reasonable strategy would be to sell high strike price oil call options when oil prices are low. The country thus receives premiums when funds are most needed, and incurs a liability that only needs to be paid when funds are most plentiful. The oil call options help to smooth the flow of funds into the country. Abken and Feinstein (1994) elaborate on the use of written call options in such a setting.

Warrants

Warrants are call options that are sold by the company whose stock is the underlying asset. If Microsoft pays its executive with Microsoft call options, those options will be called warrants. When the warrants are exercised, the total outstanding supply of Microsoft stock will rise. Warrants are valuable, even if they are not yet in the money. Clearly they must be worth something, otherwise executives would not want them and would give them away! Offering warrants as compensation to executives is not free for the firm's shareholders. Stories abound nowadays of young Internet executives who became fabulously wealthy when they exercised warrants paid to them as part of their employment compensation.

Put Options

The second type of option is a put. A put option is a contract that gives the owner the right but not the obligation to *sell* some underlying asset for a pre-specified price, on or up to a given date. Consider a put option on Microsoft stock. Suppose the strike price is $100 and the expiration date is December 15th. The put option owner has the right, but not the obligation to sell a share of Microsoft stock for $100, on or up to December 15. If the market price of Microsoft is above $100, for example $120, the put option owner would not exercise. Why should he force someone to pay $100 for the stock? He can make more money by selling the stock in the open market. Thus, a put option is out of the money if the stock price is *above* the strike price. If the stock price is below the strike price, however, then the put option is in the money. If the market price of Microsoft is $80 on December 15, the owner of the put can reap a $20 payoff. To realize this payoff, he would buy the Microsoft stock in the marketplace for $80, and then turn around and sell it for $100 by exercising his put option. Thus, a put option is in the money when the stock price is below the strike price. A put option's payoff at expiration, and its intrinsic value prior to expiration, is the strike price minus the stock price, or zero, whichever is greater.

Exhibit 13.3 presents the payoff diagram for a put option. Should the stock price fall to zero, the put option's payoff would be equal to the strike

EXHIBIT 13.3   Put option payoff diagram.

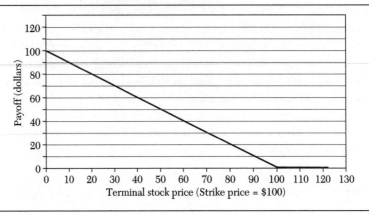

price. At that point the put option owner would have the right to sell a worthless stock for $100. From that point, the put option payoff falls one dollar for each dollar that the stock price rises. The payoff reaches zero when the stock price equals the strike price, and then remains at zero no matter how much higher the stock price goes. As is the case with call options, the put option cannot fall in value below zero. Once the put option premium is paid, the owner is never called upon to make another payment. Any subsequent cash flow is positive. It is altogether possible, however, for the buyer of the put option to lose the entire premium, so one should not think that buying a put option is a safe investment.

Notice that the put option payoff rises as the stock price falls. For this reason, puts are thought of as "bearish" instruments—instruments that are more profitable the more the underlying asset falls in value. Because of this negative relationship with the underlying asset, puts can be good hedging instruments for someone who owns the underlying asset.

Like the call option's payoff diagram, the put's payoff diagram is kinked—that is, there is an elbow at the strike price. A kinked payoff diagram is the hallmark of an option. If a payoff diagram has no kink, then the instrument depicted is not an option.

The payoff diagram for a written put option position is the mirror image of the put's payoff diagram. Such a payoff diagram is shown in Exhibit 13.4. The possible payoff reaped by the buyer of the put option is exactly equal to the possible outflow paid by the writer. Put options too are a zero-sum game. Notice that whereas the writer of a call option has unlimited potential liability, the writer of a put option has a potential liability limited to the strike price. Furthermore, notice that a long put option payoff looks nothing like a short call option. Similarly, notice that a long call option payoff is not the same as a short put. Both long puts and short calls are bearish positions, just as both short puts and long calls are bullish positions, but each of these four positions is unique in the direction, size, and timing of cash flows. Long calls and long puts

EXHIBIT 13.4   Payoff diagram for a written put option position.

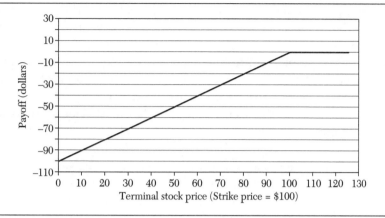

have to be paid for up front, and then receive a subsequent positive payoff depending on what happens to the underlying stock. Short calls and short puts receive all of their cash inflows up front and then become potential liabilities.

A Protective Put Strategy

A put option can be thought of as price insurance for someone who owns the underlying asset. For example, suppose you are a pension fund manager, and you hold hundreds of shares of Microsoft stock. You hold the stock because you believe the stock will rise in value. You worry, however, that the stock price can fall, and losses will be so great that the fund will be unable to meet the needs of the retirees. An effective hedging strategy would be to buy Microsoft put options. You would choose the strike price to be at a level that would guarantee the solvency of the fund. If Microsoft stock falls below the strike price of the put options, the put options will pay off the difference between the new lower market price and the strike price. If Microsoft stock rises, the put options would expire out of the money. The insurance would not pay off, but you would reap the high return of the rising stock. This strategy is known as buying a protective put. It is essentially portfolio insurance. The strategy allows for the upside appreciation of the portfolio, yet sets a floor below which the value of the portfolio cannot fall.

A protective put strategy can also be implemented by a producer who faces the risk of his product's price falling. For example, a cattle rancher can buy put options on cattle, thereby fixing the lowest price at which he will be able to sell his herd.

Swaps

The third category of derivative we will examine is swaps. A swap is an agreement between two parties to exchange cash flows over a period of time. The size and direction of the cash flows are determined by an agreed upon formula spelled out in the swap agreement—a formula that is contingent on the performance of other underlying instruments. Due to this contingency on other underlying assets, swaps are considered derivatives.

One easy type of swap to understand is the equity swap. Suppose Back Bay Investment Management owns a large block of Standard & Poor's 500 stocks. Suppose another firm, Capital Bank owns a large block of NASDAQ stocks. Back Bay would like to diversify into NASDAQ stocks, and simultaneously Capital Bank would like to diversify into S&P 500 stocks. The old fashion way of achieving the desired objectives would be for each party to sell the stocks they do not want, and reinvest the proceeds in the stocks they do want. Such an approach is very expensive in terms of commissions. A much cheaper alternative is for each party to keep their own portfolio intact, and arrange between themselves an equity swap.

The swap agreement might dictate the following terms. For every percentage point that the NASDAQ stock index rises over the course of the year, Capital Bank will pay Back Bay Investment Management $1 million. Simultaneously, for every percentage point that the S&P 500 rises over the course of the year, Back Bay will pay Capital $1 million. Thus, if the NASDAQ index rises 15% and the S&P 500 rises 11%, there will be a net payment of $4 million from Capital to Back Bay. If in the following year the NASDAQ index rises 23% and the S&P 500 rises 29%, Back Bay will pay Capital $6 million on net. The equity swap is illustrated in Exhibit 13.5.

In this equity swap, the "notional principal" is $100 million—that is, the payments equal a base of $100 million times the indexes' respective returns. The net effect of the swap is to essentially convert $100 million of Back Bay's Standard & Poor's stocks into $100 million of NASDAQ stocks. Simultaneously, $100 million of Capital Bank's NASDAQ stocks will now perform as if they were $100 million of Standard & Poor's 500 stocks. Both sides keep their assets parked where they were, but they swap exposures on the notional principal.

Some arithmetic will prove the point that Back Bay's portfolio will now perform as if it were invested in NASDAQ stocks instead of S&P stocks. If Back Bay did in fact own $100 million of NASDAQ stocks, by the end of the first year, after the 15% rise in NASDAQ stocks, this portfolio would have

EXHIBIT 13.5   An equity swap.

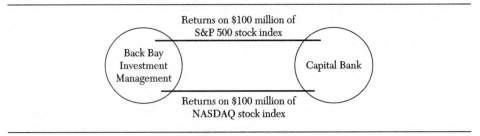

grown to be worth $115 million. But Back Bay owns $100 million of S&P stocks, and has a position in an equity swap. The $100 million of S&P stocks grows to $111 million after the 11% S&P rise in the first year. The swap, however, pays Back Bay $4 million at the end of the first year. Thus, at the end of the first year, Back Bay does have $115 million in total portfolio value. Verify, that the total value of Capital Bank's portfolio at the end of the first year will be $111 million, just as if it had invested $100 million in S&P stocks.

Since the notional principal remains fixed at $100 million, the swap will continue to convert $100 million of Back Bay's S&P stocks into $100 million of NASDAQ stocks, and visa versa for Capital Bank. Total portfolio performance in subsequent years depends on how the swap proceeds are reinvested by each party.

Interest Rate Swaps

The most common type of swap is an interest rate swap. The typical, or "plain-vanilla" interest rate swap, is a "fixed for floating swap," whereby cash flows depend on the movement of variable interest rates. For example, consider two firms Michel/Shaked Manufacturing (M) and Healing Heart Hospital (H). The swap agreement might specify that M pay H a fixed 10% per year on a notional principal of $100 million, and H pays to M the prime rate, as quoted in the *Wall Street Journal,* times $100 million. Settlement might be once per year. The prime rate quoted at the beginning of each year will determine the cash flow paid at the end. Thus, if at first the prime rate is 12%, H will pay M $2 million at the end of the first year. If by the end of the first year the prime rate has fallen to 7%, at the end of the second year M will pay H $3 million. And so the swap continues for a specified number of years. H will benefit if rates fall; M will benefit if rates rise. This interest rate swap is depicted in Exhibit 13.6.

Examples of Hedging Interest Rate Exposure with a Swap

The Keating Computer Company assembles and markets computer hardware systems. In the past several years Keating Computer has been one of the fastest

EXHIBIT 13.6   An interest rate swap.

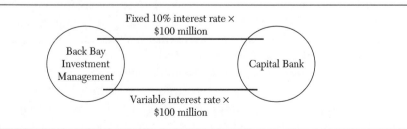

growing computer hardware companies. They borrowed extensively to finance this growth. Currently on the books is a very large long-term variable rate loan. Also on the books is a sizable amount of short-term debt. The managers of Keating Computer have observed that they are dangerously exposed to interest rate risk. If rates should rise, they will have to pay more in debt service on the variable rate loan, and they will face higher interest rates when they roll over their short-term debt. The company is currently profitable, but they worry that rising interest rates can wipe out that profit. Since the company is planning an equity offering in coming years, management is very concerned about the prospect of reporting any losses over the near term.

One solution to Keating Computer's problem would be to refinance at fixed interest rates. The transaction costs of refinancing, however, are sizable, and the rates currently offered on long-term debt are not favorable. Entering an interest rate swap is a better hedging strategy. The company should enter as the fixed rate payer, which means they would be the variable rate receiver. As interest rates rise, the company will make money on the swap, offsetting the higher payments they must make on their own debt. Since swaps are over-the-counter instruments, the company can tailor the terms of the swap so that the hedge will be in force for the exact number of years it is needed. Moreover, the notional principal can be tailored so that the money received when rates rise is closely matched to the new higher debt service obligations.

Another Example

Kayman Savings and Loan holds most of its assets in the form of long-term mortgages, mortgage backed securities, and 30-year Treasury bonds. The liabilities of Kayman Savings are mostly short-term certificates of deposits. Kayman has also sold some short-term commercial paper of its own. Stephen Kayman, the president of Kayman Savings, suddenly realizes that they are in the same precarious predicament as that of many savings and loans (S&Ls) that went bust in the 1980s. Long-term fixed income instruments are more sensitive to interest rates than short-term instruments. When interest rates rise, both long-term and short-term instruments fall in value, but the long-term instruments fall much more. Consequently, if interest rates should rise, the market value of the S&L's assets will fall farther than the market value of its liabilities. When this happens, the S&L's equity will be wiped out. The bank will be bankrupt. Even if government auditors do not shut down the S&L, the institution will experience cash flow problems. The relatively low fixed interest revenue from the long-term assets will not be enough to keep up with the rising interest expenses of the short-term liabilities. What can Kayman do to protect against the risk of rising interest rates?

The predicament faced by Kayman Savings is known as a "duration gap." The duration of the assets is greater than the duration of the liabilities. As rates rise, equity vanishes. Kayman Savings needs a hedge that will pay off when rates rise. Entering an interest rate swap as the fixed payer can close the duration gap. The swap will grow in value as rates rise, offsetting the equity losses. Again, the size, timing, and other terms of the interest rate swap can be tailored to meet the particular needs of Kayman Savings.

HOW TO CHOOSE THE APPROPRIATE HEDGE

We have now examined forwards, futures, call options, put options, and swaps. We have observed how these instruments can be used to hedge in a wide variety of risky scenarios. How does one choose which of these instruments to use in a particular situation? When is a future better than a forward? When should an option be used instead of a future? Should interest rate exposure be hedged with bond futures or swaps? The following steps will provide some guidance.

The first task in implementing a hedge strategy is to identify the natural exposures that the firm faces. Does the firm gain or lose when interest rates rise? Does it gain or lose as the dollar appreciates? Is a falling wheat price good news or bad news for the company? What about oil prices and stock prices? How about foreign stock and bond prices? Is the company exposed, and if so, which direction causes a loss?

Clearly the answers to these questions vary from firm to firm. The bakers benefited from falling wheat prices while the farmers suffered. Rising interest rates might hurt a firm that has variable rate debt, but might help a pension fund that is about to invest in bonds. A rising dollar benefits U.S. importers but hurts U.S. exporters. The first step in risk management is to identify the exposures.

Once the exposures are identified, one should narrow the search for an appropriate hedge to the set of derivatives that compensate the firm when the adverse scenario is realized. For example, an airline that purchases jet fuel will see higher costs when the price of oil rises. The airline should look for derivatives that pay off when oil prices rise. Thus, the airline should consider a long position in an oil future, or a long oil forward, or an oil call option. A bank that suffers losses when interest rates rise should consider a short position in a bond future or forward, bond put options, or the fixed-payer side of an interest rate swap. An exporter that expects to receive Mexican pesos, might wish to go short in peso futures or forwards, or buy peso puts.

The next step is to choose from among futures, forwards, options, and swaps. This is perhaps the trickiest part of the analysis. To guide the selection, it is helpful to categorize the risks and the instruments as either symmetric or asymmetric. Futures, forwards, and swaps are symmetric hedging instruments, in that they pay off money if prices move in one direction, but incur losses if prices move in the opposite direction. Options, on the other hand, are asymmetric hedging instruments. They pay off money if prices move in one direction, yet result in no cash outflows if prices should move the other way. A symmetric risk is one in which the firm is hurt if underlying prices move one way but benefits if prices move in the opposite direction. An asymmetric risk is one in which the firm is hurt if prices move in one direction, but the firm does not benefit appreciably if the price moves in the other direction. For example, a firm that exports to Japan and receives payment in yen benefits when the value of the yen rises, but is hurt when the yen falls in value. This foreign exchange risk is thus symmetric. The symmetric foreign exchange risk can be eliminated most completely with a symmetric instrument such as a future or forward, not an option.

A portfolio manager invested in stocks also faces a symmetric risk. He benefits if stock prices rise, and loses money if stock prices fall. The portfolio manager, however, might wish to modify the exposure in an asymmetric way, insuring against losses on the downside while maintaining the potential for upside appreciation. An asymmetric instrument, a put option, would be the appropriate hedge instrument in this case, since an asymmetric instrument converts a symmetric risk into an asymmetric exposure.

An automobile leasing company is an example of a commercial venture that faces an asymmetric risk. If interest rates rise, the firm's interest expenses rise. If the firm tries to offset these higher costs by charging higher prices to customers, the firm will lose business. However, if interest rates fall, buying an automobile on credit becomes a more attractive substitute for leasing unless the leasing company also lowers its prices. Thus, the leasing company suffers when rates rise, but does not benefit when rates fall. An asymmetric hedge, such as a bond put option would be the best choice of instrument in this case. The bond put option will pay off when rates rise, but will not require a cash outflow when rates fall.

The key to choosing between symmetric and asymmetric instruments is to first identify the nature of the risk that is faced, and then choose the type of instrument which will modify the risk appropriately. A symmetric risk can best be eliminated with a symmetric instrument. An asymmetric risk can best be eliminated with an asymmetric instrument. A symmetric risk can be turned into an asymmetric exposure with an asymmetric instrument.

Finally, the last step is to choose whether the instruments should be of the exchange-traded or over-the-counter variety. Forwards and swaps are over-the-counter instruments; futures are exchange-traded instruments. Options are generally exchange-traded, but they can also be bought over the counter. Exchange-traded instruments are standardized, and are thus liquid and entail low transaction costs. But since they are standardized, they may not perfectly suit the risk exposure the firm wishes to hedge. Over-the-counter instruments can be custom tailored, but they are therefore less liquid and more expensive in terms of transaction costs. The firm must weigh the costs and benefits of liquidity, differences in transaction costs, and custom fit. The correct choice depends on the particular hedging situation.

A couple of examples will illustrate the process of putting all the factors together to pick the best suited hedge. A U.S. manufacturing firm owns a production facility in Canada. Rent and wages are paid in Canadian dollars. Consequently, if the Canadian dollar rises in value, the wages and rent translated into U.S. dollars would become more expensive. If the Canadian dollar falls, the expenses in terms of U.S. dollars decline. Thus, the exposure is symmetric. If the firm wishes to completely eliminate the exposure, a symmetric instrument is called for, ruling out options. The firm should go long in Canadian dollar futures or forwards, since either of these instruments will provide positive cash flows when the Canadian dollar is rising. An exchange-traded Canadian dollar futures contract is available. The commission on the forward is greater than the commission on the futures, but the futures contract covers slightly more Canadian dollars than the firm wishes to hedge, and the timing does not exactly correspond to the timing of wage and rent payments. An over-the-counter forward contract could be constructed so that cash flows are synchronized with wage and rent payments. After weighing the two alternatives, the managers decide that the benefit from lower commissions on the futures contract outweighs the disadvantage of the futures' slight mismatch in the hedge. They go long in Canadian dollar futures.

The same manufacturing firm has many customers in Venezuela. If the Venezuelan currency (the bolivar) falls in value, the U.S. dollar value of the revenue will fall. If the Venezuelan currency rises in value, the dollar revenue will rise. Thus, the risk is symmetric, and so the list of hedging candidates is narrowed to futures and forwards. The firm benefits from a rise in the bolivar, and loses when the bolivar falls. Thus, the firm should go short in bolivar futures or forwards, so that a cash flow will be received when the bolivar falls. No bolivar futures contracts are available on exchanges, so the firm must go short in over-the-counter Venezuelan bolivar forwards.

A producer of copper wire purchases large amounts of copper as a raw material. When copper prices rise, the firm must either absorb the higher expenses, or raise the price of copper wire. Raising the price of wire, however, causes customers to cut back on purchases, and so the firm is stuck with unsold inventory. When copper prices fall, alternatively, competitors lower their prices and so the firm must also lower its price in order to sell its output. Consequently, the firm's profits suffer when copper prices rise, but profits do not increase when copper prices fall. Management would like to increase production capacity, but it is difficult to forecast how much the firm can sell, given recent copper price fluctuations. With current levels of raw copper inventory, management believes that raw copper prices can rise as much as 10% without significantly impacting the firm's bottom line. What is the appropriate hedge?

Clearly, the firm faces an asymmetric risk. The firm is hurt when copper prices rise, but does not benefit when the price falls. An option will best mitigate the risk. Since the firm is hurt when copper prices rise, a call option that pays off when copper prices rise is the best choice. Since the firm can tolerate a 10% rise in copper prices without suffering significant losses, an out-of-the-money copper call option that begins to pay off only when copper prices rise more than 10% is ideal. Exchange-traded copper call options exist, and so due to their greater liquidity and lower transaction costs, they would be the best choice.

A cellular communications firm has sold a six-year variable rate bond, where the interest payments are tied to the London Interbank Offered Rate (LIBOR). When LIBOR rises, so too do the company's interest payments. When LIBOR falls, the firm's interest payments fall. The company's interest payments are due twice a year, on the last days of February and August. The firm raised $160 million this way. With competition holding cellular telephone rates down, the firm worries that an increase in interest rates can wipe out all profits. What is the appropriate hedge instrument?

The interest rate exposure is symmetric, ruling out options. The firm needs an instrument that will pay it money when interest rates rise. Thus, the firm should go short in either bond futures or forwards, or the firm should be the fixed-rate payer in an interest rate swap. Since the cash flows that the firm is trying to hedge do not conform to those of any exchange-traded future, the correct choice is narrowed to the over-the-counter instruments—a forward or a swap. The firm must hedge twelve interest rate payments, two per year for six years. Forwards are generally constructed to provide one payment only. Swaps are designed to hedge multiple payments over longer terms. Thus, entering a six-year interest rate swap as the fixed payer is the ideal hedge in this situation.

SUMMARY AND FINAL RECOMMENDATIONS

This chapter has presented the basics of risk management using derivatives. By separating an asset's value from its exposure, derivatives allow firms to exchange exposures without exchanging the underlying assets. It is much more economical to transfer exposures, rather than assets, and thus derivatives have greatly facilitated risk management. Derivatives are indeed powerful risk management tools, but in the wrong hands they can be dangerous and destructive. It is essential that managers fully understand how much and under what conditions derivatives will provide positive cash flows or require cash outflows. If it is not absolutely clear when and how much the cash flows will be, do not enter the contract. Managers should strive to identify the nature, magnitude, and size of their risk exposures. They can then match those exposures with countervailing positions in derivatives. Managers should never forget that their job is to preserve value by reducing risk. The temptation to speculate should be avoided. Don't be greedy.

FOR FURTHER READING

Abken, Peter, and Steven Feinstein, "Covered Call Options: A Proposal to Ease Less Developed Country Debt," in *Financial Derivatives: New Instruments and Their Uses* (Atlanta: Federal Reserve Bank of Atlanta, 1994).

Bernstein, Peter, *Against the Gods: The Remarkable Story of Risk* (New York: John Wiley, 1998).

Bodie, Zvi, and Robert C. Merton, *Finance* (Upper Saddle River, NJ: Prentice-Hall, 2000).

Chance, Don M., *An Introduction to Derivatives* (New York: Dryden Press, 1998).

Chew, Lillian, *Managing Derivative Risks: The Use and Abuse of Leverage* (New York: John Wiley, 1996).

Daigler, Robert T., *Financial Futures and Options Markets: Concepts and Strategies* (New York: HarperCollins, 1994).

Dunbar, Nicholas, *Inventing Money: The Story of Long-Term Capital Management and the Legends Behind It* (New York: John Wiley, 2001).

Fraser, Andrew, "Top Banks Plan Bailout for Fund," Associated Press, September 24, 1998.

———, "Fed Key Player in Rescue of Floundering Hedge Fund," Associated Press, September 25, 1998.

Hull, John C., *Options, Futures, and Other Derivative Securities* (Upper Saddle River, NJ: Prentice-Hall, 2000).

Lowenstein, Roger, *When Genius Failed: The Rise and Fall of Long-Term Capital Management* (New York: Random House, 2000).

Various authors, "Managing Risks," special report in *Business Week*, October 31, 1994, 86–104.

NOTES

1.   Zvi Bodie and Robert C. Merton, *Finance* (Upper Saddle River, NJ: Prentice-Hall, 2000) deserve credit for this perspective on risk management techniques.

2.   Fischer Black, who helped invent the model, passed away prior to recognition from the Nobel committee.

3.   All data referring to equity positions, assets under management, exposure, and profits and losses in this section come from Roger Lowenstein, *When Genius Failed: The Rise and Fall of Long-Term Capital Management* (New York: Random House, 2000).

PART THREE

MAKING KEY
STRATEGIC DECISIONS

14 GOING PUBLIC

Stephen M. Honig

SETTING THE STAGE

It is June 2000, and recent MIT graduate John Dough and his friend, business school graduate Mary Manager, decide to pursue a software idea that Dough has conceptualized. Dough believes that he can design a relational database that will more tightly store financial information and more quickly access that information than anything now on the market.

Dough and Manager take their meager savings accounts and $20,000 of credit card advances and form Dough.com Inc., a Delaware corporation. Dough sits down at his computer and begins to program Dough-Ware.

Mary successfully approaches five business school acquaintances; each invests $4,000 and each is issued 4% of the company's stock.

By the spring of 2001, Dough has a working initial version of Dough-Ware available for testing at the sites of potential clients. The company is completely out of funds, and is without the necessary liquidity to negotiate for the test sites, install the software, and work with prospective clients. Dough and Manager have been networking at venture capital forums, and are able to induce five "angel" investors, wealthy individuals with a history of investing in emerging technology companies, to invest an aggregate of $250,000. By June 2001, each of Dough and Manager now owns 30% of their company; each of the original five investors owns 3%; the new angel investors have received a 25% common stock interest. With this new money and with modest interim payments from the first "beta site," or test customers, the company begins installation and testing of its software.

459

By June 2002 the company has refined its software into a salable product for which Dough believes there is a significant market. However, in order to produce, customize and install the software, and in order to broadly market, the company needs significant new investment. All prior financing, and the meager proceeds from the test installations, are virtually exhausted. The company is fortunate enough to induce a venture capital investor, Vulture Partners, to invest $1 million but there is a significant cost:

- Vulture Partners insists on receiving 50% of the equity in the form of convertible preferred stock that will participate in the proceeds of the sale of the company in preference to all the other stockholders, who hold only common stock.
- Vulture Partner's preferred stock will convert into common stock upon any public offering.
- Vulture Partners gets two board of directors seats.
- Vulture Partners insists upon a substantial increase in personnel in order to aggressively address the market place; John Dough is given the title of "chief scientific officer"; Mary Manager is made vice president; they hire a chief operating officer who formerly was a senior vice president at a large software firm, a chief financial officer from one of the big five accounting firms, and a sales manager with experience at Mega-Soft, the largest software development firm in the country.

The new team, properly financed, goes off to sell Dough-Ware and is fabulously successful.

It is one year later, in the spring of 2002, and everyone involved in management, including John Dough and Mary Manager, agrees that substantial additional capital is needed. It looks as though the company can reach $100 million in sales next year and have a 10% market penetration, but that's going to take an awful lot of money, something like $40 million. This money will be necessary to further refine the product, increase the engineering capacity to customize the product, and enter into sales efforts so as to speed market penetration. The directors hope that a direct approach to customers will enable the company to decrease its dependence on Big Deal Corporation, a large software company which has marketed Dough-Ware in exchange for a substantial commission. The directors call a board meeting for the end of June 2003 to discuss their options.

THE THREE OPTIONS

Dough and Manager have understood from various board members that there are three primary sources for financing company growth: raising additional money on a private basis as in the past; raising money through an initial public offering (IPO); or merging with a strategic partner (such as Big Deal Corporation), which might pay a high price to acquire Dough-Ware and add it to its stable of software products offered by its existing sales force.

Dough and Manager precede the board meeting by visiting with corporate attorney Stanley Sharp, who explains the difference between selling stock privately and selling stock in an IPO.

Both the United States government and all of the states substantively regulate the offer and sale of securities within their borders. The offer and sale of securities federally is regulated by the Securities and Exchange Commission (SEC) under authority granted by the Securities Act of 1933. Each state also has its own similar statute, administered by various state agencies; these state statutes collectively are referred to as "Blue Sky Laws." It is necessary to satisfy both federal and state law in order for Dough.com Inc. to sell shares of stock.

Whether shares of stock are sold privately or publicly, all of these laws at a minimum require full disclosure of material information. This means that in both private and public transactions the company typically must prepare an offering document which explains its business, finances, and the risks of investment. In a private offering, this booklet is often called a private placement memorandum (PPM); in an offering to the public, this booklet is called a "prospectus."

The big difference, Attorney Sharp continues, between public and private sale of securities has to do with whether the transaction by which those securities are sold is "registered" with government authorities. Registration is the process by which the offering document is filed with and reviewed by such authorities. In a private transaction or "private placement," there is little or no involvement of either the federal or state governments. A private placement generally is effected to a limited number of investors who, because of their small number or because of their financial resources or sophistication in making investments, do not trigger the registration requirements of federal or state law. Attorney Sharp explains that in a $40 million private placement, it is likely that the securities will be sold to sophisticated venture capital investors who qualify as "accredited investors" under Regulation D of the General Rules and Regulations of the SEC, which by its terms exempts such sale from the federal registration requirement. Further, in many such transactions compliance with the federal law automatically will constitute compliance with state laws.

An IPO involves selling securities in smaller minimum investments, to a greater number of people who need not meet any standard of sophistication or financial resources. These people must receive a prospectus which has been reviewed by the SEC, and in order to obtain clearance to finally utilize that prospectus in the sale of their securities, the company will have to undergo a "going public" process that is liable to take at least four months of management's time and attention.

THE BOARD OF DIRECTORS MEETING

The board of directors of Dough.com Inc. meets with its various advisers to determine how to raise the necessary capital to promote the development of Dough-Ware. Every possible solution has its advocates.

Some directors want to raise the money through a private placement of securities from venture capital firms, believing that going public is too time consuming, involves too much expense (upward of 10% of the proceeds typically will be absorbed in selling commission and out-of-pocket expenses), and that the underwriters (the investment bankers who will sell the IPO to the public investors) will attempt to value the shares at less than their true value so that the public investors will see the price rise upon conclusion of the offering.

An investment banker on the board suggests that the shares could be privately placed by selling an additional 20% of the company's common stock for $40 million, effectively valuing the company as it sits today (a "pre-money" valuation) at $160 million.

The representative from Vulture Partners has yet another strategy. He suggests that the company not raise the additional funds now, but push the current version of their product out the door and work on building volume and profitability for the next six months; then, the company can go public at a valuation which is 30 times the company's projected pretax earnings, which would value the company at $300 million pre-money. In conjunction with the IPO, Vulture Partners then would sell half of its own original shares, realizing a multimillion dollar profit while still retaining a substantial equity position.

Dough and Manager do not want to wait to raise money; they see the most important thing as capturing market share before competitors overtake the advantage that struggling Dough.com Inc. now enjoys. Company management does not care whether Vulture Partners is able to sell any equity interest at this time; they have been investors for only one year, and management does not feel that Vulture's rush to liquidity is appropriate. But some of the other early investors, the original group of five friends and the angel investors, also are intrigued with the possibility of selling some of their shares.

The investment banker warns that in an IPO, it is sometimes a negative if too many shares are sold by existing stockholders and not by the company itself; new investors like to invest their money in the enterprise and help it grow, not into the pockets of prior investors, and too many sales by previous investors indicate a lack of confidence in the future.

Some of the management team wants the company acquired by Big Deal Corporation Management, which is experienced in working with larger corporations, sees an acquisition by a strategic acquirer as increasing the value of their existing stock options, and believes that through their existing close contacts with Big Deal Corporation's management they will be able to structure attractive personal compensation packages. They point out that, whether capital is raised publicly or privately, there is far greater risk of failure if Dough.com Inc. goes it alone, as compared to joining forces with an existing multibillion dollar entity like Big Deal Corporation. Besides, if the key to success is to hit the market fast with Dough-Ware, teaming up with Big Deal Corporation is the fastest way to achieve that goal.

The investment banker says that if the desire is to sell to a strategic partner such as Big Deal Corporation, or anyone else who can pay a high price quickly and assist in the marketing of Dough-Ware, his investment banking firm will be pleased to handle the proposed sale of the company and could shop potential strategic acquirers and find the best price.

Through the afternoon, the conversation works itself toward a consensus to effect an immediate public offering. Certainly the prospect of more rapid ultimate profit which would result from a prompt IPO is intriguing to all: Vulture Partners and the other prior investors; management; and John Dough and Mary Manager as founders. All are intrigued with the advantages that being a public entity can bring:

- Relative ease of raising additional capital for expansion in the future.
- Ability to obtain debt financing at reasonable rates (not now available due to lack of hard asset collateral or proven cash flow).
- An ability of existing stockholders to partially cash out their investments at a profit.
- The ability to attract employees in a highly competitive technology marketplace by reason of public equity incentives.
- The ability to easily acquire related software companies and to make payment for such acquisitions through the issuance of additional shares of company stock.

Near the end of the meeting, the investment banker turns to Dough, Manager, and the entire executive team and says that he feels compelled to share with them some of the risks and problems, both short term and long term, that they will encounter in going public. Effecting an IPO, and living with the reality of being a public company thereafter, is not all a bed of roses. For example:

- At this particularly crucial time in the marketing of the Dough-Ware product, significant attention will be diverted from the operation of the business into the process of going public and in preparation of the prospectus.
- The full disclosure that will be required in the prospectus will cause the disclosure in detail of the company's business strategy and perhaps some of its trade secrets, and will reveal the terms of its contracts with Big Deal Corporation, and with some of its customers and suppliers.
- Any transactions between the company and its affiliates (its officers, directors, significant stockholders, and their relatives, and companies they own) must be disclosed.
- The cost of an IPO is significant; it is likely that investment banking firms will be retained as underwriters and will take 7% of the gross proceeds

right off the top, although this is an expense that will not be incurred unless the offering is successful; certain other significant expenses, particularly legal fees, accounting fees, printing fees, filing fees, and miscellaneous out of pocket fees, must be paid even if the transaction is not successful. Expenses in this size of proposed IPO could approximate $1 million.

- Once the company is public, it will be subject to public scrutiny, must make periodic filings with the SEC, and will incur an overhead in dealing with the public which does not now exist.
- There will be public pressure to achieve short-term growth on sales and profitability so as to sustain and advance the stock price, and these pressures will affect strategic decisions made by management which might otherwise be based on a long-range product-driven strategy.
- Management and the directors can incur personal liability in connection with a public offering, if it is ultimately determined that the prospectus is materially false or misleading, causing a decline in the value of investor shares (although certain protections from this risk can be obtained by the company's purchase of directors and officers [D&O] insurance).

The vote is taken. With some trepidation, the board decides to attempt a public offering, or IPO, of its shares of common stock as quickly as possible. A "team" of two directors and three members of management is established to pursue that result.

THE PROCESS OF GOING PUBLIC

While it is possible for the company to sell its shares directly to the public through a variety of mechanisms including direct offerings over the Internet, the company wants to proceed in a more traditional fashion and retain one or more investment bankers to serve as lead or "managing" underwriters for the public offering of its common stock. Through the contacts of the investment banker on the board, and the contacts of Vulture Partners, the team interviews several investment banking firms.

The entire process of going public is supervised by the managing underwriters who will head the syndicate of other investment banking firms which will sell the shares of common stock to the public.

An underwriter is either a distributor or sales agent for the shares, depending upon the type of underwriting which is undertaken. A "firm" commitment underwriting means that the underwriters agree, as a group, that if the public offering occurs, the underwriters will themselves purchase all the shares of stock and resell those shares to the public. Consequently, in the theoretical event that an insufficient public market develops for the shares, the underwriters themselves will end up owning the shares of stock as investors. As a practical matter, it is an exceedingly rare event that the underwriters cannot resell the shares after an IPO is effected.

The other kind of underwriting is a "best efforts" underwriting. This is, literally speaking, not an underwriting at all. The investment bankers agree, as agents of the company, to sell such number of shares for which they can actually find buyers. Such an underwriting may be "all or none" which means that the underwriters must find buyers for all of the shares, or a "minimum-maximum" offering (which may close if the underwriters find purchasers for a specified minimum number of shares). Most established underwriters only undertake "firm" underwritings, and are entitled to receive somewhat greater compensation under the rules of the National Association of Securities Dealers, Inc. (which regulates underwriter compensation) in consideration of undertaking a firm deal. The underwriters, even in a firm underwriting, are not required to purchase the shares until the very last moment and retain certain abilities to abort the transaction; consequently, the practical difference to the company between these two kinds of underwritings is slight, although much may be made of it in the marketplace.

The prospective managing underwriters all propose to do the same thing: organize the entire process, establish a timetable, and assign tasks to the various players; review the company's drafts of its filing with the SEC (which consists of a "registration statement" in two parts, the longest part being the "prospectus" which describes the company and its prospects and risks, and the shorter part being a Part II which contains other technical information); organize and conduct several meetings of the going public team, focused on performing "due diligence" (an examination of the company to make sure that all material facts are uncovered and disclosed), and on reviewing in detail the contents of the prospectus to make sure that there is no inaccuracy or material omission; gather other investment banking firms as part of a syndicate of underwriters or selling group so as to achieve a broader distribution of the shares; and find buyers for the shares.

The team considers several factors in discussions with prospective managing underwriters:

- The value that each underwriter is willing to place on the company, and the discount that the underwriters propose in making company shares attractive for public purchase.
- The recent track record of the underwriter, based both on general reputation and on that underwriter's success in closing similar transactions.
- Whether the underwriter has been able to structure prior IPOs so that there was a sufficient "aftermarket" for the shares, preventing the price from collapsing.
- The experience of other companies which have gone public through that underwriter, as gathered from conversations with CEOs of those companies.
- The degree to which the underwriter seems capable of placing some of the shares in the hands of larger "institutional" purchasers, so as to provide some stability in the stockholdings of the company.

- The ability of the underwriter to distribute the stock on a broad enough geographical basis that all constituencies having an interest in the company have an opportunity to participate in the public offering.
- Whether the underwriter employs well-known securities analysts within the company's industry, whose views are valued within the investment community.

Finally, the team selects two investment-banking firms as managing underwriters. A Letter of Intent, outlining the terms of the proposed public offering, is then prepared and signed by the company. Among other matters, this Letter of Intent will obligate the company to pay certain expenses of the underwriter, whether or not the IPO is successful.

One of the managing underwriters takes the lead in organizing the IPO process. First, a date is fixed for an "all hands organizational meeting." This important meeting will be attended by the managing underwriters, the lawyers for the underwriters, the company management, the lawyers for the company, and the certified public accountants who will prepare the SEC-specified financial statements. At the organizational meeting:

- It is decided that shares of voting common stock will be sold; it is expected that Vulture Partners will convert its preferred stock into common stock effective upon the public offering.
- All parties are assigned specific responsibilities with specific deadlines.
- A timetable for the offering is established, generally encompassing a 12- to 16-week period from the date of the organizational meeting to a closing of the public offering.
- The parties discuss the selection of a financial printer, and the company later will interview and negotiate price with a printer who is experienced in printing SEC filings and causing those filings to be effected electronically through the SEC's electronic filing system (called EDGAR).
- The managing underwriters present a "due diligence checklist" which is a list of numerous facts to be gathered and documents to be produced by the company; it is the task of the underwriters to perform "due diligence" to make sure that all facts are uncovered. The diligence process is outlined and materials for the checklist are contained in the NASD's "Due Diligence Examination Outline," annexed to this chapter as Appendix A.
- The participants discuss the addition of "antitakeover provisions" to the corporate structure of the company; when a company becomes publicly held, there is the possibility that third parties might attempt to obtain a controlling financial interest or voting interest. The underwriters are of the view that certain antitakeover provisions are inappropriate, as they limit the likelihood of a legitimate takeover of the company at a high price and therefore work against the interest of the stockholders. Management expresses an interest in taking reasonable steps to preserve current control. Antitakeover provisions may include: staggering the board of directors so that all directors cannot be replaced at once; limiting

the rights of stockholders to call special stockholder meetings; limiting the rights of stockholders to amend the company's bylaws; eliminating the right to remove directors except for cause; establishing voting mechanisms which do not permit the purchaser of shares immediately to affect the control of the company; and the adoption of complicated stockholder protection plans, called "poison pills," that dilute the equity interest of any unfriendly future significant stockholder.

- There is discussion concerning the number of shares to be offered, the percentage of the company to be offered, the general range of share pricing, and whether the company's shares will be listed for trading over an exchange or quoted through the facilities of NASDAQ (National Association of Securities Dealers' Automated Quotation System). It is decided that approximately 10% of the shares to be sold in the IPO will belong to Vulture Partners and other original investors in the company.

- The underwriters ask for the option to purchase from the company, for resale to the public a short time after the closing of the IPO, an additional number of shares of common stock. These shares, typically not in excess of 15% of the shares sold in an IPO, are an "overallotment" to permit the co-managing underwriters to cover short positions in the company's stock which they may have created immediately after the IPO closing in an effort to stabilize the stock price. These shares are sometimes referred to as "the green shoe," named after a securities offering which allegedly first utilized this technique.

- There is a discussion of "lockup agreements." The underwriters will require that existing stockholders contract that for some period following the IPO (most typically 180 days), they will not sell any shares; this prohibition permits the underwriters to "stabilize" or create an equilibrium in the price of the shares, and eliminates the perception that the insiders are "bailing out." Conversely, the underwriters may be asked to include a reasonable number of shares for sale by prior investors.

- Management asks to set up a "directed share program" by which friends of the company, such as key suppliers and business partners, will be given an opportunity to preferentially subscribe for shares; generally underwriters seek to limit these programs to 5% of the total offering.

- The parties discuss the inclusion of online "e-brokers" as part of the underwriter distribution group, in order to address the growing appetite of online purchasers in technology-related IPOs.

The organizational meeting sets off a time of hectic effort by management, accountants, and attorneys. Some staff is delegated to filling the due diligence checklist. The bulk of the more visible effort is directed, however, toward the preparation of the registration statement, which includes the prospectus.

The company and its attorneys are charged with the task of preparing a first draft of this registration statement. The contents of the registration statement are rigorously specified by the forms and rules promulgated by the SEC.

One of the tasks of the organizational meeting is to determine which SEC "Form" will be utilized in going public. The SEC has promulgated two additional forms, Form SB-1 and Form SB-2, for certain small businesses. The financial statements for such forms are less rigorous than for Form S-1 and require only one year of audited balance sheet and two years of audited income statements, statements of cash flows, and statements of stockholders' equity.

However, because of a combination of limitation on amount of capital to be raised and value of the company at the commencement of the process, at the organizational meeting it is determined that SEC Form S-1 must be utilized; the accountants will be required to prepare two years of audited balance sheets and three years of audited income statements, cash flows, and stockholders' equity. (Appendix B is Securities and Exchange Commission Form S-1, the most typical registration form for an IPO.)

Although audited information is required for only three years in Form S-1, the accountants also will have to put together the results of operations for a five-year comparative period (if available). Since 2001 the company has received an audit of its financial statements, but results of operations for the initial year 2000 were prepared on a review basis only. The accountants will have to go back and apply audit standards to this period. Since the objectives of an audit are to obtain and evaluate evidence to corroborate management's assertions regarding its financial statements, and to express an opinion on those financial statements, the "review" of the operating numbers will be an insufficient basis for the issuance of an audit opinion. But since Mary Manager was assiduous in financial record keeping and since the certified public accountants are familiar with the company's financial records and financial statements, the accountants will be able to complete the audit procedure at the same time that they are preparing the Form S-1 financial information and supporting schedules in the format required by the SEC.

In preparing the registration statement, the company, the underwriters, the accountants, and the attorneys are guided by specific instructions from the SEC. The textual content of the registration statement is controlled by SEC Regulation S-K; the accounting content is regulated by SEC Regulation S-X. These regulations and related pronouncements contained in the General Rules and Regulations of the SEC, may be accessed through the SEC Web site, and are made available to companies undergoing the IPO process through a series of publications provided without additional charge by most financial printers.

The process of drafting the prospectus is made more complicated by efforts of the SEC to clarify communication between the company and its potential public investors. Since October 1998, the SEC has required that the prospectus be drafted in "plain English" pursuant to the provisions of Rule 421 of the SEC's General Rules and Regulations. The entire prospectus is to be written in clear, concise, and understandable English using short sentences and paragraphs, bullet lists, and descriptive headings without either technical or legal jargon. The company will struggle to describe the technicalities of its business in language that will be clear and understandable to an intelligent but non-technologically oriented reader. The lawyers will struggle in similar fashion to convey technical information concerning the terms of the offering.

Special plain-English rules apply to the front and back cover pages, to the summary contained in the front of the prospectus, and to the section of "risk factors." Risk factors are a constant feature of IPO prospectuses, and are designed fully to apprise the potential investor of all pitfalls that the company might encounter and which might cause it to falter. These risk factors generally relate to the newness and lack of financing and operating history of the company, the experience level of management, rapid technological change for the marketplace in which the company proposes to compete, and the superior resources of the competition. These vital pages are the ones likely to be read most carefully by the investing public, and must be reviewed particularly to make sure that sentences are short, that the active voice is utilized, that concrete everyday words are employed, and that complex information is contained in tables or otherwise graphically depicted.

There will be several drafting meetings in the six to eight weeks between the organizational meeting and the filing of the first draft of a registration statement with the SEC. During these lengthy meetings, each word of the prospectus will be reviewed and considered, some on-the-spot rewriting will occur, and other sections will be designated for later rewrite. Much attention will be directed to the description of the company's business, and to the "MD&A" (management's detailed discussion and analysis of its financial operations, liquidity, and capital requirements for the past three years, as well as for the foreseeable future, if known). When all parties are confident that the description is accurate, the "preliminary prospectus" will be filed as part of the registration statement.

Contemporaneously, filings also must be made with the regulatory agencies of each state in which the IPO will be offered; state practice varies as to the degree of substantive review that state regulators will give to a registration statement, and in the past the severity of state review was more stringent than SEC review; some states involved themselves in approving or disapproving the substance of an offering ("merit review"), while SEC review typically is restricted to ensuring the adequacy and completeness of the description of the company and the attendant risks of investment.

In the case of the company, a decision has been made to apply for the immediate right to have the shares issued in the IPO quoted for trading on NASDAQ. By law, when IPO shares will be quoted on NASDAQ or listed on a national securities exchange, the states' right to insist on separate registration and review is preempted.

Now everyone waits for the SEC staff to provide comments and ask questions in a written "comment letter." It is not typical to print and distribute to the public the first filing of the preliminary prospectus, in part because no one is quite sure whether the SEC will have significant comments or request significant corrections and in part because often the managing underwriters are not ready to effect such a distribution. During the three to four weeks that it typically takes for the SEC to provide both accounting and business comments on the prospectus, several things will be occurring:

- The company's accountants will work on updating financials, so they will be "fresh" (i.e., within 135 days of filing) for the anticipated amendments to the registration statement.
- The company will be careful in its public utterances and in the contents of its Web site, to avoid the improper direct or implicit promotion of the company's stock; during this waiting period generally the only writing that may be utilized to actually offer company stock for sale is the prospectus itself, and no generally ancillary writing and no inconsistent oral presentations can be made.
- The comanaging underwriters will form a syndicate of additional underwriters who will agree to purchase a certain number of the IPO shares. These underwriters in turn will deal with the lowest tier of distribution, the "selected securities dealers" whose securities customers ultimately will be asked to purchase the shares.
- The managing underwriters will have filed with the National Association of Securities Dealers Inc. (NASD) the following: the registration statement, their underwriting agreement with the company, the agreement among the underwriters themselves, and the agreement between the underwriters and those "selected securities dealers." The NASD regulates compensation of underwriters, and must review the offering to declare that the consideration to be paid by the company to the underwriters is fair and reasonable.
- The company will prepare the information necessary to permit the company's common stock to be quoted over the NASDAQ, on completion of the IPO.

When the SEC staff issues its comment letter, a flurry of rewriting results in an amended registration statement, which is combined with updated financial statements and refiled with the SEC as promptly as possible. Typically, this version of the prospectus is then printed in large numbers and distributed by the underwriters to the investment community. This distributed prospectus is typically referred to as the "red herring." Until 1996, the SEC required that the cover of a preliminary prospectus, which was being distributed, bear in red ink a legend which advised that the prospectus was subject to change and that the SEC had not finally approved the offering. Under current practice, language to similar effect is required on the front cover and on occasion may be printed in red ink, but it need not be.

At this juncture, the underwriters together with key company management embark on a "road show," which is a key element in the marketing of an IPO. For a couple of weeks, the managing underwriters and management crisscross the United States, and sometimes travel overseas, to hold brief meetings with underwriters, brokers, securities analysts, and significant investors to present the company, discuss and answer questions concerning the prospectus, and make the company story palpable to the people whose support is essential to sell the offering. Management typically makes a highly orchestrated half hour presentation, supported by a PowerPoint or similar screen presentation. Because the company is still in the waiting period and (generally) only the prospectus can be utilized as a written presentation of the company's prospects, no written materials are distributed. The managing underwriters had booked two and a half weeks of in-person meetings, mostly at breakfast and lunch time when securities professionals and significant investors are most available, in cities all across the United States, with a brief two-day trip to London.

Perhaps the fastest evolving and most confused aspect of the going public process is the road show procedures, in light of technological advances. Road show sessions are now permitted to be accessed online with the Internet, and the SEC and the underwriting community is grappling with the ground rules for such access. At present, there are no general rules and regulations as to the types of potential investors who may participant in an Internet road show, although the trend seems to be toward opening road show participation to increasingly less sophisticated investors. It is quite possible that this trend will continue so as to open road shows to all interested parties, and if Internet road shows are open to everyone, then the in-person road show seemingly could also be fully attended. The attorneys for the underwriters have written to the SEC and obtained specific permission to permit the Internet streaming of several of the United States road shows to selected retail investors who are securities customers of the underwriting syndicate, which investors will be given a password to a Web site in order to participate. Because of the prohibition against utilizing any writing other than the prospectus during this "cooling off" period, Internet participants will be prohibited from downloading the PowerPoint presentation which will be made by the company management.

Throughout this period, the underwriters gather indications of interest for the purchase of stock. They also receive feedback as to the proposed range of pricing, which reflects the market value that will be placed on the company and will be reflected in the per share price. In dialogue with the team, and with approval of the board of directors, just prior to final clearance from the SEC the managing underwriters fix the per share price at which company common stock will be sold in the IPO.

Meanwhile, the SEC staff has reviewed the amended prospectus, and has been satisfied with the response it has received to questions it has addressed to management and to the accountants. It has indicated that the IPO can proceed. Pursuant to SEC practice, the underwriters may now file a final registration statement (with fresh financials if needed), which for the first time will contain the actual per share purchase price, the aggregate proceeds to the company and to selling stockholders, and the specific dollar amounts for the underwriter discount (the commission that the underwriters will receive on the sale of the shares). This "pricing amendment" by SEC regulation will take effect in 20 days, but in practice the company requests and the SEC will grant "acceleration," which permits the immediate offering of the stock pursuant to the final prospectus. The prospectus is printed in large numbers for distribution to investors, without the "red herring" legend on the front cover which had indicated that the prospectus was subject to change. The prospectus is now final.

At the same time that the company's registration statement under the Securities Act of 1933 has become effective, permitting the initial sale of the company's stock, the SEC also has permitted to become effective a filing made by the company under the Securities Exchange Act of 1934, which statute establishes the rules for subsequent trading of the shares on the part of the purchasers who obtain company stock in the IPO.

It is only at this time that the company and the two managing underwriters will sign the underwriting agreement by which the underwriters agree to purchase the company's shares. The agreement had been filed as an exhibit with the registration statement and had been approved by the NASD, but until the SEC has granted its approval of the registration statement the underwriters have not been contractually bound to purchase the shares. Even now, in the brief period of time it will take for the underwriters to effect the going public transaction, the underwriting agreement contains a series of "market out" provisions which permit the underwriters, over the next few days, to decline to move forward with the IPO in the event material and unexpected changes occur in the financial markets.

The underwriters and the selected dealers now are entitled to accept payment for the shares, and they sell the company's common stock to various institutional and individual investors. Approximately one week later, a closing under the underwriting agreement occurs. Before the underwriters will close, they will require a series of assurances from the company and its advisers with respect to the continuing accuracy of the contents of the registration statement. Officers of the company will deliver certifications as to the accuracy of facts, the attorneys for the company will give formal legal opinions with respect to legal matters and the absence of their awareness of contrary material facts, and the accountants will deliver a "comfort letter," which sets forth the degree of diligence utilized by the accountants, the materials which the accountants have reviewed, and the conclusion that nothing has come to the attention of the accountants to indicate that the financial statements are improperly prepared or erroneous. An example of a comfort letter approved by the American Institute of Certified Public Accountants Inc. is attached to this chapter as Appendix C.

At the closing, the company receives $33 million from the underwriters in exchange for its stock. Vulture Partners and certain other stockholders, who sold their shares along with the shares issued by the company, receive $4.2 million. The underwriters retain $2.8 million, or a 7% commission. Out of its proceeds, the company pays many additional substantial expenses: several hundred thousand dollars to each of its lawyers, its accountants, and its financial printer, as well as the legal fees and expenses of the underwriters' attorneys.

Dough.com Inc. now is a publicly held company with a couple of thousand shareholders spread throughout the United States and Britain.

THE MORNING AFTER

Although the infusion of over $30 million of net capital in the company is of major significance, the life of the company in public mode has drastically changed. The company's executives and directors have taken on both new roles and serious potential liabilities. The company itself has become obligated to feed the public's earnings appetite, and the requirements of the regulatory authorities for a continuous stream of accurate information.

As a publicly held company with shares quoted on NASDAQ and registered under the Securities Exchange Act of 1934, both the company and its executives have further become responsible for the filing of very specific and complex reporting forms.

The company itself must keep the public informed by filing within 90 days of each fiscal year-end, on Form 10-K, an extensive discussion of the company's business and financial condition. Much like a prospectus, the Form 10-K contains a description of the business, properties, and legal proceedings involving the company, an MD&A (management's discussion and analysis of financial condition and results of operations) for the three prior years, three years of audited financial statements, and a variety of other information about the company's stock, the company's management, and (typically although not specifically required by regulation) an ongoing and updated list of risk factors.

Less comprehensive but equally required by regulation, the company must file within 45 days of the end of each of its fiscal quarters (except for the year-end) a quarterly report of its financial condition on Form 10-Q, and furthermore must file periodic reports on Form 8-K within several days after the occurrence of significant events, such as a change of control, the acquisition or disposition of significant assets, a change in the auditors, or a resignation of directors because of disagreement.

The company will be required by NASDAQ to provide a written annual report with audited financial statements to all of its stockholders. Corporate practice will require the corporation to hold an annual meeting of its stockholders, generally within two or three months of the release of the annual report on Form 10-K, which will contain the financial statements for the prior year.

Now that the company's stock is widely held by a couple of thousand people in diverse locations, it is necessary for management to seek written voting authorization, through signature and return of a proxy card, by which stockholders authorize designated members of management to vote the shares of such investors for the election of directors and for any other action to be taken at the annual meeting. Proxy regulations of the SEC will require that the company send extensive written information (a "proxy statement") to each stockholder in advance of the annual meeting, and in connection with management's solicitation of proxies for the voting of shares. The SEC requires filing of this proxy statement and all related information at the same time they are sent to stockholders; in the event significant action beyond the typical election of directors is to be voted on at the annual meeting, the SEC requires advance filing of proxy materials so that the SEC staff can review and comment on such materials.

The company will have to consider whether it wishes to attempt to conduct its annual meeting online. While substantive state law controls whether a corporation can accept electronically sent proxies or electronically sent direct votes, the desire on the part of companies to communicate more completely with its stockholders will likely push the company to spend more and more time in producing online annual meetings.

Now that the company is public, the company and its management can have personal liability if materially incorrect information about the company falls into the public domain. Indeed, it is the purpose of the various formal SEC filings to make sure that accurate current information is disseminated. But often events arise which call for public disclosure on the part of the company, and if the information contained in such disclosure is both material and not previously contained in an SEC filing or other public announcement, then under SEC Regulation FD the company must make sure that contemporaneously with the making of such private disclosure there is also a broad public dissemination.

The annual meeting presents particular problems in the control of company information. Company officers answering questions at the annual meeting will have to stick to a recitation of previously announced material facts; in the event a decision is made to release previously nonpublic material information, or if such information inadvertently is provided, SEC regulations require prompt broad dissemination through filing of Form 8-K and through appropriate press releases to the public. In connection with its annual meeting, management may be briefed by attorneys and PR consultants as to how to answer questions from the floor concerning company operations and finances.

Indeed, separate and apart from its annual meeting, the company must generate some specific policies on the handling of material nonpublic information. Dough.com has already placed an ad in the newspaper for a director of investor relations, to coordinate the need of company investors for accurate information about the company. It is likely that this function within the company will grow over time and indeed likely that an outside public relations firm, experienced in the public relations and disclosure issues of public entities, will be retained. The company should anticipate adopting a constant policy of broadly disseminating public press releases about new products, and material developments in the company.

Particular problems arise in connection with dealing with rumors that may circulate in the public domain. The company may decide that it will systematically offer "no comment" with respect to questions about certain kinds of rumors or misinformation (whether raised at an annual meeting or at other times). Such a policy is difficult to sustain; once adopted it must be followed rigorously, and if in the past the company had a practice of discussing such matters, then it cannot state "no comment" in a particular case. Additionally, rules of most Exchanges and of the NASDAQ require a company affirmatively to correct, through its own public disclosure, materially inaccurate and misleading rumors which circulate in the marketplace through third parties regardless of whatever legal ground rules may exist.

The investor relations and legal advisers to the company also will now have to pay attention to the contents of the Web site, which in the past might have contained overly enthusiastic reports about the company, its potential profitability and the functionality of its products. Contents of the Web site can constitute false and misleading information upon which investors may rely to their detriment, and financial losses incurred by investors based on erroneous or dated Web site information can be recovered by lawsuit against the company and its management.

In forming a public disclosure policy, the company will work closely with legal counsel. Many of its pronouncements will contain language approved by the Private Securities Litigation Reform Act of 1995 so as to establish a so-called "safe harbor" for forward-looking statements. A company and its management will be insulated from liability in connection with any statement which later proves to be inaccurate, provided the statement is believed to be true when made and provided it is disclosed clearly that the anticipated future event is dependent on certain variables.

The company now must deal with the common practice of announcing quarterly earnings, generally by a conference call with securities analysts (securities professionals who follow the company stock and write about the stock in research reports and publications). Although quarterly financial information must be filed in the Form 10-Q within 45 days of the end of the first three fiscal quarters (or included in the annual Form 10-K within 90 days of the end of each fiscal year), it is not unusual for a company to announce its earnings by conference call or perhaps online as soon as determined. It is also during such earnings announcements that management is sometimes induced to speculate as to earning trends, and such speculation must be made carefully if it is to be protected by the "safe harbor" for forward-looking statements. The SEC is actively involved in regulating the announcement of earnings in such a private forum. The practice of releasing this information only to selected securities professionals has been criticized as fundamentally unfair to the broad investing public, and regulatory changes in this practice are likely in the near future.

Now that the company is public, management will be expected to announce its projected sales and profits; produce results that are reasonably consistent with its projections; adjust those projections in midquarter if it appears that they will prove to be materially erroneous; answer questions of securities analysts in such a way that the information which is provided is both accurate and does not materially disclose previously unknown facts; and manage the enterprise strategically with an eye toward quarter-to-quarter financial progress. The morning after the IPO closing, John Dough has already learned that there will be a monthly management meeting designed to control his budget and to narrow areas of research into the development of products with short test cycles so as to drive forward current earnings.

John Dough and Mary Manager meet for coffee a few weeks later. Each has sold a modest number of shares as part of the IPO. John has purchased a small sailboat, and Mary has made a down payment on a ski house. On paper, each is worth millions of dollars, although the remaining balance of their shares cannot now be resold because of the lockup for 180 days, and thereafter can be resold only pursuant to specific SEC regulations because they are "affiliates" of an issuer of publicly traded securities.

They have to be careful what they say to reporters, investors, and securities analysts. They even have to be careful about what they say casually in conversation with friends and relatives, lest they inadvertently leak nonpublic information which results in illegal insider trading profits. Someone who accidentally "tips" or leaks material information to someone who improperly profits from it is personally liable for that act.

Within 10 days of the IPO, Mary and John had filed with the SEC their personal report on Form 3, disclosing the amount of company stock that each owns of record and beneficially. Mary reminds John that these forms will have to be updated periodically by filing other forms, Forms 4 and 5, with the SEC whenever there is a material change in ownership. Section 16(b) of the Securities Exchange Act of 1934 will also require John and Mary to forfeit any profit they make in so-called "short swing trading"; the law requires automatic disgorgement of any profit made by corporate insiders who both buy and sell securities of their company within six calendar months as an automatic disincentive to trading by insiders based on their possible possession of material inside information.

If John and Mary do go to sell their shares, they will always possess much more information than the investing public. How can they protect themselves against a claim that they abused that information by, for example, selling just before the price of the stock fell based on poor earnings or excessive warranty claims? They may be able to sell their shares of stock only in prespecified time "windows" which follow immediately and briefly after the systematic announcement of public information by the company, such as immediately following the filing of SEC Form 10-K or SEC Form 10-Q. Alternately, they may adopt a preexisting Sales Plan under SEC Rule 10b5-1, which operates like a doomsday machine: The stockholder who wishes to trade in shares of stock of his or her company will set up in advance a program for purchasing or selling stock on a certain date or at a certain price, and then the brokerage firm will effect those transactions without the insider making any specific buy or sell decisions at the point in time that the transaction actually occurs.

Finally, John and Mary must avoid acting together in the purchase, sale or voting of stock, or joining together with others in that regard; the mere formation of such a "group" with respect to the stock of the company, if involving persons owning 5% or more of the company's stock, will trigger a requirement that such event be reported by the filing of a Form 13D with the SEC.

John and Mary agree that they are richer and have the opportunity to aggressively develop and directly market Dough-Ware, which is the reason they started Dough.com Inc. in the first place. But they are in some ways more personally restricted. They're sitting in the coffee shop, also agreeing that it is exciting and gratifying to be thought of as winners in the "new economy."

Then, glancing around, they lower their voices, because they want to make sure that no one can overhear their conversation.

FOR FURTHER READING

Arkebauer, James B., and Ron Schultz, *Going Public: Everything You Need to Know to Take Your Company Public, Including Internet Direct Public Offerings* (Chicago: Dearborn Trade, 1998).

Blowers, Stephen C., Peter H. Griffith, and Thomas L. Milan, *The Ernst & Young Guide to the IPO Value Journey* (New York: John Wiley, 1999).

Bloomenthal, Harold S., and Holme Roberts & Owen, *Going Public Handbook* (St. Paul, MN: West Group Securities Law Series, 2001).

Farnham, Brian, Bill Daugherty, and Jonas Steinman, *Codename Bulldog: How Iwon.com Went from the Idea to IPO* (New York, John Wiley, 2000).

Harmon, Steve, *Zero Gravity: Riding Venture Capital from High-Tech Start-up to Breakout IPO* (Princeton, NJ: Bloomberg Press, 1999).

Lipman, Frederick D., *The Complete Going Public Handbook: Everything You Need to Know to Turn a Private Enterprise into a Publicly Traded Company* (Roseville, CA: Prima Publishing, 2000).

Taulli, Tom, *Investing in IPOs: New Paths to Profit with Initial Public Offerings* (Princeton, NJ: Bloomberg Press, 1999).

INTERNET LINKS

www.sec.gov	The SEC Web site, links all SEC forms, regulations, and filings made by companies under EDGAR.
www.nasdaq.com/about /going_public.stm	Provides a going public summary, with discussion of fairness in underwriting compensation. This site is maintained by NASDAQ.
www.nyse.com and www.amex.com	Descriptive listing of IPO shares on the New York and American Stock Exchanges, through sites maintained by the exchanges themselves.
www.iporesources.org/ipopage.html and www.emergencepub.com /IPO07.going.publicwebs.htm	List and link a wide variety of related Web sites.

APPENDIX A

DUE DILIGENCE EXAMINATION OUTLINE

The goal of due diligence is to understand fully the business of the issuer, to identify the risks and problems it will face, and to assure that the registration statement is complete and accurate. Thoughtful analysis concerning the particular issuer as well as the experience, knowledge and care of the underwriters and their counsel in this process represent the critical ingredients of due diligence. A checklist of topics and procedures merely serve as an aid in the due diligence process when used in conjunction with thoughtful analysis and the review of applicable registration forms, rules and guides promulgated by the SEC.

The SEC and NASD Regulation both have acknowledged that attempts to define or standardize the elements of the underwriters' due diligence obligations have not been successful. The appropriate due diligence process will depend on the nature of the issuer, the level of the risk involved in the offering, and the investment banker's knowledge of and relationship with the issuer.

Checklists of the items to be covered in a due diligence investigation can be useful tools. It is not possible, however, to develop a checklist that will cover all issues or all offerings. Due diligence is not a mechanical process. The use or absence of use of a checklist does not indicate the quality of due diligence. Conversely, deviation from any checklist that is used does not taint a due diligence review any more than the following of a checklist validates such a review.

In view of the above, the following outline should not be considered a definitive statement of, or a standard recommended by, NASD Regulation regarding the due diligence issues and procedures that would be required or appropriate in any particular initial public offering.

I. **Before Commitment Is Made to Establish Investment Banking Relationship with Prospective Investment Banking Client (the "Company")**

A. Staffing the Review

1. Assign personnel who have particular competence in the business in which the issuer is engaged.

2. Consider retaining outside consultants to analyze the technology employed by the Company and others in the Company's industry.

B. Assessing Integrity of Management

1. Inquire of appropriate parties whether the corporation is being run by the type of persons with whom the investment banker would wish to be associated.

2. Determine whether any of the Company's officers, directors, or principal shareholders have been charged or convicted of any charges involving fraud, embezzlement, insider trading, or any other matter concerning dishonesty.

C. Review of Industry

1. Examine prospectuses, Form 10-Ks, and annual reports prepared by other corporations in the industry.

2. Examine research reports on major corporations in the industry as well as reports on the industry itself.

3. Become familiar with applicable regulations governing the industry.

4. Study the accounting practices followed in the industry, including any differences in accounting practices followed by different companies.

5. Determine financial ratios of the industry as a whole.

6. Become acquainted with new developments in the industry by examining trade publications.

7. Determine the industry size and growth rate.

8. Assess whether the industry is subject to cyclical influences.

9. Determine whether seasonality of demand affects the industry.

10. Determine the stage of the industry in the industry life cycle (e.g., growth, maturity).

11. Evaluate short-term and long-term prospects for the industry.

II. After Commitment Is Made to Establish Investment Banking Relationship

A. Submission of Questionnaire to Officers and Directors

The specific information to be sought includes:

1. Relationship to underwriters.

2. Voting arrangements.

3. Transactions with the companies.

4. Past and present occupations.

5. Record and beneficial ownership of the stock.

6. Compensation, direct and indirect.

7. Principal shareholders.

8. Knowledge of pending or threatened litigation.

B. Submission of Request for Company Documents

1. Regarding legal status.

   a. Charter documents (articles of incorporation and bylaws) and all amendments.

   b. Minute books for meetings of directors, shareholders, executive committee, stock option committee and the like for the past five years.

   c. Copies of applications for permits to issue stock permits, and exemption notices.

   d. Specimen stock certificates.

   e. Copies of voting trust and voting agreements.

   f. Documents previously filed with the SEC, including prospectuses, Form 10, 10-K, 9-K, 8-K, proxy statements, and supplementary sales literature.

   g. Contracts or arrangements restricting the transferability of shares.

   h. Shareholders' list indicating names, ownership, and how shares are held.

   i. Licenses to conduct business.

   j. Foreign qualifications, if any.

   k. All documents filed with any state agency affecting corporate status, including annual reports.

2. Regarding the Company's business.

   a. Promissory notes (except immaterial routine notes from persons, other than officers, directors, or 10 percent shareholders), loan agreements, trust deeds, indentures and all relevant correspondence regarding same.

   b. Financial statements and tax returns for the past five years.

   c. Stock option agreements, profit sharing and pension plans, supplementary information booklets.

   d. Annual reports.

   e. Advertising materials, brochures, and other sales literature.

   f. Leases and/or grant deeds.

   g. Description of plants and properties.

   h. Agreements with officers, directors, shareholders, or promoters (e.g., employment agreements, indemnification agreements).

   i. Documents of agreements with affiliates (e.g., lease, purchase agreement, license, covenant not to compete, etc.), insiders and other related parties, and if affiliate is other than a natural person (e.g., trust, estate, partnership, joint venture, corporation) court orders, agreements, stock book, and other documents necessary to establish precise nature of affiliation and terms thereof.

   j. All materials contracts.

   k. Copies of licenses, permits, governmental approvals, quality ratings, franchises, patents, copyrights, trademark and service mark registrations, trade secret agreements and any opinions of counsel related thereto.

   l. Distribution or agency agreements.

   m. Consignment agreements.

   n. List of major customers and suppliers, copies of their existing agreements, and copies of correspondence for the past year.

   o. All documents relating to any complaints, investigations, claims, hearings, litigation, adjudications, or proceedings by or against the Company, including copies of the material pleading.

   p. All documents relating to issuance of stock, including offering documents and documents relating to reliance on securities registration exemptions and any related litigation action or proceeding.

   q. Business plans (past five years).

   r. All written documents relating to employment policies and practices.

   s. All correspondence between the Company and legal counsel regarding responses to requests for auditors information (for five years).

   t. Copies of any pleading or other documents relating to any litigation, action, or proceeding related to any of the Company's affiliates, officers, directors, or beneficial owners of 10 percent or more of stock.

   u. All insurance documents.

   v. Affirmative action plans.

   w. Any other documents that are material to the Company.

C. Review of Basic Corporate Documents

1. After gaining an understanding of the industry, examine specific Company documents filed with the SEC during the past five years, including:

   a. Form 10-K.

   b. Form 8-K.

   c. Form 10-Q.

   d. Registration statements and private offering memoranda relating to the sale of securities and any

   e. Proxy statements for:

      1) Annual meetings,

      2) Acquisitions, and

      3) Other transactions requiring a shareholder vote.

2. Examine document and other communications sent to the shareholders during the past five years, including:

   a. Annual reports and quarterly reports, with particular attention to the president's letter, which may provide insight into any major problems faced by the corporation.

   b. Follow-up reports on annual meetings.

   c. Shareholder letters.

3. Examine public documents on the Company.

   a. News clippings.

   b. Press releases.

   c. Documents on file.

   d. NEXIS computer searches.

   e. Recent private placement memoranda and written rating agency presentation.

4. Evaluate restrictive covenants.

   a. Examine indentures and loan agreements.

   b. Consider the effect such covenants might have on the Company's operations and prospective financing.

D. Analysis of the Company and Its Industry

1. Company analysis.

   a. Compare the Company's prior business plan and financial plan with the actual results obtained.

   b. Determine the Company's principal product lines. If the Company's principal products are newly developed, it may be desirable to retain an independent consultant who can advise on the technology, the feasibility of the product, and its potential market.

   c. Examine the demographic and geographic markets in which the company sells its products.

   d. Compile a list of principal customers by products.

   e. Obtain samples of marketing and sales literature used for various products.

   f. Determine the mechanism for distribution of company products or services, i.e., wholesale and retail distributors, personal service, or Internet.

   g. Assess the technology position of the company.

   h. Compile a list of trademarks, trade names, and service marks and assess the protection obtained for such marks and names.

   i. Obtain copies of permits for conduct of business, including licenses, franchises, concessions, and distributorship agreements.

2. Strategic analysis.

   a. What are the Company's long-term goals?

   b. On what basis does the Company measure its performance?

   c. What strengths does the Company intend to exploit to be successful in its industry?

   d. What weaknesses does the Company have in the industry and what does it intend to do to overcome such weaknesses?

   e. What are the current market opportunities and how does the Company plan to exploit such opportunities?

   f. What are the risks that the Company faces in the industry? What is the likelihood that such risks will come to fruition? What would be the consequence to the Company if the risks came to fruition?

   g. What are the Company's business strategies for success in the industry?

3. Financial analysis.

   a. Compare basic financial ratios of the Company to the industry average.

      (1) Debt to equity ratios.

      (2) Liquidity ratios.

         (a) Current ratio (Current assets/current liabilities).

         (b) Quick ratio (Current assets minus inventory/current liabilities).

         (c) Earnings/fixed charges.

         (d) Price/earnings ratios.

      (3) Asset utilization ratios.

         (a) Sales turnover.

         (b) Total assets turnover.

      (4) Profitability ratios.

         (a) Return on assets.

         (b) Return on equity.

      (5) Price-earnings ratios.

4. Prepare a written memorandum setting forth questions to be asked of management and areas to be explored in greater depth.

E. Visits to Principal Facilities

1. If the Company is a manufacturing concern, visit one or more of its principal plants. Inspect the facilities to become acquainted with the Company's products and the manner in which they are produced.

2. If the Company is not a manufacturing concern, visit one or more of the Company's offices to obtain an overview of the Company's day-to-day operations.

3. Does it appear the facilities are being fully utilized?

F. Meetings with Principal Officers (after reviewing the registration statement but before engaging in a line-by-line discussion of the document)

1. Hold individual meetings with executive officers responsible for significant aspects of the Company's business.

   a. Prepare a list of questions in advance to focus the discussions.

      (1) How would you assess the flexibility of the production facilities?

      (2) Do you anticipate advances in production techniques and, if so, is the Company prepared to make such advances?

(3) Does the Company have any continuing obligations in connection with sales, such as an ongoing maintenance and repair obligation or a requirement to finance purchases by customers?

(4) How do you assess the quality and quantity of resources allocated by the Company to research and development?

(5) What are your financial projections?

(6) Have results met past projections?

(7) How do you assess the gross profit margin trends in your various product lines?

(8) How do you feel about the level of sales for each of the Company's product lines?

(9) How do you assess labor relations? Have there been any work stoppages and, if so, how have you dealt with them?

(10) What is the Company's overall advertising and marketing plan?

(11) What is the Company's acquisition policy? Explain the Company's recent acquisitions, if any.

(12) For what does the Company plan to use the proceeds of the public offering?

(13) How would you assess the inventory turnover?

(14) Have there been any delays in new product introduction?

(15) Has the Company changed accounting or legal representation within the last five years? If so, why?

(16) Has the Company lost any major customer, supplier or distributor within the last five years? If so, why?

(17) Are any of the existing shareholders antagonistic toward the current management of the Company? If so, please explain.

b. During the course of the interviews, ask the same questions of different corporate officials to evaluate the answers received and to obtain different perspectives on potential problems.

2. Hold at least one meeting with the Company's chief executive officer (CEO).

a. Ask the CEO to review the broad aspects of the Company's strategic and operational goals and its plan to achieve those goals.

b. Ask the CEO for his or her personal assessment of the Company's strengths and weaknesses.

(1) This interview should be as far reaching as circumstances warrant.

(2) It is essential to listen critically to the CEO's comments.

3. Based on the meetings, assess the competence of the officers of the Company.

a. Are the administrators organized and knowledgeable?

b. Are the financial officers skilled?

c. Are the technical personnel well-qualified?

d. Is the management structure such that it can adjust to the Company's growth beyond the current stages of operation?

G. Meetings with Company's Accountants (Out of the Presence of the Company's Officials)

Questions to Ask:

1. How would you assess the Company's internal controls?

2. Are there any unusual accounting issues in regard to the Company or the industry?

3. Are reserves adequate?

4. How would you assess the Company's aged-analysis of accounts receivable?

5. Do you note any unusual fluctuations in inventory?

6. Is the Company's method of revenue recognition in line with industry practice and applicable accounting principles?

7. How do you assess the Company's segment reporting?

8. From your dealings with the Company's accounting and financial personnel, how would you assess their capability?

H. Meeting with Company's Counsel

Questions to Ask:

1. How would you assess the pending litigation and contingent liabilities of the Company?

2. How would you assess the pending administration and regulatory proceedings that the Company is facing?

3. How would you assess the status of the Company's proprietary information and intellectual property, including any copyrights, trademarks, service marks and trade secrets?

I. Meetings with Other Third Parties

1. Suppliers/creditors/distributors. Does the Company pay its bills/debts in a timely manner?

2. Competitors and customers.

   a. What is the company's reputation?

   b. How would you rate management's reputation?

   c. What risks are present in the Company and its industry?

   d. How would you rate the quality of the Company's products and services?

J. Legal Review

1. Review of basic corporate documents.

   a. Articles of incorporation.

      (1) Obtain copies of the articles of incorporation, including any restated articles and amendments.

      (2) Determine whether all of these items were certified by the Secretary of State (by whatever name known) of the state in which the company is incorporated.

      (3) Determine whether the purposes clause of the articles is broad enough under the applicable law to include all actions previously taken and presently being contemplated.

      (4) List the dates of all amendments and summarize changes.

      (5) Were such amendments validly authorized by the shareholders?

      (6) Is the name as specified in the Charter the same as used by the Company?

      (7) Do the powers of the Company suggest any restrictions?

      (8) Is the authorized capital sufficient?

(9) Verify the description of the Company's equity stock.

(10) Do the articles provide for preemptive rights?

(11) Does the authorized number of directors conform to the minutes?

(12) Do the articles provide for the accessibility of shares?

(13) Do the articles provide for restrictions on issuance of shares?

(14) What is the county of the principal place of business?

(15) Do the articles provide for indemnification of officers and directors?

b. Bylaws.

(1) Obtain copies of the bylaws, including all amendments certified by the corporate secretary.

(2) Review for powers of officers, roles of committees, powers to amend, restrictions on actions, and other governing provisions.

c. Minutes.

(1) Obtain minutes of all meetings of directors, committees of directors and shareholders, including copies of any written notices, waivers of notices, and written consents to action without a meeting, all for the past five years.

(2) Has the Company regularly held its annual meeting of shareholders? If not, explain the circumstances. If not, were notices duly given or waivers obtained? If notices or waivers were properly obtained, indicate whether such waivers were actually signed before or during the meetings, or whether they were executed after the meetings.

(3) Indicate whether the Company holds regular periodic meetings of its directors.

(4) What is the normal frequency of such meetings?

(5) Were notices duly given or waivers obtained with respect to these meetings? If so, indicate whether such waivers were actually signed before or during the meetings, or whether they were executed after the meetings.

(6) If a meeting was not held, were resolutions adopted pursuant to proper unanimous written consent?

(7) Prepare a summary of the minutes for review by the underwriters.

d. Meetings.

(1) Indicate the date and place for meetings, both for directors and shareholders, as provided in the bylaws or articles of the corporation.

(2) What were the actual locations of the last three shareholders' meetings?

(3) What were the actual locations of the last two directors' meetings?

e. Executive committee meetings.

(1) If the Company has an executive committee, does it hold regular periodic meetings?

(2) If so, are minutes regularly prepared?

(3) If such minutes are prepared, is such preparation under the direction or approval of the office of general counsel?

(4) If no meetings are held, are resolutions properly adopted pursuant to unanimous written consent?

f. Directors' and shareholders' meetings/minutes.

(1) How are the corporate minutes and/or unanimous written consents kept? If the minutes or consents are kept looseleaf, are the pages consecutively numbered?

(2) Are previous minutes of meetings properly signed? Who signs the minutes?

(3) Do all previous minutes reflect the presence of a quorum and the names of those in attendance?

(4) Do all previous minutes indicate the approval of previous minutes?

(5) Do all previous minutes indicate the time and place of the holding of the meeting?

(6) Do all previous minutes indicate that either waivers were properly executed or notices properly given for the meeting?

g. Voting trust agreements.

(1) Obtain copies of any voting trust agreements, or shareholders' or similar agreement, and lists of the shares covered.

(2) Do such agreements terminate by virtue of the offering?

h. Minute books and stock records.

(1) Where are the minute books of the Company physically kept?

(2) Where are the stock record books of the Company physically kept?

(3) Who is the stock transfer agent for the Company? (Indicate the transfer agent's complete address.)

i. Annual reports.

(1) Obtain copies of any document sent to shareholders, including the Company's annual reports, quarterly reports, following reports on annual meetings and shareholder letters and press releases sent within the last three years.

j. Proxy statements.

(1) Obtain copies of any proxy statements of the Company for annual meetings, acquisitions or other transactions requiring a shareholder vote within the last five years.

(2) Obtain copies of the form of proxy used for the last annual meetings.

k. Annual certified audits.

(1) Obtain copies of the annual certified audits of the Company for the last three years, if any, unless contained in the annual report.

(2) Has there been any change in the accountants?

l. Election procedures.

(1) Do election procedures for directors, as used by the Company, comply with all applicable laws and regulations, including the Company's bylaws?

(2) Have directors been unanimously elected?

m. Concurrent director/officer status.

(1) Was any person who was both a director and an officer present at

the meeting at which his or her salary was set?

(2) Was such person counted as part of the quorum for such a meeting or did that person sign a unanimous written consent for same?

(3) If an affirmative answer is given to either (1) or (2), does such action create a legal problem under the applicable law?

n. Power of board of directors.
Is it the Company's policy to get the board of directors' approval for:

(1) Changes in reserves?

(2) Changes in surplus accounts?

(3) Declaration of dividends?

(4) Election of officers?

(5) The setting of officers' salaries and/ or bonuses?

(6) Amendments to the by-laws of the corporations?

(7) The granting of powers of attorney?

o. Policy-making authority of the board of directors.

(1) As a practical matter, does the Company get the board of directors' approval for all major policy decisions?

(2) If not, how much leeway does the board of directors give the Company's management in the area?

p. Indemnification.

(1) Obtain copies of any insurance policies or other agreements, other than the bylaws of the articles of incorporation, which provide for the indemnification of any officer, director, shareholder, employee, or other agent of the company.

(2) Is the indemnification agreement or policy authorized by applicable jurisdiction?

(3) Is any indemnification in the bylaws consonant with law in the applicable jurisdiction?

q. Rights of the various classes of stock.

(1) State the voting rights of the various classes of stocks.

(2) Are any dividends on preferred stock presently in arrears? If so, indicate any additional preferences that come into being because of the arrearage.

(3) Indicate any potential voting right, other than noted in Section II.J.1.b. above, held by holders of preferred, convertibles, debentures, bonds, etc., that become effective on the happening of contingent events (such as failure to pay dividends or make payments).

r. Dividends and other distributions

(1) Indicate the Company's dividend record on common stock for the past five years.

(2) Indicate any other distribution of property to shareholders by the Company over the past five years.

(3) Has the Company ever paid a dividend or made another distribution to shareholders without meeting an earned surplus or other test under applicable state law to cover it? If so, explain.

s. Pension plans/profit sharing plans/stock option plans.

(1) Obtain copies of (i) all pension plans, (ii) all profit sharing plans, and (iii) all stock option plans.

(2) If the Company has a pension plan, indicate the date on which there last was a compliance with the Federal Pension Plan Disclosure Act. (Compliance is obtained by giving a printed copy of the plan to the employees covered thereby.)

t. Reports filed with governmental agencies.

(1) Review all material reports filed with any governmental agency (state or federal) during the last 12 months.

(2) Indicate whether the narrative in all reports filed with any governmental agency, as well as the Company's annual report, is checked for accuracy by the office of general counsel.

u. Related parties.

(1) Does the Company do business with which any officer or director, including spouses and other close relatives, has an interest?

v. Insurance.

(1) Is the Company self-insured?

(2) If so, to what extent?

(3) Indicate the insurance coverage of the Company, giving the name of the carrier and the policy numbers of each type of coverage.

w. License to do business.

(1) Indicate the states in which the Company does business.

(2) Obtain copies of certificate of good standing to determine if the Company is properly licensed in each state it is doing business.

(3) Is the Company licensed to do business in any states in which it presently is not doing business? If so, indicate the tax consequences for each jurisdiction.

x. Corporate opportunity doctrine compliance.

(1) Indicate any possible violation of the corporate opportunity doctrine known to the Company's counsel.

y. Contingent liabilities.

(1) List all material contingent liabilities of the Company not otherwise set forth in this audit.

2. Documents regarding securities.

a. Stock options/stock purchases/ stock bonuses.

(1) Obtain all forms of stock option plans, stock purchase plans, and stock bonus plans, and all forms of stock option agreements, or escrow agreements that have been or may be used under any such plan, as well as all other documents relating to the issuance of securities by the Company, including other purchase agreements, registration rights agreements, and offering circulars.

b. Sources of capital.

(1) List each issue of stock, bonds, debentures, options, warrants, other convertibles, etc., indicating the amount, the authorized amount, and the applicable permit or registration of each (both state and federal), and if there is no permit and/or registration, state the claimed state and Federal exemption.

(2) List the states where such securities described in Section J.2.a., above, were issued and state the date of blue-sky authorization. If no such authorization, give the applicable exemption.

(3) Indicate the date of each federal registration, if any, and the term for which registered.

(4) Obtain copies of any agreements pursuant to which such securities were issued (e.g., stock option plans, underwriting agreements, placement agreements, bond indentures, etc.).

(5) Do any such agreements provide for registration rights? If so, describe.

(6) Obtain copies of all applications for permits, private placement memoranda and registration statements.

c. Payments for stock.

(1) Do the Company's records indicate all of its outstanding stock was properly issued for value?

(2) Is any of the Company's stock not fully paid? If so, explain; do statutes, articles and by-laws permit?

d. Stock issuance/transfer restrictions.

(1) Do all issuance and transfers comply with any rights of first refusal, preemptive rights, or other restrictions contained in the articles, bylaws or other documents, such as placement agreements?

3. Review of material contracts.

a. Various material contracts.

(1) Obtain bank lines of credit agreements, including any amendments, renewal letters, notices, default waivers, etc.

(2) Obtain other outstanding loan agreements, guarantees, indentures, or agreements with respect to indebtedness.

(3) Obtain all outstanding material leases for real and personal property.

(4) Obtain material contracts with suppliers and customers.

(5) Obtain any model sales contracts, license agreements, and dealer agreements used by the Company.

(6) Obtain agreements for loans and any other agreements (including consulting and employment contracts) for officers, directors, or employees, whether or not now outstanding.

(7) Obtain schedule for all insurance policies in force covering property of the Company and any other insurance policies, such as "key man" policies or products liability policies.

(8) Obtain partnership or joint venture agreements.

(9) Obtain copies of any bonus plans, retirement plans, pension plans, deferred compensation plans, profit sharing and management incentive agreements.

b. Mortgages, notes payable, and other liabilities.

(1) List all mortgages (including deeds of trust) of the Company on which

the anticipation is that final payment will not be made within the 36 months of the date of this examination.

(2) Indicate whether such mortgages overlap any other security interest given by the Company.

(3) List all notes and other liabilities in excess of $5,000.

c. Reports on dividends.

(1) Does the Company make reports (both federal and/or state) on dividends paid to its shareholders?

(2) If so, give the date of the last such report.

d. Corporate negotiable insurance.

(1) Indicate each institution in which the Company has authorized its agents to execute negotiable instruments, showing the authorized agents, their titles, and the limit of their authority.

(2) For each of the authorizations, indicate the date of the corporate resolution authorizing the signature.

e. Authority of corporate agent.

(1) Is a notice of limit of agent's authority given to each new account with which the Company does business?

(2) If not, what steps are taken to ensure that each agent of the Company does not exceed his/her authority?

f. Business outside the United States.

(1) If the Company does any business outside the United States, determine whether or not any activities of the Company might reasonably be construed as a violation of any statutory or regulating limitation on

doing business with specified nations or limitation on certain trading, such as trading in gold and foreign exchange.

(2) What steps have been taken to ensure that the Company does not violate any prohibitions concerning transactions between designated foreign companies or concerning transfer with respect to securities registered in the name of designated nationals, as well as importation of and dealing on certain classes of merchandise?

(3) List all corporations incorporated in a foreign country in which the Company owns 10 percent or more of the capital stock, and for each such corporation indicate (i) any outstanding powers of attorney (ii) any guarantees undertaken (iii) any liabilities created, and (iv) and contract commitments undertaken.

g. Prepaid items.

(1) List all prepaid items on the Company's book of assets when such prepayments exceed $100,000 and will continue in excess of this amount for more than 12 months.

h. Bad debts.

(1) Indicate the percentage of accounts receivable that became bad debts in each of the last three years.

(2) Ascertain trends regarding bad debts.

i. Security interests.

(1) What security interest, if any, is typically used to secure open accounts?

(2) Are such security devices properly perfected?

(3) In how many states does the Company presently have perfected security interest?

(4) What steps are taken to ensure the timely filing of continuation statements required under Article 9 of the Uniform Commercial Code?

j. Warehousing.

(1) Does the Company, as either buyer or seller, utilize the facilities of on-premises warehousing for financing purposes?

(2) Does the Company, as either buyer or seller, utilize warehouse receipts in financing?

k. Labor contracts.

(1) List all labor contracts to which the Company is a signer, indicating the bargaining unit covered, the union, the termination date, and a general statement of the company's relationship with the union, indicating specifically any major problem areas.

(2) If there are material problems, obtain copies of each labor contract.

l. Individual employment contracts.

(1) Does the Company have any individual employees with a written employment contract?

(2) If so, obtain copies of all forms used for employment contracts (including forms of contracts used for executives).

m. Minimum wage compliance.

(1) Is the Company considered to be engaged in interstate commerce?

(2) Are any employees or employees of subcontractors working on the premises currently being paid less than the applicable minimum wage per hour? If so, what justification can be given for a lower rate of pay?

(3) Are any employees covered by a state minimum wage law requiring the payment of more than the federal minimum wage per hour? If so, indicate with appropriate citation the state law, the bargaining units covered, and any other pertinent information.

(4) Is overtime paid? If not, explain when it is not paid.

n. Child labor.

(1) Does the Company employ any person under eighteen years of age on a permanent basis?

(2) What safeguards are taken to ensure that the Company does not violate either the federal or state "Child Labor Act"?

o. Compliance with fair labor standards.

(1) Has any governmental agency checked the Company within the last three years in regard to compliance with the fair labor standard act or other litigation regarding employees?

(2) If so, indicate the approximate date and result of the investigation.

p. Compliance with antidiscrimination statutes.

(1) Does the Company have procedures to assure compliance with antidis-criminatory statutes relating to age, sex, and race; and does it keep adequate records to demonstrate compliance (e.g., application forms,

records of employees, and work assignments, etc.)?

(2) Does the company, in fact, have an age limit cutoff beyond which general hiring is not done? If so, what is the age limit?

(3) What steps have been taken to ensure the compliance by the Company with federal statutes prohibiting age discrimination in hiring?

q. Salary withholding information.

(1) Does the Company maintain an up-to-date file of Form W-4 (withholding information) for each employee?

(2) Has the Company failed to comply with withholding requirements?

r. Worker's compensation.

(1) Does the Company maintain the worker compensation insurance required by the state on each employee?

(2) If not, explain.

s. Other. Assess compliance with state and Federal laws related to the environment, occupational health and safety, and antitrust/unfair trade practice regulations.

t. Material payments on contracts.

(1) List all contracts, presently in force, on which the Company, directly or indirectly, is bound, that will not be completed within 24 months, and each that involves payments (or performance of services or delivery of goods) to or by the Company of a material account.

(2) Make a schedule of all leases for real and personal property requiring payment of a material amount.

u. Contract forms and significant provisions.

(1) Do the contract forms presently in use by the Company meet the requirements of the Uniform Commercial Code?

(2) What precautions are taken to ensure that, upon acceptance, additional terms are not inserted by the other party and made part of the agreement?

(3) Obtain copies of all significant contract forms utilized by the Company.

(4) Are any required anti-discrimination provisions included?

v. Current breaches of material agreements.

(1) If any party is presently in breach of any material agreement with the Company, indicate:

(i) The default,

(ii) The contract penalty for the breach, if any,

(iii) What action presently is being taken and

(iv) What action is being contemplated.

(2) Does the Company take action in the event of breaches by others?

w. Sales of the Company's products.

(1) Indicate how the Company's sales are made (i.e., through sales agents, distributors, independent contractors, etc.).

(2) Indicate the authority each type of selling agent possesses.

(3) If sales agents have limited authority, what steps are taken to publish this authority to those with whom the agent deals?

(4) If independent contractors are used, are they permitted to set prices? Are they given a sales quota? Are they truly independent contractors?

x. Identification of agents.

(1) List the titles and positions of those who, under a reasonable interpretation of the statutory and case law of the jurisdiction in which they sell for the Company, could be considered agents of the Company.

(2) Do any such agents act through contractual relationships?

y. Sales forms.

(1) Does the Company have sales forms that are considered to be offers tendered for acceptance by the purchaser, or

(2) Does the Company have forms that are considered offers to the Company when executed by a purchaser? If the latter is used, is acceptance accomplished at the home office or by the agent in the field?

z. Direct sales.

(1) List those jurisdictions in which direct sales are made by the Company.

(2) List those jurisdictions in which direct sales are made through an independent contractor or distributor.

(3) List those jurisdictions in which direct sales are made only via communications in interstate commerce.

aa. Trade associations.

(1) Indicate whether the Company is a member of any trade association(s).

(2) List all such organizations with which the Company has any contract.

(3) Indicate the relationship between the Company and such organizations.

(4) Indicate whether any of the organizations above listed have been investigated by any state or federal group, either administrative, judicial, or legislative, for possible anti-trust violations during the last five years.

(5) If so, explain in detail the outcome of the investigation and what impact, if any, this had on the Company.

bb. Material transactions with insiders and affiliates.

(1) Obtain material of any material transactions within the last five fiscal years with any insider (i.e., any director, officer or substantial owner of the Company's securities) or any associate of, or entity affiliated with, an insider.

4. Regulation and litigation.

a. Various items relating to regulation litigation.

(1) Obtain all letters sent to the Company's independent auditors in connection with its audits for the past five fiscal years, including "litigation letters."

(2) Obtain copies of letters from the auditors to the Company regarding its internal management controls.

(3) Obtain active litigation files for material litigation, including letters asserting claims, complaints, answers, etc.

(4) Obtain any settlement documents for material litigation.

(5) Obtain any decrees, orders, or judgments of courts or governmental agencies.

(6) Obtain information regarding any material litigation to which the Company is a party or in which it may become involved.

(7) Obtain audited financial statements (five years).

(8) Obtain recent forward-looking budgets for the next two fiscal years prepared on a monthly basis (if available).

(9) Obtain recent five-year projections (if available).

b. Pricing policies.

(1) Does the Company, in its pricing policies, follow an industrial leader?

(2) If so, which competitor does the Company follow as leader?

(3) If not, how are the Company's pricing policies determined?

c. Compliance with building codes.

(1) Is the Company in compliance with all building codes (or other similar local governmental codes) that are applicable to it?

(2) If not, explain.

(3) Indicate the approximate date of the last time the Company's facilities were checked by local governmental authorities for possible violations of local governmental codes, and indicate the results of such investigation.

(4) If any of the Company's facilities are borderline, indicate any remedial steps that should be undertaken at this time.

(5) List any warnings that the Company has received within the past three years for the violation of any local governmental codes.

(6) List the date and amounts of fines, if any, paid to any local governmental authority for violation of local codes, other than the traffic code, paid by the Company during the last three years.

d. Contract defaults.

(1) Is the Company presently in default under any contractual arrangement?

(2) If so, explain the default and indicate the penalties arising out of such default.

e. Liens.

(1) List all liens presently in force against the Company's property, both real and personal.

(2) Have any actions been taken in respect to any such liens?

f. Legal action.

(1) List all legal actions presently pending or known to be contemplated in which the Company might have an involvement.

(2) Ascertain the identity of legal counsel representing the Company in such matters.

g. Assignment of patents, trademarks, and copyrights.

    (1) Obtain the form used in which employees assign to the Company any patent, trademark, and/or copyright that might arise from inventions discovered while working for the Company, together with a list of the employees who have signed the contract. If a form is not used, should it be?

    (2) Does the Company have nondisclosure agreements with employees?

h. Surety bonds.

    (1) Indicate those employees (by title or position) who are presently covered by a fidelity or other surety bonds.

    (2) What are the amounts of any such bonds?

i. Charitable contributions.

    (1) Indicate the number and amount of charitable contributions made by the Company in each of the last two years in the following categories: (i) religious, (ii) educational, (iii) other.

    (2) Does the Company have any policy regarding employee charitable contributions?

j. Lobbying activities/political campaigns

    (1) Indicate whether the Company is engaged in any lobbying activities or political campaigns and, if so, to what extent, and at what financial cost.

(2) Does the Company retain any lobbying firms?

k. Tax compliance.

    (1) Does the Company file all required tax reports?

    (2) If not, explain.

    (3) How long are tax records kept?

    (4) Does the Company have its tax records reviewed periodically for compliance with tax laws?

    (5) How often are the tax reports reviewed and by whom?

    (6) Does the Company utilize tax counsel in the planning phase of transactions?

    (7) If so, is tax advice rendered by house counsel or outside counsel?

    (8) How are audits by governmental tax authorities conducted?

l. Year 2000 compliance.

    (1) Assess the affect on the company of its compliance with the Year 2000 transition, taking into account the costs, potential disruptions of productivity, potential liabilities related to company products or services, and compliance by suppliers.

m. Subsidiary information.

    (1) Identify the Company's subsidiaries.

    (2) Where material, provide the information above with respect to each subsidiary of the Company.

K. Review Officers' and Directors' Questionnaire

1. Obtain from the Company's counsel the "officers' and directors' questionnaire" to gather information on the Company's officers and directors, their remuneration and employee benefits, and material transactions that they have had with the Company.

2. Compare the information disclosed in the questionnaire with the disclosure required by the applicable registration form, especially in regard to:

   a. Insider transactions and loans.

   b. NASD Regulation affiliations.

   c. Litigation.

   d. Cheap stock.

   e. Stock ownership.

L. Check of Order Backlogs

1. Compare oral purchase orders or oral changes to written purchase orders.

2. Do cancellation provisions exist in standard purchase orders, including any penalties for cancellation?

3. Are there indications that outstanding offers may be "soft," or subject to cancellation?

M. Detailed Review of Draft of Registration Statement

1. Read the draft of the registration statement carefully for content.

2. Read the draft of the registration statement a second time against:

   a. The items of the applicable form (e.g., Form S-1, Form S-2, Form S-3, Form S-18) and

   b. Regulation S-K (to the extent covered by the applicable form).

      (1) Item 501-Forepart of Registration Statement and Outside Front Cover Page of Prospectus.

      (2) Item 502-Inside Front and Outside Back Cover Pages of Prospectus.

      (3) Item 503-Summary Information, Risk Factors, and Ratio of Earnings to Fixed Charges.

      (4) Item 504-Use of Proceeds.

      (5) Item 505-Determination of Offering Price.

      (6) Item 506-Dilution.

      (7) Item 507-Selling Security Holders.

      (8) Item 508-Plan of Distribution.

      (9) Item 509-Interests of Named Experts.

      (10) Item 510-Disclosure of Commission Position on Indemnification for Securities Act Liabilities.

      (11) Item 511-Other Expenses of Issuance and Distribution.

      (12) Item 512-Undertakings.

3. Review the registration statement on a line-by-line basis with appropriate individuals, including:

   a. Officers of the Company responsible for preparing the registration statement.

b. The Company's counsel.

c. Representative of the Company's certified public accountants.

4. Based on the information elicited through discussions with various individuals, encourage that the registration statement be revised in an effort to improve upon its disclosure.

5. After a revised draft of the registration statement is available, see that it is distributed to all directors and key officials.

6. Review the Company's procedures for collecting and evaluating comments on the registration statement from those persons to whom it has been furnished.

N. Review of Other Documents

1. Review documents not previously furnished, including those of a confidential nature that the Company would prefer not to be taken from its offices, including:

a. Five-year plans.

b. Financial forecasts.

c. Budgets.

d. Periodic reports by operating units to senior management or the board of directors.

e. Letters of comment received by the Company in connection with prior registration statements.

f. At least the most recent management letter prepared by the accountants in connection with their audit.

SOURCE: The NASDAQ Stock Market, Inc.

O. Review During Negotiation of Underwriting Agreement

1. During negotiations on representations and warranties in the underwriting agreement, be sensitive to potential problems that arise and may need to be disclosed in the registration statement.

2. Review legal counsel's summary of the Company's minutes.

III. Summary Analysis

A. Prior to effectiveness of registration statement, prepare a memorandum summarizing the due diligence investigation, including the dates of any visits to principal facilities, meetings with management, and registration statement review sessions.

B. Have this memorandum reviewed by counsel for the underwriters.

APPENDIX B

UNITED STATES
SECURITIES AND EXCHANGE COMMISSION
WASHINGTON, D.C. 20549

FORM S-1
REGISTRATION STATEMENT UNDER THE
SECURITIES ACT OF 1933

(Exact name of registrant as specified in its charter)

(State or other jurisdiction of incorporation or organization)

(Primary Standard Industrial Classification Code Number)

(I.R.S. Employer Identification Number)

(Address, including zip code, and telephone number, including area
code, of registrant's principal executive offices)

(Name, address, including zip code, and telephone number,
including area code, of agent for service)

(Approximate date of commencement of proposed sale to the public)

If any of the securities being registered on this Form are to be offered on a delayed or continuous basis pursuant to Rule 415 under the Securities Act of 1933, check the following box: ☐

If this Form is filed to register additional securities for an offering pursuant to Rule 462(b) under the Securities Act, please check the following box and list the Securities Act registration statement number of the earlier effective registration statement for the same offering. ☐

If this Form is a post-effective amendment filed pursuant to Rule 462(c) under the Securities Act, check the following box and list the Securities Act registration statement number of the earlier effective registration statement for the same offering. ☐

If this Form is a post-effective amendment filed pursuant to Rule 462(d) under the Securities Act, check the following box and list the Securities Act registration statement number of the earlier effective registration statement for the same offering. ☐

If delivery of the prospectus is expected to be made pursuant to Rule 434, please check the following box. ☐

Calculation of Registration Fee

Title of Each Class of Securities to Be Registered	Amount to Be Registered	Proposed Maximum Offering Price per Unit	Proposed Maximum Aggregate Offering Price	Amount of Registration Fee

Note: Specific details relating to the fee calculation shall be furnished in notes to the table, including references to provisions of Rule 457 (§ 230.457 of this chapter) relied upon, if the basis of the calculation is not otherwise evident from the information presented in the table. If the filing fee is calculated pursuant to Rule 457(o) under the Securities Act, only the title of the class of securities to be registered, the proposed maximum aggregate offering price for that class of securities, and the amount of registration fee need to appear in the Calculation of Registration Fee table. Any difference between the dollar amount of securities registered for such offerings and the dollar amount of securities sold may be carried forward on a future registration statement pursuant to Rule 429 under the Securities Act.

GENERAL INSTRUCTIONS

I.   Eligibility Requirements for Use of Form S-1

This Form shall be used for the registration under the Securities Act of 1933 ("Securities Act") of securities of all registrants for which no other form is authorized or prescribed, except that this Form shall not be used for securities of foreign governments or political subdivisions thereof.

II.   Application of General Rules and Regulations

A.   Attention is directed to the General Rules and Regulations under the Securities Act, particularly those comprising Regulation C (17 CFR 230.400 to 230.494) thereunder. That Regulation contains general requirements regarding the preparation and filing of the registration statement.

B.   Attention is directed to Regulation S-K (17 CFR Part 229) for the requirements applicable to the content of the nonfinancial statement portions of registration statements under the Securities Act. Where this Form directs the registrant to furnish information required by Regulation S-K and the item of Regulation S-K so provides, information need only be furnished to the extent appropriate.

III. Exchange Offers

If any of the securities being registered are to be offered in exchange for securities of any other issuer, the prospectus shall also include the information which would be required by item 11 if the securities of such other issuer were registered on this Form. There shall also be included the information concerning such securities of such other issuer which would be called for by Item 9 if such securities were being registered. In connection with this instruction, reference is made to Rule 409.

IV. Roll-up Transactions

If the securities to be registered on this Form will be issued in a roll-up transaction as defined in Item 901(c) of Regulation S-K (17 CFR 229.901(c)), attention is directed to the requirements of Form S-4 applicable to roll-up transactions, including, but not limited to, General Instruction I.

V. Registration of Additional Securities

With respect to the registration of additional securities for an offering pursuant to Rule 462(b) under the Securities Act, the registrant may file a registration statement consisting only of the following: the facing page; a statement that the contents of the earlier registration statement, identified by file number, are incorporated by reference; required opinions and consents; the signature page; and any price-related information omitted from the earlier registration statement in reliance on Rule 430A that the registrant chooses to include in the new registration statement. The information contained in such a Rule 462(b) registration statement shall be deemed to be a part of the earlier registration statement as of the date of effectiveness of the Rule 462(b) registration statement. Any opinion or consent required in the Rule 462(b) registration statement may be incorporated by reference from the earlier registration statement with respect to the offering, if: (i) such opinion or consent expressly provides for such incorporation; and (ii) such opinion relates to the securities registered pursuant to Rule 462(b). *See* Rule 411(c) and Rule 439(b) under the Securities Act.

PART I—INFORMATION REQUIRED IN PROSPECTUS

Item 1. Forepart of the Registration Statement and Outside Front Cover Page of Prospectus.

Set forth in the forepart of the registration statement and on the outside front cover page of the prospectus the information required by Item 501 of Regulation S-K (§ 229.501 of this chapter).

Item 2. Inside Front and Outside Back Cover Pages of Prospectus.

Set forth on the inside front cover page of the prospectus or, where permitted, on the outside back cover page, the information required by Item 502 of Regulation S-K (§ 229.502 of this chapter).

Item 3. Summary Information, Risk Factors, and Ratio of Earnings to Fixed Charges.

Furnish the information required by Item 503 of Regulation S-K (§ 229.503 of this chapter).

Item 4. Use of Proceeds.

Furnish the information required by Item 504 of Regulation S-K (§ 229.504 of this chapter).

Item 5. Determination of Offering Price.

Furnish the information required by Item 505 of Regulation S-K (§ 229.505 of this chapter).

Item 6. Dilution.

Furnish the information required by Item 506 of Regulation S-K (§ 229.506 of this chapter).

Item 7. Selling Security Holders.

Furnish the information required by Item 507 of Regulation S-K (§ 229.507 of this chapter).

Item 8. Plan of Distribution.

Furnish the information required by Item 508 of Regulation S-K (§ 229.508 of this chapter).

Item 9. Description of Securities to Be Registered.

Furnish the information required by Item 202 of Regulation S-K (§ 229.202 of this chapter).

Item 10. Interests of Named Experts and Counsel.

Furnish the information required by Item 509 of Regulation S-K (§ 229.509 of this chapter).

Item 11. Information with Respect to the Registrant.

Furnish the following information with respect to the registrant:

(a) Information required by Item 101 of Regulation S-K (§ 229.101 of this chapter), description of business;

(b) Information required by Item 102 of Regulation S-K (§ 229.102 of this chapter), description of property;

(c) Information required by Item 103 of Regulation S-K (§ 229.103 of this chapter), legal proceedings;

(d) Where common equity securities are being offered, information required by Item 201 of Regulation S-K (§ 229.201 of this chapter), market price of and dividends on the registrant's common equity and related stockholder matters;

(e) Financial statements meeting the requirements of Regulation S-X (17 CFT Part 210) (Schedules required under Regulation S-X shall be filed as "Financial Statement Schedules" pursuant to Item 15, Exhibits and Financial Statement Schedules, of this Form), as well as any financial information required by Rule 3-05 and Article 11 of Regulation S-X;

(f) Information required by Item 301 of Regulation S-K (§ 229.301 of this chapter), selected financial data;

(g) Information required by Item 302 of Regulation S-K (§ 229.302 of this chapter), supplementary financial information;

(h) Information required by Item 303 of Regulation S-K (§ 229.303 of this chapter), management's discussion and analysis of financial condition and results of operations;

(i) Information required by Item 304 of Regulation S-K (§ 229.304 of this chapter), changes in and disagreements with accountants on accounting and financial disclosures;

(j) Information required by Item 305 of Regulation S-K (§ 229.305 of this chapter), quantitative and qualitative disclosures about market risk;

(k) Information required by Item 401 of Regulation S-K (§ 229.401 of this chapter), directors and executive officers;

(l) Information required by Item 402 of Regulation S-K (§ 229.402 of this chapter), executive compensation;

(m) Information required by Item 403 of Regulation S-K (§ 229.403 of this chapter), security ownership of certain beneficial owners and management; and

(n) Information required by Item 404 of Regulation S-K (§ 229.404 of this chapter), certain relationships and related transactions.

Item 12. Disclosure of Commission Position on Indemnification for Securities Act Liabilities.

Furnish the information required by Item 510 of Regulation S-K (§ 229.510 of this chapter).

PART II—INFORMATION NOT REQUIRED IN PROSPECTUS

Item 13. Other Expenses of Issuance and Distributions.

Furnish the information required by Item 511 of Regulation S-K (§ 229.511 of this chapter).

Item 14. Indemnification of Directors and Officers.

Furnish the information required by Item 702 of Regulation S-K (§ 229.702 of this chapter).

Item 15. Recent Sales of Unregistered Securities.

Furnish the information required by Item 701 of Regulation S-K (§ 229.701 of this chapter).

Item 16. Exhibits and Financial Statement Schedules.

(a) Subject to the rules regarding incorporation by reference, furnish the exhibits as required by Item 601 of Regulation S-K (§ 229.601 of this chapter).

(b) Furnish the financial statement schedules required by Regulation S-X (17 CFR Part 210) and Item 11(3) of this Form. These schedules shall be lettered or numbered in the manner described for exhibits in paragraph (a).

Item 17. Undertakings.

Furnish the undertakings required by Item 512 of Regulation S-K (§ 229.512 of this chapter).

SIGNATURES

Pursuant to the requirements of the Securities Act of 1933, the registrant has duly caused this registration statement to be signed on its behalf by the undersigned, thereunto duly authorized in the City of _____, State of _____, on _____, 20____.

_____

(Registrant)

_____

By (Signature and Title)

Pursuant to the requirements of the Securities Act of 1933, this registration statement has been signed by the following persons in the capacities and on the dates indicated.

_____

(Signature)

_____

(Title)

_____

(Date)

Instructions.

1. The registration statement shall be signed by the registrant, its principal executive officer or officers, its principal financial officer, its controller or principal accounting officer, and by at least a majority of the board of directors or persons performing similar functions. If the registrant is a foreign person, the registration statement shall also be signed by its authorized representative in the United States. Where the registrant is a limited partnership, the registration statement shall be signed by a majority of the board of directors of any corporate general partner signing the registration statement.

2. The name of each person who signs the registration statement shall be typed or printed beneath his or her signature. Any person who occupies more than one of the specified positions shall indicate each capacity in which he or she signs the registration statement. Attention is directed to Rule 402 concerning manual signatures and to Item 601 of Regulation S-K concerning signatures pursuant to powers of attorney.

APPENDIX C

COMFORT LETTER

AICPA Professional Standards
(Updated as of January 1, 2000)
Copyright © 2000, American Institute of Certified Public Accountants Inc.

[Note: dating throughout, in 1900s]

1. The contents of comfort letters vary, depending on the extent of the information in the registration statement and the wishes of the underwriter or other requesting party. Shelf registration statements may have several closing dates and different underwriters. Descriptions of procedures and findings regarding interim financial statements, tables, statistics, or other financial information that is incorporated by reference from previous 1934 Act filings may have to be repeated in several comfort letters. To avoid restating these descriptions in each comfort letter, accountants may initially issue the comments in a format (such as an appendix) that can be referred to in, and attached to, subsequently issued comfort letters.

Example A: Typical Comfort Letter

2. A typical comfort letter includes—
    a. A statement regarding the independence of the accountants (paragraphs .31 and .32).
    b. An opinion regarding whether the audited financial statements and financial statement schedules included (incorporated by reference) in the registration statement comply as to form in all material respects with the applicable accounting requirements of the Act and related rules and regulations adopted by the SEC (paragraphs .33 and .34).
    c. Negative assurance on whether—
        (1) The unaudited condensed interim financial information included (incorporated by reference) in the registration statement (paragraph .37) complies as to form in all material respects with the applicable accounting requirements of the Act and the related rules and regulations adopted by the SEC.
        (2) Any material modifications should be made to the unaudited condensed consolidated financial statements included (incorporated by reference) in the registration statement for them to be in conformity with generally accepted accounting principles.
    d. Negative assurance on whether, during a specified period following the date of the latest financial statements in the registration statement and prospectus, there has been any change in capital stock, increase in

long-term debt, or any decrease in other specified financial statement items (paragraphs .45 through .53).

Example A is a letter covering all these items. Letters that cover some of the items may be developed by omitting inapplicable portions of example A.

Example A assumes the following circumstances. The prospectus (Part I of the registration statement) includes audited consolidated balance sheets as of December 31, 19X5 and 19X4, and audited consolidated statements of income, retained earnings (stockholders' equity), and cash flows for each of the three years in the period ended December 31, 19X5. Part I also includes an unaudited condensed consolidated balance sheet as of March 31, 19X6, and unaudited condensed consolidated statements of income, retained earnings (stockholders' equity), and cash flows for the three-month periods ended March 31, 19X6 and 19X5, reviewed in accordance with section 722 but not previously reported on by the accountants. Part II of the registration statement includes audited consolidated financial statement schedules for the three years ended December 31, 19X5. The cutoff date is June 23, 19X6, and the letter is dated June 28, 19X6. The effective date is June 28, 19X6.

Each of the comments in the letter is in response to a requirement of the underwriting agreement. For purposes of example A, the income statement items of the current interim period are to be compared with those of the corresponding period of the preceding year.

June 28, 19X6

[Addressee]

Dear Sirs:

We have audited the consolidated balance sheets of The Blank Company Inc. (the company) and subsidiaries as of December 31, 19X5 and 19X4, and the consolidated statements of income, retained earnings (stockholders' equity), and cash flows for each of the three years in the period ended December 31, 19X5, and the related financial statement schedules all included in the registration statement (no. 33-00000) on Form S-1 filed by the company under the Securities Act of 1933 (the Act); our reports with respect thereto are also included in that registration statement. The registration statement, as amended on June 28, 19X6, is herein referred to as the registration statement. In connection with the registration statement—

1. We are independent certified public accountants with respect to the company within the meaning of the Act and the applicable rules and regulations thereunder adopted by the SEC.

2. In our opinion [include the phrase "except as disclosed in the registration statement," if applicable], the consolidated financial statements and financial statement schedules audited by us and included in the registration statement comply as to form in all material respects with the applicable

accounting requirements of the Act and the related rules and regulations adopted by the SEC.

3. We have not audited any financial statements of the company as of any date or for any period subsequent to December 31, 19X5; although we have conducted an audit for the year ended December 31, 19X5, the purpose (and therefore the scope) of the audit was to enable us to express our opinion on the consolidated financial statements as of December 31, 19X5, and for the year then ended, but not on the financial statements for any interim period within that year. Therefore, we are unable to and do not express any opinion on the unaudited condensed consolidated balance sheet as of March 31, 19X6, and the unaudited condensed consolidated statements of income, retained earnings (stockholders' equity), and cash flows for the three-month periods ended March 31, 19X6 and 19X5, included in the registration statement, or on the financial position, results of operations, or cash flows as of any date or for any period subsequent to December 31, 19X5.

4. For purposes of this letter we have read the 19X6 minutes of meetings of the stockholders, the board of directors, and [include other appropriate committees, if any] of the company and its subsidiaries as set forth in the minute books at June 23, 19X6, officials of the company having advised us that the minutes of all such meetings through that date were set forth therein; we have carried out other procedures to June 23, 19X6, as follows (our work did not extend to the period from June 24, 19X6, to June 28, 19X6, inclusive):

  a. With respect to the three-month periods ended March 31, 19X6 and 19X5, we have—

  (1) Performed the procedures specified by the American Institute of Certified Public Accountants for a review of interim financial information as described in SAS No. 71, *Interim Financial Information*, on the unaudited condensed consolidated balance sheet as of March 31, 19X6, and unaudited condensed consolidated statements of income, retained earnings (stockholders' equity), and cash flows for the three-month periods ended March 31, 19X6 and 19X5, included in the registration statement.

  (2) Inquired of certain officials of the company who have responsibility for financial and accounting matters whether the unaudited condensed consolidated financial statements referred to in a(1) comply as to form in all material respects with the applicable accounting requirements of the Act and the related rules and regulations adopted by the SEC.

  b. With respect to the period from April 1, 19X6, to May 31, 19X6, we have—

  (1) Read the unaudited consolidated financial statements of the company and subsidiaries for April and May of both 19X5 and 19X6

furnished us by the company, officials of the company having advised us that no such financial statements as of any date or for any period subsequent to May 31, 19X6, were available.

(2) Inquired of certain officials of the company who have responsibility for financial and accounting matters whether the unaudited consolidated financial statements referred to in b(1) are stated on a basis substantially consistent with that of the audited consolidated financial statements included in the registration statement.

The foregoing procedures do not constitute an audit conducted in accordance with generally accepted auditing standards. Also, they would not necessarily reveal matters of significance with respect to the comments in the following paragraph. Accordingly, we make no representations regarding the sufficiency of the foregoing procedures for your purposes.

5. Nothing came to our attention as a result of the foregoing procedures, however, that caused us to believe that—

a. (1) Any material modifications should be made to the unaudited condensed consolidated financial statements described in 4a(1), included in the registration statement, for them to be in conformity with generally accepted accounting principles.

(2) The unaudited condensed consolidated financial statements described in 4a(1) do not comply as to form in all material respects with the applicable accounting requirements of the Act and the related rules and regulations adopted by the SEC.

b. (1) At May 31, 19X6, there was any change in the capital stock, increase in long-term debt, or decrease in consolidated net current assets or stockholders' equity of the consolidated companies as compared with amounts shown in the March 31, 19X6, unaudited condensed consolidated balance sheet included in the registration statement, or

(2) for the period from April 1, 19X6, to May 31, 19X6, there were any decreases, as compared to the corresponding period in the preceding year, in consolidated net sales or in the total or per-share amounts of income before extraordinary items or of net income, except in all instances for changes, increases, or decreases that the registration statement discloses have occurred or may occur.

6. As mentioned in 4b, company officials have advised us that no consolidated financial statements as of any date or for any period subsequent to May 31, 19X6, are available; accordingly, the procedures carried out by us with respect to changes in financial statement items after May 31, 19X6, have, of necessity, been even more limited than those with respect to the periods referred to in 4. We have inquired of certain officials of the company who have responsibility for financial and accounting matters whether

(a) at June 23, 19X6, there was any change in the capital stock, increase in long-term debt, or any decreases in consolidated net current assets or stockholders' equity of the consolidated companies as compared with amounts shown on the March 31, 19X6, unaudited condensed consolidated balance sheet included in the registration statement or

(b) for the period from April 1, 19X6, to June 23, 19X6, there were any decreases, as compared with the corresponding period in the preceding year, in consolidated net sales or in the total or per-share amounts of income before extraordinary items or of net income. On the basis of these inquiries and our reading of the minutes as described in 4, nothing came to our attention that caused us to believe that there was any such change, increase, or decrease, except in all instances for changes, increases, or decreases that the registration statement discloses have occurred or may occur.

7. This letter is solely for the information of the addressees and to assist the underwriters in conducting and documenting their investigation of the affairs of the company in connection with the offering of the securities covered by the registration statement, and it is not to be used, circulated, quoted, or otherwise referred to within or without the underwriting group for any purpose, including but not limited to the registration, purchase, or sale of securities, nor is it to be filed with or referred to in whole or in part in the registration statement or any other document, except that reference may be made to it in the underwriting agreement or in any list of closing documents pertaining to the offering of the securities covered by the registration statement.

15 THE BOARD OF DIRECTORS

Charles A. Anderson
Robert N. Anthony

This chapter describes the nature and function of the board of directors, which has the ultimate responsibility for governing a corporation. It describes the board's activities in normal meetings, in strategy meetings, and in special situations, and it describes the work of three important board committees: the compensation committee, the audit committee, and the finance committee.

We focus on large corporations whose stock is listed on a securities exchange. These corporations must conform to regulations of the Securities and Exchange Commission. Most of the discussion is also relevant to boards of smaller corporations.

WHY HAVE A BOARD OF DIRECTORS?

Every corporation is required by law to have a board of directors. The board's legal function is to govern the corporation's affairs. However, in a small corporation in which the chief executive officer (CEO) is also the controlling shareholder, the CEO actually governs and the board acts primarily as an adviser.

When a corporation grows to a size where it needs outside capital, it may go public by selling shares of stock (as explained in Chapter 14), and the board then represents the interests of these shareholders. The shareholders, who are the owners of the corporation, have a say in the way their company is run. They expect to receive regular, reliable reports on the company's operations. If the company is profitable, they probably expect to receive dividends. If the

510

company has problems, the owners need to know about these problems so that they can take any necessary remedial action.

A corporation may have many shareholders; American Telephone & Telegraph Corporation has 2.6 million. Individual shareholders obviously can't govern the company directly; moreover, most of them are engaged in their own pursuits and will not give much, if any, time to governance. They elect people to act for them. This is the board of directors.

SIZE AND COMPOSITION OF THE BOARD

The typical board has about 11 members. Some boards, especially those in banks, are much larger. Large boards must delegate much of their work to an executive committee for overall matters and to several committees for specific topics.

Most board members typically are "outside directors"; that is, they are not employees of the corporation. At one time, most board members were "inside directors," and this is still the case in a few boards. The trend toward outside directors results from the shareholders' recognition that the board should have a significant degree of independence from the company's management. The board is responsible for selecting, appraising, and compensating management. If the board and management are the same people, the board can hardly perform its governance role in an objective manner.

Many outside board members are CEOs or senior officers of other corporations (but not competitors). Other outsiders are lawyers, bankers, physicians (on health-care boards), scientists and engineers (on high-tech boards), retired government officials, and academics. A few people are professional board members; that is, their principal occupation is serving on boards. The number of female and minority board members has increased substantially in recent years. The CEO and perhaps one or two senior members of management typically are members of the board.

Board members are compensated. Generally, they receive an annual retainer plus a fee for meetings attended. In addition, many companies offer some form of stock compensation and retirement benefits. According to a Conference Board survey, the median basic annual compensation in manufacturing companies for 1999 (not including stock components) was $35,000. When the value of the stock component was added, compensation totaled $46,000.

Board members are elected at the annual meeting of shareholders. The shareholders almost always elect the slate proposed by the incumbent board; thus, as a practical matter, the board is self-perpetuating. The process of selecting candidates for filling board vacancies is an important board function. Many have staggered terms; that is, one-third of the board members are elected each year for a three-year term. This practice is intended to make it more difficult for corporate raiders to obtain control of the company.

BOARD MEMBER RESPONSIBILITIES

In the following sections, we describe the specific activities for which the board is responsible. In this section, we describe the responsibilities of individual board members.

Board members must not personally buy stock or sell their own stock immediately after they learn of important developments at board meetings or other activities. Examples of relevant developments include current estimates of earnings, change in dividend policy, a decision to acquire another company or to buy back stock, and changes in senior management. The Securities and Exchange Commission and rules of the stock exchanges impose an "earnings blackout" period of one or two days in which such trading is prohibited.

Board members and management must not disclose any of these events to a selected group of interested parties. For example, they must not make a telephone conference call to a selected group, send an Internet message to them, or disclose information at a meeting of such a group. When this information is disclosed, it must be made available at the same time to the general public. These rules were significantly tightened in 1999 and 2000 by SEC Regulation FD.

RELATION TO THE CHIEF EXECUTIVE OFFICER

Their titles indicate that the board of directors "directs" and the chief executive officer "executes" the board's directions, but these terms are not an accurate description of the roles of these two parties. In the majority of companies, the chief executive officer is also the board's chairman and is the principal architect of policies. Executing these policies is indeed a primary responsibility. The CEO is truly the "chief."

The board selects the CEO and, therefore, wants to give the CEO its full support. The CEO is accountable to the board and may be terminated if the board decides that the individual's performance was unsatisfactory.

The appropriate relationship is one of trust. The board must believe that the CEO is completely trustworthy, provides the board with all the information it wants and needs, withholds nothing, and doesn't slant arguments to support a preconceived position. The CEO, in turn, must believe that he or she has the full support of the board.

Appraising the CEO

A board's major responsibility is to appraise the CEO. If performance is below expectations, there are two possible explanations: (1) The CEO is to blame, or (2) extraneous influences are responsible. In most cases, both factors are involved, and the directors have the extraordinarily difficult job of judging their relative importance. If they conclude that the CEO has made an incorrect decision, they may suggest a different course of action. More likely, however, they may say nothing and mentally file the incident for future reference in evaluating the CEO. The Business Roundtable, a group of CEOs of leading companies, succinctly described the directors' role vis-à-vis the CEO as "challenging, yet supportive and positive."

An important function of board meetings, conversations, and even social occasions is to give the directors a basis for continuously appraising the CEO. Directors usually cannot make constructive suggestions on the details of current operations. Occasionally, they may call attention to a matter that should be investigated. Primarily, however, they listen carefully to what the CEO says and do their best to judge whether things are going satisfactorily and, if not, where the responsibility lies.

The directors want the CEO to be frank and to give an accurate analysis of the company's status and prospects; concealing bad news is one of the worst sins a CEO can commit. Nevertheless, human nature is such that directors cannot expect the CEO to be completely objective. Incipient problems may go away, and making them known, even in the relative privacy of the boardroom, may cause unnecessary alarm. Directors, therefore, are on the alert for indications of significant problems. In many well-publicized bankruptcies of public companies, the directors were significantly responsible; they did not identify or act on the problem soon enough.

Louis B. Cabot, former chairman of the board of Cabot Corporation, had a frustrating experience with the ill-fated Penn Central Corporation. He joined the Penn Central board about a year before the company went under. From the outset, he was disturbed by management's unwillingness to furnish the information about performance that he felt he needed. A few months after joining the board, he wrote the CEO a letter that contains the following succinct description of the director's role:

> I believe directors should not be the managers of a business, but they should ensure the excellence of its management's performance. To do this, they have to measure that performance against agreed-upon yardsticks.

The Next CEO

The board cannot tell beforehand whether a candidate will make a good CEO. The best indicator is how well the individual performs in his or her current job. In most instances, therefore, the board looks to senior executives with proven track records as candidates for the CEO position. One of the most important responsibilities that a board assigns to a CEO is to develop a succession plan for the company's senior managers. The purpose of such a plan is to identify potential CEO candidates, provide them with opportunities for growth, and groom them for higher level positions. The board participates actively in this process by meeting with the CEO (usually once a year) in a meeting devoted largely to reviewing the senior management. Typical questions asked are: How is a key executive performing? What is his or her potential? Who are potential successors for the CEO, now and in the future?

At one company the authors are familiar with, the chairman and CEO held an annual meeting of the outside directors to discuss succession. He referred to it as the "truck meeting" because he always started with the question, "Suppose I am run over by a truck tomorrow. What will you do?" At this meeting, two, and sometimes three, managers were identified as potential CEOs. Individuals were added to or eliminated from the list and their relative ranking changed. When this process works properly, an agreed upon CEO candidate is available in an emergency, and a person who will take over from a retiring CEO in normal succession is identified.

If boards fail to deal effectively with succession, they may be forced to go outside the company for a new CEO. Under most circumstances, this increases the risk that the CEO will not succeed since chances for a successful succession are usually better when the CEO position is filled by a proven executive from within the organization. In some cases, an organization may need a "shaking up" and the board may elect to go outside for a CEO who can give the organization new life.

NORMAL BOARD MEETINGS

Most boards meet eight, nine, or ten times a year. Some meet only quarterly, and a few meet every month. The typical meeting lasts two to three hours, but it may go considerably longer if contentious issues arise.

Premeeting Material

Prior to the meeting, board members are sent an agenda and a packet of material on topics to be discussed. This homework usually requires several hours of work. Directors may query the CEO, in person or by a phone call before the meeting, on matters that require clarification.

Current Situation and Outlook

The first substantive topic on a meeting's agenda usually is a discussion of current information about the company and its outlook. The CEO leads this discussion, perhaps delegating part of it to another senior officer. Much of the information is financial—that is, condensed income statements for each division or for groups of division, corporate expenses, and key balance sheet items, such as inventory and receivable amounts. There are three ways to present this financial information:

1. Compare management's current estimate of performance for the whole year with budgeted performance for the year. What is the current estimate of how the company will perform for the whole year? This is the most important type of information. However, it is also the most sensitive, and many CEOs do not circulate it prior to the meeting.

2. Compare actual performance with budgeted performance for the current period and for the year to date. Because the actual numbers are firm, they provide a more objective basis for analysis than the current estimate for the whole year.

3. Compare actual current performance with performance for the same period last year. A carefully prepared budget incorporates changes in the business and the economy that have occurred since the prior year, and this is a more meaningful basis for comparison than last year's numbers. If, however, the budgeted amounts, particularly the estimate of revenue, are highly uncertain, the numbers for last year provide a firmer foundation for comparison.

Variances between actual and budgeted performance are discussed. Are unfavorable variances temporary? If not, what steps will be taken to eliminate them, or, if they result from unforeseen outside forces, what adjustments in the company's operations will be made?

By reviewing the company's financial performance and raising questions or making suggestions to management, directors form judgments regarding the company's affairs. Preparing and presenting to the board a report on the company's performance is an important discipline for management.

Other Actions

Next, a number of proposed actions are submitted for board approval. Many of these recommendations come to the full board from committees that have discussed the topics in meetings held prior to the board meeting; these are described later in this chapter. Questions may be raised about the recommendations, but usually they are requests for clarification. Board members rely on committee members to explore these matters thoroughly; there is not enough time to do so in the full board meeting. Unless new information surfaces, these recommendations typically are approved.

The board also deals with a number of routine items. These include requests for approval of capital projects, of signature authority for various banking connections, of exceptions to pension plans, and of certain types of contracts. Except for large capital projects, these items are usually referred to as "boilerplate." In most cases, they come to the board because state law, corporate bylaws, or written policy requires board action. They are approved with little discussion, sometimes en bloc, despite the fact that the minutes may state for each of them, "After a full discussion, a motion to adopt the recommendation was duly made and seconded, and the motion was approved."

Education

A division manager, assisted by senior associates, may report on the activities of the division. This is an educational experience for the directors. (Some board meetings may be held at company plants or other facilities; this also is a valuable educational device.)

The meeting itself and the informal activities that usually are associated with it are also educational. Directors have an opportunity to appraise both company officials and their own colleagues. Judgments about these individuals may be valuable if the board is required at some time to deal with a crisis situation.

Setting Standards

Partly through written policy statements, but primarily through their attitudes, directors communicate to management the standards that they believe should govern the organization's actions. There are two general types of standards; they might be labeled *economic standards* and *ethical standards*, although neither term is precisely correct.

With respect to economic standards, the directors communicate the overall goals they believe the company should attain: the relative importance of sales growth, earnings per share and return on investment, and the specific numbers that they believe to be attainable. The board also indicates the relative importance of short-run versus long-run performance. In the final analysis, board members generally rely on management's recommendations, but the enthusiasm, or lack of enthusiasm, with which they support a given recommendation conveys an important message to management.

Ethical standards are nebulous. Written policy statements are always impeccably virtuous, but directors' actual expectations are revealed in the way they react to specific ethical problems. How does the company deal with its female and minority employees? What happens to an employee who has a drinking problem? Does the company have a policy concerning support for the communities in which it operates? These and many other issues are loaded with ethics, and the manner in which the board reacts to them establishes the real policy, regardless of what is in a written statement.

It is easy to rely on counsel's answer to the question, Must we report this unpleasant development to the Securities and Exchange Commission? The answer depends on the legal interpretation of the regulations. It is much more difficult for the directors to agree, and to convey to management, that certain policies or practices, although perhaps within the letter of the law, should not be allowed or sanctioned. Examples include environmental considerations, employment practices in Third World countries, and involvement in political issues.

STRATEGY

A company should have a set of strategies that are well thought out and clearly understood by all managers. Strategies include the industry in which the company has decided to operate, its product lines within this industry, the price and quality position of these products, the targeted customers and markets (local, regional, national, international), the company's distribution channels (direct sales, dealers, distributors), marketing policies (advertising, sales promotion), manufacturing policies (in-house production, plant locations, outside sourcing), financial policies (balance among borrowing, equity financing, retained earnings), and others.

The board usually does not have the knowledge necessary to initiate a strategy or to decide among alternative strategies. It must rely on management to take the initiative, make the necessary analyses, and bring its recommendations to the board. What the board can and should do is described by Kenneth R. Andrews in *The Concept of Corporate Strategy.*[1] He writes, as a summary,

> A responsible and effective board should require of its management a unique and durable corporate strategy, review it periodically for its validity, use it as the reference point for all other board decisions, and share with management the risks associated with its adoption.

While it is unrealistic to expect directors to formulate strategies, they should satisfy themselves that management has a sound process for developing them. The strategy is probably acceptable if:

- It is based on careful analysis by people who are in the best position to evaluate it, rather than on an inspiration accepted without study.
- The reasoning seems sensible.
- No significant information has been omitted from the analysis.
- The results expected from the strategy are clearly set forth so that actual accomplishment can be compared with them.

Strategy Meetings

As a basis for considering strategic plans, many companies arrange a meeting at which directors, together with senior managers, spend one, two, or three days discussing where the company should be headed. In order to minimize distractions and provide an opportunity for informal discussion and reflection, these meetings are often held at a retreat that is distant from the corporate offices. While company practices differ widely, it is not uncommon for meetings devoted primarily to strategic issues to be held every year or two.

The primary purpose of a strategy meeting is for management to explain current and planned strategies and the rationales for them. The explanations provide useful information to the directors. The quality of the rationale for the strategies indicates the competence of senior management and the managers of the divisions concerned. Thus, the strategies provide additional insight about the abilities of the CEO and the participants who may be CEO candidates.

Once adopted, a corporate strategy must be adhered to. Management brings to the board for decision and approval many matters that may impact a company's strategy—major capital expenditures, acquisitions, divestitures, and financing proposals. The board ensures that these proposals are consistent with the adopted strategy. If they are not, the company can drift off course and may get into serious trouble.

DEALING WITH MAJOR CRISES

In addition to its regular activities, a board occasionally must deal with crises. These usually arise unexpectedly and require special board meetings. We describe two of these: terminating the CEO and dealing with takeover attempts.

Terminating the CEO

There are times when a board must replace the CEO. Failure to act in time is a major criticism of some boards. Although such criticism may be justified one should recognize that it is much easier for an outside observer to criticize than to be in the shoes of the directors who are faced with this decision.

The decision to replace a CEO is subjective and usually emotional. Sometimes there are compelling reasons for taking action—for example, when the CEO is becoming an alcoholic or when his or her corporate performance has dramatically deteriorated. In most instances, however, the case is not so clear. Earnings may not have kept pace with industry leaders because the board discouraged management from assuming additional debt that would have enabled the company to expand. Or perhaps the board supported a major acquisition that did not work out. In such instances, it is not obvious that the CEO is primarily at fault.

There are, however, several important signals that can alert a board to question the CEO's capabilities:

- *Loss of confidence in the CEO.* If a significant number of directors have lost confidence in, or no longer trust, the CEO, the individual should be replaced.
- *Continuing deterioration in corporate results.* Earnings may be significantly below industry norms or below the budget without an adequate explanation. The board must act before it is too late.
- *Organizational instability.* A CEO who consistently has problems retaining qualified senior executives probably should be replaced.

These problems are especially serious in the many new companies springing up in information technology industries. In these industries, change is rapid, competition is severe, there are no track records on which to base judgment, and stock prices may change by huge percentages in a few days, reflecting changes in investors' opinions about the company's outlook.

It is one thing for board members to begin to doubt the CEO's capabilities, but it is quite another thing for them to demonstrate the courage and consensus needed to take action. The CEO and the directors usually have worked together for some time; they are good, perhaps close, friends. For the CEO, dismissal is a catastrophic event. Taking action that will probably destroy the career of a business associate is a difficult decision.

Replacing the CEO precipitates a crisis, not only for the board but also for the entire organization. When it happens, the board must be prepared to announce a successor and to deal with the problems inherent in the transfer of executive authority. Such action puts a major burden on the outside directors. Nevertheless, this is their responsibility to the shareholders and to the other constituencies of the corporation.

For example, in early 2000, Jill E. Barad, CEO of Mattel Inc. the world's largest toy manufacturer "resigned." Ms. Barad built one of Mattel's flagship products, the Barbie doll, from $250 million in annual sales in the mid-1980s to $1.7 billion in 1999. In the late 1980s, Barbie's growth slowed, and Ms. Barad turned to acquisitions. Unfortunately, several acquisitions failed to live up to expectations. A loss of $82 million was recorded for 1999, and Mattel's stock price dropped from a high of $45 in 1998 to a low of $11 in early 2000. The board acted, and Ms. Barad "resigned." Apparently the board decided that there was no suitable successor within the company. They selected Robert Eckel, formerly CEO of Kraft Foods to be the new CEO.

The turnover of CEOs of major corporations seems to be accelerating in the twenty-first century. Mr. William Rollinick, a Mattel board member and former acting chairman, observed that when a chief executive stumbles, "there's zero forgiveness. You screw up and you're dead." The investing community puts boards under considerable pressure to act when things appear to be going wrong. Sarah Telsik, executive director of the Council of Institutional Investors, which represents 110 pension funds with more than $1.5 trillion in assets, believes that underperforming CEOs were not losing their jobs fast enough.

Too fast or too slow? A board should decide what is in the long-term best interests of the company and its stockholders. In some instances, immediate pressures should be resisted in favor of long-term considerations. In other cases, the board should "bite the bullet." The decision is not easy.

Unfriendly Takeover Attempts

Another crisis event is the hostile, or unfriendly, takeover attempt. Board decisions vital to the company's future—even its continued existence—must be made in circumstances in which emotions are high, vested interests are at stake, and advice is often conflicting. The business press reports daily the dramatic developments of offers and counteroffers, tactics, and strategies as each side in the struggle seeks to gain an advantage. Boards and management spend much time preparing offensive and defensive plans.

One of the problems in takeover situations is that the board, which represents the shareholders, may have interests that differ from those of management. In most successful unfriendly takeovers, the senior managers of the target company lose their jobs. A common accusation, therefore, is that management resists takeovers in order to entrench itself, even though the deal would result in a handsome gain for the shareholders.

In these situations, directors must exercise great care in making a decision that is in the shareholders' interests. This is not always easy to determine. What is the intrinsic value of the corporation? What is the real value of the "junk bonds" being offered to the shareholders? What consideration, if any, should the directors give to the interests of other parties—employees, communities, suppliers, and customers?

In an unfriendly takeover attempt, the directors of the target company must rely on legal advice since takeovers inevitably lead to lawsuits. The board also depends on expert advice from investment banks about the value of the company and the true value of offers to acquire it.

In practice, when a hostile takeover is initiated, the target company's lawyers, investment bankers, accountants, and other advisers, together with the board and management, become involved in a hectic struggle that can last for weeks or months. It is a sixteen-hour-day, seven-day-week effort; nearly everything else yields to the intense preoccupation with survival or striking the best possible deal.

BOARD COMMITTEES

Much of the board's work is done in committees. They meet before board meetings, hear reports, and prepare summaries and recommendations for full board action. In this section, we describe the activities of the three committees—compensation, audit, and finance—that deal with finance and accounting matters.

COMPENSATION COMMITTEE

The board determines the compensation of the CEO and the other principal corporate officers. In many boards, a compensation committee, composed of outside board members, analyzes what compensation should be and makes its recommendations to the full board.

The SEC requires that a section of the proxy statement, issued prior to the annual meeting of shareholders, must describe the work of the compensation committee, the decisions on compensating senior executives, reasons for the decision, their compensation for the past three years, and comparisons with other companies in the industry.

CEO Compensation

When the board sets the CEO's compensation, it is establishing a compensation standard for managers throughout the company. Their compensation is integrally related to the CEO's and this, therefore, is the single most important compensation decision the board must make.

In most instances this decision is not easy. Most CEOs are ambitious and competitive, and compensation is their report card. Since proxy statements disclose the compensation of all CEOs of public companies, each CEO is able to see just where he or she stands in relation to others. Virtually every CEO would like to stand higher on that list.

Compensation committees consider three principal factors. The CEO's compensation should: (1) be related to performance, (2) be competitive, and (3) provide motivation. Compensation includes not only salary but also perquisites and, in most companies, long-term incentive arrangements, such as stock options or performance-share plans. These plans, however, are far from perfect, and compensation committees constantly struggle to find new arrangements or formulas in an effort to relate compensation more closely to performance.

Performance

The CEO's compensation should be related to performance. Superior performance should be rewarded with high compensation, while poor performance, if it does not warrant dismissal, should at least result in decreases or minimal increases in compensation.

There is justification for the claim that in some companies top-executive compensation continues to climb without regard to performance. The problem is complex. In theory, the CEO should be rewarded for increasing the shareowner's wealth over the long term. Although this is a splendid generalization, the criterion is hard to measure, especially on a year-to-year basis.

Competitive Range

Compensation committees look at the CEO's compensation relative to that of competitors. They can be sure that their CEO has this information and is likely to be unhappy if the compensation is perceived as unfair or not competitive.

There are many sources for salary information. They include proxy statements from similar organizations and published surveys. Some consulting organizations specialize in executive compensation; they provide data and advice on these matters. In the end and with all of the information at hand, the committee makes its judgment as to where in the competitive spectrum they want the CEO's compensation to fall.

Motivation

Compensation committees ask themselves, How can we structure a compensation package that motivates the CEO to do what the board expects? If the company has a plan to move aggressively and take unusual risks in the near term, with the possibility of significant long-term payoff, the committee can structure a compensation plan for the CEO that will reward that kind of behavior. For example, the CEO might have a multiyear contract that provides assurance of employment during the high-risk phase, as well as a long-term stock option plan. At the other extreme, a mature company might be interested in moderate growth but steady dividends. The compensation committee might then structure a plan weighted heavily toward a fixed salary, reviewed annually, with only modest incentive features.

There are many types of compensation arrangements: base salary reviewed annually, base salary plus annual discretionary bonus, base salary with bonus based on a formula, stock option plans, performance share plans, and multiyear incentive plans. Benefits play an important part in CEO compensation arrangements, especially retirement programs. Each plan has its own motivational features, and the compensation committee attempts to structure a plan that provides the motivation for the CEO that the board wants to generate.

Compensation Reviews

In addition to deciding the CEO's compensation, the committee also determines compensation for the other senior executives—that is, corporate officers and others whose salary is above a stated level. The review process usually takes place at a meeting that brings together the compensation committee, the CEO, and the staff officer concerned with compensation and personnel policies.

At this meeting the CEO describes the compensation history of, and makes a recommendation for, each executive. Usually, a few of the recommendations are discussed, and a few changes may be made. For the most part, however, the committee accepts the CEO's recommendations. Nevertheless, the review process is important. It enables the compensation committee to be sure that the CEO is following sensible guidelines and consistent policies and is not playing favorites. It also serves to remind the CEO that recommendations to the committee must be justified.

Board Remuneration

The compensation committee also recommends compensation arrangements for the board members. Obviously, this is a delicate matter because the board is disbursing company funds (actually shareholder funds) to its members.

Directors' compensation is disclosed on the annual proxy statement. Most companies would like to see their directors "respectably" compensated and, while compensation usually is not the compelling reason for holding a directorship, directors want to feel that they are being compensated on a competitive basis. On the other hand, most directors want to feel that their compensation is not excessive and that they will never be criticized for compensating themselves improperly.

Much survey information is available on board retainer fees, board meeting fees, and compensation for committee chairs to help reach a balanced level of compensation.

AUDIT COMMITTEE

The audit committee is responsible for ensuring that the company's published financial statements are presented fairly in conformance with generally accepted accounting principles (GAAP), and that the company's internal control system is effective. Furthermore, the audit committee deals with important cases of alleged misconduct by employees, including violations of the company's code of ethics. It also ratifies the selection of the company's external auditor.

All companies listed on major stock exchanges are required to have audit committees, and most other corporations have them. The SEC requires at least three members of the audit committee to be "financial literate or to become financial literate within a reasonable period of time."[2]

Responsibility

Although the full board can delegate certain functions to the audit committee, this delegation does not relieve individual board members of their responsibility for governance. In its 1967 decision in the BarChris case, the federal court emphasized this fact:[3]

> Section 11 [of the Securities Act of 1933] imposes liability in the first instance upon a director, no matter how new he is. . . . He is presumed to know his responsibility when he became a director. He can escape liability only by using that reasonable care to investigate the facts which a prudent man would employ in the management of his own property.

Directors have directors' and officers' (D&O) insurance, but this only partially protects them against loss from lawsuits claiming that they acted improperly. Recent decisions suggest that courts are increasingly willing to examine directors' decisions. For example, the shareholders of Oxford Health Care sued the company for misleading financial statements. Oxford's stock price thereupon fell by 50%, a $14 billion drop in market value. The company reportedly agreed to settle the case for $2.83 billion. In the 1990s, there were more than 100 fraud actions annually against SEC firms and many more against smaller firms.

Audit committee members walk a tightrope. On one hand, they want to support the CEO—the person whom the board itself selected. On the other hand, they have a clear responsibility to uncover and act on management inadequacies. If they do not, the entire board of directors is subject to criticism at the very least and imprisonment at worst. Their task is neither easy nor pleasant.

Published Financial Statements

The audit committee does not conduct audits; it relies on two other groups to do this. One is the outside auditor, a firm of certified public accountants. All listed companies are required to have their financial statements examined by an outside auditor, and most other corporations do so in order to satisfy the requirements of banks and other lenders. The other group is the company's internal audit staff, a group of employees whose head reports to a senior officer, usually the CEO or chief financial officer (CFO).

Selection of Auditors

Ordinarily, management recommends that the current auditing firm be appointed for another year and that its proposed audit scope and fee schedule be adopted. After some questioning, the audit committee usually recommends approval. The recommendation is submitted to shareholders in the annual meeting. Occasionally, the audit committee gives more than routine consideration to this topic.

There may be advantages to changing auditors, even when the relationship between the audit firm and the company has been satisfactory for several years. One advantage is that the process of requesting bids from other firms may cause the current firm to think carefully about its proposed fees. However, the public may perceive that a change in outside auditors indicates that the superseded firm would not go along with a practice that the company wanted. The SEC requires that when a new auditing firm is appointed, the reason for making the change must be reported on its Form 8-K. Also, because a new firm's initial task of learning about the company requires management time, management may be reluctant to recommend a change.

Public accounting firms often perform various types of consulting engagements for the company: developing new accounting and control systems, analyzing proposed pension plans, and analyzing proposed acquisitions. Fees for this work may exceed the fees for audit work. The SEC and the stock exchanges have strict rules that prohibit a public accounting firm from conducting an audit if it has consulting engagements with the corporation that might affect the objectivity of the audit. Some auditing firms have responded to these rules by setting up a separate firm to conduct these engagements.

The Audit Opinion

In its opinion letter, the public accounting firm emphasizes the fact that management, not the auditor, is responsible for the financial statements. Almost all companies receive a "clean opinion"; that is, the auditor states that the financial statements "present fairly, in all material respects" the financial status and performance of the company in accordance with GAAP. Note that this statement says neither that the statements are 100% accurate nor whether different numbers would have been more fair.[4] The audit committee's task is to decide whether the directors should concur with the outside auditor's opinion and, occasionally, to resolve differences when auditors are unwilling to give a clean opinion on the numbers that management proposes.

Management has some latitude in deciding the amounts to be reported, especially the amount of earnings. Since managers are human beings, it is reasonable to expect them to report performance in a favorable light. Examples of this tendency, discussed next, are: (1) accelerating revenue, (2) smoothing earnings, (3) reporting unfavorable developments, and (4) the "big bath." Much of the discussion of these topics is complicated by differences in the meaning of "materiality." The SEC has tried to lessen the reliance on materiality by publishing detailed descriptions of what the term means.

Accelerating Revenue

A company may go to great lengths to count revenues actually earned in future periods as revenues in the current period, even though this decreases the next period's revenues. The following example illustrates:

> The SEC sued two executives of Sirena Apparel Group for misleading revenue estimates for the quarter ended March 31, 1999. They instructed employees daily to set back the computer clock that entered the dates on invoices until a satisfactory revenue amount was recorded. Invoices dated from April 12, 1999, were set back.[5]

Not all attempts to accelerate revenue recognition are improper. There are documented stories of managers who personally worked around the clock at year-end, packing goods in containers for shipment. This enabled them to count the value of the packed goods as revenue in the year that was about to end. Counting goods that actually were shipped as revenue is legitimate.

Smoothing Earnings

There is a widespread belief (not necessarily supported by the facts) that ideal performance is a steady growth in earnings, certainly from year to year, and desirably from quarter to quarter. Within the latitude permitted by GAAP, therefore, management may wish to smooth reported earnings—that is, to move reported income from what otherwise would be a highly profitable period to a less profitable period. The principal techniques for doing this are to vary the adjustments for inventory amounts and bad debts, and estimated returns, allowances, and warranties.

The audit committee, therefore, pays considerable attention to the way these adjustments and allowances are calculated and to the resulting accounts receivable, inventory, and accrued liability amounts. Changes in the reserve percentages from one year to the next are suspect. The audit committee tolerates a certain amount of smoothing, within limits. Indeed, it may not be aware that smoothing has occurred. Outside these limits, however, the committee is obligated to make sure that the reserves and accrual calculations are reasonable.

Management may also recommend terminology that does not affect net income but does affect income from operating activities. Examples are *earnings before marketing costs, cash earnings per share, earnings before losses on new products,* and *pro forma earnings.* None of these terms is permitted in GAAP; they appear in press releases and speeches.

Reporting Unfavorable Developments

The Securities and Exchange Commission requires that its Form 8-K report be filed promptly whenever an unusual material event that affects the financial statements becomes known. The principal concern is with the bottom line, the amount of reported earnings. Management, understandably, may be inclined not to report events that might (or might not) have an unfavorable impact on earnings. These include the probable bankruptcy of an important customer, an important inventory shortage, a reported cash shortage that might (or might not) turn out to be a bookkeeping error, a possibly defective product that could lead to huge returns or to product liability suits, possible safety or environmental violations, an allegation of misdeeds by a corporate officer, the departure of a senior manager, or a lawsuit that might (or might not) be well founded. It is human nature to hope that borderline situations will not actually have a material impact on the company's earnings.

Furthermore, publicizing some of these situations may harm the company unnecessarily. Disclosing a significant legal filing against the company is necessary, but disclosing the amount that the company thinks it might lose in such litigation, in a report that the plaintiff can read, would be foolish.

In any event, the audit committee should be kept fully informed about all events that might eventually require filing a Form 8-K. One might think that the CEO would welcome the opportunity to inform the board of these events because this shifts the responsibility for disclosure to the board. But managers, like most human beings, prefer not to talk about bad news if there are reasonable grounds for waiting a while.

Occasionally, a manager may attempt to "cook the books," that is, to produce favorable accounting results by making entries that are not in accordance with GAAP. The audit committee must rely on the auditors (or occasionally on a whistle-blower) to detect these situations.

The Big Bath

A new CEO may "take a big bath"; that is, the accounting department may be required to write off or write down assets in the year he or she takes over, thereby reducing the amount of costs that remain to be charged off in future periods. This increases the reported earnings in the periods for which the new management is responsible. Since the situation that led to the replacement of the former manager may justify some charge-offs, and since the directors don't want to disagree with the new chief executive officer during the honeymoon period, this tactic is sometimes tolerated. If the inflated earnings lead to extraordinarily high bonuses in future years, the board may regret its failure to act.

Audit Committee Activities

In probing for the possible existence of any of the situations described above, the audit committee takes two approaches. First, it asks probing questions of management: Why has the receivables-reserve percentage changed? What is the rationale for a large write-off of assets?

Then, and much more important, the committee asks similar questions of the outside auditors. The audit committee usually meets privately with the outside auditors and tells them, in effect, "If you have any doubts about the numbers, or if you have reason to believe that management has withheld material information, let us know. If you don't inform us, the facts will almost certainly come to light later on. When they do, you will be fired."

A more polite way of probing is to ask the following: "Is there anything more you should tell us? What were your largest areas of concern? What were the most important matters, if any, on which you and management differed? Did the accounting treatment of certain events differ from general practice in the industry? If so, what was the rationale for the difference? How do you rate the professional competence of the finance and accounting staff?"

Usually, these questions are raised orally. Because the auditors know from past experience what to expect, they come prepared to answer them. Some audit committees provide their questions in writing prior to the meeting.

Although cases of improper disclosure make headlines, they occur in only a tiny fraction of 1% of listed companies. Most such incidents reflect poorly on the work of the board of directors and its audit committee. Increasingly, the courts penalize such boards for their laxity. Directors are aware of the fact that when serious misdeeds surface, the CEO often leaves the company, but the directors must stay with the ship, enduring public criticism and the blot on their professional reputation. Their lives will be much more pleasant in the long run if they act promptly.

Quarterly Reports

In addition to the annual financial statements, the SEC requires companies to file a quarterly summary of key financial data on Form 10-Q. Because the timing of the release of this report usually does not coincide with an audit committee meeting, most audit committees do not review it. Instead, they ask the CEO to inform the committee chair if there is an unusual situation that affects the quarterly numbers. The chair then decides either to permit the report to be published as proposed or, if the topic seems sufficiently important, to have the committee meet in a telephone conference call or an e-mail exchange to discuss it.

Internal Control

In addition to its opinion on the financial statements, the outside auditing firm writes a "management letter." This letter lists possible weaknesses in the company's control system that have come to the auditor's attention, together with recommendations for correcting them. (In the boilerplate preceding this list, the auditor disclaims responsibility for a complete analysis of the system. The listed items are only those that the firm happened to uncover.) Internal auditors also write reports on the subject.

Audit committees follow up on these reports by asking management to respond to the criticisms. If management disagrees with the recommended course of action, its rationale is considered and is either accepted or rejected. If action is required, the committee keeps the item on its agenda until it is satisfied that the matter has been addressed.

If an especially serious problem is uncovered, the committee may engage its public accounting firm or another firm to make a special study. If the problem involves ethical or legal improprieties, the committee may engage an outside law firm. As soon as material problems are identified, they must be reported promptly to the SEC on Form 8-K.

The audit committee has a difficult problem with internal audit reports. In the course of a year, a moderate size staff may write 100 or more reports. Many of them are too trivial to warrant the committee's attention. (One of the authors participated in an audit committee meeting of a multibillion dollar company in which 15 minutes were spent discussing a recommendation to improve the computer system that was expected to save $24,000 annually.) Drawing a line between important reports and trivial ones is difficult, however. A rule of thumb, such as, "Tell us about the dozen most important matters," may be used, but what if the thirteenth matter also warrants the committee's attention?

In its private meeting with the head of internal audit, the audit committee assures itself that the CEO has given the internal audit staff complete freedom to do its work. The committee also makes it clear that the head of internal audit has direct access to the audit committee chair if a situation that warrants immediate board attention is uncovered. The internal auditor normally would report the matter in question to his or her superior first, but the auditor's primary obligation is to the audit committee. The committee, in turn, should guarantee, as well as it can, that the internal auditor will be fully protected against possible retaliation.

Internal Audit Organization

The audit committee also considers the adequacy of the internal audit organization. Is it large enough? Does it have the proper level of competence? For example, do the auditors know how to audit the latest computer systems? In many companies, the internal audit organization is a training ground where promising accountants are groomed for controllership. The audit committee may find it useful to get acquainted with the internal audit staff, as a basis for judging future candidates for the controller organization.

When campaigns to reduce overhead are undertaken, the internal audit staff may be cut more than is healthy for the organization. The audit committee questions such cuts and gets an opinion from the outside auditing firm. However, because internal auditors do much of the verifying that otherwise would be done by external auditors, at a much lower cost per hour, external auditors may not have an unbiased view of the proper size of the internal audit organization.

FINANCE COMMITTEE

The board is responsible to the shareholders for monitoring the corporation's financial health and assuring that its financial viability is maintained. The finance committee makes recommendations on these matters. (Nevertheless, as emphasized earlier, the full board cannot escape its ultimate responsibility for making sound decisions on important matters.)

The committee's agenda includes analyses of proposed capital and operating budgets and regular reviews of the company's financial performance as reported on the income statement, and its financial condition as reported on the balance sheet. The committee reviews the estimated financial requirements over the next several years and looks at how these requirements will be met. It also recommends the amount of quarterly dividends. The finance committee (or a separate pension committee) reviews matters of the pension fund as well as those of the fund for paying health-care and other post-employment benefits. It reviews the policies that determine the annual contribution to these funds and the performance of the firm or firms that invest them.

This section describes aspects of these matters that are dealt with at the board of directors level. Reviews of performance and status are described in Chapters 1 and 2. The budget preparation process is described in Chapter 6. Financial policies are discussed in Chapters 9 through 13.

In some companies, the functions described here are divided among three committees, for budget, finance, and pension, and the names may be different. Our purpose is to describe what committees do, regardless of their titles.

Analysis of Financial Policies

Financial policies are recommended by management. Tools of analysis are increasingly sophisticated. Using these tools to evaluate risk and return is the responsibility of management, not the finance committee. These tools help to quantify risk, but they are not a substitute for a definite policy on risk. An attitude toward risk is a personal matter, and the finance committee should recognize it as such. Each CEO has a personal attitude toward risk, and so does each individual director.

The committee's responsibility is to probe management's rationales for its policies and thereby assure itself that management has thought them through and that the policies are within acceptable limits.

Dividend Declaration

One financial policy specifically for the board to decide is the declaration of dividends. Dividends are paid only if the company declares them; this declaration usually is made quarterly.

Some companies regularly distribute a large fraction of earnings, while others retain a large fraction (or all) within the corporation. Although generous dividends may suit shareholders in the short run, they can deprive the corporation of resources it needs to grow and thereby penalize shareholders in the long run. Conversely, if a large fraction of earnings is retained, shareholders may be deprived of the opportunity to make profitable alternative investments of their own. Thus, the finance committee must balance the interests of the corporation with the interests of individual shareholders.

Some boards take a simplistic approach to dividends: "Always pay out X% of earnings," or "Increase dividends each year, no matter what." Both statements are acceptable guidelines, but neither is more than a guide. In some industries, a certain payout ratio is regarded as normal, and a company that departs substantially from industry practice may lose favor with investors. Good evidence suggests that a record of increasing dividends over time, or at least a record of stable dividends, is well regarded by investors. By contrast, an erratic dividend pattern is generally undesirable; it creates uncertainty for investors.

Dividend policy warrants careful analysis. The principal factors that the board considers are:

- What are the company's financial needs? These needs depend on how fast the company wants to grow and how capable it is of growing. Or, as is the case with some companies, what is needed to preserve the company during a period of adversity?

- How does the company want to finance its requirements for funds? It can meet its needs by retaining earnings, issuing debt, issuing equity, or some combination of these. Each source of funds has its own cost and its own degree of risk.

- What return does the company expect to earn on shareholder equity, and what degree of risk is it willing to assume in order to achieve this objective? The trade-off between risk and return will determine the appropriate type of financing and thus influence the extent to which earnings should be retained or paid out in dividends.

These are complex questions. Moreover, the factors involved in arriving at answers to them interact with one another. Consider the example of Cisco Systems:

Cisco was founded in 1984 and shipped its first product in 1985. The company grew rapidly. In 2000 it was a world leader in networking for the Internet, with sales of $18.9 billion and net income of $2.7 billion. The following statement is included in the company's 2000 Annual Report. "The Company has never paid cash dividends on its common stock and has no present plans to do so." Cisco retained all of its earnings to help finance its growth and used its stock to acquire other companies, which it integrated into its operations.

Cisco's dividend policy is typical of high-growth technology companies that need resources to grow but find raising equity in the financial markets expensive because they have no financial "track record" for new ventures.

Many successful companies have quite different dividend and financing policies from Cisco's. Many public utility companies, for example, have long, unbroken records of stable dividends that are a relatively high percentage of earnings, ranging from 50% to 90%. Even during the Depression in the 1930s many of these companies maintained their regular dividends, although dividends exceeded earnings in some periods.

The contrast between Cisco Systems and public utility companies indicates the extent to which dividend policy depends on an individual company's circumstances and needs. It also highlights the relationships between dividend policy, the company's need for financing, and the methods that it selects in order to meet its financial requirements.

Pension Funds

The finance committee considers two aspects of pension fund policy: (1) the amount required to be added to the fund and (2) the investment of the fund.

Size of the Pension Fund

Most corporate pension plans are defined benefit plans. In deciding the size of the fund required to make benefit payments to retirees, directors tend to rely heavily on the opinion of an actuary. The actuary calculates the necessary size of the fund using information about the size and demographic characteristics of the covered employees, facts about the provisions of the plan, and assumptions about the fund's return on investment and probable wage and salary increases over time. (With available software, the company can make the same calculation.)

There is no way of knowing, however, how reasonable are two key assumptions: the future return on investment and the future wage and salary payments on which the pensions are based. Since the actuarial calculations depend on the accuracy of these assumptions, the calculations should not be taken as gospel. Both of these variables are roughly related to the future rate of inflation, and the spread between them should remain roughly constant. That is, when one variable changes by one percentage point, the other variable also is likely to change by one percentage point.

Pension Fund Investments

The most conservative practice is to invest the pension fund in annuities or in bonds whose maturities match the anticipated pension payments. Such a policy is said to "lock in" the ability to make payments. This works out satisfactorily for employees who have already retired, but not for employees who are currently working. If the latter group's compensation increases at a faster rate than is assumed in the actuarial calculations, or if the plan itself is sweetened, the fixed return will turn out to be inadequate. Under a defined benefit plan, there is no sure way to guarantee that the cash will be available when it is needed. In any event, with such a conservative policy, the company gives up the opportunity to earn the usually greater return from an investment in equities.

Most companies hire one or more banks or investment firms to manage their pension funds. Voluminous data are available on the past performance of these managers. However, an excellent past record is no guarantee of excellent future performance. A firm is a collection of individuals. Investment performance is partly a function of the individuals doing the investing, and the performance record may change when these individuals leave or lose their skills. For many years, when it was managed by Peter Lynch, the Magellan Fund was the most successful of all mutual funds. After Mr. Lynch left, the fund's performance was not so huge (but was still above average). Performance is also partly a matter of luck.

Some companies divide the pension fund among several managers, periodically compare their performance, and replace the one with the poorest record. This may spread the risk somewhat, but it does not guarantee optimum performance. Luck and the individual who manages the fund continue to be dominant factors. It is a fact that some managers are better than others. The finance committee watches performance carefully. It is cautious about making changes based primarily on short-run performance, but it does so promptly when it is convinced that a better manager has been identified.

The finance committee also decides on asset allocation investment policies: how much in equities, how much in fixed income securities, how much in real property, how much in new ventures, how much in overseas securities, and the maximum percentage in a single company or industry.

Companies must also provide for costs of health-care and other benefits of employees who have not yet retired. The problems of estimating these costs are similar to those for pension funds, but with the additional complication that healthcare costs continue to increase at an unpredictable rate.

SUMMARY

In doing its job, the board accepts certain responsibilities. It should:

- Actively support the CEO, both within the organization and to outside parties, as long as the individual's performance is judged to be generally satisfactory.

- Discuss proposed major changes in the company's strategy and direction, major financing proposals, and other crucial issues, usually as proposed by the CEO.

- Formulate major policies regarding ethical or public responsibility matters, convey to the organization its expectation that the policies will be adhered to, and ensure that policy violations are not tolerated.

- Ensure, if feasible, that the CEO has identified a successor and is grooming that person for the job.

- Require the CEO to explain the rationale behind operating budgets, major capital expenditures, acquisitions, divestments, dividends, personnel matters, and similar important plans. Accept these proposals if they are consistent with the company's strategy and the explanation is reasonable. Otherwise, require additional information.

- Analyze reports on the company's performance, raise questions to highlight areas of possible concern, and suggest possible actions to improve performance, always with the understanding that the CEO, not the board, is responsible for performance.

- Assure that financial information furnished to shareholders and other outside parties fairly presents the financial performance and status of the company. Assure that internal controls are satisfactory.

- Replace the CEO promptly if the board concludes the executive's performance is and will continue to be unsatisfactory.

- Participate actively in decisions to elect or appoint directors.

- Decide on policies relating to the compensation of senior management, including bonuses, incentives, and perquisites. Determine the compensation of the CEO. Review recommendations of the CEO and ratify the compensation of other executives.

FOR FURTHER READING

American Bar Association Committee on Continuing Professional Education, *Corporate Governance Institute: ALI-ABA Course of Study Materials* (Philadelphia, PA: American Law Institute, 2000).

———, *Corporate Director's Guidebook* (Chicago, IL: ABA, 1994).

American Law Institute-American Bar Association, *Current Issues in Corporate Governance: ALI-ABA Course of Study Materials* (Philadelphia, PA: ALI-ABA, 1996).

American Society of Corporate Secretaries, *Current Board Practices* (New York: ASCS, 2000).

Anderson, Charles A., and Robert N. Anthony, *The New Corporate Directors* (New York: John Wiley, 1986).

Bawley, Dan, *Corporate Governance and Accountability: What Role for the Regulator, Director, and Auditor?* (Westport, CT: Quorum, 1999).

Berenbeim, Ronald, *The Corporate Board: A Growing Role in Strategic Assessment* (New York: Conference Board, 1996).

Bureau of National Affairs, *Corporate Governance Manual* (Washington, DC: Author, 1998).

Cagney, Lawrence K., *Compensation Committees* (Washington, DC: Bureau of National Affairs, 1998).

Cohen, Stephen S., and Gavin Boyd, eds., *Corporate Governance and Globalization: Long Range Planning Issues* (Northampton, MA: Edward Elgar, 2000).

Davies, Adrian, *A Strategic Approach to Corporate Governance* (Brookfield, VT: Gower, 1999).

Donaldson, Gordon, and Jay W. Lorsch, *Decision Making at the Top* (New York: Basic Books, 1983).

Ernst & Young, *Compensation Committees: Fulfilling Your Responsibilities in the 1990s* (New York: Ernst & Young, 1995).

Harvard Business Review on Corporate Governance (Boston: Harvard Business School, 2000).

Investor Responsibility Research Center, *Global Corporate Governance: Codes, Reports, and Legislation* (Washington, DC: Author, 1999).

Iskander, Magdi R., and Nadereh Chamlou, *Corporate Governance: A Framework for Implementation* (Washington, DC: World Bank, 2000).

Keasey, Kevin, and Mike Wright, eds., *Corporate Governance: Responsibilities, Risks, and Remuneration* (New York: John Wiley, 1997).

Knepper, William E., and Dan A. Bailey, *Liability of Corporate Officers and Directors,* 6th ed. (Charlottesville, VA: Michie, 1998).

Lorsch, Jay W., *Pawns or Potentates: The Reality of America's Corporate Boards* (Boston: Harvard Business School, 1984).

Mace, Myles L., *Directors: Myth and Reality,* rev. ed. (Boston: Division of Research, Harvard Business School, 1984).

Montgomery, Jason, *Corporate Governance Guidelines: An Analysis of Corporate Governance Guidelines at S&P 500 Corporations* (Washington, DC: Investor Responsibility Research Center, 2000).

National Association of Corporate Directors, *The Role of the Board in Corporate Strategy* (Washington, DC: NACD, 2000).

———, *Report of the NACD Blue Ribbon Commission on Director Professionalism* (Washington, DC: NACD, 1996).

Oliver, Caroline, ed., *The Policy Governance Fieldbook: Practical Lessons, Tips, and Tools from the Experience of Real-Word Boards* (San Francisco: Jossey-Bass, 1999).

Patterson, D. Jeanne, *The Link between Corporate Governance and Performance: Year 2000 Update* (New York: Conference Board, 2000).

Stoner, James A. F., R. Edward Freeman, and Daniel R. Gilbert, Jr., *Management,* 6th ed. (London: Prentice-Hall International, 1995).

Vancil, Richard F., *Passing the Baton: Managing the Process of CEO Succession* (Boston: Harvard Business School Press, 1987).

Varallo, Gregory V., and Daniel A. Dreisbach, *Corporate Governance in the 1990s: New Challenges and Evolving Standards* (Chicago, IL: American Bar Association, 1996).

Ward, Ralph D., *Improving Corporate Boards: The Boardroom Insider Guidebook* (New York: John Wiley, 2000).

——, *21st Century Corporate Board* (New York: John Wiley, 1997).

Weidenbaum, Murray L., *The Evolving Corporate Board* (St. Louis: Center for the Study of American Business, Washington University, 1994).

NOTES

1. Kenneth R. Andrews, *The Concept of Corporate Strategy* (Homewood, IL: Dow-Jones Irwin, 1980).

2. SEC Release 34-41982.

3. *Escott v. BarChris Construction Corp.*, 283 F. Supp. 643 (S.D.N.Y. 1968).

4. If the auditing firm cannot make this statement, it states that it is unable to give any opinion. In these circumstances, the stock exchanges immediately suspend trading in the company's stock.

5. *Investors Relation Business.* Press release October 9, 2000.

16 INFORMATION TECHNOLOGY AND THE FIRM

Theodore Grossman

INTRODUCTION

The personal use of information technology was discussed in an earlier chapter. This chapter will discuss the firm's use of information technology.

Of all the chapters in this book, the two dealing with information technology will have the shortest half-life. Because of the constant flow of new technology, what is written about today will have changed somewhat by tomorrow. This chapter presents a snapshot of how technology is used *today* in industry finance and accounting. By the time you compare your experiences with the contents of this chapter, some of the information will no longer be applicable. Change means progress. Unfortunately, many companies will not have adapted; consequently, they will have lost opportunity and threatened their own futures.

HISTORICAL PERSPECTIVE

To understand the present and future of information technology, it is important to understand its past. In the 1960s and 1970s, most companies' information systems were enclosed in the "glass house." If you entered any company that had its own computer, it was located behind a glass wall with a security system that allowed only those with access rights to enter the facility. *One* computer controlled all of a company's data processing functions. Referred to as a host centric environment, the computer was initially used for accounting purposes—accounts payable, accounts receivable, order entry, payroll, and so on. In the late 1970s and 1980s, most companies purchased in-house computer systems and stopped outsourcing their data processing. Recognizing the power and potential of information technology, companies directed the use of their technology toward operations, marketing, and sales; and they created a new executive position, Chief Information Officer (CIO), to oversee this process.

In the 1980s, many companies gradually changed from host centric to distributed computing. Instead of processing all of the information on one large, mainframe computer, companies positioned minicomputers to act as processors for departments or special applications. The minicomputers were, in many cases, networked together to share data. Databases became distributed, with data residing in different locations, yet accessible to all the machines in the network.

The personal computer had the greatest impact on the organization. It brought true distributed processing. Now everybody had their own computer, capable of performing feats that, until then, were only available on the company's mainframe computer. This created both opportunities and headaches for the company, some of which will be addressed in the section on controls. As companies entered the 1990s, these computers were networked, forging the opportunity to share data and resources, as well as to work in cooperative groups. In the mid-1990s, these networks were further enhanced through connection to larger, wide area networks (WANs) and to the ultimate WAN, the Internet. Companies are doing what was unthinkable just a couple of years ago. They are allowing their customers and their suppliers direct connection into their own computers. New technology is being introduced every day, and new terms are creeping into our language (Internet, intranet, extranet, etc.). It is from this perspective that we start by looking at computer hardware.

HARDWARE

Most of the early computers were large, mainframe computers. Usually manufactured by IBM, they were powerful batch processing machines. Large numbers of documents (e.g., invoices or orders) were entered into the computer and then processed, producing various reports and special documents, such as checks or accounts receivable statements.

Technology was an extremely unfriendly territory. In many companies, millions of lines of software were written to run on this mainframe technology. Generally speaking, these machines were programmed in a language called COBOL and used an operating system that was proprietary for that hardware. Not only was it difficult to run programs on more than one manufacturer's computer, but, because there were slight differences in the configurations and operating systems, it was difficult to run the same software on different computers, even if they were produced by the same manufacturer.

In the 1980s, technology evolved from proprietary operating systems to minicomputers with open systems. These were the first open systems, computers that functioned using the UNIX operating system. While, in the 1970s, Bell Labs actually developed UNIX as an operating system for scientific applications, it later became an accepted standard for commercial applications. Platform independent, the operating system and its associated applications could run on a variety of manufacturers' computers, creating both opportunities for users and competition within the computer industry. Users were no longer inexorably tied to one manufacturer. UNIX became the standard as companies moved into the 1990s. However, standards changed rapidly in the nineties, and UNIX has lost ground due to the development of client server technology.

In the early 1990s, technologists predicted the demise of the mainframe. IBM's stock declined sharply as the market realized that the company's chief source of margin was headed toward extinction. However, the mainframe has reinvented itself as a super server, and, while it has been replaced for some of the processing load, the mainframe and IBM are still positioned to occupy important roles in the future.

Server technology is heading toward a design in which processors are built around multiple, smaller processors, all operating in parallel. Referred to as symmetrical multiprocessors (SMPs), there are between two and eight processors in a unit. SMPs are made available by a range of manufacturers and operating systems, and they provide processor power typically not available in a uniprocessor. Faced with the demanding environment of multiple, simultaneous queries from databases that exceed hundreds of gigabytes, processors with massively parallel processors, or MPPs, are being utilized more and more. MPPs are processors that have hundreds of smaller processors within one unit. The goal of SMPs and MPPs is to split the processing load among the processors.

In a typical factory in the 1800s, one motor usually powered all of the machinery, to which it was connected by a series of gears, belts, and pulleys. Today, that is no longer the case, as each machine has its own motor or, in some cases, multiple, specialized motors. For example, the automobile's main motor is the engine, but there are also many other motors that perform such tasks as opening and closing windows, raising and lowering the radio antenna, and powering the windshield wipers. Computers are the firm's motors, and like motors, they, too, have evolved. Initially, firms used a host centric mainframe, one large computer; today, they are using many computers to perform both specialized and general functions.

In the early 1990s, Xerox's prestigious Palo Alto Research Center introduced "ubiquitous computing," a model that it feels reflects the way companies and their employees will work in the future. In ubiquitous computing, each worker will have available differing quantities of three different size computers: 20 to 50 Post-it note size portable computers, three or four computers the size of a writing tablet, and one computer the size of a six-foot-by-six-foot white board. All of the computers will work together by communicating to a network through, in most cases, wireless connections.

The progress of chip technology has been highly predictable. In the early 1960s, Gordon Moore, the inventor of the modern CPU at Intel, developed

EXHIBIT 16.1   Moore's Law—charting the power of the growth of the PC.

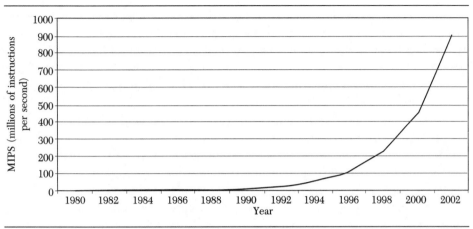

Moore's Law, which predicts that the density of the components on a computer chip will double every 18 to 24 months, thereby doubling the chip's processing power. This hypothesis has proven to be very accurate. Exhibit 16.1 shows the growth of the various Intel CPU chips that have powered the personal computer and many other machines. As can be seen, the PC's power has just about doubled every 18 to 24 months.

This growth can be seen more dramatically when the graph is plotted logarithmically, as in Exhibit 16.2.

EXHIBIT 16.2   Moore's Law—charting the growth of the PC (logarithmically).

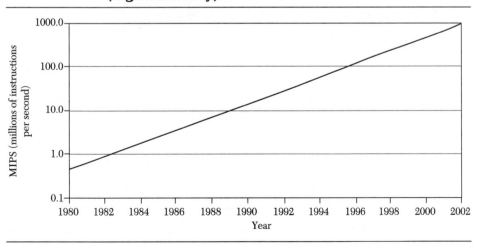

SOFTWARE

Exhibit 16.3 represents the information systems paradigm. Operational control systems, which run the company's day-to-day operations, are typically used by the lowest level of the organization, are run on a scheduled basis, and usually contain large volumes of input data, output reports, and information. These systems might be accounts payable, accounts receivable, payroll, order entry, or inventory control.

Decision support systems are generally used by middle-level managers to supply them with information that they can use to make decisions. Usually run on an ad hoc basis and involving small amounts of data, budgets, exception reporting, cash-flow forecasting, accounts receivable dunning reports, "what if" analyses, audit analysis reports, and variance analyses are examples of these decision support systems. Many of the newer applications packages come with facilities for managers without any programming knowledge to create their own decision reports.

Strategic information systems are used by senior management to make decisions on corporate strategy. For example, a retail company might use demographic census data, along with a computerized geographical mapping system, to evaluate the most appropriate locations at which it should open new stores. A manufacturing company, given its demands for both skilled and unskilled labor, might use a similar method to determine the optimal location for a new plant.

While most older hardware has given way to newer computers, most companies use a combination of newly acquired and older, self-developed software. The latter was developed over a period of years, perhaps 20 or more, using COBOL, which, until the early 1990s, was the standard programming language in business applications. Today, many companies' mission critical systems still

EXHIBIT 16.3   Types of information systems.

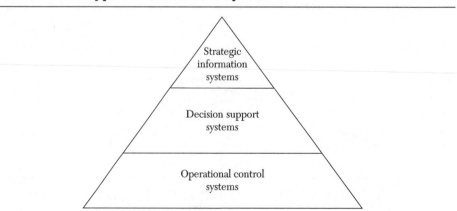

run on mainframe technology, using programs written in COBOL; in fact, there are billions of lines of COBOL programming code still functional in U.S. business.

These "legacy" systems have become a major issue for many, though, and were the key issue behind the Y2K problem. In many instances, they have grown like patchwork quilts, as they have been written and modified by programmers who are no longer with their firms. More often than not, documentation of these changes and enhancements is not available, and the guidelines for many of these software applications no longer exist. Replacing these applications is cost prohibitive, and the distraction to the organization caused by the need to retrain workers would be tremendous.

Nonetheless, as a result of the Y2K problem, many of these systems were replaced, but large volumes of them were merely patched to allow for the millennium change. These systems will eventually have to be replaced. If history is a lesson, many of these systems will not be replaced, though, until it is too late. In any event, the business community should not face the singular deadline it faced at the end of 1999.

Today, most programmers write in C++, C, or fourth-generation programming languages. C++ is an object oriented programming language; object oriented languages provide the programmer with a facility to create a programming object or module that may be reused in many applications. Fourth-generation programming languages are usually provided with sophisticated relational database systems. These database systems provide high-level tools and programming languages that allow programmers to create applications quickly without having to concern themselves with the physical and logical structure of the data. Oracle, Informix, Sybase, and Progress are some of the more popular relational database package companies.

INTERNET TECHNOLOGY

Nothing has impacted technology and society in the past 10 years more than the Internet. When Bill Clinton was inaugurated in January 1993, there were 50 pages on the Internet. Today, there are more than 200 billion pages. The underlying technology behind the Internet has its roots in a project begun by the U.S. government in the early 1970s. The network was originally developed by a consortium of research colleges and universities and the federal government that was looking for a way to share research data and provide a secure means of communicating and for backing up defense facilities. The original network was called ARPANET. ARPANET was sponsored by the Department of Defense's Advanced Research and Planning Agency (ARPA). It was replaced in the 1980s by the current network, which was originally not very user friendly and was used mostly by techies. The Internet's popularity exploded with the development of the World Wide Web and the necessary software programs that made it much more user friendly to explore.

The Internet works on a set of software standards the first of which, TCP/IP, was developed in the 1970s. The entire theory behind the Internet and TCP/IP, which enables computers to speak to each other over the Internet, was to create a network that had no central controller. The Internet is unlike a string of Christmas lights, where if one light in the series goes out the rest of the lights stop functioning. Rather, if one computer in the network is disabled, the rest of the network continues to perform.

Each computer in the Internet has an Internet, or IP, address. Similar to one's postal address, it consists of a series of numbers (e.g., 155.48.178.21), and it tells the network where to leave your e-mail, and data. When you access an Internet site through its URL (e.g., www.babson.edu), a series of computers on the Internet, called domain name servers (DNS), convert the URL to an IP address. When an e-mail, message, or data is sent to someone over the Internet, it is broken into a series of packets. These packets, similar to postcards, contain the IP address of the sender, the IP address of the recipient, the packet number of the message (e.g., 12 of 36), and the data itself. These packets may travel many different routes along the Internet. Frequently, packets belonging to the same message do not travel the same route. The receiving computer then reassembles these packets into a complete message.

The second standard that makes the Internet work is HTML, or Hypertext Markup Language. This language allows data to be displayed on the user's screen. It also allows a user to click on an Internet link and jump to a new page on the Internet. While HTML remains the underlying programming language for the World Wide Web, there are many more user-friendly software packages, like FrontPage 2000, that help create HTML code. Moreover, HTML, while powerful in its own right, is not dynamic and has its limitations. Therefore, languages such as JavaScript, Java, and Pearl, which create animation, perform calculations, create dynamic Web pages, and access and update databases with information on the host's Web server, were developed to complement HTML. Using a Web browser (e.g., Netscape Navigator or Microsoft's Internet Explorer), the computer converts the HTML or other programming languages into the information that the users see on their computer monitors.

Internet technology has radically changed the manner in which corporate information systems process their data. In the early and mid-1990s, corporate information systems used distributed processing techniques. Using this method, some of the processing would take place on the central computer (the server) and the rest on the users' (the clients') computers—hence, the term *client-server computing*. Many companies implemented applications using this technology, which ensured that processing power was utilized at both ends and that systems were scalable. The problem with client-server processing was that different computers (even within the IBM-compatible PC family) used different drivers and required tweaking to make the systems work properly. Also, if the software needed to be changed at the client end, and there were many clients (some companies have thousands of PC clients), maintaining the software for all of those clients could be a nightmare. Even with specialized tools developed for that purpose, it never quite worked perfectly.

As companies recognized the opportunity to send data over the Internet, whether for their customers or their employees, they started to migrate all of their applications to a browser interface. This change has required companies to rethink where the locus of their processing will occur. Prior to the 1990s, companies' networks were host-centric, where all of their processing was conducted using one large mainframe. In the early 1990s, companies began using client-server architecture. Today, with the current browser technology and the Internet, the locus has shifted back to a host-centric environment. The difference, though, is that the browser on the users' computers is used to display and capture data, and the data processing actually occurs back at the central host on a series of specialized servers, not on one large mainframe computer. The only program users need is a standard browser, which solves the incompatibility problem presented by distributed data processing. No specialized software is stored on the users' computers.

Internet technology was largely responsible for many of the productivity enhancements of the 1990s. Intel's microprocessors, Sun and Hewlett Packard's servers, CISCO's communications hardware, and Microsoft's Windows operating systems have all facilitated this evolution. While Windows is the predominant client operating system, most servers operate on Windows NT or 2000, UNIX or LINUX operating systems.

TODAY'S APPLICATION SYSTEMS

In the 1970s and 1980s, application software systems were stand-alone. There was little sharing of data, leading to the frequent redundancy of information. For example, in older systems, there might have been vendor data files for both inventory and accounts payable, resulting in the possibility of multiple versions of the truth. Each of the files may have contained address information, yet each of the addresses may have been different for the same vendor. Today, however, software applications are integrated across functional applications (accounts payable, accounts receivable, marketing, sales, manufacturing, etc.). Database systems contain only one vendor data location, which all systems utilize. These changes in software architecture better reflect the integration of functions that has occurred within most companies.

Accounting systems, while used primarily for accounting data, also provide a source of data for sales and marketing. While retail stores' point of sale cash registers are used as a repository for cash and to account for it, they are also the source of data for inventory, sales, and customer marketing. For example, some major retailers ask their customers for their zip codes when point of sale transactions are entered, and that data is shared by all of the companies' major applications.

Accounts receivable systems serve two purposes. On one hand, they allow the company to control an important asset, their accounts receivable. Also, the availability of credit enables customers to buy items, both commercial and retail, that they otherwise would not be able to buy if they had to pay in cash. Credit card companies, which make their money from the transaction fees and the interest charges, understand this function well. Frequently, they reevaluate the spending and credit patterns of their client base and award increased credit limits to their customers. Their goal is to encourage their customers to buy more, without necessarily paying off their balance any sooner than necessary. Information systems make it possible for the companies to both control and promote their products, which in this case are credit card transactions.

These examples of horizontally integrated systems, as well as the understanding of the strategic and competitive uses of information technology, demonstrate where industry is headed.

ACCOUNTING INFORMATION SYSTEMS

As mentioned earlier, computer-based accounting systems were, for most companies, the first computerized applications. As the years progressed, these systems have become integrated and consist of the following modules:

- Accounts Payable.
- Order Entry and Invoicing.
- Accounts Receivable.
- Purchase Order Management and Replenishment.
- Inventory Control.
- Human Resource Management.
- Payroll.
- Fixed Assets.
- General Ledger and Financial Statements.

Whereas in past years some of these modules were acquired and others were self-developed, today most companies purchase packaged software.

In the 1980s, "shrink-wrapped" software was developed and introduced. Lotus Corporation, along with other companies, was a pioneer, selling software like its 1-2-3 application in shrink-wrapped packages. The software was accompanied by sufficient documentation and available telephone support to ensure that even companies with limited technical expertise could manage their own destinies.

There are a host of software packages that will satisfy the needs of companies of all sizes. Smaller companies can find software selections that run on personal computers and networks, are integrated, and satisfy most of the companies' requirements. Quicken and Computer Associates have offerings that provide most of the necessary functional modules for small and medium size companies, respectively. The more advanced packages, like Macola and Acc-Pac, are equipped with interfaces to bar-code scanners and scales, which, together, track inventory and work in process and weigh packages as they are shipped, producing not only invoices but also shipping documents for most of the popular freight companies such as FedEx and UPS. These packages range in price from $100 for the entire suite of accounting applications for the smallest packages to approximately $800 per module for the larger packages, which, of course, have more robust features. While some of the smaller packages are available through computer stores and software retailers, the larger packages are acquired through independent software vendors (ISV), who, for a consulting fee, will sell, install, and service the software. The practice of using third party ISVs began in the 1980s, when large hardware and software manufacturers realized that they were incapable of servicing all of the smaller companies that would be installing their products, many of whom required a lot of hand-holding. Consequently, a cottage industry of distributors and value added dealers developed, in which companies earn profits on the sale of hardware and software and the ensuing consulting services.

Larger companies are following a trend toward large, integrated packages from companies like SAP and Oracle. These packages integrate not only the accounting functions but also the manufacturing, warehousing, sales, marketing, and distribution functions. These systems are referred to as enterprise resource planning (ERP) systems. Many of these ERP systems, available from companies such as SAP, Oracle, and BAAN, also interface with Web applications to enable electronic commerce transactions. SAP has spawned an entire industry of consulting companies that assist large companies in implementing its software, a process that may take several years to complete. As in any software implementation, one must always factor into the timetable the process's cost and the distraction it causes the organization. In today's lean business environment, people have little extra time for new tasks. Implementing a major new system or, for that matter, any system, requires a major time and effort commitment.

INFORMATION TECHNOLOGY IN BANKING AND FINANCE

The financial services industry is the leading industry in its use of information technology. As shown in Exhibit 16.4, according to a survey conducted in 1999 by the Computer Sciences Corporation, this sector has spent 5.0% of its annual revenue on IT, almost more than double that of any other industry, except the technology driven telecommunications industry.

This graph also illustrates how integral a role real-time information plays in the financial services industry, whether it be for accessing stock quotes or processing bank deposits. The industry has become a transaction processing

EXHIBIT 16.4   Information technology budgets by industry.

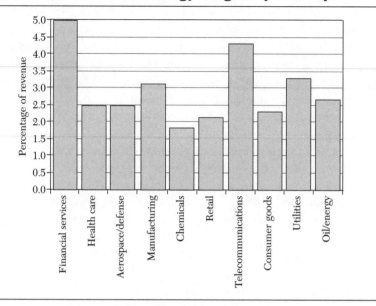

industry that is information dependent. Very little real money is ever touched. Rather, all transactions, from stock purchases to the direct deposit of workers' checks, are processed electronically. Information technology has paved the way for innovations like the NASDAQ trading system, in which, unlike the New York Stock Exchange (NYSE), all of the trades are conducted totally electronically.

NETWORKS AND COMMUNICATIONS

It is becoming increasingly common in industry to create virtual wide area networks using multiple, interconnected local area networks. These networks also connect the older mainframe and midrange computers that industry uses for its older legacy systems to the client terminals on the users' desks. Exhibit 16.5 is a model of a typical company's wide area network, and it demonstrates how all of the older technology interconnects with the newer local area networks and the Internet.

In the early 1990s, there were numerous, competing network operating systems and protocols. While Novell and its NetWare software holds the largest market share, Microsoft's Windows NT is becoming the network operating system of choice, and, because of the Internet's overwhelming success, TCP/IP is rapidly becoming the standard communications protocol. Remember, though, success is very fragile in the world of information technology. Today's standard can easily become yesterday's news. If you are always prepared for change, then you will not be surprised by it.

EXHIBIT 16.5   Model of wide area network (local area network and Internet connection using open communications protocol, c. 1997).

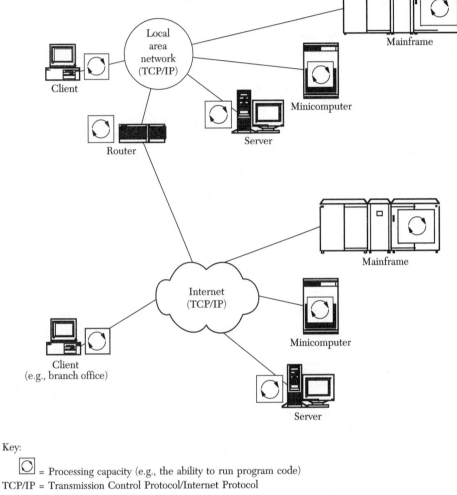

Key:

⬚ = Processing capacity (e.g., the ability to run program code)

TCP/IP = Transmission Control Protocol/Internet Protocol

Electronic Data Interchange (EDI) allows companies to communicate and conduct electronic commerce from one computer to another. EDI is one of the industry's growing uses for data communications, and many companies are using it to send purchase orders to their suppliers, thereby lessening the time it takes for purchase orders to be mailed and then entered and processed by the suppliers. Inventories are lowered by speeding up the turnaround time of ordering and receiving goods and materials. On the flip side, many suppliers use EDI to send their customers advance ship notifications (ASN), advising them of what has been shipped so that they can prepare their warehouses for the goods and materials. Lastly, some companies use EDI to transmit their invoices and then to receive the subsequent payments. While industries use different versions of EDI in different ways, their goals are always the same: minimize the processing time and lower inventory costs and overhead expenses. An industry organization in Washington, D.C., developed and maintains a standard format that dictates how all transactions are sent, ensuring that all companies that wish to implement EDI can be assured that all vendors' and customers' computers will understand each others' transactions, without requiring any custom programming. EDI, while still used quite extensively, has been eclipsed by electronic commerce, which will be discussed later in this chapter.

The 1990s has also seen the advent of virtual organizations. Virtual organizations are formed when companies join together to create products or enterprises that they could not have created individually. In most cases, information technology allows companies to create these partnerships and share information as if they were one company. Using communications and groupware products like Lotus Notes, the partners can share information with each other about their individual progress to ensure the best possible success. This will be discussed further in the section on IT strategy.

DATABASE

The following scenario depicts what information systems looked like prior to the use of database management systems. Imagine a physical office in which each person has his or her own file cabinet. The information in the file cabinets belongs to the people whose desks are closest to them. They decide what information will be in their file cabinets and how it will be organized. For example, sales might refer to gross sales in one worker's cabinet and net sales in another's. Yet, the discrepancy would be unimportant, because there was actually very little sharing of data.

Database management systems assume that information is a corporate asset to be shared by all workers in the enterprise. Database technology, therefore, allows a company to have one integrated location for the storage of all company data. These systems create a standard vocabulary, or data dictionary, by which all references are consistent (e.g., sales always means net sales). They also enable each user to have her own individual view of the data as if the information were still in the file cabinet next to her desk. Users need not concern themselves with the physical location or physical order of the data either. Database management systems are capable of presenting the data as necessary. In fact, with distributed databases, the data does not even have to reside in the same location or computer. It can be spread around the world if necessary. Database systems are sufficiently intelligent and can find the data and process it as if it were located directly on the user's personal computer.

Most of the software that was developed in the earlier years relied on data structures called flat files. While some companies utilized database technology to store information, those database management systems were, in many cases, unwieldy and very expensive to both acquire and maintain. They were usually hierarchical or network database systems that, alone, cost in excess of $200,000 and frequently required special database administrators just to constantly fine-tune the system.

Today's database technology is based on a relational model, and, on a very simplistic basis, it resembles a spreadsheet. In a relational database, there are a series of tables or files. Similar to a spreadsheet table, each table has columns with attributes and rows of data. The difference is that there is only one table in a spreadsheet, whereas there can be an almost unlimited number of tables in a database. In addition, there is a practical limit to the size of a spreadsheet, but databases can contain thousands of columns and millions of rows of data. In addition, databases also allow users to relate or connect tables that share common columns of data.

Exhibit 16.6 is an example of a very simple portion of a payroll application. There are two different tables. The employee table contains data about each of the company's employees: name, address, marital status, number of dependents, and so on. The pay table contains data about every time each of the employees is paid: their gross payroll, social security taxes, federal withholding, state tax, and so forth.

First, notice the common column between the two tables, the employee number. This column enables the database management system to relate the two tables. It allows the system, for example, to print a payroll journal that has both the weekly payroll information from the pay table and to access the employees' names from the employee table. Why not combine all the data into one table? Not only would the employees' names, social security numbers, and other information appear multiple times, requiring the unnecessary use of data storage, but also multiple versions of the truth might occur. If one of the employees should happen to change his name or address (if address were included in the employee table), the database would show one name for part of the year and another for the rest of the year. Redundant data creates opportunities for data corruption; just because data is changed in one table, that same data is not necessarily changed in all tables. Prudent systems design eliminates data field duplications wherever possible.

DATE WAREHOUSE

Data warehousing attempts to reconcile and live with past applications software, while still benefiting from today's newer technology. As mentioned earlier, industry is rife with older legacy systems that are currently cost prohibitive to replace. Most of these older systems are mission critical operational control systems (see Exhibit 16.3) and satisfy most of the operational needs of the company. However, they are built on technology that cannot support the kinds of decision support tools that management requires. Many of these

EXHIBIT 16.6 Database example.

EMPLOYEE TABLE

Employee Number	First Name	Initial	Last Name	Social Security Number	Marital Status	Number of Dependents	Date of Birth	Date of Hire	Date of Termination	Date of Last Pay Raise	Pay-Rate	Hourly or Salary
1	Mary	E	Smith	123456789	M	4	4/1/63	7/21/91		9/1/96	8.505	H
2	Tom	T	Day	234567890	M	3	3/2/55	11/15/91		1/15/96	750.000	S
3	Harry	F	Jones	345678901	S	1	11/30/71	1/15/92	9/24/96	11/6/94	12.500	H
4	Sally	D	Kraft	456789012	S	0	10/5/65	3/6/92		3/5/96	14.755	H
5	Charlie		Malt	567890123	S	1	6/6/80	6/2/93		6/17/96	900.000	S
6	John	K	Free	678901234	M	5	8/5/49	11/1/94		12/15/95	17.500	H

PAY TABLE

Employee Number	Date	Number of Regular Hours	Number of Overtime Hours	Gross Payroll	Social Security Tax	Medicare Tax	Federal Withholding Tax	Net Pay	Check Number
1	1/7/96	40.0	4.0	391.23	24.26	5.67	101.1642534	238.62	1
2	1/7/96	40.0	0.0	750.00	46.50	10.88	193.935	457.44	2
3	1/7/96	40.0	0.0	500.00	31.00	7.25	129.29	304.96	3
4	1/7/96	40.0	4.0	678.73	42.08	9.84	175.5060034	413.97	4
5	1/7/96	40.0	0.0	900.00	55.80	13.05	232.722	548.93	5
6	1/7/96	40.0	2.5	765.63	47.47	11.10	197.9753125	466.97	6
1	1/14/96	40.0	12.0	493.29	30.58	7.15	127.5549282	300.87	7
2	1/14/96	40.0	0.0	750.00	46.50	10.88	193.935	457.44	8
3	1/14/96	40.0	8.0	650.00	40.30	9.43	168.077	396.45	9
4	1/14/96	40.0	7.9	765.05	47.43	11.09	197.8257886	466.62	10
5	1/14/96	40.0	0.0	900.00	55.80	13.05	232.722	548.93	11
6	1/14/96	40.0	0.0	700.00	43.40	10.15	181.006	426.94	12
1	1/21/96	40.0	0.0	340.20	21.09	4.93	87.968916	207.49	13
2	1/21/96	40.0	0.0	750.00	46.50	10.88	193.935	457.44	14
3	1/21/96	40.0	2.4	545.00	33.79	7.90	140.9261	332.41	15
4	1/21/96	40.0	6.7	738.49	45.79	10.71	190.9581624	450.42	16
5	1/21/96	40.0	0.0	900.00	55.80	13.05	232.722	548.93	17
6	1/21/96	40.0	5.0	831.25	51.54	12.05	214.944625	507.00	18

systems use older file structures or obsolete database management systems and are almost incapable of accessing and manipulating data.

As an alternative to replacing these systems, data warehousing provides a state of the art database management system that is fed data from the older legacy systems. However, data does get duplicated, which can potentially cause a synchronization problem between the data in the warehouse and the data in the older legacy systems. Consequently, IT management must put stringent controls in place. Still, the benefits outweigh the potential problems, for the data warehouse comes with all of the high tech tools that will enable management to create a plethora of queries and reports. Most of the newer Decision Support Tools and Executive Information Systems, which will be discussed later, require a storage capability similar to the data warehouse.

CONTROLS

Because the initial software applications that were developed in the 1960s and 1970s were accounting oriented, data processing, which is what information technology was then called, typically reported to the Chief Financial Officer, creating a control atmosphere consistent with accounting controls. A central group of trained data entry operators was responsible for entering and verifying data. Access to the "glass house" was restricted, and in some cases access to the data entry and report distribution areas was also restricted. Because everything was self-contained, control was not a major issue.

In the late seventies and early eighties, online terminals began appearing on users' desks, outside of the glass house, allowing them access to data. Initially, these terminals were used for information inquiry. Yet, even this limited function was tightly controlled by strict software access control and password protection. While workers were getting additional capabilities, they were also creating opportunities for lapses in control. This was just the beginning of the Trojan horse. Eventually, data entry moved out of the glass house to the warehouse receiving dock to be used for inventory receipts; the order entry desk to be used for new orders; the purchasing department to be used for purchase orders; and, in the case of retailing, on to the sales floor for point of sale processing. No longer were trained data-entry operators responsible for the quality of the data; others were responsible for entering data, and it was just an ancillary part of their job, for which they were not necessarily even trained.

The control environment was breaking down, and the introduction of the personal computer only complicated the issue. No longer was control centralized. While access to data could be controlled, control over the use of data and the content of reports was lost. For example, two people could each issue a report on sales, and the numbers could easily be different. Yet, both reports could be accurate. How is this possible? Simple. One of the reports may have been about gross sales and the other about net sales, or one may have been based on data through Friday and the other on data through Saturday.

When all programming was controlled by a small professional group, control was much easier. Because today's spreadsheet programs are user friendly, however, and software does not require programming knowledge, everybody is his or her own programmer. Thus, it is difficult to control the consistency of the information that is being distributed.

The problems only become more complicated. Now companies allow their business partners, vendors, and even outsiders to access their computers, using the Internet and EDI. Data is interchanged and moneys are exchanged electronically often without paper backup. While technology can prevent most unauthorized access to data, as recent history has shown, even the U.S. Defense Department has not successfully prevented the best hackers from accessing its computers and wreaking havoc. What was relatively simple to control before 1990 is now a nightmare. Accountants, systems professionals, and auditors must remain forever vigilant against both inadvertent and intentional unauthorized use and abuse of company data.

INFORMATION TECHNOLOGY STRATEGY

How do companies decide how to invest their IT money? What projects get funded? Which projects are of higher priority? IT strategy is not created in a vacuum. Rather, like all of the other operational departments within a corporation, IT must support the direction and goals of the company. The Chief Information Officer's job is to educate the rest of senior management about IT's ability to create opportunities for the company and help it move in directions that make sense.

IT architecture is developed to support the IT and corporate strategy. If additional networks, workstations, or data warehouses are required, they are either acquired or developed.

In the late 1980s and early 1990s, Wal-Mart adopted an everyday low pricing strategy. To accomplish this goal, Wal-Mart needed to change the manner in which it both conducted business with its suppliers and managed the inbound logistics, warehousing, and distribution of merchandise to its stores. It needed to abolish warehousing as much as possible and quicken the process by which stores ordered and received merchandise. Also, Wal-Mart needed to eliminate any unnecessary inventory in stores and allow stores to order merchandise only as needed. Lastly, lags in its distribution centers needed to be prevented, enabling goods to be received from their suppliers and immediately shipped to stores.

As a result, Wal-Mart designed a systems and technology infrastructure that, through EDI, enables the stores to order goods, as needed, from their suppliers. Moreover, Wal-Mart permits manufacturers to access computerized sales information directly from its computers, which, in turn, allows them to gauge Wal-Mart's demand and then stage production to match it. Wal-Mart effectively shifted the burden of warehousing merchandise from its own warehouses to the vendors, eliminating the costs of both warehouse maintenance and surplus inventory. The distribution centers were automated, allowing cross docking, whereby goods being received for specific stores were immediately sent to the shipping area designated for those stores, thus putting an end to all time lags.

Wal-Mart now has the lowest cost of inbound logistics in its industry. Its selling G&A is 6% below its nearest competitor, enabling it to be the most aggressive retailer in its industry. Wal-Mart aligned its IT strategy and infrastructure to support the company's overall strategy. IT was the agent for change. Without the newer information technologies, none of the newer strategies and directions could have been successful.

JUSTIFYING THE COST OF INFORMATION TECHNOLOGY

Should companies take that giant leap of faith and invest millions of dollars in new machines and software? Can we measure the return on a company's investment in technology?

These are questions that, for years, have concerned professional technology managers. Today, information technology consumes an increasing share of companies' budgets. While we cannot live with the cost of technology, ultimately, we cannot live without the technology. Thus, when every new version of the personal computer chip or Windows hits the market, companies must decide whether it is a worthwhile investment. Everyone wants the latest and greatest technology, and they assume that, with it, workers will be more productive.

While IT is the medium for change, its costs and soft benefits are difficult to measure. As technology gets disbursed throughout a company, it becomes increasingly difficult to track costs. As workers become their own administrative assistants, each company must determine whether its workers are more or less productive when they type their own documents and prepare their own presentations. These are many of the issues that companies are facing now and will be in the future as they struggle with new IT investments.

INTERNET/INTRANET/EXTRANET

The Internet, intranets, and extranets provide companies with a plethora of opportunities to find new ways of transacting business. An alternative to some of the older technology, an intranet, a subsystem of the Internet, was developed in 1996 to allow employees from within a company to access data in the company's system. A "firewall" prevents outsiders from accessing any data that a company wishes to keep confidential. An intranet refers to those systems that are inside the firewall. Employees have the access authority to break through the firewall and access information, even though they might be using a computer outside of the company. Remember, the Internet is just one large party line on which everybody is sending around data.

One manufacturing company provides an intranet facility for its employees to learn about their health, life and disability insurance, and educational benefits. The system allows them to sign up for these programs and, in the frequently asked questions (FAQs) section, to inquire about some of the most common issues specific to the programs. When online, employees can also access and sign up for a list of in-house training courses, read an employee newsletter, and check the current price of the company's publicly traded stock.

An extranet is a version of the intranet that allows external users to access data inside of the firewall. For example, part of Wal-Mart's ordering and logistics system allows its vendors and suppliers to access Wal-Mart's store sales data directly from Wal-Mart's computer systems. If these transactions occurred over the Internet, they would be referred to as extranet transactions.

ELECTRONIC COMMERCE

Electronic commerce is changing the entire landscape in how business is transacted. While most consumers think just about business to consumer (B2C) e-commerce, the greatest potential lies in business-to-business (B2B) e-commerce. International Data Corporation estimates that B2C e-commerce will generate $300 billion annually by 2004, but B2B e-commerce will generate $2.2 trillion annually by 2004. Most of the focus of the investor community during 1999 and 2000 was on the B2C space, with millions of dollars made and lost as a result of people not understanding the business model. Most of the money raised in venture capital was used for advertising to gain brand recognition, whereas very little was invested in infrastructure. As a result, the B2C landscape is littered with the corpses of failed ventures. Those that have survived are spending money on the traditional back office functions that brick and mortar retailers have developed over the years.

All the while, bricks-and-mortar retailers have been experimenting in selling on the Internet and have adopted a hybrid model for doing so. Customers are able to order over the Internet, but they can also return merchandise to traditional stores. The Internet can also make a significant difference when products, such as music and software, can be ordered—and delivered—electronically.

These new opportunities create new challenges for those involved in the operations, accounting, and finance of these virtual-marketplace companies. The order is being not only processed electronically but also shipped automatically, sometimes from a third party's fulfillment center. Also, the payment is being processed electronically. The electronic payment, usually through a third-party clearance house, must conform to various security standards in order to protect credit card information that is transmitted over the Web. Frequently, the company selling the goods never receives the credit card number of the consumer, only an authorization number from the credit card clearance house. The tracking of the merchandise, as well as the payment, not to mention the processes for handling customer returns and credits, will present significant angst for the auditors and controllers of these firms.

Nonetheless, the financial services industry has embraced e-commerce and now offers most of its products over the Internet. Online services include, among others, the purchase of stocks and bonds, online mortgages, and life insurance and online banking. Because they are nontangible, these products and services lend themselves well to e-commerce. The Internet works well in many cases, because, while it is not delivering the product itself, it is delivering information about the product, often in levels of detail and consistency that were never available in the physical world.

As noted earlier, the real action is and will be in B2B e-commerce. Companies of every shape and size are realizing the opportunities for both ordering and selling their products over the Internet. Businesses are or will be using the Internet for both the purchasing of direct and indirect materials and MRO (maintenance, repair, and operations). General Electric runs its own auction site on which suppliers bid to provide GE's operating divisions with millions of dollars of materials per day. Their private e-auction is squeezing hundreds of millions of dollars out of purchases annually and opening their purchasing to many new vendors. Some companies, such as W. W. Grainger, long known as a supplier of MRO materials through its network of physical distribution centers, have established a giant Internet presence for the sale of MRO materials called Total MRO. They are attempting to supply any nondirect material a company could use, including office equipment and supplies.

Other marketplaces have been created to offer products for specific industries (vertical marketplaces) or across industries (horizontal marketplaces). These marketplaces provide not just buying opportunities, but selling opportunities as well. Many utilize auctions or reverse auctions. Hundreds of millions of dollars are or will be changing hands on a daily basis, totally electronically. As per legislation passed by the U.S. government in 2000, it is now possible to electronically sign purchase commitments and contracts over the Internet.

Some companies are using their Internet site to process orders, create and price custom configurations (similar to what Dell Computer is doing on its site), track orders, and assist with customer service. Some industries are creating their own marketplaces for the cooperative purchase of goods and services. The most notable of these marketplaces, Covisint, is an online auto parts exchange created by major automobile manufacturers Ford, GM, and Daimler-Chrysler. There are multitudes of B2B marketplaces and exchanges. Some are vertical, servicing specific industries like Metalsite.com for the steel industry, retailexchange.com for the retail industry, or paperexchange.com for the paper industry. Others are horizontal marketplaces, like staples.com or wwgrainger.com. There are also some hybrid models, like Verticalnet.com, that address multiple industries. Companies like Ariba and Commerce One provide the necessary software that facilitates these marketplaces and exchanges.

APPLICATION SERVICE PROVIDERS (ASPS)

ASPs are companies that provide hosted access to software applications like Microsoft Office and ERP systems. In effect, a company rents the application while the data is processed on the ASP's computer. Companies typically pay a per-user fee along with a cost-per-storage unit and access-time unit. This cost structure is similar to a model from the 1960s and 1970s, when computers were very expensive and companies used service bureaus to process their data. The difference today is that much of the data is accessed over high speed data lines or over the Internet. The downside of using an ASP is that the user is placing its destiny in another company's hands and is dependant on its security and financial health. The upside is that users are not responsible for purchasing the application, maintaining it, and having to provide the computer power to process the data.

WEB HOSTING

While many companies host their own Web site, others prefer to contract that job out to other companies. These companies provide the communications lines, Web servers, data backup, and, in some cases, Web design and maintenance services. Companies that choose to outsource their Web hosting are also protecting their main network from security breeches. However, they are still placing a great deal of their data on the Web hosting company's computer, which is still subject to security hackers. Many large companies such as Earthlink, AT&T, Qwest, along with many smaller companies, provide Web hosting services. These companies provide speed, reliability, and cost advantages, along with redundancy and technical service.

DECISION SUPPORT SYSTEMS/EXECUTIVE INFORMATION SYSTEMS

A class of software that is used mostly by middle-level and senior executives to make decisions, this software combines many of the features of traditional exception reporting with the graphical display tools available in spreadsheets. It allows users to make their own inquiries into large volumes of data, stored in databases or data warehouses, and provides for drill down reporting, or "slice and dice" analysis.

Typically, most data in a database or data warehouse is three dimensional and looks something like a Rubic's cube. Consider a database model for a chain of 300 retail stores. The first dimension may be the company's merchandise; the second dimension may be its store locations; and the third dimension may represent different points in time. An executive might examine the men's department sales. Not satisfied with the results, she might then probe to learn

EXHIBIT 16.7   Example of options screen for a decision support system.

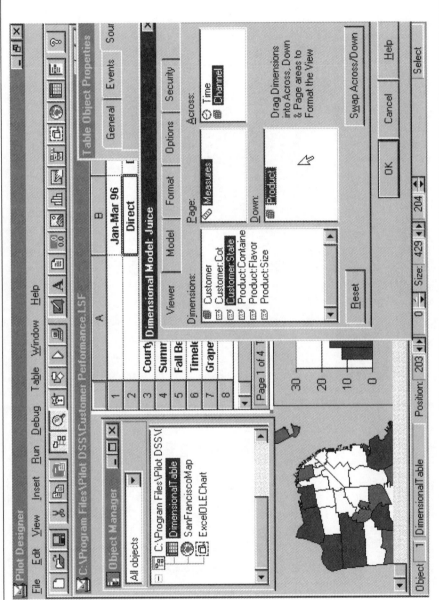

EXHIBIT 16.8 Example of output from a decision support system.

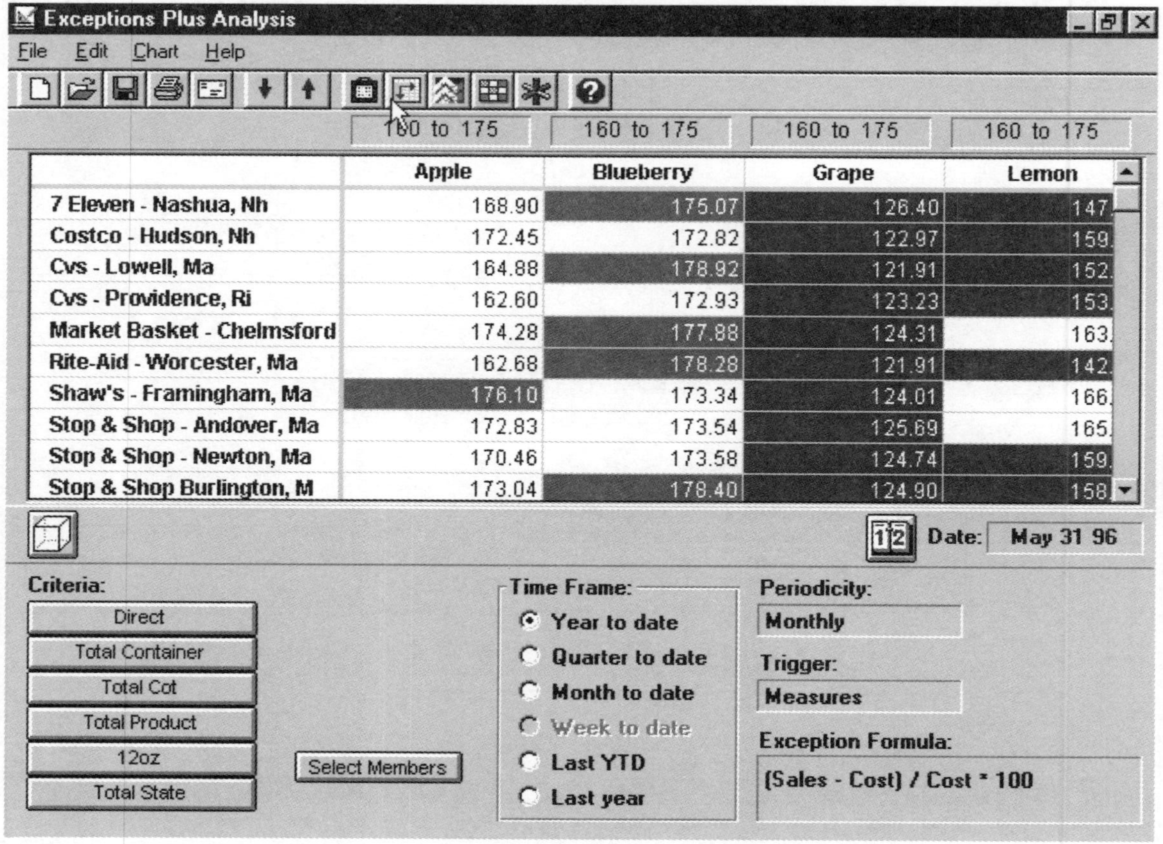

what categories of items sold better than others. After finding an underper-forming category, she may check how different groups or districts of stores performed for that category. Knowing how each store performed, she might explode down, looking at individual items, and compare their performance to that of a prior week or year. This process is like taking the Rubic's cube and continually rotating the levels, looking at each of the cube's faces. Each face of each small cube represents data for a piece of merchandise for a store for a period of time. That is why this process is referred to as "slice and dice." You can slice and turn the data any which way you desire. The data can also be viewed and sorted in a tabular or graphical mode. The same theory applies whether the database contains retailing data, stock market data, or accounting data. Exhibits 16.7 and 16.8 show examples of a decision support system's output. The output was created by Pilot Software's executive information system.

ADVANCED TECHNOLOGY

Many new technologies are on the horizon, two of which are database mining and intelligent agents. Both address the issue of information overload. In the 1970s, the average database was perhaps 100 megabytes (millions of bytes) in size. In the 1980s, databases were typically 20 gigabytes (billions of bytes). Now, databases are in the terabytes (trillions of bytes). Wal-Mart has a data warehouse that exceeds 100 terabytes. With all that data, it is difficult for a user to know where to look. It is not the question that the user knows to ask that is necessarily important, but, rather, the question that the user does not know to ask that will come back to haunt him.

These new technologies examine entire databases, scanning them for any data that does not fit the business's model and identifying any data that the user needs to examine further. These data mining techniques can be used successfully in many industries. For example, auditors might use them to scan client transaction detail to look for transactions that do not conform to company policies, and stock analysts can use them to scan data on stock prices and company earnings over a period of time in order to look for opportunities.

CONCLUSION

The world of business has changed dramatically in the past 10 years. What was unimaginable then is ordinary today. Product life-cycle times have decreased from years to months. New technology is being introduced every day. An Internet year is equal to three or four calendar months. The manager who is comfortable with and understands the practical implications of technology will be one of the first to succeed. Imagination and creativity are vital. Don't be afraid of change. Understand it, and embrace it.

FOR FURTHER READING

Amor, Daniel, *The E-business (R)Evolution* (Upper Saddle River, NJ: Prentice-Hall, 2000).

Frenzel, Carroll, *Management of Information Technology,* 3rd ed. (Danvers, MA: Boyd & Fraser, 1999).

Fried, Louis, *Managing Information Technology in Turbulent Times* (New York: John Wiley, 1995).

Kanter, Jerry, *Information Literacy* (Wellesley, MA: Babson Press, 1996).

Kanter, Jerry, *Information Technology for Business Managers* (New York: McGraw-Hill, 1998).

Kalakota, R., and M. Robinson, *E-Business 2.0* (Boston: Addison-Wesley, 2000).

Nickerson, Robert, *Business and Information Systems,* 2nd ed. (Upper Saddle River, NJ: Prentice-Hall, 2001).

Pearlson, Keri, *Managing and Using Information Systems* (New York: John Wiley, 2001).

Reynolds, George, *Information Systems for Managers* (St. Paul, MN: West, 1995).

Turban, E., E. McLean, and J. Wetherbe, *Information Technology for Management,* 2nd ed. (New York: John Wiley, 2001).

Turban, E., J. Lee, D. King, and H. M. Chung, *Electronic Commerce—A Managerial Perspective* (Upper Saddle River, NJ: Prentice-Hall, 2001).

INTERESTING WEB SITES

www.ariba.com	ARIBA
www.baan.com	BAAN
www.commerceone.com	Commerce One
www.esri.com	ESRI
www.greatplains.com	Great Plains Software
www.intel.com	Intel
www.intuit.com	INTUIT
www.macola.com	Macola Software
www.microsoft.com	Microsoft
www.microstrategy.com	Microstrategy
www.oracle.com	ORACLE
www.retailexchange.com	Retail Exchange
www.sap.com	SAP
www.staples.com	Staples
www.sun.com	Sun Microsystems
www.verticalnet.com	VerticalNet
www.wwgrainger.com	W. W. Grainger

17 PROFITABLE GROWTH BY ACQUISITION

Richard T. Bliss

The subject of this chapter is growth by acquisition; few other business transactions receive more scrutiny in both the popular and academic presses. There are several reasons for this attention. One is the sweeping nature of the deals, which typically result in major upheaval and job losses up to the highest levels of the organizations. A second is the sheer magnitude of the deals—the recently announced merger between Time-Warner and AOL, worth more than $150 billion, exceeds the annual GDP of 85% of the world's nations! Thirdly, the products involved are known to billions around the globe. Daimler-Benz, Coca Cola, and Louis Vuitton are just a few of the world-renowned brand names recently involved in merger and acquisition (M&A) transactions. Finally, the personalities and plots in M&A deals are worthy of any novelist or Hollywood scriptwriter. The 1988 acquisition of Nabisco Foods by RJR Tobacco—at that time the largest deal ever, at $25 billion—was the subject of a *New York Times* best-seller and a popular film, both called *Barbarians at the Gate*. Since then, there have been numerous other best-selling books and movies based on real and fictional M&A deals.

In spite of this publicity and the huge amounts of money involved, it is important to remember that M&A transactions are similar to any other corporate investment, that is, they involve uncertainty and the fundamental tradeoff between risk and return. To lose sight of this simple fact or to succumb to the emotion and frenetic pace of M&A deal-making activities is a sure path to an unsuccessful result. Our goal in this chapter is to identify the potential pitfalls you may face and to create a road map for a successful corporate M&A strategy.

561

We review the historical evidence and discuss some of the characteristics of both unsuccessful and successful deals. The importance of value creation is highlighted, and we present simple analytical tools that can be used to evaluate the potential of any merger or acquisition. Practical aspects of initiating and structuring M&A transactions are presented and the issues critical to the successful implementation of a new acquisition are briefly described. It is important to understand that there are many legal and financial intricacies involved in most M&A transactions. Our objective here is not to explain each of these in detail, since there are professional accountants, lawyers, and consultants available for that. Instead, we hope to provide valuable and concise information for busy financial managers so that they can design and implement an effective M&A strategy.

DEFINITIONS AND BACKGROUND

Before examining the historical evidence on acquisitions, we need to define some terminology. An *acquisition* is one form of a *takeover*, which is loosely defined as the transfer of control of a firm from one group of shareholders to another. In this context, control comes with the ability to elect a majority of the board of directors. The firm seeking control is called the *bidder* and the one that surrenders control the *target*. Other forms of takeovers include *proxy contests* and *going private*, but the focus of this chapter is takeover via acquisition.

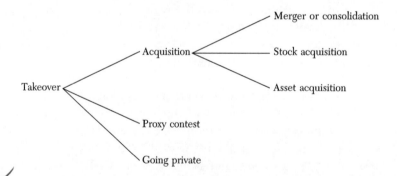

As we can see, acquisitions may occur in several ways. In a *merger*, the target is absorbed by the bidder and the target's original shareholders receive shares of the bidder. In a *consolidation*, the firms involved become parts of an entirely new firm, with the bidder usually retaining control of the new entity. All original shareholders hold shares in the new firm after the deal. The two transactions have different implications for shareholders, as the following examples make clear.

Example 1 There has recently been a wave of takeover activity in the stuffed animal industry. Griffin's Giraffes Inc. (GGI) has agreed to merge with Hayley's Hippos Inc. (HHI). GGI offers one of its shares for three shares of HHI. When the transaction is completed, HHI shares will no longer exist. The original HHI stockholders own GGI shares equal in number to one-third of their original HHI holdings. GGI's original shareholders are unaffected by the transaction, except to have their ownership stake diluted by the newly issued shares.

Example 2   Kristen's Kangaroos Inc. (KKI) wishes to take over the operations of Michael's Manatees Inc. (MMI) and Brandon's Baboons Inc. (BBI). Rather than giving its shares to the owners of MMI and BBI, KKI decides to establish a new firm, Safari Ventures Inc. (SVI). After this consolidation, shareholders of the three original companies (KKI, MMI, and BBI) will hold shares in the new firm (SVI), with KKI having the controlling interest. The three original firms cease to exist.

Another method of acquisition involves the direct purchase of shares, either with cash, shares of the acquirer, or some combination of the two. These *stock acquisitions* may be negotiated with the mangers of the target firm or by appealing directly to its shareholders, often via a newspaper advertisement. The latter transaction is called a *tender offer,* which typically occur after negotiations with the target firm's management have failed. Finally, an acquisition can be effected by the purchase of the target's assets. *Asset acquisitions* are sometimes done to escape the liabilities (real or contingent) of the target firm or to avoid having to negotiate with minority shareholders. The downside is that the legal process of transferring assets may be expensive.

Acquisitions can be categorized based on the level of economic activity involved according to the following:

- *Horizontal:* The target and bidder in a *horizontal merger* are involved in the same type of business activity and industry. These mergers typically result in market consolidation, that is, more market share for the combined firm. Because of this, they are subject to extra antitrust scrutiny. The pending acquisition of USAir by United Airlines is an example of a horizontal merger (see p. 564). Because the combined entity would be the world's largest airline and have a dominant market share in the United States, the Justice Department has demanded that certain assets and routes be divested before approval for the deal will be granted.

- *Vertical:* A *vertical merger* involves firms that are at different levels of the supply chain in the same industry. For example, stand-alone Internet service provider/portal AOL functions primarily as a distribution channel. Its pending merger with Time Warner will allow AOL to move up the home entertainment industry supply chain and control content in the form of Time Warner's music and video libraries.

- *Conglomerate:* In a *conglomerate merger,* the target and bidder firms are not related. These were popular in the 1960s and seventies but are rare

CAN THEY FLY UNITED?		
A Mammoth in Resources...		
	United	**US Airways**
'99 Revenue	$18.3 billion	$8.6 billion
Employees	100,000	40,000
Fleet	604 jets	414 jets
Daily Flights*	2,300	2,250
'99 Passengers carried	87 million	56 million
Hubs *Excluding commuter affiliates' flights*	Chicago, Denver, San Francisco, Los Angeles, Washington	Philadelphia Charlotte, Pittsburgh

That Will Dominate the Market
1999 share of U.S. passengers carried

United/US Airways	25.6%
Delta	19.3
American	13.5
Southwest	13.4
Others	11.1
Northwest	9.7
Continental	7.3

Sources: General Accounting Office, Department of Transportation, The companies

SOURCE: *The Wall Street Journal*, December 20, 2000.

today. An auto manufacturer acquiring an ice cream producer would be an example.

Armed with a basic understanding of the types of acquisitions and how they occur, we now turn our attention to the track record of M&A transactions. Be forewarned that it is spotty at best and that many practitioners, analysts, and academics believe that the odds are stacked against acquirers. We do not say this to dissuade anyone from pursuing an acquisition strategy, but rather to highlight the fact that without careful planning, there is little chance of success.

THE TRACK RECORD OF MERGERS AND ACQUISITIONS

There has been tremendous growth in the number and dollar value of M&A transactions over the last two decades (see Exhibit 17.1). In 1998, the total annual value of completed transactions exceeded one trillion dollars for the first time in history. The number of deals fell in 1999, but larger deals resulted in a total deal value of almost $1.5 trillion. Exhibit 17.2 lists the largest deal for each of the years between 1990 and 2000.

While the data in Exhibits 17.1 and 17.2 focus on large transactions, the growth trend for all M&A deals is similar. And in 1999, for the first time in history, there were more deals done abroad than in the United States. By any

EXHIBIT 17.1   M&A activity, 1981–1999.[a]

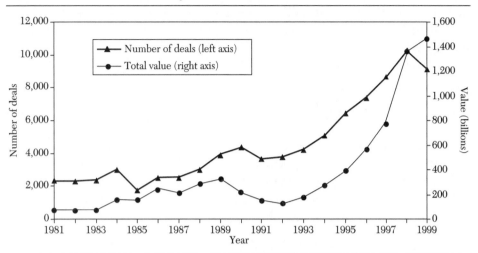

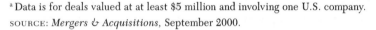

[a] Data is for deals valued at at least $5 million and involving one U.S. company.

SOURCE: *Mergers & Acquisitions*, September 2000.

measure, the 1990s was an increasingly acquisitive decade around the world. This explosion in deal making might lead one to assume that mergers and acquisitions are an easy way for corporate managers to create value for their shareholders. To assess this, we now examine the empirical evidence on mergers and acquisitions. Let's begin with the wealth of academic studies that analyze M&A performance.[1]

M&A activity has been the focus of volumes of academic research over the last 40 years. The evidence is mixed, but we can draw several clear conclusions from the data. We break our discussion into two pieces: short-term

EXHIBIT 17.2   A decade of megadeals.

Year	Bidder	Target	Price (billions)
1990	Time Inc.	Warner Communications	$ 12.6
1991	AT&T Corp.	NCR Corp.	7.5
1992	BankAmerica Corp.	Security Pacific Corp.	4.2
1993	Merck & Co.	Medco Containment Services	6.2
1994	AT&T Corp.	McCaw Cellular Inc.	18.9
1995	AirTouch Communications	US West Inc.	13.5
1996	Walt Disney Co.	Capital Cities/ABC Inc.	18.9
1997	Bell Atlantic Corp.	NYNEX Corp.	21.3
1998	Travelers Group Inc.	Citicorp	72.6
1999	Exxon Corp.	Mobil Corp.	78.9
2000	America Online Inc.	Time Warner Inc.	156.0

SOURCE: *Mergers & Acquisitions*, September 2000.

and long-term M&A performance. The short-term is a narrow window, typically three to five days, around the merger announcement. Long-term studies examine postmerger performance two to five years after the transaction is completed.

We can offer three unambiguous conclusions about the short-term financial impact of M&A transactions:

1. Shareholders of the target firms do very well, with average *premiums* between 30% and 40%.
2. Returns to bidders have fallen over time as the market for corporate control becomes more competitive; recent evidence finds bidder returns indistinguishable from zero or even slightly negative.
3. The combined return of the target and the bidder, that is, the measure of overall value creation, was slightly positive.

However, these results are highly variable depending on the specific samples and time periods analyzed. The findings on the long-term performance of mergers and acquisitions are not any more consistent or encouraging. Agrawal et al. report "shareholders of acquiring firms experience a wealth loss of about 10% over the five years following the merger completion."[2] Other studies' conclusions range from underperformance to findings of no abnormal postmerger performance. The strongest conclusions offered by Weston et al. are that, "It is *likely*, therefore, that value is created by M&As," and that, "Some mergers perform well, others do not."[3] So much for the brilliance of the academy! This level of confidence hardly seems to justify the frenetic pace of merger activity chronicled in Exhibits 17.1 and 17.2.

If the academic literature seems ambivalent about judging the financial wisdom of M&A decisions, the popular business press shows no such hesitancy. In a 1995 special report, *Business Week* carefully analyzed 150 recent deals valued at $500 million or more and reported "about half destroyed shareholder wealth" and "another third contributed only marginally to it." The article's last paragraph makes it clear that this is not a benign finding and places the blame squarely on corporate CEOs.

> All this indicates that many large-company CEOs are making multibillion-dollar decisions about the future of their companies, employees, and shareholders in part by the seat of their pants. When things go wrong, as the evidence demonstrates that they often do, these decisions create unnecessary tumult, losses, and heartache. While there clearly is a role for thoughtful and well-conceived mergers in American business, all too many don't meet that description.
>
> Moreover, in merging and acquiring mindlessly and flamboyantly, dealmakers may be eroding the nation's growth prospects and global competitiveness. Dollars that are wasted needlessly on mergers that don't work might better be spent on research and new-product development. And in view of the growing number of corporate divorces, it's clear that the best strategy for most would-be marriage partners is never to march to the altar at all.[4]

A 1996 survey of 150 companies by the Economist Intelligence Unit in London found that 70% of all acquisitions failed to meet the expectations of the initiator. Coopers and Lybrand studied the postmerger performance of 125 companies and reported that 66% were financially unsuccessful.

We now turn our attention to several specific M&A transactions. While unscientific, this approach is more informative and certainly more interesting than reviewing academic research. We purposely focus on failed deals in an attempt to learn where the acquirers went wrong. In the next section, we examine the acquisition strategy and policies of Cisco Systems, the acquirer ranked No. 1 in a recent survey of corporate M&A practices.

As you read about these dismal transactions, can you speculate on the reasons for failure? On their faces, they seemed like strategically sound transactions. While one might question AT&T's push into personal computers, the other two deals were simple horizontal mergers, that is, an extension of the existing business into new product lines or geographic markets. In hindsight, each deal failed for different reasons, but there are some common issues. The lessons learned are critical for all managers considering growth by acquisition. We now examine these colossal failures in more detail.

Analysts believe that the merger between AT&T and NCR failed due to managerial hubris, overpayment, and a poor understanding of NCR's products and markets. A clash between the two firms' cultures proved to be the final nail in the coffin. In 1990 AT&T's research division, Bell Labs, was one of the worlds premier laboratories. With seven Nobel prizes and countless patents to its name, it was where the transistor and the UNIX operating system had been invented. AT&T's executives mistakenly believed that this research prowess

---

Disaster Deal No. 1

Between 1985 and 1990, AT&T's computer operations lost approximately $2 billion. The huge conglomerate seemed unable to compete effectively against the likes of Compaq, Hewlett Packard and Sun Microsystems. They decided to buy rather than build and settled on NCR, a profitable, Ohio-based personal computer (PC) manufacturer with 1990 revenues of $6 billion. NCR did not want to be purchased and this was made clear in a letter from CEO Chuck Exley to AT&T CEO Robert Allen: "We simply will not place in jeopardy the important values we are creating at NCR in order to bail out AT&T's failed strategy." OUCH! However, after a bitter takeover fight—and an increase of $1.4 billion in the offer price (raising the premium paid to more than 100%!)—AT&T acquired NCR in September 1991 for $7.5 billion.

Aftermath: In 1996, after operating losses exceeding $2 billion and a $2.4 billion write-off, AT&T spun-off NCR in a transaction valued at about $4 billion, approximately half of what it had paid to acquire NCR less than five years before.

Disaster Deal No. 2

Throughout 1994, Quaker Oats Co. was rumored to be a takeover target. It was relatively small ($6 billion in revenue) and its diverse product lines could be easily broken up and sold piecemeal. In November, Quaker announced an agreement to buy iced-tea and fruit-drink maker Snapple Beverage Corp. for $1.7 billion, or $14 per share. CEO William Smithburg dismissed the 10% drop in Quaker's stock price, arguing "We think the healthy, good-for-you beverage categories are going to continue to grow." The hope was that Quaker could replicate the success of its national-brand exercise drink Gatorade, which held an extraordinary 88% market share.

Snapple, which had 27% of the ready-to-drink tea segment was distributed mainly through smaller retail outlets and relied on offbeat advertising and a "natural" image to drive sales. Only about 20% of sales were from supermarkets where Quaker's strength could be used to expand sales of Snapple's drinks.

Aftermath: In April 1997, Quaker announced it would sell Snapple for $300 million to Triarc Cos. Quaker takes a $1.4 billion write-off and the sale price is less than 20% of what Quaker paid for Snapple less than three years earlier. Analysts estimated the company also incurred cash losses of approximately $100 million over the same period. Ending a 30-year career with the company, CEO Smithburg "retires" two weeks later at age 58.

---

and $20 billion of annual long-distance telephone revenues, along with the NCR acquisition, would guarantee the company's success in the PC business. They were confident enough to increase their original offer price by $1.4 billion. The problem was that by this time, PCs had become a commodity and were being assembled at low-cost around the world using off-the-shelf components. Unlike the microprocessor and software innovations of Intel and Microsoft, AT&T's research skills held little profit potential for the PC business.

AT&T hoped to use NCR's global operations to expand their core telecom business. But NCR's strengths were in developed countries, whereas the fastest-growing markets for communications equipment were in developing third-world regions. And in many companies, the computer and telephone systems were procured and managed separately. Thus, the anticipated synergies never materialized.

Finally, the two companies had very different cultures. NCR was tightly controlled from the top while AT&T was less hierarchical and more politically correct. When AT&T executive Jerre Stead took over at NCR in 1993, he billed himself as the "head coach," passed out T-shirts, and told all of the employees they were "empowered." This did not go over well in the conservative environment at NCR, and by 1994, only 5 of 33 top NCR managers remained with the company.

Disaster Deal No. 3

The 1998 $130 billion megamerger between German luxury carmaker Daimler-Benz and the #3 U.S. automobile company, Chrysler Corporation, was universally hailed as a strategic coup for the two firms. An official at a rival firm simply said "This looks like a brilliant move on Mercedes-Benz's part."* The stock market agreed as the two companies' shares rose by a combined $8.6 billion at the announcement. A 6.4% increase in Daimler-Benz's share price accounted for $3.7 billion of this total. The source of this value creation was simple: There was very little overlap in the two companies' product lines or geographic strengths. "The issue that excites the market is the global reach," said Stephen Reitman, European auto analyst for Merrill Lynch in London.* Daimler had less than 1% market share in the U.S., and Chrysler's market share in Europe was equally miniscule. There would also be numerous cost-saving opportunities in design, procurement, and manufacturing.

The deal was billed as a true partnership, and the new firm would keep operational headquarters in both Stuttgart and Detroit and have "co-CEOs" for three years after the merger. In addition, each firm would elect half of the directors.

Aftermath: By the end of 2000, the new DaimlerChrysler's share price had fallen more than 60% from its post merger high. Its market capitalization of $39 billion was 20% less than Daimler-Benz's alone before the merger! All of Chrysler's top U.S. executives had quit or been fired, and the company's third-quarter loss was an astounding $512 million. As if all of this weren't bad enough, DaimlerChrysler's third-largest shareholder, Kirk Kekorian, was suing the company for $9 billion, alleging fraud when they announced the 1998 deal as a "merger of equals."

---

* "Auto Bond: Chrysler Approves Deal With Daimler-Benz," *The Wall Street Journal*, May 7, 1998.

What doomed the Quaker-Snapple deal? One factor was haste. Quaker was so worried about becoming a takeover target in the rapidly consolidating food industry that it ignored evidence of slowing growth and decreasing profitability at Snapple. The market's concern was reflected in Quaker's stock price drop of 10% on the acquisition announcement. In spite of this, Quaker's managers proceeded, pushing the deal through on the promise that Snapple would be the beverage industry's next Gatorade. This claim unfortunately ignored the realities on the ground: Snapple had onerous contracts with its bottlers, fading marketing programs, and a distribution system that could not support a national brand. There was also a major difference between Snapple's quirky, offbeat corporate culture and the more structured environment at Quaker.

Most importantly, Quaker failed to account for the possible entrance of Coca Cola and Pepsi into the ready-to-drink tea segment—and there were few barriers to entry—which ultimately increased competition and killed margins.

In this case, Quaker's management was guilty of two mistakes: failure to analyze Snapple's products, markets, and competition correctly and overconfidence in their ability to deal with the problems. Either way, their lapses cost Quaker's shareholders billions.

Although the jury is still out on the Daimler-Chrysler merger, analysts already have assigned at least some of the blame. There were culture issues from the start, and it quickly became apparent that co-CEOs were not the way to manage a $130 billion global giant. Chrysler CEO Robert Eaton left quietly at the beginning of 2000 and there were other departures of high-level American executives. Morale suffered as employees in the U.S. realized that the "merger of equals" was taking on a distinctive German flavor and in November 2000, the last remaining Chrysler executive, U.S. president James Holden, was fired.

Rather than deal with these issues head-on, Daimler CEO Jergen Schremp took a hands-off approach as Chrysler's operations slowly spiraled downward. The company lost several top designers, delaying new product introductions and leaving Chrysler with an aging line of cars at a time when its competitors were firing on all cylinders. The delay in merging operations meant cost savings were smaller than anticipated as were the benefits from sharing technology. Finally, analysts suggested that Daimler paid top dollar for Chrysler at a time when the automobile industry in the U.S. was riding a wave of unprecedented economic prosperity. As car sales began to sag at the end of 2000, all three U.S. manufacturers were facing excess capacity and offering huge incentives to move vehicles. This was not the ideal environment for quickly restructuring Chrysler's troubled operations and Daimler was facing a 35% drop in projected operating profit between 1998 and 2001.

Conclusions: These three case studies highlight some of the difficulties firms face in achieving profitable growth through acquisitions. Managerial hubris and a competitive market make it easy to overestimate the merger's benefits and therefore overpay. A deal that makes sense strategically can still be a financial failure if the price paid for the target is too high. This is especially a problem when economic conditions are good and high stock prices make it easy to justify almost any valuation if the bidder's managers and directors really want to do a deal. Shrewd managers can sell deals that make little strategic sense to unsuspecting shareholders and then ignore signals from the market that the deal is not a good one.

The previous examples make it clear that it is easy to overstate the benefits that will come after the transaction is completed. Whatever their source, these benefits are elusive, expensive to find and implement, and subject to attack by competitors and economic conditions. Managers considering an acquisition should be conservative in their estimates of benefits and generous in the amount of time budgeted to achieve these benefits. The best way to accurately estimate the benefits of the merger is to have a thorough understanding of the target's products, markets, and competition. This takes time and can only come from careful due diligence, which must be conducted using a disciplined approach that fights the tendency for managers to become emotionally attached to a deal. In spite of the time pressures inherent in any merger transaction, this is truly a situation where "haste makes waste."

A common factor in each of these transactions—and one often overlooked by managers and researchers in finance and accounting—is culture. Two types of culture can come into play in an acquisition. One is corporate or industry culture and the second is national culture, which is a factor in cross-border deals. If the target is in a different industry than the bidder, a careful analysis of the cultural differences between them is essential. Culture is especially critical in industries where the main assets being acquired are expertise or intellectual capital. Failure to successfully merge cultures in such industries can be particularly problematic because key employees will depart for better working conditions. The attempted 1998 merger between Computer Associates (CA) and Computer Science Corporation (CSC) ultimately failed when CA realized that their mishandling of the negotiations and their insensitivity to the culture at CSC would cause many of CSC's consultants to quit the merged company. We will discuss the keys to successful implementation of mergers later in the chapter. In the next section we examine the acquisition strategy of Cisco Systems Inc. We do this to make it clear that there are ways to increase your chances of success when planning and implementing an M&A strategy.

ANATOMY OF A SUCCESSFUL ACQUIRER: THE CASE OF CISCO SYSTEMS INC.

Cisco Systems Inc., the Silicon Valley-based networking giant, is one of the world's most successful corporations. Revenues for the fiscal year ending July 2000 were up an incredible 55% to $18.9 billion, while net income grew to $3.9 billion, resulting in a healthy 21% net profit margin. Even more impressive was its 10th consecutive quarter of *accelerating* sales growth, culminating in a 61% sales increase for the last quarter. At $356 billion, Cisco's market capitalization trailed only General Electric Company. What is behind such phenomenal results?

Beginning in 1993, Cisco has acquired 51 companies, 21 of them in the 12-month period ending March of 2000. Not every one of these deals has been a winner, and certainly some elements of Cisco's strategy are unique to the high-technology industry. However, in a recent survey of corporate M&A policies Cisco was ranked number 1 in the world, and there are lessons for any potential acquirer in its practices.[5]

We will focus on two aspects of Cisco's acquisition strategy: the competitive and economic forces behind it and how new acquisitions are merged into the corporate fold. The strategic imperative behind Cisco's acquisition spree is simple. Each year the company gets 30% to 50% of its revenue from products that it did not sell 12 months before. Technological change means that Cisco cannot internally develop all of the products its customers need. They have two choices; to limit their offerings or to buy the products and technology they can't or choose not to develop. In this case, the strategy is driven by their customer's demands and by the realities of the industry. Once CEO John Chambers and Cisco's board made rapid growth a priority, an effective M&A plan was the only way to accomplish this goal. To minimize risk, Cisco often begins with a small investment to get a better look at a potential acquisition and to assess it products, customers, and culture. Finally, Cisco often looks for private and pre-IPO companies to avoid lengthy negotiations and publicity.

Cisco's 1999 acquisition of fiber-optic equipment maker Cerent Corporation is a good example of this strategy. Cisco purchased a 9% stake in Cerent in 1998 as a hedge against what analysts viewed as Cisco's lack of fiber-optic expertise. Through this small investment, Cisco CEO John Chambers got to know Cerent's top executive, Carl Russo. He quickly realized that they had both come up through the high-tech ranks as equipment salesmen and had built their companies around highly motivated and aggressive sales teams. Cerent's 266 employees included a 100-member sales team that had assembled a rapidly growing customer base. Cerent also favored sparse offices—a Cisco trademark—and Mr. Russo managed the company from an eight-foot square cubicle. All of these factors gave Cisco important insights into Cerent's strengths and corporate culture.

When Mr. Chambers felt comfortable that Cerent could successfully become part of Cisco, he personally negotiated the $7 billion purchase price for the remaining 91% stake with Mr. Russo. The discussions took a total of two and a half hours over three days. When the deal was announced on August 25, 1999, the second—and arguably the most important—phase of Cisco's acquisition strategy kicked in. Over the years, including an occasional failure, Cisco had developed a finely tuned implementation plan for new acquisitions. The plan has three main pieces:

1. Don't forget the customer.
2. Salespeople are critical.
3. The small things garner loyalty.

There is often a customer backlash to merger announcements because customers' perception of products and brands may have changed. In the recent spate of pharmaceutical industry mergers, only those firms that avoided pairing up experienced substantial sales growth. As part of the external environment, customers are easy to ignore in the short term when the tendency is to focus on the internal aspects of the implementation. This is a big mistake. To allay customer fears, in the weeks after Cerent was acquired, Mr. Russo and his top sales executive attended the annual Cisco sales convention meeting and Mr. Chambers joined sales calls to several of Cerent's main customers.

This lesson did not come cheaply. When Cisco acquired StrataCom in 1996, it immediately reduced the commission schedule of StrataCom's sales force and reassigned several key accounts to Cisco salespeople. Within a few months, a third of StrataCom's sales team had quit, sales fell drastically, and Cisco had to scramble to retain customers. In the Cerent implementation, the sales forces of the two companies remained independent and Cerent's sales-people received pay increases of 15% to 20% to bring them in line with Cisco's compensation practices. As a result, there was little turnover and sales grew.

Cisco executives realized early on that the strategic rationale for an acquisition and their grand plans for the future meant little to the target's mid- and low-level employees. They had more basic concerns like job retention and changes in their day-to-day activities. Cisco had also learned that quickly winning over these employees—and keeping them focused on their jobs—was critical to a successful implementation. This process begins weeks before the deal is done, as the Cisco transition team works to map each employee at the target into a Cisco job. As each Cerent employee left the meeting where the acquisition was announced, they were given an information packet on Cisco, telephone and e-mail contacts for Cisco executives, and a chart comparing the vacation, medical, and retirement benefits of the two companies. There were follow-up sessions over the next several days to answer any lingering questions. Cisco also agreed to honor several aspects of Cerent's personnel policies that were more generous than their own, such as providing more-generous expense allowances and permitting previously promised sabbaticals to be taken. Cisco understood that these are relatively small items in the larger context of a successful and timely transition.

When the merger was actually completed, Cerent employees had new IDs and business cards within days. By the following week, the e-mail and voice-mail systems had been converted to Cisco's standards and all of Cerent's computer systems were updated. By the end of September, one month after the acquisition announcement, the new employee mapping had been implemented. Most employees kept their original jobs and bosses; about 30 were reassigned because they had positions that overlapped directly with Cisco workers. Overall, there was little turnover.

This example highlights some of the factors important to developing and implementing a successful acquisition strategy. However, all companies are not like Cisco, and what works for them may not guarantee you a winning acquisition plan. Cisco is fortunate to be in a rapidly growing industry in continuous need of new technologies and products. It also has the benefit of a high stock market valuation, which makes its shares valuable currency for making acquisitions. At the same time, the keys to successful implementation discussed previously—that is, concern for the customer, taking care of salespeople, and understanding what creates employee loyalty—are universal and must be part of any acquisition strategy. In the next section we look more closely at the question of value creation in M&A decisions.

CREATING VALUE IN MERGERS AND ACQUISITIONS

We have already presented the dubious historical evidence on the financial performance of mergers and acquisitions. This record makes it clear that a significant number destroy shareholder value, some spectacularly. In this section, we more closely examine the issue of value creation, focusing on its sources in mergers and acquisitions. We begin the discussion with an assumption that the objective of managers in initiating these transactions is to increase the wealth of the bidder's shareholders. We will ignore the reality that managers may have personal agendas and ulterior motives for pursuing mergers and acquisitions, even those harmful to their shareholders. A discussion of these issues is beyond the scope of this chapter.[6]

To be very clear, recall the source of all value for holders of corporate equity. Stock prices are a function of two things: expected future cash flows and the risk of those flows. These cash flows may come as dividends, share price increases, or some combination of the two, but the important thing to understand is that changes in share prices simply reflect the market's expectations about future cash flows or their risk—nothing more and nothing less. If investors believe a company's cash flows in the future will be smaller or riskier, ceteris paribus, the share price will decline. If the expectation is for larger or less risky cash flows, the share price goes up. Thus, when we talk about M&A decisions creating value, there can only be two sources of that value: more cash flow or less risk. Our discussion focuses primarily on the former.

Consider two independent firms, A and B, with respective values V_A and V_B. Assume that the managers of firm A feel that the acquisition of firm B, that is, the creation of a merged firm AB, would create value. That is, they believe $V_{AB} > V_A + V_B$. The difference between the two sides of this equation, $V_{AB} - (V_A + V_B)$, is the incremental value created by the acquisition, sometimes called the *synergy*. That is,

$$\text{Synergy} = V_{AB} - \left(V_A + V_B\right) \tag{1}$$

Clearly, positive synergy would be a prerequisite to going forward with the acquisition. In practice, things are a bit more complicated for two reasons: the costs of an acquisition and the target premium. The acquisition process carries significant direct costs for lawyers, consultants, and accountants. There is also the indirect cost caused by the distraction of the bidder's executives from their day-to-day operation of the existing business. Finally, the data presented in the section on mergers and acquisitions shows that target shareholders in acquisitions typically receive a 30% to 40% premium over market price. Some transactions have smaller premiums, but in almost all cases, the acquirer pays a price above the pre-acquisition market value. All of these costs can be factored into the evaluation as follows:

$$\text{Net advantage of merging} = \left[V_{AB} - \left(V_A + V_B\right)\right] - \text{Merger costs} - \text{Premium} \tag{2}$$

Example 3   Midland Motorcycles Inc. is considering the acquisition of Scotus Scooters. Midland's current market capitalization is $10 million, while Scotus has a market capitalization of $2 million. The executives at Midland feel the combined firm would be worth $14 million due to synergies. Current takeover premiums average 35% and the total cost of the acquisition is estimated at $1.5 million. Should Midland proceed with the deal?

$$\text{Net advantage of merging} = \left[14 - \left(\$10 + \$2\right)\right] - \$1.5 - \left(35\% \times \$2\right) = -\$0.2 \text{ million}$$

The deal would destroy $200,000 of value. Note that this is in spite of the fact that there are $2 million of positive synergies created by the acquisition. The reality is that this synergy is more than offset by the costs of the transaction and the premium paid for the target, a typical problem in acquisitions. For example, consider Coca-Cola's recent interest in Quaker Oats, which Coke CEO Douglas Daft felt "fit perfectly into Coke's strategy of boosting growth by increasing its share of non-carbonated drinks."[7] Even Coke's directors felt that the strategic rationale behind the transaction was sound. But the deal was ultimately rejected because of the price. Warren Buffett, a major Coca-Cola shareholder, said "Giving up 10% of the Coca-Cola Company was just too much for what we would get."[8]

Note that the bracketed term in equation 2 is just the synergy as defined in equation 1. Where does this synergy or incremental value originate? From above, we know that value can only come from two places—increased cash flows or reduced risk. In this case, the synergy can be computed as follows:

$$\text{Synergy} = \sum_{t=0}^{\infty} \frac{\Delta CF_t}{\left(1+r\right)^t} \tag{3}$$

where ΔCF_t is the incremental cash flow in period t, and r is the appropriate risk-adjusted discount rate. The total synergy is just the present value of all future incremental cash flows. Equation 3 makes it clear that changes in future cash flows or their risk are at the root of any M&A synergies. Before considering how a merger might impact cash flows, recall how they are computed:

> Incremental Revenues
> − Incremental Costs
> − Incremental Taxes
> − Incremental Investment in New Working Capital
> − Incremental Investment in Fixed Assets
> = Incremental Cash Flow

With this in mind, we can look more closely at potential sources of incremental cash flows—and therefore, value—in acquisitions. We focus on the following three areas:

1. Incremental revenue.
2. Cost reductions.
3. Tax savings.

Incremental Revenue   More revenue for the combined firm can come from marketing gains, strategic benefits, or market power. Increased revenue through marketing gains result from improvements in advertising, distribution or product offerings. For example, when Citicorp and Travelers Inc. announced their merger in 1998, incremental revenue was a key factor:

> "Finally, there is the central justification of the deal: cross-selling each other's products, mainly to retail customers. Over the next two years, Citigroup ought to be able to generate $600 million more in earnings because of cross-selling."[9]

After acquiring Miller Brewing Company in 1970, Philip Morris used its marketing and advertising strength to move Miller from the number 7 to the number 2 U.S. beer maker by 1977.

Some acquisitions provide strategic benefits that act as insurance against or options on future changes in the competitive environment. As genetic research has advanced, pharmaceutical firms have used acquisitions to ensure they participate in the commercial potential offered by this new technology. The 1998 acquisition of SmithKline Beecham PLC by Glaxo Wellcome PLC was motivated by Glaxo's fear of missing out on this revolution in the industry. SmithKline had entered the genetic research field in 1993 by investing $125 million in Human Genome Sciences, a Rockville, Maryland, biotechnology company created to commercialize new gene-hunting techniques.

Finally, the acquisition of a competitor may increase market share and allow the merged firm to charge higher prices. By itself, this motive is not valid justification for initiating a merger, and any deal done solely to garner monopolistic power would be challenged by global regulators on antitrust grounds. However, market power may be a by-product of a merger done for other reasons. American Airline's potential bid for USAir, while launched primarily to thwart a similar attempt by its competition, would also have implications for market power in the industry.

> American is particularly worried about the prospect of USAir falling into United's hands. Nabbing the carrier for itself would give American coveted slots at Chicago's O'Hare, New York's LaGuardia, and Washington's National Airport.[10]

Cost Reductions   Improved efficiency from cost savings is one of the most often cited reasons for mergers. This is especially true in the banking industry, as the recent merger between J.P. Morgan and Chase Manhattan makes clear.

> The key to executing the merger, say analysts, will be how quickly Chase can trim its expenses. It plans to save $500 million through job cuts, $500 million by consolidating the processing systems of the two institutions and $500 million by selling off excess real estate. In London, for example, the two banks have 21 buildings, and they won't need all of them.[11]

In total, there is an estimated $1.5 billion of annual savings. The link between this and value creation is easy for investors to understand and the benefits from cost reductions are relatively easy to quantify. These benefits can come from *economies of scale, vertical integration, complementary resources,* and the elimination of inefficient management.

Economies of scale result when a certain percentage increase in output results in a smaller increase in total costs, resulting in reduced average cost. It doesn't matter whether this increased output is generated internally or acquired externally. When the firm grows to its "optimal" size, average costs are minimized and no further benefits are possible. There are many potential sources of economies of scale in acquisitions, the most common being the ability to spread fixed overhead, such as corporate headquarters expenses, executive salaries, and the operating costs of central computing systems, over additional output.

Vertical integration acquisitions can reduce costs by removing supplier volatility, by reducing inventory costs, or by gaining control of a distribution network. Such benefits can come in any industry and for firms of all sizes. Waste Systems International, a regional trash hauler in the United States, acquired 41 collection and disposal operations between October 1996 and July 1999 with the goal of enhancing profitability.

> The business model is fairly straightforward. Waste Systems aims to own the garbage trucks that pick up the trash at curbside, the transfer stations that consolidate the trash, and the landfills where it's ultimately buried. Such vertical integration is seen as crucial for success in the waste business. Owning landfill space gives a trash company control over its single biggest cost, disposal fees, and, equally important, produces substantial economies of scale.[12]

One firm may acquire another to better utilize its existing resources. A chain of ski retailers might combine with golf or tennis equipment stores to better utilize warehouse and store space. These types of transactions are typical in industries with seasonal or very volatile revenue and earnings patterns.

Personnel reductions are often used to reduce costs after an acquisition. The savings can come from two sources, one being the elimination of redundancies and the second the replacement of inefficient managers. When firms combine, there may be overlapping functions, such as payroll, accounts payable, and information systems. By moving some or all of the acquired firm's functions to the bidder, significant cost savings may be possible. In the second case, the target firm managers may actually be making decisions that limit or destroy firm value. By acquiring the firm and replacing them with managers who will take value-maximizing actions, or at least cease the ones that destroy value, the bidder can effect positive changes.

The U.S. oil industry in the late 1970s provides an excellent example of this. Excess production, structural changes in the industry, and macroeconomic factors resulted in declining oil prices and high interest rates. Exploration and development costs were higher than selling prices and companies were losing money on each barrel of oil they discovered, extracted, and refined. The industry needed to downsize, but most oil company executives were unwilling to take such action and as a result, continued to destroy shareholder value. T. Boone Pickens of Mesa Petroleum was one of the few industry participants who not only understood these trends, but was also willing to act. By acquiring several other oil companies and reducing their exploration spending, Pickens created significant wealth for his and the target's shareholders.[13]

Tax Savings   Corporations in the U.S. pay billions each year in corporate in-come taxes. M&A activity may create tax savings that would not be possible ab-sent the transaction. While acquisitions made solely to reduce taxes would be disallowed, substantial value may result from tax savings in deals initiated for valid business purposes. We consider the following three ways that tax incen-tives may motivate acquisition activity:

1. Unused operating losses.
2. Excess debt capacity.
3. Disposition of excess cash.

Operating losses can reduce taxes paid, provided that the firm has operating profits in the same period to offset. If this is not the case, the operating losses can be used to claim refunds for taxes paid in the three previous years or car-ried forward for 15 years. In all cases, the tax savings are worth less than if they were earned today due to the time value of money.

Example 4   Consider two firms, A and B, and two possible states of the econ-omy, *boom* and *bust* with the following outcomes:

	Firm A		Firm B	
	Boom	**Bust**	**Boom**	**Bust**
Taxable income	$1,000	$(500)	$(500)	$1,000
Taxes (at 40%)	(400)	0	0	(400)
Net income	$ 600	$(500)	$(500)	$ 600

Notice that for each possible outcome, the firms together pay $400 of taxes. In this case, operating losses do not reduce taxes for the individual firms. Now consider the impact of an acquisition of firm B by firm A.

	Firm A/B	
	Boom	**Bust**
Taxable income	$500	$500
Taxes (at 40%)	(200)	(200)
Net income	$300	$300

The taxes paid have fallen by 50% to $200 under either scenario. This is incremental cash flow that must be considered when assessing the acquisition's impact on value creation. This calculation must be done with two caveats. Firstly, only cash flows over and above what the independent firms would ulti-mately save in taxes should be included and secondly, the tax savings cannot be the main purpose of the acquisition.

Interest payments on corporate debt are tax deductible and can generate significant tax savings. Basic capital structure theory predicts that firms will issue debt until its additional tax benefits are offset by the increased likelihood of financial distress. Because most acquisitions provide some degree of diversification, that is, they reduce the variability of profits for the merged firms, they can also reduce the probability of financial distress. This diversification effect is illustrated in the previous example, where the postmerger net income is constant. The result is a higher debt-to-equity ratio, more interest payments, lower taxes, and value creation.

Many firms are in the enviable position of generating substantial operating cash flows and over time, large cash surpluses. At the end of 1999, for example, Microsoft and Intel held a combined $29 billion in cash and short-term investments. Firms can distribute these funds to shareholders via a dividend or through a stock repurchase. However, both of these options have tax consequences. Dividends create substantial tax liabilities for many shareholders and a stock repurchase, while generating lower taxes due to capital gains provisions cannot be executed solely to avoid tax payments. A third option is to use the excess cash to acquire another company. This strategy would solve the surplus funds "problem" and carry tax benefits as no tax is paid on dividends paid from the acquired to the acquiring firms. Again, the acquisition must have a business rationale beyond just saving taxes.

The following example summarizes the sources of value discussed in this section and illustrates how we might assess value creation in a potential acquisition.

Example 5 MC Enterprises Inc. manufactures and markets value-priced digital speakers and headphones. The firm has excellent engineering and design staffs and has won numerous awards from *High Fidelity* magazine for its most recent wireless bookshelf speakers. MC wants to enter the market for personal computer (PC) speakers, but does not want to develop its own line of new products from scratch. MC has three million outstanding shares trading at $30/share.

Digerati Inc. is a small manufacturer of high-end speakers for PCs, best known for the technical sophistication of its products. However, the firm has not been well managed financially and has had recent production problems, leading to a string of quarterly losses. The stock recently hit a three-year low of $6.25 per share with two million outstanding shares.

MC's executives feel that Digerati is an attractive acquisition candidate that would provide them with quick access to the PC market. They believe an acquisition would generate incremental after-tax cash flow from three sources.

1. *Revenue enhancement:* MC believes that Digerati's technical expertise will allow it to expand their current product line to include high-end speakers for home theater equipment. They estimate these products could generate incremental annual cash flow of $1.25 million. Because this is a risky undertaking, the appropriate discount rate is 20%.

2. *Operating efficiencies:* MC is currently operating at full capacity with significant overtime. Digerati has unused production capacity and could easily adapt their equipment to produce MC's products. The estimated

annual cash flow savings would be $1.5 million. MC's financial analysts are reasonably certain these results can be achieved and suggest a 15% discount rate.

3. *Tax savings:* MC can use Digerati's recent operating losses to reduce its tax liability. Their tax accountant estimates $750,000 per year in cash savings for each of the next four years. Because these values are easy to estimate and relatively safe cash flows, they are discounted at 10%. The values of MC and Digerati premerger are computed as follows:

Company	Number of Shares	Price/Share	Market Value
MC Enterprises	3,000,000	$30.00	$90 million
Digerati Inc.	2,000,000	6.25	12.5 million

Assume that MC pays a 50% premium to acquire Digerati and that the costs of the acquisition total $3 million. What is the expected impact of the transaction on MC's share price?

Solution: We first compute the total value created by each of the incremental cash flows:

Source	Annual Cash Flow	Discount Rate	Value
Revenue enhancement	$1.25 million	20%	$ 6.25 million
Operating efficiencies	1.5 million	15	10.0 million
Tax savings	$750,000	10	2.38 million
		Total Value =	$18.63 million

The total value created by the acquisition is $18.63 million. A 50% premium would give $6.25 million of this incremental value to Digerati's shareholders. After $3 million of acquisition costs, $9.38 million remains for MC's three million shareholders. Thus, each share should increase by $3.13 ($9.38 million divided by the 3 million shares outstanding) to $33.13.

Note that the solution to Example 5 assumes the market knows about and accepts the value creation estimates described. Investors will often discount management's estimates of value creation, believing them to be overly optimistic or doubting the timetable for their realization. In practice, estimating the synergistic cash flows and the appropriate discount rates is the analyst's most difficult task.

Summary The sole motivation for initiating a merger or acquisition should be increased wealth for the acquirer's shareholders. We know from the empirical evidence presented in section III that many transactions fail to meet this simple requirement. The main point of this section is that value can only come from one source—incremental future cash flows or reduced risk. If we can estimate these parameters in the future, we can measure the acquisition's synergy, or potential for value creation. For the deal to benefit the acquirer's shareholders, management must do two things. The first is to pay a premium that is less than the potential synergy. Many acquisitions that make strategic sense and generate positive synergies fail financially simply because the bidder overpays for the target. The second task for the acquirer's management is to implement the steps needed after the transaction is completed to realize the deal's potential for value creation. This is a major challenge and is discussed further in section VII. In the next section we briefly present some of the key issues managers should consider when initiating and structuring acquisitions.

SOME PRACTICAL CONSIDERATIONS

In this section, we briefly discuss the following issues you may encounter in developing and executing a successful M&A strategy:

- Identifying candidates.
- Cash versus stock deals.
- Pooling versus purchase accounting.
- Tax considerations.
- Antitrust concerns.
- Cross-border deals.

This is not meant to be a comprehensive presentation of these topics. Rather, the important aspects of each are described with the focus on how they can influence cash flows and synergy. The goal is to make sure that you are at least aware of how each item might affect your strategy and the potential for value creation.

Identifying and Screening Candidates

Bidders must first identify an industry or market segment they will target. This process should be part of a larger strategic plan for the company. The next step is to develop a screening process to rank the potential acquisitions in the industry and to eliminate those that do not meet the requirements. This first screen is typically done based on size, geographic area, and product mix. Each of the target's product lines should be assessed to see how they relate to (a) the bidder's existing target market, (b) markets that might be of interest to the bidder, and (c) markets that are of no interest to the bidder. Keep in mind that undesirable product lines may be sold.

It is also important to evaluate the current ownership and corporate governance structure of the target. If public, how dispersed is share ownership and who are the majority stockholders? What types of takeover defenses are in place and have there been previous acquisition attempts? If so, how have they fared? For a private company, there should be some attempt to discern how likely the owners are to sell. Information about the recent performance of the firm or the financial health of the owners may provide some insight.

The original list of potential acquisitions can be shortened considerably by using these criteria. The companies on this shortened list should be first analyzed assuming they would remain as a stand-alone business after the acquisition. This analysis should go beyond just financial performance and might include the following criteria:[14]

Future Performance Forecast
Growth prospects
Future margin
Future cash flows
Potential risk areas

Key Strengths/Weaknesses
Products and brands
Technology
Assets
Management
Distribution

Industry Position
Cost structure versus competition
Position in supply chain

Financial Performance
Profit growth
Profit margins
Cash flow
Leverage
Asset turnover
Return on equity

Business Performance
Market share
Product development
Geographic coverage
Research and assets
Employees

Other popular tools for this analysis include SWOT (strengths, weaknesses, opportunities, and threats) analysis, the Porter's Five Forces model, and gap analysis. Once this process is completed, the potential synergies of the deal should be assessed using the approach presented in the previous section. The result will be a list of potential acquisitions ranked by both their potential as stand-alone companies and the synergies that would result from a combination.

Cash versus Stock Deals

The choice of using cash or shares of stock to finance an acquisition is an important one. In making it, the following factors should be considered:

1. *Risk-sharing:* In a cash deal, the target firm shareholders take the money and have no continued interest in the firm. If the acquirer is able to create significant value after the merger, these gains will go only to its shareholders. In a stock deal, the target shareholders retain ownership in the new firm and therefore share in the risk of the transaction. Stock deals with Microsoft or Cisco in the 1990s made many target-firm shareholders wealthy as the share prices of these two firms soared. Chrysler Corporation

stockholders on the other hand, have seen the postmerger value of the Daimler-Benz shares they received fall by 60%.

2. *Overvaluation:* An increase in the acquirer's stock price, especially for technology firms, may leave its shares overvalued historically and even in the opinion of management. In this case, the acquirer can get more value using shares for the acquisition rather than cash. However, investors may anticipate this and view the stock acquisition as a signal that the acquirer's shares are overpriced.

3. *Taxes:* In a cash deal, the target firm's shareholders will owe capital gains taxes on the proceeds. By exchanging shares, the transaction is tax-free (at least until the target firm stockholders choose to sell their newly acquired shares of the bidder). Taxes may be an important consideration in deals where the target is private or has a few large shareholders, as Example 6 makes clear.

Often firms will make offers using a combination of stock and cash. In a study of large mergers between 1992 and 1998, only 22% of the deals were cash-only. Stock only (60%) and combination cash and stock (18%) accounted for the vast majority of the deals.[15] This contrasts with the 1980s when many deals were cash offers financed by the issuance of junk bonds. The acquirer's financial advisor or investment banker can help sort through these factors to maximize the gains to shareholders.

Example 6   Sarni Inc. began operations 10 years ago as an excavating company. Jack Sarni, the principal and sole shareholder, purchased equipment (a truck and bulldozer) at that time for $40,000. The equipment had a six-year useful life and has been depreciated to a book value of zero. However, the machinery has been well maintained and because of inflation, has a current market value of $90,000. The business has no other assets and no debt.

Pave-Rite Inc. makes an offer to acquire Sarni for $90,000. If the deal is a cash deal, Jack Sarni will immediately owe tax on $50,000, the difference between the $90,000 he receives and his initial investment of $40,000. If he instead accepts shares of Pave-Rite Inc. worth $90,000 in a tax-free acquisition, there is no immediate tax liability. He will only owe tax if and when he sells the Pave-Rite shares. Of course in this latter case, Sarni assumes the risk that Pave-Rite's shares may fall in value.

Purchase versus Pooling Accounting

The *purchase method* requires the acquiring corporation to allocate the purchase price to the assets and liabilities it acquires. All identifiable assets and liabilities are assigned a value equal to their fair market value at the date of acquisition. The difference between the sum of these fair market values and the purchase price paid is called *goodwill.* Goodwill appears on the acquirer's books as an intangible asset and is *amortized,* or written off as a noncash expense for book purposes over a period of not more than 40 years. The amortization of purchased goodwill is deductible for tax purposes and is taken over 15 years.

Under the *pooling of interests method,* the assets of the two firms are combined, or pooled, at their historic book values. There is no revaluation of assets to reflect market value and there is no creation of goodwill. Because of this, there is no reduction in net income due to goodwill amortization. This method requires that the acquired firm's shareholders maintain an equity stake in the surviving company and is therefore used primarily in acquisitions for stock.

Weston and Johnson report that 52% of the 364 acquisitions they analyzed used pooling and 48% used purchase accounting.[16] To illustrate the difference between the two methods of accounting for an acquisition, we offer a simple example.

Example 7   Consider the following predeal balance sheets for B.B. Lean Inc. and Dead End Inc., both clothing retailers:

B.B. Lean Inc. ($ millions)				**Dead End Inc. ($ millions)**			
Cash	$ 6	Equity	$28	Cash	$ 3	Equity	$12
Land	22			Land	0		
Building	0			Building	9		
Total	$28		$28	Total	$12		$12

Now assume that B.B. Lean offers to purchase Dead End for $18 million worth of its stock and elects to use the purchase method of accounting. Assume further that Dead End's building has appreciated and has a current market value of $12 million. B.B. Lean's balance sheet after the deal appears as follows:

B.B. Lean Inc. ($ millions)			
Purchase Method			
Cash	$ 9	Equity	$46
Land	22		
Building	12		
Goodwill	3		
Total	$46		$46

Note that the acquired building has been written up to reflect its market value of $12 million and that the difference between the acquisition price ($18 million) and the market value of the assets acquired ($15 million) is booked as goodwill. Lean's equity has increased by the $18 million of new shares it issued to pay for the deal.

Now assume that the same transaction occurs, this time using the pooling method.

B.B. Lean Inc. ($ millions)

Pooling Method

Cash	$ 9	Equity	$40
Land	22		
Building	9		
Goodwill	0		
Total	$40		$40

Under the pooling method, there is no goodwill and the acquired assets are put on B.B. Lean's balance sheet at their book value.

Entire volumes have been written on the accounting treatment of acquisitions and this is a very complex and dynamic issue. In fact, as this chapter is being written, accounting-rule makers in the United States were proposing to eliminate the pooling of interests method of accounting for acquisitions. Because of this, it is important to get timely, expert advice on these issues from competent professionals.

Tax Issues

Taxes were discussed briefly in the paragraph comparing cash and stock deals. In a *tax-free transaction,* the acquired assets are maintained at their historical levels and target firm shareholders don't pay taxes until they sell the shares received in the transaction. To qualify as a tax-free deal, there must be a valid business purpose for the acquisition and the bidder must continue to operate the acquired business. In a *taxable transaction,* the assets and liabilities acquired are marked up to reflect current market values and target firm shareholders are liable for capital gains taxes on the shares they sell.

In most cases, selling shareholders would prefer a tax-free deal. In the study by Weston and Johnson (1999), 65% of the transactions were nontaxable. However, there are situations where a taxable transaction may be preferred. If the target has few shareholders with other tax losses, their gain on the deal can be used to offset these losses. A taxable deal might also be optimal if the tax savings from the additional depreciation and amortization outweigh the capital gains taxes. In this case, the savings could be split between the target and bidder shareholders (at the expense of the government). Again, it is important to get current, expert advice from knowledgeable tax accountants when structuring any transaction.

Antitrust Concerns

Regulators around the world routinely review M&A transactions and have the power to disallow deals if they feel they are anti-competitive or will give the merged firm too much market power. More likely than an outright rejection are provisions that require the deal's participants to modify their strategic plan or to divest certain assets. These concessions can have important implications for margins and ultimately cash flow and shareholder value. For example, in approving the recent megamerger between AOL and Time Warner, the U.S. Federal Trade Commission (FTC) imposed strict provisions on the new company with respect to network access by competing internet service providers. The goal of this is to increase competition, which will ultimately reduce AOL/Time Warner's margins and future cash flows.

The basis for antitrust laws in the U.S. is found in the Sherman Act of 1890, the Clayton Act of 1914, and the Hart-Scott-Rodino Act of 1976. Regulators assess market share concentration within the context of the economics of the industry. Factors such as ease of entry for competitors and the potential for collusion on pricing and production levels are also considered. In the end, antitrust enforcement is an inexact science that can have a major impact on M&A activity. When assessing potential acquisition candidates, the potential for regulatory challenges—and an estimate of the valuation impact of likely remedies—must be considered in the screening and ranking process.

Cross-Border Deals

In 1999, for the first time in history, there were more acquisitions of foreign companies (10,413) than U.S. companies (7,243). The U.S. deals were larger on average, totaling $1.2 trillion versus $980 billion for the foreign transactions.[17] By any measure, the level of international M&A activity is increasing as the globalization of product and financial markets continues. All of the issues discussed in this chapter apply to cross-border deals, in some cases with significant added complexities, which are discussed briefly next.

Each country has its own legal, accounting, and economic systems. This means that tax and antitrust rules may vary greatly from U.S. standards. While there is a move to standardized financial reporting via generally accepted accounting principles (GAAP) or international accounting standards (IAS), there is still great variability in the frequency and reliability of accounting data around the world. The problem is that developing nations, which offer some of the best acquisition opportunities, have the most problems.

Doing M&A transactions across borders brings additional risks that have not been previously discussed. These include currency exchange risk, political risk, and the additional risk of national cultural differences. If a company is going to execute an effective international M&A strategy, all of these must be identified and quantified, because they can have a significant impact on synergies and the implementation timetable. It is critical for a bidder to get capable financial and legal advisors in each country it is considering acquisitions.

SUCCESSFUL POSTMERGER IMPLEMENTATION

The section on mergers and acquisitions makes it clear that most acquisitions fail to meet the expectations of corporate managers and shareholders. This dismal record is attributable to various causes, including ill-conceived acquisition strategies, poor target selection, overpayment, and failed implementation. In a study of 45 Forbes 500 firms, Smolowitz and Hillyer ask senior executives to rate a list of reasons for the poor performance record of acquisitions.[18] The following were the five most frequently ranked factors:

1. Cultural incompatibility.
2. Clashing management styles and egos.
3. Inability to implement change.
4. Poor forecasting.
5. Excessive optimism with regard to synergy.

The last two are premerger problems, but the first three occur in the postmerger transition process. Deloitte & Touche Consulting estimates that 60% of mergers fail largely because of integration approach. Managers must understand that the acquisition closing dinner marks the end of one stage of the transaction and the beginning of the process that will determine the deal's ultimate success or failure. In this section, we briefly discuss the following key components of a successful implementation plan:

- Expect chaos and a loss of productivity.
- Create a detailed plan *before* the deal closes.
- First, keep your executives happy.
- Speed and communication are essential.
- Focus managerial resources on the sources of synergy.
- Culture, culture, culture.

The process of merging two firms creates havoc at every level of the organization. The moment the first rumors of a possible acquisition begin, an air of uncertainty and anxiety permeates the company. The first casualty in this environment is productivity, which grinds to a halt as the gossip network takes over. While the executives debate grand, strategic issues, the employees are concerned with more basic issues and need to know several key things about their new employers, their compensation and their careers before productivity will resume. Managers must understand that this "me first" attitude is human nature and must be addressed—especially in transactions where the most important assets are people.

The first step in any postmerger implementation must be a detailed plan. We saw how Cisco "maps" the future of every employee in a soon-to-be-acquired firm. For those continuing on, their new position and duties within Cisco are clearly defined from the beginning. The employees that will be relocated or terminated are also identified and a separate plan for handling them is created. Relocation and severance packages must be generous to signal retained workers that their new employer is ethical and fair. The second reason for a detailed plan is that it allows transition costs to be accurately estimated. The costs to reconfigure, relocate, retrain, and sever employees must be budgeted as they can have a significant impact on postmerger cash flows.

The detailed plan must start at the highest levels of the organization. If executives from the two firms are going to lead the transition, they must be confident of their future roles and comfortable with their compensation plans. In the Daimler-Benz-Chrysler deal, there was a good deal of animosity between executives as the German managers watched their American counterparts walk away with multimillion-dollar payoffs from their Chrysler stock options while simultaneously receiving equity in the newly merged firm. A fair incentive system must be in place at the corporation's executive suite before any implementation plan begins.

Once the key managers have been identified, retained, and given the proper incentives, they must carry the vision of the merger to the rest of the organization. To combat the productivity problems discussed above, managers have two critical weapons, speed and communication. Remember that the enemy from the employee's perspective is uncertainty, and absent timely information from above, they will usually assume the worst. Executives must move quickly to convey the vision for the merged entity and to assure key employees of their role in executing this vision.

While all employees should be part of this process, those that deal with the firms' customers should receive special attention. We saw how Cisco moves quickly to retain key salespeople and reassure important customers that the merger will only improve product offerings and services. In contrast, the 1997 merger between Franklin Planner and Covey Systems failed to heed this advice. Combining sales forces was seen as a key source of synergy, but the company was unsuccessful in merging the two compensation programs.

> Divisions were especially strong within the company's 1,700-person sales force, which marketed its seminars and training sessions. Former Covey salespeople got higher bonuses than Franklin staffers. Covey employees also kept their free medical coverage, while Franklin's had to pay part of their premiums.[19]

This situation created such sniping by sales reps on both sides that productivity plunged.

The implementation plan must focus management resources on those areas at the root of the deal's synergies. If value is going to be created, it will only be by executing on those aspects of the deal that were the original rationale for merging. Without a plan, it is too easy for managers to get bogged down in details of the implementation that have little marginal impact on shareholder wealth. In the failed AT&T-NCR merger, the hoped-for technological synergies between telecommunications and computers never materialized as managers worried more about creating a team environment.

In many cases, the disappointing performance of mergers can be traced to a failure to account for cultural differences between organizations. These differences can be based in corporate culture or national culture in the case of cross-border deals. In many transactions, both corporate and national cultural differences are present. Because they are difficult to measure and to some extent intangible, cultural differences are often ignored in the pre-acquisition due diligence. This is unfortunate since they can ultimately be the most costly aspect of the implementation process. In mergers where the firms have similar cultures, the rapid combination of the two organizations can actually be easier. However, where there are large cultural differences, executives should consider keeping the entities separate for some time period. This allows each to operate comfortably within its own culture while at the same time learning to appreciate the strengths and weaknesses of the cultural differences between the organizations. Such an arrangement may delay the realization of certain synergies but, in the end, is the most rationale plan. The key is that culture can have a huge impact on value (both positive and negative), and therefore needs to be part of the planning process from the very beginning—even before any acquisition offer is made.

To ensure success, the postmerger implementation process must be carefully planned and executed. Even when this is done, there will undoubtedly be surprises and unanticipated problems. However, a well-thought-out plan should minimize their negative impact. The most important parts of the plan are speed and communication, which are critical weapons in the fight against successful implementation's main enemies—uncertainty, anxiety, and an inevitable drop in productivity. A plan conceived and implemented swiftly by the firms' executives, with their full and active leadership, improves the chances for a successful transition. As always, we urge acquirers to seek the advice of knowledgeable experts on the implementation process.

SUMMARY AND CONCLUSIONS

Mergers and acquisitions are a popular way for firms to grow, and as economic globalization continues, there is every reason to believe their size and frequency will increase. However, it is not that case that profitable growth by acquisition is easy. The empirical data presented in this chapter makes it clear that corporate combinations have historically failed to meet the operational and financial expectations of the acquiring firm's managers and shareholders. While target firm shareholders typically earn 30% to 40% premiums, M&A transactions do not create value on average for the acquirer's stockholders. This information should make it clear that a carefully designed acquisition strategy, realistic estimates of the potential synergies, and an efficient implementation plan are critical if the historical odds are to be overcome.

Managers must understand that the only source of incremental value in corporate mergers and acquisitions is incremental future cash flows or reduced risk. These cash flows can come from increased revenues, reduced costs, or tax savings. The sum of the potential value created from these incremental cash flows is called synergy. For a deal to be successful financially the premium paid and the costs of the transaction must be less than the deal's total synergy.

Only then will the bidder's shareholders see their wealth increase. This sounds simple, but in a competitive market for corporate control, there must be a relatively unique relationship between the bidder and the target that other firms cannot easily match. The market must perceive the target as worth more as part of your firm than alone or with some other firm.

There are many practical details that potentially impact the creation of value in M&A transactions. These include the choice of payment (cash vs. stock), the accounting method (purchase or pooling), tax considerations, and antitrust concerns. Each of these may affect future cash flows and synergies and therefore must be part of the premerger due diligence process. We describe briefly how each factor can impact value creation, but refer potential bidders to investment bankers, professional accountants, tax experts, and attorneys for the most timely and customized advice.

The final and most important part of the process is the postmerger implementation plan. Managers often focus on completing the transaction, which is unfortunate, since the transition to a single organization is where the keys to value creation lie. A detailed implementation plan must be developed *before* the transaction closes and communicated quickly and effectively to employees by the firm's new leadership. The plan must focus on the roots of synergy in the deal to ensure the successful creation of the anticipated shareholder value. In deals where there are major cultural differences, special attention must be paid to smoothly integrating these differences. Failure to do so can doom an otherwise sound transaction.

In the end, profitable growth by acquisition is possible but difficult. The market for corporate control is competitive and it is easy for bidders to overestimate potential synergies and therefore overpay for acquisitions. To avoid this, managers must develop and stick to an acquisition plan that makes strategic and financial sense. Only then can they hope to overcome history, human nature, and the odds against successfully creating shareholder value through mergers and acquisitions. Our hope is that this chapter provides the basic information needed to embark on such a course.

FOR FURTHER READING

Morosini, Piero, *Managing Cultural Differences* (New York: Elsevier, 1997). A comprehensive discussion of culture's role in mergers and other corporate alliances. The focus is on cross-border deals, but the strategies for effective implementation can be used by all.

Sirower, Mark L., *The Synergy Trap: How Companies Lose the Acquisition Game* (New York: Free Press, 1997). Focuses on assessing the potential for synergies and value creation in mergers.

Vlasic, Bill, and Bradley A. Stertz, *Taken for a Ride: How Daimler-Benz Drove Off with Chrysler* (New York: HarperCollins, 2000). A fascinating behind-the-scenes look at the Daimler-Benz-Chrysler deal. Clearly shows the roles of culture, human nature, and managerial hubris in M&A transactions.

Weston, J. Fred, Kwang S. Chung, and Juan A. Siu, *Takeovers, Restructuring, and Corporate Governance* (Upper Saddle River, NJ: Prentice-Hall, 1998). An excellent reference for developing and implementing an effective M&A strategy.

INTERNET LINKS

www.cnnfn.cnn.com/news/deals	Up-to-date stories on deals, all free information
www.stern.nyu.edu/~adamodar	Academic site with numerous quantitative examples and spreadsheets that can be used to value potential synergies
www.mergerstat.com	Comprehensive source of M&A data; some good free information
www.webmergers.com	Good reports on M&A activity of internet companies

NOTES

1. For a concise summary of and more detail on empirical tests of M&A performance see chapter 7 of J. Fred Weston, Kwang S. Chung, and Juan A. Siu, *Takeovers, Restructuring, and Corporate Governance* (Upper Saddle River, NJ: Prentice-Hall, 1998).

2. Anup Agrawal, Jeffrey F. Jaffe, and Gershon N. Mandelker, "The Post-Merger Performance of Acquiring Firsms: A Re-examination of an Anomaly," *Journal of Finance* 47 (September 1992): 1605–1621.

3. Weston, Chung, and Siu, 133, 140.

4. *Business Week,* October 30, 1995.

5. *Merger & Acquisition Integration Excellence* (Chapel Hill, NC: Best Practices, 2000).

6. For a more thorough discussion of this topic, see Weston, Chung, and Siu, chapter 5.

7. *The Wall Street Journal,* November 30, 2000, B4.

8. Ibid.

9. *Business Week,* April 20, 1998, 37.

10. *Business Week,* October 16, 1995, 38.

11. *The Wall Street Journal,* September 21, 2000, C22.

12. *The Wall Street Journal/New England,* July 28, 1999, NE3.

13. See Harvard Business School case #285053, *Gulf Oil Corp—Takeover,* for a complete discussion of this value creation.

14. Adapted from Brian Coyle, *Mergers and Acquisitions* (Chicago: Glenlake, 2000), 32.

15. J. Fred Weston and Brian Johnson, "What It Takes for a Deal to Win Stock Market Approval," *Mergers and Acquisition* 34, no. 2 (September/October 1999): 45.

16. Weston and Johnson, 45.

17. "M&A Time Line," *Mergers & Acquisitions,* 35(8) (September 2000): 30.

18. Ira Smolowitz and Clayton Hillyer, *Working Paper,* 1996, Bureau of Business Research, American International College, Springfield, MA.

19. *Business Week,* November 8, 1999, 125.

18 BUSINESS VALUATION

Michael A. Crain

It has been said that determining the value of an investment in a closely held business is similar to analyzing securities of public companies. The theories are similar and not overly complex on the surface. There are even Web sites that proclaim to be able to value a private business. But like so many things in the business world, the devil is in the details. The valuation of a closely held business depends on many variables. While the theories of valuation are not overly complicated, the accuracy of the valuation result is only as good as the variables that go into it. The valuation of closely held businesses is often complicated because of the limitations of the underlying information and the way private businesses are operated. Unlike public companies, private businesses often do not have complete and accurate information available. Dollar for dollar, the time to accurately value most profitable private companies is out of proportion to the analysis of public-company securities. This is illustrated in the following case study that demonstrates the financial theories of business valuation and the level of information needed for an accurate result.

For the past 20 years, Bob has owned and operated a manufacturing business that has grown significantly since its inception. Bob is approaching 60 years of age and his children do not appear capable of taking over the company. He is contemplating the future of the business at a time when he would like to slow down. One of his options is selling his business. Bob's company, ACME Manufacturing Inc. is a manufacturer of certain types of adhesives and sealants and has revenues of approximately $50 million. It has six manufacturing locations throughout the country. Bob owns 100% of the company's common stock. He does not know what the company is worth, nor does he know how its value would be determined. Bob asked his certified public accountant (CPA) about valuing the business. The CPA tells him that it would be most appropriate to engage someone who specializes in business valuations. After interviewing several candidates, Bob hires Victoria to appraise his business. The valuation date is December 31, 2000, and the *standard of value* is fair market value. Victoria explains the appraisal process and the scope of her work.

THREE APPROACHES TO VALUE

Victoria tells Bob that the value of a business is determined by considering three approaches.

1. Income approach.
2. Market approach.
3. Asset (or cost) approach.

The income approach is a general way of determining the value using a method to convert anticipated financial benefits, such as cash flows, into a present single amount. This approach is based on the concept that the value of something is its expected future benefits expressed in present value dollars. (A simple example of present value is that a dollar received a year from now is worth less than a dollar today.)

The market approach is a general way of determining a value comparing the asset to similar assets that have been sold. For example, real estate appraisals using the market approach rely on the sales prices of comparable properties. In business valuation, it is sometimes possible to locate similar businesses that have sold and are appropriate to use as guidelines in the appraisal.

The asset approach is a general way of determining the value based on the individual values of the assets of that business less its liabilities. The company's balance sheet serves as a starting point for this approach. The proper application requires that all of the business's assets be identified. Often, the balance sheet prepared in accordance with general accepted accounting principals does not include assets that have been created within the company such as goodwill and other intangible assets. Once all the company assets and liabilities have been identified, each one is valued separately.

DIFFERENT TYPES OF BUYERS

Victoria explains to Bob that buyers have different motives for acquiring businesses and they may be willing to pay different prices for the same business. Most buyer motives can be grouped into these categories:

- *Financial buyers.* These buyers are primarily motivated by getting an appropriate rate of return on their investment. Financial buyers generally have a much broader range of investment alternatives than other types of buyers. Also, financial buyers often have an exit strategy to sell their investment at some time in the future. They usually pay fair market value (defined next).

- *Strategic/investment buyers.* These buyers probably already know the company or already operate in its industry. Therefore, the number of strategic buyers for a particular business is typically more limited than the market of financial buyers. A strategic buyer is usually looking at integrating its operations with the purchased business. Most of these buyers will pay a price that reflects certain synergies that are not readily available to financial buyers. This price is called investment value, which is different than fair market value.

The smallest of businesses, sometimes called "mom and pop businesses," often have two other groups of buyers—lifestyle buyers and buyers of employment. A lifestyle buyer is looking to acquire a business that gives him or her a desired lifestyle (e.g., a motel in the mountains). Another group of buyers of small businesses is primarily motivated to provide employment for the buyer and/or the family.

Among strategic and financial buyers, strategic buyers will usually pay a higher price because of the anticipated synergies between the two businesses.

After explaining the different types of buyers to Bob, Victoria discusses how it applies to ACME. Obviously, Bob would like to obtain the highest price possible if he sold his business. However, Victoria has no way to foresee who that buyer may be or that buyer's strategic motives for buying ACME. Therefore, she is going to determine what a financial buyer would likely pay—the company's "fair market value." Practically, determining the fair market value will assist Bob in establishing a target minimum price to accept when selling ACME. If Bob can locate a particular strategic buyer who would pay a strategic price (or investment value), he will try to obtain a higher price.

Bob asks Victoria to explain fair market value and how it differs from investment value. She tells him that *fair market value* is defined as "the price, expressed in terms of cash equivalents, at which property would change hands between a hypothetical willing and able buyer and a hypothetical willing and able seller, acting at arm's length in an open and unrestricted market, when neither is under compulsion to buy or sell and when both have reasonable knowledge of the relevant facts."[1] Fair market value contemplates what the "market" will pay. *Investment value* is the price a specific investor would pay based on individual requirements and expectations. It frequently reflects a higher price for the unique synergies between the buyer and company.

AN OVERVIEW OF THE BUSINESS
VALUATION PROCESS

Victoria explains to Bob that a complete business appraisal is both a quantitative and qualitative process involving a risk and investment return analysis. A complete valuation is more than simply analyzing the historic financial statements of the business and then making future projections. Valuations that give the most accurate results consider qualitative matters such as technology changes, the company's competition, and its customers. In addition, other areas that are considered are macro-environment issues such as the industry and the national and local economic factors that affect the particular business. A complete business valuation will consider the following areas:

- Analysis of the company.
- Industry analysis.
- Economic analysis.
- Analysis of the company's financial statements.
- Application of the appropriate valuation methodologies.
- Application of any appropriate valuation discounts or premiums.

A large part of valuing a business is the assessment of the *investment risk* of buying and owning the business. A buyer of the business assumes the risk that he or she will actually receive the anticipated economic benefits. Of course, there is no guarantee of actually receiving the projected income. A fundamental concept in business valuation is the risk-reward relationship in making any kind of investment. Rational individuals and companies make investment decisions regularly by comparing the risk of an investment to the anticipated rewards. For example, a certificate of deposit from a bank that is guaranteed from default may have a rate of return (interest) of 5%. This investment has little or no risk. Investments in large public company (large-cap) stocks have traditionally returned an average of 10% to 12% per year over the long term. Small public company (small-cap) stocks have average historical rates of return in the 15% to 20% range over the long term. These three types of investments illustrate the risk-reward relationship investors have in making decisions. Buying large-cap stocks instead of a certificate of deposit carries more risk and, thus, the market rewards the investor with a higher rate of return. Small-cap stocks over the long term have been more risky than large company stocks and have rewarded investors even more with higher returns. Simplistically, the valuation of a closely held business considers the risk of an investment in the company and compares it to alternative forms of investments.

Victoria further explains that valuation concepts are founded in several economic principles. The first is the principle of alternatives that states that each person has alternatives to completing a particular transaction. In the preceding example, the individual has the alternatives of investing funds in a bank certificate of deposit, large-cap stocks, or small-cap stocks. Investing in a business is yet another alternative. The second economic principle in valuation is the principle of substitution. This states that the value of something tends to be determined by the cost of acquiring an equally desirable substitute. For example, if a new restaurant offers steak on its menu, it will likely have a price similar to other restaurants selling steak (all things being equal). The first restaurant will probably not sell very many steaks if the price is double what the customer could buy at another restaurant. Likewise, a potential purchaser of a business is not likely to pay significantly more than the price he or she can purchase a similar business.

In business valuation, we must remember that buyers/investors have many places to invest their money and they will generally not pay significantly more for a business than the price of comparable investments. Thus, a business valuation will generally benchmark the profitable private company against alternative investments. This involves an analysis of the risk of those investments as well as those of the business being valued.

INDUSTRY ANALYSIS

ACME operates in the adhesive and sealant industry. The U.S. government's Standard Industrial Classification (SIC) is number 2891. Victoria researches this industry and finds that the segment consists of approximately 1,100 U.S. establishments primarily engaged in manufacturing industrial and household adhesives, glues, caulking compounds, sealants, and linoleum, tile, and rubber cements. The annual sales in this industry segment are $16.9 billion, and the industry employs roughly 36,000 people. Also, the industry has grown at an average annual compound rate of 6.7% over the past 10 years. Victoria finds that this industry segment is a large growing global segment. However, the U.S. portion is highly fragmented and a significant majority of the industry participants are small and regional companies. It is expected that the industry will consolidate as companies seek to enhance operating efficiencies and new product development, sales and marketing, distribution, production, and administrative overhead.

Victoria concludes that the industry outlook is positive in revenue and earnings expectations but moderated by the level of competition from numerous, smaller companies selling similar products.

THE FUNDAMENTAL POSITION OF THE COMPANY

During Victoria's management interview, she discovers that Bob founded ACME 20 years ago. The company's history has been one of relative success. It started in a small garage and grew by expanding the number of products and its customer base. Over the years, ACME acquired new facilities, not only in its hometown but in other cities as well. The company's growth was primarily funded by reinvesting its profits and with long-term financing when purchasing real estate. During the past five years, ACME's sales increased from $34 million to $50 million. ACME currently expects to expand its manufacturing capacity by adding equipment to the existing locations.

Victoria's investigation into ACME's competitors reveals competition from numerous companies, many of which are small, privately held businesses.

She also finds that ACME's customers are retail distributors of its products and the company does not have any significant customer concentration. Generally, relationships with customers have been long term.

The company currently has numerous products in the adhesives and sealants area. ACME has several trademarks and several products that are well recognized as well as ACME's name. Victoria determines through her research that the risk of product obsolescence or replacements by new products is a minimal risk to ACME.

ACME has conducted research and development activities and the costs range from $250,000 to $500,000 per year over the past five years. Management does not expect any significant product developments in the near future.

Victoria's financial analysis examines the dividend paying capacity of ACME. Because the company is closely held, special analysis of the compensation paid to family members and perquisites is necessary. Victoria determines that officers' compensation, shareholder distributions, and perquisites over the past five years have been as follows:

Officers' Compensation, Perquisites, and Shareholder Distributions

Year	$ Million
2000	$7.7
1999	5.5
1998	8.2
1997	6.3
1996	6.5

Closely held businesses are frequently operated to minimize taxable income. Publicly held companies, in contrast, are operated to maximize earnings for the benefit of the shareholders and public markets. A financial analysis of a closely held company should make adjustments so that revenues and expenses are "normalized." In this particular case, Victoria determines the amount of economic benefits the family members took from the business and compares that with the market compensation for others employed in similar positions. The difference between the two amounts is actually an economic benefit or dividend (profit) flowing to ACME's owner. Victoria's analysis strives to identify the actual profitability of the business enterprise even though it is different from what is reported on the income statement.

ACME has approximately 240 employees at its six locations. The three top individuals in management are family members including Bob. Should the company be sold, it is unlikely that the three family members would remain in the business.

Summary of Positive and Negative Fundamental Factors

As a result of Victoria's preceding analysis of ACME's fundamental position, she identifies the following key positive and negative factors for the company.

Positive

ACME has been in existence for 20 years.

ACME has a long-term history of growing sales and profits.

ACME owns several trademarks for products that are well known.

ACME has diversification in the number of its manufacturing locations.

ACME's industry outlook is moderately positive.

The demand for ACME's products is expected to continue.

Negative

ACME is highly dependent on the three family members who hold the top management positions.

ACME's products face significant competition and are regionalized.

FINANCIAL STATEMENT ANALYSIS

An analysis of a company's historic financial statements is important (unless it is a start-up business), as the past is usually relevant to estimating future business operations. If a company has had high growth in recent years, that may indicate significant growth potential in the future. If past earnings have been volatile, this is an indication of increased financial risk for a buyer of the business. While an analysis of the financial statements is important, the process does not stop with looking at the company's past performance. The ultimate goal of the quantitative analysis is estimating the future profitability of the business since that is what a prospective buyer is looking to receive. Future earnings may or may not be similar to the past.

Balance Sheet Analysis

Victoria prepares Exhibit 18.1 that presents ACME's historic balance sheets in condensed form for the most recent five years. She finds that total assets grew an average of 15% per year over the five years and a similar amount in the most recent year. The current assets consist primarily of accounts receivable and inventory. Fixed assets primarily consist of land, buildings, and improvements, machinery and equipment, factory construction in progress, and transportation equipment. As of the most recent year's end, ACME's depreciable fixed assets were depreciated to 69% of their original costs.

The most recent year reflects unamortized intangible assets, consisting primarily of goodwill (that had been recorded in accordance with generally accepted accounting principles) in connection with ACME's acquisition of a manufacturing facility.

Current liabilities consist of accounts payable and the amounts due within the next 12 months on promissory notes and obligations under capital leases.

ACME is moderately leveraged. During the past five years, ACME's interest bearing debt (both current and noncurrent portions) increased from $6.6

EXHIBIT 18.1   ACME Manufacturing Inc.: Summary of condensed balance sheets 1996–2000.

	($million)					Growth Rates	
	2000	1999	1998	1997	1996	1996–2000	1999–2000
Assets							
Current assets	$11.69	$11.56	$12.37	$ 9.43	$ 9.17	6.3%	1.1%
Fixed assets, net	13.87	10.36	9.37	7.65	6.79	19.5	33.9
Other assets	3.17	3.00	3.25	1.12	0.62	50.4	5.5
Total assets	$28.72	$24.92	$24.98	$18.20	$16.58	14.7%	15.3%
Liabilities and Equity							
Current liabilities	$11.50	$ 6.41	$ 8.78	$ 4.34	$ 4.94	23.5%	79.4%
Long-term liabilities	5.83	7.26	7.78	4.85	4.96	4.1	−19.7
Total liabilities	17.33	13.67	16.56	9.19	9.90	15.0	26.8%
Equity	11.39	11.25	8.42	9.01	6.69	14.2	1.3
Total liabilities and equity	$28.72	$24.92	$24.98	$18.20	$16.58	14.7%	15.3%

	Common Size				
	2000	1999	1998	1997	1996
Assets					
Current assets	40.7%	46.4%	49.5%	51.8%	55.3%
Fixed assets, net	48.3	41.6	37.5	42.0	41.0
Other assets	11.0	12.0	13.0	6.1	3.7
Total assets	100.0%	100.0%	100.0%	100.0%	100.0%
Liabilities and Equity					
Current liabilities	40.1%	25.7%	35.1%	23.9%	29.8%
Long-term liabilities	20.3	29.1	31.2	26.6	29.9
Total liabilities	60.3	54.9	66.3	50.5	59.7
Equity	39.7	45.1	33.7	49.5	40.3
Total liabilities and equity	100.0%	100.0%	100.0%	100.0%	100.0%

million to $10.4 million. Debt consists of real estate mortgage notes, term loans, a revolving line of credit, and obligations under capital leases.

Over the past five years, the shareholder equity increased from $6.7 million to $11.4 million. Shareholder equity decreased slightly as a percentage of total liabilities and equity over the past five years.

Income Statement Analysis

Victoria also prepares Exhibit 18.2 that presents ACME's historic income statements in condensed form for the past five years. She also prepares Exhibit 18.3, which is a graph of ACME's annual revenues for the previous five years. It graphically shows the revenue amounts from Exhibit 18.2 and more clearly shows the revenue growth trend. The company had a compounded annual growth rate in revenues of 11.1% during the previous five years and 3.5% for the most recent year. ACME's revenue growth rate over the past five years was substantially higher than the 5.6% revenue growth reported by the chemical products industry.

Cost of goods sold as a percentage of revenues fluctuated between 66.6% and 69.9% over the past five years. Operating expenses, exclusive of officers' compensation, ranged from 9.8% to 11.8%. The overall trend is up.

ACME reported consistent profitability during the past five years. In 1996, income before officers' compensation and taxes was $6.5 million ($4.31 + $2.23). For 2000, it increased to $8.7 million ($5.29 + $3.38).

Ratio Analysis

Victoria also prepares Exhibit 18.4 that presents various financial operating ratios of ACME for the past five years. The *liquidity ratios* indicate the ability of ACME to meet current obligations as they come due. The current ratio decreased from 1.9 to 1.0 during the five-year period. Working capital also decreased from $4.2 million to $190,000 during the same five-year period. These indicate the company has a greater risk in being able to pay its bills.

The *activity ratios* indicate how effectively a company is utilizing its assets. The average number of days in ACME's accounts receivable was similar over the past five years at approximately 50 days. However, the average number of days inventory remained at the plant before being sold decreased from 58 days to 47 days. The average number of days of accounts payable was similar during the five-year period at 48 days.

The *coverage ratios* indicate a company's ability to pay debt service. The number of times interest was earned, as measured by earnings before interest and taxes (EBIT) divided by interest expense, decreased from 8 to 7 times.

The *leverage ratios* generally indicate a company's vulnerability to business downturns. Highly leverage firms are more vulnerable to business downturns than those with lower debt-to-worth positions. ACME's debt to tangible worth increased in the past five years from 1.5 to 1.8. Fixed assets to tangible worth increased from 1.0 to 1.5.

EXHIBIT 18.2   ACME Manufacturing Inc.: Summary of condensed income statements 1996–2000.

	($million)					Growth Rates	
	2000	1999	1998	1997	1996	1996–2000	1999–2000
Revenues	$50.29	$48.59	$40.85	$37.94	$33.02	11.1%	3.5%
Cost of goods sold	34.80	33.95	28.45	25.25	22.63	11.4	2.5
Gross profit	15.49	14.64	12.39	12.69	10.39	10.5	5.7
Operating expenses	5.95	5.58	4.34	3.72	3.31	15.8	6.7
Officers' compensation	3.38	2.86	3.53	3.03	2.23	11.1	18.4
Operating EBITDA	6.15	6.20	4.52	5.94	4.86	6.0	–0.9
Depreciation and amortization	0.31	0.22	0.10	0.05	0.07	44.9	42.3
Operating income (EBIT)	5.84	5.99	4.42	5.89	4.79	5.1	–2.5
Miscellaneous (income)	(0.30)	(0.25)	(0.19)	(0.18)	(0.12)	26.1	17.1
Interest expense	0.84	0.74	0.55	0.47	0.59	9.0	12.6
Pretax income	5.29	5.49	4.06	5.60	4.31	5.3	–3.6
Less: Income taxes°	—	—	—	—	—	N/A	N/A
Net income	$ 5.29	$ 5.49	$ 4.06	$ 5.60	$ 4.31	5.3%	–3.6%

	Common Size				
	2000	1999	1998	1997	1996
Revenues	100.0%	100.0%	100.0%	100.0%	100.0%
Cost of goods sold	69.2	69.9	69.6	66.6	68.5
Gross profit	30.8	30.1	30.3	33.4	31.5
Operating expenses	11.8	11.5	10.6	9.8	10.0
Officers' compensation	6.7	5.9	8.6	8.0	6.8
Operating EBITDA	12.2	12.8	11.1	15.7	14.7
Depreciation and amortization	0.6	0.5	0.2	0.1	0.2
Operating income (EBIT)	11.6	12.3	10.8	15.5	14.5
Miscellaneous (income)	–0.6	–0.5	–0.5	–0.5	–0.4
Interest expense	1.7	1.5	1.3	1.2	1.8
Pretax income	10.5	11.3	9.9	14.8	13.1
Less: Income taxes°	0.0	0.0	0.0	0.0	0.0
Net income	10.5%	11.3%	9.9%	14.8%	13.1%

° ACME is an S corporation for tax purposes and taxable income is passed through to the shareholder. Thus, the corporation does not pay income taxes.

EXHIBIT 18.3   ACME Manufacturing Inc.: Revenue growth 1996–2000.

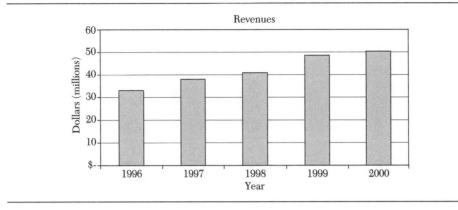

The *profitability ratios* reflect the returns earned by ACME and assist in evaluating management performance. ACME has been consistently profitable in each of the past five years. The earnings before taxes to tangible worth fluctuated between 55% and 66%. Officers' compensation ranged from $2.2 million to $3.6 million during the five years and was $3.4 million in the most recent year.

EXHIBIT 18.4   ACME Manufacturing Inc.: Ratio analysis 1996–2000.

	2000	1999	1998	1997	1996
Liquidity ratios:					
Current ratio	1.0	1.8	1.4	2.2	1.9
Quick ratio	0.6	1.1	0.9	1.3	1.1
Activity ratios:					
Revenue/accounts receivable	7.3	7.5	7.0	7.8	7.2
Days' receivable	49.8	48.6	52.4	46.9	50.4
COS/inventory	7.8	7.6	6.4	7.2	6.3
Days' inventory	46.6	47.8	57.2	50.5	58.1
COS/payables	7.6	9.4	4.9	7.4	7.6
Days' payables	47.7	39.0	73.9	49.2	48.0
Revenue/working capital	274.2	9.4	11.4	7.5	7.8
Coverage/leverage ratios:					
EBIT/interest	7.3	8.4	8.4	13.0	8.3
Fixed assets/tangible worth	1.5	1.1	1.5	0.9	1.0
Debt/tangible worth	1.8	1.5	2.6	1.0	1.5
Profitability & operating ratios:					
EBT/tangible worth	55.4%	58.8%	63.4%	62.8%	65.5%
EBT/total assets	18.4%	22.1%	16.2%	30.8%	26.0%
Revenue/fixed assets	3.6	4.7	4.4	5.0	4.9
Revenue/total assets	1.8	2.0	1.6	2.1	2.0

COMPARISON TO INDUSTRY AVERAGES

Victoria also compares ACME's key financial ratios to peer companies. The main differences between ACME and other companies of similar size in the same industry are as follows:

- ACME's liquidity is significantly less than other companies in the group. Similar companies had a ratio of 1.6 while ACME had a current ratio of 1.0. This is likely due to ACME having a significant portion of its financing due within twelve months as opposed to longer term financing.
- The average number of days in accounts payable for ACME is 48 days and is significantly more than the peer group at 32 days. This is likely due to the company taking longer to pay its expenses related to raw materials and inventory than that of its peer group because of low working capital.
- The times interest earned measure for ACME is significantly higher than its peer group. The company had a measure of 7.3 as compared to its peers at 4.0. This is likely due to ACME having a higher profit margin than its peers.
- ACME is significantly more leveraged than its peer group. Its measure of debt to tangible worth is 1.8 as compared to its peers at 1.2. Also, the company's measure of fixed assets to tangible worth is 1.5 as compared to its peers at 0.5. This assessment is related to the company having a higher level of fixed assets as compared to its tangible worth.
- ACME is more profitable than its peers. The measure of earnings before taxes to total assets was 18%, as compared to its peers' 12%. Additionally, ACME's earnings before taxes to tangible worth was 55% as compared to its peers at 22%. This is due to ACME's profit margin of 11%, as compared to its peers at 5%.

The purpose of the this part of Victoria's analysis is to assess the risk factors of owning this business as compared to an investment in the average peer company. As previously discussed in this chapter, investors have options of where to place their capital and rational investors require a higher reward (in the form of returns) for investments with higher risks.

APPRAISAL OF FAIR MARKET VALUE

Victoria tells Bob that the shares of ACME are closely held securities and there is no ready market for their sale. The three general approaches available for the valuation of private business interests were discussed earlier in this chapter. Victoria considers all relevant valuation approaches and methods and ultimately relies on two approaches to estimate the value of ACME's common stock—a market approach and an income approach. She rejects the asset approach because the premise of value is a going concern and the company has no intention to liquidate the assets. In addition, this approach does not clearly reflect the value of the business resulting from its earnings potential.

Debt-Free Analysis

She further explains to Bob that there are two ways to value the equity (stock) of a private business under the income approach. The first is the *direct equity methodology.* Under this approach a company's net income or cash flow is the basis to determine the value of the company's stock. This methodology either *capitalizes* net income or net cash flow, or it determines the present value of a series of future cash flows.

The second is the *debt-free methodology* (or invested capital methodology). How much or how little a company is leveraged can have a significant impact on the value of the company's stock. If a specific company has too little leverage or too much leverage as compared to an ideal blend of debt and equity capital, the direct equity methodology may result in a distorted valuation.

A company's *invested capital* represents all of its sources of capital to fund the business—capital from investors (equity) and lenders (debt). When we say the value of a "business," it often has a different meaning from the value of the corporation's equity. This concept is illustrated below.

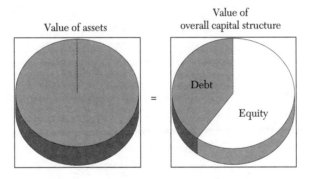

When we say the value of a "business" or "company," we are often referring to the value of the overall capital (the debt and equity capital equals the total assets). Many sales transactions are structured only to transfer the assets of a business and it is up to the buyer to raise capital from investors and/or lenders. (In an asset sale, the seller would be responsible for paying off the existing debt, usually upon the receipt of the sales proceeds.) When the objective is to value only the equity, debt is subtracted from the value of the total assets. This is the underlying model of the debt-free methodology. First, the total assets are valued based on the company's cash flow without regard to servicing the debt. Second, if the equity is being valued, then the company's debt is subtracted from the value of the assets.

The direct equity methodology determines the value of the equity by using the net cash flow *after* the company services its debt, which results in a lower cash flow. Then a discount rate or capitalization rate (multiple) is applied. The result is the value of the company's equity. The direct equity and debt-free methodologies are summarized below:

Direct Equity Methodology	Debt-Free Methodology
Net income or net cash flow to equity holders (defined later)	Net cash flow to holders of total invested capital (defined later)
Apply discount rate or capitalization rate on a cost of equity basis (discussed later)	Apply discount rate or capitalization rate on a weighted average cost of capital basis (discussed later)
Results in value of company's equity	Results in value of company's invested capital (debt and equity)
	Subtract value of debt capital to arrive at the value of the company's equity

COST OF CAPITAL

Bob asks Victoria to explain the cost of capital. She says that when a business owner or prospective buyer is raising capital, debt capital is less expensive than equity capital. Debt capital represents those monies borrowed from a lender, such as a bank, to fund the business. The lender expects a return on its investment in the form of interest. From a financial prospective, interest expense on the debt is called the *cost of debt*. Therefore, the business pays interest, or the cost of debt, which is often near the prime lending rate. ACME's cost of debt that it pays in interest is 9%. However, since ACME can take a tax deduction for the interest expense, its actual cost of debt capital is 5.4% (9% interest cost less 40% in reduced taxes). For every $100 ACME pays in interest expense to the bank, its income tax obligation is lowered by $40 because interest is a business expense that lowers taxable income. Thus, ACME's after-tax interest expense is $60 ($100 minus $40 in reduced taxes).

In order for a business to raise equity capital (selling stock to investors), it expects to provide the shareholders a rate of return. As previously discussed, stocks of large public companies have had average returns of 10% to 12% per year to the shareholders over an extended time period. Small public company stocks have traditionally yielded 15% to 20% to shareholders. Since closely held companies are frequently more risky than small public companies, most private businesses must offer a rate of return to shareholders exceeding the returns of small public stocks. Let's say that a closely held business is raising capital by selling stock. The return a company expects to give its investors (stockholders) in order to attract their capital is called the company's *cost of equity*.

Therefore, a company has a cost of debt capital and a cost of equity capital. Combined, they are referred to as a company's *cost of capital*. The cost of debt is less than the cost of equity as illustrated above. Management of a business can maximize the shareholders' returns by using a blend of debt financing (less expensive) and equity capital (more expensive). Say that a prospective buyer of a business must raise $10 million to acquire the company. If it raised the entire $10 million from the sale of stock, it would have to pay those shareholders a rate of return of, say, 20%. Or, it could raise a portion of the $10 million by borrowing from a bank at, say, an after-tax interest cost of 5%. Obviously, the cost of debt is significantly less than the cost of equity. If management borrows $5 million from the bank and raises another $5 million through the sale of stock, its overall cost of capital is significantly lower than if the company raised the entire $10 million from the sale of stock. This comparison is presented below:

Blended Capital Structure of Debt and Equity

Type of Capital	Amount ($ million)	Percent	Cost of Capital	Weighted Average Cost of Capital
Debt	$ 5	50%	5% (after-tax)	2.5%
Equity	5	50	20	10.0
Debt and Equity	10	100	N/A	12.5

No Debt in Capital Structure

Type of Capital	Amount ($ million)	Percent	Cost of Capital
Equity	$10	100%	**20%**

The above illustrates that with the proper blending of debt and equity capital, management can decrease its overall cost of capital from 20% to 12.5%. This has the effect of increasing the shareholders' rate of return. It also has a positive effect on the value of the company's stock.

(This concept of different returns for different types of capital and the respective weightings is called the *band of investment* methodology when used in real estate appraisals.)

The relevance of all this to business valuation is that if a particular company does not already have the proper blend of debt and equity capital, a valuation may be performed and have an incorrect result unless a more sophisticated debt-free analysis is done. The direct equity methodology does not take into account an optimal blend of debt and equity (unless the business already happens to have it). Consequently, the result of a valuation using the direct equity methodology may result in an incorrect value. However, if the business already has an appropriate blend of capital, the direct equity method is a simpler valuation methodology and produces a correct value result. In addition, buyers of smaller private companies do not necessarily take capital structure into account when making purchase decisions, so a debt-free analysis may not be necessary for these companies to determine fair market value.

Victoria's research indicates that ACME does not have the ideal capital structure. Therefore, she concludes that a debt-free methodology is necessary to arrive at a proper value of ACME. This methodology determines the earnings of ACME without regard to its debt service. Thus, net income on a debt-free basis will be higher than the company's net income, which typically includes interest expense. The resulting higher value using the debt-free methodology is not only for equity holders but also debt holders. This combined value of equity and debt is known as the *market value of invested capital* (MVIC). Once the value of ACME's MVIC is determined, then the value of debt capital is subtracted resulting in the value of ACME's equity. Victoria summarizes this concept for Bob. The debt-free methodology results initially in the combined value of equity and debt (total invested capital) of the business. Interest bearing debt is then subtracted to determine the value of the company's equity. This methodology is more complicated but it is frequently necessary to obtain a correct valuation when the business's debt and equity blend is not optimal.

ADJUSTMENTS TO EARNINGS FOR VALUATION PURPOSES

As previously mentioned, financial statements of private companies sometimes do not reflect the true profitability. Victoria tells Bob that valuation adjustments to the financial statements are sometimes necessary.

These adjustments fall into two categories. The first type of adjustment is the elimination of unusual or nonrecurring items. These adjustments eliminate the effect of past events that are not expected to occur again in the future, such as a profit center that has been eliminated, legal expenses that were incurred to defend an extraordinary lawsuit, or a nonrecurring capital gain from the sale of an asset. A buyer of the business does not expect these items to recur in the future and, therefore, they are eliminated. The second type of adjustment are the economic adjustments. These include adjustments to expenses that are not reflected at their market values, such as the officers' compensation being paid at an above-market amount, the company's rent expense being paid on a shareholder-owned building at an amount different than market rent, or the shareholder's extra perquisites being expensed by the business. In addition, some closely held businesses fail to report all of their revenues and these amounts should be considered in the adjustments. Any expenses related to nonoperating assets (e.g., a ski condominium) would also be eliminated.

After the valuator identifies the adjustments, the reported earnings of the company are modified to reflect the economic earnings of the business on an ongoing basis.

In the case of ACME, Victoria determines that officers' compensation actually being paid is in excess of the amount the business would need to pay by replacing the family members. Thus, officers' compensation expense is reduced to the market level and earnings increased accordingly. In addition, Bob owns some of the factory locations personally. Victoria also determines that ACME is not paying market rents to Bob, and she makes the corresponding adjustment to rent expense. As reflected in Exhibit 18.2, ACME has elected to be treated as an S corporation for income tax purposes. Thus, ACME does not pay income taxes since the income is reported on Bob's personal income tax return. Bob pays the income taxes instead of the corporation. Victoria determines that the most likely buyer of ACME would be a large corporation that would not be able to maintain ACME's S corporation tax status. (The most likely buyer is a C corporation that pays its own taxes.) Therefore, Victoria makes an economic adjustment to ACME's pro forma income statement to include income tax expense. The after-tax income is what a typical buyer expects to earn from purchasing this business. After these adjustments are made on a pro forma income statement, the result indicates ACME's true profitability to a typical buyer of the business.

Once Victoria determines ACME's actual earnings base, she continues her appraisal by applying the most appropriate valuation methodologies for the business.

INCOME APPROACH: DISCOUNTED CASH FLOW METHOD

As previously discussed, the income approach is based on the concept that the value of an asset today represents its perceived future benefits discounted to present value. Victoria uses the discounted cash flow (DCF) methodology in her valuation. This method forecasts ACME's cash flows into the future and discounts them to their present value. In addition, this method assumes that ACME will be sold at some point in the future and the owner will receive the sales proceeds at that time. The estimated future sales price, also know as the *residual value* (or terminal value), is also discounted back to present value. The sum of the present values of future cash flows and the residual value are added together to determine the value of ACME. This concept is summarized here:

> *Discounted Cash Flow Valuation Method (simplified)*
>
> Annual future cash flows, discounted to present value
>
> + Future residual value of the company, discounted to present value
> ——
> = Value (today)

This methodology can be applied to different forms of earnings—net income, cash flow to equity holders, or debt-free cash flow. Many business valuators prefer to use cash flows as the earnings base rather than net income because it is cash flow that is available for shareholder distributions. As previously discussed, cash flows may be determined after the inclusion of debt costs (referred to as *equity net cash flow*) or on a debt-free basis (referred to as *invested capital net cash flow*). The formulas for these types of cash flows are presented below. The use of either type of cash flow is valid when the appropriate discount rate is applied in the DCF model.

Equity Net Cash Flow

After-tax net income
+ Depreciation and amortization (noncash) expenses
− Capital expenditures
− Increases (or + decreases) in working capital requirements
+ Increases (or − decreases) in long-term debt

= Net cash flow to equity holders

Invested Capital Net Cash Flow

After-tax net income
+ Depreciation and amortication (noncash) expenses
− Capital expenditures
− Increases (or + decreases) in working capital requirements
+ Interest expense × (1 minus tax rate)

= Net cash flow to holders of total invested capital (debt and equity)

Application of DCF Model

Type of Income Stream	Type of Discount Rate
Equity net cash flow	Cost of equity
Invested capital net cash flow	Weighted average cost of capital

A common error in the income approach to valuation is improperly matching the income stream and discount rate. The equity net cash flow represents the return on investment to the equity holders. Thus, the appropriate discount rate in the DCF model is the company's cost of equity. The invested capital net cash flow is the rate of return to all holders of invested capital and, therefore, the company's weighted average cost of capital should be used.

Projected Financial Statements

Management of ACME prepared a financial projection and discusses it and the underlying assumptions with Victoria. Management's financial projections are presented in Exhibits 18.5, 18.6, and 18.7. Key assumptions incorporated into the projections include:

- Sales would grow 12% in 2001 and 2002, 11% in 2003 and 2004, and 10% in 2005.
- Costs of goods sold are 69% of sales.
- Operating expenses (exclusive of officers' salaries) are 12% of sales.
- Officers' salaries (at market) are 3.1% of sales.
- The 2001 capital expenditures are $2.8 million and increase thereafter 5% per year.
- The company needs a minimum cash balance of $200,000.

EXHIBIT 18.5 **ACME Manufacturing Inc.: Projected income statements 2001–2005.**

	($million)					
	Pro Forma	**2001**	**2002**	**2003**	**2004**	**2005**
Revenue	$50.29	$56.32	$63.08	$70.02	$77.72	$85.50
Cost of goods sold	34.58	38.86	43.53	48.32	53.63	58.99
Gross profit	15.70	17.46	19.56	21.71	24.09	26.50
Operating expenses	5.95	6.76	7.57	8.40	9.33	10.26
Officers' salary	1.54	1.75	1.96	2.17	2.41	2.65
Depreciation & amortization	1.00	0.88	1.01	1.14	1.28	1.43
Interest expense	0.84	1.04	1.10	1.14	1.21	1.28
Operating profit	6.37	7.03	7.92	8.85	9.87	10.88
Other expenses/(income)	(0.30)	(0.21)	(0.21)	(0.21)	(0.21)	(0.21)
Income before taxes	6.66	7.24	8.13	9.06	10.08	11.09
Income taxes	2.67	2.90	3.25	3.63	4.03	4.44
Adjusted net income	$4.00	$4.34	$4.88	$5.44	$6.05	$6.65

	Common Size					
	Pro Forma	**2001**	**2002**	**2003**	**2004**	**2005**
Revenue	100.0%	100.0%	100.0%	100.0%	100.0%	100.0%
Cost of goods sold	68.8	69.0	69.0	69.0	69.0	69.0
Gross profit	31.2	31.0	31.0	31.0	31.0	31.0
Operating expenses	11.8	12.0	12.0	12.0	12.0	12.0
Officers' salary	3.1	3.1	3.1	3.1	3.1	3.1
Depreciation & amortization	2.0	1.6	1.6	1.6	1.6	1.7
Interest expense	1.7	1.8	1.7	1.6	1.6	1.5
Operating profit	12.7	12.5	12.6	12.6	12.7	12.7
Other expenses/(income)	−0.6	−0.4	−0.3	−0.3	−0.3	−0.2
Income before taxes	13.2	12.9	12.9	12.9	13.0	13.0
Income taxes	5.3	5.1	5.2	5.2	5.2	5.2
Adjusted net income	8.0%	7.7%	7.7%	7.8%	7.8%	7.8%

- The dividend payout ratio (the amount of cash flows actually distributed to shareholders; the remainder is reinvested in the company) ranges from 55% to 65% per year.

Residual Value

The DCF valuation methodology assumes the company will be sold at some point in the future and the business owner will receive the proceeds. Victoria assumes ACME will be sold five years in the future, on December 31, 2005. (Five years is common among analysts for established businesses. Start-up businesses may require financial projections for a longer period such as 10 years until the company's earnings become stable.) The value of a company at the end of the financial forecast is the residual value. The residual value of

EXHIBIT 18.6 ACME Manufacturing Inc.: Projected invested capital net cash flows 2001–2005.

	($million)				
	2001	**2002**	**2003**	**2004**	**2005**
Projected after-tax income	$4.35	$4.88	$5.44	$6.05	$6.65
Projected interest expense	1.04	1.10	1.14	1.21	1.28
Tax shield of interest expense	(0.42)	(0.44)	(0.45)	(0.48)	(0.51)
Common stock dividend adjustment	(0.30)	(0.26)	—	—	—
Projected depreciation/amortization	0.88	1.01	1.14	1.29	1.43
After-tax gross cash flow to invested capital	5.55	6.28	7.26	8.06	8.86
± Increase/decrease in working capital (excluding interest-bearing ST debt)	(0.54)	(0.63)	(0.65)	(0.72)	(0.73)
± Increase/decrease in investments	(2.80)	(2.94)	(3.09)	(3.24)	(3.40)
± Increase/decrease in other assets	(0.13)	(0.15)	(0.16)	(0.18)	(0.20)
± Increase/decrease in other liabilities	—	—	—	—	—
Cash available for financing	2.08	2.57	3.37	3.92	4.53
– Preferred stock dividends	—	—	—	—	—
Net cash flow	2.08	2.57	3.37	3.92	4.53
+ Beginning cash balance	0.04	0.20	0.20	0.20	0.20
Preliminary cash available	2.12	2.77	3.57	4.12	4.73
– Minimum required cash balance	(0.20)	(0.20)	(0.20)	(0.20)	(0.20)
Available for dividend to invested capital, net free cash flow	$1.92	$2.57	$3.37	$3.92	$4.53

ACME is estimated based on the net cash flows in 2005 and then increasing them by the estimated sustainable (long-term) earnings growth rate. For the projection's final year, items such as interest expense and depreciation need to be stated at their stabilized ongoing amounts since the hypothetical new buyer at December 31, 2005, is expecting to receive a stabilized annual net cash flow using this residual value methodology. The result of this portion of the DCF analysis is the estimated net cash flows someone would expect ACME to earn in 2006. The presumption is that the company will be sold at the end of 2005, its earnings have stabilized, and a new owner can expect to receive the 2006 cash flows.

A multiple is applied to ACME's estimated 2006 net cash flow in order to determine the residual value at the end of 2005. The multiple is based on the inverse of the company's weighted average cost of capital less the estimated sustainable long-term earnings growth rate. This is called a *capitalization rate* (or capitalization factor) and is illustrated:

$$\text{Capitalization rate} = \text{Discount rate} - \text{Sustainable long-term earnings growth rate}$$

$$\text{Price-earnings (P/E) multiple} = \frac{1}{\text{Capitalization rate}}$$

EXHIBIT 18.7 ACME Manufacturing Inc.: Projected balance sheets 2001–2005.

	Adjusted 2000	2001	2002	2003	2004	2005
			($million)			
Cash	$ 0.04	$ 0.20	$ 0.20	$ 0.23	$ 0.24	$ 0.40
Accounts receivable	6.87	7.69	8.61	9.55	10.61	11.67
Inventory	4.45	4.98	5.58	6.19	6.88	7.56
Other current assets	0.34	0.38	0.42	0.47	0.52	0.57
Total current assets	11.69	13.24	14.81	16.44	18.24	20.20
Fixed assets	14.34	17.14	20.08	23.16	26.40	29.80
Accumulated depreciation	(2.94)	(3.82)	(4.83)	(5.97)	(7.26)	(8.69)
Net fixed assets	11.40	13.32	15.25	17.19	19.15	21.12
Other assets	1.33	1.47	1.61	1.77	1.95	2.15
Total assets	$24.42	$28.03	$31.67	$35.41	$39.34	$43.46
Accounts payable	$ 4.55	$ 5.12	$ 5.74	$ 6.37	$ 7.07	$ 7.77
Notes payable	—	0.30	0.26	—	—	—
Current portion LTD	4.58	3.28	3.45	3.63	3.85	4.07
Other current liabilities	2.37	2.66	2.97	3.30	3.66	4.03
Total current liabilities	11.50	11.35	12.42	13.29	14.58	15.87
Long-term debt	5.83	7.65	8.04	8.46	8.98	9.49
Total liabilities	17.33	19.00	20.46	21.75	23.57	25.36
Equity	7.09	9.03	11.21	13.66	15.77	18.10
Total liabilities & equity	$24.42	$28.03	$31.67	$35.41	$39.34	$43.46

Required Discount Rate (Rate of Return)

As previously discussed, since ACME is being analyzed on a debt-free basis, Victoria uses the *weighted average cost of capital* (WACC) as the discount rate. The WACC incorporates the cost of debt and the cost of equity using market evidence and weights them based on capital structure. Each element of the weighted average cost of capital as it applies to ACME is discussed in the following sections.

Cost of Equity

As discussed earlier in this chapter, an investor has many places to invest his or her funds. A rational investor expects a higher rate of return when an investment carries more risks. In developing ACME's rate of return on equity capital, Victoria uses the modified capital asset pricing model (CAPM) that is defined as:

Equity rate of return = Risk-free rate + (Equity risk premium × Beta)

+ Size risk premium + Specific company risk premium

Investments in closely held businesses are widely considered to be long-term rather than short-term investments. Accordingly, the *risk-free rate,* the first element in the modified CAPM, is based on the 20-year U.S. Treasury bond yield as of the valuation date. U.S. Treasuries are considered risk-free investments and the 20-year bond is considered a long-term investment benchmark for purposes of valuing closely held businesses. At the valuation date, the risk-free rate is 6.4%.

Victoria explains that the second element of the modified CAPM is the *equity risk premium.* The equity risk premium is the additional rate of return investors in stocks require above a risk-free rate of return because of the higher risks of investing in equities. Ibbotson Associates of Chicago, Illinois, has performed annual empirical studies of the equity risk premium that investors have received dating back to 1926. As of ACME's valuation date, the historic equity risk premium since 1926 has been 8.1% above the risk-free rate. Again, since investments in closely held businesses are considered long term, the equity risk premium is also measured on a long-term basis.

The CAPM uses the sensitivity of a company (investment) as compared to swings in the overall investment market. The risk that is common to all investment securities that cannot be eliminated through diversification is called *systematic risk.* When using CAPM, the systematic risk of a particular investment is measured by *beta.* Beta is a measure of the relationship between the returns on an individual investment and the returns of the overall market as typically measured by an index such as the Standard & Poor's 500. For example, the market prices of some investments have a tendency to rise and fall faster than the overall market. The base measure of beta is 1.0. When an investment's beta is greater than 1.0, its returns have tended to be more than the market returns. Also, the investment's losses have tended to be greater than the market's losses. An investment with a beta of less than 1.0 has had returns that tend to be less than the market returns. In summary, beta measures an investment's return volatility as compared to the overall market. If an investment has a beta greater than 1.0, its returns are more volatile and carry more risk than the market. If beta is less than 1.0, its returns are less volatile and carry less risk than the market.

One way to estimate the beta of a closely held company is to use the average beta of guideline publicly traded companies. Beta is a coefficient used by financial analysts that adjusts the general equity risk premium to a specific investment in the CAPM. A complete discussion of beta is beyond the scope of this chapter but it is widely available in finance literature. The beta of publicly traded companies is generally available from investment publications and from empirical studies such as the one conducted by Ibbotson Associates.

Victoria's research analysis indicates the average beta of publicly traded companies in ACME's industry is 0.99 as of the valuation date. She concludes that this average is a reasonable estimate of ACME's beta for use in the CAPM.

Therefore, the equity risk premium for ACME is 8.0% (the general equity risk premium of 8.1% multiplied by the beta of 0.99).

Victoria tells Bob that the capital asset pricing model is widely used by analysts for investment management where a specific investment's risks can be eliminated through portfolio diversification. Business valuation theory uses CAPM but modifies it to consider a specific company's unsystematic risks in addition to the systematic risks. *Unsystematic risk* represents those risks uniquely associated with an investment that cannot be avoided through portfolio diversification. ACME's unsystematic risks are discussed next.

Studies have shown that investments in small companies typically have more risk than those in large companies. Generally, small company earnings and stock prices are more volatile than those of larger companies. Over the long term, investors in smaller companies have received higher rates of return than investors in the larger Standard & Poor's (S&P) 500 companies. Empirical data from Ibbotson Associates shows that the smallest 20% of public companies have yielded an extra 2.2% rate of return above the returns of S&P 500 companies since 1926. Therefore, Victoria adds a premium of 2.2% to ACME's required rate of return for the risks associated with its size as compared to S&P 500 companies.

Finally, the differences between ACME and small publicly traded companies are considered. Victoria previously identified the quantitative and qualitative attributes of ACME that are considered negative and positive risk factors for the company. These were presented earlier in the chapter. After reviewing her quantitative and qualitative analyses, she determines that ACME is somewhat more risky than small public companies. In Victoria's judgment, she adds a 2% specific company risk premium as an additional required rate of return for an investor in ACME.

In summary, Victoria determines ACME's cost of equity using the modified CAPM as shown Exhibit 18.8.

Cost of Debt

Victoria analyzes ACME's audited financial statements, including the footnotes, and interviews management to determine the company's interest rate on long-term financing was 9%. This was comparable to market interest rates. Since interest paid by the company is tax deductible, the after-tax effective

**EXHIBIT 18.8   ACME Manufacturing Inc.:
Cost of equity.**

Risk-free rate		6.4%
Overall equity risk premium	8.1%	
Multiply by Beta	0.99	
ACME's equity risk premium		8.0%
Small company risk premium		2.2%
Specific company risk premium		2.0%
ACME's cost of equity		18.6%

EXHIBIT 18.9 ACME Manufacturing Inc.: Cost of debt.

ACME's borrowing rate	9.0%
Multiply by the tax effect (1 − Tax rate of 40%)	60%
ACME's cost of debt	5.4%

interest rate is less than 9%. Victoria determines that ACME is in the 40% income tax bracket. Therefore, ACME's after-tax cost of debt is 5.4% as presented in Exhibit 18.9.

Weighted Average Cost of Capital

Victoria estimates the optimal capital structure for ACME as 40% debt and 60% equity based on her analysis of the average capital structures of publicly traded companies and then considering that ACME does not have the same access to capital sources as public companies.

Based on this weighting between debt and equity, ACME's weighted average cost of capital is 13.3%. The calculation is presented in Exhibit 18.10.

Discounted Cash-Flow Calculation

As previously discussed, ACME's forecasted invested capital net cash flows for 2001 to 2005 are discounted to present value as of the December 31, 2000, valuation date. The discount rate is ACME's weighted average cost of capital—13.3%. In addition, the residual value of ACME in 2005 is discounted to present value using the same rate.

Victoria prepares Exhibit 18.11 that presents the resulting value from discounting the cash flows for the five-year period and also discounting the residual value. It assumes that the annual cash flows are earned equally throughout each year. Therefore, the present value calculation for the annual cash flows uses the middle of each year (June 30) to determine the length of time for the present value calculation. This is called the mid-year convention. For example,

EXHIBIT 18.10 ACME Manufacturing Inc.: Weighted average cost of capital.

Cost of equity (above)	18.6%	
Equity weighting	60%	
		11.1%
Cost of debt (above)	5.4%	
Debt weighting	40%	
		2.2%
ACME's weighted average cost of capital		13.3%

EXHIBIT 18.11   ACME Manufacturing Inc.: DCF method of valuation as of December 31, 2000.

Forecast Year	(Exhibit 18.6) Projected Cash Flows	WACC	Present Value
2001	$1,921,000	13.3%	$ 1,804,731
2002	2,565,000	13.3%	2,126,878
2003	3,367,000	13.3%	2,464,157
2004	3,917,000	13.3%	2,530,165
2005	4,533,000	13.3%	2,584,349
Residual value (see below)		13.3%	30,591,919
Value of invested capital			42,102,198
Less: debt capital			(10,411,554)
Value of equity			$31,690,644
Value of equity (rounded)			$31,700,000

Residual Value at December 31, 2005

2005 Projected cash flow		$4,533,000
Estimated sustainable growth rate		1.05
2006 Projected cash flow		4,759,650
Price multiple		
WACC (discount rate)	13.3%	
Less: Sustainable growth rate	−5.0%	
Capitalization rate	8.3%	
Multiple (inverse of capitalization rate)		12
Residual value at December 31, 2005		$57,115,800
Present value of residual value		$30,591,919

the first forecasted year (2001) is discounted one-half year, rather than one complete year, to the valuation date of December 31, 2000.

The residual value is based on the expected invested capital net cash flow in the last year of the projection (2005) of $4.533 million. Victoria estimates ACME's *long-term sustainable* earnings growth rate at 5% annually. Accordingly, the cash flow for 2006 is estimated at $4.760 million ($4.533 million × 1.05). The multiple Victoria applies for the residual year is 12. The calculation for the multiple is presented in Exhibit 18.11. ACME's residual value at December 31, 2005, is estimated as $57.1 million.

The present values of the five years of cash flows are added together plus the present value of the residual value. These items represent the anticipated future benefits to all capital holders at December 31, 2000. The sum of the present values represents the market value of the total invested capital (MVIC) of $42.1 million. ACME's interest bearing debt of $10.4 million is subtracted resulting in $31.7 million for the value of ACME's common stock as of December 31, 2000, on an as-if-freely-traded basis. Since this amount is based on rates of return of freely traded marketable securities, Victoria will take a valuation discount for lack of liquidity at the end of her analysis.

Because Victoria made adjustments to the 2000 pro forma income statement (see the pro forma column in Exhibit 18.5) for discretionary items (officers' compensation and rent expense) and income tax expense, the 2000 pro forma earnings and resulting value of $31.7 million represents a value for a control (rather than a minority) equity interest.

In summary, the discounted cash flow methodology determines ACME's value today, which represents an owner's perceived future benefits discounted to the present value. The DCF method forecasts ACME's cash flows into the future and discounts them to their present value. In addition, this method assumes that the owner will sell the company at some point in the future and receive the sale price. The estimated future sale price is also discounted back to present value. The present values of future earnings and future sale price are added together to determine the value of ACME.

MARKET APPROACH: PUBLICLY TRADED GUIDELINE—COMPANIES METHOD

Bob asks Victoria to explain the market approach to determining value. She says the market approach is a general way of determining a value by comparing the asset to similar assets that have been sold. In business valuation, this can be done by looking for any prior arm's-length sales of the company's stock, sales of other companies, or prices of shares in publicly traded companies. In the latter two instances, careful analysis of the other companies must be done to determine if they would properly serve as guidelines under this approach. The American Society of Appraisers describes *guideline companies* as those "companies that provide a reasonable basis for comparison to the investment characteristics of the company being valued. Ideal guideline companies are in the same industry as the company being valued; but if there is insufficient transaction evidence available in the same industry it may be necessary to select companies with an underlying similarity of relevant investment characteristics (risks) such as markets, products, growth, cyclical variability and other salient factors."[2]

In ACME's case, there have never been any prior sales of corporate stock. In addition, Victoria is unable to find any sales of guideline companies in which adequate information is available. However, she is able to identify five publicly traded companies that could potentially serve as guidelines under the market approach.

Having identified the list of potential public companies through database searches, Victoria performs a qualitative and quantitative analyses on the companies to determine whether they should serve as guideline companies. This analysis results in the selection of five companies.

Victoria's analysis looks at the public companies' balance sheets and income statements over several years, growth rates, margins, returns on assets and equity, and financial ratios. She also analyzes various share price multiples of the public companies such as:

- Market value of invested capital to sales.
- Market value of invested capital to earnings before interest, taxes, depreciation, and amortization (EBITDA).
- Market value of invested capital to earnings before interest and taxes (EBIT).
- Market value of equity to pretax income.
- Market value of equity to net income.
- Market value of equity to cash flow.
- Market value of equity to book value.

Based on her detailed analyses of the guideline companies and comparing them to ACME, Victoria determines that the following price multiples of the public companies appear to be most correlated and relevant for application to ACME: market value of invested capital to sales, market value of invested capital to EBITDA, market value of invested capital to EBIT, and market value of equity to pretax income.

The median price multiples for the five public companies are:

	Median Price Multiple
Market value of invested capital to sales	0.54
Market value of invested capital to EBITDA	5.80
Market value of invested capital to EBIT	7.26
Market value of equity to pre-tax income	6.72

Then Victoria applies the median price multiples to ACME. See Exhibit 18.12 for her calculations. Her analysis indicates a value of ACME's equity at December 31, 2000, of $35.2 million on an as-if-freely-traded basis.

Since Victoria made adjustments to the 2000 income statement (see the resulting pro forma column in Exhibit 18.5) for discretionary items (officers' compensation and rent expense), she explains that the 2000 earnings and resulting value of $35.2 million represents a value to an owner of a *control* equity interest. Thus, Victoria concludes that there is no need to add a control premium. A *control premium* is an upward adjustment to the value that reflects the power of control as compared to the value of a noncontrol equity interest. (However, many analysts believe that a control premium would be necessary simply because of the use of public minority share multiples even though the income was adjusted upward to reflect the discretionary expenses of a control owner. Many of these people, however, would not use the median multiple of the public companies as Victoria did but adjust it [usually down]

EXHIBIT 18.12 ACME Manufacturing Inc.: Publicly Traded Guideline Co. method of valuation.

			ACME ($million)				
Price Multiple	Median Multiple of Guidelines	Pro Forma Amounts[a]		Market Value of Invested Capital	Less: Debt	Market Value of Equity	Weight	Weighted Average
Market value of invested capital to sales	0.54	Sales	$50.29	$27.16	$10.41	$16.75	25%	$ 4.19
Market value of invested capital to EBITDA	5.80	EBITDA	8.21	47.62	10.41	37.21	25%	9.30
Market value of invested capital to EBIT	7.26	EBIT	7.21	52.34	10.41	41.93	25%	10.48
Market value of equity to pretax income	6.72	Pretax income	6.66	N/A	N/A	44.76	25%	11.19
Value of Equity								$35.16

[a] See Exhibit 18.5 for 2000 pro forma amounts after valuation adjustments were made.

for fundamental differences between the selected public companies and the private business. Thus, if these analysts first adjust the price multiple downward as a fundamental adjustment and then apply an upward control premium, the result may be similar to Victoria's valuation conclusion.)

However, since the $35.2 million value is based on freely traded marketable securities, Victoria will take a valuation discount for lack of liquidity at the end of her analysis.

RECONCILIATION OF VALUATION METHODS

The results of Victoria's valuation analysis are:

Method	Value
Income approach	$31.7 million
Market approach	35.2 million
Average	33.5 million

Victoria chooses to weigh each method equally resulting in an average value of $33.5 million. This value represents 100% of the common stock of ACME at December 31, 2000, on an as-if-freely-traded and control basis.

DISCOUNT FOR LACK OF LIQUIDITY

A *freely traded* basis means an investment can be sold and converted to cash within several days. When shares of stock are sold on a public exchange, the seller will usually receive cash within a few days making them freely traded investments. Under the income approach, Victoria used rates of returns from publicly traded securities. Under the market approach, she used price multiples of publicly traded shares. Thus, the values under both of Victoria's approaches result in as-if-freely-traded values. Because it would likely take Bob (or any other owner of the business) several months or longer to sell ACME and receive cash, the liquidity of an investment in ACME's shares is significantly different than the liquidity of publicly traded shares of stock. Therefore, Victoria takes a discount from the as-if-freely-traded value of $33.5 million for ACME's equity.

The preceding provides the rationale for applying a discount for lack of liquidity. However, the amount of the discount must be quantified. The closest empirical evidence to quantify the discount comes from studies of restricted public stock prices and studies of share prices just prior to companies' initial public offerings. These studies indicate discounts for lack of marketability of 35% to 45% on average. Since these studies relate to minority equity positions in the companies instead of control positions, Victoria uses a discount below the averages of the studies. Based on her analysis and judgment, she applies a 10% lack of liquidity discount to the as-if-freely-traded $33.5 million equity value. This represents the discount an investor would require for buying shares in ACME instead of an investment that is freely traded.

VALUATION CONCLUSION FOR ACME

Victoria concludes that the fair market value of the common stock of ACME as of December 31, 2000, was $30,150,000 ($33.5 million less 10% discount for lack of liquidity).

VALUING MINORITY INTERESTS

The preceding ACME case study valued 100% of the equity (stock) in the business. Had Bob owned only, say, 25% of the common stock, Victoria would have to apply some additional analysis to value his minority interest. With a 25% interest, Bob would no longer have the ability to control the company.

A *minority interest* is a business ownership of less than 50% of the voting shares. The owner of a minority interest in most private businesses cannot control the company. A *control interest* in a company has the power to direct management and policies of a business usually through ownership of enough shares to influence voting and other decisions. Intuitively, someone would rather own a control interest in a private business (51%) instead of a minority interest (49%) because of the power to control the company. Buyers would typically pay a significantly different price when comparing a 51% interest to a 49% interest. This phenomenon is called a *discount for lack of control* (or minority discount).

The second area of additional analysis for Victoria would be for the typical difficulty in selling a minority interest in a closely held business. *Marketability* is the ability to quickly convert property (an investment) to cash at minimal cost. Hypothetically, if Bob owns only 25% of ACME's stock and someone else owns the other 75%, the number of buyers interested in buying Bob's shares is significantly less than if he owns 100%. Since Bob actually owns the entire company, he has several ways to sell it. For example, he can sell the company through an investment banker or business broker. He can also take the company public. If Bob hypothetically only owns 25% of ACME's stock, these options are not realistically available to him. Therefore, his minority interest is less marketable. Intuitively, investors prefer owning marketable investments over nonmarketable ones. Therefore, buyers of minority interests in private companies typically pay less since the shares are not marketable. This is called a *discount for lack of marketability.*

In valuing a minority interest, a major consideration is the timing and amount of the anticipated future economic benefits flowing directly to the minority owner. This consists of the company's periodic distributions to the minority owner and the estimated holding period for owning the equity interest until it is sold and the sales proceeds are received. We saw through the DCF model that the value of the asset is the present value of the expected future benefits. In valuing a minority interest, the emphasis shifts toward the future benefits flowing to the minority shareholder as opposed to the business overall. For example, if a minority owner expects not to receive any distributions from the business for 10 years even though the business is profitable, this is significantly different from a business that makes annual shareholder distributions of the profits. The values in these two situations would be considerably different.

BUSINESS VALUATION STANDARDS

Professional business appraisers follow certain standards when doing business valuations. Business valuation standards include the following:

> Uniform Standards for Professional Appraisal Practice—The Appraisal Foundation.
>
> Standards issued by various membership organizations such as American Society of Appraisers, Institute of Business Appraisers, and National Association of Certified Valuation Analysts.

VALUE ENGINEERING

Just as the CEO of a public company tries to enhance the value of the shares, management of a private company can work on increasing the value of the business in anticipation of a future sale. Certain factors can have a significant effect on the value of a typical closely held business. Management can focus on these factors to potentially increase the future value of the business. Some of the factors are obvious, while some are not. They include the following:

- Decrease expenses (increases cash flow/income).
- Increase revenues (increases cash flow/income).
- Significantly increase the earnings growth rate (may increase earnings projections, lower capitalization rate due to growth factor).
- Eliminate the owners' personal expenses and perquisites (increases cash flow/ income, lowers buyer risk of inaccurate financial statements).
- Report all income on the financial statements and tax return (increases cash flow/income).
- Develop the management team for the possibility that the current owner(s) may leave the business upon a sale (lowers buyer risk of earnings volatility).
- Plan for the current owner-managers' continuing employment under the new owner for a fixed period (lowers buyer risk of earnings volatility and loss of customers, employees, and vendors).

- Have annual financial statements audited or reviewed by a certified public accountant and improve interim financial reporting (lowers buyer risk of inaccurate financial statements).

- Develop a list of potential synergistic buyers and identify the ones with the most to gain from an acquisition of the subject company (search for the highest synergistic value to be paid).

- Decrease dependency on major customers and vendors (lowers buyer risk of earnings volatility in the event of the loss of any of these customers or vendors).

- Begin assembly of key business information for potential buyers (lowers buyer risk of perceptions of potential earnings volatility without having such knowledge).

- Improve any existing poor financial statistics or ratios (lowers buyer financial risk).

Public companies report earnings and performance on a quarterly basis and the share prices frequently react quickly. On the other hand, private company values generally react more slowly to changes. Thus, management may need to work on value improvement factors one to two years in advance of marketing a business.

SUMMARY

The fair market value of a private business is essentially an estimate of the price that a willing buyer would pay and a willing seller would accept. Buyers have different motives for buying a business. Financial buyers are looking for a return on their investment. Strategic buyers are usually looking to integrate their company with the business for unique strategic reasons. Financial buyers pay fair market value while strategic buyers usually pay a price reflective of the unique strategic advantages to the specific buyer. Often, strategic buyers pay more than fair market value. Although it is possible to conduct a business valuation that is not overly complex, the question remains whether the resulting value is accurate. Many variables go into a valuation analysis. A business valuation is both a quantitative and qualitative process that is focused on assessing investment risk and investment return. It is largely an assessment of the risks a buyer is taking in acquiring and owning the company. In addition, a valuation attempts to project the earnings an owner of the business can expect in the future as a return on investment.

Author's Note.   This chapter is not intended to be a complete text on business valuation. It is meant to illustrate through examples many of the fundamentals of business valuation and their application. The proper application of valuation theory depends on the actual facts and circumstances of the investment being valued.

FOR FURTHER READING

Desmond, G. and J. Marcell, *Handbook of Small Business Valuation Formulas and Rules of Thumb*, 3rd ed. (Los Angeles: Valuation Press, 1993).

Pratt, S., R. Reilly, and R. Schweihs, *Valuing a Business: The Analysis and Appraisal of Closely Held Companies*, 4th ed. (New York: McGraw-Hill, 2000).

Pratt, S., R. Reilly, and R. Schweihs, *Valuing Small Businesses and Professional Practices*, 3rd ed. (New York: McGraw-Hill, 1998).

Reilly, R. and R. Schweihs, *Valuing Intangible Assets* (New York: McGraw-Hill, 1998).

Smith, G. and R. Parr, *Valuation of Intellectual Property and Intangible Assets* (New York: John Wiley, 2000).

Trugman, G., *Understanding Business Valuation: A Practical Guide to Valuing Small- to Medium-Sized Businesses* (New York: AICPA, 1998).

————, *Handbook of Business Valuation*, 2nd ed. T. West and J. Jones, Eds. (New York: John Wiley, 1999).

————, *Stocks, Bonds, Bills, and Inflation Yearbook Valuation Edition* (Chicago: Ibbotson Associates, published annually).

INTERNET LINKS

www.aicpa.org	American Institute of Certified Public Accountants
www.appraisers.org	American Society of Appraisers
www.appraisalfoundation.org	Appraisal Foundation
www.gofcg.org	Financial Consulting Group
www.ibbotson.com	Ibbotson Associates
www.instbusapp.org	Institute of Business Appraisers
www.nacva.com	National Association of Certified Valuation Analysts

NOTES

1. *International Glossary of Business Valuation Terms,* jointly published by the American Institute of Certified Public Accountants, American Society of Appraisers, Canadian Institute of Chartered Business Valuators, National Association of Certified Valuation Analysts, and Institute of Business Appraisers. Further terminology from this jointly published international glossary is included in glossary at the end of this book.

2. American Society of Appraisers, *Statement on Business Valuation Standards 1.*

Glossary

Accounting exposure: Increases or decreases in assets and liabilities resulting from exchange rate movements, which may not be associated with either current or prospective cash inflows or outflows. Accounting exposure is distinguished from economic exposure where cash inflows and outflows are expected to be associated with exchange rate movements.

Accrual accounting: An accounting method that recognizes revenues as they are earned and expenses as they are incurred. The timing of revenue and expense recognition is not tied to the timing of the inflow and outflow of cash. Accrual accounting is seen as essential in order to develop reliable measures of periodic financial performance.

Acquisition: The purchase—not necessarily for cash—of a controlling interest in a firm.

Activity-based costing: A process of identifying the different activities that generate costs.

Adapter: Typically, a small circuit board inside a computer that lets the computer work with hardware external to the computer. Examples: A network adapter allows a computer to be hooked into a network; a display adapter allows a computer to drive (display text, graphics) a computer monitor.

AICPA: The American Institute of Certified Public Accountants. This is the national professional association of certified public accountants (CPAs).

All-current method: A method of translating foreign-currency financial statements whereby all assets and liabilities are translated at the current (balance sheet date) exchange rate, contributed capital accounts are translated at historical exchange rates (rates in existence when the account balances first arose), and all revenues and expenses are translated at the average exchange rate in existence during the reporting period. Translation adjustments resulting from fluctuating exchange rates are accumulated and reported with accumulated other comprehensive income in shareholders' equity.

Amortization: the periodic, noncash charge used to reduce an intangible asset.

Application Service Providers (ASP): Companies that rent out applications and process data for other companies, similar to service bureaus in the 1960s and 1970s.

Asset (asset-based) approach: A general way of determining a value indication of a business, business ownership interest, or security by using one or more methods based on the value of the assets of that business net of liabilities.

Asset acquisition: an acquisition executed by purchasing the assets of the target firm.

Asymmetric risk: An exposure that results in profits or losses only if the underlying price or economic variable moves in one direction.

At-the-money: The condition of a call or put option when the strike price equals the stock price. Some economists define at-the-money as being the case when the stock price equals the present value of the strike price.

B2C e-commerce: The sale of goods and services between a company and a consumer over the Internet.

Balanced scorecard: A comprehensive set of performance measures intended to capture a more balanced picture of management's success in achieving goals than can be captured by financial measures only.

Bearish: Pessimistic. Anticipating a decrease in an asset value.

Best efforts underwriting: An agency arrangement by which underwriters agree to use best efforts to sell all, or a certain minimum number of, shares of a public offering.

Beta: A measure of systematic risk of a security; the tendency of a security's returns to correlate with swings in the broad market.

Bidder: The firm that initiates a merger or acquisition; the bidder usually retains control of the surviving firm.

Bit: The smallest gradation of data stored in a computer. Technically, a bit is either a 1 or a 0. Computers use groups of bits, called bytes, to represent character data.

Blue-sky laws: State laws regulating securities that provide for licensing brokers/dealers and registering new securities issuances.

Budget: A comprehensive, quantitative plan for utilizing the resources of an entity for some specified period of time—showing planned revenues, expenses, and resulting earnings—together with a planned balance sheet and cash flow statement. If budgets adjust for volume they are called flexible; otherwise, they are static.

Budget entity: Any accounting entity, such as a firm, division, department, or project, for which a budget is prepared.

Budget performance report: An internal accounting report that shows the difference between actual results and expected performance planned in a budget.

Budget review process: The process of evaluating budget proposals and arriving at the master budget.

Budget variance: The difference between the budgeted data and actual results.

Bullish: Optimistic. Anticipating an increase in an asset value.

Business valuation: The act or process of determining the value of a business enterprise or ownership interest therein.

Byte: Typically, eight bits in a computer, which as a unit, represent one character of data. A computer diskette can store 1,400,000 bytes of data, or 1,400,000 characters of data. This represents about 500 pages of single-spaced text.

C+, C++: Programming languages used in the 1990s to program many personal computer and UNIX based applications.

Call option: An asset which gives the owner the right but not the obligation to purchase some other asset for a set price on or up to a specified date.

Capital asset pricing model (CAPM): A model in which the cost of capital for any security or portfolio of securities equals a risk-free rate plus a risk premium that is proportionate to the systematic risk of the security or portfolio.

Capital loss carryover: The excess of capital losses over capital gains that may not be deducted currently but may be carried forward and set off against future capital gains.

Capital structure: The composition of the invested capital of a business enterprise; the mix of debt and equity financing.

Capitalization: The conversion of a single period stream of benefits into value.

Capitalization factor: Any multiple or divisor used to convert anticipated benefits into value.

Capitalization rate: Any divisor (usually expressed as a percentage) used to convert anticipated benefits into value.

Cash flow: Cash that is generated over a period of time by an asset, group of assets, or business enterprise. It may be used in a general sense to encompass various levels of specifically defined cash flows. When the term is used, it should be supplemented by a qualifier (e.g., "discretionary" or "operating") and a definition of exactly what it means in the given valuation context.

Cash settled: A future contract that does not require delivery of the underlying asset upon expiration. Instead of actual delivery, the contract is marked to market, so that one party is compensated in cash by the other for the change in the underlying asset price.

CD: A compact disk, which stores roughly 700,000,000 bytes (700 megabytes) of data in digital format. CDs used in computers and in stereos are identical. A music CD has the capacity to store roughly one hour of sound.

Changes in accounting estimates: Estimates are essential to the implementation of accrual accounting. A typical example would the estimates of useful lives and salvage values that are necessary in computing depreciation. Changes in either useful lives or salvage values would represent changes in accounting estimates.

Changes in accounting principles: A change in the accounting treatment applied to a particular area of accounting. The most common examples would be discretionary changes in inventory and depreciation accounting. A firm might change from the LIFO to the FIFO inventory method or from the accelerated to straight-line method of computing depreciation. Most accounting changes are not discretionary but rather are the result of the mandatory adoption of new accounting standards.

Charges: Commonly used in accounting in referring to expenses and losses.

COBOL: A programming language used prior to the early 1990s to program most business applications.

Comfort letter: Communication from the independent auditor to the underwriter, at the time of registration of securities, which includes information about the auditor's role, auditor's independence, compliance of the financial statements with the

Securities Act of 1933, and any changes in the financial statements subsequent to information included in the Registration Statement.

Comprehensive income: An expanded measure of income that includes items of other comprehensive income in addition to traditional realized net income.

Conglomerate merger: a combination of firms in unrelated industries.

Consolidation: A merger in which an entirely new firm is created.

Constant-dollar method: A method of inflation accounting whereby accounts, which are measured according to historical cost accounting principles, are restated into units of the same purchasing power using the same general price index.

Control: The power to direct the management and policies of a business enterprise.

Control premium: An amount (expressed in either dollar or percentage form) by which the pro rata value of a controlling interest exceeds the pro-rata value of a non-controlling interest in a business enterprise, that reflects the power of control.

Cooling-off period: That period from the filing of a Registration Statement in connection with an IPO (or other public offering) until the effective date of the Registration Statement, during which time the only written information that may be provided to prospective investors is the Prospectus itself.

Core earnings: Earnings exclusive of the effects of nonrecurring items (see sustainable earnings base). Also refers to earnings that only derive from the primary, or core, activities of the firm.

Cost approach: A general way of estimating a value indication of an individual asset by quantifying the amount of money that would be required to replace the future service capability of that asset.

Cost driver: The cause of the cost of an activity.

Cost of capital: The expected rate of return (discount rate) that the market requires in order to attract funds to a particular investment.

CPU: The Central Processing Unit of a computer. The CPU is the computer's equivalent to its brain: All logical operations occur in the CPU, and the CPU directs all other hardware associated with the computer.

Credit risk: The loss potential that would result from the inability of a counterparty to satisfy the terms of the foreign currency derivative.

CRT: A Cathode Ray Tube is very similar to the picture tube in a television set. Most computer monitors use CRT technology, which is relatively cheap.

Currency swap: An exchange of currencies between two parties with an agreement to re-exchange the currencies at a future date at the same rate.

Current-cost method: A method of inflation accounting that replaces historical cost accounting principles with current (replacement) cost as the basis for financial statement measurement.

Data warehouse: A repository for data transactions, in a database format. This technology is frequently used as a stop gap to replace older legacy systems in order to allow greater access to data.

Decision support system: An application used by middle-level and senior management to make management decisions.

Deferred tax valuation allowance: A portion of a deferred tax asset that is judged unlikely to be realized.

Derivative: An instrument whose value or contingent cash flows are a function of the value of some other asset or economic variable.

Derivative instrument: A financial instrument that derives its value from its relationship to some other financial contract, currency, commodity, or index.

Discontinued operations: Operations that constitute an entire segment of the firm's business and not, for example, simply one product line in a segment made up of a number of related product lines. Other key characteristics include: Segments engage in business and produce revenues and incur expenses; the operations of segments are regularly reviewed by the chief operating officer of the enterprise; and discrete financial information can be provided on the operations of segments.

Discount rate: A rate of return (cost of capital) used to convert a monetary sum, payable or receivable in the future, into present value.

Duration gap: A situation in which assets are more sensitive to interest rates than are liabilities. As interest rates rise, assets fall more than liabilities, wiping out equity.

DVD: Digital Video Disks are the direct descendents of CDs, but have the capacity to store roughly 10 times the amount of data as does a CD. This capacity allows a DVD to store all of the pictures and sounds that make up an entire, feature-length movie.

Economic exposure: "Derived from the risk that currency fluctuations could affect the dollar value of future cash flows at the operating income level" (Dow 1995 annual report, p. 36).

Economies of scale: the decrease in the marginal cost of production as a firm's output expands.

EDGAR: The electronic filing system by which IPOs and other filings required under the Securities Act of 1933 and the Securities Exchange Act of 1934 are effected. The public may access such filings through the World Wide Web.

EDI: Electronic Data Interchange. Used by businesses to transact commerce electronically. These transactions include purchase orders, shipping notifications, invoices, and so on.

Effective income tax rate: Total income tax provision (expense) deducted from pretax income from continuing operations divided by pretax income from continuing operations.

Effectiveness: The degree to which a goal is met.

Efficiency: A measure of the inputs needed to produce a given level of output in pursuit of a goal, or the outputs produced in pursuit of a goal by a given level of inputs.

Efficient search sequence: A pattern of searching for nonrecurring items that is designed to maximize their discovery and minimize search time.

Electronic commerce: The transacting of business over the Internet, whether for the purchase or sale of goods and services.

E-mail: Electronic mail is one of the most common and important computer applications, allowing people to communicate cheaply and quickly with other computer users almost anywhere on earth.

Encryption: Encryption is a process of encoding data to protect its confidentiality. Typically, we encrypt data before it is transmitted from one computer to another so that, should the data be intercepted by a third party during transmission, the data will be unintelligible to that third party. Secure Web sites use encryption to protect confidential data that users might send them, such as credit card numbers.

Equity net cash flows: Those cash flows available to pay out to equity holders (in the form of dividends) after funding operations of the business enterprise, making necessary capital investments, and reflecting increases or decreases in debt financing.

Equity risk premium: A rate of return in addition to a risk-free rate to compensate for investing in equity instruments because they have a higher degree of probable risk than risk-free instruments (a component of the cost of equity capital or equity discount rate).

ERP: An integrated software package that processes and controls all the functions of a company, including order processing, inventory control, purchasing, invoicing, financial systems, and customer management.

Exercise price: Same as **Strike price.**

Exotics: Engineered derivatives that contain unusual features, or nonstandard contingent cash flow formulas.

Extraordinary gains and losses: Revenues or gains and expenses or losses that are both unusual and nonrecurring.

Fair market value: The price, expressed in terms of cash equivalents, at which property would change hands between a hypothetical willing and able buyer and a hypothetical willing and able seller, acting at arm's length in an open and unrestricted market, when neither is under compulsion to buy or sell and when both have reasonable knowledge of the relevant facts.

Family limited partnership: An estate planning device which may entitle a donor to a discount on the value of gifts while allowing the donor to maintain control over the assets given away.

FAQ: Frequently asked questions. A file of questions that are frequently asked about a specific product or topic that is available to users through the Internet or intranet.

FASB: See **Financial Accounting Standards Board.**

FIFO: A method of computing cost of sales that includes the oldest inventory costs first in the computation of cost of sales. That is, the cost of goods purchased first (first-in) are included first (first-out) in the computation of cost of sales.

Financial Accounting Standards Board (FASB): The principal private sector organization with the responsibility of establishing U.S. generally accepted accounting principles (see **GAAP**).

Fire wall: A hardware and software device that protects an organization's computer systems and data from possible electronic intrusion from external sources. Computers that are connected to the Internet would be under constant threat from hackers and snoops without the protection of a fire wall.

Firm underwriting: An arrangement by which the underwriters agree themselves to purchase all the shares of a public offering.

Fixed costs: Those costs that are not responsive to changes in volume over the relevant range, but which respond to factors other than volume. Fixed costs are sometimes known as "period costs" when they depend on time (e.g., rent, depreciation, insurance).

Flexible budget: A budget prepared for more than one level of activity, covering several levels within the relevant range of activity. Also called a dynamic budget.

Foreign Corrupt Practices Act of 1997: The law that explicitly prohibits the bribery of foreign governments or political officials and requires firms to keep accurate and detailed records of company financial activities and maintain an adequate system of internal controls.

Foreign currency transaction: Any transaction (e.g., the sale or purchase of inventory, the lending or borrowing of money) that creates a balance-sheet account that is denominated in foreign currency. Examples include foreign-currency denominated receivables and loans, and foreign-currency denominated payables and long-term debt.

Form S-1: The standard form which is to be completed by a registrant and filed with the Securities and Exchange Commission in connection with an IPO (and with many other public offerings).

Forms 10-K, 10-Q, 8-K: Principal periodic reports filed by most companies registered under the Securities Acts.

Forms SB-1 and SB-2: Forms for filing an IPO or other public offering with the Securities and Exchange Commission for certain small business issuers.

Forward: A contract in which two parties agree to a deferred transaction. One party is obligated to deliver an underlying asset or commodity; the other party is obligated to take delivery and pay for it. The terms of the deferred transaction are fully specified in the forward contract.

Forward exchange contract: A privately negotiated agreement to purchase foreign currency for future receipt or to sell foreign currency for future delivery. The amount of foreign currency, the rate of exchange, and the future date of settlement are established at the time the contract is made.

Forward exchange rate: Rate at which currencies are to be exchanged at future dates.

Functional currency: The currency of the primary economic environment in which the entity operates. Typically, this is the currency of the environment in which it generates and expends cash. The functional currency may be the U.S. dollar and not the local currency of the foreign country.

Futures contract: An exchange-traded instrument with a preestablished expiration date, whose market value is linked to the relative exchange rates between two currencies. A futures contract can be purchased (a long position), resulting in a gain if the foreign currency appreciates and a loss if it depreciates. A contract can also be sold (a short position), resulting in a gain if the foreign currency depreciates or a loss if it appreciates.

GAAP: See **generally accepted accounting principles.**

Generally accepted accounting principles: The body of standards, rules, procedures, and practices that guide the preparation of financial statements. For commercial firms, the primary bodies involved with adding to or modifying existing GAAP are the Financial Accounting Standards Board, the American Institute of Certified Public Accountants, and the Securities and Exchange Commission.

Geographical information system: A computer application that uses a mapping system display on a terminal or a printer. Data, such as sales data or census data, is overlaid over the geographical information for decision-making purposes.

Giga-: The prefix given to another number which means a billion. Thus, a 10 giga-byte hard drive has the capacity to store 10 billion bytes of data.

Going private: The conversion of a public firm into a private company, usually by either a leveraged buyout (LBO) or a management buyout (MBO).

Goodwill: As it relates to valuation, that intangible asset arising as a result of name, reputation, customer loyalty, location, products, and similar factors not separately identified. The excess of purchase price over fair market value of net assets acquired under the purchase method of accounting; goodwill appears on the acquirer's balance sheet as an intangible asset and is amortized over a period of not more than 40 years.

Hedge: To reduce risk by taking a position that offsets some preexisting risk exposure.

Hedging: Steps taken to protect the dollar value of a foreign-currency asset or to hold constant the dollar burden of a foreign-currency liability, in the presence of fluctuating exchange rates, by maintaining offsetting foreign-currency positions.

Horizontal merger: A merger of firms producing similar goods or services.

Hypertext: Hypertext is the data-connecting protocol of the Internet that allows a document on the World Wide Web to connect with (or link to) other documents on the Web.

Income (income-based) approach: A general way of determining a value indication of a business, business ownership interest, security, or intangible asset using one or more methods that convert anticipated benefits into a present single amount.

Income from continuing operations: A measure of financial performance for the period that excludes the effects of discontinued operations, extraordinary items, and the cumulative effect of accounting changes. All other revenues, gains, expenses, and losses are included in the computation of income from continuing operations.

Intangible assets: Nonphysical assets (such as franchises, trademarks, patents, copyrights, goodwill, equities, mineral rights, securities, and contracts as distinguished from physical assets) that grant rights, privileges, and have economic benefits for the owner.

International Accounting Standards Committee (IASC): An organization representing accounting bodies from over 70 countries whose mission is to harmonize accounting standards internationally.

In-the-money: An option is in-the-money when exercise would be profitable. For a call option this is when the underlying stock price is above the strike price. For a put option, this is when the stock price is below the strike price.

Intrinsic Value: The amount of money earned when an option is exercised, or zero, whichever is greater. For a call option, intrinsic value is the maximum of zero or the stock price minus the strike price. For a put option it is the maximum of zero or the strike price minus the stock price.

Invested capital: The sum of equity and debt in a business enterprise. Debt is typically (a) long-term liabilities or (b) the sum of short-term interest-bearing debt and long-term liabilities.

Invested capital net cash flows: Those cash flows available to pay out to equity holders (in the form of dividends) and debt investors (in the form of principal and interest) after funding operations of the business enterprise and making necessary capital investments.

Investment risk: The degree of uncertainty as to the realization of expected returns.

Investment value: The value to a particular investor based on individual investment requirements and expectations.

IPO: An initial public offering; such transaction is registered with the Securities and Exchange Commission and permits a company, called a "registrant," first to offer to the public its shares of common stock or other securities.

Irregular items of revenue, gain, expense, or loss: See **nonrecurring items.**

ISP: An Internet service provider is an organization that sells connectivity to the Internet. An ISP has a permanent, high capacity connection to the Internet. Customers of the ISP use a telephone or cable modem to connect themselves to the ISP, and, thereby, the Internet. America OnLine is the largest ISP in the world.

Kilo-: The prefix given to another number which means a thousand. Thus, a 10 kilobyte document contains 10,000 bytes or characters of data.

Labor variance: A measure of the change in the cost of labor, analyzed according to wage changes and changes in labor productivity.

LAN: A local area network is a group of computers, usually within one or a few nearby buildings, which are connected to each other to allow the sharing of data, printers, e-mail, and other capabilities.

LCD: A liquid crystal display is a method of displaying data using a relatively flat panel. Many digital watches use LCDs to show time. LCD technology competes with CRT technology in computer monitors. LCDs take up less space than CRTs, but cost more.

Leading and lagging: A foreign-currency hedging technique that involves the matching of cash flows associated with foreign currency payables and receivables by speeding up or slowing down their payment or receipt.

Legacy systems: Older systems that were developed prior to the 1990s using older technologies. Usually mission critical systems, they are both costly and difficult to replace.

LIBOR: The London interbank offered rate. The interest rate used in Euromoney transactions between London banks. It is widely used as the benchmark floating rate in swaps.

LIFO inventory method: A method of computing cost of sales that charges the most recent inventory costs to cost of sales. The most recent (last-in) inventory items go into the cost of sales computation first (first-out).

LIFO liquidation: A reduction in the physical quantity of inventory by a firm using the LIFO method. Typically, older and lower costs will be associated with the liquidated quantities. This has the effect of reducing cost of sales and increasing earnings. This earnings increase is treated as nonrecurring in the computation of sustainable earnings.

LIFO reserve: The excess (typically) of the replacement cost of a LIFO inventory over its LIFO carrying value.

Link: A connection from one World Wide Web document to another. Typically, one navigates the Web by following a series of links.

Liquidity: the ability to quickly convert property to cash or pay a liability.

Long: To enter a future or forward as the long party. Also known as "buying" the future or forward.

Long party: The party in a forward or future contract that will take delivery of the underlying asset and make payment, that is, the buying party. The party in a forward or future contract that benefits from a rise in the price of the underlying asset.

Management's Discussion and Analysis of Results of Operations and Financial Condition (MD&A): A report required under Securities and Exchange Commission regulations, constituting part of an S-1 for an IPO and an annual report on Form 10-K. The discussion of operations is required to include material nonrecurring items of revenue, gain, expense, and loss.

Mark to market: The process by which at the end of each trading day, a payment is made from one party in a futures contract to the other, based on that day's movement in the futures price. When the futures price rises, the short party pays the long party the amount of the price rise. When the futures price falls, the long party pays the short party the amount the price fell.

Market (market-based) approach: A general way of determining a value indication of a business, business ownership interest, security, or intangible asset by using one or more methods that compare the subject to similar businesses, business ownership interests, securities, or intangible assets that have been sold.

Marketability: The ability to quickly convert property to cash at minimal cost.

Master budget: The total budget package of an organization, including both the operating and financial budgets. Sometimes referred to as the profit plan.

Material items: Items of sufficient size to have the potential to influence decision makers or other users of financial statements.

Material variance: A measure of the change in cost of materials used, analyzed according to price changes and changes in material efficiency.

MD&A: See **Management's Discussion and Analysis of Results of Operations and Financial Condition.**

Mega-: The prefix given to another number which means a million. Thus, a 10 megabyte file contains 10,000,00 bytes or characters of data.

Merger: The combination of two or more companies into a single entity

Minority discount: A discount for lack of control applicable to a minority interest.

Minority interest: An ownership interest less than 50% of the voting interest in a business enterprise.

Modem: A device used to allow computers to communicate with each other over wires not originally designed for computer communications. The most common form of modem allows computers to communicate over regular voice telephone wires. Cable modems allow computers to communicate using wires originally designed for cable TVs.

Monetary assets and liabilities: Assets and liabilities that represent a fixed number of monetary units. Monetary assets include cash and accounts receivable; monetary liabilities include accounts and notes payable. During inflationary periods monetary assets (liabilities) result in purchasing power gains (losses), respectively.

Multimedia: The simultaneous use of multiple forms of media on a computer. If you were to watch a football game on your computer that is coming to you over the Internet, you would be simultaneously using both video and sound media.

Multistep income statement: An income statement format that includes one or more profit subtotals such as gross profit and operating profit (also see single-step income statement).

NASD: See **National Association of Securities Dealers Inc.**

NASDAQ: National Association of Securities Dealers Automated Quotation System. An organized, electronically linked over-the-counter market for stocks. The NASDAQ stock index comprises stocks that trade on NASDAQ. These stocks are generally smaller, less capitalized stocks than those that compose the S&P 500.

National Association of Securities Dealers Inc: A self-regulatory organization which regulates the business of broker/dealers, including underwriters who sell securities to the public. In an IPO or any other public offering, the underwriters must obtain approval of the NASD of their compensation as "fair and reasonable."

Net cash flow: A form of cash flow. When the term is used, it should be supplemented by a qualifier (e.g., "Equity" or "Invested Capital") and a definition of exactly what it means in the given valuation context.

Net operating loss carry-forward: Under U.S. tax law, operating losses can be carried back and set off against profits in the previous three years. A refund of taxes can be obtained. If the loss is greater that the profits in the three previous years, then the loss can be carried forward for 20 years and set off against the profits of future years. The carrying forward of a loss may produce a future tax savings. In contrast, the carrying back of a loss produces a tax refund.

NetWare: The network operating system standard through the early and mid-1990s. Developed by Novell.

Network: The connecting together of two or more computers, typically with the purpose of sharing resources, such as printers, data, or an Internet connection.

Nonrecurring items: Items of revenue, gain, expense, and loss that appear in earnings on only an infrequent or irregular basis, fluctuate significantly in terms of amount and or sign, and are often not related to the core operational activities of the firm.

Notional principal: The principal amount specified in a swap agreement, which though not exchanged, serves as the benchmark to determine all cash flows. The cash flows generally equal the difference between two interest rates, multiplied by the notional principal.

Operating income: An intermediate, pretax measure of financial performance. Only operations-related items of revenue, gain, expense, and loss are included in the computation of operating income.

Operational control system: Systems that run the company's day-to-day operations.

Opportunity cost: A benefit forgone as a result of pursuing an alternative action.

Option contract: The right, but not the obligation, to purchase foreign currency at a fixed price (a call option), or the right, but not the obligation, to sell foreign currency at a fixed price (a put option).

Other comprehensive income: A set of unrealized income elements that are added to conventional net income to arrive at comprehensive income. The key other comprehensive income items are foreign currency translation adjustments, unrealized gains and losses on certain securities, and adjustments related to underfunded pension plans.

Out-of-the-money: An option is out of the money when exercise would generate a loss. For a call option this is when the underlying stock price is below the strike price. For a put option this is when the stock price is above the strike price.

Overhead variance: A measure of the change in the cost of overhead items, analyzed according to price and salary changes and changes in labor productivity.

Over-the-counter: Description of contracts that are negotiated between two parties, often with the help of an intermediary. Over-the-counter derivatives are custom-tailored to meet the needs of the parties involved. Over-the-counter derivatives are not traded on exchanges.

Participative budgeting: The process of preparing the budget using input from managers who are held responsible for budget performance.

PDA: Personal Digital Assistants are small, pocket-sized computers, usually with LCD screens, which allow users to keep their calendar, list of contacts, play games, and, in some cases, send and receive e-mail.

Physical delivery: A future contract that stipulates actual delivery of the underlying asset upon expiration of the contract.

"Plain English": The standards for clarity in drafting various portions of a Prospectus, as set forth in SEC Rule 421.

Plain vanilla: The most common type of swap. It is a fixed for floating interest rate swap, where LIBOR is the floating rate. The fixed rate is the current rate of the Treasury bond with the same maturity as the swap.

Pooling method: After the acquisition, the bidder and target firm balance sheets are combined simply by adding book values

Premise of value: An assumption regarding the most likely set of transactional circumstances that may be applicable to the subject valuation (e.g., going concern, liquidation).

Premium: The amount paid to the target over current market price to execute an acquisition.

Premoney valuation: The valuation ascribed to a business enterprise prior to the issuance of additional equity securities, for the purpose of pricing those securities to their public or private purchasers.

Private placement: An offering of securities to a sufficiently small or to a sufficiently sophisticated group of purchasers, such that registration of the transaction is not required with the Securities and Exchange Commission.

Private Securities Litigation Reform Act of 1995: A U.S. statute that establishes a safe harbor for forward-looking statements by public companies, insulating the company and management from liability for statements that ultimately prove to be inaccurate if they are believed to be true when made and if the contingencies on which their accuracy depend are properly articulated.

Productivity: Output divided by input. Productivity rates measure the input required for a unit of output. Compare the definition of efficiency.

Profit plan: A company's total budget used in achieving a desired profit goal. Sometimes the term refers only to the operating budget, and sometimes it is used synonymously with the term master budget.

Prospectus: Part I of a Registration Statement filed by a company offering its securities to the public, which Registration Statement is filed with and must be approved by the Securities and Exchange Commission. The Prospectus describes the registering company, its business and finances, and the risk factors the company faces.

Proxy: The grant by a shareholder to another party of the right to vote the stockholder's shares of stock.

Proxy contest: An attempt to gain control of a corporation by soliciting shareholder votes.

Purchase method: After the acquisition, the target firm's assets are put on the bidder's balance sheet at their fair market value.

Put option: An asset that gives the owner the right but not the obligation to sell some other asset for a set price on or up to a specified date.

RAM: Random access memory is the hardware which a computer uses for storing programs and data that the computer is currently using. In human terms, you can think of RAM as the memory storing part of your brain. When you are thinking about a problem, you are using your own RAM to work through various calculations and thoughts.

Rate of return: An amount of income (loss) and/or change in value realized or anticipated on an investment, expressed as a percentage of that investment.

Red herring: A preliminary, nonfinal Prospectus distributed by underwriters for the purpose of generating interest in shares of stock to be offered to the public.

Registration statement: A filing made with the SEC by a company issuing its securities to the public, which describes the company and its financial condition. Part I consists of the Prospectus.

Regulation FD: A Securities and Exchange Commission Regulation which among other matters requires a company which purposely or inadvertently releases previously unknown material information to promptly further distribute that information to the public.

Regulation S-K: A Regulation of the Securities and Exchange Commission that sets forth the standards for drafting the body of a Prospectus.

Regulation S-X: A Regulation of the Securities and Exchange Commission that sets forth the standards for the preparation of financial statements to be included in documents filed with the Securities and Exchange Commission.

Remeasurement: See **temporal translation procedure.**

Reporting currency: The currency in which a firm prepares its financial statements.

Residual value: The prospective value as of the end of the discrete projection period in a discounted benefit streams model.

Restructuring charges: Expenses typically recognized in conjunction with downsizings, reengineerings, reorganizations, and comparable activities. The expenses are usually made up of cash costs, accruals of obligations for future expenditures, as well as the write-down of assets.

Risk factors: That section of a Prospectus, or of a Form 10-K or other SEC filing, which lists the operational and financial risks faced by a company.

Risk-free rate: The rate of return available in the market on an investment free of default risk.

Risk premium: A rate of return in addition to a risk-free rate to compensate the investor for accepting risk.

Road show: A trip, generally of two or more weeks' duration, by underwriters and company management to meet with underwriters, brokers, and investors in different cities in order to explain a proposed public offering of securities.

Roll over: To enter a new future or forward contract to replace a contract that is expiring.

ROM: Read-only memory are forms of data storage which cannot be written to (or changed), but from which data can only be retrieved. A music CD (and, hence, CD ROM) is a device from which you can play back music, but you cannot record your own music to a CD ROM. (If you *can* record to a CD, the device is called a CD-R (for *recordable*), not a CD ROM.)

Securities Act of 1933: The U.S. statute that permits the private placement or private sale of securities without registration provided full and fair disclosure is made and that requires the registration of public offerings of securities.

Securities and Exchange Commission (SEC): An agency of the U.S. government which regulates the public issuance of securities under the Securities Act of 1933 and the conduct of trading markets and brokerage firms under the Securities Exchange Act of 1934, so as to protect investors from fraud and misleading or inadequate corporate and financial information.

Securities Exchange Act of 1934: The U.S. statute which established the Securities and Exchange Commission and regulates the operation of broker/dealers. Under this statute, companies with publicly held securities are required to make periodic reports to the public on various forms, most typically Forms 10-K, 10-Q, and 8-K. Officers, directors, and significant shareholders of publicly held companies are required to report purchases and sales of securities and the formation of "groups" for the holding, voting, purchase, or sale of publicly traded securities.

Short: To enter a future or forward as the short party. Also known as "selling" the future or forward.

Short party: The party in a forward or future contract that will deliver the underlying asset and receive payment (i.e., the selling party). The party in a forward or future contract that benefits from a decline in the price of the underlying asset.

Single-step income statement: An income statement format that simply deducts expenses and losses from revenues and gains in arriving at a single measure of income from continuing operations.

Speculate: Attempt to profit by taking on a risk exposure.

Spot market: The market in which transactions are executed for immediate delivery of an asset.

Spot price: The price to be paid for immediate delivery of an asset or commodity.

Spot rate: Rate at which currencies are exchanged for immediate delivery.

Standard and Poor's 500: A stock portfolio consisting of 500 large corporations. The composition and value of the stock portfolio is tracked and reported by the Standard and Poor's publishing company. The S&P 500 value is widely used as a benchmark index of overall stock market performance.

Standard of value: The identification of the type of value being utilized in a specific engagement (e.g., fair market value, fair value, investment value).

Standards: Predetermined, expected levels of efficiency or measures of desired performance (e.g., a budget amount, a standard cost, or a nonquantitative statement of desired performance). A standard cost is the predetermined cost of an input per unit of output. Standards may be unchanging (basic), perfect (ideal), or currently attainable.

Statements of Financial Accounting Standards (SFAS): Pronouncements of the Financial Accounting Standards Board that are the central elements of generally accepted accounting principles.

Stock acquisition: The purchase of a controlling interest in a firm by buying its outstanding equity.

Strategic information system: An application used by senior management to create a company's strategy.

Streaming media: Typically, refers to Internet sites that send out a continuous flow of sound or video signal to user. An example might be www.radiotango.com, which plays tangos 24 hours per day.

Strike price: The prespecified purchase or sale price for the underlying asset in an option contract.

Sustainable earnings base: A revised historical earnings series from which the effects of all nonrecurring items have been removed (see **core earnings**).

Sustainable earnings worksheet: A worksheet used to organize and summarize nonrecurring items so that their effects can be removed from as-reported net income in order to arrive at a sustainable earnings base.

Swap: An agreement between two parties to exchange cash flows over a period of time. Cash flows are determined by an agreed upon formula specified in the swap agreement—a formula that is contingent on the performance of other underlying instruments.

Symmetric risk: An exposure that results in profits when an underlying price or economic variable moves in one direction, and proportional losses if the variable moves in the opposite direction.

Synergy: The incremental value generated by the combination of two or more firms.

Synthetic stock portfolio: A portfolio that consists of Treasury bills and a long position in equity futures contracts. A properly constructed synthetic stock portfolio behaves the same as a portfolio consisting of actual stocks.

Systematic risk: The risk that is common to all risky securities and cannot be eliminated through diversification. When using the capital asset pricing model, systematic risk is measured by beta.

Takeover: The transfer of corporate control from one group of shareholders to another.

Target: A firm that is the subject of takeover or acquisition activities.

Tau: The amount of time remaining prior to an option's expiration.

Taxable transaction: An acquisition in which the target firm shareholders are immediately subject to capital gains on their sale of shares.

Tax-adjusted nonrecurring items: Pretax nonrecurring items of revenue, gain, expense, and loss that are multiplied by one minus a representative income tax rate. The result is the after-tax effect of each of these items on net income.

Tax-free transaction: An acquisition in which the primary consideration paid to the target's shareholders is the acquirer's common stock, thereby deferring capital gains taxes until the new shares are sold.

TCP/IP: The communications standard that is used by the Internet. A protocol is the understanding that computers have for how information will be delivered over the communications network, which enables computers with different operating systems to communicate with each other and to eliminate errors in data.

Temporal (remeasurement) translation procedure: A method for translating foreign currency financial statements in which monetary assets (including assets valued at market) and liabilities are translated at current exchange rates. Nonmonetary assets, liabilities, and paid-in capital accounts are translated at historical exchange rates; cost of sales and depreciation expense are translated at the rates in existence when the related inventory or fixed assets were acquired; and revenues and other expenses are translated at the average exchange rate in existence during the reporting period. Translation gains and losses are reported as a component of net income.

Transaction exposure: The potential for gains and losses as foreign-denominated assets and liabilities (e.g., accounts receivable, accounts payable, notes payable), increase or decrease in value with changes in exchange rates.

Transfer prices: Prices charged when goods or services are transferred either within firms (e.g., from one division of a firm to another) or between related firms (e.g., between a parent and its subsidiaries).

Translation exposure: Typically, the excess of foreign-currency assets over foreign currency liabilities of foreign subsidiaries. Translation gains result from increases in the value of the foreign currency and losses in the event of decreases.

Translation of foreign currency financial statements: The restatement of the financial statements of a foreign entity from its local currency to the reporting currency of its parent.

UNIX: An open operating system running on many manufacturers' computers. The first successful nonproprietary operating system. It was developed by Bell Labs in the 1970s.

Unsystematic risk: The portion of total risk specific to an individual security that can be avoided through diversification.

Unwind: To close out a future or forward position.

URL: Universal Resource Locator is the Internet address for a given Web site. The URL for the president of the United States is www.whitehouse.gov.

Valuation date: The specific point in time at which the valuator's opinion of value applies (also referred to as "Effective Date" or "Appraisal Date").

Variances: Measures of the difference between actual costs and standard costs. They are favorable if costs are less than expected and unfavorable otherwise. Variances may be analyzed by the effect of changing prices (price variances) or changing usage (quantity or usage variances).

Vertical merger: A merger in which the two firms are from different stages of the same industry or production process (e.g., an automobile manufacturer purchases a steelmaker).

WAN: A wide area network is a connection of two or more computers which are geographically distant from each other. The typical purpose of a WAN is to send data or communicate with distant facilities. Thus, an airline might have a WAN connecting all of its airports world wide to allow for the quick communications of scheduling changes between its various facilities.

Weighted average cost of capital (WACC): The cost of capital (discount rate) determined by the weighted average, at market value, of the cost of all financing sources in the business enterprise's capital structure.

Windows NT or 2000: Quickly becoming the network operating system standard of the industry. Developed by Microsoft.

Write an option: Sell an option. The writer is paid the option premium up front. The writer of a call must later sell the underlying asset if the call option owner exercises. The writer of a put must later buy the underlying asset if the put option owner exercises. The writer of the option is essentially liable for any future payoffs received by the option owner. Also known as shorting the option.

About the Authors

Charles A. Anderson's career includes academic and business experience. He has been a faculty member of both the Harvard Business School and the Stanford Business School. He was the president, chief executive officer, and a director of Walker Manufacturing Co., J.I. Case, and the Stanford Research Institute. He has served on a number of corporate boards of directors, including NCR Corp., Owens-Corning Fiberglas Corp., Boise-Cascade Corp., and the Eaton Company.

Robert N. Anthony is Ross Graham Walker Professor of Management Control, Emeritus, at Harvard Business School. He has been a director and chairman of the audit committee of Carborundum Company and Warnaco, Inc. He has been a director of several smaller organizations and a trustee (including chairman of the board) of Colby College, and of Dartmouth-Hitchcock Medical Center. He is the author or coauthor of some 20 books and 100 articles on management subjects, especially management control; his books and articles have been translated into 12 languages. He is a past president of the American Accounting Association.

Richard T. Bliss has been involved in corporate financial analysis since 1987 and is currently on the finance faculty at Babson College. He teaches at the undergraduate, MBA, and executive levels, specializing in the areas of Corporate Financial Strategy and Entrepreneurial Finance. Prior to coming to Babson, Dr. Bliss was on the faculty at Indiana University and he has also taught extensively in Central and Eastern Europe, including at the Warsaw School of Economics, Warsaw University, and the University of Ljubljana in Slovenia.

With publications in the areas of corporate finance, entrepreneurship, and banking, Dr. Bliss has an active research agenda. His recent work on the impact of bank mergers on CEO compensation has been cited in *Fortune* magazine and numerous other business publications and will be published in the *Journal of Financial Economics*.

Dr. Bliss holds a PhD in Finance from Indiana University. He also received his MBA in Finance/Real Estate from Indiana University and graduated with honors from Rutgers University, earning a BS degree in Engineering and a BA degree in Economics

Edward G. Cale Jr. is a professor of information systems at Babson College in Wellesley, Massachusetts. Dr. Cale holds a BS in electrical engineering from Stanford University and an MBA and a DBA from the Harvard Business School. After working for five years in the aerospace and integrated circuits industries, Dr. Cale has spent the past 20 years in academia, teaching, conducted research, and consulting in the management of information technology.

Eugene E. Comiskey received his PhD from Michigan State University and his professional qualifications include both Certified Public Accountant (CPA) and Certified Management Accountant (CMA). Professor Comiskey taught from 1965 to 1980 at the Krannert Graduate School of Management at Purdue University and also as a visiting faculty member during 1972 and 1973 at the University of California, Berkeley. While at Purdue, he twice received the Salgo Noren Foundation Award as the outstanding professor in the Graduate Management Program. Since arriving at Georgia Tech he has six times been recognized as Professor of the Year by the Graduate Students in Management organization. In 1999, Professor Comisky was the recipient of the Educator of the Year award from the Georgia Society of CPAs.

Professor Comiskey has published over 60 papers in a wide range of professional and scholarly journals and edited books. A book, with Charles W. Mulford, *Financial Warnings* (478 pages), was published in 1996 by John Wiley & Sons and is now in its fifth printing. Another book, *Guide to Financial Reporting and Analysis* (624 pages), also with Charles W. Mulford, was published by John Wiley & Sons in 2000. A third book, *The Financial Numbers Game,* is under contract with John Wiley and should be published in late 2001 or early 2002. Current research interests center on financial analysis and financial reporting practices, financial early warnings, international financial reporting practices, and the role of financial data in credit decisions. For over 25 years, Professor Comiskey has worked with commercial banks, both in the United States and in Europe and Asia, in the design and delivery of educational programs to improve the financially oriented credit analysis skills of lenders. Since 1988, he has been a partner in Financial Training Associates, a financial training and consulting firm that he founded with his colleague Charles W. Mulford.

Professor Comiskey served from 1978 to 1980 as Director of Research for the American Accounting Association. He also served (1995–1996) as president of the Financial Accounting and Reporting Section of the American Accounting Association. The Section has a membership of over 1,500 and is made up of scholars and practitioners who have a primary interest in matters related to the measurement and disclosure of financial information. Professor

Comiskey served two terms on the editorial review board of the *Accounting Review*—the second term was as an editorial consultant, or under current nomenclature, an associate editor. He has also served a term on the editorial review board of *Issues in Accounting Education* and is now serving a three-year term on the editorial board of *Accounting Horizons*.

Michael A. Crain, CPA/ABV, ASA, CFE, MBA, is a business appraiser and litigation consultant practitioner in Ft. Lauderdale, Florida. He is an Accredited Senior Appraiser in business valuation awarded by the American Society of Appraisers and he is Accredited in Business Valuation from the American Institute of Certified Public Accountants (AICPA). He has served on the examination committee for the AICPA's business valuation accreditation and on other AICPA national committees. He has been retained as an expert witness and testified on numerous occasions. His articles have appeared in the *Journal of Accountancy, CPA-Expert,* and other professional publications, and he has spoken on numerous occasions to national audiences.

Steven P. Feinstein, PhD, CFA, is an associate professor of finance at Babson College and a consultant with the Michel/Shaked Group in Boston. He holds a PhD in economics from Yale University. Prior to entering academia, Dr. Feinstein served as an economist at the Federal Reserve Bank of Atlanta. Dr. Feinstein's primary areas of research are financial valuation and the use and pricing of derivatives. He has presented his research at numerous academic conferences including the annual meetings of the American Finance Association and the Financial Management Association. His articles have appeared in *Derivatives Quarterly,* the *Journal of Risk, Risk Management,* the *Atlanta Federal Reserve Bank Economic Review,* the *American Bankruptcy Institute Journal,* and the *Journal of Financial Planning.* Dr. Feinstein conducts professional seminars for executives and has consulted for a wide variety of institutions. Clients have included Bankers Trust, Cho Hung Bank of Korea, Chrysler, Honeywell, ITT, Lehman Brothers, Nippon Life Insurance, Travelers Insurance, and numerous law firms.

Theodore Grossman is a member of the faculty of Babson College, where he teaches information technology and accounting. He lectures on various information technology topics such as Web technologies, e-commerce, strategic information systems, managing information technology, and systems analysis and design. He also performs extensive consulting for food and nonfood retailers, suppliers of technology products to the retail industry. He is called upon frequently to act as an expert witness in complex litigation in matters relating to technology and cyber law. Prior to joining Babson College, he was the founder and CEO of a computer software company for the retail industry. He holds a BS degree in engineering from the University of New Hampshire and an MS in management from Northeastern University.

Robert Halsey has an MBA in finance and a PhD in accounting from the University of Wisconsin—Madison. During his business career, he managed the commercial lending division of a large Midwestern bank, and served as the Chief Financial Officer of a privately held retailing and manufacturing company. Prior to joining the faculty of Babson College, Dr. Halsey taught at the University of Wisconsin—Madison where he received the Douglas Clarke Memorial Teaching Award. His research interests are in the area of financial reporting and include firm valuation, financial statement analysis, and disclosure issues. He has published in *Advances in Quantitative Analysis of Finance and Accounting*, the *Journal of the American Taxation Association*, and *Issues in Accounting Education*.

Stephen M. Honig is senior partner with the Boston office of the national law firm of Schnader, Harrison, Segal & Lewis, LLP. A holder of a BA from Columbia College and an LLB from Harvard University, Mr. Honig has worked in the private and public finance of emerging technology companies since 1966. He was assisted in the preparation of his chapter by his partner Albert Dandridge, formerly on the staff of the Securities and Exchange Commission, and associate Craig Circosta, both of Schnader's Philadelphia office.

William C. Lawler is an Associate Professor of Accounting at Babson College, Wellesley, Massachusetts, and Director of the Consortium for Executive Development at Babson College's School of Executive Education. Dr. Lawler did his undergraduate work at the University of Connecticut and his graduate studies at the University of Massachusetts. His teaching and research focus on two areas: financial footprints of business unit strategy and the impact of new technologies on cost systems design.

Professor Lawler has authored several papers and given numerous professional presentations. His primary focus is on aiding operational managers in understanding the financial consequences of their decisions. He has run seminars on this topic for such diverse groups as telecom managers in China, production managers in the Czech Republic, and R&D managers in the United States. Dr. Lawler consults with a number of companies, ranging from small biotechs to Fortune 100 computer companies, concerning the design and use of cost information systems for management decision support rather than external financial reporting. His most recent publications in this area are chapters on Activity Based Accounting and Profit Planning for the third edition of *The Portable MBA in Finance and Accounting*.

John Leslie Livingstone earned MBA and PhD degrees from Stanford University. He is a CPA, licensed in New York and Texas, and a CVA (certified in business valuation). Les directs a nationwide business consulting practice, headquartered in West Palm Beach, Florida. He has been a partner in Coopers & Lybrand (now PricewaterhouseCoopers), an international accounting firm, and in The MAC Group, an international management consulting firm specializing in business strategy with offices in Boston, Chicago, Los Angeles, New York, San Francisco, Washington, D.C., London, Paris, Munich, Rome, Madrid, and Tokyo (since acquired by Cap Gemini/Ernst & Young). He has consulted to major corporations and other organizations such as the U.S. Postal Service and the SEC. He was the Arthur Young Distinguished Professor of Accounting at Ohio State University, Fuller E. Callaway Professor of Accounting at Georgia Institute of Technology, and Chairman of the Department of Accounting and Law at Babson College. He has authored or coauthored 10 books, several chapters in authoritative accounting handbooks, and many articles in professional journals.

Richard P. Mandel is an associate professor of law at Babson College, where he teaches a variety of courses in business law and taxation on the undergraduate and graduate school levels and has served as chairman of the Finance Division. He is also a partner in the law firm of Bowditch and Dewey, of Worcester and Framingham, Massachusetts, where he specializes in the representation of growing businesses and their executives. Mr. Mandel has written a number of articles regarding the legal issues encountered by small businesses. He holds an AB in Government and Meteorology from Cornell University and a JD from Harvard Law School.

Charles W. Mulford is Invesco Chair and professor of accounting in the DuPree College of Management at Georgia Tech. Since joining the faculty in 1983, he has been recognized nine times as the Core Professor of the Year and once as the Professor of the Year by the Graduate Students in Management. In 1999 the Graduate Students in Management voted to rename the Core Professor of the Year Award the "Charles W. Mulford Core Professor of the Year Award." An additional teaching award received in 2000 was the university-wide W. Roane Beard Class of 1940 Outstanding Teacher Award.

Dr. Mulford's scholarly pursuits include the publication of numerous papers in scholarly as well as professional accounting and finance journals. His research interests center on the effects of accounting standards on investment and credit decision making, earnings forecasts, the relationship between accounting-based and market-based measures of risk and international accounting and reporting practices. More recently, his research interests have turned to the use of published financial reports in the prediction of financial distress. He has coauthored a book on the subject, *Financial Warnings*, published in 1996. A second book on financial analysis, *Guide to Financial Reporting and Analysis*, was published in July 2000. A third book on how accounting is used to mislead investors, *The Financial Numbers Game: Identifying Creative Accounting Practices*, is scheduled for publication in 2001. All three books were or will be published by John Wiley & Sons, New York.

In addition to his work at Georgia Tech, Professor Mulford regularly consults with major domestic and international commercial banks on issues related to credit decision making.

Charles Mulford has a doctorate in accounting from Florida State University and is professionally qualified as a Certified Public Accountant (CPA) in Florida and Georgia. Prior to joining the Georgia Tech faculty, he practiced public accounting with the firm of Coopers & Lybrand. He was an audit senior in the firm's Miami office.

Michael F. van Breda teaches at Southern Methodist University where he was chair of the accounting department for a number of years. He is currently Director of the Graduate Certificate Program in Finance and Accounting. His courses have included cost and managerial accounting at the graduate level. He obtained his PhD in Accounting from Stanford University and his MBA from the University of Cape Town. He was previously on the faculty of MIT and has held positions at the University of Cape Town, the University of the Witwatersrand, and at University College, Oxford. He is the author of numerous scholarly publications one of which won the Lybrand silver medal for its contribution to managerial accounting. He is the coauthor (with Eldon S. Hendriksen) of the fifth edition of *Accounting Theory* (Richard D. Irwin, 1991). In addition he has consulted to a number of major corporations.

Andrew "Zach" Zacharakis, PhD, is the Paul T. Babson Term Chair in Entrepreneurship and an associate professor of entrepreneurship with the Arthur M. Blank Center for Entrepreneurship at Babson College. Professor Zacharakis received a BS (finance/marketing), University of Colorado; an MBA (finance/international business), Indiana University; and a PhD (strategy and entrepreneurship/cognitive psychology), University of Colorado. At Babson, he teaches the business plan preparation course at both the MBA and undergraduate levels. He also actively advises entrepreneurial start-ups and venture capital firms. His primary research areas include the (1) venture capital decision-making process and (2) entrepreneurial growth strategies. Professor Zacharakis has articles appearing in *Journal of Business Venturing, Entrepreneurship: Theory and Practice, Journal of Small Business Management, Venture Capital: An International Journal of Entrepreneurial Finance, Journal of Private Equity Capital, International Trade Journal, Academy of Management Executive, Journal of Business Strategies, Case Research Journal,* as well as *Frontiers of Entrepreneurial Research.* Professor Zacharakis has been interviewed in newspapers nationwide including the *Boston Globe* and the *Los Angeles Times.* He has also appeared on *Bloomberg Small Business Report.* Professor Zacharakis's dissertation, *The Venture Capital Investment Decision,* received a Certificate of Distinction from the Academy of Management and Mr. Edgar F. Heizer recognizing outstanding research in the field of new enterprise development. Professor Zacharakis's actively consults with entrepreneurs and small business start-ups. His professional experience includes positions with The Cambridge Companies (investment banking/venture capital), IBM, and Leisure Technologies.

Index